New Systems and Architectures for Automatic Speech Recognition and Synthesis

NATO ASI Series

Advanced Science Institutes Series

A series presenting the results of activities sponsored by the NATO Science Committee, which aims at the dissemination of advanced scientific and technological knowledge, with a view to strengthening links between scientific communities.

The Series is published by an international board of publishers in conjunction with the NATO Scientific Affairs Division

A **Life Sciences** Plenum Publishing Corporation
B **Physics** London and New York

C **Mathematical and** D. Reidel Publishing Company
 Physical Sciences Dordrecht, Boston and Lancaster

D **Behavioural and** Martinus Nijhoff Publishers
 Social Sciences Boston, The Hague, Dordrecht and Lancaster
E **Applied Sciences**

F **Computer and** Springer-Verlag
 Systems Sciences Berlin Heidelberg New York Tokyo
G **Ecological Sciences**

New Systems and Architectures for Automatic Speech Recognition and Synthesis

Edited by

Renato De Mori and Ching Y. Suen
Department of Computer Science, Concordia University
Montréal, Québec H3G 1M8, Canada

Springer-Verlag Berlin Heidelberg New York Tokyo
Published in cooperation with NATO Scientific Affairs Division

Proceedings of the NATO Advanced Study Institute on New Systems and Architectures for Automatic Speech Recognition and Synthesis held at Bonas, Gers, France, 2–14 July 1984

ISBN 3-540-15177-X Springer-Verlag Berlin Heidelberg New York Tokyo
ISBN 0-387-15177-X Springer-Verlag New York Heidelberg Berlin Tokyo

Library of Congress Cataloging in Publication Data. NATO Advances Study Institute on New Systems and Architecture for Automatic Speech Recognition and Synthesis (1984 : bonas France) New systems and architecture for automatic speech recognition and synthesis. (NATO ASI series. Series F, Computer and system sciences ; vol. 16) "Proceedings of the NATO Advanced Study Institute on New Systems and Architecture for Automatic Speech Recognition and Synthesis held at Bonas, Gers, France, 2–14 July 1984" — T.p. verso. "Published in cooperation with NATO Scientific Affairs Division." Includes indes. 1. Automatic speech recognition — Congresses. 2. Speech synthesis — Congresses. I. De Mori, Renato. II. Suen, Ching Y. III. North Atlantic Treaty Organization. Scientific Affairs Division. IV. Title. V. Series: NATO ASI series. Series F, Computer and system sciences ; no. 16. TK7895.S65N375 1984 629.8'92 85-17228 ISBN 0-387-15177-X (U.S.)

Printing: Beltz Offsetdruck, Hemsbach; Bookbinding: J. Schäffer OHG, Grünstadt
2145/3140-543210

TABLE OF CONTENTS

LIST OF PARTICIPANTS IX

FOREWORD XIII

I. REVIEW OF BASIC ALGORITHMS

An Overview of Digital Techniques for 1
Progessing Speech Signals
Murat Kunt and Heinz Hugli

Systems for Isolated and Connected Word Recognition 73
Roger K. Moore

II. SYSTEM ARCHITECTURE AND VLSI FOR SPEECH PROCESSING

Systolic Architectures for Connected Speech Recognition 145
Patrice Frison and Patrice Quinton

Computer Systems for High-Performance Speech Recognition 169
Roberto Bisiani

VLSI Architectures for Recognition of Context-Free Languages 191
K. S. Fu

Implementation of an Aeoustical Front-End for Speech 215
Recognition
Michele Cavazza, Alberto Ciaramella and Roberto Pacifici

Reconfigurable Modular Architecture for a Man-Machine Vocal 225
Communication System in Real Time
D. Dours and R. Facca

A Survey of Algorithms & Architecture for Connected Speech 233
Recognition
D. Wood

III. SOFTWARE SYSTEMS FOR AUTOMATIC SPEECH RECOGNITION

Knowledge-Based and Expert Systems in Automatic 249
Speech Recognition
Jean-Paul Haton

The Speech Understanding and Dialog System EVAR 271
H. Niemann, A. Brietzmann, R. Mühlfeld, P. Regel and G. Schukat

A New Rule-Based Expert System for Speech Recognition 303
G. Mercier, M. Gilloux, C. Tarridec and J. Vaissiere

SAY — A PC Based Speech Analysis System 343
P. R. Alderson, G. Kaye, S. G. C. Lawrence, D. A. Sinclair, B. J. Williams
and G. J. Wolff

Automatic Generation of Linguistic, Phonetic and Acoustic 361
Knowledge for a Diphone-Based Continuous Speech Recognition System
Anna Maria Colla and Donatella Sciarra

The Use of Dynamic Frequency Warping in a 389
Speaker-Independent Vowel Classifier
W. A. Ainsworth and H. M. Foster

Dynamic Time Warping Algorithms for Isolated and 405
Connected Word Recognition
J. di Martino

An Efficient Algorithm for Recognizing Isolated Turkish Words 419
Nese Yalabik and Fatih Ünal

A General Fuzzy-Parsing Scheme for Speech Recognition 427
Enrique Vidal, Francisco Casacuberta, Emilio Sanchis and Jose M. Benedi

IV SPEECH SYNTHESIS AND PHONETICS

Linguistics and Automatic Processing of Speech 447
John J. Ohala

Synthesis of Speech by Computers and Chips 477
Ching Y. Suen and Stephen B. Stein

Prosodic Knowledge in the Rule-Based Synthex Expert System 495
for Speech Synthesis
A. Aggoun, C. Sorin, F. Emerard, M. Stella

Syntex — Unrestricted Conversion of Text to Speech 517
for German
Wolfgang Kulas and Hans-Wilhelm Rühl

Concatenation Rules for Demisyllable Speech Synthesis 537
Helmut Dettweiler and Wolfgang Hess

On the Use of Phonetic Knowledge for Automatic 569
Speech Recognition
Renato De Mori and Pietro Laface

Demisyllables as Processing Units for Automatic 593
Speech Recognition and Lexical Access
G. Ruske

Detection and Recognition of Nasal Consonants in 613
Continuous Speech — Preliminary Results
R. Gubrynowicz, L. Le Guennec and G. Mercier

AUTHOR INDEX 629

List of Participants

Mr. A. Aggoun
C.N.E.T.
B.P. 40
22301 Lannion
France

Dr. W. A. Ainsworth
Dept. of Communication and Neuroscience
University of Keele
Keele, Staffs. ST5 5BG
England

Mr. J. M. Benedi Ruiz
Departamento de Electronicae Informatica
Universidad de Valencia
Burjasot — Valencia
Spain

Prof. R. Bisiani
Carnegie-Mellon University
Dept. of Computer Science
Schenley Park
Pittsburgh, Pa 15213
U.S.A.

Dr. A. Cappelli
Istituto di Linguistica Computazionale
Via della Faggiola, 32
56100 Pisa
Italy

Dr. G. Chollet
E.N.S.T.
46, Rue Barrault
75634 Paris Cedex 13
France

Dr. A. Ciaramella
CSELT
Via G. Reiss Romoli 274
Torino 10148
Italy

Prof. G. Danserau
Université de Quebec à Hull
Dept. Informatique
CP 1250 succ. B
Hull, Quebec J8X 3X7
Canada

Prof. R. De Mori
Dept. of Computer Science
Concordia University
Montreal, Quebec H3G 1M8
Canada

Mr. Di Martino
C.R.I.N.
B.P. 239
54506 Vandoeuvre
France

Dr. D. Dours
U.E.R. de Mathématiques - Informatiques-Gestion
Université Paul Sabatier
118, Rue de Narbonne
31062 Toulouse Cedex
France

Mr. D. Fohr
C.R.I.N.
B.P. 239
54506 Vandoeuvre
France

Mr. N.J.A. Forse
British Telecom Research Laboratories
Martlesham Heath
Ipswich IP5 7RE
England

Dr. P. Frison
I.R.I.S.A.
Campus de Beaulieu
35042 Rennes Cedex
France

Prof. K. S. Fu
School of Electrical Engineering
Purdue University
West Lafayette, Ind.   47907
U.S.A.

Dr. R. Gubrynowicz
Université de Provence, Institut de Phonétique
29, Avenue Robert Schuman
13621 Aix en Provence Cedex
France

Prof. J. P. Haton
C.R.I.N.
Université de Nancy 1
B.P. 239
54506 Vandoeuvre
France

Dipl. Ing. H. Heckl
Siemens AG,
ZTI INF
Otto-Hahn-Ring 6
D 8000 München 83
West Germany

Dr. W. Hess
Lehrstuhl Für Datenverarbeitung
Technische Universität München
Arcisstr. 21
8000 München 2
West Germany

Prof. J. L. Houle
Ecole Polytechnique de Montréal
C.P. 6079 Succ "A"
Montreal, Que. H3C 3A7
Canada

Dr. A. Ingegnoli
C/O FACRC
Via Della Magione
00040 Pomezia (Rome)
Italy

Ing. B. Kammerer
Siemens AG, ZTI INF 111
Otto-Hahn-Ring 6
D 8000 München 83
West Germany

Dipl. Ing. W. Kulas
Lehrstuhl Fuer Allgemeine Elektronik
und Akustik
Ruhr-Universität Bochum
Universität Str. 150
D-4630 Bochum
West Germany

Prof. M. Kunt
Laboratoire de Traitement de Signaux
Ecole Polytechnique Fédérale de Lausanne
16, Chemin de Bellerive
1007 Lausanne
Switzerland

Prof. P. Laface
Departimento di Automatica e Informatica
CORSO Duca Degli Abruzzi 24
10129 Torino
Italy

Mr. L. Leguennec
C.N.E.T.
B.P. 40
22301 Lannion Cedex
France

Prof. H. Leich
Faculté Polytechnique e Mons
31 Boulevard Dolez
7000 Mons
Belgium

Mr. P. Lockwood
Laboratoire de Marcoussis
91460 Marcoussis
France

Mr. U. Macdonald
Dept. of Computational
University of Saint Andrews
North Haugh, St. Andrews
Scotland

Dr. J. Manley
Centre for Research on Perception
and Cognition
University of Sussex
Brighton BN1 9QG
England

Dr. J. P. Martens
Laboratorium voor Electronica
St-Pietersnieuwstraat 41
9000 GENT
Belgium

Dr. G. Mercier
C.N.E.T.
B.P. 40
22301 Lannion Cedex
France

Dr. R. K. Moore
Royal Signals and Radar Establishment
St. Andrews Road
Great Malvern, Worcs. WRI4 3PS
England

Mr. J. Mudler
Institut für Nachrichtentechnik
TU Braunschweig
Postfach 3329
West Germany

Mr. R. L. Muhlfeld
IMMD 5
Universität Erlangen
Martensstr. 3
8520 Erlangen
West Germany

Dr. E. Mumolo
FACE RC
Via Della Magione 10
00040 Pomezia (Rome)
Italy

Dr. H. Ney
PHILIPS Gmbh
Forschungslaboratorium Hamburg
P.O. Box 540840
2000 Hamburg 54
West Germany

Prof. H. Niemann
Universität Erlangen-Nurnberg, IMMD
Martensstr. 3
8520 Erlangen
West Germany

Prof. J. Ohala
Phonology Laboratory
Department of Linguistics
University of California
Berkeley, CA   94720
U.S.A.

Dr. M. Ohala
Linguistics Program
California State
University at San Joseé
San Jose, CA   95192
U. S. A.

Mr. W. Ronnebrinck
Institut Für Nachrichtentechnik
Technische Universität Braunschweig
Schleinitzstr. 23
3300 Braunschweig
West Germany

Dipl. Ing. H. W. Rühl
Lehrsuhl für Allg. Elektrotechnik
und Akustik
Ruhr-Universität Bochum
Postfach 102148
4630 Bochum 1
West Germany

Dr. G. Ruske
Lehrstuhl für Datenverarbeitung
Technische Universität München
Franz-Joseph Str. 38
8000 München 40
West Germany

Prof. B. Sankur
Bogazici University
Dept. of Electrcal Engineering
Bebek, Istanbul
Turkey

Mr. E. G. Schukat
Universität Erlangen-Nurnberg
IMMD 5
Martensstr. 3
8520 Erlangen
West Germany

Dr. D. Sciarra
Electronica San Giorgio
Via Puccini 2
16154 Genova Sestri Ponente
Italy

Mr. N. Sedgwick
Acorn Computers Ltd.
Fulbourn Road
Cherry Hinton
Cambridge CB1 4JN
England

Dr. D. Sinclair
IBM Science Center
Athelstan House
St. Clement Street
Winchester, S023 9DR
England

Prof. W. Steenaart
Electr. Eng. Dept.
University of Ottawa
Ottawa, Ontario K1N 6N5
Canada

Prof. Ching Y. Suen
Dept. of Computer Science
Concordia University
1455 de Maisonneuve Blvd., West
Montreal, Quebec H3G 1M8
Canada

Mr. A. Tassy
E.N.S.T.
46, Rue Barrault
75013 Paris
France

Mr. E. Verdonck
Katholieke Universitat Leuven
CME — ESAT
De Croylaan 52
3030 Heverlee
Belgium

Mr. J. Verhoeven
University of Antwerp (UIA)
Dept. of Didactics & Criticism
Universiteitsplein 1
2610 Wilrijk
Belgium

Dr. E. Vidal Ruiz
Centro de Informatica
Universidad de Valencia
Burjasot — Valencia
Spain

Mlle. Nadine Vigouroux
Laboratoire CERFIA
(mr. Perennou)
118, Rte de Narbonne
31062 Toulouse, Cedex
France

Mr. D. Wood
GEC Research Laboratories
East Lane
Wembley, Middx
England

Prof. N. Yalabik
Computer Engineering Dept.
Middle East Technical University
Ankara
Turkey

FOREWORD

It is an established tradition that researchers from many countries get together on the average every three years for a two week Advanced Studies Institute on Automatic Speech Recognition and Synthesis. According to ASI policies the Institute is financed by NATO. This book contains the texts of lectures and papers contributed by the attendees of the ASI which was held July 2 — 14, 1984, at Bonas, Gers, France. Focussed on New Systems and Architectures for Automatic Speech Recognition and Synthesis, this book is divided into 4 parts:

(a) *Review of basic algorithms*

(b) *System architecture and VLSI for automatic Speech*

(c) *Software systems for automatic speech recognition,*

(d) *Speech synthesis and phonetics.*

Due to the international nature of the Institute, the readers will find in this book different styles, different points of view and applications to different languages. This reflects also some characteristics of the International Association for Pattern Recognition (IAPR) whose technical committee on Speech Recognition has organized this ASI.

Proposed contributions have been reviewed by an Editorial Committee composed of W. Ainsworth (Kent), R. Bisiani (Pittsburgh), J. P. Haton (Nancy), W. Hess (Munich), J. L. Houle (Montréal), P. Laface (Turin), R. Moore (Malvern), H. Niemann (Erlangen) and J. Ohala (Berkeley).

Typesetting of the book was performed using SYMSET facilities developed entirely by the Department of Computer Science at Concordia University. Special thanks are due to L. Lam, H. Monkiewicz and L. Thiel.

Montreal, Canada   R. De Mori and C. Y. Suen

May 1985

AN OVERVIEW OF DIGITAL TECHNIQUES FOR PROCESSING SPEECH SIGNALS

Murat Kunt

Signal Procesing Laboratory

Swiss Federal Institute of Technology

16 Ch. de Bellerive

CH - 1007 Lausanne, Switzerland

and

Heinz Hugli

Mircrotechnique Institute

University of Neuchatel

Rue de la Maladière 71

CH - 2007 Neuchatel, Switzerland

ABSTRACT

This paper discusses major digital signal processing methods used in processing speech signals. Basic tools, such as the discrete Fourier transform, the z transform and linear filter theory are briefly introduced first. A general view of fast transformation algorithms and most widely used particular fast transformations are given. Linear prediction is then described with a particular emphasis on its lattice structure. A brief introduction to homomorphic processing for multiplied and convolved signals and to its applications in speech processing is given. Recalling some fundamentals of the speech signal, various speech analysis and synthesis models are described, showing which kind of processing methods are

NATO ASI Series, Vol. F16
New Systems and Architectures for Automatic Speech
Recognition and Synthesis. Edited by R. De Mori and C. Y. Suen
© Springer-Verlag Berlin Heidelberg 1985

involved. Finally, two aspects of speech recognition are presented: feature traction and pattern matching using dynamic time warping.

1. INTRODUCTION

Because of its multidisciplinary character, digital signal processing became increasingly important in a number of scientific and technical areas. Continuous interaction between the methods and the particular applications have led to an avalanche on both sides. Increasingly sophisticated methods are developed to fulfil wider needs of a large number of applications. There is no doubt that one of the major application areas of digital signal processing is speech signals. Over the last two decades, considerable effort has been devoted to analyse, code, model, synthesize and recognize speech signals. A dozen of books are already available, presenting various aspects of digital speech processing.

This paper attempts to give a tutorial review of major digital signal processing methods used in processing speech signals. Because of space limitations and the wide range of the subject, in depth treatments are omitted. Essence of the methods and insight for the interpretation of the results are indicated whenever possible. In section two, basic methods are defined such as the discrete Fourier transform, correlation functions, the z transform, the convolution, and the linear system theory. A general view of fast transformation algorithms is given, showing structures for hardware and software. Commonly used fast transformations are also briefly indicated. The last part of this section presents the linear prediction models and tools for one dimensional signals and introduces its lattice structure, a structure that is modular and hence suitable for various implementations. In section three, homomorphic processing of multiplied and convolved signals is discussed with particular emphasis on its applications to speech signals, particularly for deconvolution. Section four gives an overview of the speech analysis and synthesis methods using previously defined tools. Speech recognition is summarized in section five with a particular emphasis on pattern matching. The objective, in these last two sections, is to point out particular digital signal processing methods used for reaching the goals.

2.0 BASIC METHODS

In this section basic signal processing methods are defined and their use in speech processing are discussed. Analysis and synthesis tools for digital signals, such as the discrete Fourier transform and the correlation function, and for systems, such as the z transform and the convolution are described first. A brief discussion on linear filters and fast transformations is presented next. The section ends with a rather detailed description of linear prediction. For more detail, the reader may consult [1] and [2].

THE DISCRETE FOURIER TRANSFORM

The discrete Fourier transform of a digital signal x(k) is a complex series defined by:

$$X(n) = \sum_{k=k_0}^{k_0+N-1} x(k)exp(-j2\pi kn/N) \tag{1}$$

with n = -N/2, ..., N/2-1

In this definition, only N consecutive samples of the signal are used starting at k = k0. The series X(n) is periodical in n with a period of N. The integer variable n represents discrete frequencies. For example n = 0 is the DC component and n = N/2 is the folding frequency, i.e. half of the sampling rate.

The inverse transform is given by:

$$x(k) = (1/N) \sum_{n=-N/2}^{N/2-1} X(n)\ exp(j2\pi nk/N) \tag{2}$$

with k = k0, ..., k0 + N - 1

Eq. (1) is referred to as the analysis of the signal, whereas eq. (2) is used to synthesize the signal from its Fourier Transform. From the complex numbers X(n) two real sequences are obtained. The magnitude X(n) plotted as a function of n is the magnitude spectrum. The argument arg[X(n)] is the phase spectrum. They inform on the frequency distributions of complex exponential signals composing the analysed signal x(k). If the number of samples N is small compared to the total length of the signal, these spectra are called short term spectra. On a long signal, such as a speech signal, several short term spectra can be computed. Sections of the signal used in these computations may partially overlap or may be apart. If these spectra are plotted in three dimensions as a function of the frequency n and of the time (for example time instants corrresponding to the beginning of each signal section), the resulting surface is called spectrogram. It is usually represented as a black-and-white two level image on the (n,k) plane. Additional grey levels, if available, give more precise and detailed information on the frequency variations of various components of the signal. In section 1.6 fast algorithms for computing spectrograms will be discussed.

2.2 CORRELATION FUNCTIONS

The similarity of two signals x(k) and y(k) is measured by their cross correlation function defined by:

$$\varphi_{xy}(k) = \sum_{1=-\infty}^{+\infty} x(1) \ y(k+1) \tag{3}$$

For a given delay k of the second signal y(k) with respect to the first signal x(k), the cross correlation function is just the integral of the product of these two signals. It reaches its maximum value for the greatest similarity. If x(k) is identical to y(k), the cross correlation function is called autocorrelation function. It is given by:

$$\varphi_x(k) = \sum_{1=-\infty}^{+\infty} x(1)\ x(k+1) \tag{4}$$

Its maximum is at the origin $k = 0$. If this function is normalized by dividing it by the variance of the signal $x(k)$, the result is called correlation coefficient. Its values lie between +1 and -1.

An equivalent way of computing correlation functions is obtained by taking the discrete Fourier transform of both side of eq. (3) or eq. (4). One obtains respectively;

$$\Phi_{xy}(n) = X^*(n)\ Y(n) \tag{5}$$

and

$$\Phi_x(n) = X^*(n)\ X(n) = |X(n)|^2 \tag{6}$$

These results can be proved easily. They are left as exercises to the reader.

2.3 THE z TRANSFORM

The discrete Fourier transform is a very powerful tool for analysing and synthesizing signals. It is not, however, suitable for studying signal processing systems. A more general transformation is needed. The z transform fulfils this need and becomes identical to Fourier transform in a particular case. The z transform of a signal is defined by:

$$X(z) = \sum_{k=-\infty}^{+\infty} x(k)\ z^{-k} \tag{7}$$

where z is a complex variable. A power series, such as this one, may not converge for all the possible values of z. The area of the complex plane z containing all the values for which eq. (7) converges is called convergence region.

The inverse transform is a complex integral given by:

$$x(k) = (1/2\pi j) \oint X(z) \, z^{k-1} \, dz \tag{8}$$

The integration contour must lie in the convergence region. Usually, the inverse z transform is computed by using partial fraction decomposition in which the inverse transform of each term is known. Since this transformation is linear, the sum of these partial signals gives the desired result.

It is interesting to note that if the z transform is computed on the unit circle of the z plane, i.e. for $|z| = 1$, the result is the continuous Fourier transform:

$$X(z)\Big|_{|z|=1} = X(f) = \sum_{k=-\infty}^{+\infty} x(k) \, \exp(-j2\pi kf) \tag{9}$$

If now, the continuous variable f is replaced by a discrete variable n with $f_n = n\Delta f = n/N$, or equivalently, if the z transform is computed on equally spaced points of the unit circle, the result is the discrete Fourier transform (1).

2.4 CONVOLUTION

Let us consider a signal processing system S which acts on the input signal x(k) to produce an output signal y(k):

$$y(k) = S[x(k)] \tag{10}$$

If it is required from the system to be linear, the superposition principle is satisfied, i.e.:

$$S[ax_1(k) + bx_2(k)] = aS[x_1(k)] + bS[x_2(k)] \tag{11}$$

An additional constraint may be required to be shift invariant. In this case, if the response to x(k) is y(k), the response to x(k-k0) is y(k-k0). Linear shift invariant systems are completely specified with their response to a unit sample, i.e. by their impulse response g(k). To see this, let us write the input signal in terms of unit samples:

$$x(k) = \sum_{1=-\infty}^{+\infty} x(1) \ d(k-1) \tag{12}$$

where d(k) is the unit sample having the value 1 at the origin k=0 and 0
elsewhere. Using eq. (12) as the input signal, we have:

$$y(k) = S[x(k)] \quad = \sum_{1=-\infty}^{+\infty} x(1) \ S[d(k-1)]$$

$$= \sum_{1=-\infty}^{+\infty} x(1) \ g(k-1] = x(k) * g(k) \tag{13}$$

where g(k) is the response of the system to d(k). Eq. 13 is called convolution
product or convolution. Notice the similarity between correlation and convolution.

By taking the Discrete Fourier transform of both sides of eq. (13) a simpler
form is obtained:

$$Y(n) = X(n) \ G(n) \tag{14}$$

where G(n) is the frequency response of the system or the discrete Fourier
transform of its impulse response.

A similar result is obtained by taking the z transform of both sides of eq.
(13):

$$Y(z) = X(z) \ G(z) \tag{15}$$

where G(z) is the transfer function of the system.

2.5 LINEAR FILTERS

A linear shift invariant system with an impulse response g(k) is a filter. This terminology results directly from eq. (14). Since X(n) and the frequency response G(n) are simply multiplied, the selection of a particular function G(n) may attenuate or amplify some frequency components of the input signal to the detriment of others. For example, if G(n) is zero beyond a certain value of n, the output signal will not have any components at these frequencies. These components are filtered by the system.

Digital filters are divided into two broad classes depending on their impulse response. If the length of the impulse response is finite, i.e. if g(k) has only a finite number of non zero samples, the filter is called Finite Impulse Response (FIR) filter. In contrast, if the length of the impulse response is infinite, the filter is called Infinite Impulse Response (IIR) filter.

There are three equivalent ways of implementing a digital filter: 1) By convolution, using eq. (13) with finite number of samples. 2) By discrete Fourier transform, using eq. (14) and then taking the inverse transform of Y(n). 3) By using a difference equation of the following type

$$\sum_{n=0}^{N} a(n)\ y(k\text{-}n)\ =\ \sum_{m=0}^{M} b(m)\ x(k\text{-}m) \tag{16}$$

Eq. (16) seems to come out of the blue, but it is not. It is simply the inverse z transform of eq. (15) where the transfer function G(z) is a quotient of the polynomials in z, i.e..:

$$G(z)\ =\ \frac{\displaystyle\sum_{m=0}^{M} b(m)\ z^{-m}}{\displaystyle\sum_{n=0}^{N} a(n)\ z^{-n}} \tag{17}$$

Almost every transfer function can be written in this form. The rare cases where this is not possible, an approximation in the form of eq. (17) can be established by choosing N and M large enough. FIR filters are usually implemented using the convolution eq. (13). It is a simple form which can be analyzed easily. In contrast IIR filters are more suitable for a difference equation. In this case some cares must be taken. In particular, if the dynamic range of the input signal is bounded, it is desirable for the dynamic range of the output signal to be also bounded. Filters of this type are stable filters. Unstable filters do not produce any useful output, because the output signal diverges continuously.

So far, the filters that are described were shift invariant. Their characteristics (impulse response or frequency response or the coefficients of the difference equation) do not vary in time. These filters are convenient for processing stationary signals, i.e. signals whose statistical characteristics do not vary in time also. For nonstationary signals, however, such as the speech signal, it might be desirable to vary the characteristics of the filters. In this case, these filters are called time varying or adaptive. Rules must be established, of course, to find the new characteristics. Often, these rules are derived from the input signal itself, after detecting changes in its characteristics.

The main problem in filtering is to find samples of the desired impulse response or the coefficients of the differences equation in accordance with the filtering requirements. Methods for designing FIR and IIR filters are quite different. They have been investigated quite extensively over the last two decades. Because of their variety and the complexity of some of them, they will not be discussed in this text. The reader may consult [1] or [3] for detailed discussion of the subject. Presently, research efforts in digital filtering are rather oriented into implementation technologies such as VLSI and into multi-dimensional filtering. A brief discussion is included herein to emphasize basic problems related to the design and to the structures of digital filters.

When filtering is required, the frequency response of the desired filter is often a binary function: all the components within a frequency band should be completely attenuated and others in a different band should not be modified at all. Accordingly, the frequency response is a binary function switching between 0 and 1 on each cutoff frequency. These responses are impossible to match in practice. That is why they are called ideal frequency responses or ideal filters. Implementable filters can only approximate this behaviour according to an error criterion. Fig. 1 indicates major ideal frequency responses. In Fig. 2 tolerances

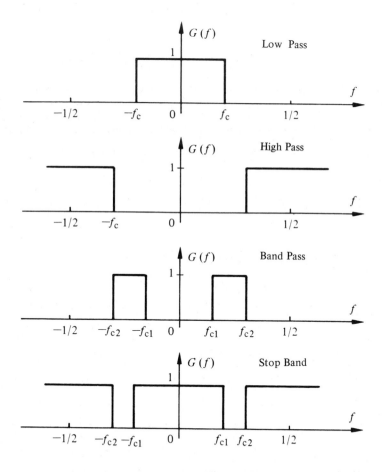

Fig. 1   Ideal frequency responses

are shown for a high pass filter. Instead of an ideal constant 1 in the passing band, oscillations within a band whose width is controlled by the parameter δ_2

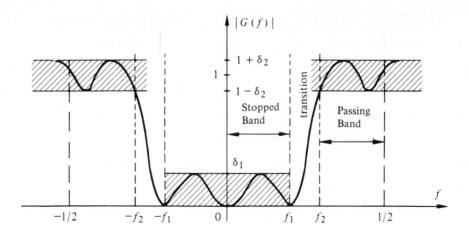

Fig. 2   Tolerance bands for a high pass filter

are tolerated.   Similarly, in the stopped band, other oscillations are tolerated as regulated with the parameter δ_1.   Finally, the transition between these two bands cannot occur at a unique frequency fc, but over a small frequency interval controlled with f1 and f2.   Algorithms are then designed to find the impulse response or the transfer function of an implementable filter whose frequency response falls within this tolerance band.

Fig. 3 shows the block diagram of an FIR filter.   This structure is quite simple and may conveniently be used with a variety of technologies (surface acoustic waves, switched capacitor circuits, charge coupled devices and VLSI).   If a similar effort is produced to draw a block diagram for a difference equation, a structure is obtained as shown in Fig. 4a.   This structure is not efficient because of the redundant number of delay elements.   With a little algebra on the difference equation, it is possible to show that this structure is equivalent to that shown in Fig. 4b in which the number of delay elements is minimized.   The big disadvantage of this last structure is its sensitivity to finite arithmetic.   In fact, all the coefficients a(n) and b(m) and the signal samples must be quantized at a finite number of levels.   Quantization error on one coefficient influence the entire frequency response and may unstabilize a stable filter.   For this reason, especially when the number of quantization levels are not too large, this structure is divided

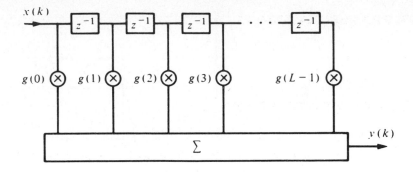

Fig. 3 Implementation structure for a transversal FIR filter

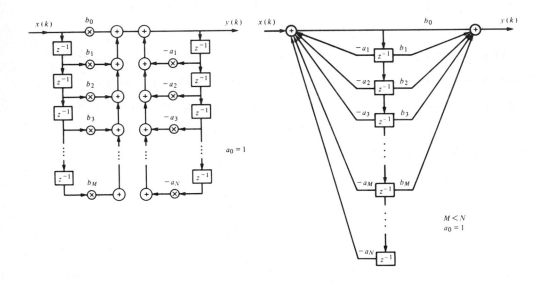

Fig. 4   Implementation structure for a recursive IIR filter. (a) structure
as derived directly from a difference equation. (b) one equivalent
canonical form.

into the cascade of first and second order sections.

2.6 FAST TRANSFORMATIONS

2.6.1 PRELIMINARY COMMENTS

Fast transformations play an increasingly important role in signal analysis, synthesis and coding. Since the reinvention of the fast Fourier transform in 1965, a number of complex methods that have not been used because of their computational cost, find increasingly wide applications and helped to solve various signal processing problems. With continuous progress in technology, a one-chip fast transform will soon find its socket in commonly used equipments.

What is meant by fast transformation is an algorithm which computes a linear transformation by using a minimum number of multiplications and additions. For example all the so-called fast Fourier transforms (FFT) compute the discrete Fourier transform given by eq. (1). Other linear transformations can also be computed with fast algorithms.

2.6.2 LINEAR TRANSFORMATIONS

A linear transformation of size N, transforms N samples of a signal into a set of N transform coefficients, each of them being a linear combination of the signal samples. From a mathematical point of view, a linear transformation can be expressed as:

$$X(n) = \sum_{k=0}^{N-1} a(n,k) \ x(k) \tag{18}$$

with $n = 0, ..., N-1$

where x(k) are the signal samples, a(n,k) the kernel of the transformation and X(n) the transformed coefficients. By comparing this equation with eq. (1), it can be shown that the discrete Fourier transform is a particular case of eq. (18) with $a(n,k) = \exp(j2\pi nk/N)$.

In order to compute each transformed coefficient independently from the others, the kernel a(n,k) is required to have othogonal or orthonormal rows, i.e.:

$$\sum_{k=0}^{N-1} a(n,k)a^*(m,k) = \hat{o}(n,m) = \begin{cases} 1 \text{ if } n = m \\ 0 \text{ otherwise} \end{cases} \tag{19}$$

where * represents the complex conjugate and ô(n,m) the Kronecker symbol. If X and x denote the coefficient and sample vectors respectively with:

$$X = (X(0), X(1), ..., X(N-1))^T \tag{20}$$

and

$$x = (x(0), x(1), ..., x(N-1))^T \tag{21}$$

Eq. (18) can be written as matrix vector product:

$$X = A x \tag{22}$$

where A is the matrix containing all the a(n,k). To recover the signal samples from the transform coefficients, A is required to be inversible. In this case, the following equation holds:

$$A A^{-1} = I \tag{23}$$

where I is the unit matrix. The matrix form of eq. (19) is:

$$A^H A = I \tag{24}$$

where H represents Hermitian transpose. Since A is unique, we have $A^H = A^{-1}$ and hence:

$$A A^H = I \tag{25}$$

If this last equation is written in series form, one obtains:

$$\sum_{n=0}^{N-1} a(n,k)\ a^*(n,1) = \delta(k,1) = \begin{cases} 1 \text{ if } n = m \\ \\ 0 \text{ otherwise} \end{cases} \tag{26}$$

This equation implies that the columns of A are orthonormal too. A matrix A for which eqs. (19) and (26) hold, is called unitary. The transformation (18) is then a change in the N dimensional coordinate system in which x and X are expresed as vectors.

2.6.3 FAST ALGORITHMS

If the number of multiplications and additions required by a linear transformation such as (18) is counted, it is found to be $Nc = N.N = N^2$. Then, how this number can be reduced to a more or less theoretical minimum ? In general, this number is the minimum, unless there is some redundancy in the kernel so that some entries can be computed as functions of the others. Fast transform algorithms exist only for those transform matrices which have a structured redundancy. The discrete Fourier transform is one example.

Two classes of fast algorithms can be established based on the factorization of the number of samples N. In the first class, a repetitive basic structure in the algorithm, and hence in the corresponding hardware, can be found if N is an integer power of a small number such as $N = 2^m$, or $N = \alpha^m$. These algorithms are more suitable for VLSI implementations. In the second class, algorithms are designed for N factorized as a product of a series of various integer numbers such as $N = N1.N2.N3....Nk$. In this case the basic structure exists but changes its size according to the particular Nj in the factorization.

To see how a structured redundancy can be introduced in a transform matrix, let us consider the successive tensorial product of a set of ρ by ρ basic matrices Bi. We have:

$$A_n = \overset{n-1}{\underset{i=0}{\boxtimes}} \; Bi \otimes Bn\text{-}2 \otimes \ldots \otimes B0 \tag{27}$$

where x represents the tensorial product defined by $C = A \otimes B$:

$$A = \begin{pmatrix} a11 & a12 \\ a21 & a22 \end{pmatrix} \qquad B = \begin{pmatrix} b11 & b12 \\ b21 & b22 \end{pmatrix}$$

$$C = \begin{pmatrix} a11b11 & a11b12 & a12b11 & a12b12 \\ a11b21 & a11b22 & a12b21 & a12b22 \\ a21b11 & a21b12 & a22b11 & a22b12 \\ a21b21 & a21b22 & a22b21 & a22b22 \end{pmatrix} \tag{28}$$

The matrix A_n is of size ρ by ρ with only $n\rho$ non redundant entries. It can be shown [1] that A_n obtained with successive tensorial products can be factored into n matrices Cj, each of size ρ by ρ and having only ρ non zero entries per line. This result is known as Good's theorem and is expressed by:

$$A_n = \overset{n-1}{\underset{j=0}{\prod}} \; Cj = Cn\text{-}1.Cn\text{-}2\ldots C0 \tag{29}$$

Eqs. (27) and (29) can be illustrated with the following example with $n = \rho = 2$.

$$A_2 = \begin{pmatrix} b_{1,0,0} & b_{1,0,1} \\ & \\ b_{1,1,0} & b_{1,1,1} \end{pmatrix} \otimes \begin{pmatrix} b_{0,0,0} & b_{0,0,1} \\ & \\ b_{0,1,1} & b_{0,1,1} \end{pmatrix}$$

$$= \begin{pmatrix} b_{1,0,0} & b_{1,0,1} & 0 & 0 \\ 0 & 0 & b_{1,0,0} & b_{1,0,1} \\ b_{1,1,0} & b_{1,1,1} & 0 & 0 \\ 0 & 0 & b_{1,1,0} & b_{1,1,1} \end{pmatrix} \cdot \begin{pmatrix} b_{0,0,0} & b_{0,0,1} & 0 & 0 \\ 0 & 0 & b_{0,0,0} & b_{0,0,1} \\ b_{0,1,0} & b_{0,1,1} & 0 & 0 \\ 0 & 0 & b_{0,1,0} & b_{0,1,1} \end{pmatrix} \tag{30}$$

A transformation using A_η as the transform matrix can be written as:

where the products should be carried out from right to left. A flow chart can be derived from eq. (31) which can be used to design various fast algorithms. Fig. 5 shows the chart of eq. (31). A basic structure is used twice. It is

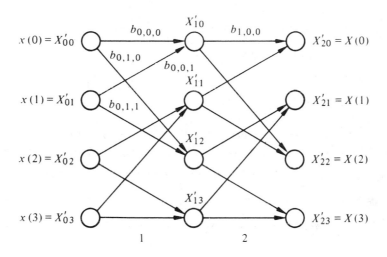

17

$$
\begin{pmatrix} X(0) \\ X(1) \\ X(2) \\ X(3) \end{pmatrix} = \begin{pmatrix} b_{1,0,0} & b_{1,0,1} & 0 & 0 \\ 0 & 0 & b_{1,0,0} & b_{1,0,1} \\ b_{1,1,0} & b_{1,1,1} & 0 & 0 \\ 0 & 0 & b_{1,1,0} & b_{1,1,1} \end{pmatrix} \cdot \begin{pmatrix} b_{0,0,0} & b_{0,0,1} & 0 & 0 \\ 0 & 0 & b_{0,0,0} & b_{0,0,1} \\ b_{0,1,0} & b_{0,1,1} & 0 & 0 \\ 0 & 0 & b_{0,1,0} & b_{0,1,1} \end{pmatrix} \begin{pmatrix} x(0) \\ x(1) \\ x(2) \\ x(3) \end{pmatrix} \quad (31)
$$

Fig. 5   Flow chart for a fast transform algorithm according to eq. (29).

possible to modify the flow charts provided that the information flow is not altered. For example, if the 2nd and 3rd lines of the rightmost matrix in (31) are swapped, the 2nd and the 3rd columns of the second matrix should also be permuted to keep the result unchanged. The corresponding flow chart is shown in Fig. 6. The basic structure of this flow chart is known as the butterfly operation which allows 'in-place' computation, i.e. the storage for input data is used for intermediary and final results.

In this scheme, the total number of multiplications and additions is reduced to $Nf = \rho N\log N$ if N is an integer power of ρ compared to $Nc = N$. For example, for $N = 1024$, which a very commonly used transform size, the saving is larger than a factor of 50 !

18

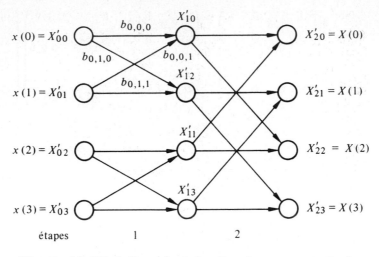

Fig. 6 Modified flow chart for 'in place computation'.

2.6.4 PARTICULAR FAST TRANSFORMS

Elaborating the general principles outlined in the previous paragraph, fast algorithms can be designed for the following particular transforms. Algorithms are not described due to the limited space of this text.

1) The discrete Fourier transform

Several fast algorithms exist for this transformation given by eq. (1). They are too specialized to be cited here. The reader may find details in [1] or [3].

2) The Hadamard transform

The Hadamard transform is perhaps the simplest transformation. Its transform matrix contains only +1's and -1's as entries. It is given by:

$$X(\beta) = (1/\sqrt{2}^{n}) \sum_{\alpha=0}^{N-1} (-1)^{\sum_{k=0}^{n-1} \alpha(k)\beta(k)} x(\alpha) \qquad (32)$$

with $\alpha \leftrightarrow \alpha(\text{n-1}) \ ... \ \ \alpha(1)\alpha(0)$

$\quad \beta \leftrightarrow \beta(\text{n-1}) \ ... \ \ \beta(1)\beta(0)$

and $\alpha(\text{k})$, $\beta(\text{k}) = 0$ or 1.

The coefficients $X(\beta)$ given by this equation are in the so-called natural order, as naturally given by the definition. They can be ordered in various ways such as bit-reversed order, sequency order or cal-sal order. Fast algorithms exist for each type ordering. A particular order is selected depending on the problem. For example, if even or odd symmetries are searched in the signal, cal-sal order is the appropriate ordering. If a parallel is made to the frequency as in Fourier transform, then sequency order should be used.

3)   The R transform

This transformation is almost identical to Hadamard transform except that absolute values are taken after each substraction in the Hadamard transform flow chart. Because of this nonlinearity, this transform has no inverse. An interesting property of this transform is that the transform coefficients remain unchanged under cyclic translation of the input samples.

4)   The Haar transform

A closed form analytical expression for this transform is cumbersome to write. The general form (18) remains valid here, where each a(k,n) are replaced by samples from the orthogonal set of Haar functions shown in Fig. 7.

5)   The sine transform

The closed form analytical expression of the sine transform is the following:

$$S(n) = \sum_{k=0}^{N-1} x(k) \ \sin[\frac{(k+1)(n+1)}{N+1} \ \pi] \tag{33}$$

A similar form can be used depending on the even or odd numbers involved. This transform, along with the cosine transform as defined below, are used often for speech coding.

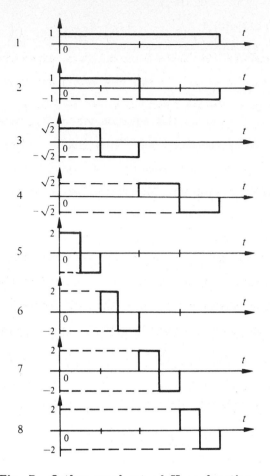

Fig. 7   Orthonormal set of Haar functions.

6)   The cosine transform

The cosine transform is defined by:

$$C(n) = \sum_{k=0}^{N-1} x(k) \cos[\frac{\pi}{2N} (2k+1)n] \tag{34}$$

Note that sine and cosine transforms are byproducts of the discrete Fourier transform. Because they require real coefficients, instead of complex exponentials used in Fourier series, they are faster to compute and hence more suitable for real-time applications.

7)   Slant transform.

As the Haar transform, the closed form analytical exprression for this transform is cumbersome to write.   In this case a(n,k) are replaced by samples from the orthogonal set of slanted functions shown in Fig. 8.

2.6.5 THE KARHUNEN LOEVE TRANSFORM

Although there is no fast algorithm for this transformation, it is useful to describe it briefly because, in many cases, it is considered as the 'best' linear transform; best meaning whatever the reader thinks it means.   The Karhunen Loeve transform, by definition, produces statistically uncorrelated cocfficients, i.e. :

$$E[X(n)X_*(m)] = \lambda_\eta \delta(n,m) \tag{35}$$

Substituting the general form (18) in (35), we have :

$$E[X(n)X_*(m)] = E[\ \sum_k a(n,k)\ x(k)\ \sum_l a_*(m,l)x_*(l)\ ]$$

$$= \sum_k \sum_l E[x(k)x_*(l)]\ a(n,k)\ a_*(m,l) = \lambda[\eta]\delta(n,m) \tag{36}$$

The expectation $E[x(k)\ x^*(l)]$ is, by definition, the general entry of the correlation matrix $\varphi_x(k,l)$ of the signal.   Eq. (36) is then :

$$\sum_k \sum_l \varphi_x\ (k,l)\ a(n,k)\ a^*(m,l) = \lambda_\eta \delta(n,m) \tag{37}$$

Comparing this result to eq. (19), we have :

$$\sum_k \varphi_x\ (k,l)\ a(n,k) = \lambda_\eta a(n,l) \tag{38}$$

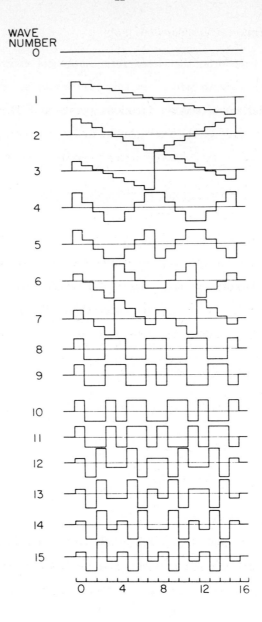

Fig. 8 Othonormal set of functions used in the slant transform.

In matrix notation, the equivalent form is :

$$\varphi_x \, A = \lambda_\eta A \qquad (39)$$

which is the classical eigen-vector, eigen-value problem. The solution of eq. (39) gives the transform matrix which guarantees (35). To derive this transformation, the correlation matrix $\varphi_x(k,l)$ of the signal must be estimated first. Then a linear tranform requiring $Nc = N^2$ operations should be computed. Because of this computational load, the Karhunen Loeve transform is not very often used in practice. It gives an indication about the upper bound of what other transform cited earlier, computationally more efficient, should attempt to reach for decorrelating data samples.

2.7 LINEAR PREDICTION

2.7.1 PRELIMINARY REMARKS

There are several ways to introduce the linear prediction. The one which will be discussed here is based on the convolution, the z transform and linear systems described previously. Let us consider a linear system and its associated equations :

$$y(k) = x(k)*g(k) = \sum_{-\infty}^{+\infty} g(1) \; x(k\text{-}1) \qquad (40)$$

and

$$Y(z) = X(z) \; G(z) \qquad (41)$$

along with the convergence region.

The transfer function $G(z)$ is then the ratio $Y(z)/X(z)$. The roots of $Y(z)$ is also the roots of $G(z)$. In contrast, the roots of $X(z)$ are the poles of $G(z)$. The desired transfer function is often so idealized that various approximation forms are the followings :

1) Polynomial approximation.

In this case, the practical transfer function is given by :

$$G(z) = \sum_{i=0}^{M} b(i) \, z^{-i} \tag{42}$$

Substituting this particular form in (41) and taking the inverse z transform of both side of this equation, we have :

$$y(k) = \sum_{i=0}^{M} b(i) \, x(k-i) \tag{43}$$

which is nothing else than a particular form of the convolution (12) for FIR filters or systems. Note that in this case, each output sample is a weighted sum of a finite number of past and present input samples. The system is entirely described by m coefficients $b(i)$. This type of system is also called all zero system since the transfer function has M zeros.

2) Inverse polynomial approximation

In this case, the practical transfer function is given by :

$$G(z) = \frac{1}{\displaystyle\sum_{j=0}^{N} a(j) \, z^{-j}} \tag{44}$$

It is possible to introduce a gain factor GO in (5) to replace the unity numerator. Substituting this particular form in (41) and taking the inverse z transform of both sides of this equation, we have :

$$y(k) = - \sum_{j=1}^{N} a(j) \ y(k\text{-}j) + x(k) \qquad (45)$$

assuming $a(0) = 1$.

which is a particular form of the difference equation (16) for IIR filters or systems. Note that in this case, each output sample is a weighted sum of a finite number of past output samples and the present input sample. The system is entirely described by N coefficients $a(j)$. These systems are also called all pole systems since the transfer function has N poles.

3)   Ratio of polynomials

In the most general case, the practical transfer function is a ratio of two polynomials in z^{-1}. This is the case discussed in section 2.5 leading to the difference equation :

$$y(k) = - \sum_{j=1}^{N} a(j) \ y(k\text{-}j) + \sum_{i=0}^{M} b(i) \ x(k\text{-}i) \qquad (46)$$

assuming again $a(0) = 1$

In this most general case, the output sample is a weighted sum of the past output samples plus a weighted sum of the present and past input samples. It is a mixed, pole-zero system.

In each of the preceeding approximations, the present output sample is expressed as a linear combination of past (and one present) samples. If the signal under investigation is associated to $y(k)$, or equivalently if it can be viewed as the output of a known linear system (coefficients $a(j)$'s and $b(i)$'s known) whose input is a known signal $x(k)$, eqs. (5), (6) or (7) can be used to predict the present sample of the output signal. Iterating these equations, the entire signal $y(k)$ can be predicted. Since this prediction is done as a linear combination of other samples, it is called linear prediction.

There are several possible framework to study in detail linear prediction such as covariance method, autocorrelation method, lattice structures, inverse filtering, spectral estimation, maximum likelihood method, dot product method, etc.

Mathematical developpments for each of them are quite simple. But each step of the computation offer a pletore of possible interpretations. This results in a very rich, precise, reliable and robust technique.

2.7.2 LINEAR PREDICTION WITH ALL POLE SYSTEMS

Linear prediction with all pole systems has the most widespread use because of the following general properties.

Let y(k) denote the signal under investigation. If N past samples of this signal are used to predict its present value, we have :

$$\hat{y}(k) = \sum_{i=1}^{N} a(i) \ y(k\text{-}i) \tag{47}$$

It is hoped that $\hat{y}(k) \approx y(k)$. The predicted signal $\hat{y}(k)$ is thus produced with a linear system excited by y(k) and whose transfer function is P(z) given by :

$$P(z) = \sum_{i=1}^{N} a(i) \ z^{-i} \tag{48}$$

This result is obtained by just taking the z transform of both sides of eq. (47) and solving for the transfer function.

The prediction error e(k) is simply the difference between y(k) and $\hat{y}(k)$:

$$e(k) = y(k) - \hat{y}(k) = y(k) - \sum_{i=1}^{N} a(i) \ y(k\text{-}i) \tag{49}$$

Again, by taking the z transform of both sides of this equation, we obtain the transfer function Q(z) of the linear system that produces the prediction error signal when excited with the signal y(k). We have :

$$Q(z) = 1 - \sum_{i=1}^{N} a(i) \ z^{-i} = 1 - P(z) \tag{50}$$

Let us assume now the hypothesis that the signal y(k) is produced according to a linear prediction model given by :

$$y(k) = \sum_{i=1}^{N} \alpha(i) \ y(k\text{-}i) + GO \ x(k) \qquad (51)$$

where the coefficients $\alpha(i)$'s are not known. The transfer function H(z) of this production model is obtained by taking the z transform of both sides of eq. (51) :

$$H(z) = \cfrac{GO}{1 - \sum_{i=1}^{N} \alpha(i) \ z^{-i}} \qquad (52)$$

If the signal y(k) is produced with eq. (51) and if $a(i) = \alpha(i)$ with $i = 1,...,N$, then Q(z) is the inverse filter of H(z) :

$$H(z) = \frac{GO}{Q(z)} \qquad (53)$$

In other words, systems characterized by the transfer functions H(z) and Q(z) have opposite effects. The first one produces the signal y(k) from a signal GO x(k), whereas the second produces the prediction error $e(k) = GO \ x(k)$ from the signal y(k). This discussion is illustrated in Fig. 9. In this context, the prediction problem consists in finding the set coefficients a(i) from y(k) in order to represent this signal in the best possible way — according to a criterion — by eq. (52). Since in this equation Q(z) is a denominator polynomial, we have an all pole system for H(z).

2.7.3 COMPUTING THE PREDICTION COEFFICIENTS

The prediction coefficients are obtained by minimizing the energy of the prediction error e(k). This energy is given by :

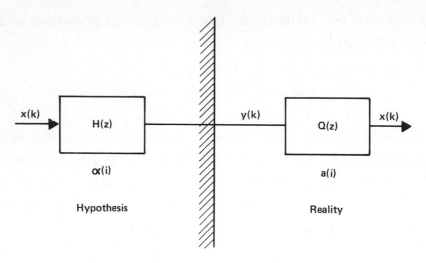

Fig. 9   Illustrating the prediction model.

$$W = \sum_{k=k_1}^{k_2} e^2(k) \tag{54}$$

Eq. (49) can be rewritten as :

$$e(k) = - \sum_{i=0}^{N} a(i) \ y(k\text{-}i) \tag{55}$$

with $a(0) = -1$.

Substituting (55) in (54), we have :

$$W = \sum_{k} \sum_{i} \sum_{j} a(i) \ y(k\text{-}i) \ y(k\text{-}j) \ a(j) \tag{57}$$

Defining the quadratic form

$$C(i,j) = \sum_{k=k_1}^{k_2} y(k\text{-}i) \ y(k\text{-}j) \tag{58}$$

we have

$$W = \sum_i \sum_j a(i) \; C(i,j) \; a(j) \tag{59}$$

Setting to zero all the derivaties of W with respect to a(i)'s :

$$C(0,j) = \sum_{i=1}^{N} a(j) \; C(i,j) \tag{60}$$

Particular cases are defined by constraining k_1, k_2 and y(k). For example, if C(i,j) is computed over an infinite interval ($k_1 = -\infty$ and $k_2 = +\infty$) and the signal y(k) is observed over a finite interal from k = 0 to k = N-1 (implicit rectangular window), the quadratic form C(i,j) becomes :

$$C(i,j) = \sum_{-\infty}^{+\infty} y(k\text{-}i) \; y(k\text{-}j) = \sum_{-\infty}^{+\infty} y(k) \; y(k+|i\text{-}j|)$$

$$= \sum_{-\infty}^{+\infty} y(k) \; y(k+|i\text{-}j|) = \varphi_y(|i\text{-}j|) \tag{61}$$

In this case C(i,j) is the autocorrelation function and the method used to solve (60) for a(i)'s is called autocorrelation method.

If $k_1 = M$ where M is the order of the predictor to start the prediction with M initial conditions and $k_2 = N\text{-}1$, C(i,j) behaves like a covariance matrix. The method using this case to solve (60) is called covariance method.

Different polynomials Q(z) are obtained with different methods and analysis conditions. The autocorrelation method guarantees in theory the stability of H(z) given by (52) but requires a window on the signal which reduces the frequency resolution. On the other hand, the covariance method does not require any window, but does not guarantee the stability. The lattice method overcomes these problems, provides a quite general solution and guarantees the stability.

2.7.4 LATTICE METHOD [2]

The lattice method is obtained by computing two predictions on the signal, one for the future (which will be denoted by +) and one for the past (which will be denoted by -). Fig. 10 shows a signal x(k) and its samples to illustrate these predictions. Starting with the sample x(k-m) the future prediction is

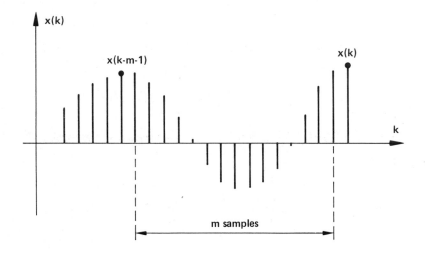

Fig. 10   Illustrating past and future predictions.

computed according to :

$$\hat{x}_{m+}(k) = - \sum_{i=1}^{m} a(m,i) \ x(k-i) \qquad (62)$$

where m is a parameter taking the values 1, 2, ..., M.   The prediction error is :

$$x_m^+(k) = x(k) - \hat{x}_{m+}(k) = \sum_{i=0}^{m} a(m,i) \ x(k-i) \qquad (63)$$

with a(m,0) = 1.   The past prediction is computed similarly :

$$\hat{x}_{m-}(k) = - \sum_{i=1}^{m} b(m,i) \ x(k-i) \qquad (64)$$

leading to the past prediction error :

$$x_m^- = x(k-m-1) - \hat{x}_{m-}(k) = \sum_{i=0}^{m} b(m,i)\ x(k-i) \tag{65}$$

with $b(m,m+1) = 1$.

Note that in eq. (65) the error is computed at $x(k - m - 1)$ to have causal systems. The criterion used is the simultaneous minimization of the past and future prediction error energies, computed over the interval $[k0,k1]$:

$$W_+(m) = \sum_{k=k_0}^{k_1} |x_m^+(k)|^2 \quad \text{and} \quad W_-(m) = \sum_{k=k_0}^{k_1} |x_m^-(k)|^2 \tag{66}$$

with $m = 1, ..., M$

The transfer functions of the future and past predictors (62) and (64) are given respectively by :

$$A_m(z) = \sum_{i=0}^{m} a(m,i)\ z^{-i} \quad \text{and} \quad B_m(z) = \sum_{i=0}^{m} b(m,i)\ z^{-i} \tag{67}$$

It can be shown [2] that the simultaneous minimization of prediction error energies given by (66) leads the orthogonality of the polynomials $A_m(z)$ and $B_m(z)$ to z^{-j} :

$$\{A_m(z),\ z^{-j}\} = 0 \quad \text{and} \quad \{B_m(z),\ z^{-j}\} = 0 \tag{68}$$

where $\{.,.\}$ represents the dot product.

The lattice structure is obtained by establishing iteratively the form of the polynomials $A_m(z)$ and $B_m(z)$ for $m = 1,...,M$ using two initial conditions $a(0,i) = b(0,i) = 1$. Iterations are governed by :

$$A_m(z) = A_{m-1}(z) + k_m B_{m-1}(z) \tag{69}$$

and by :

$$B_m(z) = z^{-1}[B_{m-1}(z) + k_m A_{m-1}(z)] \qquad (70)$$

where k_m is given by :

$$k_m = (-1/W_{m-1}) \sum_{k=k_0}^{k_1} x_{m-1}^+(k) x_{m-1}^-(k) \qquad (71)$$

and can be interpreted as partial correlation coefficient.

Taking the z transform of both sides of (63) and (65), substituting in this result (69) and (70) and taking the inverse z transform, we obtain the equations of the lattice structure :

$$x_m^+(k) = x_{m-1}^+(k) + k_m x_{m-1}^-(k) \text{ and } x_m^-(k) = x_{m-1}^-(k) + k_m x_{m-1}^+(k) \qquad (72)$$

Fig. 11 shows the lattice structure of a filter equivalent to the filter characterized by the transfer function $Q(z)$ given by (50) and producing the prediction error $e(k)$. Because of the modularity contained in it, this structure is very suitable for hardware implementations.

2.8 HOMOMORPHIC PROCESSING OF SIGNALS

Homomorphic processing is a convenient tool to be used for processing signals combined by convolution or multiplication (modulation). Let us assume that the observed signal is given by $z(k) = x(k) \cdot y(k)$ or $z(k) = x(k) * y(k)$ where $x(k)$ is the signal to be recovered. Clearly, in these cases linear filtering theory cannot be used, independently from its well known and powerful techniques. Two approaches can be envisioned. The first one consists in developing special methods to solve these problems, whereas the second attempts to transform these problems into other problems already solved, for example by using linear system theory. The second approach seems to be easier to develop and to apply, because it benefits from the large amount of available results in linear system

33

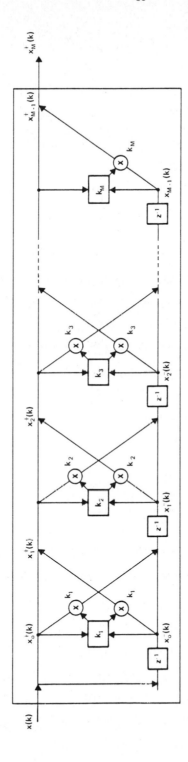

Fig. 11 Lattice structure for linear prediction

theory.

2.8.1 MULTIPLIED SIGNALS

If the observed signal is of the form :

$$x(k) = [x_1^{a_1}(k)] \ [x_{x[2]}^{a_2}(k)] \tag{73}$$

where a1 and a2 are two arbitrary constants, the well known way to transform this signal into a weighted sum is the use of logarithm. The real logarithm may be too restrictive because it can be used only for strictly positive signals or for signals which have been previously rescaled with the addition of a constant value to render them positive. The complex logarithm, however, can be used for bipolar or complex signals. In polar coordinates, a complex signal x(k) can be written as :

$$x(k) = |x(k)|\exp \ [jarg(x(k)]$$

$$= \exp[\ln|x(k)| + jargx(k)] \tag{74}$$

The complex logarithm, denoted by ln[.], is then :

$$\ln[x(k)] = \ln|x(k)| + jargx(k) \tag{75}$$

As defined, the complex logarithm has an important disadvantage. It is not a one-to-one transformation. Its argument is defined modul 2π, i.e. adding multiples of 2π to the argument in (75) does not change the result. In other words, the phase is wrapped around the unit circle. To remove this ambiguity from the argument of the complex logarithm, all the arguments to be used need to be defined as continuous functions of x(k). With a continuous argument, the complex logarithm becomes a one-to-one transform. If ever, the former form of the argument is required, it is sufficient to compute it modulo 2π. Usually, what is given in the first place is the argument modulo 2π. There are several algorithms to transform such an argument into a continuous function. This operation is known as phase unwrapping. Fig. 12 shows wrapped and unwrapped versions of an argument.

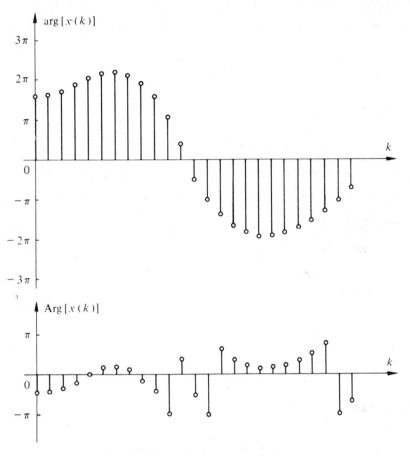

Fig. 12 Wrapped and unwrapped phase curve.

If the complex logarithm is now applied to the input signal x(k) given by eq. (73), the result is :

$$\hat{x}(k) = \ln[x(k)] = a1 \ln[x_1(k)] + a2 \ln[x_2(k)]$$

$$= a1 \; \hat{x}_1(k) + a2 \; \hat{x}_2(k) \qquad (76)$$

Notice that, now, the input signal x(k) is transformed into a signal $\hat{x}$ (k) which is a linear combination of other signals. Hence, according to the frequency content of $\hat{x}_1(k)$ and $\hat{x}_2(k)$, linear filtering may be used to recover for example $\hat{x}_1(k)$ or $\hat{x}_2(k)$ to the detriment of the other. Once the transformed version of the signal we are looking for is obtained, the signal itself is simply given by the inverse transform, i.e. :

$$x(k) = \exp[\hat{x}(k)] \qquad (77)$$

The results of this section show that with a nonlinear one-to-one transformation, it is possible to transpose a multiplicative combination of signals into an additive combination, a familiar situation in which linear system theory can be used. Fig. 13 shows the block diagram of a homomorphic system for multiplied signals.

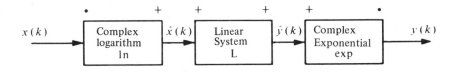

Fig. 13   Block diagram for homomorphic processing of multiplied signals.

As an example related to speech signals, let us consider the dynamic range handling. Whenever a speech signal changes its physical support, dynamic ranges on both supports should be measured and compared. Very often they are not compatible. It is therefore necessary to compress or expend the dynamic range before changing the recording media. The speech signal can be viewed as a low frequency envelope e(k) modulated with a high frequency carrier p(k). Hence, the input signal is :

$$x(k) = e(k) \cdot p(k) \qquad (78)$$

Since e(k) is strictly positive, the complex logarithm leads to :

$$\hat{x}(k) = \ln e(k) + \ln|p(k)| + j \arg[p(k)] \tag{79}$$

A linear filter can be used to compress or to expand the dynamic range of e(k) as given by :

$$\hat{y}(k) = a \ln e(k) + b \ln|p(k)| + jb \arg[p(k)] \tag{80}$$

In practice, $b = 1$ because the carrier does not influence too much the dynamic range of e(k). If a is larger than 1, the dynamic range is expended. In contrast, if a is less than 1, the dynamic range is compressed.

2.8.2 CONVOLVED SIGNALS

In this case, the observed signal x(k) is the convolution of two signals x (k) and x (k), the former being the signal of interest.

$$x(k) = \sum_{1= - \infty}^{+ \infty} x_1(1) \, x_2(k\text{-}1) = x_1(k) * x_2(k) \tag{81}$$

The problem is now to recover $x_1(k)$ from x(k). Remembering eq. (14), if the discrete Fourier transform is applied to both sides of eq. (81), the result is a simple product :

$$X(n) = X_1(n) \cdot X_2(n) \tag{82}$$

Notice that the use of the discrete Fourier transform for convolved signals, transform this problem into a problem that has just been solved, ie. the problem of multiplied signals. Since the discrete Fourier transform of a signal can be viewed as a complex signal, all that has to be done is to take the complex logarithm of both sides of eq. (82). We have :

$$\ln [X(n)] = \ln [X_1(n)] + \ln [X_2(n)] \tag{83}$$

Now, the convolved input signal is transformed into a linearly combined signal for which the linear system theory may again be applied. Notice also that, in constrast with eq. (76), in this case signals are function of the frequency and not of the time. If a linear filter is to be used for eq. (83), it should be a filter whose impulse response is expressed in the frequency domain and its frequency response in the time domain. This is rather an uncomfortable situation in which it is not difficult to mix up time and frequency. To overcome this difficulty, the inverse Fourier transform of both sides of eq. (83) can be taken, leading to :

$$\hat{x}(k) = \mathcal{F}^{-1} \ln [X(n)]$$

$$= \hat{x}_1(k) + \hat{x}_2(k) \tag{84}$$

which is now a time domain equation for linearly combined signals. Linear filtering can be applied to this equation to recover $\hat{x}_1(k)$ or $\hat{x}_2(k)$. Then, to transform everything back to the original representation, a discrete Fourier transform should be computed first. Its result is then exponentiated and inverse Fourier transformed. Fig. 14 shows the block diagram of a homomorphic system for convolved signal. Notice that solving eq. (81) for $x_1(k)$ is the inverse of convolution. This operation is commonly referred to as deconvolution. Homomorphic processing is one of the possible ways to deconvolve a signal. The inverse Fourier transform of the complex logarithm of the Fourier transform of a signal is called cepstrum; a word obtained by scrambling the letters of the word spectrum. It finds a rather large number of applications in speech processing such as echo removal, pitch detection, speech parameters estimation and restoration.

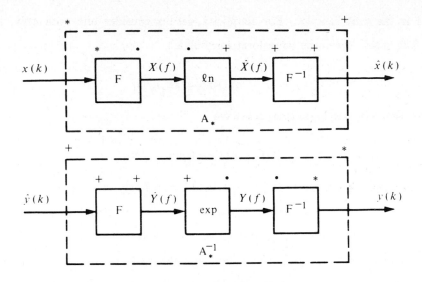

Fig. 14   Block diagram for homomorphic processing of convolved signals.

2.8.3 MAJOR APPLICATIONS OF THE CEPSTRUM

In this section three major applications of the cepstrum are given.

As a first case, let us consider a recorded signal x(k) resulting from several echos of the same initial signal $x_1(k)$:

$$x(k) = x_1(k) + \sum_{i=1}^{M} \alpha(i)\, x_1(k\text{-}ki) \tag{85}$$

where $\alpha(i)$'s are different attenuation factors and ki's the corresponding delays. Eq. (85) can be viewed as the convolution of the signal $x_1(k)$ given by :

$$x_2(k) = d(k) + \sum_{i=1}^{M} \alpha(i)\, d(k\text{-}ki) \tag{86}$$

where d(k) is the unit sample. For simplicity, let us consider one echo only, i.e. M = 1. The discrete Fourier transform of (86) is :

$$X_2(n) = 1 + \alpha(1)\exp[-j2\pi k_1 n/N] \qquad (87)$$

Taking the complex logarithm, we have :

$$X_2(n) = \ln[1 + \alpha(1)\exp(-j2\pi k_1 n/N)] \qquad (88)$$

This function is periodical of period $1/k_1$. Accordingly, the cepstrum $\hat{x}_2(k)$ will be nonzero only for integer multiples of k_1. In the cepstrum of the recorded signal, the non zero values of $\hat{x}_2(k)$ will appear as peaks. To surpress the echo, these peaks should be eliminated. This can be done with a comb filter applied to the cepstrum $\hat{x}(k)$ which recovers only the contribution of $\hat{x}_1(k)$. The inverse transform gives the original signal without any echo. Fig. 15 shows various functions involved in filtering the cepstrum for echo removal.

The second application of the cepstrum is its use in pitch detection and speech parametres estimation. A voiced portion of a speech signal can be modeled as shown in Fig. 16. The excitation signal e(k) containing a pulse train is filtered with a time-varying filter whose impulse response is h(k). A prefilter is also introduced to better represent vocal cords. Its impulse response is denoted by g(k). Accordingly, the produced speech s(k) is given by :

$$s(k) = e(k) * g(k) * h(k) \qquad (89)$$

over a short period of time (10-30 ms). To avoid discontinuities at the ends of each speech segment, a window function w(k) is introduced, producing the windowed speech x(k) :

$$\begin{aligned} x(k) &= s(k) \cdot w(k) \\ &= [e(k)*g(k)*h(k)]w(k) \end{aligned} \qquad (90)$$

Assuming that the window w(k) is smooth enough over the variation of g(k) * h(k), we have :

$$x(k) = e_w(k)*g(k)*h(k)$$

with

$$e_w(k) = e(k) \cdot w(k) \qquad (91)$$

If the pitch period is k0, then :

$$e_w(k) = \sum_{m=0}^{M-1} w(mk0) \, d(k-mk0) \qquad (92)$$

where M is the number of pulses seen through the window. The discrete Fourier transform of eq. (92) is given by :

$$E_w(n) = \sum_{m=0}^{M-1} w(mk0) \, \exp(-j2\pi nmk0/N) \qquad (93)$$

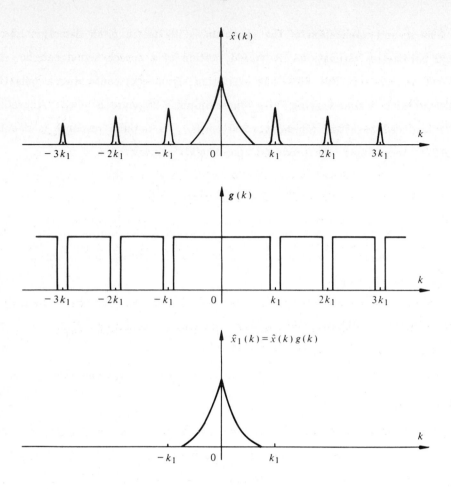

Fig. 15 Echo removal by deconvolution

This function is periodical with a period of 1/k0. The Fourier transform of the cepstrum ê(k) will also be periodical with the same period, since the logarithm is a memoryless monotonic function. Accordingly, the cepstrum ê(k) will be non zero only at integer multiples of k0. On the other hand, the duration of the composite impulse response g(k) ∗ h(k) does not exceed a few dozens of milli seconds. In the cepstral domain, the contribution of this composite impulse response is non negligible only over a short time interval around the origin. A high-pass time filter applied to the cepstrum will isolate e(k), whereas a low-pass time filter recovers the composite impulse response g(k) ∗ h(k). Fig. 17 illustrates, on a voiced speech section, various steps of this procedure.

The last application which will be described here concerns the restoration of old recordings. If s(k) denotes a speech signal or a song produced by an artist, its recorded version can be modeled as a convolution :

$$x(k) \; = \; s(k){*}g(k) \tag{94}$$

where g(k) is the impulse response of the recording system. The only assumption of this method is that the length of the impulse response g(k) is much shorter than that of the signal s(k). If the recording is done with old equipment and if there is no way to repeat the recording with modern equipment, it is necessary to recover s(k) to avoid the effects of the recording system contained in g(k). In general s(k) is a nonstationary signal which excludes the use of classical filtering techniques. Homomorphic deconvolution can be applied in this case also. Taking the complex logarithm of the Fourier transform of both sides of (94) leads to :

$$\ln[X(n)] \; = \; \ln[S(n)] \; + \; \ln[G(n)] \tag{95}$$

The difficulty of this problem is that not only s(k) is not known but also g(k), and hence G(n). A possible way to estimate G(n) is the use of eq. (95) for several, uncorrelated recordings, so that after averaging the right side of eq. (95) will converge to G(n). The problem is that it is difficult, if not impossible, to find a large number of old recordings recorded with the same equipment under

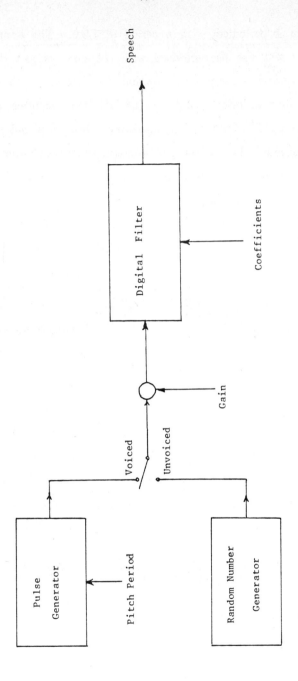

Fig. 16 Voiced speech production model

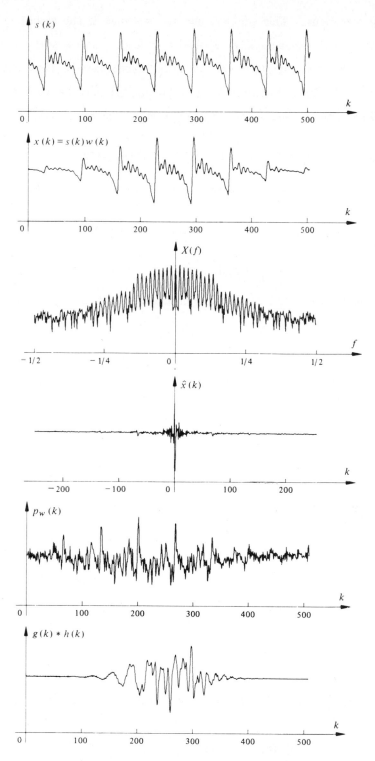

Fig. 17 Pitch period and parameter estimation

comparable conditions. This problem can be overcome if the recording $x(k)$ is divided into several segments $x_i(k)$ of moderate length, a few seconds for example, longer than that of the impulse response $g(k)$. Since each of these sections contains different $s(k)$'s, statistical filtering (averaging) may be applied. A given section $x_i(k)$ can be viewed as a windowed part of the signal $x(k)$, i.e. :

$$x_i(k) = w_i(k)\ x(k) = w_i(k)[s(k)*g(k)] \tag{96}$$

Assuming that the window is smooth enough over $g(k)$, we have :

$$x_i(k) = [w_i(k)s(k)] * g(k)$$

$$= s_i(k)*g(k) \tag{97}$$

The complex logarithm of the Fourier transform of both sides of eq. (97) leads to :

$$\ln[X_i(n)] = \ln[S_i(n)] + \ln[G(n)] \tag{98}$$

If M denotes the number of section $x_i(k)$ in $x(k)$, the average of both sides of eq. (98) gives :

$$(1/M) \sum_{i=1}^{M} \ln[X_i(n)] = (1/M) \sum_{i=1}^{M} [\ln[S_i(n)] + \ln[G(n)]] \tag{99}$$

The first term in the right hand side of eq. (99) is the estimate of the logarithmic power spectrum of $s(k)$. It can be estimated by using a contemporary recording of the same song or speech recorded with modern equipment. For these systems $G(n)$ is flat over a wide frequency range and equal to 1. So, if eq. (99) is used for a new recording, $\ln[G(n)]$ is zero and hence :

$$\frac{1}{M} \sum_{i=1}^{M} \ln[s_i(n)] = \ln[s(n)] \tag{100}$$

Substituting this in eq. (99) and solving with respect to $G(n)$, we have :

$$\ln[G(n)] = (1/M) \sum_{i=1}^{M} \ln[X_i(n)] - \ln[S(n)] \tag{101}$$

Since the logarithm used is complex, eq. (101) should be written for the magnitude and for the phase. Neglecting the phase as a first approximation, we have :

$$\ln|G(n)| = (1/M) \sum_{i=1}^{M} \ln|X_i(n)| - \ln|S(n)| \qquad (102)$$

The deconvolution is then obtained with a filter whose frequency response is the inverse of G(n), i.e. :

$$|G_r(n)| = 1/|G(n)| \qquad (103)$$

The phase of $G_r(n)$ can either be obtained with the Hilbert transform or be neglected. Stokham used this method to restore old recodings from E. Caruso done in 1907 and obtained spectacularly good results [4].

To conclude this paragraph, notice that all the applications of the cepstrum are related to the deconvolution problem. The same ideas are also used for two dimensional signals, i.e. digital images.

3. SPEECH ANALYSIS-SYNTHESIS

In this section, we present principles and models of speech analysis and synthesis and show the use of signal processing methods in this context. After recalling the fundamentals of the speech signal, the principle of speech analysis-synthesis and speech short-time processing, we treat speech analysis and synthesis in two main sections. The first of them, spectral analysis, explores spectral envelope analysis and synthesis in the various speech synthesis models. The second is dedicated to pitch detection and pitch period measurement.

3.1 SPEECH SIGNAL

The speech signal is modeled after the speech production mechanism.

3.1.1 SPEECH PRODUCTION

Major elements of the vocal apparatus are: the lung, the larynx and the vocal tract:

a)   The lung is the source of energy in form of air under pressure.

b)   The larynx consists of three cartilages supporting the vocal cords which is an opening of variable size through which air from the lung flows. Voiced sounds are produced by adjusting the vocal cords in a way that they vibrate and modulate the air flow. Unvoiced sounds are produced by keeping the vocal cords open.

c)   The vocal tract consists of: 1)   the pharynx and oral tract which together from a tube, 17 to 20 cm in length, whose cross section varies with jaw, tongue and lips position; and 2)   the nasal tract, 12 cm in length and of fixed cross section, which lies in parallel with the oral tract and is made active or inactive by displacing the velum.

Speech is the product of an original excitation, later modified by the vocal tract.

A first type of excitation, responsible for producing voiced sounds, is the airflow modulation produced by vibrating vocal cords. The excitation signal is periodic (pitch) and its spectrum displays harmonics whose power spectrum decreases with an average of 12 dB/octave.

A second type of excitation, responsible for producing unvoiced sounds, is the air turbulence provoked by a constriction somewhere in the vocal tract. The signal has noise characteristics.

The vocal tract acts as a resonator and modifies the excitation signal. For voiced sounds, the vocal tract usually shows 4 resonances which are called formants and which characterize the sound. Fig. 10 shows a typical spectrum of a voiced sound where both the periodic excitation spectrum and the formants are visible. When the nasal tract is also active then the overall transfer function also includes zeros call antiformants.

3.1.2 SPEECH MODEL

All speech production models have in common the separation of excitation features, which are accounted for by two pulse train generators and resonator features, which are accounted for by a time-varying linear system. Thus speech production is modeled after Fig. 18.

3.1.3 SPEECH ANALYSIS AND SYNTHESIS

The basic schema of a vocoder is given in Fig. 19. There are four main functions. The analysis functions are: detection and measurement of the pitch of fundamental frequency F_o, and analysis of the spectral envelope. The two synthesis functions are: generation of the excitation and restitution of the spectral envelope. Next sections will describe this function more in detail. However, compression of the data flow between analyser and synthesiser is not described further.

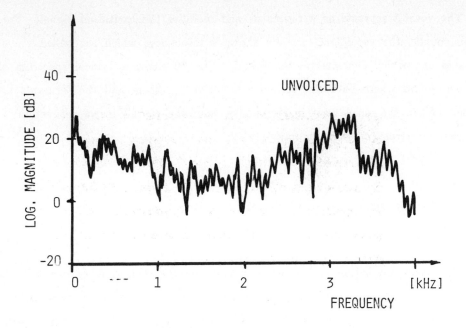

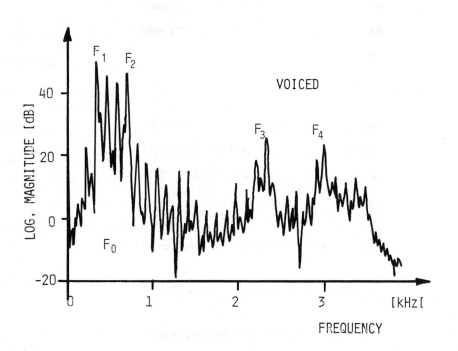

Fig. 18 Spectrum of a voiced sound

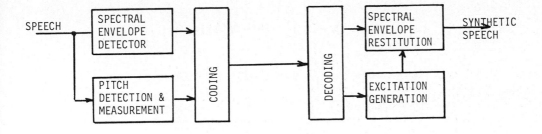

Fig. 19   Main functions of speech analysis and synthesis

3.1.4 SHORT-TIME SPEECH ANALYSIS

The properties of the speech signal change relatively slowly with time.   This leads to short-time processing methods in which speech segments called frames are isolated and processed as if they had fixed properties.   Such segments can be isolated by multiplication with a window sequence w(k) positioned at a location k = ℓ.   Windowing the speech signal x(k) using the time-domain window w(k) leads to the analysis sequence:

$$x_\ell(k) \; = \; x(k) \cdot w(\ell\text{-}k) \tag{104}$$

Two examples of short-time parameters are given.   The short-time average magnitude is defiend by :

$$M(1) \; = \; \sum_{k=\ell}^{\ell+N\text{-}1} x(k) \cdot w(\ell\text{-}k) \tag{105}$$

The short-time average zero-crossing rate is defined by :

$$Z(k) = \sum_{k=\ell}^{\ell+N-1} c(k) \cdot w(\ell-k) \qquad (106)$$

where : $c(k) = \begin{cases} 1 & \text{if } sign(x(k)) \neq sign(x(k-1)) \\ 0 & \text{else} \end{cases}$

3.2 SPECTRAL ANALYSIS-SYNTHESIS

We describe here the analysis and restitution of the spectral envelope. The various interpretations of short-time Fourier analysis are given and three vocoders are described.

3.2.1 SHORT-TIME FOURIER ANALYSIS

Three interpretations of the short-time Fourier transform are given. First it is defined as the normal Fourier transform of a sequence which is limited in time. Using the window sequence $w(k)$ which is 0 outside the significant range $k = 1..N$, we find, using the definition of eq. (1), the short-time Fourier transform in its discrete form:

$$X_\ell(n) = \sum_{k=\ell}^{\ell+N-1} w(\ell-k) \cdot x(k) \cdot exp(-j2\pi kn/N) \qquad (107)$$

with : $n = -N/2, ..., N/2-1$

where N is the maximum width of the window sequence $w(k)$. Note that it is a function of both the discrete frequency n and the position ℓ of the window. A first interpretation of $X(n)$ is as follows. Eq. (107) can be seen as the DFT of a sequence $w(\ell-k) \cdot x(k)$ which itself, according to eq. (104) is the $x(k)$ sequence observed through a window with impulse response $w(k)$ displaced at position ℓ.

The second interpretation derives directly from eq. (107) by considering it as the convolution defined in eq. (3).

$$X_\ell(n) = [x(k) \cdot \exp(-j2\pi kn/N)] * w(k) \tag{108}$$

We thus obtain $X_\ell(n)$ by cascading a modulation of $x(k)$ by $\exp(-j2\pi kn/N)$ and a filter with impulse response $w(k)$.

To catch the third meaning of $X_\ell(n)$, we transform the equation above into the equivalent form:

$$X_\ell(n) = \exp(-j2\pi kn/N) \sum_{k=\ell}^{\ell+N-1} x(\ell-k) \cdot w(k) \cdot \exp(j2\pi kn/N) \tag{109}$$

which interprets as the result of modulating $(\exp(-j2\pi kn/N))$ the output of a complex bandpass filter whose impulse response is $w(k) \exp(j2\pi kn/N)$. The practical consequence of this interpretation is that $X_\ell(n)$ can be obtained by filtering $x(k)$ with a bandpass filter followed by a modulator. Moreover, in vocoders we are satisfied with the amplitude of the complex value $X_\ell(n)$. Using equation above, we find :

$$|X_\ell(n)| = |\sum_{k=\ell}^{\ell+N-1} x(1-k) \cdot w(k) \cdot \exp(j2\pi kn/N)| \tag{110}$$

which now has the following interpretation: $|X_\ell(n)|$ is obtained by cascading a bandpass filter with impulse response $w(k)\exp(j2\pi kn/N)$ and a RMS circuit. Also, it can be shown that an equivalent result is obtained if an envelope detector is used instead of the RMS circuit.

As a way to compare the interpretations given, we emphasize the respective role of the window in each form. It appears as a simple window function $w(1-k)$ first, then as (low-pass) impulse response $w(k)$ and finally as (bandpass) impulse response $w(k)\exp(j2\pi kn/N)$.

3.2.2 ANALYSIS AND SYNTHESIS METHODS

Spectral analysis is the transform of eq. (107). As shown right above, it can be realized either by linear filtering of x(k) according to eq. (110) or by FFT of w(1-k) · x(k).

Spectral synthesis is given by the inverse DFT of X (n) according to eq. 2. Three synthesis methods are now shown. To each corresponds a particular vocoder structure.

3.2.3 CHANNEL VOCODER

Principally, the speech spectrum is divided by a number of continguous bandpasses at the input and reconstructed by addition at the output. A channel is affected to each bandpass.

Practically, either a filter bank to implement digital filtering or FFT to implement DFT is being used both for analysis and synthesis. An other practical aspect is the division of the spectrum in several bands. Both uniform and non-uniform spectrum division is used. In the case of non-uniform spectrum division, the channel bandwidth increases with frequency (exponential law for instance) to account for the characteristics of the human ear.

Fig. 20 shows the principle of a channel vocoder using filter banks both for analysis and synthesis.

55

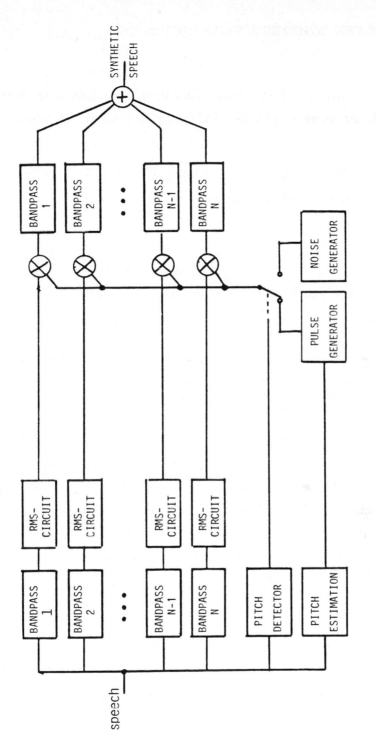

Fig. 20 Channel vocoder

3.2.4 FORMANT VOCODER

Rather than dividing the spectrum envelope in fixed contiguous bandpasses, this approach characterizes the spectral envelope by more specific information like the position, the amplitude and width of the formants. A better speech quality or better compresion factor is expected by this more specific approach.

Starting from a speech synthesis model which uses a cascade of digital resonators as a time-varying digital filter, the basic step is to find the model parameters fulfilling the following criteria: best match of the spectral envelope found by analysis, with the DFT of the system impulse response. For example, a system can use a 5 pole digital filter to account for voiced sounds and a 1 pole-1 zero digital filter for unvoiced sounds. The variable filter parameters are the pole positions F_1, F_2, F_3 for the voiced component and both the pole and zero position Fp and Fz for the unvoiced component.

A first analysis method directly finds the first three maxima of the short-time spectrum by simple peak detection. Practically, a rather large number of channels (30 to 50) is required in order to obtain a high enough spectral resolution to make those maxima detectable. Note that some kind of smoothing must be applied to the spectrum in order to remove the periodic pitch structure. By one method call cepstral smoothing, the pitch signal is filtered out from the cepstrum x (k).

A second, more simple analysis method divides the spectrum in three analysis channels by bandpass-filtering. The bandpasses are designed such as to capture each, one of the first formants F_1, F_2, F_3 and also, they are selected broad-banded enough to allow a sufficiently large variation of formant position. Then, the exact formant position and power is obtained by measurement of both the average zero-crossing rate eq. (106) as well as the average power in each channel.

A third method, called analysis-by-synthesis, proceeds by successive approximation. The model parameter are varied as long as to get, at the output, a good approximation of the input function.

Fig. 21 shows also an example of pole-zero locations for the two time-varying digital filters of the formant synthesizer.

3.2.5 LINEAR PREDICTION VOCODER

To remedy certain shortcomings encountered with the formant synthesizer, the filter model is now changed in that the cascade of second-order filters is replaced by a higher order linear system. The purpose of this system is to model together the excitation pulse shape, the vocal tract and other effects as well. The transfer function of the filter is of the form:

$$H(z) = \frac{1}{1 - \sum_{i=1}^{M} a_i \cdot z^{-i}} \tag{111}$$

where M is the filter order, typical values being 10 or 12; and $\{a_i, i = 1 \cdot M\}$ are the model parameter called the predictor coefficients. Their determination was shown in section 2.7.3.

Fig. 22 illustrates the corresponding linear predictive (LPC) synthesizer.

3.3 PITCH DETECTION AND PITCH PERIOD ESTIMATION

The purpose of pitch analysis is to provide the two pitch dependant parameters of the model: excitation mode (voiced/unvoiced) and pitch period value. The corresponding analysis procedures are pitch detection respectively pitch period estimation.

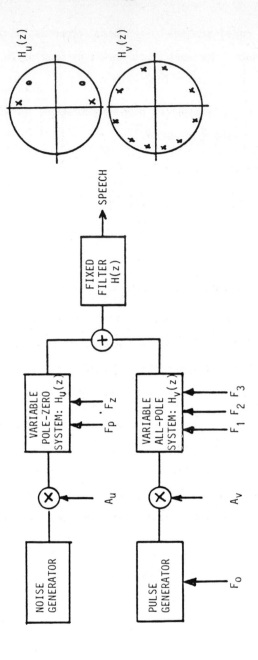

Fig. 21 Formant vocoder and typical pole-zero diagrams

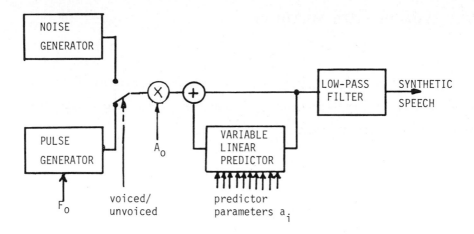

Fig. 22   Linear prediction synthesizer

Both because the human ear is very sensitive to the pitch and because the pitch contributes much to the naturalness of speech, correct pitch analysis and restitution is decisive for the quality of synthesized speech.

Pitch analysis methods are numerous and various and practical algorithms often combine seveal of them.   For a comparison see for example [6] or [7].   We restrict this presentation to the basic methods.   Also, note that for most practical methods, the effective processing is preceded by preprocesing like normalization, low-pass filtering or clipping and followed by postprocessing like smoothing, correction etc.

Pitch detection method can be divided in three categories: time-domain, frequency domain and hybrid methods.

3.3.1 TIME DOMAIN METHODS

The basic idea is to preprocess the quasiperiodic speech signal such as to reduce sufficiently the formant structure and then to use simple time domain methods to estimate the pitch.

3.3.1.1 ZERO CROSSING

The principle is: low-pass filtering followed by zero-crossing (eq. 106) measurements. A particularity however is that the useful pitch and the filter cut-off frequency are related, with the practical consequence of a limited pitch frquency range for a given filter configuration. To remedy that, adaptive filtering as a function of F can be performed.,

3.3.1.2 PEAK AND VALLEY MEASUREMENTS

The principel is: low-pass filtering followed by peak and valley detection and a final decision for the choice of the pitch. Practically, there are 6 parallel detectors: peak, valley, peak-to-valley, valley-to-peak, peak-to-previous-peak and valley-to-previous-valley detectors. The decision is made to guarantee correct pitch measurement in the case of a signal with both fundamental and second harmonic.

3.3.1.3 AUTOCORRELATION FUNCTION

This method uses the property of autocorrelation: the autocorrelation function of a periodic signal is periodic with the same period, i.e. it will show a peak at a lag value equal to the signal period. Further, the peak has same amplitude as the peak at the origin. For quasiperiodic signals, the peak is slightly reduced.

Practically, a window (eq. 104) is applied to the speech signal and the autocorrelation function from eq. 4 is computed:

$$\varphi_\ell(m) = \sum_{k=\ell}^{\ell+N-1} x(k) \cdot w(\ell\text{-}k) \cdot x(k+m) \cdot w(\ell\text{-}k\text{-}m) \qquad (112)$$

which can be computed directly or by FFT (see eq. 6). The lag value m corresponding to the first maximum of $\varphi_\ell(m)$ indicates the pitch period value.

The performance of this method is significantly improved by a non-linear preprocessing called central clipping which sets small relative values to 0.

Computation of the autocorrelation function can be simplified by quantizing the signal to the three levels +1, 0, -1. This eliminates all multiplications encountered with the normal computation of eq. 4 or 6.

3.3.1.4 AVERAGE MAGNITUDE DIFFERENCE FUNCTION

As the one just described, this method is a simple to implement approach to pitch detection. Compared to the autocorrelation function, it uses subtractions instead of multiplications. It takes advantage of the fact that for a periodic signal, $x(k)\text{-}x(k+p) = 0$ when p is a delay equal to one or several periods. The average magnitude difference function (AMDF) thus writes:

$$\text{AVDF(m)} = \sum_{k=\ell}^{\ell+N-1} [x(k) \cdot w(\ell-k) - x(k+m) \cdot w(\ell-k-m)] \qquad (113)$$

The detected pitch period is the lag value m for the first minimum of AVDF(m).

3.3.2 SPECTRAL METHODS

Frequency-domain pitch detectors use the property that, if the signal is periodic in time, then the frequency spectrum of the signal will consist of a series of impulses at the fundamental frequency and its harmonics. This harmonic structure, only present with voiced sounds, must be detected and the frequency interval between two lines must be measured.

3.3.2.1 CEPSTRUM METHOD

As we have seen, a basic step of the cepstrum computation is the logarithmic transform of the amplitudes in the spectral domain. The speech spectrum X(n) which is the product of the excitation spectrum E(n) and the vocal tract spectrum R(n) is thus transformed in the sum of two signals:

$$\ln|E(n) \cdot R(m)| = \ln|E(n)| + \ln|R(n)| \qquad (114)$$

After inverse DFT we get the cepstrum $\hat{x}(k)$ which now, is the sum of the cepstra of e(k) resp. r(k): $\hat{x}(k) = \hat{e}(k) + \hat{r}(k)$. As the excitation e(k) is periodic, its cepstrum $\hat{e}(k)$ will display a strong peak, indicating the position of the pitch period, whereas the slow and aperiodic oscillation r(k) give raise to a much flatter curve.

Practical cepstral computation requires a good resolution in the spectral domain. Therefore difficulties arise for small values of F_o where the spectral lines are close to each other.

3.3.2.2 COMB FILTERING IN THE SPECTRAL DOMAIN

The principle is to filter the short-time speech spectrum $X_\ell(n)$ with a variable comb filter in the spectral domain. The comb filter is a function $C(n,n_o)$ where n_o is the interval between two teeth of the comb. The method looks for the maximum of the cross-correlation when the teeth interval n_o is varied. When this maximum is reached, the comb lies exactly on the harmonic lines of $X_\ell(n)$, and thus: $F_o = n_o$. This writes formally:

$$F_o = \underset{n_o}{\operatorname{argmax}} \left[\sum_{n=0}^{N/2-1} X_\ell(n) \cdot C(n,n_o) \right] \tag{115}$$

3.3.3 HYBRID METHOD

Hybrid methods use features of both the time- and the spectral domain.

3.3.3.1 SIMPLIFIED INVRESE FILTERING TECHNIQUE

The basic idea here is to first eliminate or reduce the effect on x(k) of the spectral envelope (which is a characteristic of the vocal tract, not the pitch) and then to detect the pitch by the autocorrelation method. Because the second of these two steps is described above, we concentrate on step one only.

Here then, the way adopted eliminates the effect of the spectral envelope by flattening it, which is also called signal whitening. Practically, this can be done in the time-domain by inverse filtering, i.e. by a filter which whitens the spectrum of x(k).

3.3.4 CONCLUSION

Basic pitch detection methods have been presented to give the reader an idea of principles and processing methods involved. To the subject, we keep in mind that pitch detection remains a difficult task.

4. SPEECH RECOGNITION

This section presents two aspects found in most speech recognition application: feature extraction and pattern matching.

4.1 FEATURE EXTRACTION

The most versatile methods can and have been used to extract features from the speech signal. Because most of them have already been encountered in this text, we give here just a list of feature extraction methods.

Time-domain methods:

— Average energy or amplitude
— Average zero-crossing rate
— Autocorrelation function

— Parcor or LPC coefficients

— Voiced/unvoiced, pitch value

— Amplitude distribution function

Transform methods:

— Fourier spectrum

— Hadamard transform

— Cepstrum coefficient

— Formants

4.2 PATTERN MATCHING

In either speech or speaker recognition, the basic principle of recognition used is pattern matching: the unknown speech pattern is compared to already available speech reference patterns, then, the best match is detected. If we denote $D(T,Ri)$ the pattern distance measure for the unknown test pattern T and a reference pattern Ri, $i = 1...I$, then the recognition decision is:

$$i * = \underset{i}{\text{argmin}} \ [D(T,Ri)] \tag{116}$$

Considering speech patterns as time sequence of feature vectors, i.e.:

$$T = \underline{t}(1), \ \underline{t}(2), \ ..., \ \underline{t}(m), \ ..., \ \underline{t}(M) \tag{117}$$

$$Ri = \underline{r}_i(1), \ \underline{r}_i(2), \ ..., \ \underline{r}_i(n), \ ..., \ \underline{r}_i(N) \tag{118}$$

and defining the distance measure of two feature vectors:

$$d_i(m,n) = \delta[\ \underline{t}(m),\underline{r}_i(n)\ ] \tag{118}$$

where δ is some adequate distance function, we will present the basic methods for matching the sequences.

The most obvious method establishes a one-to-one correspondence between both sequences (which thus must be of equal length M = N) so that the overall distance is :

$$D(T,Ri) = \sum_{i=1}^{M} d_i(m,m) \qquad (119)$$

4.3 DYNAMIC TIME WARPING

The Dynamic time Warping (DTW) algorithm provides a procedure to align optimally in time the test and reference sequence and to find the optimal distance D (T,Ri) associated to the optimal warping path. The algorithm uses the principle of Dynamic Programming which is the theory telling how to find optimal paths in graphs. It operates in the two-dimensional field of $d_i(m,n)$ distances shown is Fig. 23, and finds under given constraints the optimal path leading from $d_i(1,1)$ to $d_i(M,N)$. If we define the cumulated distance at a given point of the path as :

$$C_i(m,n) = \sum_{j=1}^{J} d_i(m(j),\ n(j)) \cdot w(j) \qquad (120)$$

where the pairs $[k(j),l(j)]$, $j = 1...J$, describe a given path and $w(j)$ is a given associated weighting function, then the optimal path is the one which minimizes $C_i(M,N)$, the cumulated distance at $d_i(M,N)$. Formally,

$$D_1(T,Ri) = \min_{path} C_i(M,N)] \qquad (121)$$

The constraints used are various and fulfill two basic purposes: locally, limiting the range of the path slope; globally, limiting the path domain as shown for example in Fig. 23.

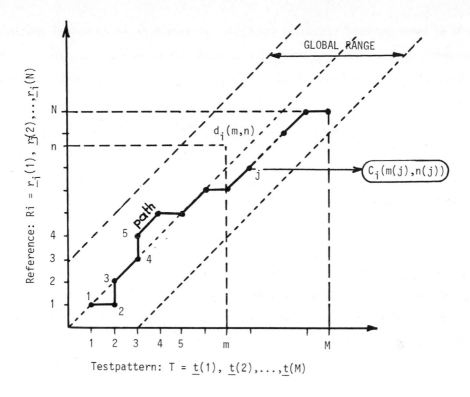

Fig. 23   Principle of DTW

4.4 CONNECTED PATTERN MATCHING

Connected pattern matching is useful to recognize connected speech patterns like connected phonemes or connected words. Again we consider the set of refrences 'Ri" and the unknown pattern T which, now, stands for a single pattern made of other patterns connected together. T must now be compared with all compound reference patterns made of connected references Ri. We call superrefernce R∗ such a compound reference. Using the notation and definition of :

$$R_i \otimes R_j = r_i(1),r_i(2),...,r_i(N_i),r_j(1),...,r_j(N_j) \qquad (122)$$

for connected time sequences, we write the genral superreference as :

$$R * (q) = R_{q(1)} \otimes R_{q(2)} \otimes \ ... \ \otimes R_{q(L)} \qquad (123)$$

where $q = [q(1),q(2),q(3),q(4),...q(L)]$ is the vector of reference indices.

With the brute force matching approach, the test pattern is compared by DTW with all possible superrefrences built from the reference set {Ri, i = 1...I}, resulting in $I + I^2 + I^L$ single matching operations.

4.5 TWO-LEVEL DTW

Starting from the DTW schema between T and Ri explained above, two levels are built by normalizing all references to a constant length $N_1 = N_2 = ... = N_0$ and thus considering fixed boundaries in the superreference. We give the indices 1 = 1,2,...,L to the boundaries. They appear as horizontal lines in Fig. 24. We call lower level processing, the one performed in-between the lines and upper level processing, the one which applies to operations performed on the boundary lines.

The principle of the algorithm is as in the case of simple DTW. The two-dimensional distance field can now be written as $d_i(m,n,1)$, m = 1,...,M; n = 1...N_0; 1 = 1...L. We search the optimal path leading from $d_i(1,1,1)$ to $d_i(M,N,1)$ where 1 = 1...L.

69

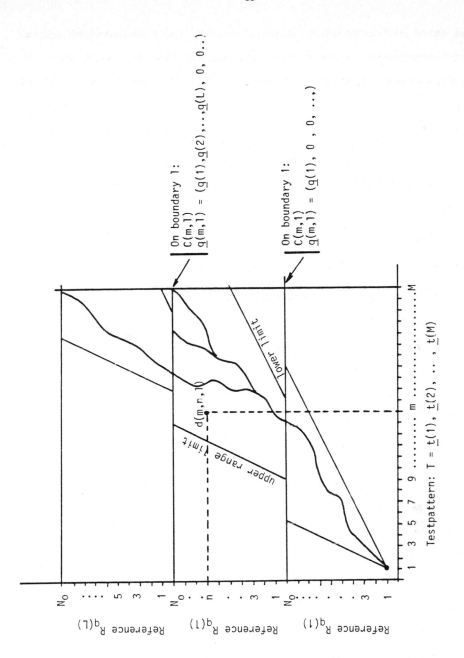

Fig. 24 Principle of two-level DTW

The upper level keeps track, at each boundary line 1 and for each position m of the test sequence, of the optimal path reaching that position in the form of the optimal cumulated distance C (m,1) as well as a path descriptor which can be the partial reference index vector q (m,1), by which we mean that, at the boundary 1, the vector components are defined up to component number 1.

The lower level performs normal DTW between T and {Ri} in the field bounded by two boundaries 1 and 1-1 with given boundary constraints. It finds, among all paths starting from the boundary 1-1 the best path reaching each position m of the boundary 1. Each lower level is repeated for each reference {Ri, i = 1...I} which ensures the optimality of the path found.

Upper and lower level processing once performed for each boundary 1 = 1...L, the final optimal path is the one given by :

$$D[T,R_*(q)] = \min[C (M,1)] \tag{124}$$

D [T,R$_*$(q)] is the optimal distance for the two-level DTW and q is the index vector giving the optimal matching.

The advantage of Two-Level DTW compared to the brute force method is to drastically reducing the number of computations and to making thus connected pattern recognition possible. It requires computing I basic DTW whereas this number is $I+I^2+...+I^L$ in the case of brute force.

5. CONCLUSION

In this paper a short tutorial review of major digital signal processing methods used in processing speech signals is given. In depth treatments are omitted to the detriment of the essence and insight for interpretation. Following more than two decades of efforts in designing methods and algorithms, the present trend is in transposing these methods and algorithms into VLSI implementable architectures for better, faster and more reliable practical systems.

It seems reasonable to expect that now, algorithm designers and circuit designers will collaborate increasingly to design algorithms more suitable for VLSI and to develop technological tools and architectures more convenient for digital signal processing and hence speech processing.

REFERENCES

1. M. Kunt, "Traitement numérique des signaux" Presses Polytechniques Romandes, Lausanne, Switzerland, 1980.
2. J. D. Markel and A. H. Gray, "Linear prediction of speech" Springer-Verlag, New York, 1976.
3. L. R. Rabiner and B. Gold, "Theory and application of digital signal procesing", Prentice Hall, Englewood Cliffs, 1975.
4. T. G. Stockham, T. M. Cannon and R. B. Ingebretsen, "Blind deconvolution through digital signal processing" Proc. IEEE, VolL. 63, No. 4, April 1975, pp. 678-692.
5. L. R. Rabiner and R. W. Schafer, "Digital processing of speech signals", Prentice-Hall, N. J., 1978.
6. L. R. Rabiner et al., "A comparative study of several pitch detection algorithms", IEEE Trans. ASSP-24, pp. 399-413.
7. W. Hess, "Algorithmes ct methodes pour la determination du fondamental", 12eme Journees d'Etude sur la Parole, Montreal, May 25-27, 1981.

SYSTEMS FOR ISOLATED AND CONNECTED WORD RECOGNITION

Roger K. Moore

Royal Signals and Radar Establishment

St. Andrews Rd., Malvern, U.K.

SUMMARY

This lecture is intended to provide an insight into some of the algorithms and techniques that lie behind contemporary automatic speech recognition systems. It is noted that, due to the lack of success of earlier phonetically motivated approaches, the majority of current speech recognizers employ whole-word pattern matching techniques. It is pointed out that these techniques, although rather shallow in concept, have enabled the development of commercial recognizers which exhibit useful and practical capabilities. A range of whole-word pattern matching algorithms are discussed, and in particular, key techniques such as dynamic-time-warping and hidden Markov modelling are explained in some detail. It is also shown how techniques for isolated word recognition may be extended to recognize connected speech. Each of the various methods is reviewed in the context of their computational implications as well as their recognition performance. It is also shown how suitable modifications to the basic algorithms can facilitate real-time operation. Where possible, specific techniqes are highlighted by reference to existing commercial recognition equipment. The lecture concludes by focusing on the key factors which limit the performance of current recognition tchniques, and by outlining some of the research work which may be relevant to future automatic speech recognition systems.

NATO ASI Series, Vol. F16
New Systems and Architectures for Automatic Speech
Recognition and Synthesis. Edited by R. De Mori and C. Y. Suen
© Springer-Verlag Berlin Heidelberg 1985

1. INTRODUCTION

In 1952 Davis, Biddulph and Balashek published the first paper to describe a technique for recognizing spoken words automatically. Over thirty years later, related techniques still dominate the speech recognition field.

The purpose of this lecture is to review such techniques and to mark the progress of the latest developments. However, before doing so it is necessary (and illuminating) to note that many different approaches to automatic speech recognition have been attempted over the past thirty years, and of particular interest is the traditional pattern recognition approach, popular during the 1950's and 60's.

This early scheme was based on the apparently reasonable assumption that speech was a highly redundant signal consisting of a sequence of invariant information bearing elements called phonemes. As a consequence, the classical speech recognizer took the form of: a pre-processor to selectively reduce the quantity of data whilst retaining the relevant information, a feature extractor typically to identify formant frequencies, a segmentor to divide the signal into phonemic segments, and a classifier to recognize the individual phonemes from their features (see figure 1). Recognition of words was then simply a matter of looking up the sequence of recognized phonemes in a pronouncing dictionary.

Schemes of this type abounded, but all failed to a greater or lesser extent because of the basic inadequacy of the initial assumptions; a speech signal is not as easily characterized as one might wish. Indeed it exhibits properties which still make automatic speech recognition a major research topic.

The reasons why speech recognition is not such a straightforward endeavour may be summarized into four main problem areas:

First, speech signals are normally continuous. That is, there are no regular pauses between the words in a spoken sentence, nor are there any other acoustic markers to indicate where the word boundaries are. For example, figure 2 shows

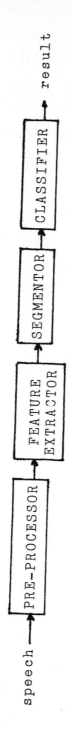

Figure 1   Typical structure of an early automatic speech recognizer.

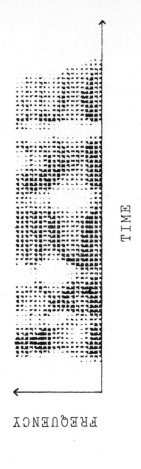

TIME

FREQUENCY

Figure 2 Speech spectrogram of the phrase "we were away a year ago".

a speech spectrogram for the phrase "we were away a year ago"; the only pause in this sentence is in the middle of the "g" in "ago", the rest is a continuously changing sound pattern. A recognition algorithm must therefore be able to recognize words even when embedded within a surrounding sentence.

Second, speech signals are highly variable in a number of ways. Obviously one person's voice can be very different to another's due to factors such as different sex, age or accent. But even a given speaker's voice will be different at different times since a speaker may speak softly or loudly or whisper, or might have a cold or be tense. In fact, it is virtually impossible for a speaker to say the same word in exactly the same way on two different occasions. For example, figure 3 shows the word "helicopter" spoken three times by the same person; note how the patterns are similar but not identical.

The continuity of speech is another source of variability. Since words flow smoothly one into another, the beginnings and ends of words can change significantly. For example, the phrase "bread and butter" may become "breb'm butter" if spoken quickly.

The inherent variability of speech is thus a very big problem for any technique which relies on invariance in the signal. A recognition algorithm must therefore be able to deal with pattern similarities rather than rely on the preservation of absolute identity.

The third problem area is ambiguity. For example, there is no acoustic difference between the words "to", "too" and "two". Similarly, "grey tape" sounds almost exactly the same as "great ape". A recognition algorithm must therefore be able to decide on the identity of a particular word whilst taking into account the identity of surrounding words.

The fourth problem area results from the fact that speech is just one component in the complex system of human language. Often it is the intention behind a message that is more important than the message itself. For example, the most useful answer to the question "Can you tell me the time?" is "10:15" not "Yes, I can".

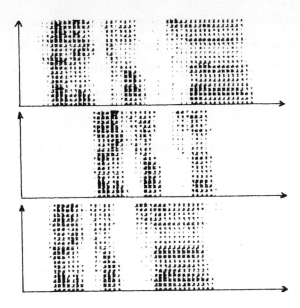

Figure 3   Three versions of the word "helicopter".

Faced with these problems, automatic speech recognition appears to be an almost unattainable goal. However, it turns out that by minimizing one's assumptions about the nature of speech signals, and by developing the rather simple principle exemplified by the 1952 recognizer, it has been possible to begin to derive some powerful (albeit only partial) solutions.

The basic principle underlying almost all current commercial speech recognition equipment is illustrated in figure 4. Speech which is to be recognized is compared with a set of pre-stored reference words (often referred to as 'templates'), and the identity of the stored patterns which most resemble the unknown pattern determines the result. In this scheme a pre-processor transforms the speech signal into some useful representation, a segmentor isolates the speech from the surrounding silence, and then a comparison module compares the unknown words with each of the templates, and outputs the result. Prior to recognition, such a recognizer is 'trained' by presenting it with examples of each of the words in its vocabulary at least once. The entire procedure is known as 'whole-word pattern matching'.

Notwithstanding the problems posed by variability and continuity, this approach relies on the patterns for different words being separable, and for words to be recognizable in context.

The rest of the lecture describes techniques for 'whole-word pattern matching' in detail.

2. PRE-PROCESSING

The range of signal processing techniques which may be applied to speech signals is very large [Schafer and Rabiner 1975, Flanagan 1972, Holmes 1982]. However, only a few have established themselves as standard techniques for automatic speech recognition. This section describes briefly the most popular techniques for producing a useful representation of a speech signal, and also the

80

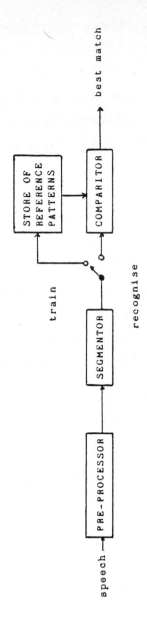

Figure 4   Structure of a contemporary automatic speech recognizer.

most common techniques for reducing the data rate of the pre-processor output.

2.1 Signal Representation

One of the most crucial factors which determines the success or failure of an automatic speech recognizer is the nature of the representation presented to the recognition algorithms.

Short-time Spectrum

The most common way to analyze a speech signal is to measure its short-time spectrum. This is possible because a speech signal can be considered to be stationary over a short time interval. Hence the spectrum can be estimated using the Fourier transform. One of the simplest methods for implementing short-time Fourier analysis is a bank of bandpass filters. Such an analysis is the basis of the UK channel vocoder analyzer [Holmes 1980] (see figure 5) which is used as a front-end to several automatic speech recognizers (and which was used to generate the spectrograms and other data presented in this paper).

In general, filter bank analyzers are easy to construct with analogue circuitry and the distribution of frequency bands can be readily modelled on the critical bands of the human ear. However, unless a very large number of channels is used, it is difficult to estimate the spectrum shape around spectral peaks.

Cepstral Analysis

The most useful spectral representation for speech recognition is the wide-band spectrum (which does not preserve pitch information). Such an analysis requires a short data window. However an alternative approach, which is able to use a wider time window is homomorphic or cepstral processing. This process is based on the assumption that speech is a convolution of an excitation function with a vocal tract impulse response. Figure 6 illustrates the scheme for separating these two components by liftering the cepstrum to obtain a smooth spectrum. In practice, the first few terms (excluding zero frequency) of a cosine

82

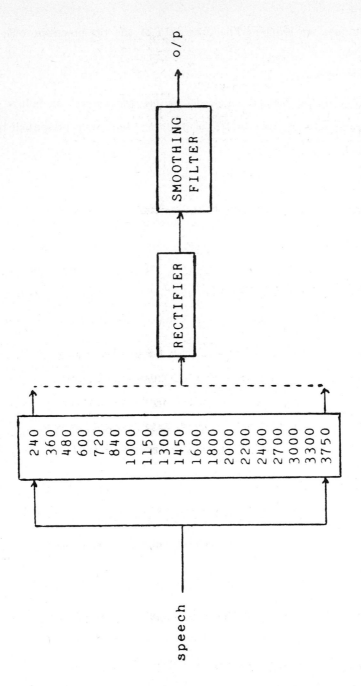

Figure 5   The JSRU channel vocoder analyser.

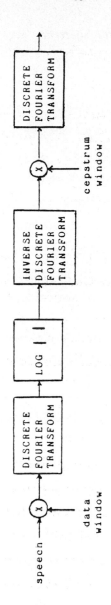

Figure 6 Cepstral analysis.

transform of the short-time log power spectrum may be used [Bridle and Brown 1974, Hunt et al 1980].

Linear Predictive Analysis

Linear predictive coding (LPC) is an analysis technique which is particularly attractive from the computational point of view. In this scheme the autocorrelation characteristics of the speech signal are exploited by estimating the value of the current sample using a linear combination of the past n samples. Figure 7 illustrates the principle. The all-pole properties of LPC analysis enable accurate estimations of spectral peaks to be made. However this is only true during speech sounds which conform to an all-pole model. During nasals and many consonant sounds LPC tends to overestimate the bandwidths of spectral peaks.

2.2 Data Reduction Techniques

The output of a typical front-end analyzer is thus framed data consisting of a sequence of vectors of a given size occurring a certain number of times each second. This data rate may be too high for subsequent processes to handle, hence techniques can be used for reducing the data rate by various forms of coding scheme.

Vector Quantization

Speech coding by vector quantization (or 'character string encoding' [White 1972]) is a technique whereby each frame of spectral data is coded in terms of the identity of a prestored reference vector called a 'codeword'. The collection of possible codewords is referred to as a 'codebook'. The spectral shape of an input vector is thus coded by identifying the particular codeword from the codebook that minimizes some predefined distortion measure. This means that a speech signal can be represented by a sequence of codewords with a bit-rate of b bits per vector if there are 2^b vectors in the codebook.

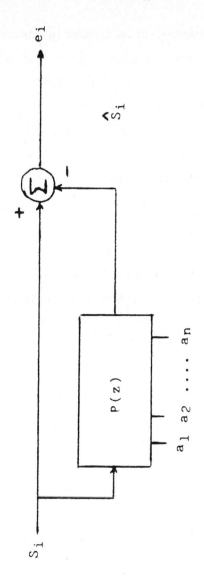

Figure 7 Liner predictive analysis.

A codebook is normally generated by a training procedure which minimizes the average distortion resulting from coding a suitably long sequence of vectors. This training procedure is essentially a cluster analysis; more codewords are allocated where the population of vectors is more dense.

Trace Segmentation

Trace segmentation is a 'data-adaptive frame rate' technique for reducing the number of vectors in a sequence. Each vector is viewed as a point in n-dimensional space (where n is the size of each vector) and the trace is the sequence of points drawn out by an utterance. The n-dimensional trace is subsequently resampled by calculating the total length of the trace, and then dividing the trace into a fixed number of uniformly spaced segments. By suitable choice of the new sampling rate, fewer vectors are required to represent a speech signal, and those vectors are better distributed (there will be more allocated when the spectrum is changing quickly than when it is changing slowly).

Variable Rate Coding

Variable frame rate coding is similar to trace segmentation in that the net result is a resampling of a speech signal according to the changing spectrum. However, trace segmentation relies on being able to determine the beginning and end of a trace. In circumstances where this might not be known (for example in the middle of a section of speech) variable rate coding techniques may be utilized.

The simplest scheme is to set a threshold such that a vector in a sequence is only retained if the distance between it and the last retained vector exceeds the threshold. Hence by adjusting the value of the threshold, the resampling rate can be varied to suit the circumstances; the higher the threshold, the fewer samples there will be in the more stationary regions of the signal.

More complex schemes have involved averaging vectors [Piereccini and Billi 1983] or multiple thresholds [Bridle and Brown 1982].

3. ISOLATED WORD RECOGNITION

Any approach to automatic speech recognition must overcome the continuity problem outlined in section 1. However, the simplest and most effective solution is obvious; ask the speaker to put artificial pauses between his words, thereby sacrificing naturalness in favour of greatly simplifying the recognition process. Each word is thus 'isolated' from its neighbours, and can be recognized individually.

Even for isolated words, the key to the success of the whole-word pattern matching approach lies in the comparison process (see figure 4). The rest of this section is concerned with techniques for implementing the comparison.

3.1 Absolute Pattern Match

The most basic comparison process is simply to correlate the time-frequency word patterns producd by the pre-processor in order to determine the 'distance' between an unknown word and each template. Unfortunately this is not possible because words are often different durations, hence their corresponding patterns are different sizes. However, by aligning the beginnings of all the patterns, and by corrclating only over the areas of overlap, it is possible to generate a suitable measure of correlation (or distance: for example, the sum of the squares of the differences). The length difference can also be taken into account separately [White and Fong 1975].

Although rather simple minded, such a technique requires the minimum of computation: N vector comparisons per pattern match, where N is the number of vectors in the smallest pattern.

The performance of the technique can be gauged from White and Fong's experiments: the error rate for a test using a 54 word vocabulary, six band-pass filters (sampled every 10 ms) and vector quantization (32 codewords) was 7%. White identified misalignment of the beginnings of words as a source of some of the errors.

3.2 Best Absolute Time Alignment

An alternative to aligning the beginnings of words in order to perform an absolute comparison, is to adjust their relative timing to maximize the correlation of the overlap. This means starting with the beginnings aligned, then shifting the patterns with respect to each other until the ends align. The similarity of the pattern overlap is calculated at each shift, and the highest similarity is the output of the comparison.

Computationally this scheme is much more expensive: M*(N-M) vector comparisons, where N is the number of vectors in the longer pattern, and M is the number of vectors in the shorter pattern.

Recognition performance on the ten digit vocabulary, with a 16 channel filter bank (10 ms frame rate) was found to be only 82% using this technique [Moore 1980]. However, this level of performance is to be expected, since the behaviour of the algorithm for comparing different words is somewhat unpredictable.

3.3 Linear Time-Normalization

The problem with the two previous techniques is that they do not accommodate the fact that the same word is very rarely the same duration on different occasions. For example, in figure 3 it can be seen that the three versions of "helicopter" all have different lengths. A solution therefore, is to uniformly 'time-normalize' each pattern in order to make them the same size. Such a technique is referred to as 'linear time-normalization'.

Figure 8 illustrates the process on a pair of utterances of the word "helicopter". The two original patterns are shown at right angles to each other so that the two time scales can be compared. It is clear that the vertical utterance is much longer than the horizontal one. The rectangle on the right is prescribed by the lengths of the two words, and the diagonal line is the linear time-normalization relationship between the two. The third pattern is the result of stretching the horizontal one to the same length as the vertical one. The net result is that the two vertical patterns are more similar than the originals.

In practice, either the template patterns are time-normalized to the unknown word, or all patterns are time-normalized to a standard duration. In both cases the distance calculation involves a constant number of vector comparisons: N vector comparisons per pattern match, where N is the number of vectors in the input word (or in the standard length pattern).

The recognition performance of linear time-normalization can be quite useful if the vocabulary is kept reasonably small, 10 to 30 words for example. For the ten digits, one could expect recognition accuracies up to about 97% under ideal conditions. The actual performance obtained depends, amongst other things, on the inherent confusability of the words, the consistency of the speakers, the exact nature of the pre-processing and the number of training examples allowed per word.

In practice, the level of performance is such that several commercial speech recognizers employ the linear time-normalization principle.

EXAMPLE SYSTEM: Interstate Electronics VRM

Pre-processing:
- 16 channel analogue filter bank
- bandwith: 200 Hz to 7000 Hz
- 5 ms frame rate
- variable rate coding (user definable threshold)
- minimum number of frames per word: 16 (80 ms)
- maximum number of frames per word: 250 (1250 ms)

Segmentation:
- endpoint detection by spectral energy change
- user definable threshold
- minimum pause between words: 40 ms to 320 ms (user definable; default 160 ms)

Training:

    — 40, 70 or 100 reference word patterns (depending on model)

    — 32 bytes (256 bits) per reference pattern

Recognition:

    — linear time-normalization (linear conversion from 250 frames to 256 bits)

    — recognition based on number of bits in agreement between standard length patterns

    — user definable reject threshold

Computation:

    — CPU plus 4K ROM and up to 4K RAM (for references)

    — processing time is $25+N$ ms, where N is the number of references

    — response time is pause length plus processing time

Recognition accuracy:

    — 2.9% error on Doddington-Schalk [1981] Texas Instruments (DSTI) data (20 word vocabulary; "zero" to "nine" plus ten command words, 8 men and 8 women, 5120 test tokens in total)

Cost:

    — $2400

    — latest product: VRT300 (512 bits/word, 200 words, $1295)

3.4 Non-Linear time-Normalization

For larger vocabularies, the recognition accuracy of linear time-normalization can drop significantly. The reason is that linear timescale distortion is not an adequate model of what actually happens when people make words longer or shorter. In reality some sounds are lengthened (or shortened) more than others. This effect is apparent from figure 8; although linear time-normalization has made the patterns the same lengh, it has still not made them particularly similar. In particular the technique is susceptible to 'endpoint detection' errors since correct normalization depends on the first and last frames being correctly aligned. In

91

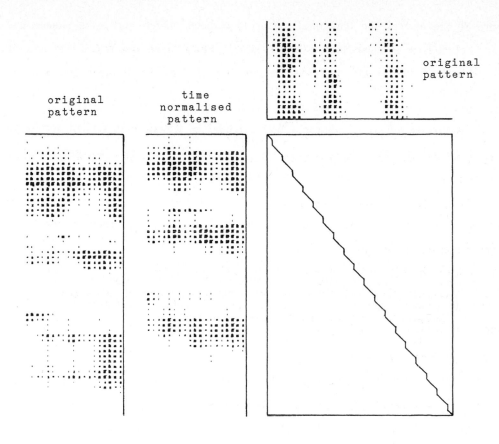

Figure 8   Demonstration of linear time-normalisation between two versions of the word "helicopter".

figure 8, the end of the horizontal pattern has been missed and extra silence has been included; it is clear that a better match would have resulted if the end of the horizontal pattern had been determined more accurately [Rabiner and Sambur 1975].

However, as suggested above, a better model of timescale distortion would be one which allows different sounds to be distorted differentially. By eye one can see from figure 8 that the patterns do have similar structures, and one can imagine that by distorting the horizontal pattern non-linearly, it could be made to look more like the original vertical pattern. Figure 9 shows such a non-linear time-normalization or 'time registration path'.

In fact, the time registration path in figure 9 was determined by eye, and it is obvious that it could be further modified to achieve a better match. Of course in practice it is necessary to find such a path automatically, but this involves a search space of many millions of possible paths! Luckily it is possible to use the mathematical technique of 'dynamic programming' (DP) to solve this optimization problem using only N*M operations (where N and M are the number of frames in the two patterns), and since DP is guaranteed to find the best solution, the result is optimal non-linar time-normalization or 'dynamic time warping' (DTW).

Figure 10 shows the result of using dynamic programming to find the best path; note how similar the vertical time-distorted version of the original horizontal utterance is to the original vertical utterance.

Dynamic time Warping

DTW is essentially a two-stage process; figure 11 illustrates the first stage. Two abstract speech-like patterns are shown, one vertically and one horizontally. Each pattern has time frames consisting of 3-element vectors; the vertical pattern has four frames, and the horizontal has five. The matrix in the centre is known as the 'distance matrix' and it contains numbers which correspond to the distance between each frame in one pattern and each frame in the other pattern. For example, the number "20" in the top right hand corner indicates that the first

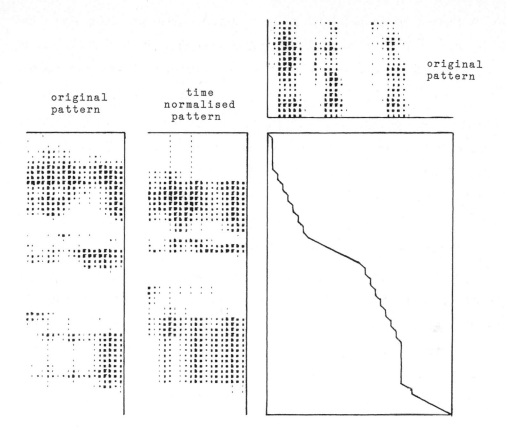

Figure 9 Non-linear time-normalisation (obtained by hand).

94

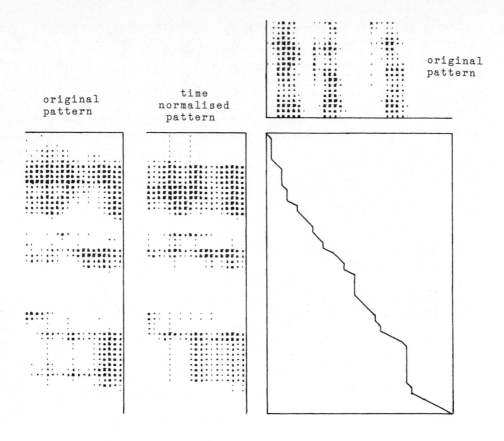

Figure 10 Optimal non-linear time-normalisation obtained using dynamic programming.

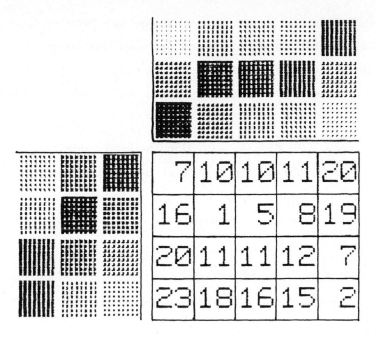

Figure 11   Distance matrix obtained by comparing two abstract speech patterns.

frame of the vertical pattern is quite different to the last frame of the horizontal pattern. Similarly, the "1" in row-2 column-2 indicates that the second frames of each pattern are very similar. The distances are actually calculated by taking the sum of the squares of the differences between each element of each pair of frames.

The second stage is to find the path through the distance matrix, from the top left hand corner to the bottom right hand corner, which has the minimum accumulated sum of distances along its length. This path is the required non-linear relationship between the timescales of these two patterns, and it is found by dynamic programming.

Dynamic programming involves the regular application of a local optimization procedure which ultimately leads to an overall global solution. In this case a 'local decision function' is used, together with the distance matrix, to construct a second matrix called the 'cumulative distance matrix'. Figure 12 illustrates the process. The local decision function is shown in figure 12a, and it defines that a path may arrive at any particular point either vertically, horizontally or diagonally. It is applied as follows:

For each point in the cumulative distance matrix, add the cheapest cost of getting to that point to the cost of being at that point, and enter it in the matrix. The cheapest cost of getting to a point is the smallest of the values in the previous entries (as defined by the local decision function) and the cost of being at a point is simply the value taken from the corresponding position in the distance matrix. Hence, if this process is applied iteratively, starting at the top left hand corner of the matrix, it is possible to complete all the entries in the cumulative distance matrix.

Figure 12b shows the cumulative distance matrix in the process of being filled in. The "?" indicates the point being considered, and the three previous points are highlighted. The cost of getting to the point is the minimum of 19, 13 or 21, and the cost of being at that point is 12 (from the distance matrix in figure 11). Hence the cumulative distance entered at that point is 25 (13+12).

Figure 12c shows the cumulative distance matrix completely filled in.   The number in the bottom right hand corner is highlighted because this is the overall distance between the two patterns; it is the sum of distances along the least-cost path through the distance matrix.   To find the path it is necessary to remember at each point in the calculation exactly which local decisions were made (horizontal, vertical or diagonal).   Figure 12d shows all of these decisions and it can be seen that they form a tree radiating from the top left hand corner (where the calculation started).   The actual minimum cost path is found by tracing back along the local decisions, starting at the bottom right hand corner (where the calculation ended).

Referring back to the distance matrix (figure 11), the calculation shows that the least-cost path takes the route 7+1+5+12+2; no other path has a cumulative sum less than 27.

The formulation for this dynamic programming calculation is the following recursive expression:

$$D(i,j) \; = \; d(i,j) \; + \; \min[D(i\text{-}1,j), D(i\text{-}1,j\text{-}1), D(i,j\text{-}1)]$$

where $1 \leq i \leq I$ and $1 \leq j \leq J$ (I and J are the numbers of frames in the two patterns being compared), d is a distance measure between two frames, and the initial condition is $D(0,0) = 0$.   The overall distance between the two patterns is $D(I,J)$.

As an example of the same process applied to real speech patterns, figure 13 shows the comparison of two versions of the phrase "joe took father's shoe bench out".   In this case the values in the distance matrix are shown as point densities; similar regions give rise to the highest density of points.   From figure 13 the most likely route for the optimal time registration path can easily be seen by eye.

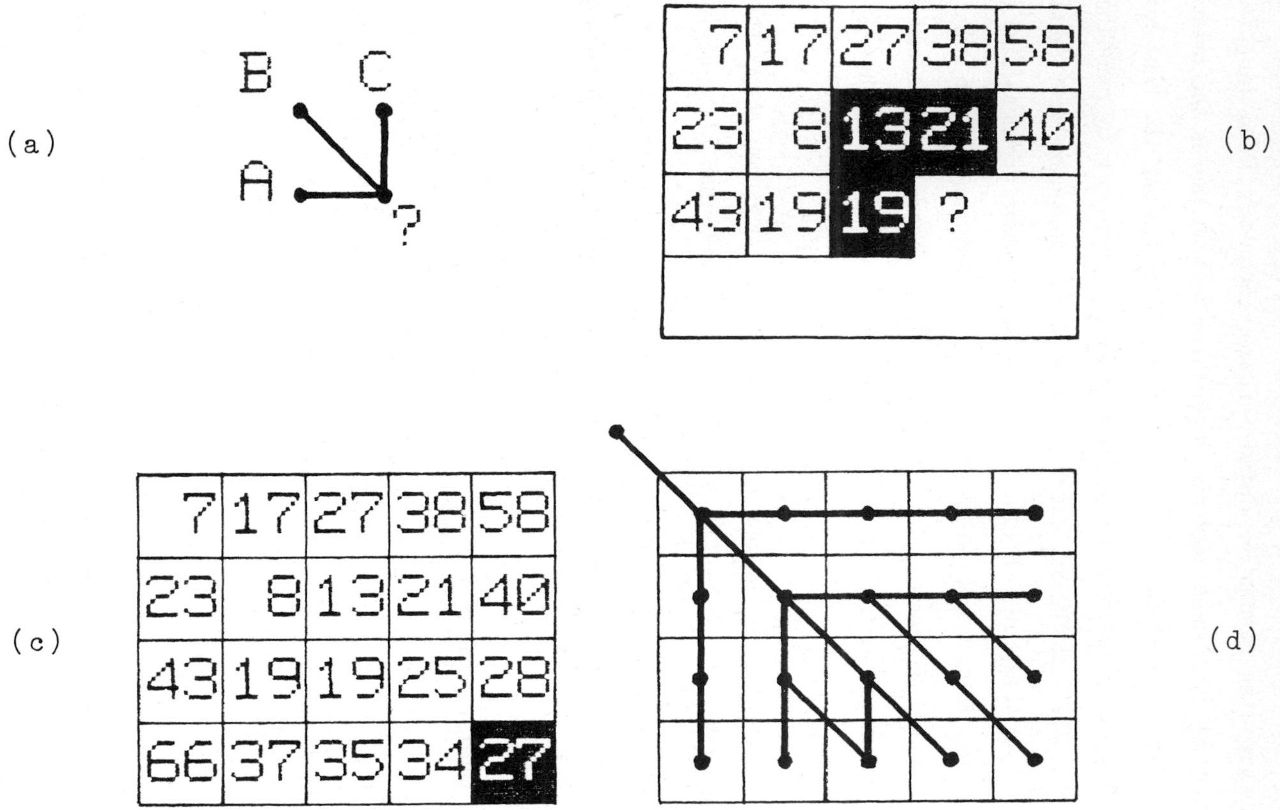

Figure 12 Demonstration of dynamic time warping; (a) local decision function, (b) partially completed cumulative distance matrix, (c) completed cumulative distance matrix and (d) record of local decisions.

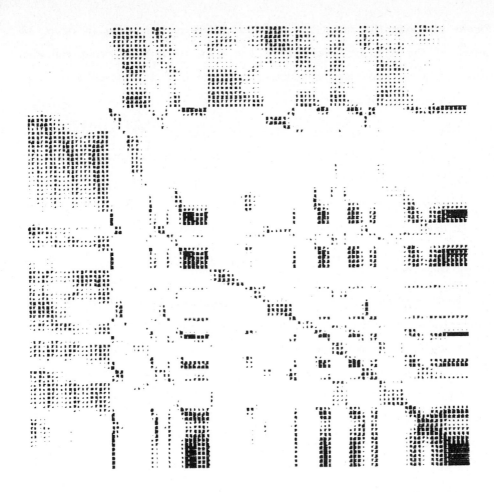

Figure 13   Distance matrix obtained by comparing two versions of the phrase "joe took father's shoe bench out".

Figure **14** shows the cumulative distance matrix corresponding to figure **13**. The effect of the dynamic programming has been to form a rising valley of cumulative distances since high cumulative distances tend to lie well away from the likely route of the optimal path.

The matrix of local decisions is shown in figure **15**. The complete tree is shown, and the best path, obtained by backtracking from the bottom right hand corner, is clearly visible. The result indicates that the "joe" in the vertical utterance was said much slower than in the horizontal, but the rest of the phrase has a more nearly linear temporal relationship.

Local Path Constraints

The technique described above is perhaps the simplest variant in the range of possible DTW algorithms, and it is termed the 'basic symmetric' algorithm. This refers to the shape of the local decision function which in this case is very simple, but in general may take many different shapes. For example, figure 16 shows several local decision functions which have been found to be useful. Essentially the local decision function determines the shape of possible time registration paths and hence the nature of the optimization that will be achieved. By varying the shape of the function, different properties can be introduced. For example, the basic symmetric function allows paths to have long horizontal or vertical stretches, and this might be considered to be undesirable. In this case it is possible to introduce extra limbs to the decision function such that a horizontal or vertical step can only be taken after a diagonal (see the 3rd function in figure 16).

In these circumstances the slope of the path is constrained by the shape of the local decision function, hence this property is referred to as the 'local path constraint' or 'slope constraint'. Similarly, the consequences for the total time registration path are that certain areas of the distance matrix are never visited. This effect is referred to as the 'global path constraint'.

Figure 14   Cumulative distance matrix for the example shown in figure 13.

Figure 15 Local decision tree for the example shown in figure 13 and figure 14.

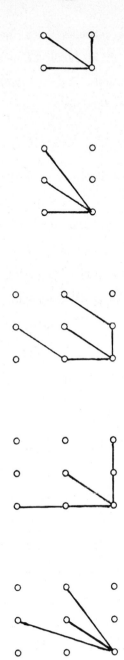

Figure 16   A selection of local decision functions.

In order to generalize these concepts, each limb of a local decision function is termed a 'production' [Myers et al 1980]. Hence a local decision function can be described as a list of productions, and a complete time registration path can be described by a sequence of productions.

Production Weighting

A softer form of path control is achieved by weighting the various productions in a local decision function. For example, in the case of the basic symmetric function, there is a natural bias towards paths which have more diagonal productions (since these paths will naturally have fewer distances) and this might be an undesirable property. Weighting the diagonal production by a factor of two cancels out this bias [White and Neely 1976, Sakoe and Chiba 1978].

In general each production may be weighted differently according to some predetermined path constraint requirement.

Path Length Normalization

The total cumulative distance along the optimal path will obviously depend on the total number of distances (and productions) which make up the path. Hence comparisons between long word patterns are bound to give rise to larger overall distances than comparisons between short patterns. To avoid this causing a problem, it is possible to normalize the final cumulative distance such that it represents the average distance per unit length of path.

Various normalizations are possible; Sakoe and Chiba suggest dividing the cumulative distances by I+J, where I is the length of one pattern, and J is the length of the other. It is also possible to divide by the actual length of the path, if such information is available.

Distance Measure

The entire DTW process ultimately depends on the choice of a suitable distance measure between two speech frames or vectors. Various alternatives may be used; for filter bank analyzer frames it is common to use either the 'city-block' metric, or the 'squared-Euclidean' metric. (The latter is squared so that the cumulative distance between two patterns can be interpreted as a global Euclidean distance between them.) In the case of an LPC analysis, it is common to use the log likelihood distance ratio proposed by Itakura [1975].

Isolated Word Recognition Using DTW

Figure 17 shows an example of isolated word recognition using optimal non-linear time-normalization. In the example there are three reference patterns, the digits "one", "two" and "three", shown vertically. The horizontal pattern is the word to be recognized (actually a "one"). The unknown word is compared with the three reference patterns using the techniques described above, and the three resulting non-linear time registration paths are shown. Also shown are the cumulative distances between the unknown pattern and each of the reference patterns. The best match is determined by the smallest distance, hence the unknown word is correctly recognized as "one".

The algorithm used in the example is the basic symmetric with no slope constraints and no path length normalization. To interpret the non-linear time registration paths, it should be noted that when matching two words which are the same, the distortions tend to be subtle variations on an essentially linear theme. On the other hand, when two different words are compared, the time registration paths tend to be extremely non-linear. This is because it takes a severe distortion of the timescales of two different words to make them even remotely similar. In fact, this is why slope constraints may sometimes increase recognition performance; in-class time registration paths will be unaffected, but out-class matches will be forced to be non-optimal (in comparison with the unconstrained condition) and thus further apart — hence less confusion.

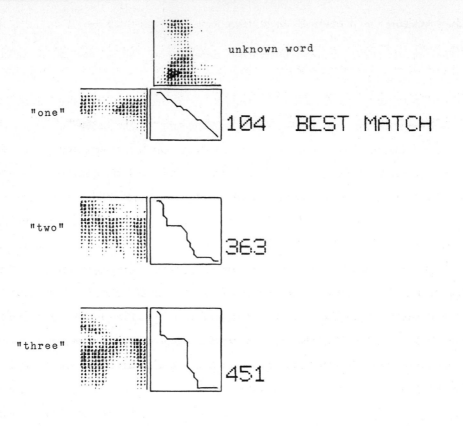

Figure 17 An example of isolated word recognition using dynamic time warping.

In practice it is possible to have more than one reference per word, and this enables more variability in pronunciation to be captured. Similarly, some training procedures involve averaging different examples to obtain a suitably representative reference pattern. The Bell laboratories 'robust' training procedure is a hybrid of the two, combining averaging with a statistical clustering technique [Rabiner and Wilpon 1980].

The computational requirement for DTW is composed of two parts: calculation of the distance matrix, and calculation of the dynamic programming optimization. It is not necessary for these two processes to be kept entirely separate (as in the example given above), but care must be taken to avoid calculating any of the distances more than once. A comparison of a word pattern of length M and a word pattern of length N therefore consists of M*N vector comparisons (the distance matrix) and M*N DP minimizations if there are no slope constraints. If there are slope constraints, then there will be fewer operations. The split between the distance matrix and DP calculation is approximately 80%:20% of the total time taken.

The recognition performance of isolated word recognizers based on DTW techniques is significantly better than that obtainable from linear time-normalization. This is because DTW provides a far more realistic timescale compensation process; greater variability can be accommodated, hence larger vocabularies may be used. Also by using relaxed endpoint constraints (the position where the timescale registration path is allowed to start and end), DTW does not suffer from the same dependency on endpoint detection as linear time-normalization. Hence the segmentor can be much simpler, and it is left to the DTW process to decide precisely where the words begin and end.

Typically, for the ten digits, one could expect recognition accuracies greater than 99% (the NEC DP-100 DTW based recognizer scored 98.8% on the DSTI test).

EXAMPLE SYSTEM: VOTAN V5000

Pre-processing:

— 16 channel filter bank

— bandwidth: 150 Hz to 4000 Hz

— 1000 bits for every 0.5 seconds of speech

— incorporates voice store and forward facility

Segmentation:

— pause between words: 500 ms

Training:

— 500 seconds of template storage

— maximum vocabulary: 256 words

Recognition:

— dynamic time warping

— second choice available

Recognition accuracy:

— 0.55% errors on DSTI data (test performed by **VOTAN**)

Cost:

— $5000 (V1000 board alone: $3200)

3.5   No Time-Normalization

The developing theme so far in section 3 has been the progressive relaxation of timescale registration constraints.   Therefore, the next logical step from non-linear time normalization is to allow any assignment of time aligned points, without regard for temporal ordering at all — in other words, no time-normalization!

Although this idea sounds trivial, it is at least interesting to know how well it is possible to do by ignoring temporal information completely. In fact the very first recognizer (mentioned in the introduction) correlated word patterns without regard to the temporal sequence. More recently, Shore and Burton [1982] have pursued this concept in more detail.

The basic idea is that by using vector quantization, it is possible to set up a separate codebook for each word in the vocabulary. Recognition is then simply a question of which codebook best fits an unknown word (the fit being determined using the average distortion resulting from coding a word).

Computationally, each input vector has to be compared with all of the codewords in each codebook.

Surprisingly, the recognition performance obtained by Shore and Burton was excellent; 0.8% error on part of the DSTI database (which is comparable with the performance of DTW based techniques). The implications of this result are therefore important since it raises questions about whether DTW algorithms make the best use of the extra temporal information which they have at their disposal.

3.6 Stochastic Modelling

Perhaps one reason why Shore and Burton found such superior performance for recognition without time-normalization is that vector quantization is essentially a statistical data collection process. Hence by training their vector quantizer on all of the available training material, they were in a better position than DTW recognizers which could only use part of the training material. The implication is thus that automatic speech recognizers might achieve much better performance if they were statistically based; indeed one would be foolish to expect a recognizer to perform outstandingly well if its entire knowledge about speech is a single example of each word in its vocabulary. The recognizer ought at least to be given some information about the variability in the patterns.

One simple way of providing variability information is to use more than one example of each word. However, this leads to a large increase in the amount of computation required. An alternative is to use 'average' templates, but what this means for DTW based techniques is not absolutely clear. It is more constructive, however, to consider the statistical assumptions underlying the entire whole-word pattern matching process [Bridle 1979].

Statistical Pattern Recognition

In the completely general case, it would be possible to obtain the best classification of an observation vector 0 in terms of a set of classes C by finding for which j P(Cj|0) is a maximum:

$$0 \text{ is from Ci if } P(Ci|0) = \max_{j} P(Cj|0)$$

Unfortunately it is difficult to measure P(C|0) directly, but using Bayes' theorem:

$$P(Cj|0) = P(0|Cj) * P(Cj) / P(0)$$

Thus by substituting, and by ignoring the a-priori frequencies of occurrence of the classes, a 'maximum likelihood classifier' is obtained: 0 is from Ci if

$$P(0|Ci) = \max_{j} P(0|Cj)$$

The advantage of this statement is that P(0|Cj) is easily measurable for each class. Hence, for an observation pattern which is a speech pattern 0(N,T) (where N is the size of the analysis frame and T is the number of time-frames in a word), if N and T are fixed (T being fixed by using time-normalization of some description), then it would be possible to construct the optimal statistical classifier. In practice, such a high dimensionality problem (N*T) would require an inordinate amount of training data and would therefore be unfeasable.

Therefore, to make the problem tractable it is necessary to introduce some assumptions·

a)   assume multivariate normal distributions — this means that it is only necessary to measure class means and covariance matrices,

b)   assume each frame and each element of the analysis vector are independent — this means that the covariance matrices are diagonal,

c)   assume all variances are equal, and equal to 1.

These assumptions lead to the following consequences; 0 is from Ci if

$$P(0|Ci) = \max_{j} \prod_{n,t} P(0(n,t)|Cj)$$

where $0(n,t)$ is the scalar value of the speech pattern at element n of the vector at time t. Hence from the one-dimensional form of the normal distribution:

$$P(0(n,t)|Cj) = 1/\sqrt{2\pi} * \exp[-(0(n,t)-M(n,t|Cj))^2/2]$$

where $M(n,t|Cj)$ is the mean value of the class j speech pattern at element n of the vector at time t. If, for convenience, logs are taken (and constant terms are ignored) then $\log P(0(n,t)|Cj)$ becomes $\log \exp[-(0(n,t)-M(n,t|Cj))^2$ which is:

$$-(0(n,t)-M(n,t|Cj))^2$$

and the product of terms becomes a sum. Hence 0 is from Ci if

$$\log P(0(n,t)|Ci) = \max_{j} - \sum_{n,t}(0(n,t)-M(n,t|Cj))^2$$

$$= - [\min_{j} \sum_{n,t}(0(n,t)-M(n,t|Cj))^2]$$

and this is the familiar nearest neighbour squared Euclidean distance. Hence such a classifier functions by finding the pattern match which results in the smallest sum of the squared differences over the entire patterns.

Thus whole word pattern matching is already operating in a statistical framework where a time-normalized example of an actual word is used to provide the values for M(n,t). So the question is not how to introduce statistics into whole word pattern matching, but how to relax some of the built-in assumptions.

However, more important is the reliance of the above statistical analysis on the use of time-normalized patterns. It explains how DTW is able to use minimum squared Euclidean distance as an optimization criterion, but it does not give an insight into capturing the average statistical behaviour of variable length patterns. A technique which does address this problem is 'hidden Markov modelling'.

Hidden Markov Models

Levinson et al [1983] describe a hidden Markov model (HMM) as follows: "A probabalistic function of a (hidden) Markov chain is a stochastic process generated by two interrelated mechanisms: an underlying Markov chain having a finite number of states, and a set of random functions one of which is associated with each state. At discrete instants of time, the process is assumed to be in a unique state and an observation is generated by the random function corresponding to the current state. The underlying Markov chain then changes states according to its transition probability matrix. The observer sees only the output of the random functions associated with each state and cannot directly observe the states of the underlying Markov chain, hence the term hidden Markov model."

Typically, hidden Markov models of speech employ vector quantization in order to reduce the random functions associated with each state to non-parametric distributions over a finite set of output symbols.

If H is a hidden Markov model with N states and M symbols, then $H = (\pi, A, B)$ where π is an initial state probability vector (Nx1), A is a transition probability matrix (NxN), and B is a state output symbol probability matrix (NxM). These matrices completely specify the model. For example, $\pi(i)$ is the probability of starting at state i, a(i,j) is the probability of moving from state i to state j, and b(i,o) is the probability of observing output symbol o from state i.

To recognize a speech pattern, it is necessary to compare the sequence of observations 0 (0=o(1),...,o(T)) with each of the word models in order to find Hj which maximizes P(0|Hj). P(0|H) is found as follows:

A model can only generate an observation sequence of length T via a state sequence of length T. Hence if S is a state sequence (S=s(1),...,s(T)), then the joint probability of 0 and S given the model H is

$$P(0,S|H) \; = \; P(S|H) \; * \; P(0|S,H)$$

Now:

$$P(S|H) \; = \; \pi[s(1)]^*a[s(1),s(2)]^*a[s(2),s(3)]^*...^*a[s(T\text{-}1),s(T)]$$

and

$$P(0|S,H) \; = \; b[s(1),o(1)]^*b[s(2),o(2)]^*...^*b[s(T),o(T)]$$

which by combining leads to:

$$P(0,S|H) \; = \; \pi[s(1)]^*b[s(1),o(1)]^* \prod_{t=2}^{T} a[s(t\text{-}1),s(t)]^*b[s(t),o(t)]$$

To obtain the probability P = P(0|H) it is necessary to sum the probabilities P(0,S|H) over all state sequences of length T, and this may be achieved efficiently using dynamic programming. The required recursive expression is:

$$F(t,i) = [\sum_{j=1}^{N} F(t-1,j)*a[s(j),s(i)]] * b[s(i),o(t)]$$

where F(t,i) is the probability of o(1),...,o(t) finishing in state i at time t given the model H, and the initial condition G(1,i) is π(i)*b[s(i),o(1)]. Hence, since F(T,i) is the probability of 0 finishing in state i at time T:

$$P(0|H) = F(T,i)$$

Or, if H is a left-right model (one for which a(i,j) = 0 for j ≤ i: no backward transitions), then the final observation must come from state N and P(0|H) becomes F(T,N).

There are two distinct advantages of this type of statistical model for speech patterns. First, in addition to the variability within an analysis vector, it can model the temporal variability of speech data.
Second, there is an established technique for training the model: the 'Baum-Welch algorithm'.

The training procedure involves re-estimating the parameters of a model H in order to make P(0|H) larger, where 0 is now a training sequence. Intuitively, a good way to re-estimate the state transition probability from state i to state j, would be to measure the average number of transitions from i to j (given 0 and H) and to divide by the measured number of transitions out of i (given 0 and H). Similarly, the state output symbol probability of symbol s at state i can be re-estimated by counting the average number of observations of symbol s from state i, and dividing by the average number of observations of all symbols from state i.

Baums theorem [1972] gives a rigourous backing to these intuitive notions and proves that for the re-estimated model H′:

$$P(0|H') \geq P(0|H)$$

In order to perform the re-estimation, it is necessary to introduce a second dynamic programming pass, but in the reverse direction. It is then possible, by a suitable combination of the forward probabilities F with the (new) backward probabilities to re-estimate the parameters of a model. This process is commonly referred to as the 'forward-backward' algorithm.

Isolated Word Recognition Using HMM

In the experiments described by Levinson et al [1983], a five state left-right model was used with limited, but regular, allowable state transitions. Figure 18 illustrates the model. The vector quantizer used a codebook containing 64 codewords.

The experiment itself consisted of a data base of two sets (training and test) of 1000 spoken words; one example of each of the ten digits, spoken by 50 men and 50 women. The training set was used to estimate the parameters of the vector quantizer and of the hidden Markov model, and the test set was then recognized. In addition, a comparison was made with a DTW based system using the same vector quantized data.

The results showed that there was almost no difference in recognition accuracy between the two approaches, both achieving slightly more than 96%. However, from a computational point of view the HMM requires an order of magnitude less storage and execution time.

The implications of hidden Markov modelling for automatic speech recognition are thus very important. Whereas DTW based techniques have a very simple training phase (just data collection) and a very complicated recognition phase, HMMs are just the reverse. It can be argued therefore that an HMM provides the correct balance for any practical system.

116

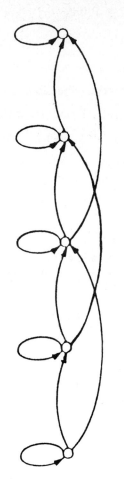

Figure 18   Typical structure of a 5-state hidden Markov model.

EXAMPLE SYSTEM: Dragon Systems

Pre-processing:

— 8-bit A/D conversion

— time domain featues

Training:

— 16/32 word vocabulary (Mark II: 96 words)

— any number of repetitions of each word (typically four)

Recognition:

— isolated words

— hidden Markov modelling

— result may be output before word is finished

Computation:

— software system

— runs on 6502 microprocessor (also 8086)

— response time may be negative

Recognition accuracy:

— 0.7% error on DSTI data (test performed by Dragon Systems)

Cost:

— $10 per unit to original equipment manufacturers

4.   CONNECTED WORD RECOGNITION

The use of dynamic programming related techniques is obviously very important to achieving practical recognition performance from isolated word recognizers.   However, this is not the only useful attribute; it turns out that it is possible to extend the techniques from isolated to connected words using relatively simple modifications to the algorithms.

To understand the principle behind these modifications, consider the isolated word recognition result illustrated in figure 17. Three time registration paths are shown, the best path (for the correct match) and two sub-optimal paths. If it were the case that only the best path were displayed, then it can be seen that the DTW process is one which finds the best explanation of the relationship between the unknown word and one of the reference patterns. Therefore, to recognize a sequence of connected words, it is necessary to find a time registration path which best explains the relationship between the unknown phrase and a sequence of reference patterns (a 'super' reference pattern).

This optimization can be achieved by a number of different techniques.

4.1 One-Pass Algorithm

Perhaps the simplest (yet very effective) connected word recognition algorithm has been described by Bridle and Brown [1979]. In this scheme the dynamic programming calculation is arranged such that the time registration path may leave the end of one reference pattern and enter the beginning of another. To do this it is necessary to use a slightly more complicated local decision function on the edges of the dynamic programming matrices than in the middles. Figure 19 illustrates the point. Essentially those productions on the top edge of a matrix, which would normally refer to non-existant data outside of the matrix, are duplicated and attached to the trailing edges of all the other matrices (including the same one). Paths are thus able to enter and leave reference patterns according to the local minimizations. As before, the best path is not known until all of the local decisions have been made; backtracking then reveals the result.

To avoid complicated recursions and also path length normalization problems, the local decision function is chosen to be asymmetric (in fact the second example in figure 16). The asymmetry is arranged such that each production takes a path from one input vector to the next. Hence all possible paths will have the

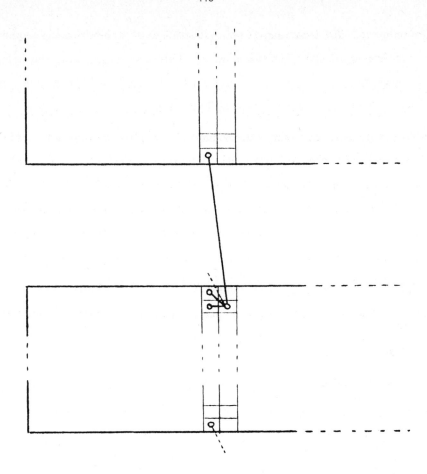

Figure 19   Arrangement of the local decision function at word boundaries in the one-pass connected word recognition algorithm.

same number of distances along their length, that number being equal to the number of frames in the unknown phrase. This also means that the computation may be performed on a column by column basis, hence processing one input vector with all of the reference data at each step.

Figure 20 shows an example of connected word recognition using the one-pass algorithm. The reference patterns are the same words as in figure 17, but the unknown pattern consists of a sequence of words (actually "11213"). The best path, determined by DTW, is shown, and it can be seen jumping around from template to template. The trajectory reveals that the phrase is correctly recognized as "11213".

(In comparing figure 20 with figure 17 it should be noted that there is only one path in figure 20: the optimal path, whereas in figure 17 three paths are shown: the optimal one and two sub-optimal ones.)

The computational requirement of the one-pass connected word recognition algorithm is exactly the same as for a DTW based isolated word recognition algorithm apart from the small amount of extra work needed to process the additional productions at template boundaries. Hence there are $T*R*V$ vector comparisons, and the same number of DP minimizations, where T is the number of frames in the test pattern, R is the average number of frames per reference pattern and V is the number of reference patterns.

The recognition accuracy of the technique depends on a number of factors. First, the algorithm assumes that continuous speech is made up of isolated words spoken in sequence. Obviously this is not the case, hence the recognition accuracy will only be high if the user speaks carefully and avoids coarticulation effects at the word boundaries. Second, the asymmetric local decision function imposes a 2:1 slope constraint which can easily be broken when comparing connected speech with isolated training examples.

One way to overcome both of these problems is to use an 'embedded' training procedure whereby reference words are extracted from a carrier sentence [Rabiner et al 1982]. The beauty of this technique is that a connected word

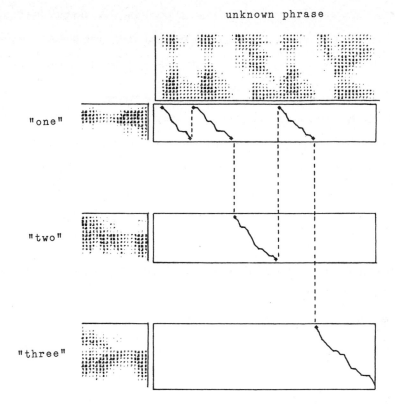

Figure 20   An example of connected word recognition using the one-pass algorithm.

recognition algorithm can be used to do the extraction. A simpler technique is to train such a connected word recognizer on isolated reference patterns which are spoken rather abruptly.

EXAMPLE SYSTEM: Marconi SR128

Pre-processing:

    — 19 channel filter bank

Training:

    — 128 seconds of template storage

    — maximum number of templates: 240

    — maximum length of a template: 2 secs.

    — built-in digital mini-cassette recorder for long term storage

Recognition

    — one-pass connected word recognition algorithm

    — maximum length of a phrase: 8 secs.

Computation:

    — recognition response time: 50 ms

Cost:

    — £ 10000

4.2 Two-Level Algorithm

The two-level connected word recognition technique of Sakoe [1979] was the first practical attempt to extend DTW beyond isolated words. It operates by first finding the optimal reference pattern to match any part of the unknown phrase and then by finding the optimal way to connect together the partial matches. Consequently, two dynamic programming processes are required, one at the word level and one at the phrase level, hence the term 'two-level'.

At the first level a standard isolated word DTW algorithm is used to find the minimum cumulative distance between each reference pattern (r) and all possible start frames (s) and all possible end frames (e) in the test pattern: $D(r,s,e)$.

At the second level a dynamic programming algorithm is used to find the path through $D(r,s,e)$ which minimizes the total distance starting with s as the first frame of the test pattern, and ending with e as the last frame of the test pattern:

$$D'(n,e) = \min_{s} \; [\min_{r} \; [D(r,s,e)] + D'(n-1,s-1)]$$

where $D'(n,e)$ is the cumulative distance obtained by matching the best concatenation of n reference patterns to the portion of the test pattern between frame 1 and frame e, and $\min[D(r,s,e)]$ over r is the distance resulting from the best reference pattern match between frames s and e of the test pattern.

The computation may be stopped once n is large enough to cover the maximum number of words expected in a phrase. The result can then be found by selecting the minimum value of $D'(n,E)$ (where E is the last frame in the test pattern), and then backtracking through the local decisions (at the second level) to find the best sequence of n words.

Computationally the two-level algorithm is much more complicated than the one-pass algorithm (due to all the $D(r,s,e)$ partial distance calculations); approximately $T*R^{4}*V$ DP minimizations, where T is the number of frames in the test pattern, R is the average number of frames per reference pattern and V is the number of reference patterns. However, the result of the different approaches should be identical. This is because ultimately they are both minimizing the same thing. However, the two-level algorithm does have the advantage that it is very easy to extract the recognition result for each value of n, that is, the scores for different length word hypothesese. Also, if required, it is easy to specify in advance how many words are in the unknown phrase.

Hence, errors of word deletion or insertion may be avoided. (It is possible to do the same for the one-pass algorithm, but it is much more complicated.)

EXAMPLE SYSTEM: Nippon Electric Company DP200

Pre-processing:

- 16 channel filter bank
- bandwidth: 120 Hz to 6000 Hz

Training:

- 4K bits per word
- vocabulary: 50 or 150 words
- built-in mini-floppy disk for template storage

Recognition:

- two-level connected word recognition algorithm
- up to five words per phrase
- 0.2 to 4.0 seconds per phrase

Computation:

- recognition result 300 ms from end of phrase

Recognition accuracy:

- 1.2% error rate on DSTI data (DP100 results)

Cost:

$15000

4.3 Level Building Algorithm

The level building connected word recognition algorithm, proposed by Myers and Rabiner [1981], is another technique for optimizing the match between a sequence of reference patterns and an unknown phrase. It is thus functionally identical to both the one-pass algorithm and the two-level algorithm.

In this scheme the term 'level' refers to the number of words in a hypothesized sequence. So to recognize a sequence of n words, at least n levels must be built. The first level corresponds to hypothesizing that the unknown phrase consists of a single word, the second level corresponds to two word hypothesese etc. Conceptually, at each level, DTW is performed between all of the reference patterns and all of the test patterns, and the results from each level are taken as inputs to the DTW calculations of the next level.

This means that at the end of the calculations for the first level, there will be associated with each frame of the test pattern a cumulative distance resulting from the best time registration path out of all of the references, and a pointer indicating which reference pattern it was. The time registration paths in this case will trace back to the first frame of the test pattern and the first frame of a reference pattern. This information then provides the starting point for the next level, and the new time registration paths will trace back to the first level, and so on.

The level building algorithm is computationally an order of magnitude more efficient than the two-level algorithm, but it has N times more dynamic programming minimizations than the one-pass algorithm (where N is the number of levels). However, like the two-level algorithm, the level building algorithm can easily find the best sequence of a given length.

4.4 Hidden Markov Models

The principle of hidden Markov modelling was in fact applied to connected word recognition before it was applied to isolated word recognition. Jelinek's team at IBM used HMMs to model phonetic speech segments, which could then be connected together to make words and then sentences [Jelinek et al 1982, Bahl et al 1983].

Exactly the same techniques may be applied to the connection of whole-word models, and the process is analogous to the one-pass algorithm described above. The advantage of this approach is that it becomes possible to train the word boundary information in context. However, the negative consequences of this feature are that the combinatorics require a large amount of training data.

EXAMPLE SYSTEM: Verbex 1800

Pre-processing:

— 32 channel filter bank

— bandwidth: 300 Hz to 3000 Hz

— autocorrelation coefficients

— eight input channels

Training:

— multiple training passes

— can train on word sequences

— vocabulary: 10 - 39 words

Recognition:

— connected word recognition

— hidden Markov models

Recognition Accuracy:

— 0.2% errors on DSTI isolated word data (best in the DSTI test)

Cost:

— $80000

5.   REAL-TIME CONSIDERATIONS

Most of the algorithms discussed so far have been described without due regard to any short-cuts or other efficiency modifications. This section outlines some techniques which may be used to cut down the computational load and which may also affect the recognition performance (either for the better, or for the worse). For most of the algorithms, the introduction of efficiency usually means sacrificing optimality. Therefore, overall performance is often raised at the expense of making a few serious errors from time to time.

5.1 Syntax

As well as a definition of the words in the vocabulary, there will also be rules which govern the ordering of the words in most applications of automatic speech recognition. These rules define a grammar (or syntax) which may be used to reduce the computational requirement for an isolated or a connected word recognizer by limiting the number of alternative words at each point in a sentence.

The implementation of syntax for an isolated word recognizer is very easy; after each word is recognized, the active vocabulary is switched according to the rules of the grammar. For connected word recognition the process is more complicated, but it is possible to modify the algorithms such that time registration paths only connect words if such a connection is legal in the syntax. In this situation the syntax becomes an integral part of the overall optimization process, hence connected word recognizers with this facility are able to find the best syntactically valid interpretation of a connected utterance.

There are a number of ways of specifying a syntax, but the most common is in the form of a state transition diagram. Figure 21 shows a syntax for a voice controlled calculator. It can be seen that the diagram describes sentences such as "what is two plus four compute" and "put nine times alpha into beta compute". The overall vocabulary size is twenty-three, but the maximum number of words that need to be considered at any point is fourteen; in some places only one word is valid. The average number of legal words at any point is eight and this is known as the 'branching factor'. The ratio of branching factor to total vocabulary size gives an indication of the reduction in computation.

A low branching factor will also increase recognition accuracy because the number of potential word confusions is reduced. (In general, variability means that recognition performance goes down as the number of choices goes up.)

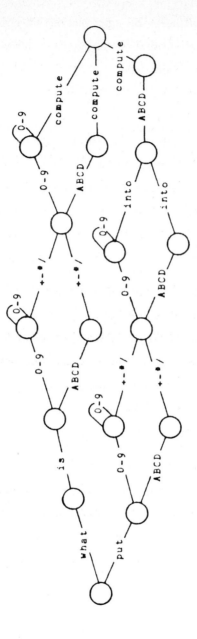

Figure 21 Syntax for a voice controlled calculator.

However, this gain in performance is balanced by the requirement that a user must be able to remember and use only allowable sequences of words. If a user says a word which is syntactically illegal, then a recognizer may be forced to misrecognize it, even if the word is in the overall vocabulary.

5.2 Fixed Search Window

In DTW based recognition algorithms the search for the optimal solution can often extend into regions which are extremely unlikely. Of course it is only by doing so, that the optimal solution can be guaranteed. Nevertheless, it is possible to achieve a reasonable reduction in computation, with only a small risk of reaching a non-optimal solution, by restricting the search in some way.

One way of achieving this restriction is to impose a fixed search window on the DTW process. Typically this might take the form of a range restriction on the total amount of time registration slippage that is allowed at any point. Hence in the calculation of the distance and cumulative distance matrices for isolated word recognition, the indices would be limited such that $|i-j| < W$, where i and j are the indices and W is the window width. Figure 22 illustrates the process (in this example the optimal path found in figure 15 has been lost).

For isolated word recognition it is possible to speed up the computation by a factor of 1.6 with no degradation in recognition accuracy [Moore 1980]. The same process may be applied to the two-level and the level building connected word recognition algorithms, and in these cases even larger savings in computation may be achieved.

5.3 Beam Search

A second technique for reducing the DTW search is not to have a fixed search window, but to have a dynamic window which is controlled by the search process itself. This technique is known as 'beam search' and it is based on the principle that at any point during the DTW process it is possible to measure the value of the best solution (minimum distance or maximum probability) so far. This means that on the next iteration of the processs, the search can be limited

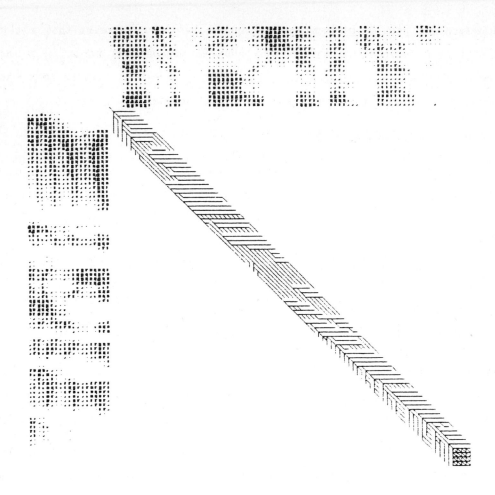

Figure 22　The effect of a fixed search window on dynamic time warping.

to solutions which lie within a given range of the current best solution.

The beauty of this technique is that when there is ambiguity there will be a range of solutions all fairly close to each other and the beam will be wide, but when there is little ambiguity there will be few competing solutions and the beam will be narrow. Hence the scheme ensures that most of the computation takes place where it is most needed. Figure 23 illustrates the effect on a single DTW word match.

The danger with the beam search technique is that if the beam is too narrow, then the optimal solution might be lost if there is a momentary bad fit in the data (after all, the main reason for using dynamic programming based algorithms is to exploit their property of overcoming local deficiencies). However, for isolated word recognition the technique is capable of speeding up computation by a factor of four without affecting recognition performance [Moore 1980].

5.4 Partial Traceback

Partial traceback is another technique for exploiting the intermediate properties of a dynamic programming type search [Spohrer et al 1980]. It is based on the idea that by continually tracing back during the DTW process (rather than waiting until the end) it is possible to discover a point in the past to which all backtraces lead. When such a point is found, no amount of further processing will change the trajectory of the path up to that point. Hence, the results of the DTW process up to that point may be output. Figure 24 illustrates the principle for an isolated word comparison.

The technique is particularly relevant to connected word recognition. If partial traceback is used in this situation, it becomes possible to output the initial words in a long sentence before the sentence has finished being spoken. More importantly, it is possible to run the entire DTW process continuously; the DTW optimization can continually take in new data, and the results are output (after a delay) by means of partial traceback [Bridle et al 1983]. (The amount of delay between input and output in such a system will depend on the ambiguity present in the signal.)

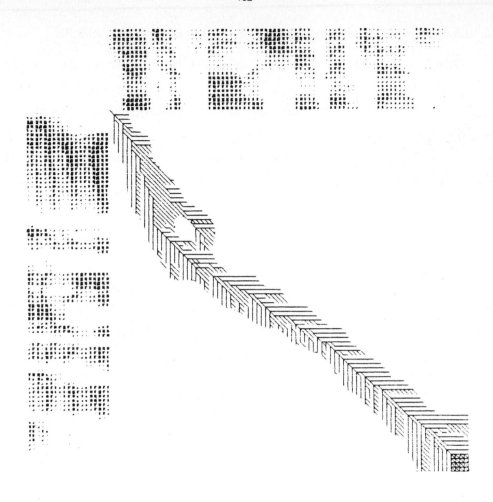

Figure 23   The effect of beam search on dynamic time warping.

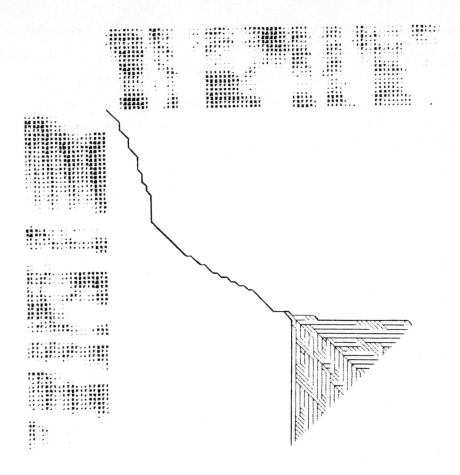

Figure 24   The effect of partial traceback on dynamic time warping.

If partial traceback is combined with beam search, then it is even possible to output the identity of a spoken word before it has been completely uttered. This will occur when competing words are sufficiently different that the beam falls totally within only one word. Partial traceback can detect this occurrence and output the word. However, if the beam is too narrow in this situation, it is possible to have a recognizer discriminating between two similar words before the deciding sounds have occurred.

EXAMPLE SYSTEM: Logica LOGOS

Pre-processing:

- 19 channel filter bank
- 200 frames per second
- variable rate coding

Training:

- embedded training (may be embedded in silence)
- uses concept of 'wildcard' frame
- storage for up to 2000 templates (minimum 64K bytes: 120 templates)

Recognition:

- continuous connected word recognizer
- one-pass connected DTW algorithm
- beam search
- partial traceback
- 5 second input buffer
- syntax (up to 256 nodes)
- number of active words: 20 (expandable up to 300 maximum)
- keyword spotting

Computation:

- separate DP processors for section of total vocabulary
- response: typically one or two words delay (depends on ambiguity)

Cost:

—£ 35000

6. FUTURE METHODS AND SYSTEMS

The foregoing sections have concentrated on established techniques for automatic speech recognition. This section is intended to focus on some of the key issues relating to future methods and systems.

From a user's point of view, perhaps the most immediate requirement is for systems with a high level of reliability for reasonable sized vocabularies regardless of whether they are isolated or connected word recognizers. Hence, work aimed at improving the discrimination power of recognizers is important. Second, users would ideally like not to have to spend too long training systems. Hence, work which is aimed at introducing more speech knowledge into systems is also important.

6.1 More Useful Representations

The beauty of the whole word pattern matching approach is that it provides a single (easy to characterize) interface between the speech patterns and the matching process. However, the performance of the approach ultimately depends on the exact nature of this interface and the quality of data that it uses. It can be seen from the preceding sections that nearly all of the recognizers employ a fairly coarse representation of the speech signal, usually equivalent to the analyzer section of a vocoder system.

Obviously such representations are in some sense appropriate for speech recognition (it is possible to understand the re-synthesized speech), but in no sense could they be described as high quality. It is therefore possible that one bottleneck in the performance of current systems is this reliance on low data rates at the front-end.

The question as to what constitutes a high enough quality representation is open to some debate, but it is reasonable to expect that work on auditory modelling has some relevance [Lyon 1982].

It might also be sensible to break away from the straightforward use of the 'raw' speech pattern, and instead to re-address the question of a suitable low-level featural description. Such an approach is currently being pursued by Cole et al [1983] using statistical pattern recognition techniques.

6.2 Better Models

In section 3.4 it can be seen how DTW is not a single well defined algorithm, but rather a principle which underlies a collection of alternative options and implementations. A lot of research effort has been directed towards manipulating the various parameters in a DTW algorithm, but it has resulted in very few insights into the meaning of DTW as a model of speech variability. On the other hand, hidden Markov modelling does provide a useful theoretical framework, but to what extent is it a 'good' model?

(It should be remembered that the purpose of a 'good' model is to take knowledge (perhaps in the form of training data) and 'generalize' that knowledge appropriately to assess previously unseen events. This can only be done by a proper understanding of the variabilities involved.)

Work at RSRE on 'timescale variability analysis' [Moore et al 1982 and Russell et al 1983] is an example of introducing into a DTW processs, knowledge about the expected local variation in the temporal structure of speech patterns. Essentially, the techniques replaces global path constraints with probabalistically conditioned local path constraints (it is analogous to training the state transition probabilities in an HMM). The result of providing DTW with a good model of temporal variability is that it is then better able to discriminate between different words, and is also able to discriminate between words where the difference is entirely temporal (something that normal DTW is unable to do). For example, using the 'locally constrained dynamic time warping' (LCDTW) algorithm, error rates for the two pronunciations of "close" (/kləʊs/ and /kləʊz/) were reduced from 40% (using DTW) to 1.5% (using LCDTW).

6.3 Improved Optimization

Assuming it is possible to arrive at a 'good' model, it is still necessary to train it (to optimize its behaviour). Hidden Markov models have an advantage here because they employ an algorithm (the Baum-Welch) which is guaranteed to improve the behaviour of the model. However, such an optimization is not guaranteed to find the 'best' solution, merely to find the best local optimum. As a consequence, the apparently straightforward handle-turning optimization process, is in fact rather more complicated.

In general, optimization techniques are becoming inherent to advanced automatic speech recognition algorithms. Hence, a better understanding of these processes is essential. An optimization technique which is able to avoid becoming trapped in local optima has been described by Kirkpatrick et al [1983]. In this scheme ideas based in statistical mechanics are used to implement an algorithm which simulates the cooling behaviour of a physical system: the annealing process. By introducing the notion of 'temperature' into an optimization problem, Kirkpatrick shows how the process can escape from local optima.

6.4 More Speech Knowledge

The performance of an automatic speech recognizer ultimately depends on the amount and quality of the training material. However, if the dimensionality of the representation is raised then recognizers are almost always going to be undertrained. It is therefore vital to know how the knowledge embedded in the training material can best be structured and hence utilized. One technique for obtaining this structured knowledge is to extract it from a human 'expert'. Unfortunately this raises questions about the usefulness of the knowledge thereby gained.

In theory, it ought to be possible to extract a great deal of structural information from the speech signal itself (humans seem to do it). So the question is how to use available speech data to the maximum advantage.

The work on 'discriminative networks' at RSRE [Moore et al 1983] shows how some of the problems associated with undertraining may be avoided. The technique is directed at the problems which arise from attempting to distinguish between two very similar words using whole-word pattern matching. Such similar sounding words are characterized by having extremely localized differences (for example, "stalagmite" and "stalactite") which are swamped by the irrelevant variability contained in the rest of the patterns.

If a recognizer was fully trained, then this variability would be characterized and it would be possible to optimally discriminate between the two words. However, since a recognizer is always undertrained (particularly if it has only one example of each word as a reference pattern), then it is possible to circumvent the undertraining by forcing the regions of the pattern which are irrelevant to the distinction to be identical. This is equivalent to deriving a network-type data structure for the two patterns (the discriminative network) which is able to focus the recognition process onto those regions of the patterns which are relevant to the distinction. The result is that the undertraining is supplemented with the a-priori knowledge that the two word patterns are supposed to be different.

The RSRE algorithm is able to derive the network structure for any pair of words automatically, and the networks assume the shapes one would expect given the phonetic structure of the component words. Figure 25a illustrates the expected discriminative network for "stalagmite"/"stalactite", and figure 25b shows the speech pattern network derived by the technique. For the same pair of words, a 40% error rate for normal DTW was reduced to no errors using the network shown.

6.5 Better Architectures

All of the techniques described in this lecture tend to be a mixture of sequential and parallel processes. Dynamic programming is essentially a sequential process since a set of partial results is needed before the next iteration can proceed. On the other hand, distance calculations may all be done in parallel since one distance does not depend on another. Suitable processing architectures

(a)

(b)

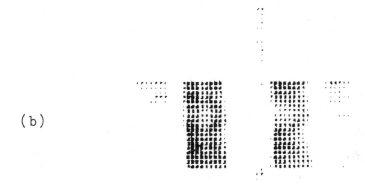

Figure 25   Discriminative network for the words "stalagmite" and "stalactite"; (a) the expected network and (b) the experimentally derived speech spectrogram network.

are needed to exploit this mix, and in particular the parallelism that is possible.

A specific example of DTW being implemented on a parallel processing architecture is described by Simpson and Roberts [1983]. A highly parallel single-instruction multiple-data (SIMD) array signal processor with 32x32 processing elements and a 100 ns cycle time (the ICL distributed array processor: DAP) is shown to be capable of handling a 600 word vocabulary in real-time using the one-pass connected word recognition algorithm.

7. CONCLUSIONS

This lecture has attempted to describe in some detail many of the techniques which underlie contemporary isolated and connected word recognition systems. The main conclusion is that, far from being a 'dead-end', whole-word pattern matching techniques provide a baseline from which to develop new methods and systems.

The key to success in this area appears to be a proper separation between the knowledge which one might have about speech signals, the models in which one chooses to embody such knowledge, and the optimization techniques which are needed to load the knowledge into the models.

ACKNOWLEDGEMENT

I am particularly indebted to my colleague Dr. Martin Russell for his many helpful contributions to this lecture.

REFERENCES

1. L. R. Bahl, F. Jelinek and R. L. Mercer, "A maximum likelihood approach to continuous speech recognition", IEEE Trans. Pattern Analysis and Machine Intelligence, Vol. 5, 1983, pp. 179-190.
2. L. E. Baum, "An inequality and associated maximization technique in statistical estimation for probabalistic functions of a Markov process", Inequalities, Vol. 3, 1972, pp. 1-8.
3. J. S. Bridle and M. D. Brown, "An experimental automatic word-recognition system", JSRU Research Report No. 1003, 1974.
4. J. S. Bridle, "Pattern recognition techniques for speech recognition", Proc. NATO ASI on Spoken Language Generation and Understanding, 1979.
5. J. S. Bridle and M. D. Brown, "Connected word recognition using whole word templates", Proc. Inst. Acoustics Autumn Conf., 1979.
6. J. S. Bridle and M. D. Brown, "A data-adaptive frame rate technique and its use in automatic speech recognition", Proc. Inst. Acoustics Autumn Conf., 1982.
7. J. S. Bridle, M. D. Brown and R. M. Chamberlain, "Continuous connected word recoognition using whole word templates", The Radio and Electronic Engineer, Vol. 53, 1983, pp. 167-175.
8. R. A. Cole, R. M. Stern, M. S. Phillips, S. M. Brill, A. P. Pilant and P. Specker, "Feature-based speaker-independent recognition of isolated English letters", Proc. IEEE Conf. Acoustics, Speech and Signal Processing, 1983, pp. 731-733.
9. K. H. Davis, R. Biddulph and S. Balashek, "Automatic recognition of spoken digits", J. Acoust. Soc. Amer., Vol. 24, 1952, pp. 637-642.
10. G. R. Doddington and T. B. Schalk, "Speech recognition: turning theory to practice", IEEE Spectrum, Vol. 18, 1981, pp. 26-32.
11. J. L. Flanagan, *Speech Analysis, Synthesis and Perception*. New York: Springer-Verlang, 1972.
12. J. N. Holmes, "The JSRU channel vocoder", IEE Proc. Communications, Radar and Signal Processing, Vol. 127, Pt.F, 1980, pp. 53-60.
13. J. N. Holmes, "A survey of methods for digitally encoding speech signals", The Radio and Electronic Engineer, Vol. 52, 1982, pp. 267-276.
14. M. J. Hunt, M. Lennig and P. Mermelstein, "Experiments in syllable-based recognition of continuous speech", Proc. IEEE Conf. Acoustics, Speech and Signal Processing, 1980, pp. 880-883.
15. F. Itakura, "Minimum prediction residual principle applied to speech recognition", IEEE Trans. Acoustics, Speech and Signal Processing, Vol. 23, 1975, pp. 67-72.
16. F. Jelinek, R. L. Mercer and L. R. Bahl, "Continuous speech recognition: statistical methods", Handbook of Statistics, Vol. 2, Krishnaiah and Kanal, eds., North-Holland, 1982, pp. 549-573.
17. S. Kirpatrick, C. D. Gelatt, Jr. and M. P. Vecchi, "Optimization by simulated annealing", Science, Vol. 220, 1983, pp. 671-680.

18. S. E. Levinson, L. R. Rabiner and M. M. Sondhi, "Speaker independent isolated digit recognition using hidden Markov models", Proc. IEEE Int. Conf. Acoustics, Speech and Signal Processing, 1983, pp. 1049-1052.

19. R. F. Lyon, "A computational model of filtering, detection and compression in the cochlea", Proc. IEEE Conf. Acoustics, Speech and Signal Processing, 1982, pp. 1282-1285.

20. R. K. Moore, "An investigation into some fundamental problems in the automatic recognition of continuous speech", Unpublished Technical Report, 1980.

21. R. K. Moore, M. J. Russell and M. J. Tomlinson, "Locally constrained dynamic programming in automatic speech recognition", Proc. IEEE Conf. Acoustics, Speech and Signal Procesing, 1982, pp. 1270-1273.

22. R. K. Moore, M. J. Russell and M. J. Tomlinson, "The discriminative network: a mechanism for focusing recognition in whole word pattern matching", Proc. IEEE Conf. Acoustics, Speech and Signal Processing, 1983, pp. 1041-1044.

23. C. Myers, L. R. Rabiner and A. E. Rosenberg, "Performance tradeoffs in dynamic time warping algorithms for isolated word recognition", IEEE Trans. Acoustics, Speech and Signal Processing, Vol. 28, 1980, pp. 623-635.

24. C. S. Myers and L. R. Rabiner, "A level building dynamic time warping algorithm for connected word recognition", IEEE Trans. Acoustics, Speech and Signal Processing, Vol. 29, 1981, pp. 284-297.

25. R. Pieraccini and R. Billi, "Experimental comparison among data compression techniques in isolated word recognition", Proc. IEEE Int. Conf. Acoustics, Speech and Signal Processing, 1983, pp. 1025-1028.

26. L. R. Rabiner and M. R. Sambur, "An algorithm for determining the endpoints of isolated utterances", Bell Syst. Tech. J., Vol. 54, 1975, pp. 297-315.

27. L. R. Rabiner and J. G. Wilpon, "A simplified, robust training procedure for speaker trained isolated word recognition", J. Acoust. Soc. Amer., Vol. 68, pp. 1271-1276.

28. L. R. Rabiner, A. Bergh and J. G. Wilpon, "An improved training procedure for connected-digit recognition", Bell Syst. Tech. J., Vol. 61, 1982, pp. 981-1001.

29. M. J. Russell, R. K. Moore and M. J. Tomlinson, "Some techniques for incorporating local timescale variability information into a dynamic time-warping algorithm for automatic speech recognition", Proc. IEEE Conf. Acoustics, Speech and Signal Processing, 1983, pp. 1037-1040.

30. H. Sakoe and S. Chiba, "Dynamic programming algorithm optimization for spoken word recognition", IEEE Trans. Acoustics, Speech and Signal Processing, Vol. 26, 1978, pp. 43-49.

31. H. Sakoe, "Two-level DP-matching — a dynamic programming based pattern matching algorithm for connected word recognition", IEEE Trans. Acoustics, Speech and Signal Processing, Vol. 27, 1979, pp. 588-595.

32. R. W. Schafer and L. R. Rabiner, "Digital representations of speech signals", Proc. IEEE, Vol. 63, 1975, pp. 662-677.

33. J. E. Shore and D. Burton, "Discrete utterance speech recognition without

time normalization — recent results", Proc. 6th Int. Conf. Pattern Recognition, 1982, pp. 582-584.

34. P. Simpson and J. B. G. Roberts, "Speech recognition on a distributed array processor", Electronics Letters, Vol. 19, 1983, pp. 1018-1020.

35. J. C. Spohrer, P. F. Brown, P. H. Hochschild and J. K. Baker, "Partial traceback in continuous speech recognition", Proc. IEEE Int. Conf. Cybernetics and Society, 1980, pp. 36-42.

36. G. M. White, "Speech recognition with character string encoding", Proc. IEEE Conf. Decision and Control, 1972, pp. 111-113.

37. G. M. White and P. J. Fong, "k-nearest-neighbour decision rule performance in a speech recognition system", IEEE Trans. Systems, Man and Cybernetics, Vol. 5, 1975, pp. 389.

38. G. M. White and R. B. Neely, "Speech recognition experiments with linear prediction, bandpass filtering, and dynamic programming", IEEE Trans. Acoustics, Speech and Signal Processing, Vol. 24, 19776, pp. 183-188.

SYSTOLIC ARCHITECTURES FOR CONNECTED SPEECH RECOGNITION

Patrice FRISON
Patrice QUINTON

IRISA, Campus de Beaulieu,
35042 RENNES-CEDEX
FRANCE

July 1984

ABSTRACT

Systolic algorithm concept is introduced and three speech recognition algorithms are presented together with a systolic version. The first algorithm is based on the dynamic time warping algorithm which is applied directly on acoustic feature patterns. The second algorithm is the probabilistic matching algorithm which requires that the input sentence be preprocessed by a phonetic analyzer. The third algorithm is the connected word recognition algorithm that find the best matching word sequence. Finally, the architecture of a speech recognition machine using a VLSI chip, called API89, as the basic processor is presented.

NATO ASI Series, Vol. F16
New Systems and Architectures for Automatic Speech
Recognition and Synthesis. Edited by R. De Mori and C. Y. Suen
© Springer-Verlag Berlin Heidelberg 1985

SYSTOLIC ARCHITECTURES FOR CONNECTED SPEECH RECOGNITION

Patrice FRISON
Patrice QUINTON

IRISA, Campus de Beaulieu,
35042 RENNES-CEDEX
FRANCE

1. INTRODUCTION

Speech recognition is a computationally intensive task which can be handled on conventional architectures only for small vocabularies. The use of pipeline and parallel architecture organizations increases the speed of the algorithms thus making realistic recognition of much larger vocabularies and broadening the range of application of vocal input.

Over the past few years, numerous attempts to map speech recognition algorithms on parallel architectures or to design dedicated parallel architectures supporting speech tasks have been reported [1]. Advances in VLSI have shown to be a determinant factor in this evolution as VLSI makes it feasible to implement complex parallel architectures on a few integrated circuits. Among the various parallel organizations that have been considered for that purpose, systolic array is a particularly appealing structure. A systolic array [2] is a special-purpose architecture made out of simple processing elements organized as a regular network. Processors are locally connected, operate synchronously, and data circulate throughout the network in a pipeline fashion.

Systolic arrays for speech recognition have been described recently. Weste, Burr and Ackland [3] present an orthogonal array of processors (40 × 40) that can support the dynamic time warping algorithm. The performances of this array permit real time isolated word recognition of a 20,000 word vocabulary. They also describe the VLSI implementation of the basic processor of this array. Yoder and Siegel [4] present various systolic schemes for dynamic time warping, including the use of a linear array. More recently, Feldman et al. [5] consider a wafer scale implementation of a two-dimensional systolic array for connected speech recognition.

This paper is based on an effort undertaken since the end of 1980 at IRISA to explore the potential of systolic architectures for connected speech recognition [6]-[9]. The algorithm that was originally considered in [6] is a probabilistic matching algorithm based on Bahl and Jelinek linguistic decoder [10]. The main difference with the dynamic time warping approach is that the speech signal must be preprocessed before applying the recognition, in order to recognize the phonemes in the speech. Our purpose in this paper is to present and discuss various systolic algorithms for connected speech recognition. In section 2 the systolic architecture concept is defined and an example presented. Moreover, a systematic design approach is shown. Section 3 presents three algorithms for which a systolic solution has been proposed: the dynamic time warping algorithm, the probabilistic matching and the connected speech recognition algorithm. In section 4, we describe a VLSI implementation of a continuous speech recognition systolic machine under developpement at IRISA.

2. SYSTOLIC ARCHITECTURE AND DESIGN METHODOLOGY

2.1. Definition and example

According to KUNG [2], a systolic architecture is defined in the following way:
- it is a special purpose parallel machine, made out of a small number of processor types (usually one);
- processors are regularly and locally connected;
- parallelism and pipeline processing are extensively used;
- computation is carried out in a synchronous way.

The convolution product is a good example to illustrate the systolic concept. Given a sequence $x(0), x(1), \cdots, x(i), \cdots$ and coefficients $w(0), w(1), \cdots, w(K)$, the convolution algorithm consists in computing the sequence $y(0), y(1), \cdots, y(i), \cdots$ where $y(i)$ is given by the following equation

$$y(i) = \sum_{k=0}^{K} w(k)\, x(i-k) \tag{1}$$

Fig. 1 shows a systolic architecture with three linearly connected processors ($K = 2$). For communication purpose, each cell is provided with four communication ports. The x values flow from left to right on the top communication lines and the partially computed y values flow on the bottom communication lines. Note that a delay is inserted on the x lines. Each processor contains a coefficient w. At each step of the computation, each cell receives two values, namely an x value and a y value. Internally, the following calculation is done:

$$y := y + w\, x$$

Then the two values x and y are sent out of the processor.

It is easy to show that the last processor gives the right sequence $y(i)$ assuming that K+1 cycles before, the values $x(i)$ and 0 were input on the first processor.

The above example is just an illustration of what a systolic machine is and how it works. It should be pointed out that the systolic concept is not a new architecture type since numerous parallel machines have been designed before the systolic term was proposed. The main idea is to combine efficiently parallel and pipeline processing and to use such machines as peripherals of a host computer in order to speed-up some very time-consuming tasks.

Moreover, the systolic idea is tightly related to the new types of applications highlighted by the VLSI technology. Indeed, a systolic machine has to be custom-designed for a given task. With new design methodologies [11], powerful and low design-cost integrated circuits can be fabricated. As explained in the following, the systolic concept is well-suited to VLSI:
- fast computation is obtained via parallelism instead of very fast technology;
- regular structure reduces the design task because only a few types of cells or processors need to be designed and tested;
- synchronisation problems are simplified due to local communications and

synchronous computation;
 - by allowing multiple use of the same data, pipelining reduces communication bandwidth with the host computer, a major issue with most of the parallel computers.

2.2. Designing systolic algorithms

In this section, it is shown how systolic algorithms can be designed in a systematic way. The process of finding systolic arrays go through several steps that will be examplified on the convolution product. The first step, which unfortunately must be done by hand right now, consists in transforming the equations of the problem to be solved in such a way that they become a uniform recurrent system of equations. For some problems (like the convolution, or the matrix product), this is not very difficult. For other, in particular problems involving recursive computations, this may be very tricky. The second step consists in finding a timing-function for the uniform recurrent system. Finally, the last step consists in allocating the computations on a finite, regular array of processors. At IRISA, a system named DIASTOL based on these ideas is being implemented. In the next sections, starting from the example of the convolution product, we will examine these three steps in turn.

2.2.1. Transforming the equations

A first transformation of (1) consists in expanding the $\sum$ operator in such a way that only remain elementary calculations. These elementary calculations actually define the structure of the elementary cells of the systolic array. Equation (1) may be rewritten as:

$$\forall i, 0 \le i \; ; \; \forall k, 0 \le k \le K: \; y(i,k) = y(i,k-1) + w(k)\, x(i-k) \qquad (2)$$

$$\forall i: 0 \le i, \; y(i,-1) = 0$$

where $y(i,k)$ are partial accumulated values for $y(i)$. The basic idea is to consider these computations to be associated with points (i,k) of the plane, and more generally, to integer coordinate points of the Euclidean space. For any integer coordinate point (i,k) lying in the domain $D = \{\, 0 \le i \; ; \; 0 \le k \le K \,\}$, we have to perform the elementary computation $y_{out} = y_{in} + w_{in}\, x_{in}$, the result of which will be $y(i,k)$ provided that y_{in}, w_{in}, and x_{in} are given correct values $y(i,k-1)$, $x(i-k)$ and $w(k)$.

As we want to express the computation as a flowgraph, it is necessary that each variable in (2) appear with all the indexes. We can see that w appears only with index k, and x only with index $i-k$. There are generally several ways to do that. Let us denote as $W(i,k)$ the new variable w, and $X(i,k)$ the new variable x. Equation (2) may be replaced by:

$\forall i: 0 \le i \; ; \; \forall k: 0 \le k \le K$

$y(i,k) = y(i,k-1) + W(i-1,k) \, X(i-1,k-1)$

$W(i,k) = W(i-1,k)$ (3)

$X(i,k) = X(i-1,k-1)$

with the following initial conditions:

$\forall i, \, 0 \le i; \, \forall k, \, 0 \le k \le K$:

$y(i,-1) = 0; \quad W(-1,k) = w(k); \quad X(i-1,-1) = x(i); \quad X(-1,k-1) = 0$

Such a system of recurrent equations is said to be uniform, since computation at point (i,k) depends only on values computed at points that are obtained by a translation which does not depend on i or k [12]. This system may be represented by a graph such as that of Fig. 2. The nodes of this graph represent the computations to be achieved and the edges represent values that are to be transmitted from one node to another.

2.2.2. Timing-functions

The next step consists in finding a schedule for the computations, called a **timing-function**. A timing-function is a integer mapping $t(i,k)$ which gives the time at which the computation associated with point (i,k) can occur. In DIAS-TOL, we only consider linear (or more exactly affine) functions for timing-functions.

In [12], it is explained formally how one can find a timing-function. Intuitively, there are two kinds of constraints to be considered. The first kind of constraints has to deal with the equations. If we want to be able to evaluate computation associated with point (i,k), it is necessary that all the computations involving input arguments of the equation be already done. Consider equation (3), computation at point (i,k) depends on results of computations at points $(i-1,k)$, $(i,k-1)$, and $(i-1,k-1)$. Therefore we must have:

$t(i,k) > t(i-1,k)$

$t(i,k) > t(i,k-1)$

$t(i,k) > t(i-1,k-1)$

The second type of constraints on the timing-function is related to the domain. If we want to be able to implement the problem on a real machine, it is necessary that the computation start once, i.e, that $t(i,k)$ have a minimum value over the domain of computation. Also there must be a bounded number of points to be computed simultaneously.

The timing-function is not unique but obviously some solutions are better than others (see [12] for details). For instance in the example we are dealing with, we obtain the timing-function:

$$t(i,k) = i + k$$

Fig. 3 shows the resulting schedule of the equations.

2.2.3. Allocation function

Once we have the schedule of the computations, it remains to map these computations on a finite machine, in a "systolic" way. A very convenient way to do so is to project the domain of computations along a direction defined by some conveniently chosen vector u. Each point of the resulting projected domain will represent a processor of the systolic architecture. Before giving more details about this step, consider again the convolution product example. A convenient way to project the domain (see Fig. 2), is to project it along the i-axis. In this way, all the points lying on lines parallel to the i-axis will be computed by the same processor. Since these points are computed at different times according to the timing-function we have chosen, a processor will never have more than a computation to do at a given time. The resulting architecture is the one already depicted on Fig. 1. To see how this architecture can be derived from the system, the timing-function, and the mapping, one can look at Fig. 3. Since the domain of computation has three lines parallel to the i-axis, there are only three processors. Let us call cell K the processor which takes care of the computations associated with points lying on line $k = K$. The data movement between the cells result from the data dependences shown on Fig. 2. Coefficients w stay on each processor. Values y and x go from processor 0 to processor 1 to processor 2. Note also that the x's move slower than the y's. This appears clearly by examining Fig. 2, since the x's move diagonally and therefore, reach a processor (i.e., a line $k=K$) every other time. This is the reason why the x's have to be delayed between two processors.

We denote as $a(i,k)$ the function that tells which processor execute the computation associated with point (i,k). This function is called the **allocation function**.

2.3. Another Example

To demonstrate the power of the previously explained method, and show that multiple solutions can be found for a specific problem, another systolic architecture for the convolution product is presented.

From the equation (1), there is another way to derive a system of recurrent equations. The idea is to expand the $\sum$ operator with the k indexes running from K to 0. Equation (1) may be rewritten as:

$$\forall i: 0 \le i \ ; \ \forall k: 0 \le k \le K$$

$$y(i,k) = y(i,k+1) + W(i-1,k) X(i-1,k-1)$$

$$W(i,k) = W(i-1,k)$$

$$X(i,k) = X(i-1,k-1)$$

with the following initial conditions:

$$\forall i, 0 \le i; \ \forall k, 0 \le k \le K:$$

$$y(i,K+1) = 0; \quad W(-1,k) = w(k); \quad X(i-1,-1) = x(i); \quad X(-1,k-1) = 0$$

Fig. 4 shows the dependence graph for that case with the corresponding timing function. The systolic array shown on Fig. 5 is obtained by projection along the i axis. Note that x and y values are input in the array every two cycles therefore indicating that each processor is idle every other cycle. Such an array would be convenient to compute two convolutions in interleaved way.

3. SYSTOLIC ALGORITHMS FOR SPEECH RECOGNITION

The systolic architecture concept presented above seems very attractive for applications such as signal processing as well as speech processing. In the following, we will see how this concept has already been used in the speech recognition area. We will also show that the systematic method for systolic architecture design can be applied very easily on realistic examples. In particular, we will see that the definition of the allocation function can depend on some constraints linked to the application.

Fig. 6 presents together the block-diagram of two connected speech recognition methods. The first one (Fig. 6A) is based on the DTW algorithm, and the second one (Fig. 6B) on a probabilistic matching algorithm. In both methods, the analog signal which results of an utterance is filtered, and acoustic features are extracted at constant intervals. Depending on the acoustic analysis method which is used, these features may be band energies, formant frequencies, cepstral coefficients, or linear prediction coefficients. Each vector of features, called a **frame,** encodes usually 20ms of speech signal and contains 8 to 15 values. Endpoints of the utterance are then determined by examining variations in the energy of the speech signal. At this point, the pronounced utterance is represented by a sequence of frames called the **acoustic test pattern.** Two different approaches are then possible. In the first one (Fig. 6A), reference words are memorized as acoustic patterns. Distance measures between reference words and every subsequence of the test pattern are calculated using the dynamic time warping algorithm. These distances are then combined in order to retrieve the original sentence. The other approach (Fig. 6B) consists in preprocessing the acoustic test pattern in order to encode it as a string of phonemes called the **phonetic test pattern.** The reference words, also represented as strings of phonemes, are then matched against the phonetic test pattern resulting in probabilities that are then used for the sentence recognition.

From the point of view of recognition accuracy, the DTW approach is superior to the probabilistic matching because the phonetic analysis that must be carried out before the probabilistic matching is a very inaccurate process. This explains why up to now only the DTW algorithm has been considered for practical application of speech recognition. However, in the long term, the second approach presents the two advantages of being less computation intensive and of needing less memory to store the reference words.

In the following, we describe in more detail the algorithms underlying each of these approaches. The DTW algorithm is first presented. Then we describe the connected word recognition algorithm based on DTW. Finally, the probabilistic matching algorithm is explained.

3.1. The dynamic time warping algorithm

The dynamic time warping algorithm is an application of the dynamic programming principle [10] to speech recognition. The following description is based essentially on the paper of Sakoe and Chiba [14].

3.1.1. Algorithm

Let $R = R(1) \cdots R(N)$ be a **reference word** and $T = T(1) \cdots T(M)$ be a **test utterance**. Given a pattern R, (word or connected word sequence), we shall denote as $R(i:j) = R(i) \cdots R(j)$ the subpattern of R from frame i to frame j and by $|R|$ the number of frames of R. Let $d(i,j) = ||\, R(i) - T(j)\,||$ denote a distance between frame i of R and frame j of T. This distance may be the Chebischev distance, the Euclidean distance, or the log spectral distance depending on the type of acoustic feature considered.

Let C be a parametric curve of the plane defined by $C(k) = (i(k), j(k))$, $k = 1 \cdots K$, where $C(1) = (1,1)$ and $C(K) = (N,M)$ (Fig.7). The dynamic time warping distance between R and T is defined by:

$$D(R,T) = \min_{C} \left[\frac{\sum\limits_{k=1}^{K} d(c(k)) \cdot w(k)}{\sum\limits_{k=1}^{K} w(k)} \right] \qquad (4)$$

where $w(k)$ are weighting coefficients.

Various recurrent schemes have been proposed to compute $D(R,T)$ depending on restrictions made on the curve C. In the following, for sake of clarity, we will only consider a very simple recurrent scheme. Equation (4) may be solved by solving the following recurrence:

$$D(i,j) = \min \begin{bmatrix} D(i-1,j) + d(i,j) \\ D(i-1,j-1) + d(i,j) \\ D(i,j-1) + d(i,j) \end{bmatrix} \qquad (5)$$

with the following initial conditions:

$$D(0,0) = 0 \; ; \; D(i,j) = \infty \; \text{ if } i \le 0 \text{ and } j \ge 1 \; \text{or if } i \ge 1 \text{ and } j \le 0$$

Assuming that $w(k) = 1$, It results immediately that:

$$D(R,T) = \frac{D(N,M)}{K}$$

Finally, a very common heuristics is that values $D(i,j)$ are computed only for the points (i,j) which lie in the band defined by:

$$|\, i - j \,| \le r$$

where r is a given constant. This restriction avoids unreasonable stretching or compression of the reference pattern, and reduces the amount of computations to be carried out.

3.1.2. Systolic algorithm

The speech recognition algorithm that has been described has the property to be very regular in the sense that the basic computation to be executed at point (i,j) depends only on results provided by computations at neighboring points. This property makes it possible to implement the algorithms on systolic arrays. Fig. 8 shows the computation flow graph. The dependency graph for each point is depicted on Fig. 9. It shows that each point of the computation domain has to receive the previously computed D values as well as a reference frame R

and a test frame T. The distance value is then calculated and sent to the next points. The reference frame has to be sent to the next point to the right and the test frame is sent to the next point down. The timing function is:

$$t(i,j) = i + j$$

At this point, various systolic structure implementations are possible. The purpose of the next section is to explain how a two-dimensional array as well as a linear array can support this algorithm.

3.1.3. 2-D systolic implementation

The following presentation is based on [3]. The basic idea is to associate one processing element to the computation of each value $D(i,j)$. Consider an array of processors denoted $P_{i,j}$ connected as indicated by Fig. 10: $P_{i,j}$ has two input ports denoted I_v (vertical input) and I_h (horizontal input), and two output ports O_v and O_h (respectively vertical and horizontal output ports). I_v of $P_{i,j}$ is connected to O_v of $P_{i-1,j}$ and I_h is connected to O_h of $P_{i,j-1}$. Note that there is no diagonal connections since data flowing diagonallly have to be delayed during one systolic cycle before they are used (due to the timing function). Therefore, distance $D(i-1,j-1)$ may be routed through $P_{i,j-1}$, and then to $P_{i,j}$. In order to illustrate the explanation of the following, we assume that each processor has the architecture depicted by Fig. 11. A set of registers memorize the partial calculations performed by the arithmetic unit. We assume that the I/O operations are performed synchronously on the whole array. In the following, we successively describe the operation of the array on a single reference pattern and the pipeline mode.

3.1.3.1. Single reference operation

Consider the comparison between a reference pattern R and a test pattern T. The overall operation of the two-dimensional systolic array for the DTW algorithm is made on a diagonal basis. Assuming that the computation starts at time 0, then at time t, all the processors $P_{i,j}$ such that $i + j = t$ are active. In such a way, it can be easily checked that all the arguments needed for the computation of equation (5) have already been computed and have been routed correctly. The results $D(N,j)$ are obtained by the processors of the bottom row: $P_{N,j}$ delivers $D(N,j)$ at time $N + j - 1$.

In order to cope with variable length reference patterns, the array is dimensioned according to the longest reference word. Let $N_m = \max_{1 \leq v \leq V} N_v$ be the maximum number of frames of the reference words. The array has thus N_m rows and $N_m + r$ columns. The process remains essentially the same if the length N_v of the reference is smaller than N_m. In such a case, the final values $D(N_v,j)$ are computed by processors of row N_v, and must be transmitted to the bottom of the array. One way to solve this problem is to associate a flag with each reference frame $R(i)$. This flag is set to 1 for $i \geq N_v$ and set to 0 otherwise. A processor receiving this flag set to 1 from its left neighbor transmits the value $D(i,j)$ instead of $D(i-1,j)$ to its bottom neighbor, and $+\infty$ instead of $D(i,j)$ to $P(i+1,j+1)$. In such a way, the processors of the rows N_v, N_v+1, etc., propagate the final values $D(N_v,j)$ to the bottom boundary of the array.

3.1.3.2. Pipelining the reference words

Since only one diagonal of this network is active at a time for the computation of the DTW algorithm, several computations may be pipelined into the array as illustrated on Fig. 12. The pipeline operation of the array allows all the distances between any reference and any sub-pattern of T to be computed very efficiently. A sub-pattern $T(\,b : b + N_m + r - 1\,)$ that enters the top of the array remains constant, and the successive reference patterns R_v, $1 \leq v \leq V$ enter the left part of the array. It can be seen that after a certain delay, each processor $P_{N_m,j}$ of the bottom row of this array will output values $D(R_v, T(b:b+j-1))$, for $1 \leq v \leq V$, one during each systolic cycle. For word spotting purpose, when all the vocabulary has been matched against the test pattern, it remains to shift the test pattern one position to the left before repeating the process. In the following, we will refer to the process of comparing the whole vocabulary with a sub-pattern of the test utterance as a **vocabulary cycle.**

3.1.4. 1-D implementation

Consider the comparison between a reference pattern R of N frames, and a test pattern T of M frames. We have to compute $D(i,j)$ for (i,j) such that $1 \leq i \leq N$, $1 \leq j \leq M$ and $|i-j| \leq r$. For the sake of simplicity, we assume $r = 2q$ to be even. We have seen in section **3.1.2** that a simple way to order the calculations is to have $D(i,j)$ computed at time $t(i,j) = i+j$. A first linear systolic implementation is obtained by projecting the computation domain along the diagonal $j=i$. The architecture derived is made out of processing elements numbered P_i, that are two-way linearly connected as depicted on Fig. 13. Each processing element has two input ports denoted as I_l (input from the left) and I_r (input from the right) and similarly two output ports, O_l and O_r. The allocation scheme shows that processor P_k carries out all the computations $D(i,j)$ such that $i-j = k$. However, this implementation has the drawback that each processor is only working every other time. Another more interesting implementation consists in having P_k compute the values $D(i,j)$ such that $\left\lfloor \frac{i-j}{2} \right\rfloor$ (where $\lfloor x \rfloor$ denotes the greatest integer lower than or equal to x) as depicted on Fig. 14 (a). In such a way, the linear array has $r+1$ processors numbered P_{-q} through P_q.

3.1.4.1. Permanent regime

Let us first examine the operation of each processor when permanent regime is attained. P_k executes two different cycles depending on whether $i-j = 2k$ or $i-j = 2k+1$.

Case 1: $i-j = 2k$ (Fig. 14 (b))

In this situation, P_k has already the value $R(j)$ that was needed for the calculation of $D(i-1,j)$ during the previous cycle. It contains also the value $D(i-1,j-1)$ which was used two cycles before. Value $T(i)$ is provided by processor P_{k+1} and value $T(i-1)$ is sent to processor P_{k-1}. Well shall refer to this cycle as a T-cycle (for T transmit cycle) later on.

Case 2: $i-j = 2k+1$ (Fig. 14 (c))

Symmetrically, P_k contains already value $T(i)$ obtained during the previous cycle, and $D(i-1,j-1)$ obtained two cycles before. It remains to get $R(j)$ from processor P_{k-1}. This cycle is called a R-cycle (for R transmit cycle).

3.1.4.2. Initialization and termination

The initialization and termination process need to be examined carefully, since it is very important to keep the overall process regular: in particular, it is most important that data enter or leave the array only through the extremal processing elements, namely P_{-q} and P_q, in such a way that the number of connections with the other parts of the system are minimized.

During the initialization cycles, data enter the array in such a way that all the processing elements reach a consistent state and thus become able to perform their first computation. This is achieved by performing particular initialization cycles referred to as TI-cycle and RI-cycle. During a TI-cycle, processor P_k reads a test frame $T(j)$ from P_{k+1}, and initialization values for the registers D_v, d_v, D_d and D_p. During a RI-cycle the processor P_k reads a reference frame $R(i)$ and initialization values for the registers D_h and d_h. The initialization sequence consists of $q-1$ TI-cycles and q RI-cycles.

The termination process is carried out by making the final values $D(N,j)$ move to processor P_{-q} so that they may be output. After a processor has received the last reference frame $R(N)$, the processor does not compute value $D(i,j)$ which is not significant any more, but instead propagates during the T-cycles the value $D(i,j)$ it receives from its right neighbor. This termination scheme has the advantage that the data are output only by P_{-q} and also that no extra hardware is needed to send the results. However, since the last result $D(N_v,N_v+r)$ is produced by P_q, $2r$ cycles are necessary before this result reaches P_{-q}, introducing a significant overhead. Another way to proceed is to have each processor access a common output bus so that the results are sent directly to the outside. This is possible, since at a given time, at most one processor produces a final result.

The number of processors required to implement this scheme is $r+1$. The comparison between a reference R_V and a pattern T consists in $r-1$ initialization cycles and $2N_v+r-1$ calculation cycles, assuming that the results are output directly by each processor. Therefore, the total number of systolic cycles for one comparison is $2(N_v+r)$. This means that the array has $V\times2(N_v+r)$ systolic cycles to perform for each test frame.

3.2. Probabilistic speech recognition

As mentioned earlier, another way to recognize speech is to preprocess the input data in order to identify the phonemes that have been pronounced. This process, called **phonetic analysis** is independent of the vocabulary chosen for the application, and reduces by approximately a factor of 5 the amount of information to be processed later on. Fig. 15 gives an example of the result of the phonetic analysis. The ideal transcription of the French sentence "liste des connecteurs" is presented together with the results of the phonetic analysis, as performed by the KEAL speech understanding system [15]. Each frame $T(i)$ contains a few phoneme candidates (three to five usually), with each of which is attached a probability (the probabilities are not represented on the figure for the sake of clarity). We denote as $x(i,k)$ the kth candidate phoneme of frame $T(i)$ and $p(i,k)$ the probability associated with this phoneme.

3.2.1. Algorithm

Let R_v be the words of the vocabulary, where the frames of R_v are now the phonemes of the ideal phonetic transcription of the word. The algorithm consists in retrieving the reference R that is most likely to have produced the test pattern T. Such a process may be carried out by the DTW algorithm provided that a distance is defined between frames of the reference words and of the test utterance. However, the information lost during the phonetic analysis makes it impossible to achieve a high recognition accuracy in this way.

Another way to proceed is to describe the behavior of the phonetic analyzer more accurately using the concept of Probabilistic Finite State Machine (PFSM) introduced by Bahl and Jelinek [10].

To each phoneme y is associated a PFSM (Fig. 16a) which describes how the phonetic analyzer is likely to deal with it. The PFSM has two states $S(0)$ and $S(1)$. Before reading y, it is in state $S(0)$, and may choose between three possibilities, namely **insertion, confusion** or **omission**. With each of these three possibilities is associated a probability denoted respectively $P_i(y)$, $P_c(y)$, and $P_o(y)$. If the insertion is chosen, the PFSM remains in state $S(0)$, and produces a phonetic label x, with a conditional probability $q_i(x \mid y)$. In the case of a confusion, the PFSM reads the phoneme y and outputs x with conditional probability $q_c(x \mid y)$. Finally, if the omission is chosen, the PFSM skips the phoneme y with probability $P_o(y)$. In order for the model to be consistent, we must have the following relationships for every phoneme y:

$$P_i(y) + P_c(y) + P_o(y) = 1$$

$$\sum_x q_i(x \mid y) = 1$$

$$\sum_x q_o(x \mid y) = 1$$

These probability distributions can be estimated from the actual results of the phonetic analyzer.

From the elementary PFSM's associated with each individual phonemes, it is possible to modelize the behavior of the phonetic analysis when dealing with a reference word $R_v = R_v(1) \cdots R_v(N_v)$ by concatenating the PFSM's associated to $R_v(1), \ldots, R_v(N_v)$ (Fig. 16b). It is convenient to assume that every reference word ends with a special marker denoted] whose PFSM is such that $P_i(]) = P_c(]) = 0$. This prevents the PFSM to produce any result when reading this special marker.

The recognition process may be carried out from this model as follows. Consider the likelihood that a test pattern T has been produced by analyzing a given reference $R = R(1). \cdots .R(N)$. Let us denote by $L(i,j)$ the probability for the PFSM to enter state $S(i)$ after having produced $T(1{:}j)$. The PFSM may enter $S(i)$ after either inserting any candidate phoneme of $T(i)$ before reading $R(j)$, or after confusing $R(j)$ with one of the candidate phoneme of $T(i)$, or finally after skipping $R(j)$. As a consequence, $L(i,j)$ is given by the following recurrence equations:

$$L(i,j) = L_i(i,j) + L_c(i,j) + L_o(i,j) \tag{6}$$

$$L_i(i,j) = L(i,j-1) \times P_i(R(i+1)) \times \sum_k p(j,k) \, q_i(x(j,k) \mid R(i+1)) \tag{7}$$

$$L_c(i,j) = L(i-1,j-1) \times P_c(R(i)) \times \sum_k p(j,k) \, q_c(x(j,k) \mid R(i)) \tag{8}$$

$$L_o(i,j) = L(i-1,j) \times P_o(R(i))) \tag{9}$$

where $L_i(i,j)$, $L_c(i,j)$ and $L_o(i,j)$ denote respectively the probability for the PFSM to enter state $S(i)$ after inserting $T(j)$, confusing $T(j)$ and $R(i)$, or missing $R(i)$. Equation (6) is valid when $1 \leq i \leq N$ and $1 \leq j \leq M$. If we add the following conditions:

$$L_c(i,0) = 0 \ \text{if} \ i > 0$$

$$L_c(0,j) = 0 \ \text{if} \ j > 0$$

$$L_c(0,0) = 1 \tag{10}$$

$$L_j(i,0) = 0 \ \forall i$$

$$L_o(0,j) = 0 \ \forall j$$

then (6) is still valid if $i = 0$ or $j = 0$.

As in the case of the DTW algorithm, one can restrict the computation of $L(i,j)$ to the points (i,j) which lie into a band of width r, i.e. such that $|i - j| \leq r$.

3.2.2. Systolic implementation

In order to apply the design methodology described in section 2, the computation of the values $L(i,j)$ must be represented as a regular computation flow graph. In the case of the previous algorithm, finding the flow graph is not straightforward. Indeed, equations 6, 7, 8 and 9 altogether show that computation at point (i,j) $(L(i,j))$ depends on neighboring points $(i-1,j)$, $(i-1,j-1)$, $(i,j-1)$ (values $L(i-1,j)$, $L(i-1,j-1)$, $L(i,j-1)$ and $R(i)$, $T(j)$). However this computation needs also the value $R(i+1)$. Unfortunetly this does not agree with the flow graph approach since values $R(i)$ and $R(i+1)$ are needed for the point (i,j). To overcome this problem, computation at point (i,j) is done in a different way. Fig. 17 describes the dependency graph at point (i,j). Point (i,j) receives $T(j+1)$ and $L_o(i,j)$ from point $(i-1,j)$, $L_c(i,j)$ from $(i-1,j-1)$, and finally $R(i+1)$ and $L_i(i,j)$ from $(i,j-1)$. Using equation (6), point (i,j) computes $L(i,j)$. Then using equations (7), (8) and (9), it computes $L_o(i+1,j)$ which is sent together with $T(j+1)$ to $(i+1,j)$, then $L_c(i+1,j+1)$ which is sent to $(i+1,j+1)$, and finally $L_i(i,j+1)$ which is sent together with $R(i+1)$ to $(i,j+1)$. To summarize, R and L_i flow horizontally, T and L_o flow vertically and finally L_c flows diagonally.

3.2.3. 2-D implementation

The first systolic implementation of the algorithm is to assign a processor to each point (i,j). The overall operation of the array is similar to that of the DTW-algorithm. In particular, the pipelining scheme remains the same. Consider the comparison between a reference pattern R containing N phonemes (including the end of word marker]) and a test pattern T having M frames. We assume that the last test frame $T(M)$ is composed uniquely of the end-of-word marker], with probability 1. The array needed to implement such a computation has N rows and M columns. Processors are numbered $P_{i,j}$ where $0 \leq i \leq N-1$ and $0 \leq j \leq M-1$.

Note that this process still remains valid for processors at the boundaries of the array. As far as processors of the top row and the left column are concerned, equation (10) defines the initial values L_o, L_c and L_i that must enter these processors. Consider now processors $P_{N-1,j}$ for $j < M-1$. Since we assume that each reference word is terminated with a special marker], and since $P_c(]) = 0$, we can deduce from (9) that:

$$L(N,j) = L_o(N-1,j) \tag{11}$$

Therefore, the final value $L(N,j)$ is delivered by $P_{N,j}$ on its O_v port. Finally, consider the processors $P_{i,M-1}$ of the right column. Provided that we have $q_c(]|y) = q_i(]|y) = 0$ for all phoneme y, it can be seen that $P_{i,M-1}$ still delivers $L_o(i+1,M-1)$ on its vertical output port O_v. Therefore, from (11), $P_{N-1,M-1}$ provides $L(N,M-1)$ on its O_v port.

Note that this operation assumes that each processor knows the probabilities distributions P_o, P_c, P_i as well as q_o, q_c and q_i. However, the pipelining scheme described in the previous section helps to reduce significantly the amount of memory required, since the test pattern remains unchanged during a whole vocabulary cycle. As a consequence, processor $P_{i,j}$ receives the same frame $T(j+1)$ during V consecutive systolic cycles. This suggests loading the processors with the probabilities $q_c(x|y)$ and $q_i(x|y)$ only for the phonemes x which are in $T(j+1)$. Before every vocabulary cycle, these parameters are loaded into the first row of the array, then the second, etc., until the whole array is initialized.

3.2.4. 1-D implementation

Although it is possible to use the diagonal scheme to implement the probabilistic matching algorithm, this scheme has the main drawback that the probability values q_c and q_i have to be left-shifted every cycle, since the test frames flow from right to left.

A better scheme is to have processor P_j compute values $L(i,j)$, $(i = 1, \cdots, N)$, in such a way that frame $T(j)$ stays in P_j during a whole vocabulary cycle, thus minimizing data transfers between processors. In this implementation, called the **row scheme**, the linear array emulates successive rows of the two-dimensional array described in the previous section. Therefore, the linear array has M processors numbered P_0 through P_{M-1}. Fig. 18 shows the linear array for the probabilistic matching algorithm. Solid arrows indicate the communication lines during a vocabulary cycle. On these lines values R, L_i and L_c flow from left to right. Dashed arrows indicate the communication lines for the T values. Indeed, as explained before, the T values do not need to move during a vocabulary cycle. They have to be left shifted before a new vocabulary cycle.

To explain in more details the operation of the array, consider the comparison between a reference pattern of N frames and a test pattern T; assume that processor P_j is already loaded with $T(j+1)$ and the probabilities $q_c(x|y)$ and $q_i(x|y)$ for x in $T(j+1)$. During a basic cycle, P_j has to compute $L(i,j)$ according to equations (6), (7), (8) and (9) (see Fig. 18). $L_o(i,j)$, which has been computed by P_j during the previous cycle is already in P_j. Values $L_c(i,j)$, $R(i+1)$ and $L_i(i,j)$ are obtained from P_{j-1}. Processor P_j computes then $L(i,j)$, $L_i(i,j+1)$, $L_c(i+1,j+1)$ and $L_o(i+1,j)$. Values $L_i(i,j+1)$ and $R(i+1)$ are then sent to P_{j+1}. The probability $L_c(i+1,j+1)$ has to stay in processor P_j, since P_{j+1} will need it only two cycles later. Instead, $L_c(i,j+1)$ which was kept from the previous cycle is sent to P_{j+1}.

If we assume that the computation of $L(0,0)$ is done at time 0, then processor P_j computes $L(i,j)$ at time $i+j$. Final results $L(N,j)$ $(0 \leq j \leq M)$, are thus obtained respectively by $P_0, \cdots, P_j$ at time $N+j$.

In the context of connected speech recognition, as we will see in section 3.3, these results need not to be sent outside the array. During a vocabulary cycle, processor P_j computes successively the probabilities $L(N,j)$ for all the reference words of the vocabulary. P_j can therefore compute the maximum probability over the whole vocabulary.

The row scheme requires N_m+r+1 processors, assuming that N_m is the maximum number of phonemes of the reference words (final marker excluded). The number of systolic cycles for a single comparison is $2(N_v+1) + r$. Note however that the vocabulary cycles may be overlapped, since as soon as a processor P_j ends a vocabulary cycle, it can start the next one. In such a way, N_v+1 cycles are in fact needed for each comparison. Therefore, the array does $V \times (\overline{N}+1)$ cycles for each test frame, where $\overline{N}$ denotes the average number of phonemes of the reference words.

3.3. Connected speech recognition

The DTW algorithm may be used either for isolated word recognition, or as a basis for connected word recognition. We shall only consider the later case here. Algorithms for connected word recognition have been described by Banatre et al. [7], Bridle et al. [16], Myers and Rabiner [17], and Sakoe [18]. The algorithms described in [17] and [18] find the best matching connected word sequence considering successively sequences of one word, then two words, etc. The results are then compared and the best connected word sequence is determined. In [7] and [16], the best connected word sequence is found in a single pass of the algorithm. In [14], the DTW algorithm and the connected word algorithm are merged, which results in a very efficient but memory consuming algorithm. In [7], the DTW algorithm and the connected word algorithm are done separately. The following description is based on [7].

3.3.1. Algorithm

Let T be the pattern resulting from the acoustic analysis of a sequence of words taken from a given vocabulary. We denote as V the number of reference words of the vocabulary, and denote as R_v the vth reference word. The length of R_v is denoted as N_v. (The index v will be omitted when understood by the context). We call **super-reference** and denote as R^s the pattern obtained by the concatenation of a finite number of words R_v of the vocabulary. $||R^s||$ denotes the number of words of R^s (not to be confused with $|R^s|$, which is the number of frames of R^s).

With the above notations, the connected speech recognition algorithm consists, given a test sentence T, in finding the super-reference R^s which minimizes the distance $D(R^s,T)$. This process consists in two steps. First, one computes the quantity:

$$D^* = \min_{R^s} D(R^s,T)$$

Then one finds out the sequence of words whose concatenation achieves the distance D^*.

Let $D^+(b,e)$ be the minimal distance between any reference word and a sub-pattern $T(b:e)$ of T, i.e:

$$D^+(b,e) = \min_{1 \le v \le V} D(R_v, T(b:e)) \tag{12}$$

We denote as $v^+(b,e)$ the number of the reference pattern which minimizes (12). Let $D^*(e)$ be the minimum distance between any super-reference and $T(1:e)$, defined by:

$$D^*(e) = \min_{R^s} D(R^s, T(1:e))$$

Finally, let $D^{*L}(e)$ be the distance between a L-word length super-reference and $T(1:e)$. Since the recurrence scheme of equation (5) is considered, a L-word super-reference can match only a pattern having at least L frames. As a consequence, we have:

$$D^*(e) = \min_{1 \le L \le e} D^{*L}(e) \tag{13}$$

On the other hand, $D^{*L}(e)$ obey the following recurrence equation:

$$D^{*L}(e) = \min_{1 \le b \le e} \left[D^{*L-1}(b-1) + D^+(b,e) \right] \tag{14}$$

Substituting (14) into (13) gives:

$$D^*(e) = \min_{1 \le L \le e} \left[\min_{1 \le b \le e} \left[D^{*L-1}(b-1) + D^+(b,e) \right] \right]$$

By inverting the two minimum operations, we obtain:

$$D^*(e) = \min_{1 \le b \le e} \left[\min_{1 \le L \le e} \left[D^{*L-1}(b-1) + D^+(b,e) \right] \right]$$

or, equivalently:

$$D^*(e) = \min_{1 \le b \le e} \left[\left[\min_{1 \le L \le e} D^{*L-1}(b-1) \right] + D^+(b,e) \right]$$

which gives finally:

$$D^*(e) = \min_{1 \le b \le e} \left[D^*(b-1) + D^+(b,e) \right] \tag{15}$$

In this equation, the quantity $D^+(b,e)$ may be obtained by applying the DTW algorithm given by equation (5). For a given value b and a given word R_v, a single application of the algorithm allows all the quantities $D(R_v, T(b:e))$ to be computed for all values e lying in the interval $[e_1, e_2]$ where

$$e_1 = b - 1 + N_v - r$$

$$e_2 = b - 1 + N_v + r$$

According to equation (12) a first minimization over the index v gives then the distance $D^+(b,e)$. Finally, a second minimization over b by applying equation (15) gives the final result.

In order to retrieve the string of reference word numbers that minimizes $D^*(e)$, it is sufficient to keep track during the calculation of (15) of the index

$b^+(e)$ which achieve the minimum as well as the number $v^+(b,e)$ of the word which achieves the minimum distance $D^+(b,e)$. The string of word numbers $v^*(e)$ which minimizes $D^*(e)$ is then obtained by the following recurrence:

$$v^*(e) = v^*(\ b^+(e)\ )\ .\ v^+(\ b^+(e) + 1\ ,\ e\ )$$

where $x.y$ denotes the concatenation of strings x and y.

The probabilistic model may be also adapted to connected speech recognition, in a very similar way as explained previously for the DTW algorithm. Suppose now that T has been produced by the phonetic analysis of a super-reference R^s. Denote as $L^*(e)$ the maximum probability of a super-reference R^s given a test $T(1:e)$, and as $L^+(b,e)$ the maximum probability of a single reference word given the test $T(b,e)$. By a similar reasoning, $L^*(e)$ can be estimated by:

$$L^*(e) = \max_{1 \le b \le e}\left[L^*(b-1) \times L^+(b,e)\right] \qquad (16)$$

This equation is very similar to equation (15). The recurrent scheme for retrieving the pronounced utterance is the same as explained previously.

3.3.2. Systolic implementation

The computation of $D^*(e)$ given by (15) can be computed in exactly e steps with the following iterative scheme:

$$U_0(e) = +\infty$$

$$U_k(e) = \min\left[U_{k-1}(e),D^*(k-1) + D^+(k,e)\right] \qquad (17)$$

with $D^*(0)$ initialized to 0. It is then clear that $D^*(e)=U_e(e)$. Replacing $D^*(k-1)$ by $U_{k-1}(k-1)$ in (17) gives:

$$U_k(e) = \min\left[U_{k-1}(e), U_{k-1}(k-1) + D'(k,e)\right]$$

The dependency graph for the calculation of terms $U_k(e)$ is depicted on Fig. 19a. Fig. 19b is another representation of the same calculation but in this case data broadcasting has been removed. The timing function associated with this last flow graph is shown on Fig. 20. A systolic implementation is obtained by projecting the calculation domain along a diagonal.

The computation of $D^*(e)$ (defined by equation (15)) is carried out by a linear row of processors as depicted on Fig. 21. Every cell of the systolic array is structured as displayed on Fig. 22. It contains an adder and a comparator. The cell computes $U_k(e)$ using values $U_{k-1}(e)$, $U_{k-1}(k-1)$ and $D^+(k,e)$. Computation is achieved in the following way. In a first step, the cell inputs $D^+(k,e)$, $U_{k-1}(e)$ and $U_{k-1}(k-1)$. It computes $U_k(e)$. In a second step, the cell outputs values $U_k(e)$, $U_{k-1}(k-1)$.

3.3.3. Connected word recognition machine

Functionnally, the overall organization of a connected word recognition DTW machine is depicted on Fig. 23. The machine is built with three main array:
- the DTW array is used to compute distances between the reference patterns

and the test patterns sequences (values $D(R_v, T(b:b+j-1))$, see Fig. 12);
- the D^+ array computes during a vocabulary cycle, the best distances and memorize the words associated with them, that is:

$$D^+(b,b+j-1) = \min_{1 \le v \le V} D(R_v, T(b:b+j-1))$$

and $v^+(b:b+j-1)$;
- the D^* array is the CWR array described above.

In such a way, each step of the minimization is carried out in turn by the processors of the bottom row, from the left to the right. Note that the D^* array does not work according to the optimal timing function (Fig. 12). The reason is that the D^+ values that are necessary for the computation (Fig. 22) are provided by the D^+ array at the end of a vocabulary cycle. This shows that the computation is not done in parallel since the processors are activated in turn from the left to the right. A real implementation would be more efficient if both the D^+ and D^* were merged in a single array.

4. A VLSI IMPLEMENTATION CASE STUDY

4.1. The API89 chip

The following section is devoted to the structure of a special-purpose chip named API89 which implements one basic processor of the probabilistic matching systolic organization [9]. The design of this chip was made having in mind the following goals:
- try to have the maximum speed by using special-purpose elements required by the algorithms;
- reduce the layout space by implementing only the functions that are needed;
- keep the processor general enough to support the different variations that are commonly used in the class of speech recognition methods presented above.
- finally, choose a structure simple enough to avoid difficulties in designing and testing the chip.

4.1.1. Overall organization and Control

These ideas lead to the organization depicted by Fig. 24. The various elements of the circuit are organized around a single bus. These elements are:

a) Two input registers denoted as VR (vertical register) and HR (horizontal register);

b) One output register OR;

c) An Arithmetic Unit (AU) capable of performing addition, subtraction and incrementation on 16-bit values; the AU has an accumulator (ACC) and an input register (AR);

d) An array of 16 general purpose registers R[0] to R[15];

e) A 60 12-bit word memory with a Memory Address Register (MAR), a Memory Read Register (MR) and a Memory Write Register (MW);

f) A look-up table called the Z module, implemented using a PLA, for the summation of logarithms; this look-up table has an input register IZ and an output register OZ.

All the registers and the data paths are 16-bit wide in order to provide enough precision for the calculations as well as fast I/O. Operation of the processor is entirely synchronous and based on a two-phase nonoverlapping clock scheme. These two phases are denoted as φ_1 and φ_2 in the following.

The operation of the circuit is controlled by 10-bit micro-instructions which are generated outside the chip and expanded inside using a very simple control unit. Two types of micro-instructions have been defined as displayed on table 1. Microinstructions of the first type are executed during φ_1, and concern the transfers of data between the different modules through the bus. Microinstructions of the second type are synchronized on φ_2 and are used for I/O, memory and arithmetic operations. In order to increase speed, instructions are latched in a pipeline register thus allowing instruction decoding and execution to overlap. One instruction is thus executed every clock phase.

4.1.2. Description of the modules

Three modules of the chip need to be explained in more detail.

4.1.2.1. The memory

The memory is organized in such a way that the parameters necessary for the probabilistic matching algorithm can be memorized. We have seen that a processor need to keep track of the probabilities $q_c(x\,|y)$ and $q_i(x\,|y)$. However, since there are about thirty-five phonemes in a language as English or French, the amount of memory needed is too large to be reasonably implemented using the currently available technology. Hopefully, as explained in section 3.2.3., only a small amount of memory is used during a vocabulary cycle because only three phonemes x need to be considered at the same time. Moreover, two simplifications of the model are made according to an earlier software implementation of the algorithm [19]. First of all, it is assumed that the probability to insert a phoneme x is independent of the phonetic symbol y. Secondly, the probability to confuse a vowel and a consonant is assumed to be null. Therefore, for a given candidate phoneme x, it is only needed to memorize the quantities $q_i(x\,|y)$ and $q_c(x\,|y)$ for phonemes y which are of the same type (consonant or vowel) as x. Since we consider only three candidate phoneme for each test frame, the memory contains only 60 12-bits words, each candidate phoneme being represented on 20 words (this value has been chosen since there are 20 consonants in French). Each 12-bit word has two fields: a flag indicating the type of the phoneme, and a probability value coded on 11 bits.

The instructions for the memory are given by table 1. The RM instruction has a particular effect: if the type of the phoneme which has been loaded into the memory address register MAR and the type of the phoneme memorized in the memory word addressed are identical, then the value contained in that memory is loaded into the memory read register MR. Otherwise, the number representing probability 0 is loaded. In such a way, only one cycle is required to read a value $q_c(x\,|y)$ whatever the type of x and y are. Since the memory is implemented using dynamic memory cells, a particular instruction called RR is provided for memory refreshment.

4.1.2.2. Arithmetic Unit

The arithmetic Unit can perform addition, subtraction and incrementation as indicated on table 1. Two conditional instructions denoted as STR (star) and SBS (substar) are provided: STR complements the accumulator if the AU flag is set to 1; SBS subtract the AU input register to the ACC if the AU flag is set to 1. The AU flag is set to 1 when an arithmetic operation results in a negative number. As a consequence, the AU is capable to emulate comparison and absolute value instructions.

4.1.2.3. The Z module

Since the probabilistic matching algorithm has to perform multiplications, and manipulate very small values, the probabilities are coded using radix-2 logarithms. However, examining formulas (7), (8), and (9) reveals that we have to perform the calculation of $Log(a+b)$ given $Log\ a$ and $Log\ b$. This problem has been solved in the following way. Let Z be the real mapping defined by:

$$Z(t) = Log(1 + 2^t)$$

We have then:

$$Log\ (a+b) = Log(a) + Z(Log\ b - Log\ a) = Log(b) + Z(Log\ a - Log\ b)$$

Given the value of the function Z on the interval $[\ 0\ ,\ +\infty\ ]$, it is possible to compute $Log(a+b)$ from $Log(a)$ and $Log(b)$. Since the values are coded on 16 bits, it has been possible to implement the function Z using a PLA having only 128 product terms, with a good accuracy.

4.1.3. VLSI design of the chip

Two sets of chips have been fabricated. The first one using 4.5μ-NMOS technology was fabricated by the French MPC (Multi Project Chip) organization. The second set was fabricated by MOSIS using 4μ-NMOS technology. The chip contains approximately 12,000 transistors and measures 5mm by 6mm. The chip is housed in a 64-pin package since 16-bit wide parallel ports are used. The pin out is the following:

- 32 pins for the two input ports;
- 16 pins for the output port;
- 10 pins for the instructions;
- 4 pins for power and clocks.

Since the processor is microprogrammable, and since the inside decoding is reduced, access to the internal elements is relatively easy. A micro assembler has been written to compile tests programs and generate bit patterns for the circuit. Moreover, this micro-assembler is used for simulating the processor and thus generate a print out of the bit patterns expected on the output pads.

A first run has been returned from fabrication and tested. The test has been carried out easily as expected. Most of the modules of the chip work correctly except some minor details. The basic clock cycle has been measured to be about 700 ns for the 4.5μ version. This is slower than estimated (500ns) due to a bus design error. A new version has recently been sent for fabrication.

4.2. Example of systolic array implementation using API89

As an example, we show in this section how the chip can be used to implement the two-dimensional array for the probabilistic matching algorithm. Fig. 25 depicts the interconnection of the array, for $N = M = 3$. We assume, moreover, that the full array is implemented. The operation of the array is fully synchronous. A control unit (CU) broadcasts the microinstructions to all the processors of the array, and provides a separate flow of microinstructions for the connected word recognition array. Control lines are indicated by dashed arrows in the figure. Note that although each processor has only two input ports and one output port, all the logical connections needed can be emulated on this network, since the operation are synchronous. For example, vertical transmissions of data between processors are done by having all the processors load the output register with the value to be transmitted, and then read during the next cycle on the vertical input register. On the other hand, the left-to-right interconnection between the processors of the bottom row (see Fig. 21) is needed only for the broadcasting of the values $L^{*}(b)$ to compute equation (16). This can be emulated by having these values enter the last row of the array, move from left-to-right on this row, and be sent to the bottom processors.

A last remark that should be made concerns the synchronization of the connected word recognition row. Since the references are pipelined in the array, the operation of processor P^{*}_{j+1} is the same as the operation of P^{*}_{j} but occurs one cycle later. However, since each processor look for the maximum of the results $L(N,j)$ sent by the last row of the array, it is possible to align in time the connected word recognition array by having the network deliver values 0 when no significant comparison is done.

5. CONCLUSION

We have described several systolic arrays architectures which can implement two basic connected speech recognition methods.

The two-dimensional systolic array for the DTW algorithm leads to a 2,000 processor network when the full array is implemented, and to 925 processors when only the band of processors $P_{i,j}$ whith $|i - j| \le r$ is implemented. This estimation is based on $N_m = 40$ and $r = 10$. Such a device would permit real-time recognition for a vocabulary of 5,000 words, based on a systolic cycle time of 4 microseconds, and a feature extraction interval of 20 milliseconds. This implementation is rather unrealistic for practical purpose due to the number of processors. It could only be considered if the number of processors were reduced by folding the computations. However, the control of this array would then be much more complicated.

The probabilistic matching algorithm may be run on a two-dimensional array having 180 processors if the full array is implemented, and 104 processors if the band is implemented. This estimation is based on $N_m = 10$ and $r = 4$. Executed on the API89 chip, the systolic cycle time is $s=50$ microseconds. Based on this parameter and assuming an average phoneme duration of 100 milliseconds, vocabularies of up to 2000 words could be handled in real time. The probabilistic matching implementation would be a good candidate for wafer-scale integration as presented in [5].

The linear systolic arrays are more realistic. The DTW algorithm implementation would permit a real time recognition of approximately 70 words, using 11 processors. On the other hand, 15 processors would allow the recognition of 250 words using the probabilistic matching algorithm. The difference of performances between these two systolic implementations comes from the fact that the initialization overhead is very significant in the case of the diagonal scheme. Although the row scheme could also be considered for the DTW algorithm, the number of processors would then be much higher, since $N_m + r$ processors are needed. Both systolic arrays could be implemented on a single chip with the current available technology.

The API89 VLSI chip has been presented and it has been shown how such a chip can be used as the basic processor of these architectures. This study shows that there are many different ways to implement in parallel tasks such as connected speech recognition, even if one restricts oneself to a single type of architectures. Choosing between the different possibilities implies investigating in great details how the algorithm may be implemented, taking into consideration parameters such as the number of processors, the communications between the processors, and the complexity of the control. Our belief is that the new avenues opened by VLSI technology for special purpose hardware will become more and more practical, provided that more is known about the various ways to map an algorithm onto a parallel architecture.

REFERENCES

[1] L.J. Siegel, "Highly Parallel Architectures and Algorithms for Speech Analysis," *1984 Int. Conf. Acoustic., Speech, Signal Processing*, San Diego, March 1984, pp. 25A.1.1-25A.1.4 .

[2] H.T. Kung, "Why Systolic Architectures ?," *Computer*, Vol. 15, No 1, Jan 1982, pp. 37-46.

[3] N. Weste, D.J. Burr, and B.D. Ackland, "Dynamic Time Warp Pattern Matching Using an Integrated Multiprocessing Array," *IEEE Trans. Comp.*, Vol. C-32, Aug. 1983, pp. 731-744.

[4] M.A. Yoder and L.J. Siegel, "Dynamic Time Warping Algorithms for SIMD Machines and VLSI Processor Arrays," *1982 Int. Conf. Acoustic., Speech, Signal Processing*, Paris, May 1982, pp. 1274-1277.

[5] J.A. Feldman, S.L. Gaverick, F.M. Rhodes, and J.R. Mann, "A Wafer Scale Integration Systolic Processor for Connected Word Recognition," *1984 Int. Conf. Acoustic., Speech, Signal Processing*, San Diego, March 1984, pp. 25B.4.1-25B.4.4.

[6] J.P Banatre, P. Frison, and P. Quinton, "A Network for the Detection of Words in Continuous Speech," *Proceedings of the VLSI 81 Int. Conference*, Edimburg, Aug. 1981.

[7] J.P. Banatre, P. Frison, and P. Quinton, "A Systolic Algorithm for Speech Recognition," *1982 Int. Conf. Acoustic., Speech, Signal Processing*, Paris, May 1982, pp. 1243-1245.

[8] J.P. Banatre, P. Frison, and P. Quinton, "A Network for the Detection of Words in Continuous Speech," *Acta Informatica 18, pp. 431-448*.

[9] P. Frison, "Un Processeur Integre pour la Reconnaissance de la Parole," INRIA Research Report No. 215, July 1983.

[10] L. R. Bahl, and F. Jelinek, "Decoding for Channels with Insertions, Deletions, and Substitutions with Applications to Speech Recognition," *IEEE Trans. Informat. Theory*, Vol IT-21, No 4, pp 404-411, 1976

[11] C. Mead, L. Conway, *Introduction to VLSI Systems*, Addison Wesley Publishing Company Inc., 1980.

[12] P.Quinton, "The Systematic Design of Systolic Arrays," MCNC Technical Report, TR84-11, May 84.

[13] R. Bellman, S. Dreyfus, *Applied Dynamic Programming*, Princeton University Press, New-Jersey, 1962.

[14] H. Sakoe and S. Chiba, "Dynamic Programming Algorithm Optimization For Spoken Word Recognition," *IEEE Trans. Acoust., Speech, Signal Processing*, Vol. ASSP-26, No. 1, Feb. 1978, pp. 43-49.

[15] G. Mercier, A. Nouhen, P. Quinton, and J. Siroux, "The Keal Speech Understanding System," In: Spoken Language Generation and Understanding, J.C. Simon (Ed), Proc. NATO ASI, Bonas, 1980.

[16] J. Bridle, M. Brown, and R. Chamberlain, "An algorithm for Connected Word Recognition," *1982 Int. Conf. Acoustic., Speech, Signal Processing*, Paris, May 1982, pp. 899-902.

[17] C. Myers, and L.R. Rabiner, "A Level Building Dynamic Time Warping Algorithm for Connected Word Recognition," *IEEE Trans. on Acoust., Speech, Signal Processing*, Vol ASSP-29, No. 3, April 1083, pp. 351-363.

[18] H. Sakoe, "Two-Level DP-Matching - A Dynamic Programming-Based Pattern Matching Algorithm for Connected Word Recognition," *IEEE Trans. Acoust., Speech, Signal Processing*, Vol. ASSP-28, No. 4, Aug. 1980, pp. 588-595.

[19] L. Buisson, G. Mercier, J.Y. Gresser, M. Querre, and R. Vives, "Phonetic Decoding for Automatic Recognition of Words", *Speech Communication Seminar*, Stockholm, Aug. 1974

COMPUTER SYSTEMS FOR HIGH-PERFORMANCE SPEECH RECOGNITION

Roberto Bisiani*

Carnegie-Mellon University

Pittsburgh, PA 15232, USA

ABSTRACT

The object of this review and position paper is to draw a parallel between the field of high-performance speech recognition systems on one side and the field of computer systems (in particular computer systems for Artificial Intelligence applications) on the other. This paper gives a characterization of the computational requirements of speech recognition systems, and describes and exemplifies the classes of machines that could be useful in speeding up speech recognition systems.

---

*This research was sponsored by the Defense Advanced Research Projects Agency (DOD), ARPA Order No. 3597, monitored by the Air Force Avionics Laboratory Under Contract F33615-81-K-1539.
The views and conclusions contained in this document are those of the author and should not be interpreted as representing the official policies, either expressed or implied, of the Defense Advanced Research Projects Agency or the US Government.

1. INTRODUCTION

The object of this paper is to present the inter-relationship between the state-of-the-art of system architecture research and speech recognition research. Our concern here is with the interplay of the recognition algorithms and the structure of the machines that execute them. We are therefore not concerned with the advancement of electronic technology per-se but with the possibilities of effectively exploiting the capabilities offered by such technology improvements.

Better computer systems can only improve the *cost* and the *speed* of a recognition system. We will immediately dismiss the cost issue, since it becomes relevant only in the context of a particular application and when a system with the correct accuracy has been demonstrated. Cost reduction is achieved by "simplifying" the algorithms while trying to keep accuracy constant; therefore, cost reduction is only meaningful when the required accuracy goal has already been achieved.

As far as speed is concerned, one should ask: *Why is speed relevant? Is it reasonable to consider optimizing the speed of recognition systems before having settled all the "speech science" issues?* The answer is a strong yes; it is indeed very important to be concerned with the speed of such systems in order to limit the turn-around time in the evaluation experiments since many are required simply to evaluate one version of a system. Moreover, the number of experiments required increases when the accuracy increases. For example, if one needs to measure the error rate with a confidence interval of 30% and a confidence level of 90%, 30 statistically independent errors are required. If a system has a .1% accuracy, it will need to process 30,000 sentences in order to get 30 errors. At 2 seconds per utterance, a real time system will take about 16 hours for each experiment. When we consider that most changes in a system influence the behavior of other parts of the system, we see that the number of experiments required grows combinatorially. Past experience has shown that if a system does not run close to real time, the feedback is not quick enough to allow researchers to efficiently evaluate their solutions. For example, if the Hearsay II system [11] had been two orders of magnitude faster, much more insights could have been gained from the effort by performing experiments that had been specified but were never carried out because of lack of time.

Section 2 describes the computational requirements of speech recognition systems. Two reasons prevent Section 2 from being as complete and conclusive as one might desire: first, the requirements of speech recognition systems change widely and in non-trivial ways when the task domain changes; second, there is no "correct" way to perform certain tasks and either worst-case analysis or highly speculative analysis are the only possible ways to proceed. Section 2 is structured according to one of the many possible system decompositions. It is virtually impossible at this point in time to prove or disprove that the speech recognition techniques suggested are the correct ones. However, unless some radically different approach is invented (a possibility that will appear unlikely to anybody that has worked with the speech problem for some time), the techniques evaluated are representative of future recognition systems.

Section 3 describes the classes of machines that might have an impact on speech recognition research. The classes considered are: *language-oriented machines, production system machines, general-purpose parallel machines, massively parallel machines* and *task-oriented machines*. For each class, the paper gives the underlying ideas, the expected performance of members of the class, and their typical applications.

2. CHARACTERIZATION OF THE SPEECH RECOGNITION TASK

The goal of this Section is to characterize the requirements of speech recognition systems from the point of view of the computer system that executes them. No matter what kind of system one considers, the computation required varies widely among the different components of the same system (e.g. signal processing vs. word hypothesization). The computation required is also influenced by the recognition task (number of words, grammar, etc.) that a system can deal with. For example, although numeric computation is usually a significant part of the computation, as the complexity of the task increases, memory access operations become prevalent. As of now, there is no agreement on which modules will constitute a satisfactory speech recognition system. For the sake of this paper, the computation performed by a speech recognition system will be divided into four components: Parameter Extraction, Acoustic/Phonetic Analysis, Word Recognition, Sentence Recognition. A realistic, high performance speech recognition system will have many more modules and much more refined intermediate representations of partial results; nevertheless, the four modules chosen are likely to be representative of most of the computation.

The computation characteristics are divided into three major categories:

- The *structure of the computation* includes all the features of the computation that interact with the architecture of a computer system. For example, the *kinds* of operations performed more often or the behavior of the control-flow.

- *The amount of computation and storage* are a (somewhat coarse) way of representing the raw requirements of a system. These characteristics depend at times on the *size* of the task a system can work with.

- *The available parallelism* is a fundamental characteristic since, in many cases, the amount of computation is beyond the capabilities of sequential systems.

The goal of creating a reasonable and meaningful picture is complicated by the fact that some of the requirements are influenced by the recognition task features and some of these features, like confusability of words, are hard to quantify. The parameters used in this paper are the number of vocabulary words and the word-grammar branching factor as defined by Goodman [14].

The characterization data presented in the paper is summarized in Tables 2-1 and 2-2. Each table is divided in four sections corresponding to the four major components that we are considering: *parameter extraction, acoustic/phonetic analysis, word recognition and sentence recognition.* The different categories in which each table is divided will become clear when the characteristics of the modules are explained.

2.1 PARAMETER EXTRACTION

Parameter extraction is the most tractable part of speech recognition because the computational problems it raises are shared by a large number of other, more mature applications and have therefore been studied in depth. With parameter extraction we indicate the initial transformations that are performed on the signal after it is sampled. This process is often identified with *signal processing* since most of the techniques employed are derived from classic signal processing algorithms (e.g. Fast Fourier Transform). Some form of parameter extraction is used in all systems and for many years most of the activity in speech processing was exclusively concerned with this kind of processing. The two mostly used parameter extraction procedures are (in chronological order) filter banks [19] and Linear Predictive Coding [22]. Initially, filter bank processing was mainly performed with analogic techniques (analogic filter bank processing has resurfaced for economic reasons with single-chip filter bank analyzers [7]). In both cases, a number of additional parameters like zero crossing and amplitude are often computed. The FFT is also often used in systems that need to extract very detailed information from the signal (e.g. FEATURE [8]).

Parameter extraction algorithms are highly regular and their control pattern is mostly data independent. This characteristic opens the possibility of using computer systems that are optimized for a given sequence of operations and data-flow. In the simplest case, the optimal computer structure for parameter extraction will have data paths optimized for vector and matrix operations and pipelined multiply-add. In the most complex and effective case, the architecture will have multiple functional units and data paths tailored for a given algorithm. For example, the systolic WARP processor [31] is one of such machines.

CHARACTERISTICS COMPONENT	Control structure	Needs fast arithmetic integer / floating point		Needs efficient symbolic processing	Complexity of data structures	Data memory bandwidth
PARAMETER EXTRACTION	mostly regular and data independent	yes	no	no	low	medium
ACOUSTIC/ PHONETIC ANALYSIS	both regular and data dependent	yes	no	no	medium	low
WORD & SENTENCE RECOGNITION	mostly data dependent	no	no	yes	high	high

CHARACTERISTICS COMPONENT	amount of computation in MIPSS				amount of storage	
	number of words				number of words	
	1,000		10,000		1,000	10,000
	branching factor					
	low	high	low	high		
PARAMETER EXTRACTION	30	30	30	30	less than 64K bytes	less than 64K bytes
ACOUSTIC/ PHONETIC ANALYSIS	.5	.5	.5	.5	less than 64K bytes	less than 64K bytes
WORD & SENTENCE RECOGNITION	3	30 to 300	15	100 to 1000	.5M bytes	.5M bytes

Figure 2-1 Tentative assessment of the requirements a speech recognition system poses on a computer system

CHARACTERISTICS	parallelism			
	computation		communication	
COMPONENT	granularity size	number of parallel operations	structure	traffic
PARAMETER EXTRACTION	a few operators	up to 0(100) (in practice only a few)	regular	a few times signal bandwidth in samples/sec
ACOUSTIC/ PHONETIC ANALYSIS	large	a few	regular	low
	medium	0 (number of phonemes)		
WORD SENTENCE RECOGNITION	large	0(10)	random	high
	small	0(words)		

Figure 2-2   Tentative assessment of the requirements a speech recognition system poses on a computer system (cont.)

The most widely used primitives are integer arithmetic operators. Speech processing seldom requires more than 16 bits of precision (the input signal has a dynamic range of less than 11 bits). The reason why "floating point array processors" have been widely used for speech processing has to do with the ease of programmability that machines like the Floating Point Systems' AP-120B have when compared with most of the fixed point machines that have been built in the past. Therefore, recent technology improvements in integrated circuit design, that produced single chip processors like the Texas Instruments TMS32010, fulfill almost all the requirements of parameter extraction.

As one might expect, parameter extraction algorithms do not need very efficient symbolic (e.g. list) processing operators. The data structures used are very simple, mainly arrays, but the amount of load/store operations is very high. Since the access patterns are regular but at times complicated (e.g. the shuffling of FFT's) the performance of a system executing parameter extraction procedures depends on its ability to efficiently perform (or avoid) address calculations. For example, the author has observed an increase by a factor of 5 in the performance of an implementation of the FFT algorithm on a TMS32010 when the address computation and some of the data shuffling have been improved by additional hardware.

The amount of computation and storage is independent from the complexity of the task and ranges from about 1 to about 30 Millions of Instructions per Second of Speech (MIPSS). In some commercial systems, analog processing has been used in order to reduce cost but when detailed parametrization is required as in the Feature system [8], analog processing is not sufficient. The amount of memory that is necessary can be extremely small and is never much more than the number of samples that have to be kept around if non-local processing has to be performed (e.g. pitch tracking) or if the signal has to be re-examined in the context of some higher level constraint. The 64K byte figure in Table 2-1 is derived by assuming that a full 4-second-long utterance (16 bit values sampled at 16KHz) is kept in memory for delayed re-examination.

The parameter extraction computation can be easily parallelized because of its regular, predictable control and data-flow. When the control-flow is not data dependent, a very small granularity (e.g. "butterfly" operators) can be efficiently used. The degree of parallelism can also be very high, for instance in the order of hundreds of parallel operations. The communication structure can be quite complicated if the parallelism is pushed to its maximum, e.g. a fully parallel FFT. In practice, it is not necessary to exploit such parallelism because the necessary performance is already available from commercial high speed processors. In conclusion, speech recognition is not in the class of applications that one would define "signal processing intensive" by current standards.

2.2 PHONETIC ANALYZER

The phonetic analyzer comprises all the techniques that transform the parametric representation of the input speech into a phonetic description of the utterance. This component is not present in small systems that perform a template matching directly at the parameter level. Typically, this component contains a mixture of arithmetic computation (e.g. computation of distance) and data-dependent, branching programs (e.g. segmentation algorithms). The typical data structures that are used in this component are neither too complex (they would require special instructions to work fast) nor too simple (a signal processing architecture could be used). Therefore, this component is the one that matches best with "general-purpose" architectures.

The amount of computation and memory required are independent of the task characteristics and depend on the level of refinement necessary. For example, the Harpy segmenter and labeler used about .5 MIPSS and used less than 64K bytes of memory. Most current systems perform little or no phonetic analysis, relying on pattern matching of some kind of parameters, e.g. LPC coefficients. When feature extraction and classification techniques are used, as in the Feature system [8], there is the possibility that a lot of computation be required if complex combinations of features that vary over time have to be evaluated.

A limited amount of parallelism could be exploited in this module. For example, a number of "segment detectors" could work in parallel on the incoming data, each segment detector specialized in identifying a different set of acoustic characteristics. Each segment detector could be independent or cooperate very little with other segment detectors. A continuous speech acoustic front end that has these characteristics has never been built, and it is impossible to accurately evaluate the amount of computation involved since it will depend on how well one will be able to exploit the acoustic and phonetic knowledge.

2.3 WORD AND SENTENCE RECOGNITION

The word and sentence recognition component is the biggest unknown, both from the speech science point of view and from the computation point of view. The analysis is complicated by the fact that the computational requirements are influenced in a complex way by the characteristics of the task domain. We will examine increasingly complex techiniques that are used to perform this task. Although different techniques have different capabilities and performance from the point of view of recognition accuracy, this paper will not comment on this issue.

2.3.1 TEMPLATE MATCHING

In most of the current commercial systems and in some research systems, word and sentence recognition is performed by some kind of template matching. In the simplest (and cheapest) systems the pattern matching is performed at the parametric level, e.g. using LPC parameters [25]; in other cases the template matching is performed at a higher level [13]. In all these instances, highly regular architectures can be devised. For example see [30,6].

2.3.2 SEARCH-INTENSIVE SYSTEMS

For the purpose of this paper, search-intensive systems comprise all the systems that search a single large data structure in order to identify the "best matching" utterance. Usually these systems use an intermediate representation at the level of phonemes. Examples of this kind of systems are Harpy [21] and the IBM system [18].

One way to attack the analysis of the complexity of such systems is to extrapolate from the behavior of existing systems. For example, the Harpy system is a good example of a computationally very efficient, albeit limited system. The analysis of the Harpy system that was performed in order to build a tailored architecture [4] showed that:

- arithmetic operations were a small part of the total computation ($< 5\%$);

- comparisons were also less than 10% of the total computation;

- more than 50% of the time was spent in accessing data structures;

- a static parallel decomposition was impossible because of the data dependent behavior of the algorithm.

Since the performance is a function of the task, one should be concerned with how the requirements will change when the task complexity increases. In the case of the Harpy system, the branching factor of the grammar and the number of words were the main factors controlling the number of instructions per second of speech required. Table 2-1 shows how the performance of the Harpy system (expressed in Millions of Instructions per Second of Speech, MIPSS) is influenced by changes in the number of vocabulary words or in the branching factor. The data shown are from [1] and were corrected to take into account the improvements to the Harpy system (about one order of magnitude) that we were able to obtain after the publication of [1].

The table shows a factor of three increases in the amount of computation when the number of words increases by a factor of four (from approximately 1 MIPSS and 250 words to 2.6 MIPSS and 1000 words). An increase of the static branching factor with the number of words (250) held constant caused an equal increase in the amount of computation required (.7 MIPSS to 6 MIPSS).

In order to extrapolate the results of these experiments to a 1000-word vocabulary where any word can follow any other word, we have to multiply the amount of computation (2.6 MIPSS) by the branching factor ratio of the two tasks (1000 versus 9.5 for the AIX05 grammar). This brings us to about 270 million instructions per second of speech. This should be considered an upper bound on the computational requirements of any system of this kind for such a

Grammar	MIPSS	Static branching factor	Vocabulary size
AIS10 (Harpy)	1	8.2	250
AIM12 (Harpy)	1.7	10.5	500
AIX05 (Harpy)	2.6	9.5	1000
AIX05 (Hearsay II))	60	9.5	1000
AIS06 (Harpy)	.73	4.6	250
AIS10 (Harpy)	1	8.2	250
AIS15 (Harpy)	1.4	11.9	250
AIS30 (Harpy)	4.5	33.3	250
AIS40 (Harpy)	6	39.5	250

Table 2-1:   Effect of the vocabulary size and grammar branching factor on the performance of the Harpy and Hearsay II systems. The performance is measured in Millions of Instructions per Second of Speech (MIPSS)

task. In practice, the use of filtering based on coarse phonetic features and prosodic patterns can reduce the effective vocabulary size by one to two orders of magnitude with a corresponding decrease in the amount of computation required. Better parameter extraction and phonetic transcription modules will also help in limiting the amount of computation required. In general, a number of factors will contribute to reduce the amount of computation required, and will counterbalance the growth of computational requirements caused by the increase in the vocabulary size and in the branching factor.

2.3.3 HYPOTHESIZE-AND-TEST SYSTEMS

From table 2-1 we see that the Hearsay-II system needed much more computation than Harpy on the same task. Part of this increase in the computation was due to the less constrained recognition paradigm of Hearsay-II. For example, Hearsay-II could start searching an utterance at many different places while Harpy always performed a left-to-right search. The remaining difference in the amount of computation is due to inefficiencies encountered in executing a parallel system on a single processor. We can expect all the systems that use the same paradigm to incur a similar overhead. On the other hand, a system like Hearsay-II could benefit from executing on a really parallel system as suggested in Section 3.

Some more sophisticated algorithms that could exploit a large amount of parallelism have been proposed [10] but their effectiveness and their implementability still remain to be demonstrated.

3.   COMPUTER SYSTEMS

In this Section, we will briefly describe a few classes of machines that might have an impact on the improvement the computational cost effectiveness of the previously described speech recognition system components. Machine classes will be presented in the order of their increasing departure from conventional "general-purpose" single-processor systems.

3.1 LANGUAGE-ORIENTED MACHINES

When executing a given algorithm, the easiest most cost-effective way to increase the performance of a machine is to tailor the instruction set to the task at hand. This generates a new "general-purpose" machine that behaves much better for some kinds of algorithms but can still be programmed to execute almost any kind of algorithm. This is at the basis of the current breed of LISP machines [15].

LISP machines make it reasonable to run large LISP based systems that require a lot of computation. For example, Boley [5] reports 3 to 12 fold improvement in speed by using a LISP machine instead of a "typical" LISP mainframe like the DECSystem-10. However, the success of LISP machines might in part be due to other features like their "window" system and their user interface.

LISP machines can be very good at executing some of the algorithms that might arise at the Word and Sentence Level (and sometimes at the Phonetic Analyzer Level), but their current value is more in the possibility to very quickly implement and test algorithms that is offered by a language like LISP when it is executed in a rich environment. This is currently one of the most important characteristics that a system for speech research should have.

The importance of the environment and the language are demonstrated by fine speech tools like SPIRE [26] and ISP [20]. LISP machines are necessary for tools like SPIRE because of their very good programming and user interface environment and not because of their processor. As a matter of fact SPIRE needs an attached array processor to perform some of its functions at an acceptable speed.

Prolog machines are also being proposed [32]. Since these efforts are trailing by a few years the similar LISP efforts, Prolog machines are not a possible research tool at this point. Some of the proposed parallel Prolog machines, if they will ever see the light, might be useful at the word and sentence level because of the processing power they will make available.

In conclusion, AI-oriented high-level language architectures are likely to have an impact on speech research not as an ultimate engine for speech recognition but rather as a very effective research tool, especially if integrated with other specialized computation engines and task-oriented architectures.

3.2 PRODUCTION SYSTEM MACHINES

Production Systems are widely used to build expert systems and to model intelligent behavior. In many respects, Production Systems could be a viable way of building speech recognition systems for which experts (e.g. spectrogram readers) channel their knowledge into rules that are executed by the system. It is hard to judge if this will ever be possible since the slow speed of execution of such systems has prohibited their use in domains requiring high performance and real-time response. This situation might change in the future if some ongoing research on machines for production systems [16, 23, 27] is successful.

A production system program contains rules (productions) that are activated depending on whether some conditions, that are specified with the rule, are satisfied. Production systems are constantly executing a three phase algorithm:

- *match*: the conditions are examined to identify the rules that can be executed;

- *conflict resolution*: one of the executable productions is selected;

- *act*: the production is executed, i.e. the memory is modified.

These three phases must be executed sequentially and cannot be "unfolded" as one might do with certain kinds of loops, since it is hard to predict whether any computation in a given iteration will depend on the result of previous iterations or not. The second and third phases require very little computation and are never a problem. The first phase seems to contain a large amount of parallelism since each condition could in principle be examined in parallel. Recent analysis of existing systems [16, 23] has shown that the amount of parallelism available is limited by the fact that a small set of productions (a few tens) is affected by the act phase. This result, if common to all kinds of production systems, would put the burden of speeding-up production systems on the improvement of the performance of the processors used in the match phase.

In conclusion, production systems are currently not a viable solution for speech processing but could become interesting in the future if suitable architectures are designed and built.

3.3 GENERAL-PURPOSE PARALLEL MACHINES

The next logical step away from language-oriented systems is to exploit parallelism as much as possible. We have already seen (in production systems) that this might not be easy and that the expected parallelism might not be there at the expected level. It is convenient to distinguish between algorithm level parallelism and machine level parallelism. Algorithm level parallelism is explicitly expressed *and managed* by the application algorithm, while machine level parallelism is visible only at a level different from the algorithm level and is *transparent* to the application algorithm. This distinction is important because the former kind of parallelism requires a known parallel algorithm, while the latter can improve any kind of algorithm.

If we exclude some massively parallel and hypothesize-and-test paradigms, most speech recognition paradigms are inherently non-parallel and even hypothesize-and-test can be truly parallel only if a satisfactory focus-of-attention policy is devised. It is therefore necessary to either restructure the algorithm in a parallel fashion *that fits the characteristics of a given multiprocessor* or to use a machine that can take advantage of the existing parallelism at a lower level.

In the past, the most taxing problem in adapting an algorithm to a general purpose multiprocessor has been the high overhead required for the synchronization of tasks. This required the algorithm to be partitioned in fairly large components which, in turn, caused poor load sharing and, ultimately, a speed-up curve that would sharply deviate from the linear speed-up after more than a few processors were used in the system [4]. For example, speech algorithms had the worst behavior over a number of other application-oriented algorithms when run on C.mmp and Cm* [24, 28].

One might ask if more modern multiprocessors would behave better. It is hard to tell at this point since no speech experiment has been performed on systems like the Denelcor's Heterogeneous Element Processor, the C-MU Parallel Processor Architecture (a shared memory multi-Vax system now being designed at C-MU in cooperation with an industrial partner) and the Ultracomputer [29]. Most likely these systems will require less synchronization overhead but, because of their "general-purpose" structure, their performance will be less than it could be obtained with a task-oriented system [4].

Modern general-purpose multiprocessors might, on the other hand, become the best vehicle for speech research if an hypothesize-and-test paradigm with independent knowledge source is used. The reason is that in this case the recognition process is implemented as a set of independent processes (the knowledge sources) whose interconnections can be implemented with protocols that do not guarantee complete correctness of the communication and, therefore, can be very efficient. For example, this paradigm is suitable for a distributed system of processors connected by a local area network.

Some machine level parallelism techniques like CPU pipelining and vector instructions do not make any use of the information contained in the representation of the algorithm and attain a limited parallelism regardless of the algorithm representation. If we describe an algorithm using a data-flow style language, the inherent parallelism is available all the way to the level of the atomic functions. Data-flow machines could efficiently exploit all this parallelism (if they have enough resources) and could therefore attain maximum effectiveness. Moreover, since computation resources in a data-flow machine are assigned while the machine is running, algorithms that have a control-flow that is highly data dependent can be dealt with as effectively as any other algorithm. For an in-depth treatment of data-flow machine issues see Arvind's article [2].

In conclusion, the highly data-dependent behavior of some speech algorithms seems to indicate that general-purpose data-flow machines might be more appropriate for speech recognition than vonNeumann style multiprocessors. Unfortunately, working data-flow machines are an almost empty class at this time. If one desires to use existing general-purpose multiprocessors, the use of an hypothesize-and-test paradigm can make it possible to build a recognition system on a loosely connected set of processors.

3.4 MASSIVELY PARALLEL MACHINES

Parallelism, rather than raw speed, seems the way the brain gets most jobs done and speech recognition is obviously one of these jobs. Massively parallel architectures are machines with a very large number of (perhaps small) processing elements connected by some ad-hoc network. Most of the computation consists in sending information to other elements and combining the incoming information. The connections between the elements are part of the "program" or the "knowledge" present in the machine.

These kinds of machines can be classified by the type of information that is passed among the elements: some simply exchange a marker [12], some exchange values [17], some exchange arbitrary messages [9]. Some components of a speech recognition system seem very suitable to massively parallel architectures. For example, word hypothesization could be performed by a system in which

- elements represent words or phonemes,

- phoneme-nodes are connected to word-nodes to represent the lexical knowledge, and

- "phoneme likelihoods" (values) *activate* words which, in turn, inhibit each other (e.g. sending negative values).

Massively parallel algorithms are not here yet and neither are massively parallel machines. In some way, even if the effectiveness of massively parallel algorithms could be demonstrated on a small task, massively parallel algorithms would become useful only if a machine could be built to execute them effectively.

3.5 TASK-ORIENTED MACHINES AND VLSI

With the advent of Very Large Scale Integration (VLSI) comes the advent of the phrase: "With the advent of Very Large Scale Integration" (alas)*

The first part of this section dealt with the impact that various general-purpose architectures might have on the execution of speech algorithms. It is clear, though, that the current technology allows ultimate cost effectiveness to be obtained only if an architecture is specifically tailored to a given algorithm. Unfortunately, tailoring makes sense only when an algorithm has become well established. This does not mean that the algorithm cannot be further improved but simply that it has reached a satisfactory performance from the recognition accuracy standpoint. Among speech recognition components, parameter extraction techniques and template matching techniques are now sufficiently stable to be candidate for the design of dedicated architectures. Parameter extraction has been tackled by designing analog/digital components like filter banks [7] and specialized digital processors (e.g. LPC processors on a single chip). Template matching is dealt with in detail elsewhere in this book, suffice it to say that a regular and data-dependent control structure is the major characteristic of the Dynamic Programming algorithms that their systolic implementations exploit.

---

*From Mike Foster's plan file, Carnegie-Mellon University VLSI Vax

Some work has been done by the author at Carnegie-Mellon University in designing and building an architecture for the Harpy recognition system. This experiment showed that tailoring can dramatically improve the cost-effectiveness of a system. The system (Harpy Machine [4]), using five Digital LSI-11 multiprocessors executed in real time a task that a large mainframe like the Decsystem-10/KL-10 executed in double real time. The author is now working on a set of VLSI chips [3] that will improve the performance of the Harpy Machine by about two orders of magnitude. These chips will be used in the word hypothesizer of a connected, speaker independent system now being designed at C-MU. The reason why in this particular case it is reasonable to design VLSI chips for a partially unsettled algorithm is that a set of tools is being built at the same time allowing us to quickly design similar chips once the speech algorithms have stabilized.

VLSI, by itself, has little to do with improving the performance of speech recognition systems. The importance of VLSI stems from two facts: first, VLSI technology has made available fast signal processing devices that have satisfied all the requirements for signal processing including the case when an extremely high cost effectiveness is required (e.g. in a low performance, low cost application). Second, the possibility of designing and building a new architecture down to the logic circuit level (instead of the off-the-shelf microprocessor level) has given us the possibility to make real-time speech recognition in the context of complex tasks a reality.

4. SUMMARY

This paper has discussed the computational side of the speech recognition problem and described how some of the currently known computer architectures can influence the performance of speech recognition systems. Although speech recognition opinions take sometimes the flavor of articles of faith, too little is known about speech recognition to take any side and too little is known for the computer architect to design the ultimate speech recognition machine. Enough is known, though, to build increasingly interesting and fast systems.

REFERENCES

1. Speech Group, Summary of Results of the Five-year Research Effort at Carnegie-Mellon University, Computer Science Department, Carnegie-Mellon University, 1977.
2. R. A. Iannucci Arvind, "A critique of multiprocessing von Neumann style," 10th Annual International Symposium on Computer Architecture, 1983.
3. T. Anantharaman, M. Annaratone, R. Bisiani, "A family of custom VLSI circuits for speech recognition," IEEE International Conference on Acoustics, Speech and Signal Processing, March 1984.
4. R. Bisiani, H. Mauersberg and R. Reddy, "Task-oriented architectures," Proceedings of the IEEE, July 1983.
5. H. Boley, "A preliminary survey of artificial intelligence machines," SIGART, 72, July 1980.
6. R. A. Kavaler, T. G. Noll, M. Lowy, H. Murveit and R. W. Brodersen, "A dynamic time warp IC for a one thousand recognition system," ICASSP '84, IEEE, San Diego, March 1984.
7. R. D. Fellman and R. W. Brodersen, "A switched capacitor adaptive lattice filter," Journal of Solid State Circuits, February 1983.
8. R. A. Cole, R. M. Stern, M. S. Phillips, S. M. Brill, P. Specker, and A. P. Pilant, "Feature-based speaker-independent recognition of English letters," ICASSP '83 Proceedings, IEEE, 1983, pp. 731-734.
9. W. D. Hillis, *The Connection Machine*, MIT, 1981.
10. R. De Mori, R. Giordana, A. Laface, P. Saitta, "Parallel algorithms for syllable recognition in continuous speech," to be published.
11. L. D. Erman, F. Hayes-Roth, V. R. Lesser, D. R. Reddy, "The Hearsay-II speech-understanding system: integrating knowledge to resolve uncertainty," ACM Computing Surveys, 12, 2, June 1980.
12. S. E. Fahlman, NETL: A system for representing and using real world knowledge, Ph. D. Th., MIT, 1979.
13. P. Frison and P. Quinton, "A VLSI parallel machine for speech recognition," ICASP '84, IEEE, San Diego, March 1984.
14. R. G. Goodman, Language design for man-machine communication, Ph. D. Th., Carnegie-Mellon University, 1976.
15. R. Greenblatt, T. Knight and J. Holloway, *A LISP Machine, Fifth Workshop on Architectures for Non-numeric Processing*, Asilomar, March 1980.
16. A. Gupta and C. L. Forgy, *Measurements on Production Systems*, Carnegie-Mellon University, 1983.
17. S. E. Fahlman, G. E. Hinton and T. J. Sejnowski, "Massively parallel architectures for AI: NETL, THISTLE and Boltzmann machines," AAAI-83,

AAAI, Washington, DC, 1983.

18. L. R. Bahl, Das Das, P. V. De Souza, F. Jelinek, S. Katz, R. L. Mercer, M. A. Picheny, "Some experiments with large-vocabulary isolated word sentence recognition," ICASSP '84, IEEE, San Diego, March 1984.

19. J. N. Holmes, "The JSRU channel vocoder," IEEE Proceedings 127, February 1980.

20. G. E. Kopec, "The integrated signal processing system ISP," ICASSP '84, IEEE, San Diego, March 1984.

21. B. T. Lowerre, The Harpy Speech Recognition System, Ph. D. Th., Computer Science Department, Carnegie-Mellon University, 1976.

22. J. Makhoul, "Linear prediction: A tutorial review," Proc. IEEE 63, April 1975.

23. K. Oflazer, Partitioning in Parallel Processing of Production Systems, Computer Science Dept., Carnegie-Mellon University, Thesis Proposal 1984.

24. P. N. Oleinick, The Implementation and Evaluation of Parallel Algorithms on C.mmp. Ph. D. Th., Carnegie-Mellon University, Computer Science Department, 1978.

25. L. R. Rabiner, A. E. Rosenberg, S. E. Levinson, "Considerations in dynamic time-warping algorithms for discrete word recognition," IEEE Trans. ASSP ASSP-26, 6, December 1978.

26. D. W. Shipman, "SpireX: statistical analysis in the spire acoustic-phonetic workstation," ICASSP '83, IEEE, March 1983.

27. S. Stolfo, D. Miranker and D. F. Shaw, "Architecture and applications of DADO: A large scale parallel computer for artificial intelligence," International Joint Conference on Artificial Intelligence, 1983.

28. R. J. Swan, The Switching Structure and Addressing Architecture of an Extensible Multiprocessor: Cm*, Ph. D. Th., Carnegie-Mellon University, Computer Science Department, August 1978.

29. A. Gottlieb, C. P. Grishman, K. P. Kruskal, L. McAuliffe, L. Rudolph, "The NYU ultracomputer — designing an MIMD shared memory parallel computer," IEEE Trans. on Computers C-32, 2, February 1983.

30. J. A. Feldman, F. M. Gaverick, F. M. Rhodes and J. R. Mann, "A wafer scale integration systolic processor for connected word recognition," ICASSP '84, IEEE, San Diego, March 1984.

31. H. T. Kung, "Systolic algorithms for the CMU warp processor," Proceedings of the Seventh International Conference on Pattern Recognition, Quebec, Canada, July 1984.

32. D. H. D. Warren, "A view of the Fifth Generation and its impact," The AI Magazine, Fall 82.

VLSI ARCHITECTURES FOR RECOGNITION OF CONTEXT-FREE LANGUAGES

K. S. Fu

School of Electrical Engineering

Purdue University

W. Lafayette, Indiana 47907

U.S.A.

ABSTRACT

This paper presents two VLSI architectures for the recognition of context-free languages based on Cocke-Younger-Kasami's and Earley's algorithms. By restricting the context-free grammar to be free of null rule, it is possible to implement the two algorithms on triangular shape VLSI systems. For both parsing algorithms, the designed VLSI systems are capable of recognizing a string of length n in 2n time units. Extensions to the recognition of regular tree languages and finite-state languages are also discussed.

1.   INTRODUCTION

The speed of formal languages recognition is frequently considered to be important in many applications such as syntactic pattern recognition [8], artificial intelligence [9], natural language processing [10], syntax analysis of programming languages [11], pattern matching [12], etc. With the continuing advances in Very Large Scale Integration (VLSI) technology making circuitry smaller and faster, many processors can now be put together on a single chip and communicate with

---

This work was supported by the NSF Grant ECS 80-16580.

NATO ASI Series, Vol. F16
New Systems and Architectures for Automatic Speech
Recognition and Synthesis. Edited by R. De Mori and C. Y. Suen
© Springer-Verlag Berlin Heidelberg 1985

each other at on-chip speeds. This offers the opportunity in building low-cost, high-performance, special-purpose multiprocessor architectures to aid in the rapid solution of sophisticated language recognition of general context-free languages. These languages are most commonly used in the mentioned areas and their recognition methods have been well studied [1]. The recognition methods employed in this paper will be based on the Cocke-Younger-Kasami (CYK) algorithm and Earley's algorithm [1]. Multiprocessing and pipelining techniques are used in the architectures to execute the algorithm in parallel and they will be presented in the following sections.

The definition for context-free language is taken from [1]. N and Σ represent nonterminal and terminal sets, and $V = N \cup \Sigma$. Throughout this paper, Roman capitals A, B, ... denote elements of N while lower case a, b, ... are elements of Σ. Yet, n should always be the length of the string. Greek letters α, β, ... are elements of V^*, however, λ is specifically designated as the null or empty string.

Definition 1. A context-free grammar is a 4-tuple

$$G = (N, \Sigma, P, S)$$

where N is the set of nonterminal symbols denoted by upper case letters, Σ is the set of terminal symbols denoted by lower case letters, P is the set of productions of the form $A \rightarrow \alpha$, $A \in N$, $\alpha \in (N \cup \Sigma)^*$, and S is the start symbol. The grammar is said to be in Chomsky normal form if the productions are all of the form $A \rightarrow BC$ or $A \rightarrow a$. If α, β and γ are strings of terminals and nonterminals, then $\alpha A \beta \rightarrow \alpha \gamma \beta$ if and only if $A \rightarrow \gamma$ is a production. The language generated by the grammar is the set of strings of terminals w such that $S \overset{*}{\rightarrow} w$ where $\overset{*}{\rightarrow}$ is the transitive closure of $\rightarrow$.

2. VLSI ARCHITECTURE FOR CONTEXT-FREE LANGUAGES RECOGNITION BY CYK ALGORITHM

2.1 THE CYK ALGORITHM

Two major methods for context-free language recognition are known [1,2]. The first was proposed independently by Cocke, Younger and Kasami [1]. It requires a grammar in Chomsky normal form [1] with no null rule. The second major method was developed by Earley [3] which will work for context-free grammar of any form. Although the two algorithms appear to be quite different, both have the same time bound of $O(n^3)$ for general context-free languages. Valiant [14] had shown that the computation performed by CYK algorithm can be related to boolean matrix multiplication, and came up with a recognizer running in time $O(n^{2.81})$. This is the fastest known method on a sequential machine. About the same time, Kosaraju [15] showed that CYK algorithm can be used to recognize context-free languages in time $O(n)$ on two-dimensional array automata, and in time $O(n^2)$ on one-dimensional array automata. In this section, the CYK algorithm for context-free language recognition will be discussed.

Algorithm 1 — CYK algorithm

Let $G = (N, \Sigma, P, S)$ be a context-free grammar in Chomsky normal form (with no null rule) and let $w = a_1 a_2 \ldots a_n$, $n \geq 1$, be a string where, for $1 \leq k \leq n$, $a_k \in \Sigma$. Form the strictly upper-triangular $(n + 1) \times (n + 1)$ recognition matrix T as follows, where each element $t_{i,j}$ is a subset of N and is initially empty. (note: 0-origin addressing convention is used for matrices).

```
Begin
    loop1:For i = 0 to n-1 do
        t      = {A|A→a     is in P};
         i,i+1          i+1
    loop2:For d = 2 to n do
        For i = 0 to n-d do
            Begin
                j = d = i;
                t    = {A|there exists k, i + 1 ≤ k ≤ j-1
                 i,j
                        such that A→BC is in P for some
                        B ε t   , C ε t  }
                             i,k      k,j
            End
End
```

If the element $t_{0,n}$ of the recognition matrix contains the start symbol S then the string is accepted, otherwise the string is rejected.

2.2 THE VLSI IMPLEMENTATION

The VLSI architecture for implementing the CYK algorithm in parallel can be divided into two parts: The preprocessing requirement and the hardware design. Preprocessing requirements are those tasks that are mostly input independent and therefore they are required to compute only once in the beginning. The hardware design is the part that uses the preprocesed results and performs the recognition in 2n time units.

(A) Preprocessing requirement

The preprocessing requirement has three parts. First, each distinct nonterminal of the grammar are numbered in ascending order. That is, if the nonterminal set is {S, A} then the corresponding numbered nonterminal set will be $\{A_1, A_2\}$ where $A_1 = S$ and $A_2 = A$. Similarly, we also number the terminals of the grammar in this way. That is, if the terminal set is {b, a} then the corresponding numbered terminal set will be $\{a_1, a_2\}$ where $a_1 = b$ and $a_2 = a$. With the production rules rewritten according to the numbered terminal and nonterminal sets, we can proceed to the next stage of the preprocessing requirement.

The next stage of preprocessing requirement is to construct a coded production table for the hardware. Assume we have s distinct nonterminals in the grammar labeled A_1, A_2, ... , A_s, then form the permutation of all possible nonterminal pairs in order (i.e. $A_1 A_1, A_1 A_2$, ..., $A_1 A_s, A_2 A_1$, ..., $A_2 A_s$, ..., $A_s A_1$, ... $A_s A_s$). Following this order, for each of these pairs find the set of nonterminals that derives that pair. For example, if $A_1 \rightarrow A_2 A_3$, and $A_4 \rightarrow A_2 A_3$ then the set of nonterminals corresponding to the pair $A_2 A_3$ is $\{A_1 A_4\}$. Coded each of these sets with a corresponding binary word or bit vector of length s, if A_i is in the set then set bit i of the word to 1, otherwise set it to 0. For example, if the length of the binary word s is 4, the set $\{A_1, A_4\}$ will be coded as 1001. This bit vector representation will be used throughout the design. After completing the coding, we have a coded production table for the production matching operation. The table will then be loaded into the memory module of each cell in the architecture during the initialization phase. This will be further discussed when we come to the hardware design.

The last preprocessing requirement is to code every input string according to a special format. This task is corresponding to loop 1 of the CYK algorithm. First we build a code table similar to the one before except we use terminals this time. That is, assume we have n terminals labeled a_1, a_2, ..., a_n then for each terminal find, in the order of labels, the corresponding set of non-terminals that derives it and code the set the same way as before. Now we can use this table to code the input strings by using table scanning. This table scanning job can be done either in the host computer or it can be done on-the-fly by a simple content addressable memory [4] which contains this code table.

Except the table scanning, all the other pre-processing tasks are input independent. Therefore, they are required to compute only once in the beginning and the rest of the recognition tasks will be carried out by the hardware.

(B) Hardware design

In order to implement the CYK algorithm efficiently in hardware, the VLSI structure is chosen to be the same as the strictly upper triangular recognition matrix T (See Figure 1). In this way, the data paths which are determined by the recognition matrix and the algorithm are explicitly incorporated in the processors' organization. On the other hand, data in each matrix element are represented by using a s-bit bit vector as described in the preprocessing tasks. In this way, the set membership representation of nonterminals can be done efficiently. The hardware design can be subdivided into two portions: The dataflow requirement and the functional units design. The dataflow requirement and the functional units design. The dataflow requirement takes care of the necessary data communications between cells whereas the functional units design handles the required operations on input data within a cell.

a) Dataflow requirements

The dataflow requirement is specified in loop2 of the CYK algorithm. It is easy to see that element (i,j) of the recognition matrix needs to receive data from elements (i,k) and (k,j), for $i < k < j$. Observe also that there is no data dependency among the elements on a particular diagonal of the recognition matrix, therefore we can compute the elements on a diagonal in parallel if the required data for each element is arranged to arrive at the right moment. It happens that this dataflow requirement is the same as the optimal parentization problems in [5]. Therefore, we have adopted their algorithm for such a dataflow requirement. An informal description of the algorithm is given as follows:

Let $t = j-i$ be the distance between cell (i,j) and the boundary (See Figure 1). The result of a cell at distance t will be ready at time 2t, the cell then transmits its result upwards and to the right. This result travels at a rate of one cell per time unit for t additional time units and then slows down to one cell in every two time units until the recognition is finished. Using this algorithm, a network with $n(n+1)/2$ cells will require 2n time units for the final result to be available.

To implement such a dataflow pattern, the method used in [5] is also adopted. Referring to Figure 1, each cell has three types of channel for data communications between its neighbors. The first one is called the fast belt, it can transmit one data value at a rate of one cell per time unit. The second one is known as the slow belt, it can transmit one data value at a rate of one cell

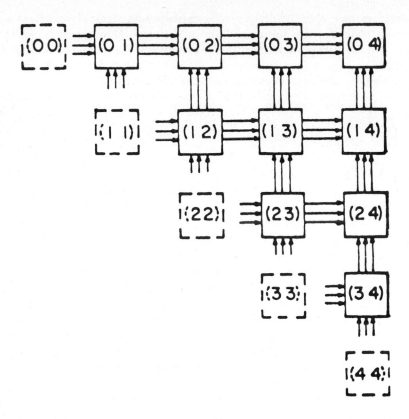

Solid square = cell
Dotted square = boundary location

Figure 1. VLSI architecture for fast recognition of context-free
languages (the case of n = 4 is shown).

in every two time units. The third one is a single bit control line, it is used for transmitting control signals between cells. There are five registers in each cell (See Figure 2): The accumulator (ACCUM.) where the current value of an entry of the recognition matrix is maintained, the horizontal fast (HORI.FAST) and vertical fast (VERT.FAST) registers for the implementation of the fast belts, and similarly the horizontal slow (HORI.SLOW) and vertical slow (VERT.SLOW) registers for slow belts implementation. Each of them is s-bits in length, where s is the number of distinct non-terminals in the grammar. In each time unit, the horizontal fast register receives data from its left neighbor while sending its old content to its right neighbor. On the other hand, the vertical fast register receives data from its neighbor below while sending its old content to its neighbor above. The horizontal slow and vertical slow registers behave exactly the same way except that the operation is done in two time units. That is, each of these registers has two stages. The incoming data enter the first stage, move the next stage at the next time unit and finally exit the cell at the following time unit. In each unit of time, a cell takes part in the belt motion as well as updating its accumulator. The new value of the accumulator is updated by the functional module FM (See figure 3) using the current contents of the five registers. This will be discussed later when we come to the functional units design. In addition, if the cell is at distance t away from the boundary, then at time 2t it will copy the contents of its accumulator into its fast horizontal and vertical registers. This is done by the data transfer module DT1. And finally, if it is at an even distance t == 2s from the boundary, then at time 3t/2 it will load the first stage of its horizontal (and vertical) slow register from the horizontal (resp. vertical) fast belt, ignoring its slow belts entirely. This is done by the data transfer module DT2. The timing of these transfers is controlled by the horizontal control line (HCTL) and vertical control line (VCTL) respectively. The accumulator to fast belt transfer (DT1) that occurs in cell (i,j) at time j-i is controlled by a rightward moving signal (HCTL) that moves at a rate of one cell every two time units. The fast to slow belt transfer (DT2) that occurs at time 3(j-i)/2 is controlled by an upward moving signal (VCTL) that moves at a rate of two cells every three time units. Using this implementation, the dataflow requirement is fulfilled.

b)   Functional units design

In this part of the discussion, the emphasis will be on the design of the Functional Module (FM) such that the architecture can produce the required recognition matrix. Other functional units such as data transfer modules and various registers can be easily designed by using a few pass transistors and/or buffers [4], therefore they will not be further discussed.

The design of the Functional Module (FM) is shown in Figure 3. In order to simultaneously process data received from the register pair horizontal fast (HF) and Vertical Slow (VS) as well as the register pair horizontal slow (HS) and vertical fast (VS), the Functional Module has employed two Permutation Modules (PM1 and PM2). They are used to compute all possible right-hand side non-terminal pairs induced by data in each register pair (one PM for each pair).

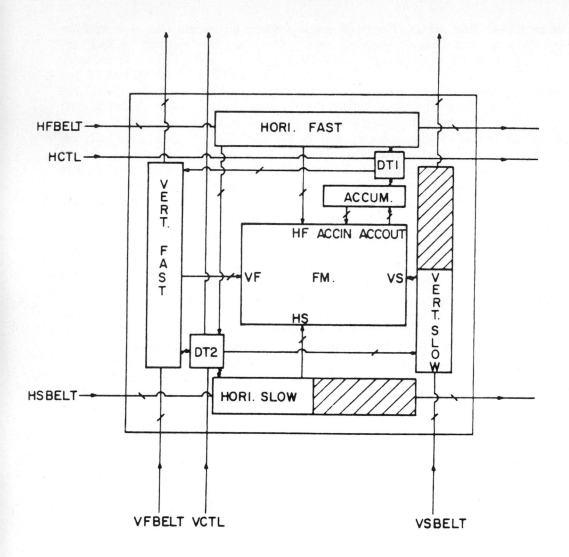

Figure 2. Cell design for CYK algorithm

Each Permutation Module simply performs the Boolean function $a_{ij} = b_i$ AND c_j for $1 \leq i, j \leq s$, where s is the number of distinct non-terminals in the grammar. Each b_i is from the input of its horizontal register whereas each c_i is from its vertical register and the output a_{ij} is arranged in the same order as the storage of the coded production table. Since we are interested in the right hand side non-terminal pairs induced by both of the register pairs together, the output of the two PM's are union together by the upper OR module in Figure 3 to form a single output of s^2 bit in length. That is, bit b_{ij} of PM1 is ORed with the corresponding bit c_{ij} of PM2 for $1 \leq i, j \leq s^2$. Now, in order to find the corresponding left-hand side non-terminal set simultaneously for each non-terminal pair, a Memory Module (MM) which stored the coded production table is used. The Memory Module has s^2 one-bit inputs and s^2 s-bit outputs, it will output the content of the memory cell (s bits in length) if the input is one and output zeroes otherwise. The outputs of the upper OR Module are directly connected to the inputs of the Memory Module so that the production table scanning process can be done simultaneously. The results of the table scanning (i.e. the outputs of MM) are then union together with the content of the accumulator (from ACCIN) to form the s-bit final result. This is done by the lower OR module (See Figure 3) which ORed bit i of every s-bit output of MM and ACCIN together, for $1 \leq i \leq s$. The output of the OR module (ACCOUT) will be sent to update the accumulator. In this way, the Functional Module in each cell will incorporate with the dataflow algorithm and produce the required recognition matrix in 2n time units.

To initialize the system so that it can behave properly, one requires to store the coded production table into the MM of every cell, reset every register in each cell to zero and have the coded input string loaded in the first diagonal. The loading can be done by sharing input data lines in each cell during the initialization phase. Now, start every control signal at the boundary (See Figure 1) and the architecture will run as desired. The next input string can be loaded overlappingly after the architecture has executed two time units and the next execution can start right after the completion of the present by properly resetting the registers and control signals. In this way, we can reduce the pin count by multiplexing input data lines and still can keep the system running continuously.

What is left now is to check the output of cell (0,n) and see if its non-terminal set contains the start symbol. This can be done by creating a mask with bit i equals to one if A_i is the start symbol and zero otherwise. We can then ANDed the output of cell (0,n) with this mask and test for zero. If the result indicates non-zero, we accept the string, otherwise we reject it. These operations can be done by using another simple module, we call this the Decision Module (DM). A simple design for such module is shown in Figure 4. Bit i of the input (IN) from the output of cell (0,n) is ANDed with bit i of the mask, for $1 \leq i \leq s$. The s bits result is then ORed together to form a single bit

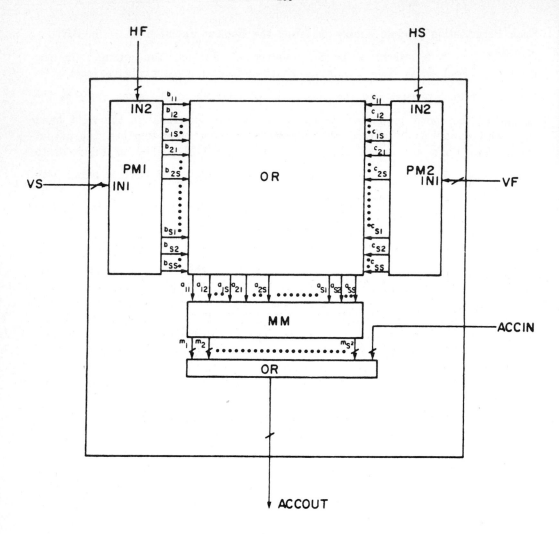

Figure 3.   Functional Module (FM)

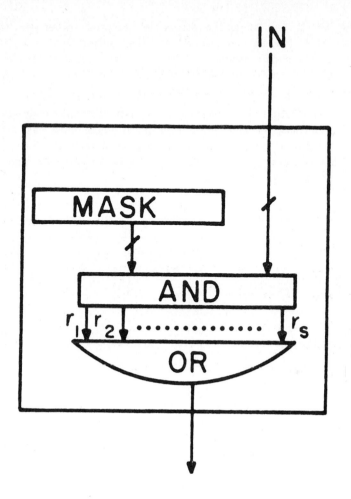

Figure 4.   Decision Module (DM).

output. If the bit is one then the string is accepted, otherwise the string is rejected. With this module connected to the output of cell (0,n) of the architecture, the system can provide a 'yes' or 'no' answer in every 2n time units. In this case, the mask of DM is required to be computed and loaded by the host computer in the initialization phase.

A computer simulation has been carried out on the logic of the VLSI architecture. The purpose of this simulation is to make sure that the logic and the various timings of the architecture are designed correctly. The result of the simulation has demonstrated that the architecture is correctly designed to provide the recognition matrix in 2n time units [13].

A parse for a given input string is sometimes useful in syntactic pattern recognition because it provides the structural descriptions of the input string. Since the recognition matrix is generated during the recognition process, it is not hard to obtain a parse for an accepted input string by a simple parsing algorithm.

3. VLSI ARCHITECTURE FOR CONTEXT-FREE LANGUAGE RECOGNITION BY EARLEY'S ALGORITHM

It is known that Earley's algorithm recognizes general context-free languages in time $O(n^3)$. In 1976, Graham, et al [16] derived from Earley's algorithm a new on-line context-free language recognition algorithm. This algorithm allows an implementation with only $O(n^2/\log n)$ operations on bit vectors of length n, or $O(n^3/\log n)$ operations on a RAM. In the same year, Weicker came up with a similar result [17]. These two recognition algorithms are the fastest ever known.

Definition 2. For any rule $A \rightarrow \alpha\beta$ in P we will call $A \rightarrow \alpha \cdot \beta$ a *dotted rule*. The dot "." is a symbol not found in V and is used as a marker to indicate the position.

Definition 3. If $X \in V$, the predecessors of $X = \{A|A \overset{*}{\Rightarrow} X, A \in N\}$.

Definition 3. The $\times$ operator. Let Q be a set of dotted rules, then

$$Q \times R = \{A \rightarrow \alpha U\beta \cdot \gamma| A \rightarrow \alpha \cdot U\beta\gamma \in Q, \beta \overset{*}{\Rightarrow} \lambda \text{ and } U \in R\}, \text{ when } R \subseteq V.$$

$$Q \times R = \{A \rightarrow \alpha U\beta \cdot \gamma| A \rightarrow \alpha \cdot U\beta\gamma \in Q, \beta \overset{*}{\Rightarrow} \lambda \text{ and } U \rightarrow \delta. \in R\},$$ when R is a set of dotted rules.

Definition 5. The $*$ operator. Let Q and R be sets of dotted rules, then

$$Q * R = \{A \rightarrow \alpha U\beta \cdot \gamma | \ A \rightarrow \alpha \cdot U\beta\gamma \ \epsilon \ Q, \ \beta \overset{*}{\Rightarrow} \lambda$$

and there is some $U' \rightarrow \delta.$ in R such that $U \overset{*}{\Rightarrow} U'\}.$

Definition 6. Let $R \subseteq V$, define

$$\text{PREDICT}(R) = \{C \rightarrow \gamma \cdot \delta | C \rightarrow \gamma\delta \text{ is in P}, \ \gamma \overset{*}{\Rightarrow} \lambda,$$

$B \overset{*}{\Rightarrow} C\eta$ for some B in R and some $\eta\}.$

Graham, et al [16] rewrote Earley's algorithm in terms of dotted rule notation and the $\times$, $*$ operators. We called their algorithm the GHR algorithm as shown below:

Algorithm 2 — GHR Algorithm

$\quad t_{0,0} = \text{PREDICT}(\{S\})$

$\quad \textit{for } j = 1 \textit{ to } n \textit{ do}$

$\quad \textit{begin } [\text{build col. } j, \text{ given cols. } 0,1,...,j\text{-}1]$

$\quad [\text{Scanner:}]$

$\qquad \textit{for } 0 \leq i \leq j\text{-}1 \textit{ do}$

$\qquad\qquad t_{i,j} = t_{i,j-1} \times \{a_j\}$

$\quad [\text{Completer:}]$

$\qquad \textit{for } k = j\text{-}1 \textit{ downto } 0 \textit{ do}$

$\qquad \textit{begin } t_{k,j} = t_{k,k} * t_{k,j}$

$\qquad\qquad \textit{for } i = k\text{-}1 \textit{ downto } 0 \textit{ do}$

$\qquad\qquad\qquad t_{i,j} = t_{i,j} \cup t_{i,k} \times t_{k,j}$

$\qquad \textit{end}$

$\quad [\text{Predictor:}]$

$\qquad t_{j,j} = \text{PREDICT} (\cup_{0 \leq i \leq j\text{-}1} t_{i,j}$

$\quad \textit{end}$

Algorithm 2 constructs a recognition matrix $T = \{t_{i,j}\}$. All of its elements are sets of dotted rules. As Graham et al claimed, this algorithm has several advantages. The straightforward control and data structures used make it conceptually simpler than Earley's version. This algorithm also combined many steps in the Earley's version into one step. Therefore, Algorithm 2 can be implemented so as to take $O(n^2/\log n)$ bit vector steps on a bit vector machine or $O(n^3/\log n)$ steps on a RAM [16].

3.1 A PARALLEL EARLEY'S ALGORITHM

The computation in Algorithm 2 has one restriction, that is, no element of column $j + 1$ can be processed until $t_{j,j}$ is processed, and hence until all elements of column j are processed. This restriction is enforced by the Predictor, which ensures that $A \rightarrow \alpha \cdot \beta$ appears in the ith row only if $S \overset{*}{\Rightarrow} a_1 \ldots a_i A \gamma$. Because of this restricted order in computation, Algorithm 2 can not be performed in parallel. However, it was mentioned by Graham [16] that with a weakened Predictor, Algorithm 2 will have the same form as CYK algorithm, except that the operation between elements is different. Based on this suggestion we developed a parallel version of Earley's algorithm and implemented it on a VLSI architecture.

(A) Removal of predictor

The function of the Predictor is to build up $t_{j,j}$ in the jth column after other elements in that column all have been processed. Suppose that we add some extra dotted rules which are not ordinarily there, the subsequent normal Scanner, Completer and Predictor operations may introduce extra dotted rules into columns to the right of j, but not above row j. In other words, this addition would have no effect on $t_{0,n}$, so we still have a correct recognizer. As a matter of fact, the Predictor can be replaced by the statement

$$t_{j,j} = \text{PREDICT(N)}$$

and the correctness is preserved. In doing so, the characterization theorem [1] would be changed to "$A \rightarrow \alpha \cdot \beta \in t_{i,j}$ if and only if $\alpha \overset{*}{\Rightarrow} a_{i+1} \ldots a_j$", which is analogous to the one for CYK algorithm. Since the diagonal elements would be all the same, independent of the input, they could be eliminated by a suitable combination of the operations $\times$ and $\cdot \, \cdot$. Earley's algorithm without the Predictor restriction is called *weakened Earley's algorithm*.

(B) Operator " × · "

From Algorithm 2, we realized that eliminating the diagonal elements $t_{k,k}$ will also eliminate the * operation and leave the algorithm with only × operation. The × operation is the main computation for constructing the matrix elements and the * operation only applies to the element after it has completed its own computation and ready to assist the computations of other elements above it. Therefore, we can combine these two operations by attaching the * operator to a × operator. The formal definition is given below. Let Q and R be sets of dotted rules and Y = PREDICT(N), which replaces every central diagonal element.

$$Q \times \cdot R = \{A \rightarrow \alpha U\beta \cdot \gamma | A \rightarrow \alpha \cdot U\beta\gamma \in Q, B \overset{*}{\rightarrow} \lambda \text{ and } U \rightarrow \delta. \in R\}$$

and

$$\{B \rightarrow \delta C\xi \cdot \eta | \gamma = \lambda, B \rightarrow \delta \cdot C\xi\eta \in Y, \text{ and } \xi \overset{*}{\rightarrow} \lambda, C \overset{*}{\rightarrow} A\}$$

if $R \subseteq V$, then

$$Q \times \cdot R = \{A \rightarrow \alpha U\beta \cdot \gamma | A \rightarrow \alpha \cdot U\beta\gamma \in Q, \beta \overset{*}{\rightarrow} \lambda, U \in R\}$$

and

$$\{B \rightarrow \delta C\xi \cdot \eta | \gamma = \lambda, B \rightarrow \delta \cdot C\xi\eta \in Y, \text{ and } xi \overset{*}{\rightarrow} \lambda, C \overset{*}{\rightarrow} A\}$$

(C) The parallel weakened Earley's algorithm

After removing the Predictor restriction and substituting the central diagonal elements, we can write the weakened Earley's algorithm in terms of " × * " operator.

Algorithm 3 — Weakened Earley's Algorithm

for i = 1 to n do

$$t_{i-1,i} = Y \times \cdot \{a_j\}$$

for j = 2 to n do

begin

[Scanner:]

for $0 \leq i \leq j-2$ do

$$t_{i,j} = t_{i,j-1} \times \cdot \{a_j\}$$

[Completer:]

$for \ k = j\text{-}1 \ downto \ 0 \ do$

$\quad for \ i = k\text{-}1 \ downto \ 0 \ do$

$$t_{i,j} = t_{i,j} \cup t_{i,k} \times \cdot \ t_{k,j}$$

end

This algorithm builds up a $(n+1)X(n+1)$ upper triangular matrix. Figure 5 depicts the detailed computations of the algorithm. The Completer operation is to calculate $t_{i,j}$ based on the information from $t_{i,k}$ and $t_{k,j}$. Noted that for the maximum value $k = j\text{-}1 < j$ and $i = k\text{-}1 < k$, $t_{i,k}$ and $t_{k,j}$ are either to the left or below $t_{i,j}$. This characteristic suggests that we can construct the same matrix by calculating one diagonal from another and moving from the central diagonal towards the upper right corner as described in the following algorithm.

Algorithm 4

$for \ i = 1 \ to \ n \ do \ in \ parallel$

$$t_{i\text{-}1,i} = Y \times \cdot \{a_i\}$$

$for \ j = 2 \ to \ n \ do$

$\quad for \ i = 0 \ to \ n\text{-}j \ do \ in \ parallel$

begin

[Scanner:]

$$t_{i,i+j} = t_{i,i+j-1} \times \cdot \{a_{i+j}\}$$

[Completer:]

$\quad for \ k = 1 \ to \ j\text{-}1 \ do \ in \ parallel$

$$t_{i,i+j} = t_{i,i+j} \cup t_{i,i+k} \times \cdot \ t_{i+k,i+j}$$

end

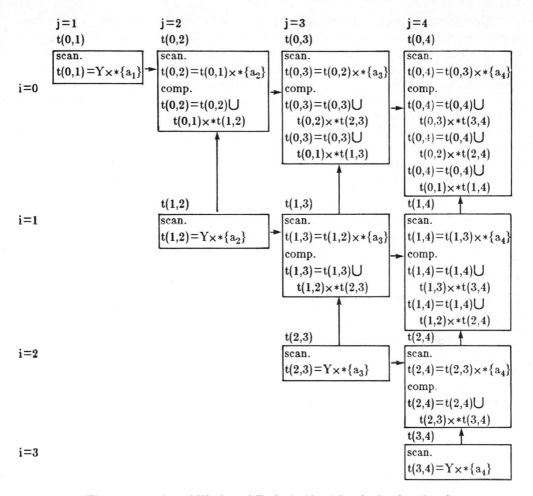

Figure 5. The computation of Weakened Earley's Algorithm (string length=4).

Algorithm 4 constructs the same matrix as Algorithm 3 does. From this parallel algorithm, we can see that j loop executes n times. Within j loop, all the i and k can be executed in parallel, provided we have enough processors to do so, hence this algorithm has time complexity O(n). Although we can break down the computation into (n-j+2) × (j-1) independent subjobs for each j loop and execute the algorithm on a MIMD system [18], yet it is not practical in real applications. For instance, if n = 50, when j = 20 the algorithm requries 608 processors to work simultaneously and when j = 50, only one processor is required while other processors have to be idled. This is a tremendous waste. Of course we can ease this situation by setting a loop for k = 1 to j-1 instead of executing in parallel. This arrangement reduces the number of required processors in the sacrifice of increasing the time complexity to $O(n^2)$. Besides, the rather complicate data exchange may also degrade the performance of this algorithm. A more efficient and promising architecture is still needed.

3.2 VLSI IMPLEMENTATION

For Algorithm 3, a direct implementation is to use the same VLSI system as the one for the CYK algorithm. Algorithm 3 has a regular communication geometry as shown in Figure 5, and the data movement can be kept simple and regular but, each processor does not perform constant-time operations.

(A) Constant-time operation

In Algorithm 3, only " × · " operator was used. Recall the definition of " × · " we notice that λ-production was considered in the operation, that is, we will add a dotted rule $A \rightarrow \alpha U \beta \cdot \gamma$ to the result instead of $A \rightarrow \alpha U \cdot \beta \gamma$, provided $\beta \overset{*}{\rightarrow} \lambda$. Since the length of β is not known, we have to check the following symbols until the decision is made. This variable length of β makes the operation time different with different data and therefore hinders the implementation on a VLSI architecture. However, if we restrict our grammar to be λ-free, the " × · " operation can easily be implemented on a dedicated hardware.

(B) Data representation

Bit vectors [20] are used to represent symbols in V and the matrix elements $t_{i,j}$. The former is easy to understand but the latter deserves further explanations. As we know, every matrix element $t_{i,j}$ is a set of dotted rules. Each dotted rule conveys the information about one production rule and its associated dot position. Since the production rules are given by the grammar, the matrix elements can only cover the dot position by bit vectors. For instance, one dotted rule with 5 symbols at its right hand side (RHS) and a dot between the second and the third symbol can be reprresented by a 6-bit bit vector with a 1 appears in the third bit and all the other bits are 0's. The extra one bit is reserved for the end marker of the RHS. Consequently, the matrix elements $t_{i,j}$ can be represented by an array of bit vectors. The dimension of the array equals the number of the production rules. We call this array of bit vectors the *cell data*, which represents the matrix elements and is transferred from cell to cell through data buses. This data structure contains all the information we need and has equal length for all elements hence indicates the uniform data transfer.

(C) Preprocessing

During the preprocessing stage, there are some information needed to be put into the VLSI system in certain forms. The grammar is coded into group of bit vector arrays and every array represents one grammar rule. If V has k symbols and each rule has at most m RHS symbols, then the array has m+1 bit vectors, each bit vector has k+1 bits. We also need to convert all the left hand side (LHS) symbols and its corresponding predecessors into array of bit vectors. Let Y = PREDICT(N) be a set of dotted rules. Since Y only depends on grammar, it can be calculated and converted into r(m+1)-bit bit vectors before hand, where r is the number of productions.

(D) The VLSI architecture

The VLSI system is similar to the one shown in Figure 1 except one extra vertical INP bus was used here to transfer input symbols. Every cell has identical structure. The system is controlled under a system clock (or unit time). It is assumed that during each system unit time, every cell can finish its computation and every bus can complete its data transfer operation. There are three vertical buses. VFB (vertical fast bus), VSB (vertical slow bus) and INP (input symbol bus), and two horizontal buses, HFB (horizontal fast bus) and HSB (horizontal slow bus). The fast buses and slow buses have the same transfer rate as discussed in the CYK algorithm, and INP bus has a transfer rate as that of a slow bus.

Each cell has three functions, namely, computing the " $\times$ $\cdot$ " opeation, loading the data onto fast buses and shifting the data from the fast buses to the slow buses. The last two functions are essential for keeping the bus system work and are controlled by two control lines, VC (vertical control) and HC (horizontal control). The control lines only transfer one bit at a time. The transfer rate and functions of VC and HC are the same as the one mentioned in the previous section.

Initially, every cell has the information about grammar rules, LHS symbols and its predecessors and Y. Start from time 1, the input symbols are read into the system in parallel, as shown in Figure 1, and all the data buses are sending 0's except HFB is loaded with Y. The control lines start to send 1 from the central diagonal cells (which are not physically exist). The system is running in a pipelining and multiprocessing fashion. After 2n unit times the tester receives data from cell (0,n) through HFB and after one more time unit, the tester will tell whether or not the input string can be generated by the grammar. The tester stores a mask which contains the information $\{S \rightarrow \alpha. | S \rightarrow \alpha \in P\}$ in terms of array of bit vectors. After it receives data from cell (0,n), a simple AND operation can give us the result.

(E) Cell structure

In this section, we will discuss the implementation of the main cell function, the computation of " $\times$ · ". Let us assume Q is a set of dotted rules. For convenience, when we say R1 of Q, we mean that R1 is an array of bit vectors and each vector represents the symbol appearing to the right of the dot, the dot position is specified by the cell data Q. Again, Y = PREDICT(N) and we can write Q $\times$ · R into an eight-step procedure.

(1) Find the dotted rules which have the form $U_i \rightarrow \delta$. from R and record the union of the LHS symbols U = union of U_i's.

(2) Compare U with R1 of Q and mark the dotted rule whenever a match occurs.

(3) Change Q by shifting those marked bit vectors one bit to the right and clear the other bit vectors.

(4) Find the dotted rules which have the form $U_i \rightarrow \delta$. from Q and record the union of the LHS symbols U = union of U_i's.

(5) Find the predecessors for U.

(6) Compare predecessors with R1 of Y and mark the dotted rule whenever a match occurs.

(7) Change Y the same way as in step (3).

(8) Q $\times$ · R = Y bit by bit ORing Q.

Recall from Figure 5, the Scanner operation only applies to the data from the left neighbor cell $t_{i,j-1}$ $\times$ · b and the same data is used in Completer operation as $t_{i,j-1}$ $\times$ · $t_{j-1,j}$. It is very easy to combine the Scanner with the Completer, that is, after forming the U for $t_{i,j-1}$, we can OR U with the input symbol b and the remaining calculations are still the same. Therefore, instead of building up a Scanner, we can modify step (1) as follows:

(1) Find the dotted rules which have the form $U_i \rightarrow \delta$. from R and record the union of the LHS symbols and the INP, U = union of U_i's and b.

The above procedure can be executed by the device shown in Figure 6. Figure 7 illustrates the architecture of the cell. In Figure 7, Operation 1 has the same structure as the one in Figure 6 while Operator 2 does not have the INP bus. The ACC will OR the results from both operators and itself. When the HC signal arrives, it will load the results to both HFB and VFB.

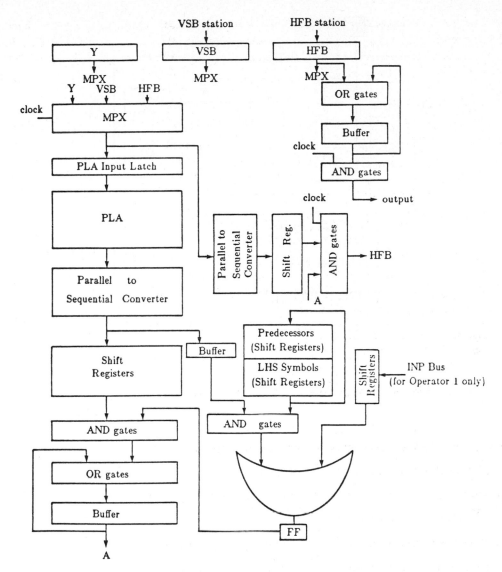

Figure 6. Structure of the operator for Earley's algorithm

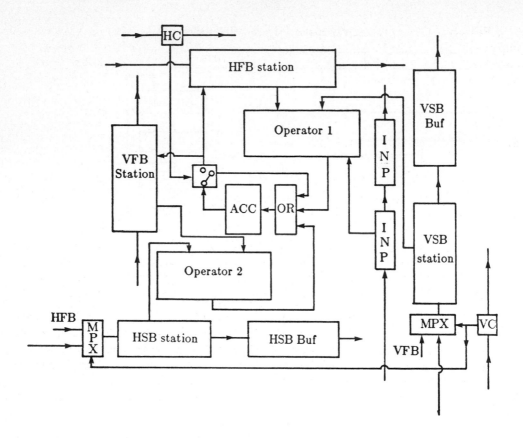

Figure 7.   Structure of the cell (Earley's algorithm)

Following the parse extraction algorithm given in [1], it is possible to implement the algorithm on a processor array [21]. It is also possible to implement the minimum-distance error-correcting parse (a modified Earley's algorithm) on a VLSI system [21].

4. CONCLUDING REMARKS

It is interesting to see that although the VLSI systems for CYK algorithm and Earley's algorithm use the same triangular matrix structure, the cell designs in each system are different. Notice that the VLSI system for CYK algorithm has simpler cell design; however, the algorithm requires the grammar to be convered into Chomsky normal form. On the other hand, a more complex cell design is required in the VLSI implementation for Earley's algorithm that, however, has imposed no specific restrictions on the form of the grammar.

Since finite-state languages form a subset of context-free languages, the context-free parsing algorithms and hence the VLSI architectures described in Section 2 and Section 3 can also be used for the recognitin of finite-state languages. A more efficient method for finite-state language recognition, derived from the CYK algorithm, has recently been proposed. The VLSI architectur using this algorithm can be made to recognize a string of length n in constant time [13].

Tree languages are often used in sytactic pattern recognition for description of high dimensional patterns [8]. It has been shown that for a given regular tree grammar one can effectively construct an equivalent expansive tree grammar [8], and this equivalent grammar will have a form of context-free grammar in Griebach normal form [1]. Consequently, the VLSI architectures proposed in this paper can be employed for the recognition of regular tree languages.

Since Earley's parsing algorithm (or modified Earley's algorithm) has been commonly used in many fields, the proposed VLSI architecture for Earley's algorithm should find applications also in error-correcting parsing and high dimensional language recognition [8,22].

REFERENCES

1. A. V. Aho and J. D. Ullman, *The Theory of Parsing, Translation and Compiling*, Vol. I, Prentice-Hall, 1972.
2. M. A. Harrison, *Introduction to Formal Language Theory*, Addison-Wesley, 1978.
3. J. Earley, "An efficient context free parsing algorithm", Comm. ACM,

13(1970), pp. 94-102.

4. C. A. Mead and L. A. Conway, *Introduction to VLSI Systems*, Adison-Wesley, 1980.

5. L. J. Guibas, H. T. Kung and C. D. Thompson, "Direct VLSI implementation of combinatorial algorithms", Proc. Conf. on VLSI, Caltech, Jan. 1979, pp. 509-526.

6. H. T. Kung, "Let's design algorithms for VLSI systems", Proc. Conf. on VLSI, Caltech, Jan. 1979, pp. 65-90.

7. K. Q. Brown, "Dynamic programming in computer science", Carnegie-Mellon Univ., Tech. Report, CS-79-106, Feb. 1979.

8. K. S. Fu, *Syntactic Pattern Recognition and Applications*, Prentice-Hall, 1982.

9. N. J. Nilsson, *Principles of Artificial Intelligence*, Tioga publishing company, 1980.

10. D. L. Waltz and B. A. Goodman, "Writing a natural language database system", Coordinated Science Lab., Univ. of Illinois, Urbana, IL 61801.

11. A. V. Aho and J. D. Ullman, *Principles of Compiler Design*, Addison Wesley, 1978.

12. R. L. Hasin, "Hardware for searching very large text databases", Proc. 5th Workshop on Computer Architecures for Non-Numeric Processing, March 1980.

13. K. H. Chu and K. S. Fu, "VLSI architectures for high speed recognition of general context-free languages and finite-state languages", Proc. 9th Annual International Smposium on Computer Architecture, April 26-29, 1982, Austin, Texas.

14. L. Valiant, "General context free recognition in less than cubic time", J. Computer and System Science, Vol. 10, 1975.

15. S. R. Kosaraju, "Speed of recognition of context-free languages by array automata", SIAM J. Comput., Vol. 4, No. 3, Sept. 1975.

16. S. L. Graham, M. A. Harrison and W. L. Ruzzo, "On line context-free language recognition in les than cubic time", Proc. of the 8th Annual ACM Symposium on Theory of Computing, May 1976.

17. Reinhold Weicker, "General context free language recogntion by a RAM with uniform cost criterion in time $n^2 \log n$", Tech. Rpt. No. 182, Feb. 1976. Computer Science Dept., Pennsylvania State University.

18. Y. T. Chiang and K. S. Fu, "Parallel Processing for Distance Cmputation in Syntactic Pattern Recognition", Proc. IEEE Workshop on CAPAIDM, Nov. 1981.

19. M. J. Foster and H. T. Kung, "The design of special-purpose VLSI chips", Computer, Vol. 13, No. 1, Jan. 1980.

20. A. V. Aho, J. E. Hopcroft and J. D. Ullman, *The Design and Analysis of Computer Algorithms*, Addison Wesley Co., Reading, Mass., 1974.

21. Y. T. Chiang and K. S. Fu, "Parallel algorithms and VLSI implementation for syntactic pattern recogntion", IEEE Trans. Pattern Analysis and Machine Intelligence, Vol. PAMI-6, May 1984.

22. Q. Y. Shi and K. S. Fu, "Efficient error-correcting parsing for (attributed and stochastic) tree grammars", Information Sciences, Vol. 26, 159-188, 1982.

IMPLEMENTATION OF AN ACOUSTICAL FRONT-END FOR SPEECH RECOGNITION

Michele Cavazza, Alberto Ciaramella e Roberto Pacifici
CSELT - Centro Studi e Laboratori Telecomunicazioni
via Reiss Romoli, 274 - 10148 Torino, Italy

ABSTRACT

We describe the implementation of a programmable general-purpose acoustical front-end for speech recognition; its design keeps into account, as an example, the algorithm of centisecond cepstrum extraction for an acoustical signal sampled at a maximum rate of 12.8 kHz.

It consists of three boards, a master board controlled by a general purpose microprocessor, a slave board containing two digital signal processors working in parallel and an input/output analog board.

The overall system is connected to a general-purpose minicomputer, which constitutes the system host. The implementation details and its rationale (mainly reprogrammability and performance) are outlined. In cases of more demanding applications, the system could also be hardware reconfigured with cascade or parallel sections.

1. Introduction and requirements

In a speech recognition system, techniques for feature extraction have unusual interest. The algorithms used [1,2] are typical not only of most speech recognition systems [3] but also of systems used for speaker recognition [4] or certain kinds of speech coding systems [5], that is, in systems using a parametric representation of speech. Nevertheless, the algorithms for features extraction, though computationally rather demanding in a real time system, are highly regular and data dependent and use regularly structured data [6]. These algorithms are mainly spectral estimations [7] or LPC (linear prediction coded) parameter extractions [8] or cepstrum estimations [9].

Today DSP (Digital Signal Processor) technology is appropriate to the real time implementation of parameter extraction algorithms for speech and several types of these processors are presently available [10]. However, given the present memory and speed limits of these components, in several cases a number of DSP's is needed in order to perform a more complex algorithm [11] or to perform various kinds of parameter extraction in parallel. Moreover, in some cases of speech recognition the capability of changing the set of extracted parameters, depending on the context, would be welcome.

Taking these points into account, we implemented an acoustical front end for speeech recognition with the following requirements:

- high performance in a reduced space using current technology

- capability of being reprogrammed

- adequately modularized, so that every single block could also be used in different contexts, as described later.

Another requirement is a general-purpose interface to the host computer.
This acoustical front-end implements, as an example, the algorithm of cepstrum extraction via the FFT calculation followed by the DCT for an acoustical signal sampled at a maximum rate of 12.8 kHz. The computations are made over a window of 20 ms. with an overlap of 10 ms. This is useful from the recognition performance point of view [12], and exploits the computation and memory capability of the machine.

2. Architectural basic choices

The reprogrammability requirement (even in real time) leads to a software reconfigurable design and to a choice of a DSP based on an external program RAM. We chose the TMS320 [13] which, at the start of this project, was the only DSP with this characteristics. However, this DSP had other interesting characteristics,too, which have been exploited in many applications [14,15,16,17]. The basic configuration of the implementation is composed of three boards:

- a master board controlled by a general-purpose processor (Z80 in this case) and connected with the host through a high speed serial link,

- a slave board,containig two twins sections, each controlled by a TMS320,

- an input-output analog board.

This three board arrangement is the standard one, but, as we noted before, it can be not satisfactory for more demanding jobs. In these cases we can rearrange the same boards, basically in two ways:

- in "cascade" (or ripple) mode,

- in "parallel" mode.

The "cascade mode" has n blocks; the first is fed by the analog input and feeds the second; the second feeds the third and so on, this mode is useful when several stages are needed for a more complex computation (e.g. formant extraction for the sake of spectral evaluation). In "parallel mode", the analog input feeds in parallel all blocks performing different independent computations (e.g. spectral coefficients and pitch extraction).

3. Implementation details

The master is controlled by an 8-bit general purpose microprocessor, and can interface to external devices with two serial links controlled by a SIO (Serial Input Output): the first is used to communicate to the host (initially for program downloading and then for parameter passing), the second is used to communicate to a local terminal, mainly for debugging purposes. Data interchange with the slaves is controlled by two parallel input/output ports. Each also transforms the 8-bit data of the master into 16-bit data of the slave. A control register to the slaves issues suitable commands (e.g. for slave resetting). Direct data interchange is also possible from the A/D to the master and from the master to the D/A, although in the application implemented, this possibility is only used for initializing and debugging. A programmable counter (CTC) is used not only to control the speed of the serial line from/to host, but also to generate a programmable window for data acquisition. In fact, one input of the CTC is the sampling frequency, coming from the converter. The CTC and the surrounding logic divide this waveform by a programmable constant, generating two complementary square wave outputs, sent to slave 1 and slave 2, respectively, where the program synchronizes itself with the rising edge of this signal. In this way a programmable window rate (in every case the 50% overlap of windows is fixed) is obtained.

The slave board contains two twin TMS320. Since our goal was to build an efficient real time general purpose acoustical front end, we had to increase the basic input and memory capabilities of the signal processor. Regarding the first point, we note that the TMS320 has two basic input capabilities: an input line for interrupt and an input line (BIO) for sensing another status via a special conditional skip instruction, named BIOZ. Given that in our application there are many interrupting conditions, for example data ready from converter, data accepted by master, special signalling from master etc., all interrupts are suitably put in OR and then are polled by the BIO input via a multiplexer addressed by the program. This function is quite simple from the hardware point of view and introduces some overhead, though acceptable, as we will see later, in software implementation.

For the second pont, we augmented the basic program memory capabilities of the TMS320, since we relied fundamentally on software memory intensive techniques for giving general purpose real time efficiency to our system. In fact where needed we used "in line coding" [21] for increasing the efficiency of program control and "table look up" for increasing the efficiency of some address and data computations. These techniques are of course memory intensive.

In fact we chose not to add special purpose hardware to the system (e.g. for program control or address computation) for FFT only, since the front-end had to be general-purpose.

For our reference application, 4K words of program memory were not enough; hence the standard configuration was increased via bank switching. In fact, two output instructions select bank 1 and bank 2 of program memory respectively; however the first 1K of program memory is independently accessed by this selection and constitutes the bank 0 of program memory: in this way 1K of program memory is lost, but a flexible mailbox area is obtained for interchanging data between programs, independently of program page. This common area contains also, in a small ROM, the bootstrap. Bank 0 can allocate the bootstrap, interrupt programs and data to be exchanged between programs. In the first location of bank 1 and bank 2 we write the main program, which implements a loop. In this main program we can jump from page 1 to page 2 and vice versa, issuing suitable bank switching output instructions. Of course, we jump to the same address of the opposite page, for example from 4FF (hexadecimal) address in bank 2 to 4FF (hexadecimal) address in bank 1. At appropriate points of the main program, it jumps to a suitable subroutine, allocated of course in the same page (for example the routine for FFT computation). In practice the subroutines are allocated into pages 1 and 2, and then the main program is suitably written so as to allocate the calls to subroutines in the same page of the subroutine.

Details of the converter board are as follows. Strictly speaking, only the A/D section is needed for recognition purpose, although a D/A can be useful for prompting messages and diagnostic purposes. Furthermore it adds generality to the architecture for eventual uses in speech coding applications (analysis,synthesis). The board has multiple inputs and outputs for various purposes (microphone, loudspeaker, telephone) and is software reconfigurable via two command registers. By suitably loading these registers, various kind of transfers can be programmed, for example the digital loop, the A/D-D/A loop, the D/A-A/D loop. We can also program the sampling rate (8kHz. , 10kHz. ,12.8 kHz.), the input and output attenuation, and other options.

4. Programming and performance

After initial loading and testing, the master sends the calculated coefficients to the host; in our application we calculate 18 cepstral coefficients each centisecond frame. Given that each coefficient is represented with a word of 16 bits, we have to transmit to the host a net flux of 28.8 Kbit/s. over the serial link.

The computations performed by a slave can be distinguished into input/output programs, done in interrupt mode, and all the remaining computations, done in background mode. Two rotating buffers allocated in program memory are used for inputting samples: in fact, in interrupt mode one buffer is filled with samples which comprise frame n while at the same time the background program uses the contents of the other buffer which contains samples of frame n-2 in order to calculate cepstral coefficients. Of course, at the end of the frame, the contents of the buffer used for computation are not needed anymore, so this buffer becomes the input buffer for frame n+2 and the contents of the other buffer with frame n is used in background mode for computing cepstral coefficients.

Background programs perform:

- transfer of the buffer chosen for computing cepstral coefficients into a common buffer, with pre-emphasis,

- Hamming windowing of these data,

- 256 point complex FFT transform,

- modulus computation,

- band grouping,

- logarithm,

- direct cosine transform (DCT).

Given the data memory constraints of the TMS320, we performed the 256 point complex FFT transform by suitably combining 64 points complex FFT transforms (in fact this is the maximum block that can be contained in 144 words data memory); the elementary butterfly is a 4-points butterfly [18] (see also [19] for an example of efficient implementation on the TMS320).

We calculate logarithms via table look up, that is, the integer part of the logarithm is determined by searching for the most significant "1" in the binary word [20]; then the fractional part is calculated by using the remaining bits, suitably aligned, as addresses to a transform table, which in our case is composed of 128 entries.

Interrupt programs perform the input of the data and the output of calculated coefficients. There are also routines for handling special messages for master to host an vice-versa.

Fig.1 and Fig.2, respectively, summarizes program memory allocation and time performance of the application.

Memory has to be allocated to data and programs. Data in program memory are mainly the two rotating input buffers (maximum length for each: 256 words, for a 20 ms. window of signal sampled at 12.8 kHz.) and the intermediate buffer of 512 words (its double length is due to the fact that for increasing generality the input data for FFT are intended to be complex). All of these buffers together take 1K words of program memory. Tables for windowing data and for calculating logarithms via table look up plus other constants and data (e.g. output buffers) require a maximum of 0.5K words.

The program requiring the most memory is the FFT which is coded "in line" [21] for maximum speeed: this program therefore requires 2.5 K words of memory. All other programs taken together (that is, pre-emphasis, windowing, band grouping, modulus and logarithm computation, and DCT evaluation) occupy 1.9 K words, while the main and interrupting programs take a total of 0.4 k words.

Hence the total memory required is 6.3 K words. This a posteriori justifies the augmentation of the initial 4K words of available program memory to 7K words of bank switched program memory.

We also have to evaluate the computational load of the system in order to verify the fitness of the architecture for the real time implementation of the task. We can distinguish between the computational load due to background programs, independent of the sampling rate, and the computational load due to interrupting programs, proportional to the sampling rate. As we can see from Fig.2, the computational load due to background programs is 13 ms., and that due to interrupt programs is 3.2 ms. at the maximum sampling speed of 12.8 kHz. This comes from the fact that in this case every 78 μs. we use 14 μs. for the acquisition of the sample via interrupt (interrupt polling, loading of the data in the proper buffer location, controlling the advancement of buffer pointer). Hence, in total, we require 16.2 ms. every 20 ms. for the intended computation, which therefore can be done in real time.

We point out also that if data acquisition were done more automatically in hardware (with external FIFO for example) we would not still achieve a significant improvement in performance and in any case we would also need 2 DSP's.

5. Conclusions

The implementation detailed here stresses the limits of the state of the art in digital signal processing. Since we found that for the rather demanding but important task of cepstrum extraction, one DSP was not sufficient, we designed an efficient system based on two DSP, each of which controlling via bank switching an extended program memory, capable of performing the intended task, and of course less demanding tasks, as for example LPC coefficients extraction.

However in cases where the computational load overflows the basic system capability, the system is also expandable both in ripple, both in parallel way.

Acknowledgments

We acknowledge our colleagues M. Oreglia and F. Raineri, who have implemented the FORTRAN simulation of the logarithm via table look-up and who have succesfully compared its performance in a recognition task to the performance obtained via normal logarithm computation.

References

[1] Schafer R.W. and Markel J.D. (editors)
Speech Analysis
IEEE Press 1978

[2] Rabiner L. and Schafer R.
Digital Process of Speech Signals
Prentice Hall 1979

[3] Rabiner L. and Levinson S.E.
Isolated and Connected Word Recognition. Theory and Selected Applications
IEEE Trans. on Communication, vol. COM-29, N.5, May 1981, pp.621-659

[4] Foil J.T. and Johnson D.H.
Text Independent Speaker Recognition
IEEE Communication Magazine, Dec. 1983, pp.22-25

[5] Flanagan J.L., Schroeder M.R., Atal B.S., Crochiere R.E., Jayant N.S. and Tribolet J.M.
Speech Coding
IEEE trans. on Communications, Vol. COM-27, n.4, April 1979, pp.710-737

[6] Bisiani R.
Computer Systems for High Performance Speech Recognition
This issue of NATO Advanced Studies on New Systems and Architectures for Automatic Speeech Recognition and Synthesis, Bonas, July 1984

[7] Oppenheim A.V.
Speech Spectrograms Using the Fast Fourier Transform
IEEE Spectrum, August 1970, pp.57-62

[8] Makhoul J.
Linear Prediction: a Tutorial Review
IEEE Proceedings, vol 63, n.4, April 1975, pp.561-580

[9] Childers D.G.   Skinner D.P.   and Kemerait R.C.
The Cepstrum: a Guide to Processing
IEEE proceedings, vol. 65, n.10, October 1977, pp.1428-1443

[10] Burky D.
Digital Signal Processing Chips Move off the Designer's Wish
List and Enter into Everyday Use
Electronic Design, May 17,1984, pp.100-122

[11] Crochiere R.E.   and Flanagan J.L.
Current Perspectives in Digital Speech
ICC 82- Philadelphia -June 1982

[12] Davis S.B.   and Mermelstein P.
Comparison of Parametric Representations of Monosyllabic
Word Recognition in Continuously Spoken Sentences
IEEE trans. ASSP-28 (1980) pp.357-366

[13] Caudel E.R., Hester R.K. and Khen-Sang Tan
A Chip Set for Audio Frequency Digital Signal Processing
ICASSP-82 (Paris) , pp.1065-1068

[14] Daly D.F.   and Bergeron L.E.
A Programmable Voice Digitizer Using the T.I.   TMS320 Microcomputer
ICASSP-83 (Boston) 11.2 (pp.   475-478)

[15] Mehrgardt S.
Signal Processing with a Fast Microcomputer System
Signal Processing II: Theories and Applications- pp.351-354
EURASIP-1983

[16] Bryden B.   and Hassanein H.
Implementation of a Full Duplex 2.4 kbps LPC Vocoder on a Single TMS320
Microprocessor Chip
ICASSP-84 (San Diego) 44.12

[17] Sweitzer S.
A Low Cost FFT Chip Set
ICASSP-84 (San Diego) 44.3

[18] Brigham E.O.
The Fast Fourier Transform
Prentice Hall 1974

[19] Morris L.R.
Digital Signal Processing Software
1983 DSPS

[20] Weste N.   , Burr D.J.   and Ackland B.D.
Dynamic Time Warp Pattern Matching Using an Integrated Multiprocessor
Array
IEEE trans. on Computers, vol. C-32, n.8 , August 1983, pp.731-744

[21] Morris L.R.
Automatic Generation of Time Efficient Digital Signal Processing Software
IEEE trans. ASSP, vol. ASSP-25, n.1, February 1977, pp.74-79

Data or programs	Kind of data or of program	words	V= variable F = fixed }area
data	– buffer 1	256	V
"	– buffer 2	256	V
"	– internal buffer	512	V
"	– Hamming window coefficients	256	F
"	– Table for calculating logarithms	128	F
"	– other data and constants	≤128	V, F
data	partial total for data	≤1.5k	V, F
programs	– main and interrupts	0.4k	F
"	– FFT computations	2.5k	F
"	– other computations, that is,	1.9k	F
	– pre-emphasis	≃ 40(*)	
	– windowing	≃ 30(*)	
	– modulus	≃ 132(*)	
	– band grouping	≃ 312(*)	
	– logarithm via table look up	≃ 260(*)	
	– DCT	≃1076(*)	
programs	partial total for programs	4.8k	
	total memory requirements	6.3k	

(*) data already taken into account in partial sum

Fig. 1 – Program memory requirements (in words)

Background or interrupt	Kind of function	Time
background " "	windowing FFT other background computations; that is - pre-emphasis - modulus - band grouping - logarithm - DCT	1 ms 7 ms 5.0 ms 1.4 ms (*) 2.3 ms (*) 0.3 ms (*) 0.6 ms (*) 0.4 ms (*)
background	partial for background	13 ms
interrupt	acquisition at sampling rate 12.8 kHz	3.2 ms
	total for background and interrupt	16.2 ms

(*) data already taken into account in partial sum

Fig. 2 - Time requirements (in ms) per frame

RECONFIGURABLE MODULAR ARCHITECTURE
FOR A MAN-MACHINE VOCAL COMMUNICATION SYSTEM
IN REAL TIME

D. DOURS - R. FACCA

CERFIA : Université Paul Sabatier
118, route de Narbonne
31062 TOULOUSE - FRANCE

ABSTRACT

The man-machine vocal communication requires autonomous, application-adaptable real time systems, whose cost is both reasonable and proportional to their efficiency.

The realisation of a vocal terminal having such characteristics, makes it necessary to choose a parallel architecture.

We present one architecture which is a combination of parallelism and pipelining. It makes it possible to get the best of the execution parallelism proper to the application class treating a continuous data flow.

It is a modular architecture, staticly reconfigurable, functionally distributed, monitored by the data and with a multi-levelled hierarchic control.

1. INTRODUCTION

We are on the eve on a new era where everyday-extending applications of man-machine vocal communication systems will change working conditions in the most diverse fields. But to avoid limiting their use, we shall have autonomous real time systems, adaptable to application so that their cost should be reasonable and proportional to their efficiency.

As far as we know there is no vocal terminal capable of such performances on the market today. However it would be interesting to have a flexible and modular machine structure, allowing on the one hand to implement in real time methods already existing in the field of man-machine spoken communication, and on the other hand to progressively take into account the

NATO ASI Series, Vol. F16
New Systems and Architectures for Automatic Speech
Recognition and Synthesis. Edited by R. De Mori and C. Y. Suen
© Springer-Verlag Berlin Heidelberg 1985

recent results of fundamental research.

But to have at one's disposal a vocal terminal functioning in real-time which would be at the same time evolutive and of a reasonable cost imposes constraints on the treatment methods as well as on the architecture that supports them.

Once discretised, the vocal signal can be considered as a continuous data flow and its treatment in real-time necessitates a dynamic treatment mode. The dynamic treatment is different from static methods in which the data dynamic is suppressed through their memorisation, which allows backtracking to reactivate treatments. In a dynamic method, the results must appear progressively as the data arrive which implies that only current data and data concerning a recent past can be treated, but that data concerning the future cannot be utilized at all. Speech recognition methods, analysing a vocal signal from left to right without backtraking, after the strategy of the "few best" in which only the most plausible solutions are kept and treated in parallel, are dynamic methods which can be implemented in real-time.

Thus the realization of a vocal terminal imposes constraints in the writing of algorithms and also in the choice of the architecture that executes them.

As soon as some vocal terminals, however elaborate they may be, are being studied, the treatments become so complex that it is no longer possible to execute them in real-time on a classical computer. One must then turn towards parallel structure systems on which several treatments can be run simultaneously.

This has been first attempted with the Cmmp multicomputers network [1] and the CM* multiprocessors network [2] of Carnegie Melon University on which the Harpy system [3] has been implemented. It seems that the performances of these systems are insufficient for speech recognition in real time. The main reason for the relative failure appears to be the lack of adequation of the architectures used to the considered application. For, as Fennel and Lesser have underlined it, in their study on the measure of the parallelism that can be obtained by simulating the functioning in parallel of their Hearsay II system [4], the treatment speed may decrease when the number of processors increases, if the interconnections do not respect constraints related to the structure of treatments. Thus in order to satisfy these constraints, it seems preferable to define an architecture that takes into account the specificity of the data to be treated and of the derived treatments, rather than try to adapt the application to a predefined machine structure.

Overspecialized architectures, though they offer the advantage of being simple to implement, should be avoided, because their rigid structure does not allow future further system evolutions. One must then turn towards the definition of an evolutive modular structure.

This has been the aim of the "Architecture des Systèmes Parallèles" team, a section of the "Traitement Automatique de la Parole" group from the C.E.R.F.I.A. laboratory in Toulouse, whose studies have been first the definition and then the realization of a Reconfigurable Modular Architecture whose features meet the defined requirements.

2. RECONFIGURABLE MODULAR ARCHITECTURE

The discretized vocal signal can be considered as a continuous data flow which must be treated in transactional mode. The functional decomposition of this type of application brings to light treatments without any relation with each other, and treatments depending on the preceding ones only through the results obtained by them. Thus we have an application in which a continuous data flow may be treated by going through a series of stages each one being in charge of one part of the treatment. The successive pieces of information take each other's place according to the producer-consumer mode.

To define the architecture we took into account the specificity of the application. This architecture is indeed adaptable to the functional decomposition of the application to be implemented. The machine is built as a "Kit" starting from basic elements which are associated as required by the application.

We shall not give here any further detail about the architecture [5] and the physical realization [6] - [7], we shall only describe the general structure of a treatment processor as well as the way it works and the principle of an application implementation on this architecture.

2.1. STRUCTURE OF A TREATMENT PROCESSOR

The structure of a treatment processor is defined inductively from basic elements which are :
- a treatment processor (TP)
- an exchange processor (EP)
- a control processor (CP).

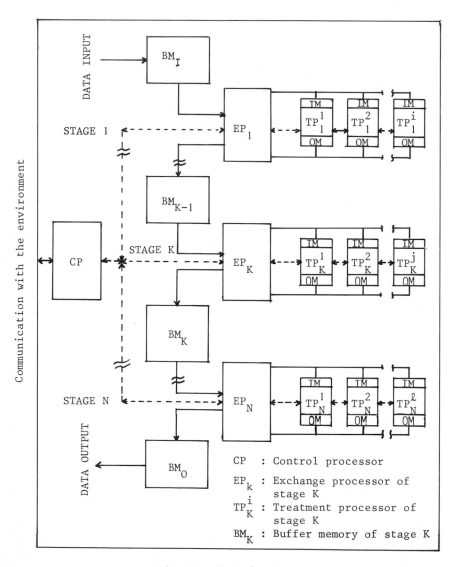

Fig. 1 - Functional structure

These elements are interconnected according to the topology defined in fig. 1. Treatment processors of the same level are linked to an exchange processor and constitute one treatment stage. Each processor ignores the other's presence and communicates only with the exchange processor. The communication is realized by a ring network for events and by two memories : the input memory (IM) in which the data to be treated are stored and the output memory (OM) in which the results to be transmitted are stored.

The distribution system in a stage is organized around two common buses, one for the input and one for the output, which allows a total parallelism for these two types of transfers.

A buffer memory (BM), with a double access port in mutual exclusion, makes it possible to store the data between two consecutive stages. The exchange processors are linked to the control processor by a ring network.

2.2. WORKING OF A TREATMENT PROCESSOR

When a treatment processor has finished carrying out the order for which it is specialized, it sends a data transfer request to the associated exchange processor and then waits. The latter transmits the request to the control processor which checks if the conditions for transfer are fulfilled.

For a stage K, these conditions are :

- input transfer possible if data have been stored in BM_{K-1} by EP_{K-1}

- output transfer possible if the data stored in BM_K have been taken by EP_{K+1}.

The control processor sends back an acknowledgement message to the exchange processor indicating the possible transfers. When receiving the message the exchange processor carries out the data transfers according to a description which specifies the links between two consecutive treatment. Afterwards, the exchange processor communicates with the treatment processor so that the task can be carried out again. Once all the data transfers in the stage have been carried out, the exchange processor informs the control processor so that the state progress, between the stages, can be updated.

When BM_I is empty or when BM_O has received some data, the control processor sends a message to the environment indicating either that some results are available or that some other data are required to carry out another treatment.

2.3. IMPLEMENTATION OF AN APPLICATION

The communication-execution-synchronisation separation simplifies the task of the user wanting to implement an application on this architecture. Indeed, he has to do only with the execution part and the descriptive processing relation between the different treatments. The synchronization and the communication are monitored by the system.

For a given application, the machine configuration principle is as follows :

Each functional task of the application is associated to a treatment processor. These processors are connected with exchange processor to make an upper level treatment processor.

The grouping of these processors must be made according to the topology defined by fig. 1 and adapted to the task to be executed. This approach is inductive. At the lowest level, to a so called elementary task (there is no subtler decomposition of the task) is associated an elementary treatment processor. At the highest level, a treatment processor is connected to I/O peripheral devices adapted to the application. For example, in the case of a vocal terminal monitoring an industrial process, a microphone and a loud-speaker, will be found for the vocal input and output, a specialized board for the system command and control, interface cards for the process control.

An elementary treatment processor is built with a MC 6809 microprocessor and its accessory circuits. Furthermore it has an input memory (I.M) and an output memory (O.M) a 128 K bytes ($16 \times 8k$ pages) memory where it is possible to plug either PROMs or RAMs (indifferently). A parallel I/O line makes it possible to connect specialized cards (FFT, LPC, filters,...) or cards to interface with peripheral devices or data processing systems. The treatment processor then behaves as a host computer.

When the machine is configured, a program is implanted on the PROMs, this program being associated to a treatment as well as the descriptive precising the connections between the different treatments. The control system then adapts itself automatically according to the number of implanted treatment processors and to the chosen configuration.

3. ADVANTAGES OF THIS ARCHITECTURE

The creation of a reconfigurable modular architecture which is adapted to the functional decomposition of the treatments allows the treatments to be carried out faster by increasing the degree of parallelism.

In effect, in this structure, a data flow undergoes a treatment by going through a series of stages, each of which being responsible for carrying out one part of the treatment, the information moving successively through the stages.

It should be noted that this type of parallelism can be particularly well adapted to the treatment of a continuous data flow.

The solution used here for processor interconnection reduces the complexity of the system from the point of view of topology, communication protocols, control and task sequencing.

The principles used here simply regulate the problems linked to parallelism :
- control of the flow of information,
- conflicts for access to the same unit,
- precedence and synchronization conflits.

The repetitive structure at all levels has the double advantage of modularity and flexibility. It is possible to increase the power of the system or to introduce new treatment algorithms without modifying the communication system. Furthermore, the repetitive structure has evident economic advantages since it minimizes the cost of the development and commercialization of a system designed with a small numbers of different cards.

4. CONCLUSION

The reconfigurable modular architecture which has just been described is that of a functionally distributed system, directed by the data and with hierarchy control over several levels.

The ease with which such a system can be realised allows us to think that there will be widespread developments of adapted systems making full use of the parallelism of one class of applications.

This is the reason why the CERFIA Laboratory thought of realising a parallel machine, based on this architecture, adapted to real time speech treatment. A prototype is now operational and the realization of a real time recognition system of isolated multi-speakers is in its final phase. The realisation of a real time analysis and recognition system for continuous speech (ARIAL project) is being studied. But this architecture can be used too for other applications, whether for image treatment, robot command or also in parallel compilation and more generally in any application treating a continuous data flow in real time.

REFERENCES

1   W.A. WULF, X.B. BELL : "C.mmp, a Multi-Mini-Processor" ; Proceeding AFIPS. FJCC. 1972

2   R.J. SWAN : "The Switching Structure and Adressing Architecture of an Extensible Multiprocessor" ; CM*, PH.D. Thesis, Carnegie Mellon University. 1978.

3   B.T. LOWERE : "The Harpy Speech Recognition System" ; PH.D, Thesis, Carnegie Mellon University, Pittsburg, USA. 1976.

4   R.D. FENNELL, V.R. LESSER : "Parallelism in Artificial Intelligence Problem Solving : A case Study of Hearsay II", IEEE Trans. Computer, Vol C26, n° 2, pp 98-111. 1977.

5   D. DOURS, R. FACCA, M. DALMAU : "ARMOR : Architecture Modulaire Reconfigurable pour le traitement d'un flot continu de données en temps réel ; "Rapport de contrat ATP-CNRS. 1983.

6   A. ALSUBAIDI, S. SOULAIMAN : "Système Multi-microprocesseur pour le traitement d'un Flot Continu de Données. Thèses de 3ème cycle, U.P.S. Toulouse. 1981.

7   M. DALMAU : "Système d'Exploitation pour la machine multiprocesseur ARMOR. Thèse de 3ème cycle, U.P.S. Toulouse, 1984.

A SURVEY OF ALGORITHMS & ARCHITECTURE FOR CONNECTED SPEECH RECOGNITION

D. Wood

GEC Research Laboratories

Hirst Research Centre

Wembley

U.K.

HA9 7PP

ABSTRACT

The paper surveys dynamic programming based connected speech recognition algorithms and architectures. A discussion of the computational complexities of the algorithms is given and suggests that the single pass algorithm of Bridle et al is the most suitable for real time operation. Currently available architectures for dynamic programming are discussed and it is shown that these are not suitable for the single pass algorithm in their present form. An alternative linear systolic architecture is described which is capable of matching vocabularies of up to 25000 words, in real time, using the single pass algorithm. The linear array has simpler data flows and uses fewer processing elements than most existing systolic structures.

NATO ASI Series, Vol. F16
New Systems and Architectures for Automatic Speech
Recognition and Synthesis. Edited by R. De Mori and C. Y. Suen
© Springer-Verlag Berlin Heidelberg 1985

INTRODUCTION

Dynamic time warping (DTW) has become a popular technique for pattern matching in some speech recognition systems. It has found application in both isolated and connected word recognition and good recognition accuracies have been reported. However, the DTW algorithm has a very high computational requirement and this can be a limiting factor when designing high vocabularies systems for real time operation. In such systems it becomes necessary to optimize computational throughput by exploring special purpose hardware structures and matching them to current algorithms. In this way, the most optimal combination can be identified.

DTW algorithms have a high degree of parallelism which can be exploited by using regular (or systolic) hardware structures. Over recent years, a variety of different options for systolic architectures have been proposed, such as Burr et al [1], Ciminiera et al [2] and Banatre et al [3]. These architectures have application in both isolated and connected speech recognition but vary with respect to the degree that parallelism and pipelining have been exploited. This leads to solutions with differing hardware requirements and complexities. It is apparent, when a global view is taken, that some architectures are only useful with certain algorithms and that some combinations may not be optimal in terms of number of processing elements, throughput and control complexity. It is important that the algorithm and architecture are considered together, the choice of algorithm can significantly affect the architecture (and vice versa!).

To give an architecture which is computationally efficient, simple to control and using the minimum of hardware requires that the right algorithm is chosen. This is reasonably straightforward with isolated word recognition but not so with connected word recognition because of its significantly higher complexity. A number of connected word matching strategies have been proposed, such as Banatre et al [3], Myers & Rabiner [4], Sakoe [5] and Bridle et al [6] which have differing architectural implications. A good algorithm is one which leads to a simple architecture that is as independent as possible of vocabulary and application. Computational flow should be simple and not too dependent on boundary functions (global path constraints) since this leads to simpler control.

The following sections summarize the considerations pertaining to the choice of algorithms and architecture comparing some of the available techniques. The first section discusses some of the alternative matching strategies with emphasis on their hardware implications. The second section discusses the available architectures with emphasis on their applicability to the algorithms and their practicality. The third section briefly describes an alternative, systolic architecture which implements Bridle's et al algorithm and shows that a very high throughput is possible. The final section concludes the paper with a summary of the most important points arising from this discussion.

ALGORITHMIC CONSIDERATIONS

The correct choice of algorithm is important since this can affect the complexity of the final implementation. This choice is not so straightforward in connected speech recognition because of the variety of matching strategies which can be employed. Matching strategy has a direct effect on computational complexity and the amenability of an algorithm for a hardware implementation. This section considers four algorithms covering a broad range of matching strategies and briefly assesses their suitability for an efficient hardware implementation.

Sakoe's [4] matching strategy, depicted in Figure 1, involves a two level process, the first level being word level matching, the second level being phrase level matching. Word level matching attempts to isolate the best word decision over each possible segment of the input speech. Segment boundaries are determined using an adjustment window. Phrase level matching uses the word level scores to determine the best concatenated sequence of word decisions over all possible concatenations and lengths.

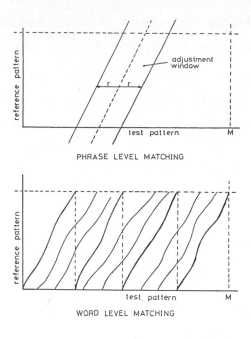

Figure 1: Sakoe's Matching Strategy

Myers' & Rabiner's [5] strategy, depicted in Figure 2, using a level building process.   The number of levels is dependent on the maximum phrase length. Each level corresponds with an isolated word matching which is computed 'in strips'.   The best scoring template ending at each strip is found and the scores used as initial conditions into the next level.   Thus matching proceeds from level to level building up a series of word decisions at each level.   Phrase level matching is implicit in the algorithm and the best phrase can be traced back from the end.   A boundary function is used to restrict word level matching to a reasonable area of the warp grid.

Bridle's et al [6] algorithm, depicted in Figure 3, computes the best concatenated sequence of templates in a single pass through the input sequence. The strategy assumes templates can start and end at any input frame. Transitions between templates are from the end of the best scoring template ending at one frame to the start of all templates in the next frame (for a simple syntax).   Phrase level matching is implicit in the process and the best sequence

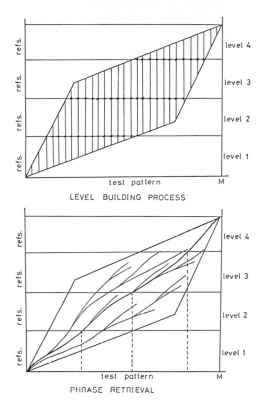

Figure 2: Myers' Matching Strategy

can be found by tracing back from the end.

Banatre's et al [3] algorithm, depicted in Figure 4, is similar to Sakoe's except that word level matching is not restricted by an adjustment window (although it can be). The vocabulary is matched to the input sequence and the best scoring template between a start point and a range of endpoints is found for all possible start and end points. The range of endpoints is determined by the dimensions of an isolated word warp grid. This grid slides through the input sequence in a similar fashion to the adjustment window of Sakoe's algorithm. Phrase level matching is done separately and concatenates the word decisions to form the best word sequence. Phrase length need not be specified.

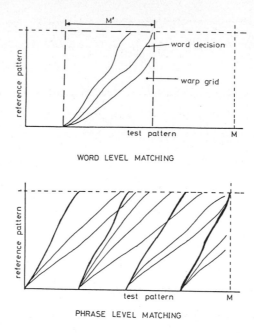

Figure 3: Bridle's Matching Strategy

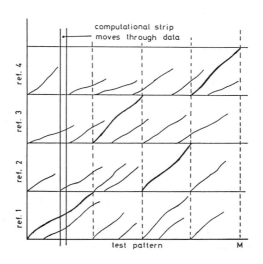

Figure 4: Banatre's Matching Strategy

The matching rate of a connected speech recognition system is dependent on how fast isolated word matching can be done. This depends on the matching strategy. Sakoe's algorithm (in 'real time mode') computes word decisions backwards from an end frame to a range of start frames given by the adjustment window. The width of the adjustment window depends on the template length. In hardware it is necessary to fix this width so that the largest template can be accommodated. A number of previous input frames must be saved and the same interframe distances re-calculated a number of times. This leads to computational inefficiency. A further restriction is that a maximum phrase length must be specified.

Myers' algorithm computes word level matches over varying lengths of the input sequence depending on the level. This is because isolated word matching is done in strips and the number of strips varies because of the boundary function. This leads to vocabulary dependent variability which is unsuitable in hardware for control complexity reasons. A further problem, especially for real time operation, is that a section of the input sequence must be entered before matching can start. Some interframe distance calculations are repeated since levels 'overlap', this leads to computational inefficiency. The removal of the boundary function may remove some of these problems. Finally, the specification of a phrase length introduces a further restriction.

Bridle's algorithm is perhaps the most efficient since interframe distances are only computed and used once. Input frames need not be saved since a single sweep is used and it is not necessary to return to an earlier section of input. Computational flow is sequential which can further simplify hardware.

Banatre's algorithm is as computationally expensive as Sakoe's algorithm since the same interframe distance must be calculated and used a number of times. The warp grid dimensions are determined by the length of the longest reference, this determines the number of PEs required. Input frames must also be saved.

ARCHITECTURAL CONSIDERATIONS

The choice of architecture has the most effect on the size of the final implementation, i.e. number of processing elements (PEs). However, the algorithm can also influence this by restricting the applicability of each structure. The final choice of algorithm and architecture should lead to a solution with a low number of PEs and simple control complexity but still offer high computational throughput. This section considers the mapping of the algorithm into an architecture using the architectures described by Burr et al [1], Ciminiera et al [2] and Banatre et al [3] as examples.

Banatre [3] described an architecture to implement the systolic algorithm, which is based on similar ideas to Burr et al [1]. This is shown in Figure 5 and

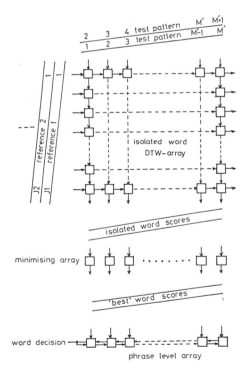

Figure 5: Banatre's Architecture

consists of the three arrays. The first is a two dimensional DTW array whose dimensions are determined by the height and width of the warp grid, these depend on the length of the longest template, Rmax. This DTW array calculates the isolated word matches. The second array takes the isolated word scores and finds the minimum over all templates. The third array computes the phrase level match. The disadvantage with this architecture is that it requires a huge number of PEs, approximately Rmax.M′, where M′ is the width of the grid, and also requires three types of processing element to be designed. If there are V vocabulary words then the time taken to complete the match is 0 (VM) 'operations', where M is the length of the input sequence and one operation is a distance calculation and a DP match. A reduced array (say a single strip) would require Rmax PEs but the time taken to complete the match would be $0(VM^2)$ operations. The number of PEs can also be reduced by removing those which lie outside of an adjustment window but this does not affect time complexity. However, the architecture integrates phrase level and word level matching quite well with a very regular data flow but is only suitable for Banatre's algorithm, and possibly Sakoe's.

Sakoe's [4] algorithm would probably be best computed using a single diagonal of processing elements as proposed by Ciminiera et al [2] since this is more appropriate to calculation of isolated word matches using an adjustment window. A further array must be added which minimizes the DP scores between start and endpoints and computes the phrase level match. The width of the window, and hence the diagonal, is (2r+1) where r is a fraction, x, of the length of the longest reference. The phrase level array would probably consist of the same number of PEs. A possible configuration is given in Figure 6. The time taken for the architecture to match V vocabulary words to an input sequence of M frames is 0((1+x)RmaxMV) operations, i.e. much slower than Banatre's architecture, but using fewer PEs. Data management and control could be a problem since the architecture must 'move through the data' hence the correct timing must be provided.

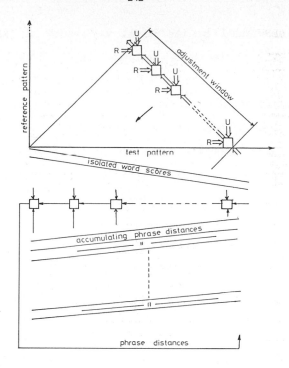

reference pattern

test pattern

isolated word scores

accumulating phrase distances

phrase distances

Figure 6:   Possible Architecture for Sakoe's Algorithm

Myers' algorithm is practically unimplementable (in hardware) in its standard form.   However, with the boundary function removed the ideas of Burr et al [1] may be appropriate here.   A number of possible array configurations have been described by Burr, the most amenable to this algorithm seems to be a horizontally moving reduced array, see Figure 7.   This sweeps out each level taking input conditions from the lower level and passing final scores to the higher level.   Some means of minimissing the 'strip' scores over all templates must be incorporated.   The number of sweeps is equal to the number of levels.   The array height is governed by the length of the longest template and the width is two processing elements, giving a total of 2Rmax PEs.   The time taken for a complete match is 0(1VM) operations where 1 is the number of levels.   Control and data management could be expensive since the architecture requrires that

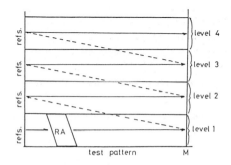

best template scores
to next level

U= Utterance
R = Reference

best template scores
from previous level

BURR's REDUCED ARRAY

Figure 7: Possible Architecture for Myers' Algorithm

frame interactions are correctly synchronized. A further disadvantage is that the whole input sequence must be saved.

Bridle's algorithm is more sequential than the others because of its single pass nature. The pass is done one input frame at a time hence true real time operation is possible if all calculations can be done between successive input frames. None of the architectures proposed by Burr et al [1] or Ciminiera et al [2] appear suitable for this algorithm since they require the whole or part of the input sequence to be saved. The next section describes an alternative architecture and shows it to outperform those considered above.

SYSTOLIC ARCHITECTURE FOR THE SINGLE PASS ALGORITHM

The single pass algorithm of Bridle's et al [6] requires an architecture which can compute path scores using only the present input frame. Square array architectures or single diagonals are not suitable since these require a number of input frames in the calculation. This section describes such an architecture and compares its performance.

The architecture is a linear chain of PEs, shown in Figure 8, which has a

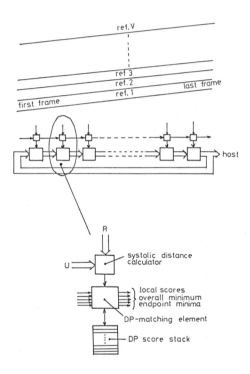

Figure 8: Architecture for Bridle's Algorithm

length determined by the longest template (Rmax). The input frame enters the left hand end of the array and meets with each frame of the reference templates as it is passed along the chain. Template frames enter in reference serial/frame parallel starting with the first frame of each template. At each PE, the interframe distance is calculated and added to the local minimum. The score is then stacked for use at the next input frame. The length of the stack is the same as the number of vocabulary words and all memory is sequentially accessed. The score is also used to find an overall minimum score and a minimum endpoint score (if the present template frame is an endpoint). Each PE performs the same operations simultaneously and passes local scores overall minimum and endpoint scores to the next PE on the right for updating the next frame. When all templates frames have passed through, the last PE contains the overall minimum and the endpoint minimum. These are passed to the left hand end of the chain as initial conditions to start templates at the next input frame. Tracepoint labels are also passed to host to aid phrase retrieval. Matching rate is independent of the number of frames in each reference. The architecture is described in more detail in [7].

The highest performance results when fixed hardware is used although this is very restrictive on the algorithm's 'internal' flexibility. The slowest computation is distance calculation which can be speeded up in the case of city block and squared Euclidean, using architectures similar to those described in [8]. The PE can thus be split up into a special purpose distance calculator plus a DP-matcher. The systolic array distance calculator can compute the distance in a time independent of the data dimensionality. However, time is dependent on data bit precision. The DP matcher must complete its calculations between successive distances. Any structure can be used assuming it is fast enough. A serial structure interfaces well with the distance calculator but requires a fixed algorithm. A parallel, ALU based architecture interfaces well with the stack memory and offers some algorithmic flexibility. In either case, latency is not important since the architecture operates sequentially. The architecture computes the complete match in a time of 0(VM) operations. Only V matches must be performed between successive input frames. If data widths are B bit then distances can be calculated in 2B cycles.

Assuming a 20 ms frame rate and B=8 bits then a vocabulary of approximately 12500 words can be matched at a 10 MHz clock frequency. With a serial structure it may be possible to push this to 20 MHz hence giving a maximum matching rate of 25000 words. Thus it can be seen that this architecture outperforms those described in the previous section on a throughput per processing element basis.

CONCLUSION

This paper has shown there is more to defining hardware for real time connected speech recognition systems than just specifying an architecture. It is not much use specifying an architecture with a high computational throughput which is then wasted on a computationally inefficient algorithm. This means that a large number of PEs must be used or low matching rates result. It is unfortunate, for instance, that Banatre et al, having developed a good regular architecture for the connected speech problem chose an inefficient algorithm to work from. For a solution which has a low number of procesing elements, low control and data management complexity, and high performance both the algorithm and the architecture must be carefully chosen.

A comparison of the algorithms shows that Bridle's, Sakoe's and Banatre's are suitable for true real time operation. Myers' algorithm requires the whole of the input sequence to be stored before matching commences. Bridle's algorithm, however, is much more efficient than Sakoe's and Banatre's since all the matching computations use only a single input frame, hence no computations are repeated. Sakoe's and Banatre's algorithm, requires that a number of previous input frames are stored since matching is 'guided' by an adjustment window or a warp grid. Banatre's, Sakoe's and Myers' algorithms also repeat inter-frame distance computations, the former two being the worse examples. Myers' algorithm also suffers because matching is guided by a boundary function which cannot be efficiently mapped into hardware. A final restriction imposed by Myers' and Sakoe's algorithms is that a maximum phrase length must be specified. Hence it can be concluded that Bridle's single pass algorithm is the most computationally efficient and the least dependent on vocabulary and application. The single pass nature allows simple and easily controllable sequential operation with low storage requirements (only one DP score and word link per frame must be stored).

A comparison of architectures shows that square arrays as proposed by Burr and also Banatre have the dual disadvantages of only implementing the less efficient algorithms and requiring inordinately large numbers of processing elements. Full size square arrays not only restrict template length (as do other hardware structures) but also restrict input sequence length. Reduced arrays and 'diagonals' of processing elements as proposed by Burr and also Ciminiera require fewer PEs and are less restrictive on input sequence length. However, the application of these types of array is still restricted to the less efficient algorithms and also require increased data management complexity to ensure that frames interact correctly. All the above structures require the input pattern to be stored over a number of input frames or the whole sequence.

Since none of the hardware structures proposed to date are suitable for implementing Bridle's algorithm an alternative structure based on a linear systolic array has been described. The architecture efficiently maps the sequential nature of the algorithm and is capable of very high throughput, i.e. 25000 words at input frame rates.

Such high throughputs suggest applications in systems with high computational requirements, such as:

(a) systems using multiple templates per word for (limited) speaker independence.

(b) systems for multi-channel operation using a single, multiplexed recognizer

(c) systems which require the tracking of sub-optimal paths for improved accuracy

(d) combinations of the above.

Incidentally, if very high throughput is not important, the length of the chain may be reduced with a proportional reduction in throughput. Other applications of this architecture are in isolated word recognition and string matching using the Levenshtein distance.

REFERENCES

1. D. J. Burr, B. D. Ackland, N. Weste, "Array configurations for dynamic time warping" IEEE Trans. ASSP, Vol. 32, No. 1, pp. 119-127, February 1984.
2. L. Ciminiera, C. Dematini, A. Serra, "A VLSI structure for pattern matching" Proc. 6th Int. Conf. on Pattern Recognition, 1982, pp. 380-383.
3. J. P. Banatre, P. Frison, P. Quinton, "A systolic algorithm for connected word recognition" Proc. ICASSP, pp. 1243-1246, 1982.
4. H. Sakoe, "Two-level DP-matching — a dynamic programming-based pattern matching algorithm for connected word recognition", IEEE Trans. ASSP, Vol. 27, No. 6, pp. 588-595, December 1979.
5. C. S. Myers, L. R. Rabiner, "A level building dynamic time warping algorithm for connected word recognition", IEEE Trans. ASSP, Vol. 29, No. 2, pp. 284-297, April 1981.
6. J. S. Bridle, M. D. Brown, R. M. Chamberlain, "An algorithm for connected word recognition", Proc. ICASSP, pp. 899-902, 1982.
7. D. Wood, R. B. Urquhart, "An architecture for a connected speech recognition algorithm" Proc. 7th Int. Conf. on Pattern Recognition, pp. 1197-1200, 1984.
8. R. B. Urquhart, D. Wood, "Efficient bit-level systolic arrays for inner product computation", GEC Journal of Research, Vol. 2, No. 1, 1984, pp. 52-55.

KNOWLEDGE-BASED AND EXPERT SYSTEMS IN AUTOMATIC SPEECH RECOGNITION

Jean-Paul Haton

CRIN - Université de Nancy 1

B. P. 239

54506 Vandoeuvre, France

I   INTRODUCTION

Artificial Intelligence (AI) has recently advanced to the point that practical applications are now existing in several domains. Most of the results obtained are not due to general problem solving techniques but to the use of specific, domain-dependent knowledge. Formalizing and incorporating specific knowledge into a system makes it possible to reach the level of expertise comparable to that of a human expert in some specialized field. Such knowledge-based and expert systems have been extensively used in various domains like chemistry, medicine, geology, etc. The basic idea in these systems is to clearly distinguish between the knowledge base which usually incorporates rules and meta-rules about the domain of expertise and the control structures which manipulate this knowledge. That ensures great modularity and flexibility and makes it easy to modify and update a system [11].

This approach is very attractive in all cases where knowledge is incomplete or ill-formalized and where it does not exist algorithmic solutions. Automatic Speech Recognition and Understanding (ASR) obviously represents a typical example in which, moreover, it is necessary to combine many diverse knowledge sources.

NATO ASI Series, Vol. F16
New Systems and Architectures for Automatic Speech
Recognition and Synthesis. Edited by R. De Mori and C. Y. Suen
© Springer-Verlag Berlin Heidelberg 1985

This chapter is devoted to the discussion of the impact of knowledge-based approaches in ASR. In section II the principles and interest of knowledge-based and expert systems are briefly exposed. The areas of ASR in which these approaches could be used are also presented.

Section III concerns the use of expert systems at the phonetic and phonological processing levels whereas section IV addressses the more general problem of designing and implementing an ASR system by using knowledge-based architectures.

II KNOWLEDGE-BASED SYSTMES

II.1. Basic principles

It is now widely admitted — although it has not been the case for years — that the automatic recognition and interpretation of a spoken sentence can only be achieved through the optimal use of a large number of very diverse knowledge sources, from acoustics to pragmatics. A similar situation can be found in others domains of AI such as computer vision or natural language understanding. The cooperation and synchronization of as many knowledge sources as available make it possible to emit and/or cancel hypotheses until reaching the final solution, according to the general paradigm of hypothesis-and-test.

It is not easy to give a definition of knowledge as useful in a knowledge-based system. A first characteristic is that knowledge is highly domain-dependent. Abstractly speaking knowledge is made up of descriptions, relationships and procedures corresponding to a given domain of activity. In practice knowledge can take many diverse forms. It roughly consists of the symbolic descriptions of "objects" and their relationships in a domain together with the procedures and heuristics for manipulating these descriptions. We will see later on that a very popular and efficient way of expressing and manipulating knowledge is under the form of simple production rules.

Three main problems are associated with the design of knowledge-based systems in any domain:

- *knowledge acquisition* — it is very difficult and time-consuming to extract knowledge from human experts. This remains an open problem in AI and the best that can be hoped is a computer-assisted system since a fully automatic acquisition of human knowledge by a system seems far ahead. Knowledge acquisition necessitates a long and careful interaction between the expert(s) and a knowledge engineer. Efficient schemes have been designed in specific domains, e.g. in speech spectrogram reading. The use of an expert system can be of valuable help since that makes it easier to test and update the knowledge, to detect contradictions, etc. In the case of speech recognition knowledge acquisition implies collecting and observing large data bases. This work is made easier by the use of dedicated computer facilities such as automatic segmentation or semi-automatic labelling of the speech wave, digital spectrograms display, etc.,

- *knowledge representation* — one is usually faced with the two complementary problems of what is to be represented and how. Classical AI representation techniques such as logic, semantic nets, production rules can be used, according to the peculiarities of the domain. An important aspect is the necessity of incorporating a certain amount of meta-knowledge, i.e. knowledge about knowledge. Meat-knowledge constitutes a fundamental aspects of human expertise and it is directly related to the reasoning strategies used by the expert,

- *control structures* — this point is related to the manipulation of knowledge and of its optimal use in order to solve a given problem. Once again techniques developed in other areas of AI can be used successfully.

II.2. An overview of expert systems

Instead of the usual two-tiered organization (data structures and program) knowledge-based and expert systems introduce a more flexible, three-level structure: data, knowledge and control structures. These systems therefore introduce a clear separation between knowledge and the programs which manipulate it.

Figure 1 illustrates the overall organization of such a system.

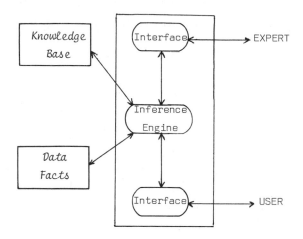

Figure 1   Architecture of a Knowledge-Based System

The data level stores a priori knowledge and facts about the domain and the particular problem to solve together with pieces of information which have been gained or deduced during the problem-solving process.

The control structures, or inference engine, constitute the heart of the system. They use the knowledge available in the knowledge base and carry out inferences from this knowledge.

The optimal use of an expert system necessitates friendly interfaces with the experts on one hand and the users on the other hand. Since these people are usually not specialists of computers these interfaces integrate a certain amount of natural language processing.

The ability of such systems to solve a problem is mainly related to the quality of the knowledge base. This knowledge is usually represented in a declarative form by using one of the classical representation schemes. It is often given under the form of "pattern-invoked" operators. At each time the applicable operators are applied and produce changes in the knowledge base. This process is repeated until the problem is solved. Such pattern-directed knowledge invocation has proven to be very efficient in a number of applications. The operators we have just introduced may be complex programs. However the most popular form for operators is the so-called production rule paradigm [6]. A production rule is of the form

IF Condition THEN Action

when "Condition" generally consists of a conjunction of predicates and "Action" means a change in the knowledge base, i.e. the current state of the problem. Production rules make it possible to split a complex expertise into a large number of small knowledge parcels. This formalism presents several advantages: modularity, readability, ease of modifying or updating, possibility for the system to explain its reasoning. Moreover, a human expert often seems to use a production rule scheme while reasoning. The method presents however some drawbacks: production rules are not very powerful in terms of speed and efficiency, at least with present, general-purpose computers and it is sometimes difficult, if not impossible, to split knowledge in a particular domain into very small pieces.

The control structures of knowledge-based systems use classical AI techniques that can be classified into three categories:

— state-space search including backtracking and the use of heuristics in order to speed up the search,

— problem reduction which consists of decomposing a problem into several subproblems that can be solved separately; this technique was used in the MYCIN expert system for medicine [23],

— constraints propagation, related to state-space search but without the necessity of backtracking since each partial solution must satisfy the various constraints which appear during the rule applications. EL, an expert system in electricity, uses this kind of control structures [25].

Another issue in expert system design concerns the chaining of rules. There are basically two different solutions:

— a forward reasoning scheme which consists of starting from the data and of making successive deductions with the knowledge base (in case of production rules that corresponds to a left-to-right application of these rules),

— a backward reasoning scheme which consists of starting from the goal to be reached and of defining subgoals in relation with the technique of problem reduction.

It is often interesting to combine these two basic schemes in order to improve the overall efficiency of the system.

The development of a knowledge-based or expert system is a long and difficult task. Besides the problem already mentioned of the automatization of knowledge acquisition this development itself necessitates the use of specific, sophisticated tools. Several tools already exists and are widely used, such as EMYCIN, OPS 5, AGE, HEARSAY III, etc. However a large amount of work is still needed in this area.

II.3. Applications to Automatic Speech Recognition

Automatic Speech Recognition, like other fields of AI such as computer vision, is characterized by a close interaction between a low-level processing, i.e. the acoustic-phonetic decoding, which represents the perceptive aspect of the problem, and a high-level (linguistic) interpretation which represents the cognitive aspect (figure 2). Knowledge engineering techniques can be helpful at both levels even though they must be considered carefully and constitute by no ways a miraculous solution for yet unsolved problems. In fact these techniques can be considered at two levels:

— they represent a flexible tool for solving specific problems especially when human experts possess an explicit knowledge about the domain (e.g. acoustic-phonetic decoding, phonology, prosody, etc.),

— they provide a general framework for designing the architecture of a speech recognition system, e.g. blackboard-like systems, production systems, expert societies, etc.

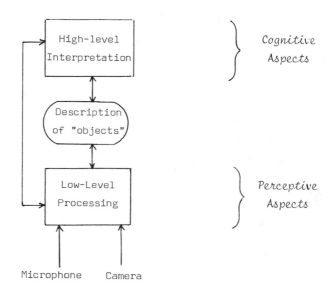

Figure 2   Principles of a Computer Understanding System (Speech or Vision).

We will now review with more details these different aspects.

III PHONETIC AND PHONOLOGICAL ASPECTS OF SPEECH RECOGNITION

III.1. Acoustic-Phonetic Decoding of Speech

The acoustic-phonetic decoding of speech, i.e. the mapping of the acoustic speech wave into discrete phonetic units, constitutes a major bottleneck in the design of large scale speech recognition systems, especially in multi-speaker environment. Prototype-based approaches using classical pattern-matching methods have proved to be unsufficient in order to obtain a high accuracy. On the other hand a rule-based recognition yields good results but cannot take into account large amounts of training data which are necessary for getting better performances. That can be done either by using a stochastic approach (for instance with a hidden Markov model) or by capturing the expertise accumulated over the years by phoneticians and speech scientists especially in reading speech spectrograms [27] or other kinds of parametric representations of speech such as LPC spectra, tables of numerical measurements [3] or temporal evolution of energy and formants [19].

There are several strong motivations for adopting a knowledge-based approach in phonetic decoding:

— first of all the existence of human expertise: a trained phonetician can transcribe a sentence by inspecting its spectrogram with a 85% accuracy which is far better than the present recognition rate of automatic systems and, moreover, this knowledge is to a large extent speaker-independent,

— this human expertise is conscious and can be formalized by a set of rules and meta-rules,

— the expertise will be useful not only for phonetic decoding but also for very important tasks such as segmentation or gross phonetic classes determination.

In the SYSTEXP project we are presently developing in our group [5] we aim at developing an expert system for automatic reading of speech spectrograms in order to improve our present speech recognition systems and eventually develop new sytems. A major point concerns the acquisition of human expertise in close interaction with the expert. We have particularly emphasized this aspect of the problem and we have developed special procedures for this purpose [4].

It is interesting to see how the expert proceeds. His process is usually made up of two successive steps:

— a global overlook on the spectrogram in order to determine the energy variations and a mean vowel duration (directly related to the speech rate of the speaker). These parameters are then integrated in the strategy of the expert,

— a local analysis which is carried out either by direct pattern matching or (most commonly) by visual analysis and reasoning on one phonemic segment and its two neighbours (whenever the segmentation seems reliable, otherwise an island-driven strategy is adopted).

According to the characteristics of the task the following guidelines have been used in the implementation of our expert system:

— most rules are contextual since the decision of the expert on a given segment relies on its neighbourhood,

— it is necessary to implement both a forward and a backward chaining of the rules,

— several kinds of rule are used concurrently [12]:
• gross phonetic class identification rules,
• exclusion rules,
• phoneme identification rules,
• meta-rules related to the knowledge of the expert about his own phonetic knowledge and enabling him to choose a strategy,

— at the strategy level any hypothesis never relies on just one, even very strong, cue. More generally it is necessary to postpone any decision until enough certainty exists. This "delayed decision" strategy is of general interest in speech recognition, not only at the acoustic-phonetic level.

It should also be noted that rule-based reasoning does not exclude in some cases the use of pattern-matching techniques with stored prototypes. The human expert sometimes uses this method and, therefore, both methods have to be mixed in the implementation of a system.

SYSTEXP is presently implemented in LISP on a Motorola 68000 machine and extensive tests are now being performed.

We have already mentioned several projects on related topics. [18] proposes a slightly different approach which consists of implementing an expert system using the expertise of a specialist of automatic speech recognition with a channel vocoder. [15] describes an interesting architecture for a speech spectrogram reading expert system. The model is based on the idea of experts cooperation and it is made up of three complementary modules:

— a visual reasoning expert which finds or verifies visual features on the spectrogram,

— an acoustic-phonetic expert which has to relate visual features to phonetic units,

— a phonetics expert which reasons about possible phoneme sequences and phoneme transformations.

Another actual application of expert systems in phonetic transcription is in the recognition of large vocabularies (several thousand of words). It is obvious that such systems have to be speaker-independent and cannot be handled by global pattern recognition techniques such as dynamic time warping. It is therefore necessary to take an analytical approach which consists of transcribing a word into a phonetic lattice and of matching this lattice against the phonetic transcriptions of the words in the lexicon. For sake of efficiency it is interesting to limit this comparison to a small subset of the lexicon. Experiments carried out for English [14] and for French [12] have shown that the selection of a sub-vocabulary for an unknown word can be done by describing the words in terms of gross phonetic classes (vowel, voiced plosive, sonorant, etc.). The results for a 1000 word vocabulary show that the mean size of the subvocabulary is around 10 for about 6 phonetic classes [17]. A rule-based decision is well suited for such a gross phonetic classification and it is then very attractive to use an expert system approach. In fact many rules used by expert phoneticians are expressed in terms of phonetic classes, e.g.

* IF Formant 1 ϵ [250 - 325 Hz]
    AND Formant 2 ϵ [1200 - 1500 Hz]
        THEN NOT Vowel

* IF Visible Energy $=$ Voicing Bar
    AND Global Energy Decreases Rapidly
        THEN Voiced Plosive

Moreover these broad classes usually related to the manner rather than the place of articulation. They tend therefore to be more robust and speaker-invariant. Figure 3 shows the architecture of our large vocabulary isolated word recognition system with the role played by the knowledge-based system both for gross phonetic classification and phonetic transcription of a word.

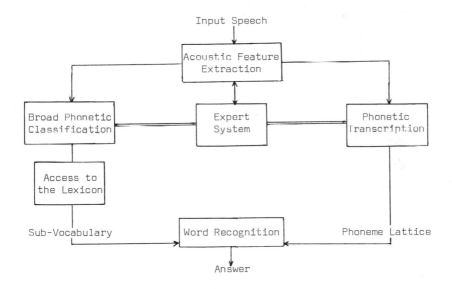

Architecture of a Large Vocabulary Isolated Word Recognition System

Figure 3

III.2. Use of frame grammars in control structures

We have just seen that the acoustic-phonetic knowledge base can be splitted into a large number of production rules. An alternative approach, though not exclusive, consists of defining the control structures of a knowledge-based system as a grammar of frames. In that case the selection of a rule or operator to be applied at any time is controlled by a planning system described by a frame grammar.

Frames were initially introduced for natural language understanding. A frame can be defined as a basic knowledge structure composed of a frame name and of a variable number of slots. The slots are the holder of particular pieces of information. The frame language is used for representing knowledge and how to use it.

There are several advantages to adapt this formalism to speech recognition. First that allows the activation of different acoustic analyses according to the context. Second these control structures are compatible with a rule-based description of knowledge. Third that makes it possible to introduce the important notion of planning in the speech recognition process.

De Mori [7] has proposed a frame language for extracting acoustic cues from the speech signal. Good results have been obtained for English, French and Italian. We are presently developing in Nancy a more general system using a frame language for the phonetic decoding of speech in relation with our phonetic expert system.

III.3. Phonology and Lexicon

A major activity in automatic speech recognition consists of emitting word hypotheses. The lexical level therefore plays a central role in a system. The great amount of variation in normal, continuous speech makes this process difficult since a word can be realized in a number of diverse ways according to the context, speaker characteristics, rate of speech, etc.

Fortunately, much of this variation appears systematically and can be formalized in contextual production rules called phonological rules [24]. In fact phonological knowledge links together the phonetic segments given by lower processsing levels and the morphological units used in the lexicon to describe the words.

A knowledge-based approach can be adopted in order to capture and use phonological rules [21]. An important contribution can be expected at the levels of knowledge acquisition in interaction with linguists and of sophisticated control structures for activating phonological rules.

There are roughly two extreme solutions for incorporating phonological knowledge in a speech rrecognition system:

— an analytical method which consists of applying the rules to the output of the acoustic-phonetic decoder at each access to the lexicon,

— a generative method which consists of expanding the lexicon by precompilation of the phonological rules. That yields a "phonological lexicon" including the various allophonic forms of words in context.

The latter is much more efficient in terms of processing time but it also presents some important drawbacks. First it is expensive in memory space (the expansion factor of the lexicon can be as large as 8). Second it is difficult to assign a likelihood measure to each production in the lexicon and a problem appears for inter-words rules. Finally the nature of phonetic variability is lost during the expansion process (for instance unstressed syllables are usually more sensitive to variations than stressed syllables).

It can be considered that a certain amount of rules should be used for generating the lexicon whereas other analytical rules should be applied during the recognition process.

IV KNOWLEDGE-BASED ARCHITECTURES FOR SPEECH UNDERSTANDING

IV.1. General Overview

We have already seen that the automatic recognition and interpretation of a sentence can only be achieved through the cooperation of all available knowledge sources, from acoustics to pragmatics. An important issue in the design of a system is therefore to define architectures which allow such an interaction between very diverse knowledge sources KSi each having its own monitor Mi, as illustrated in figure 4. Each knowledge source contains its own knowledge representation scheme and its own procedures for making hypotheses.

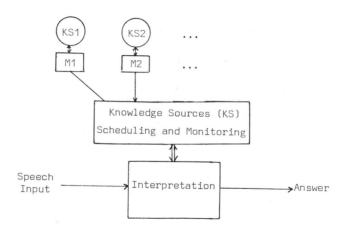

General Architecture of a Speech Understanding System

Figure 4

Various approaches have been proposed to solve this problem. Although it is an oversimplification we can distinguish between three classes of approaches:

— the first class consists of integrating all available knowledge sources into a simple structure. This is for instance the case of HARPY system which integrates a finite state network as will be seen later on,

— the second class uses some kind of stochastic modeling. We have already mentioned the use of Markov models at the phonetic level. This approach can be generalized to all knowledge sources, as for instance in the system developed by IBM [1] or in the DRAGON system [2],

— the third class is based on the classical AI paradigm of hypothesis-and-test which consists of emitting hypotheses on the basis of available knowledge and of verifying these hypotheses. This process is made necessary by the various errors and ambiguities which may be produced by a nonperfect pronunciation or during the word boundaries detection, etc. This "AI approach" is the one we are most concerned with in this paper. It clearly involves three kinds of problems which are not yet completely solved:

- knowledge representation,
- hypothesis evaluation,
- interpretation control and scheduling.

In fact the cooperation of various knowledge sources emitting hypotheses at various levels and at different instants during the interpretation of a sentence can be viewed as a parallel, synchronous or asynchronous access to a three-dimensional data base which contains the various concurrent hypotheses. The three dimensions are time, levels of interpretation and hypotheses.

IV.2. Distributed knowledge sources

There are basically two extreme models in order to implement the architecture suggested in figure 4, i.e. a heterarchical model in which each KS is connected to and interact with all other KSs and a hierarchical model in which a supervisor controls the operation and interaction of all KSs.

A straightforward implementation of a heterarchical model is not interesting for efficiency and cost reasons though attractive on a theoretical point of view. A good compromise is the blackboard model as used in HEARSAY II [16]. In this system the various knowledge sources are considered as independent processes which, theoretically, are not aware of each other and which asynchronously post hypotheses at their own level (acoustic feature, phoneme, syllable, word, phrase, sentence) to a global data base called the blackboard. This complex data structure thus contains a description at different levels of the sentence to be recognized. The blackboard constitutes the only link between the knowledge sources and its role is twofold:

— it transmits a message (i.e. an hypotheses) between two knowledge sources. An hypothesis emitted by KSi can trigger KSj. The activation of a KS is therefore data directed: a certain number of preconditions have to be fulfilled in the blackboard in order to enable a given knowledge source to access the blackboard for creating, modifying or cancelling one or several hypotheses. The action of a KS on the blackboard makes it possible to activate new KS_s, and so on,

— it contains the representation of the current interpretation of a sentence under the form of a set of hypotheses and of their relationships.

The global structure of a knowledge source in the blackboard model is thus of type "Condition-Action". It constitutes in that sense a generalization of the production rule models. However there exist considerable differences between HEARSAY II and production rule expert systems like for instance MYCIN, especially at the levels of reasoning schemes, control, etc.

In HEARSAY II the activities of the KSs are scheduled by using a strategy called "focus of attention". This strategy makes it possible to assign priorities to the different competing KS tasks according to the value of a weighting function based on several principles concerning the validity of data, the reliability of a KS, etc.

The general architecture of the HEARSAY II system is illustrated in figure 5.

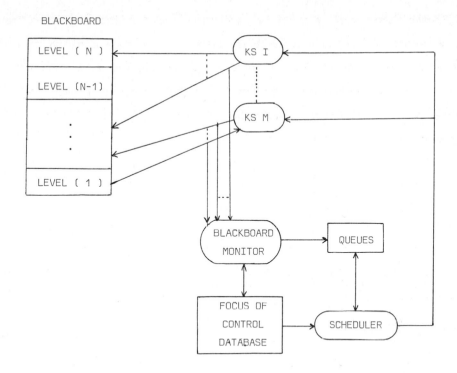

Figure 5   Architecture of HEARSAY II (after [Erman 80])

This architecture can be successfully used for implementing expert systems in complex domains with multiple, uncertain knowledge sources such as computer vision [22].

In a hierarchical model of speech understanding architecture the processing is controlled by some kind of supervisor. The supervisor activates the various available knowledge sources in contrast with the pattern-invocation of the blackboard model. This model is the most commonly encountered in practical systems.

A good example illustrating this model is the HWIM system [26]. This system uses a bottom-up, top-down strategy with island-driven focus of attention which appears to be one of the most powerful strategies available.

Another interesting way of implementing the distributed problem solving scheme necessary in automatic speech recognition is to define a society of experts. Each expert in the society is assigned a particular task which has been identified during a preliminary task decomposition [8]. That makes it possible to have a parallel execution of tasks suitable for real-time operation, with an efficient cooperation of the various experts different of the one which exists in the blackboard model. This model has been used for implementing a phonetic feature hypothesizer in the framework of a continuous speech recognition system [9]. It has now to be extended to the overall recognition process.

IV.3. Finite state networks and production rules

We have seen in par. IV.1. that a method for representing the various knowledge sources necessary in the speech recognition process was to integrate this knowledge into a single finite state network. To each state in this stochastic network is associated a phone template and a set of transitions to states representing phones that can follow it in time. The network therefore represents all allophonic variations of all possible sentences in the language. The interpretation of an input sentence consists of finding the path through the network with maximum likelihood according to the phone transcription of this sentence. In order to reduce the computational complexity of the recognition a beam search strategy has been adopted in order to keep active only a limited number of the possible states at each step of the search. Although non admissible this strategy is very efficient for speech recognition.

The stochastic network of HARPY contains all the available knowledge. It can be described by a set of stochastic rules

$$S(i) \quad \xrightarrow{P(i,j)} \quad h \ S(j)$$

where $P(i,j)$ is the transition probability of going from state $S(i)$ to state $S(j)$ and h a current hypothesis. Such stochastic rules represent pieces of knowledge which can be transformed into production rules of the type [20]:

> IF S(j)   is an active state
>
> AND h   is a hypothesis
>
> THEN Compute the likelihood of reaching S(j) from S(i).

HARPY can therefore the rewritten into a production system. Production rules can thus be applied not only for solving specific problems (phonetic decoding, phonological variations, etc.) but also for implementing speech recognition architectures. However the complexity of the task does not guarantee the efficiency of a pure production system for recognizing and interpreting a sentence.

V   CONCLUSION

Knowledge-based and expert systems have been successfully used during the past few years in a number of domains. An important aspect of such systems is to provide a functional distinction between the knowledge base concerning the domain of expertise considered and the control structures which manipulate this knowledge.

Knowledge engineering techniques can be also very helpful in ASR. On one hand they help solving specific problems where there exists an important but ill-formalized human expertise. A typical example is the acoustic-phonetic decoding of speech, a major bottleneck in the design of ASR systems. Capturing the expertise of phoneticians reading speech spectrograms makes it possible to substantially improve the phonetic decoding of speech as well as speech segmentation or gross phonetic class identification. Similar techniques can be used for formalizing and using phonological knowledge in ASR.

On the other hand knowledge-based systems provide a good framework for implementing ASR system architectures. The blackboard model used in HEARSAY II is an efficient way for having multiple knowledge sources cooperation. Other schemes, like production systems or expert societies present also interesting features.

In conclusion knowledge engineering techniques do not solve all open problems in ASR but they definitely help getting substantial improvements in the domain.

REFERENCES

1. L. R. Bahl et al, "A maximum likelihood approach to continuous speech recognition", IEEE Trans. PAMI, Vol. 5, No. 2, pp. 179-190, 1983.
2. J. Baker, "The DRAGON system: An overview", IEEE Trans. ASSP, Vol. 23, pp. 24-29, 1975.
3. M. A. Bush, G. E. Kopec and V. W. Zue, "Selecting acoustic features for stop consonant identification", Proc. IEEE Int. Conf. ASSP, Boston, pp. 742-745, 1983.
4. N. Carbonell, M. O. Cordier, D. Fohr, J. P. Haton, F. Lonchamp, J. M. Pierrel, "Acquisition et formalisation du raisonnement dans un système expert de lecture de spectrogrammes vocaux", colloque A.R.C., 1984a.
5. N. Carbonell, D. Fohr, J. P. Haton, F. Lonchamp, J. M. Pierrel, "An expert system for the automatic reading of French spectrograms", Proc. IEEE-ICASSP, San Diego, 1984b.
6. R. Davis and J. King, "An overview of production systems", Machine Intelligence, Vol. 8, pp. 300-332, 1977.
7. R. De Mori, "Extraction of acoustic cues using a grammar of frames", Speech Comunication, Vol. 2, pp. 223-225, 1983a.
8. R. De Mori, *Computer Models of Speech Using Fuzzy Algorithms*, Plenum Press, 1983b.
9. R. De Mori et al, "Phonetic feature hypothesization in continuous speech", IEEE-ICASSP 83, Boston, pp. 316-319, 1983c.
10. L. D. Erman et al, "The HEARSAY II speech understanding system. Integrating knowledge to resolve uncertainty", Computing Surveys, Vol. 12, No. 2, pp. 213-253, 1980.
11. F. Hayes-Roth et al, editors *Building Expert Systems*, Addison-Wesley, 1983.
12. J. P. Haton, "Present issues in continuous speech recognition and understanding", in *Towards Robustness in Speech Recognition*, W. A. Lea, editor, in pres, 1984a.
13. J. P. Haton, "Accès lexical et reconnaissance de grands vocabulaires", 13èmes Journées d'Etude sur la Parole, GALF, Bruxelles, 1984b.
14. D. P. Huttenlocher and V. W. Zue, "Exploring phonotactilexical constraints in word recognition", J. Acoustic. Soc. Am. Suppl. 1:74, 1982.
15. J. Johannsen et al, "A speech spectrogram expert", IEEE ICASSP 83, Boston, pp. 746-749, 1983.

16. V. R. Lesser et al, "Organization of the HEARSAY II speech understanding system", IEEE Trans. ASSP, 23, pp. 11-23, 1975.

17. J. F. Mari and J. P. Haton, "Some experiments in automatic recognition of a thousand word vocabulary", Proc. IEEE ICASSP, San Diego, 1984.

18. G. Mercier et al, "From KEAL to SERAC: a new rule-based expert system for speech recognition", NATO ASI on New Architectures and Systems for Speech Recognition, Bonas, July 1984.

19. R. Mizoguchi and O. Kakusho, "Continuous speech recognition based on knowledge engineering techniques", Proc. 7th Int. Conf. Pattern Recognition, Montreal, pp. 638-640, 1984.

20. A. Newell, "HARPY, Production system and human cognition", in *Perception and Production of Fluent Speech*, R. A. Cole, ed., Erlbaum Associates, 1980.

21. B. Oshika, "Phonological rules for continuous speech recognition", in *Towards Robustness in Speech Recognition*, W. Lea, editor, Prentice-Hall, in press, 1984.

22. J. Prager et al, "Segmentation processes in the VISIONS system", Proc. 5th IJCAI, Cambridge, 1977.

23. E. H. Shortliffe, "Computer-based medical consultation: MYCIN", American Elsevier, 1976.

24. J. E. Shoup, "Phonological aspects of speech recognition", in *Trends in Speech Recognition*, W. Lea, editor, Prentice-Hall, 1980.

25. R. M. Stallman and G. J. Sussman, "Forward reasoning and dependency-directed backtracking in a system for computer-aided circuit analysis", Artificial Intelligence, Vol. 9, pp. 135-196, 1977.

26. W. A. Woods et al, "Speech understanding systems" Final Technical Progress Report, Report No. 3438, Vol. I.V., BBN, 1976.

27. V. Zue and R. Cole, "Experiments in spectrogram reading", Proc. IEEE Int. Conf. ASSP, Washington, pp. 116-119, 1979.

THE SPEECH UNDERSTANDING AND DIALOG SYSTEM EVAR

H. Niemann, A. Brietzmann, R. Mühlfeld, P. Regel, G. Schukat

Lehrstuhl für Informatik 5 (Mustererkennung)

Universität Erlangen-Nürnberg

Martensstr. 3

8520 Erlangen

West Germany

ABSTRACT

This paper gives an overview of a research effort whose goal is to develop a system which can carry out a dialog concerning a particular task domain using continuous German speech for input and output. The main processing phases are initial segmentation and labeling, finding words, understanding the meaning and giving an answer. Specialized processing modules for handling these four phases were developed or are being developed. The processing modules communicate via a common database.

1. INTRODUCTION

Speech is considered to be the most distinguishing human capability [1] — highly developed vision capability can be observed in many animals, but speech is mastered by human only; speech is also considered to be the most natural and efficient means of human communication [2]; and speech offers a communication channel which is fairly independent of hand and eye [3]. Therefore, it is no wonder that automatic speech recognition is an area of intensive research since

NATO ASI Series, Vol. F16
New Systems and Architectures for Automatic Speech
Recognition and Synthesis. Edited by R. De Mori and C. Y. Suen
© Springer-Verlag Berlin Heidelberg 1985

several years, partly because of mere scientific interest, partly because of promising applications.

Basic tasks are recognition of isolated words or of a spoken text fairly independent of the speaker, and recognition of a speaker fairly independent of the spoken text. Recognition of a spoken text usually requires continuous speech recognition and the representation of the meaning of the speech. This field was initiated and treated with great engagement in the ARPA Speech Understanding Research Project. The role of high level syntactic, semantic, and pragmatic knowledge was stressed in this work, new system structures emerged in the HEARSAY II and HARPY architectures and several operational laboratory systems were completed. This work is reviewed in [4]. In addition, continuous speech recognition was investigated in many laboratories all over the world, and a review is given in [5]. Although this work brought significant contributions and improvements, additional work is needed in several respects, for example, more reliable phonetic segmentation, speaker independence, larger vocabularies, dialog strategies, syntactic, semantic and pragmatic reasoning and real time performance. A broad account of recent achievements is presented in [6]. It should be mentioned that also the isolated word recognition problem is treated furtheron, in particular the problems of speaker independence and large vocabularies [7].

At our institute research on understanding continuous German speech started around 1979. Our present research goals are as follows:

1. Develop a complete dialog system covering the tasks of recognition (of words), understanding (of the meaning), generation of further inquiries to the user, and generation of an answer, see Fig. 1.
2. Use a flexible system structure suited to carry out basic research.
3. Achieve speaker independence.
4. Limit the bandwidth to telephone quality.
5. Use a vocabulary of about 2000 words.
6. Apply high level syntactic, semantic and pragmatic knowledge.
7. Allow a large subset of German language.

8. Exclude dialects.

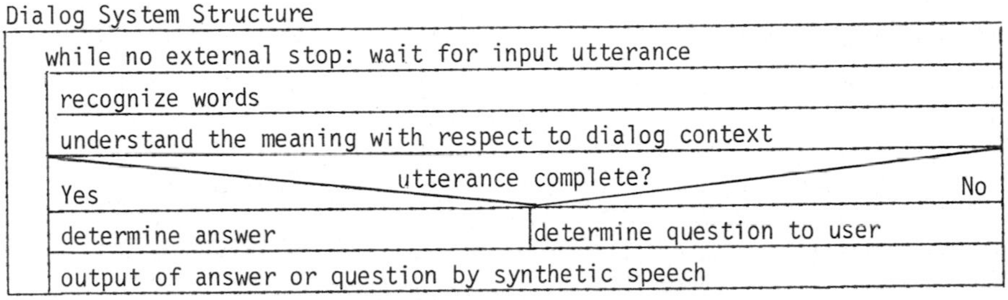

```
Dialog System Structure
  while no external stop: wait for input utterance
  recognize words
  understand the meaning with respect to dialog context
                      utterance complete?
  Yes                                                      No
  determine answer              determine question to user
  output of answer or question by synthetic speech
```

Fig. 1   The basic structure of a dialog system using continuous speech for input
and output.

The system is called **EVAR** according to the German words for the four tasks mentioned in point 1 above. It should be noted that the 2000 words in point 5 are to be understood as cardinal forms. Since flexions of a word often sound very different from the cardinal form, all flexions of a word are also included in the lexicon and the total number of entries will be about 5 - 6000.

The system structure adopted for EVAR is according to a stratified linguistic model similar to the one given in [8], and the coordination of system modules is via a centralized data base and a control strategy as suggested first in HEARSAY II [4]. Fig. 2a,b show the present structure of the system, and this was also the structure used in former work about two years ago [9,10], but with some modifications. The two modules Word Hypothesization and Word Verification in Fig. 2a formerly were combined in only one module Lexicon. Furthermore, the module application meanwhile was split into the three modules Dialog, Retrieval, and Answer. The system as documented in [9,10] consisted of a relational data

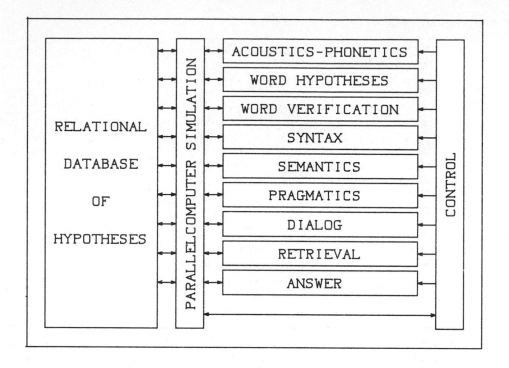

Fig. 2a   The present structure of the speech understanding and dialog system
          EVAR

base, an Acoustics — Phonetics Module [11], a Lexicon Module, and a simple
Control Module; a first version of a Syntax Module was available, but not yet
integrated into the system.   Inquiries about schedules of German intercity trains
were chosen as an example of a task domain.

Incorporated in the system EVAR is the following knowledge:

1.   A sample of hand-segmented and hand-labeled continuous German speech.
2.   A lexicon with spelling, pronunciation, syntax and semantics.
3.   Rules for generating inflexions.
4.   Rules for generating pronunciation variants.
5.   An ATN-grammar of German language.
6.   Semantic classification and compatibilities of some word classes.
7.   A semantic net representation of the task domain.

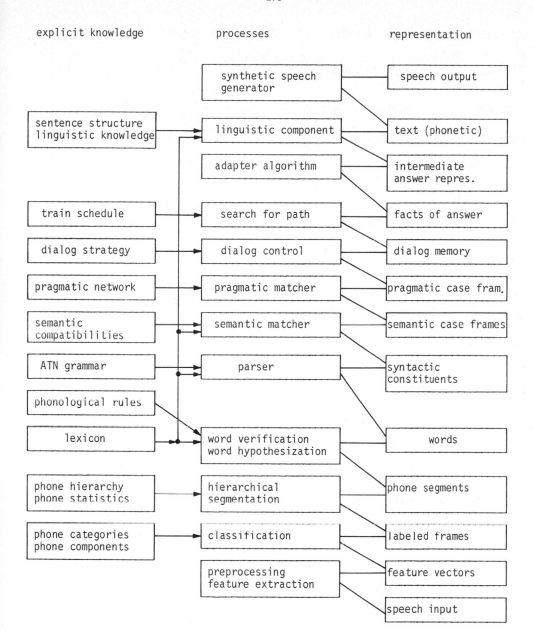

explicit knowledge · processes · representation

explicit knowledge	processes	representation
	synthetic speech generator	speech output
sentence structure linguistic knowledge	linguistic component	text (phonetic)
	adapter algorithm	intermediate answer repres.
train schedule	search for path	facts of answer
dialog strategy	dialog control	dialog memory
pragmatic network	pragmatic matcher	pragmatic case fram.
semantic compatibilities	semantic matcher	semantic case frames
ATN grammar	parser	syntactic constituents
phonological rules		
lexicon	word verification word hypothesization	words
phone hierarchy phone statistics	hierarchical segmentation	phone segments
phone categories phone components	classification	labeled frames
	preprocessing feature extraction	feature vectors
		speech input

Fig. 2b   The stratified linguistic model used in the system EVAR

8.   An Inter City train schedule.

9.   An ATN representation of the dialog strategy.

10. Linguistic knowledge for text generation.

This paper gives an account of the present status of EVAR. In Section 2 the initial segmentation and labeling of speech is treated which is performed by the Acoustics-Phonetics Module. The problem of finding words is handled by the Word Hypotheses and Word Verification Modules and discussed in Section 3. Section 4 gives an account of understanding the meaning of an utterance which is done in the Syntax, Semantic and Pragmatic Modules. First approaches to answer generation are treated in Section 5; this is done by the Dialog, Retrieval and Answer Modules. The concluding remarks in Section 6 give some directions of further work which we should like to explore. Because the intent of this paper is to give a survey of our recent and current work, mathematical details, which may be found in other and forthcoming papers, had to be omitted.

2.   INITIAL SEGMENTATION AND LABELING OF SPEECH

In our system speech is bandlimited to 0.1 - 3.4 kHz, sampled at 10 kHz, and quantized with 12 bit per sample value. Segmentation of the speech into phones is done by the "classification, then segmentation" approach. This means that the whole utterance is subdivided into a number of frames, in our system frames are repeated every 12 ms and contain 20 ms of speech passed through a Hamming window. In a first classification step each frame is classified into the four categories silence, voiceless, voiced fricative and voiced nonfricative. In a second classification step the categories of a frame are classified into phone components. Examples of phone components are M, I, L, O in category voiced nonfricative, Z in category voiced fricative, and S, F, burst of t, aspiration of t in category voiceless. In most cases a phone component coincides with a phone, for example, the phone component I coincides with the phone I; but in some cases they do not, for example, the plosive [t] has the phone components silence, burst of t, and aspiration of t.

In both classification steps several alternative classifications are allowed. Since a Bayes classifier is used for classification, posterior probabilities are used to measure the reliability of alternatives. Each category of a frame which has a posterior probability greater than 2% is considered in further processing. Reliability of a phone component assigned to a frame is measured by the product of the posterior probabilities of the category and the phone component of this frame. The five most reliable phone components are used for further processing. Finally, several frames are combined to one segment which corresponds to a phone. This is done by several rules which merge adjacent similar frames to a segment part, determine essential segment parts, and extend essential segment parts as far as possible. Again, up to five alternative phone classes may be assigned to one segment. The final output is a string of segments, each labeled with up to five alternative phones and each phone rated by an assigned reliability. In addition, each segment also is assigned a measure of loudness and, if applicable, the pitch frequency. These two parameters are provided as prosodic features, but they are not used in the system presently. The structure of the Acoustics-Phonetics Module is given in Fig. 3, a labeled speech wave is shown in Fig. 4.

Acoustics-Phonetics Module

input: speech wave from microphone in unprepared room
0.1 - 3.4 kHz band pass filtering, 10 kHz sampling
mean energy normalization in time intervals
10 mel cepstrum features plus loudness
1. classification stage: 4 categories
2. classification stage: 40 phone components
obtain phone segments by hierarchical syntactic composition of phone components
output: string of segments, each with up to 5 phone labels and reliability, each with measure of loudness and pitch

Fig. 3   An overview of initial segmentation and labeling

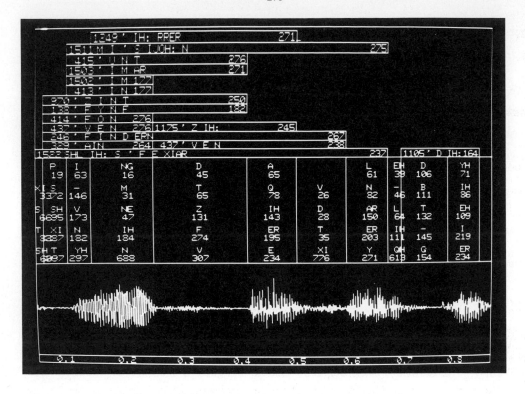

Fig. 4 An interval of continuous speech, showing the German word "Schließfächer (lockers)", its initial segmentation and labeling, and some of the word hypotheses generated.

An early version of the Acoustics-Phonetics Module is described in [11]. Meanwhile several additions, improvements and further investigations were carried out.

1. The sample of hand segmented and labeled speech was enlarged from 100 s spoken by 6 speakers to 600 s spoken by 12 speakers (6 male, 6 female).

2. Energy normalization was improved.

3. Several speaker normalization techniques reported in the literature were tested.

4. The number of phone classes was enlarged from about 30 to 40.

5. Experiments with several feature sets were made.

6.   The suitability of nearest neighbour classification was tested.

7.   Segments were built from frames by a hierarchical syntactic approach.

A detailed treatment of these points will be given in a forthcoming dissertation [12]. Only a short account of the major points can be given here.

Hand segmentation and labeling was done by one person who knew the spoken sentence, could listen to it and observe the speech spectrogram on a display. The sample of 600 s of speech spoken by 12 speakers is used to design the above mentioned classification stages for categories and phone components. Speaker independence is simulated by designing the system using data from 11 speakers and testing it with data from the one remaining speaker. This process is repeated 12 times in order to test all 12 speakers. Of course, 12 speakers probably are insufficient to judge system performance if many speakers are involved. But the present sample gives first estimates of system performance and may be the basis for obtaining larger samples by more automated approaches.

In the first experiments energy was normalized with respect to the whole utterance. This turned out to be less useful because usually energy tends to decrease at the end of an utterance. Therefore, energy now is normalized in time intervals whose length is small compared to the length of an utterance and large compared to the length of a phone segment. A time interval of 400 ms was found useful in several experiments.

Normalization of frequencies of the first two formants and of vocal tract length was employed in order to improve speaker independence. However, in our experiments the effect of these normalization procedures was negligible.

The initial set of phones consisted of 30 phones. This set was enlarged to 40 phones. A fairly complete list of phones used in German language contains about 60 phones. Nevertheless, a condensed set of only 18 phones is presently used in word hypothesization and is completely sufficient as mentioned in the next section. This condensed set is covered by the presently available 40 phones.

Initially, LPC based features were used for classification [11]. In addition mel-frequency and mel-cepstrum coefficients (mcc) were tested. The best results were obtained using mcc, and this result is in accordance with [13]. However, a slight modification was necessary in order to make mcc optimal also for classification of categories — loudness has to be used as an additional feature in this case. In our experiments the first 10 mcc turned out to be sufficient.

In [14] one finds the sentences "we should stop doing research on statistical decision theory ..." and the NN-rule is "simple to understand and to program, essentially distribution-free, and powerful in terms of performance". Since we have, in fact, evidence that there are deviations of feature distribution from the Gaussian distribution and since a more powerful classification procedure is always welcome, the NN-rule was tried as an alternative to simple Bayes classification using the normal distribution hypothesis. NN-rule prototypes were selected by editing a sample of speech spoken by 4 speakers, then condensing it and then reducing it. Tests were made with the sample from the remaining speakers, and this was compared to a Bayesian classifier designed and tested with the same samples [15]. Design time for NN-Prototypes far exceeds design time of the Bayes classifier, and recognition rate of the NN-rule was 45% with editing only and 41% with editing, condensing, and reducing compared to 51% of the Bayes classifier. A preliminary test gave no significant difference between NN-rule and edited NN-rule. Of course, there are some points which could be improved: we did not use Voronoi diagrams, and 4 speakers are not a representative sample.

A significant problem is the combination of phone components (that is classified speech frames) into larger phone segments. Initially a heuristic set of rules was used [11]. Meanwhile relaxation labeling and hierarchic syntactic combination was tested. Best results were achieved by the last approach. It starts on level 4 of the hierarchy with two broad classes of phone components which are voiced non-fricative and others. Frames are combined on this level by a formal grammar. Levels 3, 2, and 1 refine the classes to 7 vowels, 6 fricatives, 3 liquids, 3 nasals, 3 plosives, and silence and another formal grammar is used on every level. Finally on level 0 51 phone components are distinguished. A comparison using 23 phone components gave 47% correct segments with relaxation and 55% with syntactic segmentation; using 40 phone components we obtained 40% correct segments with heuristic segmentation and 46% with syntactic.

To summarize: The presently used version of the Acoustics-Phonetics Module distinguishes 40 phone classes, the first alternative is correct in 46%, errors consist of 12% insertions, 12% deletions, and 42% wrongly classified segments. The training set consisted of 520 seconds continuous speech spoken by 6 male and 3 female speakers, the test set consisted of 85 seconds spoken by 2 female speakers who were not in the training set.

Further work should explore the followig problems:

1. Steps towards automated sample set acquisition.
2. Speaker clusters to improve speaker independence.
3. Use of phonological rules and of larger time context.
4. Further improvement of classification and segmentation.
5. Some additional phone classes, in particular diphthongs and perhaps nasals.

3. FINDING WORDS

If an initial segmentation is available, the next step is to find words in the segmented speech. This requires that a lexicon of known words is prepared and made available to the system. The first approach to word recognition was a straight-forward dynamic programming algorithm which compared every word in the lexicon starting with every position in the utterance [9]. This allowed us to obtain first results, but, of course, is not sufficient for solving the word rcognition problem. Meanwhile the status reported in [9,10] was changed and improved as follows:

1. The lexicon was enlarged.
2. Word finding is done in the two phases of word hypothesization and word verification.

3. The algorithm and the data structure for word hypothesization was improved.

4. A first set of rules was developed to account for variations of pronunciation.

An initial version of the lexicon consisted of a basic vocabulary covering the most frequent German words, a task oriented vocabulary concerning the task domain of German Inter City trains, and an augmenting vocabulary containing numbers, cities, and week-days. This gave 306 cardinal forms. Adding all possible inflexions resulted in a lexicon with 1380 words. The lexicon is being augmented continuously and contains presently 3600 words. A word in the lexicon is represented by (spelling, number, pronunication, syntax, semantic). The number is a unique identification of every word, the spelling gives the usual text form, the pronunciation the standard phonetic representation. The entry syntax lists all possible syntactic classes and features of this word. The entry semantic lists, for every syntactic class, all relevant meanings together with case and valency information. Therefore, the information in the lexicon is a link between acoustics-phonetics, word finding, syntactic and semantic processing. Due to the large amount of syntactic and semantic information it is fairly time consuming to build up the lexicon. Up to now inflexions were added manually to the lexicon, but now it will be sufficient to enter the cardinal form and the inflexions will be generated by a program. Inflexions do not contain syntactic and semantic information, but have a pointer to the cardinal form where this information can be found. In addition a lexicon of about 8000 words without syntactic and semantic information is available [16] and is used up to the word recognition level.

The lexicon is to be considered as a raw information from which specialized knowledge used by various modules is derived. The type of specialization depends on the module and its processing algorithm and will be discussed as necessary.

As suggested, for example, in [3] the problem of finding words was split into the two problems of hypothesizing a small subset of words and verification of that subset. The subset should be hypothesized quickly, be as small as possible, and should contain the correct word with high probability. A word hypothesis consists of the three essential components (position, word, score),

and several auxiliary components like syntactic word class, status of the hypothesis, or a unique number. The three essential components have to be determined in the process of word hypothesization. After a subset of words is obtained all the words in it are carefully verified with respect to the utterance. Basically, the verification process should refine the essential components of the word hypothesis, in particular give high score to the correct word and low to the wrong ones.

Two approaches to word hypothesization are investigated which will be referred to as compressed lexicon tree (CLT) and feature addressed lexicon (FAL). A CLT is obtained by combining similar phone classes to superclasses. This reduces the number of confusions and also reduces the size of the lexicon since certain words become identical if they are represented by phone superclasses. Compression of the lexicon by means of broad phonetic classes was also suggested in [17] and the set of words becoming identical after compression was called a cohort. After some comparisons we obtained best results by using the transinformation as a criterion for deriving phone superclasses — in fact, this criterion is much better than error rate and also gave better results than a heuristic approach. The derivation of superclasses starts with a phone confusion matrix provided by the Acoustics-Phonetics Module. One may view the spoken phones as symbols entered into a channel and the recognized phones as symbols at the output of a channel. The transinformation gives the amount of information passed correctly from the input to the output, and it may be computed from the phone confusion matrix. Phone superclasses are obtained by merging two or more rows and columns of the phone confusion matrix in such a way that the transinformation is maximized. If the error rate is used as a criterion, rows and columns are merged to minimize error rate. Experiments showed that the error rate as a criterion tends to yield very few and very large superclasses whereas transinformation yields fairly many and small superclasses. This is a first hint that phone superclasses derived from maximization of the transinformation should be useful; this idea was confirmed by experiments with compression of the lexicon and by several cohort statistics. The size of a cohort, that is the number of words becoming identical when represented by phone superclasses, should be small. Table 1 gives some cohort statistics for superclasses obtained from maximization of transinformation, minimization or error rate, and a heuristic approach. This shows clearly the superiority of transinformation with

List of tables

	transinformation phone super classes		error rate phone super classes		heuristic
	5	18	5	18	5
Maximal cohort size	9	13	157	31	14
average cohort size	1.31	1.09	10.1	1.6	1.58
number of cohorts	928	1113	122	755	770

Table 1 Some cohort statistics obtained from a lexicon with 1222 words using 5 and 18 phone superclasses derived by three criteria

respect to cohort statistics. But also the five heuristically determined classes of vowels, fricatives, plosives, nasals, and remainder is quite satisfactory.

Presently, experiments are made using 18 phone superclasses which contain 87% of the initial transinformation in the full set of 40 phonemes (5 superclasses contain 58% of the initial transinformation). The lexicon is compressed to cohorts using these 18 classes and represented by a tree which is stored as a linear string of phonetic symbols together with some bookkeeping information; in particular, for each node of the compressed lexicon tree (CLT) representing a cohort this information contains a number identifying the cohort. From the cohort number the set of words in it can be determined. The CLT is matched with the phonetic string of the input utterance and for each word we compute the probability of observing the phonetic string when this word is pronounced [18]. This computation takes care of insertion and deletion errors in the phonetic string. The various transition probabilities are trained iteratively [19]. The result is a position of the word within the phonetic string and a probability of the word. The main steps of the algorithm are given in Fig. 5. However, the

Word Hypothesization Module

input: string of phone segments
transcription of phones to superclasses
match cpmpressed lexicon tree with input by stochastic automaton approach
select n best word positions
expand cohort hypotheses into word hypotheses
computation of word score
output: m best scoring word hypotheses

Fig. 5   The main steps of word hypothesization in the CLT

probability of a word is not used as a measure of priority for further processing because it depends highly on the length of a word. Instead, a score is computed by estimating mean and variance of word probabilities for each length and then normalizing probabilities with respect to mean and variance.

A first experiment with 20 sentences and a small lexicon of 100 words gave an average inverse rank [20] of word hypotheses equal to 0.46. Computation time on a PDP11/34 is about 2 minutes per sentence with a lexicon of about 1400 words. An example of some word hypotheses is shown in Fig. 4.

The CLT approach described above is basically a top-down approach because every cohort in the CLT is matched to the input utterance. A truly bottom-up approach is the feature addressed lexicon (FAL). The idea is to use phonetic features like phone tripels as entries in a FAL where each entry gives the set of words having this feature. By using several features, for example several phone tripels, the set of words having these features will become smaller. This approach is now being implemented and tested and results will be reported later.

The set of word hypotheses is then verified using the full set of phones and taking into account variations of pronunciation. Since word hypotheses contain the three components (position, word, score), the verificiation process can concentrate on a particular word and a particular interval of the utterance. Two versions of a Word Verification Module are under investigation; the first uses the string of phonetic segments provided by the Acoustics Phonetics Module, the second uses the string of labeled speech frames. The structure of the first version is given in Fig. 6. A set of about 140 phonological rules was developed

Word Verification Module (segment level)

input: string of phone segments, word hypotheses
select high scoring unverified word hypothesis
apply phonological rules to obtain pronunciation graph
match graph to interval of utterance
the word score is that of the best scoring pronunciation variant
output: (position, word, score, auxiliary information)

Fig. 6   The main steps of word verification on the segments level

to generate pronunciation variants of words from the standard phonetic representation contained in the lexicon. An average number of three variants per word is generated. The pronunciation variants and the standard pronunciation are represented by a pronunciation graph. Pronunciation variants occur often at word endings, voiced plosives and some frequently used words like articles, conjunctions and prepositions.

The pronunciation graph is used as input of a stack-decoding algorithm [18] which matches the graph to the relevant interval of the utterance by means of dynamic programming. This results in drastic improvements of scores of the correct word hypotheses in some cases, but also may result in improvements of the wrong word. This effect, which occurs if the correct word is pronounced clearly, needs further investigation and may require changes in some of the rules. The approach to word verification by matching a word hypothesis with labeled speech frames is presently being implemented and tested.

Further work should explore the following points:

1. Incorporation of pronunciation variants already on the hypothesis generation level.

2. Phonological rules to account for pronunciation variants between successive words.

3. Thorough experimental investigation of the performance of the various modules using lexicons of varying size.

4. Improved estimates of various parameters used in the matching algorithms, for example deletion, insertion, and confusion probabilities.

5. Take care of top-down word hypotheses generated from the Syntax Module, for example.

4. UNDERSTANDING THE MEANING OF AN UTTERANCE

The result of word matching is a set of word hypotheses which may have gaps, competing and erroneous hypotheses, and also may span the utterance by one or several sequences of (nearly) adjacent words. In the three main steps of syntactic, semantic and pragmatic analysis it is tried to find one unambiguous meaning for a spanning sequence of words or for some disjoint groups of words. This serves two goals. The first goal is to reduce the ambiguity of word hypotheses by using additional knowledge and thereby improving recognition of words. The second goal is to relate a sequence of words to the system's internal representation of linguistic knowledge, and by "understanding" we mean this process of relating an input to internal knowledge of the system.

In this paper the terms syntax, semantics, and pragmatics are used as defined in [21]. Syntax studies the formal relations of signs to one another. Consequently, the Syntax Module only treats properties of and relations between words and word classes. Semantics studies the relation of signs to the objects to which the signs are applicable. Therefore, the Semantics Module considers properties and relations of words and word classes resulting from their signifying certain objects, events, and concepts. Pragmatics deals with the relation of signs to interpreters. Therefore, the Pragmatics Module analyzes a word sequence with respect to the particular task domain. No task specific knowledge is available in the Semantics Module, and no knowledge about the general meaning of words is available in the Syntax Module. The advantage of this approach is a clear conceptual structure of the system and independence of modules — a change of the task domain would require a redesigned Pragmatics Module but no changes in syntax or semantics (probably the lexicon would have to be augmented by a task specific vocabulary, too). A disadvantage is a certain loss of processing efficiency. The three modules form a representational hierarchy in the sense that the Pragmatics Module requires a semantically interpreted word string, and the Semantics Module requires a syntactically analyzed string.

At present, the three modules are in different states of completion; the most advanced module is the Semantics Module, and this one will be described in some detail below. The early version of the Syntax Module is presented in [9,10]. It used a fairly elaborate ATN-grammar of German language and an island parser. The problem with this approach is the combinatoric explosion due to the fairly large number of word alternatives and the rigid constraints imposed by the ATN-rules, for example the case-number-gender agreement in noun groups. Therefore, we plan a redesign of the module according to Fig. 7. The two main points are that a fast prescanning of words will be done to detect a few sequences of words belonging to syntactically allowed word classes and that the rigidity of syntactic constraints will be dependent on the score of words. For example, the case-number-gender agreement may depend only on some endings of words which are hard to recognize and, therefore, this should be checked only for

289

Syntax Module

input: verified word hypotheses
determine triples of words with syntactically allowed sequences of word classes
determine larger sequences of words with syntactically allowed word class sequences
select some high scoring sequences of words
perform syntactic analysis with score - dependent rules
generate top-down word hypotheses in gaps of syntactic analysis
output: syntactic constituents of sentences represented in a syntax analysis tree

Fig. 7   The structure of the module for syntactic analysis

very high scoring words.

As shown in Fig. 8, the Semantics Module takes as input syntactic constituents and gives a semantic interpretation represented in a semantic net structure. Fig. 8 treats the case that a syntactic constituent spans the utterance,

Semantics Module

input: syntactic constituents spanning the utterance
select high scoring syntactic constituent
perform local interpretation of immediate constituents
instantiate case frames of the verb
match immediate syntactic constituents to case frames
interpretation of adjuncts
determine top-down word or constituent hypotheses from open case slots
select best scoring case frame
output: semantic net representation of interpreted constituent structure

Fig. 8   The structure of the module for semantic analysis of syntactic constituents spanning an utterance

but also constituents spanning only part of the utterance can be processed. The semantic nets are structured as suggested in [22]. Two basic components of a semantic net are the concept and the instance. Both consist of attributes which describe parts as well as properties (both may be concepts themselves). A concept is a definition of a word like 'tomorrow', or a class of objects like 'mammals', or an action like 'to eat', or a relation like 'left to'. An instance represents an individual member of a class defined by a concept. It is also possible to derive a concept as a specialization from a more general concept. The specialization inherits all attributes of all those concepts which are more general, except the attributes which are explicitly modified or differentiated. The semantic nets were implemented using GRASPE as an extension of SIMULA.

The 'raw knowledge' about semantic properties is manually prepared and stored in a dictionary, where each word has an entry as described in Section 3. By semantic analysis the dependencies and relations within a sentence are investigated and a formal representation of the meaning is obtained. The meaning concerns functional and logical or deep case relations within a sentence, the dependency structure or the valency of word groups, and aspects of text consistency and coherence. The main idea is that the structure of a sentence is determined by the leading verb, the so called nucleus. This is the topic of the valency and case theory. The nucleus has the ability to attach dependent constituents, and this ability is called its valency. The obligatory and optional dependent constituents of the nucleus largely determine the structure of a sentence. Often, different meanings of a verb give rise to different structures. In case theory the functional roles and logical relations of parts of a sentence are treated with respect to the nucleus. The structure implied by a certain meaning of the nucleus is represented in a case frame, and an example is given in Fig. 9. A case frame of a verb is a concept in a semantic net and obtained by a preprocessor from the lexicon containing the raw semantic knowledge.

The tasks of semantic analysis are to choose an appropriate meaning of a word out of the different meanings represented in the dictionary (different meanings of 'to get', for example, in 'get up', 'get started'), to recognize semantic ambiguities (in sentences like 'he wants a train to go to Munich'), to point out semantic anomalies (which may arise due to competing alternatives in word

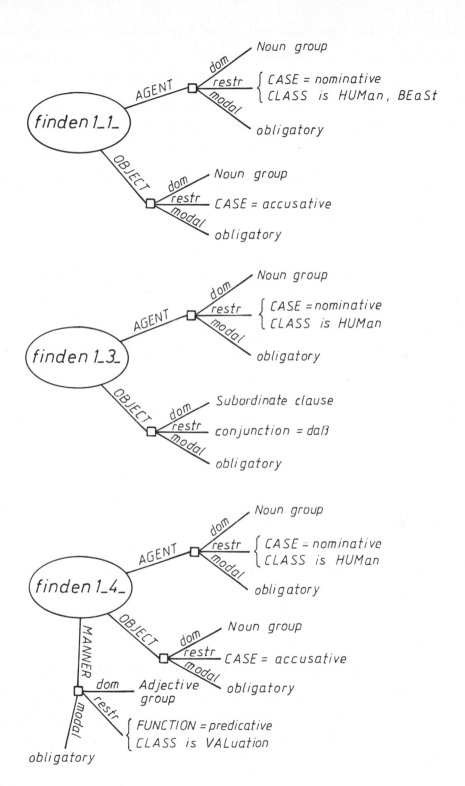

Fig. 9

recognition), to relate paraphrases (that is to map differently worded sentences with equivalent meaning to the same representation), and to support recognition by generation of top-down hypotheses. This is accomplished by three fundamental operations of the Semantics Module which are local interpretation, contextual interpretation, and top-down hypotheses. The realization and performance of these operations will be treated in the following. The reader should note that all examples which follow are taken from German language and are translated word by word. Therefore, the examples may sound awkward to the English speaking reader.

Local interpretation operates on syntactic constituents provided by the Syntax Module. Presently the five constituent types noun group NG, prepositional noun group PNG, adjective group ADJG, verbal group VG, and sentence S are available. The basic idea with local interpretation of the first three constituent types is that certain word classes (like prepositions) impose semantic constraints on other word classes (like nouns) with which they can be combined. These constraints are expressed in the dictionary by the feature SELECTION, which means that a preposition used with a certain meaning 'selects' a noun with a certain meaning.

For example, in the PNG 'mit der Bahn (with the train)' the word 'mit (with)' has four meanings in the dictionary, among them only one with class 'INSTRUMENT' and selection 'THING'. The word 'Bahn (train)' has five meanings, among them only one with class 'TRANSPORT'. Class TRANSPORT is a specialization of class THING, and therefore, the INSTRUMENT meaning of 'mit' is compatible with the TRANSPORT meaning of 'Bahn'. By checking all possible combinations of the different classes and selections, all consistent interpretations are obtained. In the above example it turns out that there is only one compatible combination. Even without a larger context the compatible alternative meanings of a constituent are much less than the combinatorial number. A compatible combination is given two features, the semantic class of the noun and that of the preposition.

Local interpretation of a constituent type VG only consists of generation of case frames of the form shown in Fig. 9. For each meaning of a verb in the dictionary a separate case frame is generated by a preprocessor. This is all that can be done by using the local information of VG only. If a constituent type S is locally interpreted, each individual constituent, that is NG, PNG, ADJG, and VG, is locally interpreted as described above.

The basic idea of contextual interpretation of a sentence or a major part of a sentence is to take the case frame obtained from local interpretation of a VG and to try to match the constituents PNG, NG, ADJG, also obtained from local interpretation, to attributes of the case frame. For a particular verb there usually will be several meanings associated with different case frames. The word 'finden (to find)' has five meanings listed in the dictionary, and the case frames of three of them are shown in Fig. 9. When matching constituents to case frames the number of successful matches will depend on whether a case frame fits to the intended meaning of the verb in the sentence or not. Therefore, a score is computed for each contextual interpretation, and the best scoring interpretation is selected.

The contextual interpretation is realized by three main functions: Frame Sentence Match (FSM), Frame Constituent Match (FCM), and Supplement Contextual Interpretation (SCI). We discuss these functions using the example sentence 'Er findet seine Fahrkarte nicht (word by word translation: He finds his ticket not)'. The Syntax Module yields a syntactic representation which is mapped to the network structure shown in Fig. 10. Since word recognition of the system is not perfect, there may be competing and erroneous word hypotheses which will give rise to several competing syntactic hypotheses. Every syntactic hypothesis has a score which is an estimate of its reliability and importance. The function FSM selects a good scoring syntax hypothesis of type S (sentence), which already was processed by the local interpretation operation. For every case frame of the verb in S an inexact matching operation of type 'concept-instance' is started. The type 'concept-instance' means that the concept of the case frame is matched with the instance S, and as many empty attributes of the case frame

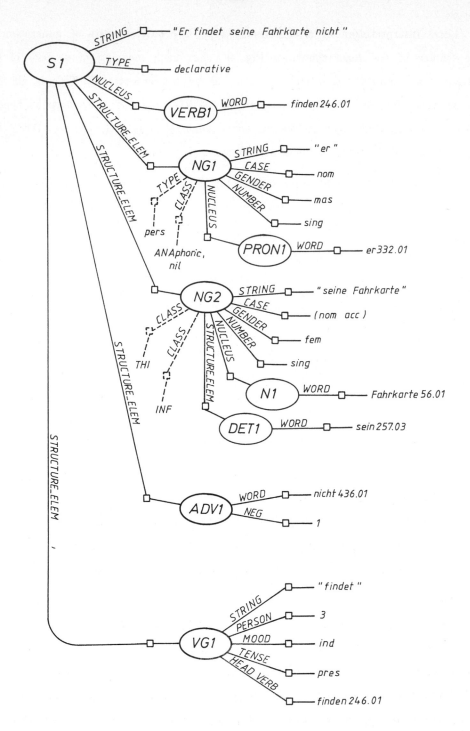

Fig. 10 Network representation of the syntax of an example sentence

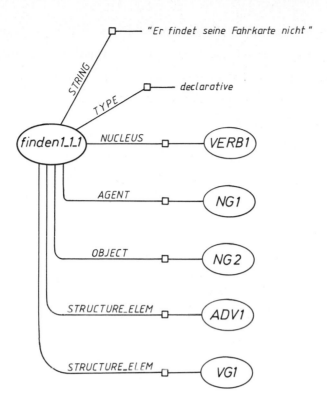

Fig. 11 Result of matching a sentence to a case frame of a verb

are filled by constituents in S as possible. The result is shown in **Fig. 11.** It is apparent that the agent and object attribute of the case frame 'finden 1_1' is matched by NG1 and NG2, respectively, of the sentence S. If 'finden 1_4' were used, the obligatory attribute 'manner' of the case frame could not be matched by S. Therefore, this match is scored less than that of 'finden 1_1' and the meaning of 'finden 1_1' is selected.

Whereas the function FSM requires a syntax hypothesis of type S, the function FCM also accepts syntactic constituents and does not require a complete sentence. FCM was implemented in order to process also intermediate results of the syntax module. The function SCI is used to attach constituents which are not part of the case frame but occur additionally in the sentence (see ADV1 in Fig. 11).

The semantic interpretation is done by local and contextual interpretation as described above. Generation of top-down semantic hypotheses is a feature which is supposed to be useful in speech undertanding but whose performance was not yet tested. The idea is to make predictions on the basis of so far unmatched obligatory attributes of a case frame.

The Pragmatics Module has not yet been implemented, but its operation is specified as shown in Fig. 12. Whereas the Semantics Module extracts general

Pragmatics Module

input: instantiated case frames
select high scoring case frame instance
perform matching of semantic categories to domain dependent concepts
perform matching of semantic deep cases to pragmatic concept roles
infer inquiry type from role structure and from situation dependent expectations
try to fill obligatory attributes of the inquiry concept by inferences and data base requests
output: semantic net representation of user inquiry

Fig. 12   The main steps of pragmatic analysis

linguistic information, the Pragmatics Module relates this to internal task specific knowledge. In our system we chose inquiries about train schedules as an example of a task domain. The relevant knowledge is represented in a semantic net containing five general concepts for five general types of inquiries, for example, inquiries about train connection or seat reservation. Each of the concepts has several obligatory and optional attributes. For example, the concept 'train connection' has obligatory attributes 'source' and 'goal'. Pragmatic analysis will try to match the obligatory attributes of a concept in the pragmatics net to attributes found by semantic analysis (see Fig. 11, where, for example, no source or goal attribute is present). If an obligatory attribute cannot be matched, this will be used to derive a question which the system asks the user.

Pragmatic analysis completes what is meant here by understanding the meaning of an utterance. If this analysis is successful, the acoustic signal is related to the system's internal knowledge.

Future work should explore the following points:

1. Efficient realization of syntactic and pragmatic analysis.
2. Refinement of the ATN grammar.
3. More general and powerful semantic analysis.
4. Thorough experimental investigation of the three modules.

5. GIVING AN ANSWER

Up to now the system always considered only one utterance and tried to recognize and understand it. Obviously this is not sufficient for a system which is supposed to carry out a dialog with a user. In the following short example S refers to utterances of the system, U to those of the user:

U1: When is there a train to Munich?

S1: At what time would you like to start?

U2: As soon as possible.

S2: You may take the train at 12:30 hours.

U3: When does it arrive there?

S3: At 13:45 hours.

U4: Does it have a dining car?

S4: Yes.

These few utterances demonstrate that a dialog is possible only if both partners can assume that some general and common knowledge is available and if they both relate and understand a sequence of utterances, not just one isolated utterance at a time. For example, in U1 the user assumes that the system has a reasonable default value for the starting point of the journey, and so does the system because it does not ask back. In U2 the user also assumes that the system has knowledge about time. Furthermore, U2 (or also S3, S4) are not understandable as isolated utterances, but only in the context of the dialog. The objects referred to by "it" and "there" in U3 have to be determined from S2. With S1 the system pursues a certain intention which is to give the user the train best fitting to the user's goals. There is a uniform topic through U1 to S3 which may be called "inquiries about train schedules", and there is a change of the topic in U4, S4 to "inquiries about an object", in this case about a particular train.

The above few examples demonstrate that finding an answer by the system raises a bulk of new problems. In EVAR these problems are treated by the following modules:

1. The Dialog Module. — It memorizes the context and meaning of a sequence of utterances and relates a new utterance to the former ones, and it determines the components of an adequate answer.

2. The Retrieval Module. — It retrieves the facts (in our case, for example, a departure time) meeting the requests determined by the Dialog Module.

3. The Answer Module. — It translates the internal representation of an answer to a German text. The text may then be printed or spoken by a speech synthesis device. The Dialog Module is specified and an interactive test facility was realized. The main structure of the module is shown in Fig. 13. Some of its functions still have to be realized. The Retrieval Module is presently under development. A version of the Answer Module using an intermediate representation of the answer was realized, but the translation of the output of the Dialog Module to this intermediate representation is not yet available. Fig. 14 gives the main steps of answer generation. Since finding an answer still needs a good deal of additional work, it seems premature to give further details in this paper.

Dialog Module

input: semantic net representation of user inquiry generated by the Pragmatics Module
resolve references and complete elliptic phrases
update memories of syntactic and semantic structures, of actual topic, and of mentioned objects
draw inferences from expectations on actual discourse move
match utterance to discourse scheme in order to determine actual dialog state
choose system reaction: determine content of answer if inquiry is complete, else ask back
update memories by system utterance
output: internal semantic network representation of system utterance

Fig. 13   An overview of the dialog facility in EVAR

Answer Generation Module

input: internal network representation of system utterance
translate network representation to caseframe-oriented intermediate structure
determine morphological surface structure from valency features and deep case rules: noun inflection; pro-form, question form, article selection
generate ellipsis and anaphora
inflect verb by tense and mood
determine phrase order
transform dependency tree to terminal string
output: textual form of answer

Fig. 14   An outline of answer generation

6. CONCLUDING REMARKS

We are convinced that speech understanding and dialog systems will become standard devices at some time, but we are careful not to predict at what time because this will depend to a good deal on the effort of research and development which can be afforded.

The modular structure of EVAR makes the system extremely suited to a multiprocessor realization, but we do not have the resources to achieve this. Presently, the processing up to the word level is done on a DEC PDP 11/34, the remaining processing is done on a CDC CYBER 845.

Concerning the whole system future work will have to consider the following points:

1. Enlargement, refinement, and correction of available linguistic data bases from which specialized knowledge of the modules is derived.
2. Incorporation of prosodic information.
3. Evaluation of user parameters (speak too loud, too fast and so on).
4. More efficient common data base.
5. Investigation and comparison of different control strategies.
6. Improvement of the available processing modules.

ACKNOWLEDGEMENT

The work reported here was partly sponsored by the German "Bundesministerium für Forschung und Technologie (BMFT)" under grant 08 IT 1019. Only the authors are responsible for the contents of this publication.

REFERENCES

1. K. R. Popper, J. C. Eccles, "Das Ich und sein Gehirn," R. Piper, München Zürich, P2.15 und E4.31, 1982.
2. A. Chapanis, "Interactive Human Communication," Scient. American, 232, No. 3, 36-42, 1975.
3. W. A. Lea (ed.), *Trends in Speech Recognition*, Prentice Hall, Englewood Cliffs, N. J., 1980.
4. D. H. Klatt, "Review of the ARPA Speech Understanding Project," J. Acoustical Soc. of America, 62, 1345-1366, 1977.
5. R. De Mori, "Recent Advances in Automatic Speech Recognition," Proc. 4, Int. Joint Conf. Pattern Recognition, Kyoto, Japan, 106-124, 1978.
6. R. De Mori (ed.), Special Issue on Speech Understanding, Information Sciences.
7. L. Bahl, "Recognition of Isolated Word Sentences from a 5000-Word Vocabulary Office Correspondence Task," Proc. ICASSP 83, Boston Mass., 1065, 1983.
8. T. Winograd, *Language as a Cognitive Process*, Vol. 1, Syntax, Addison Wesley, Rading Mass., 1983.
9. H.-W. Hein, Das Erlanger Spracherkennungssystem, Dissertation Universität Erlangen-Nürnberg, Arbeitsberichte des IMMD Band 15, Nr. 15, Erlangen 1982.
10. H. Niemann, "The Erlangen System for Recognition and Understanding of Continuous German Speech," in J. Nehmer (ed.), GI - 12. Jahrestagung, Informatik Fachberichte 57, Springer Berlin, Heidelberg, New York, 330-348, 1982.
11. P. Regel, "A Module for Acoustic-Phonetic Transcription of Fluently Spoken German Speech," IEEE Trans. ASSP-30, 440-450, 1982.
12. P. Regel, Akustisch phonetische Transkription für die automatische Spracherkennung, Dissertation, in preparation.
13. S. B. Davis, P. Mermelstein, "Comparison of Parametric Representations for Monosyllabic Word Recognition in Continuously Spoken Sentences," IEEE Trans. ASSP-28, 357-366, 1980.
14. J. Kittler, K. S. Fu, L. F. Pau, *Pattern Recognition Theory and Applications*, D. Reidel Publ. Comp., Dordrecht Boston London, 569, 1982.
15. J. John, R. Mühlfeld, P. Regel, G. Siller, "Vergleich von Klassifikatoren für die Lauterkennung," to appear in Proc. DAGM-84.
16. F. W. Kaeding (ed.), Häufigkeitswörterbuch der deutschen Sprache, Steglitz bei Berlin 1897-1898. We are grateful to Dr. Ruske who made available to us a tape with 8000 words.
17. D. W. Shipman, V. W. Zue, "Summary of Research in Speech Recognition," Res. Lab. of Electronics, M.I.T., Cambridge Mass., 1982.
18. L. R. Bahl, F. Jelinek, "Decoding for Channels with Insertions, Deletions, and Substitutions with Applications to Speech Recognition," IEEE Trans. IT-21, 404-411, 1975.
19. L. R. Bahl, F. Jelinek, R. L. Mercer, "A Maximum Likelihood Approach to Continuous Speech Recognition," IEEE Trans. PAMI-5, 179-190, 1983.

20. A. R. Smith, Word Hypothesization in a Large-Vocabulary Speech Understanding System, Ph.D. Dissertation Dept. Computer Science, Carnegie Mellon University, Pittsburgh, PA, 1977.
21. H. Niemann, *Pattern Analysis*, Springer Series in Information Sciences 4, Springer, Berlin Heidelberg New York, 1981.
22. R. J. Brachman, A Structural Paradigm for Representing Knowledge,

A NEW RULE-BASED EXPERT SYSTEM FOR SPEECH RECOGNITION

G. Mercier, M. Gilloux, C. Tarridec and J. Vaissiere

CNET

Route de Trégastel

22301 Lannion

FRANCE

I   INTRODUCTION

SERAC (Expert System for Acoustic-phonetic Recognition) is an Expert System that applies Artificial Intelligence techniques to Automatic Speech Recognition.

Rule-based Speech Recognition Systems like the KEAL C.N.E.T. System MERCIER 82 have now become too much complicated to be implemented in the form of classical sequential programs. A new methodology is required to express the knowledge of human experts which is not always well formalized. Furthermore computer programs must be developed in an environment that makes it possible an incremental improvement of the knowledge.

The Experts Systems methodology has been successfully applied to such different problems as medical diagnosis MYCIN SHORTLIFE 76, mass spectrograms interpretation (DENDRAL BUCHANAN 71), geological classification (PROSPECTOR DUDA 82) and speech understanding (HEARSAY-II HAYES-ROTH 77, CARBONELL 84, DE MORI 82). These studies have shown that it is possible to build tools that can take into account great amounts of empirical knowledge to solve problems in very specific domains.

NATO ASI Series, Vol. F16
New Systems and Architectures for Automatic Speech
Recognition and Synthesis. Edited by R. De Mori and C. Y. Suen
© Springer-Verlag Berlin Heidelberg 1985

The SERAC system was designed to structure the knowledge acquired with previous experience with the KEAL system and to provide a flexible tool for maintaining, improving and growing this knowledge. Since the whole knowledge required to build a Speech Understanding System is too wide to be taken into consideration all at once we decided to restrain our domain to the acoustic-phonetic analysis of the speech signal as a first step.

Our first task was to define a representation language for the KEAL acoustic phonetic knowledge. An object-oriented problem-driven rule-based language of the class of the OPS family (FORGY 81) appeared to be the most appropriate for this purpose. The production rule formalism was chosen for its ability to express domain expertise in a declarative way. A problem-driven forward chaining inference engine was introduced for encoding the problem resolution strategy into the language.

II REVIEW OF THE KEAL SYSTEM

II-1 SYSTEM ORGANIZATION

The KEAL Speech Understanding System has been developed to investigate the possibility of using voice as a communication support between a user and a computer for several tasks.

The present version of this system (Fig. 1) can be described as a set of components which successively perform the acoustic, phonetic, lexical and syntactic analysis in order to reconstitute the uttered sentence from the speech signal.

The comprehension part of the system involves a semantic interpreter and a dialogue manager able to perform automatic inquiry in a limited domain.

The speaker adaptation component of the system involves a matching program for extracting the new phonetic segment references and adjusting of the phonetic parameter representing the acoustic-phonetic knowledge. In the case of mapping errors (less than 10%) the limits of the segments have to be adjusted by

305

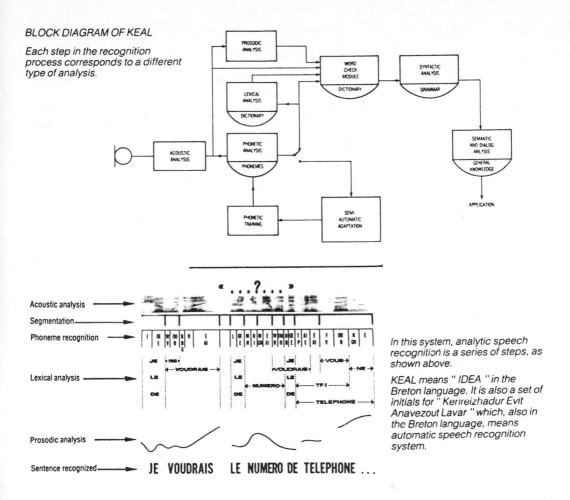

BLOCK DIAGRAM OF KEAL

Each step in the recognition
process corresponds to a different
type of analysis.

Acoustic analysis

Segmentation

Phoneme recognition

Lexical analysis

Prosodic analysis

Sentence recognized ——→ JE VOUDRAIS LE NUMERO DE TELEPHONE ...

In this system, analytic speech
recognition is a series of steps, as
shown above.

KEAL means " IDEA " in the
Breton language. It is also a set of
initials for " Kenreizhadur Evit
Anavezout Lavar " which, also in
the Breton language, means
automatic speech recognition
system.

Fig. 1   THE KEAL SYSTEM

hand.

II-2 ACOUSTIC-PHONETIC DECODING

II-2-1 PREPROCESSING AND FEATURE EXTRACTION

Acoustic-phonetic decoding transforms the continuous speech signal into a series of discrete hypotheses. The units currently taken into account by the Keal phonetic analyzer are the syllable, the phoneme, the phone and the feature.

In a first step, a spectral analysis of the digitized signal is made every 13.3 ms using a simulated channel vocoder (14 or 16 filter banks). The energies within each frequency band are computed by a signal processing routine computing a 256-point D.F.T. and using a 20 ms window. This analysis results in a series of vectors with n components called samples or frames. In parallel, a few additional parameters are associated with each 13.3 ms frame, namely signal amplitude, pitch, energy and spectral center of gravity measurements within selected frequency bands.

The other parameters used are the spectral derivative with respect to time and the frequencies and amplitude of the first three maxima of the vocoder spectrum and the zero-crossings measurements.

Segmentation of continuous speech into phonetic units as well as labelling are progressively refined through the following steps (Fig. 2) by using this set of parameters.

II-2-2 CENTISECOND FRAME LABELLING

Based on a set of acoustic cues derived from these parameters, a set of phonetic features such as vowel, consonant, silence, fricative, open, closed, front, back, voiced, unvoiced, buzz-bar is assigned to each centisecond frame. The rules used for this primary labelling based on spectral information are speaker-independent and relatively simple.

SEGMENTATION AND RECOGNITION

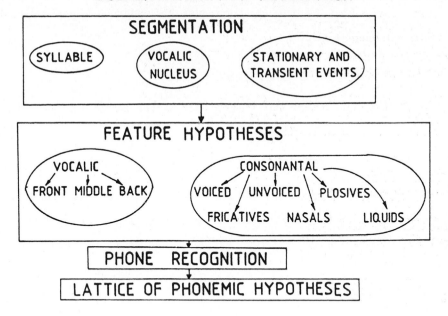

Figure 2

By computing linear decision functions between phone prototypes and a speech frame represented by the spectrum plus the additional parameters this classification is refined (Fig. 3).

II-2-3 SEGMENTATION INTO PSEUDO-SYLLABLES

The basic principle behind this segmentation is the search for the syllable's vowel nucleus; this is done in three steps:

1. First, the energy curve measuring the weighted energy in the frequency band 250-4200 Hz is split into consecutive segments computed each containing an energy maximum (Fig. 4). Consecutive segments, for which there is not a significant maximum of energy in low frequency (250-850 Hz) are concatenated.

2. These segments or pseudo-syllables, are then investigated in order to see whether or not they contain a vocalic nucleus. The following acoustic features are computed:

   — The low frequency energies measured at four instant of time corresponding respectively, to the peaks of the preceeding and current pseudo-syllables and to the minima of energy before and after the current peak of energy.

   — The amplitudes of the first formant computed at the same instants of time.

   — The number of "vowel" frames in the pseudo-syllables.

   — A measure of dissimilarity between the current potential vocalic nucleus and the preceeding one.

   — A feature indicating the presence of a significant proportion of "voiced" frames surrounded by "unvoiced" frames.

CENTISECOND PHONE LABELLING

SELECTION OF THE NUMBER OF PHONES: m
SPECTRAL FEATURE EXTRACTION AND SAMPLE
   VECTOR REPRESENTATION: $\chi(t)$
USE OF LINEAR DECISION FUNCTIONS: $Fi(t)=Ki(\chi(t))$
SELECTION OF THE THREE LARGEST VALUES $Fi(t)$,
   GIVING THE THREE MOST LIKELY PHONETIC
   LABELS.

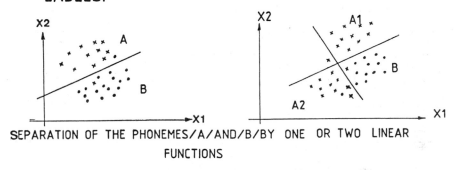

SEPARATION OF THE PHONEMES/A/AND/B/BY ONE OR TWO LINEAR
FUNCTIONS

Figure 3

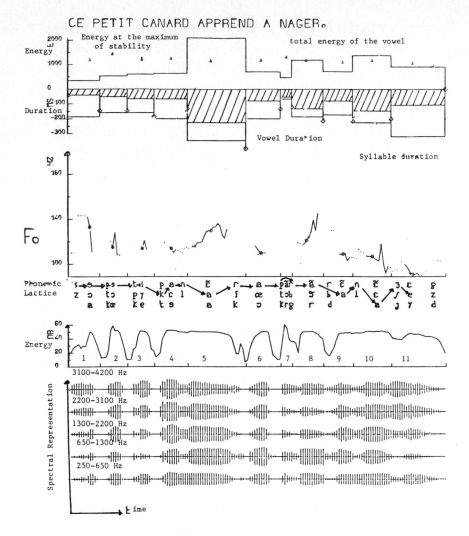

Segmentation into Syllables (after D. Bigorgne)

Figure 4

A value measuring the plausibility of there being a vocalic nucleus in the "potential" pseudo-syllable is computed by means of a linear combination of these features. When this plausibility value is equal to zero, the current segment is merged with the preceeding pseudo-syllable.

3.   At the end of this process, the boundaries of the pseudo-syllable are determined. This is done by taking the stationary portion between two vocalic nuclei which contains the least energy and designating its first frame as the boundary.

Segmentation is about 95% correct when sentences are uttered normally. Results are little lower for rapid speech.

II-2-4 SEGMENTATION INTO PHONES

An obvious property of the speech signal is that it is composed of a sequence of stationary or transient events that can be displayed for instance, by the magnitude of the derivative with respect to time, P(t), of the spectral envelope (Fig. 5). Consecutive low values of P(t) delimit a stationary portion in the signal, which may contain the main features for certain phonemes, whereas high values of this curve indicate a transient event between phones which may include essential features of one or both of these phones.

In Keal, vowels are first located within the stationary zone around the maximum of energy of each syllable. In addition this zone must contain a sufficient proportion of vowel "frames". Then sequences of stationary and transient events are located between each vocalic nucleus. These segments form the new framework within which the main phonetic features will be identified.

II-2-5 VOWEL RECOGNITION

Based upon an idea proposed by STEVENS (1981) and adapted to our spectral data by R. Gubrynowicz (1983) acoustic cues measuring spectral areas between a line coresponding to the amplitude of the first formant (or the second formant) and the spectrum curve between some frequency band are used for

PHONETIC RECOGNITION

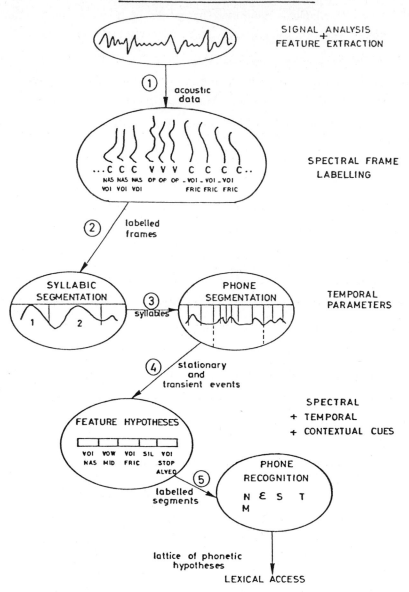

Figure 5

separating the french vowels into the following categories: open, closed, mid and front, back, central. A second algorithm [ROSSI 81] based on the notion of distinctive vowel features, permits a hierarchical recognition of vowels. In a vowel recognition experiment using isolated words pronounced by three speakers, ROSSI found that the correct vowel was among the top two choices about 90% of the time.

This feature-based vowel recognition, which has to be improved for continuous speech, is not still completely integrated in the KEAL system. Speaker-dependent linear decision functions are used to assign one or more labels to each 13.3 ms frame. Labels that are assigned with a high frequency in the vocalic segments are stored in the final phonetic lattice. This procedure of frame labelling also makes it possible to detect diphthongs and sequences of two vowels that have been incorrrectly merged into a single segment (Fig. 6). We compute the temporal center of gravity along the time axis for each of the phone candidates. If the temporal center of gravity of any the phone candidates within a segment is sufficiently far away in time from those of other candidates, two segments may be detected. In order to confirm the existence of two segments in such a case, center of gravity, degree of opening or place of articulation parameters must have changed within the segment.

II-2-6 CONSONANT RECOGNITION

The following procedure is used for recognizing "consonant" segments.

— For each stationary segment placed between two vocalic nucleus, the proportion of "voiced" and "unvoiced" frames is measured. If this segment corresponds to a phone, then the degree of voicedness or voicelessness is given by this measure. Conversely, for stops, for instance, a second cue of voice onset time (V.O.T.) may be necessary when there is no buzz-bar. This cue is measured within the transient segment. In KEAL, V.O.T. is a function of the number of voiced or unvoiced frames at the beginning of the burst. The percentage of correct identification of the voiced-unvoiced feature is about 95%.

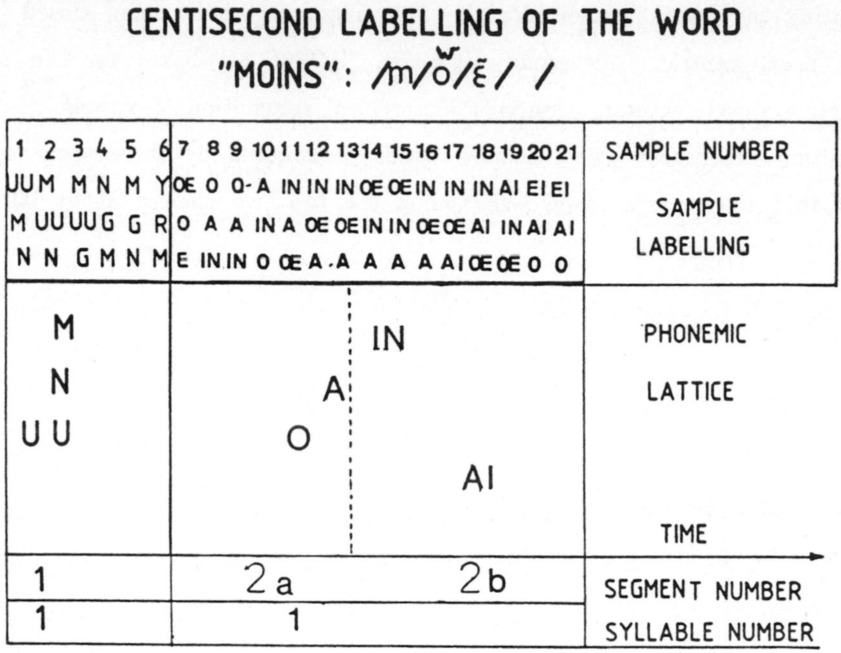

CENTISECOND LABELLING OF THE WORD
"MOINS": /m/õ̆/ɛ̃/ /

1 2 3 4 5 6	7 8 9 10 11 12 13 14 15 16 17 18 19 20 21		SAMPLE NUMBER
UUM M N M Y	Œ O O- A IN IN IN Œ ŒIN IN IN AI EI EI		SAMPLE
M UUUUG G R	O A A IN A Œ ŒIN IN Œ Œ AI IN AI AI		LABELLING
N N G M N M	E IN IN O Œ A . A A A A A AI Œ Œ O O		
M N U U	O	IN A AI	PHONEMIC LATTICE TIME
1	2 a	2 b	SEGMENT NUMBER
1	1		SYLLABLE NUMBER

Figure 6

315

— The feature "stop is detected when a zone of silence or weak low frequency energy (buzz-bar) is included in the stationary segment and followed by a strong burst and a sudden variation of the spectral parameters (energies and centers of gravity of formants). The percentage of incorrect identification of this feature is about 5%.

— The feature "fricative" is assigned if the segment is composed of enough frames with the label "fricative"; and the rule condition for assigning the "fricative" label to a frame is: "The spectral center of gravity and zero-crossings must be higher than some fixed thresholds".

— A stationary segment will be labelled "nasal" if it is composed of enough "potentially nasal spectral frames" and if some contextual and temporal criteria hold for each frame (GUBRYNOWICZ, 1984).

— A liquid /l/ or /r/ will be detected after a plosive sound if there is at least one maximum in the energy curve together with enough energy at low frequencies. Fig. 7 gives performance of recognition of a few feature classes.

— Recognition of the place of articulation of plosives is under way. For the moment, three main cues are taken into consideration: change in the first spectral center of gravity, the frequency region in which the spectral maximum of energy of the burst is located and change in the amplitude of the signal during the burst. The current performance is about 70% correct identification for a few speakers continuous speech.

— A refinement of this ordered labelling and final generation of phonetic hypotheses is provided by a "pattern matching" approach where prototypes depend upon a speaker or upon a category of speakers if they are obtained by clustering methods.

PERFORMANCE OF A FEW FEATURE CLASSES

	TOTAL NUMBER OF SEGMENTS	NUMBER OF ERRORS	NO DECISION	NUMBER OF MISSED SEGM.	NUMBER OF SPEAKERS
VOICING	145	10	6		3: 1F, 2M
NASAL CONSONANT	116	16	0		8: 3F, 5M
VOICELESS FRICATIVE	77	0	1	1	5: 1F, 4M
VOICELESS STOP	78	1	1	1(Spreading)	3: 1F, 2M
VOICED STOP	39	2	15	0	3: 1F, 2M

DATA: Different Kinds of Continuous Speech Utterances
(Mostly Phonetically Balanced French Sentences

Figure 7

Linear discriminant functions for the phone inventory are computed from twenty phonetically balanced sentences. These functions divide the R^n space where the phone references are represented and make it possible to assign a phone label to each phonetic segment found in the utterance. Within each segment, multiple phones candidates are ranked by their degree of confidence.

Following this procedure, a new set of rules combines the decisions of the feature-based hierarchical process and of the discriminant approach in order to get the final phonemic label.

II-2-7 BUILDING THE PHONEMIC LATTICES

The output of the phonetic analyzer is given in the form of segments, each with the following information: reliability value, beginning and ending time of the segment, candidate phonemes ranked by likelihood score, number of the syllable to which the segment belongs. This lattice is then given to a word spotter able to make hypotheses or verifications about the possible sequence of words in an utterance.

Fig. 8 gives an example of phonetic recognition obtained by the phonetic analyzer.

II-2-8 PHONETIC KNOWLEDGE ACQUISITION AND SPEAKER ADAPTATION

In order to evaluate the coefficients of the linear discriminant functions used to separate the phoneme classes, the following procedure has been designed.

— The phonetic segment references necessary for building the learning set are automatically extracted by using a matching program that maps the acoustic phonetic lattice given by the phonetic analyzer onto an ideal phonemic transcription of the words or sentences of the refrence data set and onto their corresponding acoustic representation (Fig. 9). In case of mapping errors (less than 10%) the limits of the segments have eventually to be adjusted (or deleted) by hand, then providing the correct acoustic samples (Fig. 10).

318

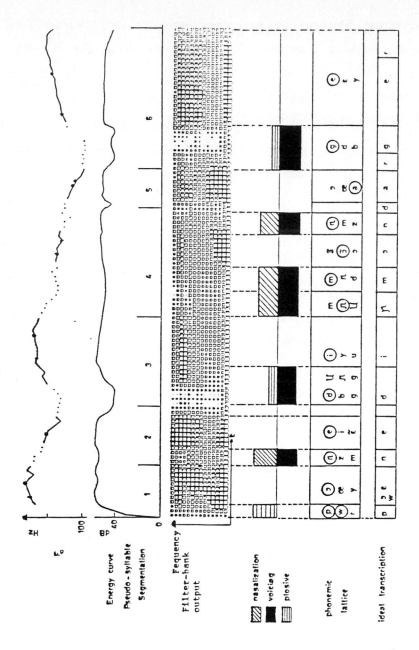

Results of applying KEAL to a Breton sentence : "poent eo din
mont d'ar guer"...) "it is time to go home".

Figure 8

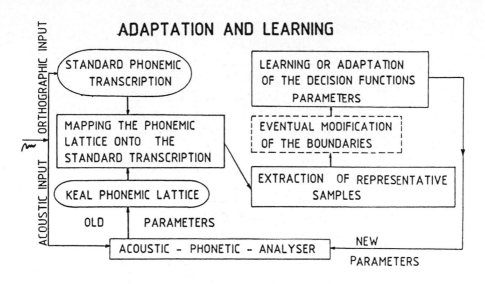

Figure 9

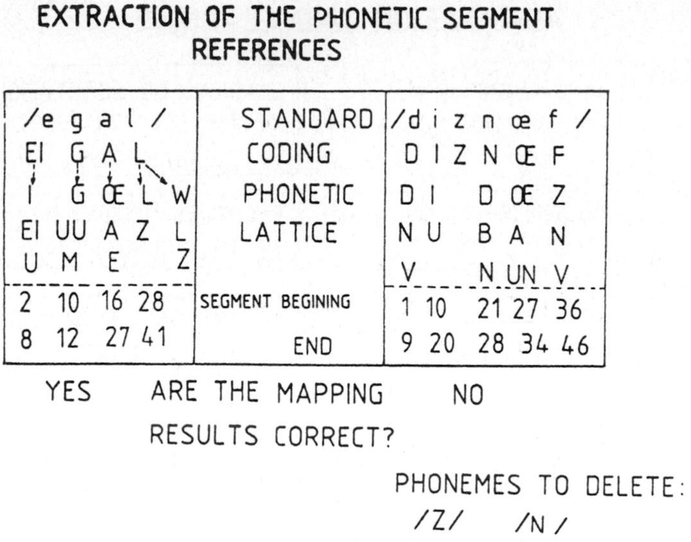

EXTRACTION OF THE PHONETIC SEGMENT REFERENCES

/e g a l /	STANDARD	/d i z n œ f /
EI G A L	CODING	D I Z N Œ F
I G Œ L W	PHONETIC	D I D Œ Z
EI UU A Z L	LATTICE	N U B A N
U M E Z		V N UN V
2 10 16 28	SEGMENT BEGINING	1 10 21 27 36
8 12 27 41	END	9 20 28 34 46

YES   ARE THE MAPPING   NO

RESULTS CORRECT?

PHONEMES TO DELETE:

/Z/   /N /

Automatic alignment of Speech with a
Standard Phonetic Transcription

Figure 10

II-2-9 RESULTS

A recognition experiment was run on a few speakers' productions of continuously spoken, phonetically balanced sentences, without top-down information and using only the best choice for each segment in the phonemic lattice, a phonemic recognition rate of 55 to 60 percent was achieved. This rate is still too low, but what is interesting is that the recognition rate rises to 70% and 80% when the top two and three choices within the phoneme lattice are taken into consideration, respectively. Fig. 11 shows percentage of phonetic recognition and syllabic segmentation.

II-4 LEXICAL ANALYSIS

The role of the lexical analyzer is to match each word of the task vocabulary against the phonemic lattice, in order to detect the word in the sentence.

For achieving this goal, each word of the task vocabulary is given an ideal phonemic representation. If a word can have many pronunciations, phonological rules are used to expand the lexicon in order to include all possible pronunciations.

During the matching process, a matrix is built, its rows corresponding to the phonemes of the word to be searched and its column to the consecutive segements of the phonetic lattice. An element (i, j) of the matrix is set to 1 if the phoneme lying in the ith row appears in the list corresponding to the jth column. Each 1 denotes a possible starting point for a detection of the word. Each 1 is a possible end point. The whole matrix is searched for paths which connect a starting point and an end point and pass through a set of (i, j) cells of the matrix. These cells must contain the number one and have increasing values of i and j. Each such path corresponds to a word detection. Each detection then receives a similarity score w (with $0 \leq w \leq 1$) which takes into account the degree of confidence for each segment and for each phoneme in the segment. Phoneme deletion, phoneme insertion, spreading or merging are also taken into account for computing this similarity score. The detection boundaries

PERCENTAGE OF PHONETIC RECOGNITION AND SYLLABIC SEGMENTATION

TOTAL NUMBER	220	385	695	635
RECOGNITION PERCENTAGE :1	60%	65%	55,1%	59 %
RECOGNITION PERCENTAGE :1+2	78,1	85,5%	74,6%	73.5 %
RECOGNITION PERCENTAGE :1+2+3	86,8	94,7%	85%	78.7
NUMBER OF SYLLABLES	85	232	275	
SYLLABIC SEGMENTATION	97,7%	96%	97,5%	
SPEAKER	1	1	2	3
TASK	RECOGNITION OF NUMBERS			30 PHONETICALLY BALANCED SENTENCES

Figure 11

are then adjusted to the syllable boundaries in order to simplify the sentence recognition process. Only detections with scores higher than a fixed threshold are kept for the sentence recognition step, in a word-lattice.

II-5 PROSODIC ANALYSIS

Using both fundamental frequency values and the duration of the vocalic nuclei determined by the phonetic analyzer, the prosodic module is able to find the main boundary of a sentence in which no pause has been automatically detected. This algorithm works like this (Fig. 13).

— A window of the size of three syllables is used to determine whether the central syllable is carrying a basic prosodic primary (P.P.C.) in terms of the durational variations of the three successive nuclei within the window and in terms of a particular shape of Fo contour across the nuclei: the vocalic nuclei corresponding to a local peak of durational contrast, and/or to a local peak of Fo contrast, and the vocalic nuclei with using Fo modulation are selected.

— Then they are ranked by order of decreasing value at the level of the sentence.

— The vocalic nucleus of the sentence with the longest duration is selected and if this nucleus is located at the end of the sentence, then it is replaced by the second largest nucleus.

— If this vocalic nucleus contains the highest or the second highest Fo peak, or the largest or the second largest Fo rise on a vowel, then it is interpreted as the main boundary in the utterance.

On a total number of 253 sentences of various types spoken by 7 speakers this algorithm has correctly detected the main boundary for 80% of the sentences; 15% have not been segmented and there is 5% errors (VAISSIERE 83).

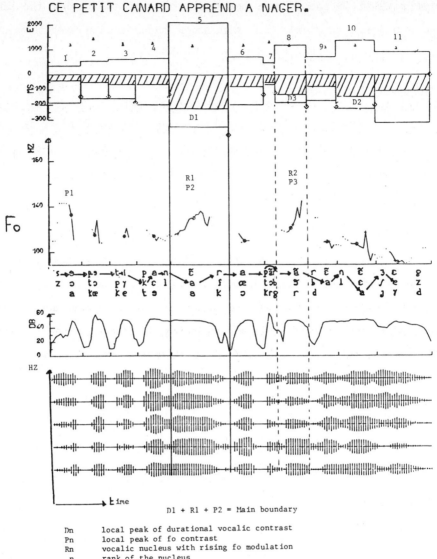

Figure 13

II-6 SYNTACTIC ANALYSIS

The role of the sentence recognizer is to search for the best sequence of word-detections of the word-lattice satisfying the grammatical constraints and to build the syntactic tree of the sentence. This algorithm has already been described in great detail (QUINTON, 1976). Briefly the language is described by a semantic context-free grammar and the parsing is based on EARLEY's algorithm. In addition, in order to avoid looking through the whole lexical lattice, only the best partial solutions are kept at each step, according to either a beam-search or a sequential decoding strategy. The result of the parsing, if any, is the recognized sentence associated with a score and a parse-tree.

Then the role of the semantic interpreter is to get from the parse-tree the information needed for the dialogue-controller. This is achieved by a set of transformation rules associated with the syntactic rules. The result of these transformations is a set of n-uplets containing only that in the sentence which is relevant to the dialogue. This comprehension part of KEAL has been described in detail in GILLET 1982.

II-7 RECOGNITION OF WORDS AND SENTENCES

Preliminary results, when using the lexical analyzer of KEAL, give a word recognition rate varying from 88% to 98% on a limited vocabulary (19 French digits and operands).

The programs corresponding to phonetic analysis, phonetic training, speaker adaptation and lexical word spotting are presently written in Fortran IV language and implemented on a SEMS M.225 mini computer. The speech data are digitalized through an A/D connected to a PDP 11/34 computer converter and the program simulating the channel vocoder and the pitch detection are implemented on an A.P. 120 B connected to the PDP 11/34. The spectral data are then transferred to the M-225 mini-computer.

Another version of KEAL including the syntactic analyzer is available on the U.T.S. systems of the new computer IBM 308 3/B of the computer center. It is written in C language. A Fortran version of this system has been tested on a set of randomly selected numbers composed of one to six digits spoken by three speakers. The results are shown in Fig. 14. Further testing will be necessary with this new version.

III SERAC SYSTEM ARCHITECTURE

III-1 GENERAL ORGANIZATION,

The SERAC system architecture uses the classical features of a rule production system. Rules that encode domain knowledge are stored in a data base, called Rule Memory, which is partitioned into sub-bases, each sub-base corresponding to a problem.

Objects that represent facts or event hypotheses are stored in an Object Memory which is divided into sub-memories corresponding to the different classes of objects.

Problem Memory contains interpretation problems whose solution will generate phonetic hypotheses such as segment boundaries detection, feature hypotheses, pseudo-syllable segmentation, vocalic nucleus detection and so on ...

Remaining entities like functions, parameters and acoustic data are encoded respectively under the form of Lisp functions, Lisp special variables (parameters) and files.

An inference Engine matches rules against problems and objects and decides which rules have to be triggered in a given circumstance.

The dialog between the user and the system is managed by an Interactive Editor. Edition of partial or complete results and triggering traces are handled by a special module.

SENTENCE RECOGNITION RESULTS

TASK	NUMBERS 0,...1000		
RECOGNITION PERCENTAGE	90%	75%	85%
NUMBER OF SENTENCES	50	40	40
SPEAKER	A	B	C

Figure 14

Fig. 15 shows the general organization of the SERAC system.

III-2 ACTIVATION

The "SERAC" phonetic recognition is decomposed into a sequence of step activations: initialization, labelling, segmentation and primary phonetic feature recognition.

The principal phases of these step activations are summarized in Fig. 16. Each module communicates with each other by means of acoustic objects like samples syllables, phonetic events and so on ... which are in the data base: these different steps are detailed in section VI.

IV THE LANGUAGE FOR EXPRESSING KNOWLEDGE

The expert's knowledge of acoustic-phonetic recognition consists of the following:

1. knowledge of domain objects (acoustic signal, samples, syllables, phonemes, etc...).

2. knowledge of the methods for phonetically transcribing the acoustic signal (algorithms, heuristics, etc...).

The objects represent the hypotheses elaborated or facts established during the recognition process and define, at a given instant the state of advancement of this process.

These objects are created or transformed through type 2 knowledge.

They are explicitly represented in a memory called the object memory.

Type 2 knowledge is coded in the form of:

— production rules
— Lisp functions evaluated in the rules

ORGANIZATION OF SERAC

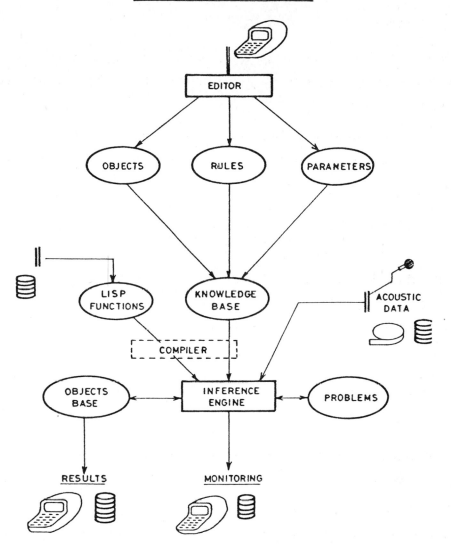

Figure 15

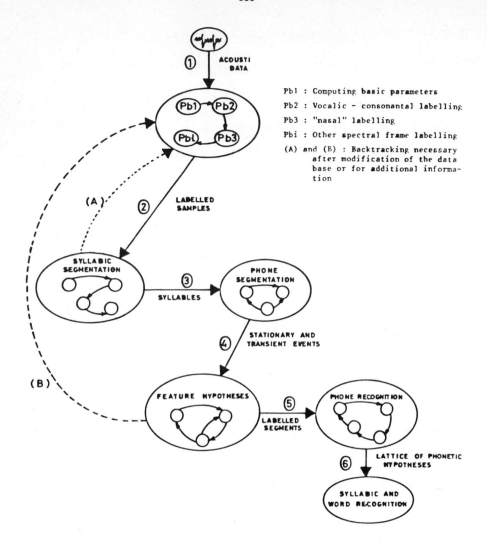

Pb1 : Computing basic parameters
Pb2 : Vocalic - consonantal labelling
Pb3 : "nasal" labelling
Pbi : Other spectral frame labelling
(A) and (B) : Backtracking necessary
    after modification of the data
    base or for additional informa-
    tion

Main step activations of a rule-based phonetic
recognizer

Figure 16

IV-1 THE OBJECTS

The objects are representatives or instances of structures in the form:

(< class > < atttribute 1 > ... < attribute n >)
as for a sample, for example:
(sample beginning end energy-vector ...)
A given sample will then be an object :
(sample 11 22 (1 2 0 3 4 0 2 3 2) ...)

Object structures are declared in a file (See functional architecture of the system) according to the syntax:

class = / attribute /+

IV-2 THE FUNCTIONS

IV-2-1 PRIMITIVE OPERATIONS OF THE LANGUAGE

Certain operations stem more from general knowledge than from expertise in the domain; these are, for example, arithmetic operations $(+, - x, :)$, logical operations (and, or, negation), arithmetic predicatives $(>, <, =, <>, \geq, \leq)$.

The operations are the primitives of the language expression knowledge, used as their Lisp equivalent.

IV-2-2 EXTENSIONS OF PRIMITIVES

Some expert knowledge corresponds to a purely algorithmic and procedural basic know-how of the domain which can easily be expressed in the form of Lisp functions, such as the computation of energy in a frequency band [f1, fh] from the vector v of energies in a sample,

This computation is made by the Lisp evaluation of:

(energy in the band fl fh v)

This use of functions permits access to value through computation rather than explicit storage, in the form of object attributes.

The expertise itself is expressed in the form of production rules:

condition ——————— action

Modular knowledge can be easily expressed with this type of representation. Its accumulation can constitute a veritable expertise.

Moreover, the knowledge base, composed of the set of rules, evolves easily by removal or addition.

Lastly, each elementary part of the knowledge appears by itself within a rule and is therefore not lost, as an instruction would be in the heart of a fortran program, for example.

Rules are in the form:

NAME	sequence of characters used as mnemonic name for the rule in question
EXPERT	expert
PROBLEM	problem
IF	context
AND	condition
THEN	conclusion

Such a rule expresses that, for a data base situation (object memory, list of problems) which can be described by < expert >, < problem >, < context > and < condition >, this data bsse can be updated in compliance with < conclusion > directives.

IV-3-2-1 THE EXPERT

The knowledge base can be divided up into sub-bases made up of rules having the same expert name.

Each sub-base must both be able to be activated in parallel with the other sub-bases and to dialogue with them through the object memory.

Examples of sub-bases (or experts):

— beginning-and-end-of-speech-detector
— pseudo-syllable-detector.

IV-3-2-2 THE PROBLEM

Each expert possesses a list of current problems.

Each of these problems can be procesed by one of the expert's subsets of rules.

At a given instant only those rules for which the problem is one of the expert's current problems can be activated.

Example of problems for the "pseudosyllable-detector" expert:

— detection-of-the-beginning-of-a-pseudosyllable.
— detection-of-the-pseudosyllable-maximum.
— detection-of-the-end-of-the-pseudosyllable.

IV-3-2-3 THE CONTEXT

The context part tests the presence in the data base of objects described by patterns.

A data base situation can be described by the context part if:

— for each of the patterns, there exists an object in the data base which can be described by it.

— for each of the negative patterns, there is no object existing in the data base which can be described by it.

In these cases, the variables contained in the context part are related to the values of the objects or attributes which they describe.

IV-3-2-4 THE CONDITION PART

When the presence of certain objects in the data base has been tested by the context part, all of the pattern variables are bound.

The condition part, a logical conjunction of conditions, verifies then certain relationships between these variables.,

If, for example, the variables ?a and ?b are respectively bound to 10 and 20, the condition part:

(> ?b ?a)

is verified and the rule is applicable.

IV-3-2-5 THE CONCLUSION PART OR DIRECTIVES

When a rule is triggered, it carries out a certain number of actions (modifications in the object memory, list of problems, edition of results, etc...). These are expressed in the form of directives using the instanciations of variables realized in the context part : The main directives are : ADD, REMOVE, MODIFY objects; DO procedures; PRINT patterns; STOP; ADD, NEW or REMOVE Problems.

There is another very useful directive which allows to search for one or more objects within the data base by "pattern matching". This directive is the directive "FIND". It is possible for instance to find all the samples with the attribute "Fricative true" within the data base.

V THE RULE ACTIVATION

The rule interpreter is that part of the system which decides upon and carries out the activation of certain rules.

V-1 THE BASIC CYCLE

The basic cycle discussed in this paragraph is specific to a given expert and does not take into account the simultaneous activation of the different experts.

1. As long as there remains an applicable rule R

> 1.1 search for the set of applicable rules
>
> 1.2 choose one of these rules (conflict resolution)
>
> 1.3 trigger the chosen rule (modifications in the object memory, in the list of problems).

2. Stop

V-2 APPLICABLE RULES

A rule is applicable if the problem that it deals with belongs to the current list of problems of the expert concerned and if the facts memory can be described by its context and conclusion parts.

V-3 CONFLICT RESOLUTION

When several rules are applicable during a given cycle of the rule interpreter, one of them must be selected for activation: this is the conflict resolution procedure.

This choice may be arbitrary or it may depend upon meta-knowledge.

The current version of SERAC (the first rule found) uses an arbitrary conflict resolution.

VI IMPLEMENTATION OF PHONETIC AND PROSODIC ANALYSIS IN SERAC

In the current version of SERAC two main experts corresponding to the first part of phonetic and prosodic knowledge have been implemented.

Current state of the phonetic analysis expert which includes more than three hundred rules is shown on Figure 17.

The phonetic recognition proceeds sequentially by step:

1. Reading each spectral sample and computing its attributes: spectral center of gravity, spectral standard deviation, low and high frequencies energies, derivatives, etc...
2. Detecting the sentence onset.
3. Setting the centisecond sample attributes: vowel, front, back, open, closed, consonant, nasal, fricative, silence.
4. Grouping of samples into pseudo-syllables.
5. Locating vocalic nuclei, detecting syllabic boundaries and computing their attributes.
6. Detecting the boundaries of stationary and transient events between the vocalic nuclei.
7. Computing the rudimentary phonetic attributes of these events: silence part, burst zone, fricative zone, nasal part, buzz-bar location, voicing segment...

These different steps are iterated each time it is possible until the sentence offset is detected and until the directive stop is given by one of the rules.

The implementation of the rules for discriminating between vowel attack and plosive burst, for recognizing the place of articulation of plosives and nasals and for refining the vowel identifiction is under way.

About fifty prosodic rules for detecting within a sentence the maxima and the minima of the vocalic durations, the peaks and the valleys of Fo, for ranking these attributes by decreasing order and for detecting the type of the sentence and its main boundary has been written in SERAC with the results given in Section II.5.

An example showing how the phonetic knowledge is represented in a rule is given in Figure 18.

VII FUNCTIONING OF SERAC

SERAC is written in NIL on a VAX 11-780 running VMS. An interactive editor allows us to add, create, modify rules, objects and parameters: During the running session it is also possible to have partial or complete traces of the instanciations of the rules and objects, to stop the execution, to save the data base memory, to modify rules or objects and to start again. Backtracking is also possible; i.e., it is possible to start one, two or n cycles before we stop. All these facilities are obtained through a "menu" organized like a tree.

The SERAC language is also compilable; each file can be compiled simultaneously or separately. This compilation makes an execution of the program much faster. For instance, the "SERAC" phonetic recognition as described in Fig. 17 takes about 1′ CPU time for analyzing a sentence composed of about 12 syllables. Digitalization and channel vocoder simulationa are done before and off-line on the PDP 11/34 and AP/120B processor. Current percentage of correct segmentation and primary phonetic feature recognition is similar to that obtained with the KEAL system.

CONCLUSION

Work is going on for including into SERAC the remaining rules which already exist in KEAL, for improving them and adding new ones possibly elaborated by other human experts. Then this new phonetic and prosodic knowledge base will be evaluated on a practical task.

'SERAC' PHONETIC RECOGNITION

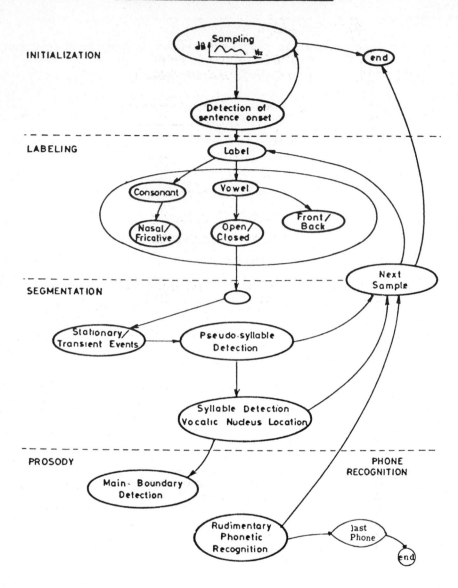

Figure 17

(DEFRULE R1-NASALITY
    SAMPLE
    LABELLING
	name of the rule
	name of the module
	current problem

IF
(SAMPLE ?ECH (ENERGIES ?EN)
  (ENERGY-LOW-FREQUENCY ?PEB)
  (CENTER-OF-GRAVITY ?CDG)
	CONTEXT PART OF THE RULE
	If there exists a sample represented by the variable ?ech, with spectral energies represented by the vector ?en, with the low frequency energy (250-450 Hz) represented by ?EB and with a spectral center of gravity represented by ?CDG

AND (> (— ?EB (MAX-ENERGY 450 1600 ?EN)) 1)	CONDITIONS: 1. The difference between the energy in the frequency range 250-450 Hz and the energy in the frequency range 450-1600 Hz must be higher than 1 (that is higher than 4 dB because the unit step of coding the energies is 4 dB)
(≥ (— ?EB (ENERGY 650 850 ? EN)) 3)	2. $E_{250\text{-}450HZ} - E_{650\text{-}850HZ} \geq 3 \times 4db$
(≥ (— ?EB (MAX-ENERGY 1600 4200 ?EN)) 2)	3. $E_{250\text{-}450HZ} - MAX(E_{1600\text{-}4200}) \geq 2 \times 4db$
(≥ (+ (— (ENERGY 450 650 ?EN) (ENERGY 650 850 ?EN)) 1) 0)	4. $E_{450\text{-}650HZ} - E_{650\text{-}850} \geq 4db$
(OR (≥ (— ?EB (ENERGY 850 1050 ?EN)) 2) (≥ (— ?EB (ENERGY 1050 1300 ?EN)) 2)))	5. one of the 2 following conditions must be satisfied: $E_{250\text{-}450} - E_{850\text{-}1050} \geq 8db$ OR $E_{250\text{-}450HZ} - E_{1050\text{-}1300} \geq 8db$

Then
  (MODIFY (SAMPLE ?ECH
      (NASAL1 TRUE)))
	Conclusion part
	The attribute NASAL 1 of the sample ?ECH becomes "TRUE"

(NEWPB (LABELLING-CONTINUE)))	The new problem to be considered is LABELLING-CONTINUE

Fig. 18   An example of rule detection "nasality"

The SERAC system itself will be improved:

— A meta language will be included in order to make easier for an user to express the global strategy of phonetic recognition.

— The actual version does not take into account the parallel organization of speech recognition algorithms; this point will be integrated in the next version in order to speed up the recognition process and to distribute the knowledge over separated modules called experts. Cooperation between the different experts will be studied. A new implementation of SERAC into the special processor SM 90 is under way making possible to study this parallelism and cooperative aspects within an expert society.

ACKNOWLEDGEMENTS

We are very grateful to Jean Monne and Michel Querre for their assistance in implementing the KEAL programs on the PDP11/34, AP/120B and SEMS Mitra 225, allowing us to use this system on-line. We thank also M. Rossi, R. Vivès, D. Gillet, P. Quinton, J. Siroux, D. Bigorgne, M. Cloatre, L. Le Guennec for having written important modules in KEAL.

Many thanks also to M. Gerard and M. A. Simon for implementing a number of rules in SERAC.

We would like also to thank C. Cagnoulet, R. De Mori, R. Gubrynowicz, M. Vailly, M. Hautin, R. Descout, M. Cartier for helpful discussions and criticisms on this work.

Many thanks to M. N. Le Gall for printing this paper and to J. Le Denmat for her help along the year for making easier our work.

RFERENCES

1. B. Buchanan, R. O. Duda, "Principles of rule-based expert systems," Stanford University Comp-Science, STAN-CS-82-926, 1982.
2. P. Carbonell, D. Fohr, J. P. Haton, J. M. Pierrel, F. Lonchamp, "Systeme expert de decodage acoustico-phonetique et invariance," 13èmes J.E.P. Bruxelles, 1984.
3. R. De Mori, A. Giordana, P. Laface and L. Saitta, "An expert system for speech decoding," Proc. AAAI Conference, Pittsburg, P.A., pp. 107-110, 1982.
4. R. O. Duda, "The prospector consultation system," Final Report SRI 8172, 1982.
5. C. L. Forgy, "OPS5 user's manual," Department of Computer Science, C.M.U., Pittsburg, 1981.
6. D. Gillet, M. Gerard, "Integration of acoustic, phonetic, prosodic and lexical knowledge in an expert system for speech understanding," ICASSP 84, Vol. III, pages 42-9-1 to 42-9-4, San Diego, 1984.
7. D. Gillet, P. Quinton, J. Siroux, "From speech recognition to speech understanding: a case study of KEAL," IEEE ICASSP meeting, Paris, May 1982.
8. R. Gubrynowicz, "La détection des consonnes nasales dans le système de reconnaissance de la parole continue KEAL," R. A. CNET, Vol. II, pp. 91-107, 1983.
9. F. Hayes-Roth, V. R. Lesser, "Focus of attention in the HEARSAY II Speech Understanding System," 5th IICAI, pp. 27-35, 1977.
10. G. Mercier, A. Nouhcn, P. Quinton, J. Siroux, "The KEAL speech understanding system," J. C. Simon, ed. *Spoken Language Generation and Understanding*, D. Reidel Publishing Company, Dordrecht, pp. 525-543, 1980.
11. P. Quinton, "Contribution à la reconnaissance de la parole, Utilisation d'heuristiques pour la reconnaissance de phrases," Thèse d'Etat, Université de Rennes, 1980.
12. M. Rossi, Y. Nishinuma, G. Mercier, "Indices acoustiques multilocuteurs et indépendants du contexte pour la reconnaissance automatique de la parole," Speech Com., Vol. 2, pp. 215-218, July 1983.
13. E. H. Shortliffe, *MYCIN: Computer Based Medical Consultations*, American Elsevier, New York, 1976.
14. R. N. Stevens, "Constraints imposed by the auditory system on the properties used to classify speech sounds: data from phonology acoustics and psycho acoustics," The Cognitive Representation of Speech, Myers, Laver, Anderson, North-Holland, pp. 61-74, 1981.
15. J. Vaissiere, "Suprasegmental effect on the velum movement in sentences," Abstract of the Tenth International Congress of phonetic sciences, Foris Publications, Dordrecht-Holland/Cinnamirson, U.S.A., 1983.
16. J. Vaissiere-Maeda, "A suprasegmental component in a speech recognition system," 104th ASA meeting, Florida, November 1982.
17. R. Vives, "Utilisation de l'information phonémique et syllabique pour la reconnaissance de mots prononcés isolément ou dans les phrases," Proc. 10 èmes J.E.P. Grenoble, pp. 375-384, 1978.

SAY - A PC based Speech Analysis system

P R Alderson, G Kaye, S G C Lawrence, D A Sinclair
B J Williams and G J Wolff

IBM UK Scientific Centre
Athelstan House
St Clement St
Winchester S023 9DR
ENGLAND

MOTIVATION FOR BUILDING A SPEECH ANALYSER

This paper is concerned with an experimental system of value to anyone interested in speech research in general, and in particular to those interested in speech input and output by computer. At the IBM UKSC we are building a system capable of converting text data to natural sounding speech. This embodies many of the features of an expert system since the system must understand and use the same rules of spelling, syntax, intonation, pronunciation and phonetics that a human speaker draws upon when talking. In building this system we must have a detailed understanding of normal human speech and a means of analysing synthetic speech to enable us to quantify the factors that determine intelligibility and acceptability. To achieve this we need a knowledge of both the physics and anatomy of speech production in the human articulatory system, and of the speech signal itself. We will need techniques for analysing synthetic speech and comparing it with its natural counterpart. An understanding of the process of speech perception, and of which parts of the speech signal carry the important perceptual information, is also relevant. A suitable system for the analysis of speech signals is thus an essential tool in this project and it is the development of such a speech analyser that is the subject of this paper.

NATO ASI Series, Vol. F16
New Systems and Architectures for Automatic Speech
Recognition and Synthesis. Edited by R. De Mori and C. Y. Suen
© Springer-Verlag Berlin Heidelberg 1985

INTRODUCTION

SAY is an IBM Personal Computer (PC) based speech analysis tool intended for a diverse set of users engaged in the evaluation of natural and synthetic speech. The challenges involved in developing such a system include

o   the recording, storage and manipulation of unlimited lengths of speech,

o   provision of a flexible, easily understood interface for a very diverse set of users (eg linguists, phoneticians, speech therapists, engineers).

o   provision of a high level of signal processing function (eg spectral and Linear Prediction Coefficient (LPC) analysis),

o   provision of a simple method of extending the system function to fulfill a particular user's requirements.

The SAY system consists of a 640 Kbyte IBM PC-XT with 20 Mbyte hard disk, IBM 370 host connection together with special purpose digitisation and display hardware.   Speech may be recorded and replayed from the hard disk at sampling rates up to 20 KHz.   A vector display capable of showing two waveforms of up to 1024 points each is provided, together with waveform scrolling and editing facilities.   There are two possible ways of editing the waveform:

1.   The user may select, copy, delete or modify portions of the speech waveform - using a special control panel while viewing the results of this editing on the display and also listening to the results as required; or

2.   System macros may be invoked to perform more complex operations on the selected portions of the waveform (eg cepstral analysis).

In the editing mode the user is provided with a special-purpose control panel containing keys allocated to the most common editing functions. These permit the user to display or replay portions of the edited or unedited wave and to scroll these waves across the display, selecting and manipulating portions by the use of a joystick and on-screen cursors.   The system may either be menu or command driven according to the expertise of the user.   The menu system provides a flexible interface for feedback of information to enhance ease of use.

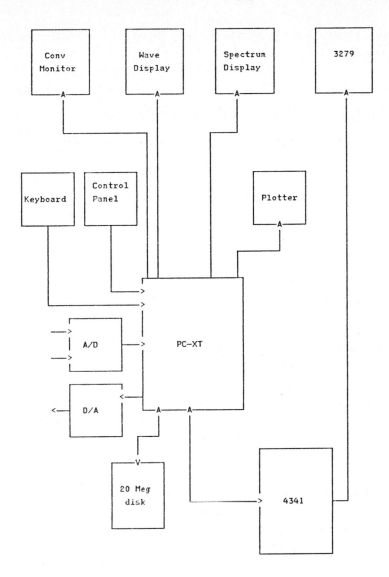

Figure 1. System Components

SAY provides a wide range of sophisticated signal processing facilites via a host link to the IBM UKSC IAX signal processing package (refs 2,3). These facilities include spectral and cepstral analysis, grey scale and colour spectrogram display, LPC analysis and pitch contour extraction. As the system is developed some of the signal processing facilites will move from the host into the PC. This will be achieved by the use of specialist signal processing hardware including a Discrete Fourier Transform (DFT) unit based on a prime radix transform and the attachment of a raster colour display.

SAY - SPEECH ANALYSER FUNCTIONAL DESCRIPTION

SAY provides the following facilities:

º   Digitisation
º   Editing
º   Analysis
º   Storage
º   Replay

of speech signals. Since all its facilities, except for the actual speech acquisition and replay, can be applied to any one-dimensional digital signal, the system could usefully be applied to a range of non-speech applications eg seismic processing, time domain reflectometry, vibrational analysis.

It is intended that the system will have a wide range of users extending from computer specialists to linguists and phoneticians. Consequently it has a user interface that balances the flexibility needed by the computer professional with the ease of access appropriate to a linguist or other person with less computational experience.

This was achieved by adopting a largely menu driven system and by the provision of a special keypad containing dedicated controls for cursor functions, waveform scrolling and speech editing and playback. The more experienced user may overide the menu system and use a single or full screen command mode while still retaining the dedicated control panel key functions where required. Many of the more sophisticated facilities are built up from basic operations using this command interface (and interactions with the menu system where necessary). These facilities are provided by a library of system functions.

Examples are:

º   Cepstrum processing to extract the vocal tract response
º   Linear prediction to obtain vocal tract response
º   Spectrum generation
º   Pitch contour extraction

In implementing these functions extensive use has been made of the host resident signal processing functions provided by IAX. To this end a modified form of the PC Personal Editor has been produced. This can be invoked from SAY. It acts both as a command editor and an interface to the external command processors such as the PC DOS, the CMS environment in the host, and the interpretive IAX command processor within CMS in the host.

A block diagram of the system is shown in Figure 1and the main functional units are:

- ° Analog audio recording equipment
- ° Speech digitiser and playback
- ° Waveform display and editor
- ° Speech and waveform analysis system
- ° Spectrum display
- ° Speech synthesisers

The **PC-XT** controls all digitisation, editing, wave storage and playback functions. It is also used for the entry of all system commands and for the display of guidance information and alphanumeric feedback. It is connected to an IBM 370 host computer via a highspeed link. It is intended to enhance the function of the PC-XT with a specialist digital signal processing hardware to make a stand-alone system in the near future.

Conversational monitor

This is the PC monochrome display. It is used to display system menus and status information, such as the number of waves being edited, time of day. A typical menu is shown in Figure 2. Here the dual display mode is being used on the waveform to display two different sections of the same waveform. The top waveform shows an expanded region (along the time axis) of the waveform while the bottom regions shows a compressed region. The user is provided with information on the position of the cursors within the wave, the relative position of the cursor on the display and the position of the display window relative to the start of the wave. The overall duration of the wave in seconds, the original sampling rate and the total number of samples in the wave are also shown, together with an indication of the amount of horizontal and vertical scaling currently being applied to the display window. The user should be able to read all the facts he needs to know about the wave directly from the screen thus removing the need for tiresome mental arithmetic, say for instance in calculating the wave duration from the sample rate and total number of samples.

```
Speech Editing/Replay                                    26 Jun 1984 03-53pm
                      Number of waves being edited :  1
                                              LEFT            RIGHT
                                         edge   cursor   cursor   edge
Wave name . : POLITELY          Display :      0     60      183    255
Sample rate : 10 Khz            Wave. . :   9049   9109     9221   9304
Duration. . : 2.50 sec 25037 samples  Scaling : Horizontal :  4 Vertical :  1

Wave name . : POLITELY          Display :      0                   2047
Sample rate : 10 Khz            Wave. . :  15033                  17079
Duration. . : 2.50 sec 25037 samples  Scaling : Horizontal : -2 Vertical :  1

The information above shows:-

      1.  How many waves are being edited.
      2.  The name of the wave being edited.
      3.  The sample number of the right and left displayed samples.
      4.  The location of each cursor on the wave display and in the wave.
      5.  The scaling currently active.
                                                        More ...

 F1 HELP  F3 EXIT  F4 WAVE  F6 DROP  F7 PLAY  F8 COMMAND  F9 STORE  F10 EXEC  SAY
```

Figure 2.   Conversational monitor menu showing HELP facility.

At the bottom of all the system menus is a prompt line which indicates which of the PC keyboard programmable function keys are active at that time and what their effect is.

In the example menu it has been assumed that the user has pressed PF1 to obtain the HELP information for that menu. This displays information on the various options available within that menu. This is carefully positioned on the conversational monitor screen so that it does not obscure the primary menu fields.

Speech Digitisation

The speech sources are:

° Microphone
° Pre-recorded tape
° Output from a synthesiser

Digitisation sampling rate and filter can be selected under the control of commands issued from the PC keyboard. At present digitisation is performed by a Tecmar Labmaster attached to the PC. The input signal is low pass filtered by an analog antialiasing filter with an appropriate cut-off to allow 10kHz and 20kHz sampling. A new digitisation system that uses fast dual port memory to buffer the ADC into the PC memory space is currently being developed. This will allow digitisation concurrent with hard disk activity and will permit records of virtually unlimited lengths of speech at sampling rates of up to 40 kHz. Lower sampling rates are obtained by digital low pass filtering and downsampling to the required sample rate. In this way linear phase may be preserved in the overall system response.

The RECORD menu displayed on the conversational monitor is shown in Figure 3. All fields are initially filled in with defaults. The user may overtype these with new values if required. A simple recording level meter also appears

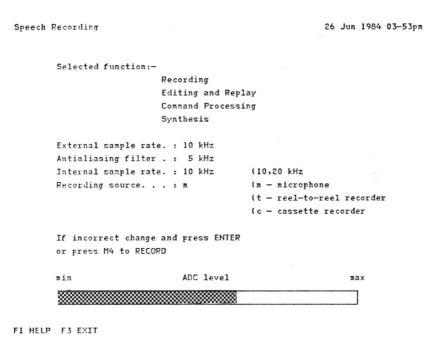

Figure 3. Record menu

on this menu so that the user may set the input level at an appropriate position to utilise the full ADC range.

Playback is through an appropriate reconstruction filter selected by the system according to the original sample rate. A dual port memory buffer (similar to that needed for digitisation) will be implemented to accomodate speech output direct from the hard disk.

The PLAYBACK menu displayed on the conversational monitor during replay of speech is shown in Figure 4.

Waveform Display

This is a high resolution X-Y directed-beam vector display capable of displaying one or two 1024 point windows on a speech waveform. The window may be scrolled along the waveform by the operation of a joystick on the control panel. The display has four levels of brightness (off, low, medium and high) and points may be made to blink as well. These brightness attributes are useful for delineating sections of the waveform that are being processed (eg deleted or copied).

Vertical zoom and horizontal zoom and compression are implemented using scaling factors of 2,4,8,16 and 32. It is very convenient being able to display two waveforms simultaneously at different resolutions, since this permits the user to have a global view of the speech waveform as well as a high resolution view of the particular area he is working with. A typical example of this is shown in Figure 5.

A pair of cursors are associated with each wave being edited. These may be manipulated from the control panel or by program control. They are used to mark sections of a wave for editing or replay purposes.

Help facilities

Help is provided for each function and facility in the system. It is displayed in either the lower or upper part of the conversation monitor screen as is most appropriate for the menu currently being displayed, and can be read whilst the user is completing the appropriate fields, or using the control panel. In general HELP is additive to what is currently displayed, and never overwrites a response field.

3279 Display

This is a colour output-only device and is used primarily as a 'soft' graph plotter. It is attached to IAX via the Grapical Data Display Manager (ref 4). Its primary purpose is to provide a rapid means of viewing, in graphical form, the results of various signal processing calculations eg to show a waveform and its corresponding pitch profile.

Graph Plotter

This is an A3 size eight-pen IBM Instruments XY-750 digital plotter. Its support software runs on the PC-XT. It provides a hard copy facilities as a counterpart to the 3279.

```
Speech Editing/Replay                                    26 Jun 1984 03-53pm
                        Number of waves being edited :  1
                                                 edge    cursor    cursor    edge
Wave name . : POLITELY              Display :       0                        255
Sample rate : 10 Khz                Wave. . :     9049                      9304
Duration. . : 2.50 sec 25037 samples    Scaling : Horizontal :  4 Vertical :  1

Wave name . : POLITELY              Display :       0     546     1845     2047
Sample rate : 10 Khz                Wave. . :   15033   15579    16877    17079
Duration. . : 2.50 sec 25037 samples    Scaling : Horizontal : -2 Vertical :  1

            Replay mode. . : s        (S,s Single / R,r Repeated
            Pause. . . . . : 0.5 secs
            Recorder . . . : 1        (t reel to reel recorder
                                      (c cassette recorder
                                      (1 loudspeaker


    F1 HELP  F3 EXIT  F4 WAVE  F6 DROP  F8 COMMAND  F9 STORE
```

Figure 4. Playback prompts on the conversational monitor: Replay of speech normally occurs when editing that speech.

Control Panel

The control panel provides a means of scrolling waveforms and of moving cursors. It also provides single key access to the commonest system functions. This means that the majority of editing activity can be performed under the control of one hand (usually the left) which leaves the other hand free for taking notes, adjusting tape recorder controls. It consists of 16 keys, a one dimensional joystick, two tracker wheels with rotary encoders and two sets of thumbwheel switches. The joystick is used for scrolling the active displayed waveform, the rate of scroll being proportional to the amount of joystick displacement. The tracker wheels are used to move the cursors on the waveform display. Two 3 digit thumbwheel switches are provided and these are used for specifying scaling factors for the region of the wave within and outside the area marked by the cursor. The function of each control panel switch is detailed below. The active action key mode is indicated on the control panel.

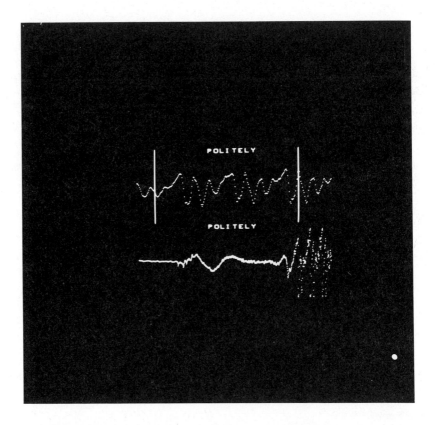

Figure 5. Waveform display: The top waveform shows the schwa at the end of 'better' in the digitised waveform of the utterance 'He had better speak politely'. The bottom waveform is an expanded view of the start of 'politely' showing the strong low frequency transient at the onset of the heavily aspirated 'p'.

M1   toggle to alternative function for A1-A8
M2   move to next wave in edit ring
M3   toggle between top and bottom displays
M4   select extended cursor mode
           record start/stop

P1   playback unedited active wave
P2   playback wave between cursors
P3   playback wave outside cursors
P4   playback displayed wave

A1   display edited wave
           select region between cursors
A2   display only selected regions within wave
           copy region between cursors
A3   display all but selected regions within wave
           mark point at left cursor
A4   toggle between dual and single wave display
           delete region between cursors
A5   increase wave vertical scaling
           reset cursor positions
A6   decrease wave vertical scaling
           reset selections
A7   increase wave horizontal scaling
           reset marked points
A8   decrease wave horizontal scaling
           select extended cursor mode

Figure 6. Control Panel Functions

354

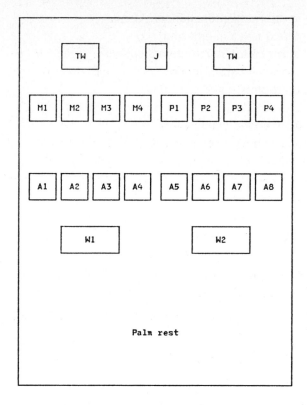

```
J          Joystick
TW1 — TW2  Thumbwheels
M1  — M4   Mode setting keys
P1  — P4   Playback keys
A1  — A8   Action keys
W1  — W2   Tracker wheels
```

Figure 7.   Control Panel

Speech Editing

A full range of waveform editing functions are provided. Up to six waves may be involved in the editing process at any one time. Sections may be copied and deleted from each of these waves freely.

The waveform editing facilities include:

º   Delete a wave section
º   Copy a section of a wave from one wave to another or within the wave
º   Move sections of a wave within the wave
º   Store wave on hard disk
º   Select a segment of a wave for subsequent processing e.g.
  ▪ Compute the Fourier transform of the segment
  ▪ Play back only the selected segments
  ▪ Play back ignoring the selected segments
  ▪ Mark points in the wave for reference in subsequent processing

Spectrogram Computation and Display

Speech spectrograms can be computed using IAX and then displayed on a raster graphics display or on the 3279 colour terminal at present. It is intended to provide this facility eventually within the PC environment by the use of dedicated Fourier transform hardware.

Signal Processing

An extensive range of signal processing functions are available within IAX (refs 2,3) at the host. The user can invoke these functions directly from the speech analyser. In the first version the results may be displayed on the 3279, or on the wave and spectrogram displays. The command interface is via a modified form of the IBM PC Personal Editor. It provides both a command editor and a means of executing a single command or command list. Eventually it is intended to move the signal processing function provided by IAX into the PC environment by installing specialist digital signal processing hardware.

356

```
/* Routine to compute the spectrogram of a speech waveform */
/* Parameters :   1st  name of file containing speech waveform
                  2nd  width of FFT window
                  3rd  amount by which FFT window is stepped along waveform
                       for each spectrum time slot
                  4th  file name to receive calculated spectrum     */


/* first get parameters from command line */

"IAXLSTR"; IF RC¬=0 THEN EXIT RC; PULL name
"IAXLSTR"; IF RC¬=0 THEN EXIT RC; PULL width
"IAXLSTR"; IF RC¬=0 THEN EXIT RC; PULL ' step_size '_size
"IAXLSTR"; IF RC¬=0 THEN EXIT RC; PULL spectrum_file

/* compute Hamming window for selected FFT size */
'hamming=hamm('width')'
/* pad out the Hamming window with 0s to make overall window 512 points */
'pad= 0.('width' :511)'
/* reserve array space for resultant sonogram */
'r=0. (0:255 , 0:xs(' name ' )/'' step_size '_size'-1)'

/* main loop */
/* select the current portion of the speech waveform */
/* apply the Hamming window and take the FFT of the result */
/* take the log of the absolute magnitude and put in the result array */
/* repeat the loop, moving the FFT window slowly along the speech waveform */

'do i=0 by ' step_size ' to xs(' name ' )-' step_size '-1'
    'b=' name ' (i:i+' width ' -1)*hamming || pad'
    'c=ft(b)'
    'r(*,i/' step_size ')= log abs c(0:255)'
    'end'
/* orientate songoram + make max energy correspond to black rather than white */
'r=-r'
'r= cl range( r )'
'r=tr mir r'
/* put final sonogram in destination file */
'put r, ' spectrum_file ', IAX1,keep,repl'
```

Figure 9.   Command list for the calculation of a spectrum

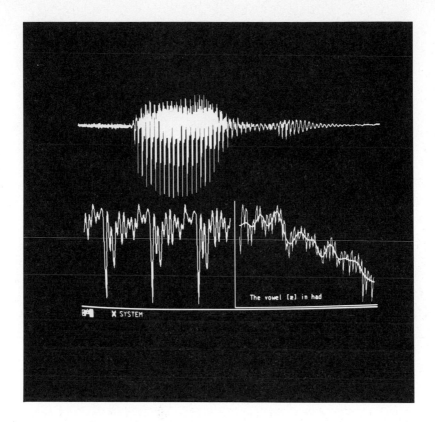

Figure 10. **Cepstral calculation of the vowel a: in 'hard'**

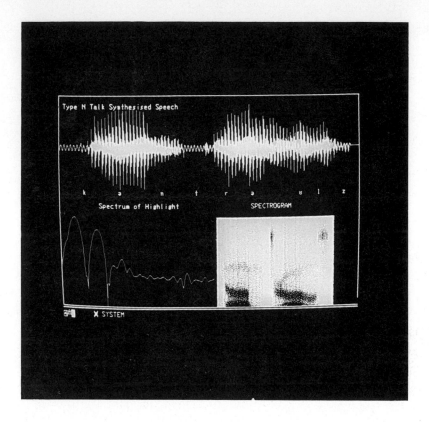

Figure 11. Analysis of phoneme synthesiser spectrum: The synthetic waveform is shown at the top. Bottom left is the spectrum of a portion of the dipthong in the second syllable of 'controls' while bottom left is a half tone spectrum of the entire word.

EXAMPLES FROM A SAY SESSION

SAY offers a wide range of signal processing functions. Here we will illustrate some of the simpler and more commonly used features. The spectrogram for the utterance 'Good morning how are you' is shown in Figure 8. This spectrogram was taken from the high resolution spectrogram display system within SAY and was computed using the hopping FFT technique shown in the SAY command list of Figure 9. The command list shows the simple, readable, high level form of the IAX language.

Figure 10 shows the type of graphical output that may be obtained from the 3279 soft graph plotter. Here the two formant peaks in the cepstrum of the vowel a: in hard can be clearly seen. (Note that this display would normally be in several contrasting colours but due to printing restraints a black and white image is shown here). By using a grey scale half-toning technique the 3279 can display spectrograms, albeit at rather lower resolution than the dedicated spectrogram display. This is useful when speech processing is being carried out under IAX but outside the normal SAY environment. An example is shown in Figure 11. This is a piece of synthetic speech - the word 'controls' generated by a simple phoneme synthesiser. It can be seen that the lower formants in the synthesiser output are approximately correct but the higher formant information is rather less well defined.

CONCLUSIONS

We have developed a multi-function speech analysis system, based on an IBM PC-XT, which is capable of a wide range of speech processing functions. The system function is being expanded to include local spectrographic calculation and processing of unlimited lengths of speech. The system is currently being used to evaluate human and synthetic speech in relation to our text to speech work.

Acknowledgements

We should like to thank all our colleagues at the UKSC for their help and

Figure 8.   Narrowband spectrum of 'Good morning how are you'

criticism. We are especially grateful to Dr Paul Jackson for the help he has given us with the IAX package and to Nick Allen and Dilbagh Singh for the significant contribution they made in implementing the SAY code.

References

1. Tomorrow's Computers, IEEE Spectrum, vol 20 no 17, Nov 1983.

2. The IAX Image Processing Language. P H Jackson, UK Science Centre Report no 113, Feb 1983.

3. The IAX Image Processing Language - Functions and Commands. P H Jackson, UK Science Centre Report no 114, May 1983.

4. The GDDM General Information Manual. GC33-0100.

AUTOMATIC GENERATION OF LINGUISTIC, PHONETIC AND ACOUSTIC KNOWLEDGE FOR A DIPHONE-BASED CONTINUOUS SPEECH RECOGNITION SYSTEM

Anna Maria Colla

Donatella Sciarra

Central Research Department

Elettronica San Giorgio, ELSAG S.p.A.

Via G. Puccini, 2

16154 Genova Sestri

ITALY

ABSTRACT

An important issue in template-matching continuous-speech recognition systems is the right choice of the language model, together with an appropriate definition of the basic units to be recognized. The advantages of using a hierarchical transition network model with diphones and diphone-like elements as basic units are illustrated in the paper. However, a severe drawback in the use of sub-word units is an increased complexity in producing and managing the overall knowledge relating to language representation and template definition and extraction. An efficient solution to this problem is required especially when the recognition system is to be used by unskilled users in actual applications. For this purpose we have developed an automatic procedure for generating the linguistic, phonetic and acoustic data bases expressing the whole information required by the diphone-based system.

NATO ASI Series, Vol. F16
New Systems and Architectures for Automatic Speech
Recognition and Synthesis. Edited by R. De Mori and C. Y. Suen
© Springer-Verlag Berlin Heidelberg 1985

1. INTRODUCTION

An important issue in template-matching continuous-speech recognition (CSR) systems is the choice of the basic units to be recognized. Economy and invariance with the surrounding units are the main requisites to be evaluated. We found that the diphones, as defined in the following, completely fulfil these requirements. In fact fewer than 400 diphones are sufficient to describe the whole Italian lexicon; moreover their fairly high insensibility to the context ensures that very few templates can adequately represent each unit. In this way the speaker-dependent template dictionaries are quite manageable even for complex applications. In fact such dictionaries need not comprise all the Italian diphones, but are tailored to a particular language: they only comprise the diphones appearing in the words of the lexicon, plus some elements that may be present at the junction between two fluently spoken words.

We have implemented two diphone-based CSR systems, obtaining satisfactory performances. One of them is described in [14]; the other one, which is referred to in this paper, has a real-time oriented, very simple architecture, consisting of two modules: an acoustic front-end and a linguistic decoder. The key point in this system is the choice of a good model of the spoken language: a *hierarchical transition network* (HTN), where the basic speech units are diphones [16]. The HTN language representation smoothly integrates the different knowledge sources involved: syntax and semantics describe the permitted sequences of words, while phonetic and phonological knowledge is used for generating the diphone subnetworks corresponding to words and for dealing with junctions. Acoustic knowledge is finally present in the sequences of spectra that make up the basic units and in the sound similarity measure.

With such a language representation, the recognition problem, formulated as that of finding the acceptable sequence of basic units that best fits the input signal [4], is turned into the search for the path through the network that obtains the maximum cumulative similarity score [16]. This task is accomplished by the *linguistic decoder*.

Such a diphone-based system led to high recognition performances [16] and proved to be more suitable for the treatment of complex languages than whole-word template matching systems; this is due particularly to the good discrimination between similar words, the small storage requirements and the fast training on new speakers. On the other hand, a drawback common to all systems that apply sub-word units is an increased complexity in producing the overall knowledge relating to language representation and template definition and extraction. With an HTN representation all the knowledge relating to an application must be conveyed into the linguistic, phonetic and acoustic data bases, corresponding to the high level networks, the diphone subnetworks and the template set, respectively (see Fig. 1). Both the building of the networks and the creating of the template set, which requires the identification, acquisition and extraction of the necessary units, are long and difficult tasks when complex languages are involved. It is hardly worth saying that manual network generation and template extraction are completely inadequate for practical applications. This spurred us to develop a completely automatic procedure (sketched in Fig. 1) that derives all the data bases relating to any language associated with a regular grammar, starting from the vocabulary and a Backus-Naur form (BNF) representation of the grammar. Besides building the high level and diphone networks, the procedure solves the problems of drawing up the inventory of the necessary diphones and correctly creating a set of templates, tasks which are not as straightforward as when dealing with whole words. The procedure derives a set of sentences containing occurrences of all the needed prototypes, which, uttered by any speaker, constitute the training material for that speaker from which the template extraction is finally accomplished by means of a *diphone bootstrapping* module.

The knowledge generation procedure, which produces all the pieces of information relating to an application and actually trains the system on new speakers, is the main subject of this paper. The diphones are defined, and their properties are illustrated in Section 2; the relevant phonological rules are described in Section 3. In Sections 4 and 5 the HTN language model and the linguistic

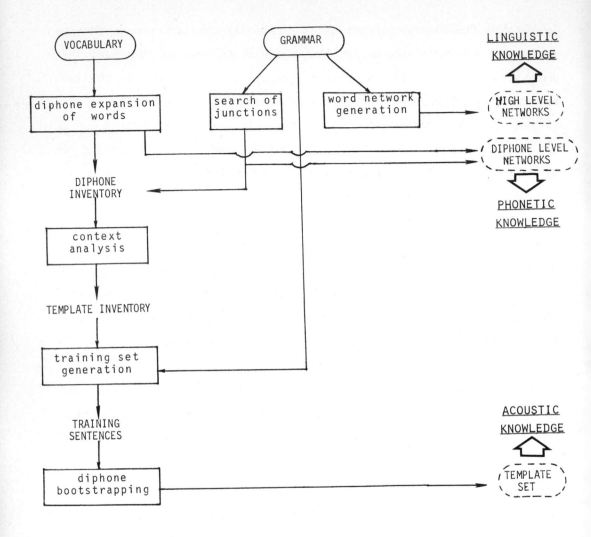

FIG. 1 :   Generation of the linguistic, phonetic and acoustic knowledge for a given application from its vocabulary and grammar.

decoder are presented. The training phase of the system, consisting of the automatic generation of the training set and the extraction of the templates, is discussed in Section 6. Finally some experimental results obtained with data bases generated by means of our procedure are presented in Section 7.

2. THE DIPHONES: DEFINITION AND PROPERTIES

Diphone is a general name, used in order to avoid the proliferation of new terms, referring to three different types of units, whose common and major characteristic is the insensibility to coarticulation effects with the surrounding sounds. This means that a diphone keeps its identity regardless of the context in which it happens to be embedded; that is to say, a diphone is not influenced by adjacent diphones (although it may be influenced by prosodic factors such as the location within a word or the stress level). An important consequence of this feature is the economy of the diphone dictionaries, due to the very small number of templates required in order to represent each diphone adequately. In addition, the number of the diphones themselves is small (much smaller than that of syllables, for instance).

The different types of diphones are related to the main parts of fluent speech: steady-state sounds and transitions. With regard to the latter, we have chosen to take into account only the very transitions, that is, very short portions of the signal. Thus, as will be shown in the following, the matching with transition templates does not require any time warping [10] capability, necessary with longer units (words, demisyllables, and so on), which may sometimes cause misrecognition because of the allowance to skip spectral states. The resulting definition of "diphone" [15] is somewhat different from the classical one of "interval between the centres of adjacent phonemes" [8, 12, 17]. Our diphone dictionaries are made up of units representing:

1) stationary sounds corresponding to the steady-state part of some phonemes: vowels, silence and consonants other than plosives (we will

describe in Sect. 3 how plosives are dealt with);

2) true diphones, that is, transitions between two adjacent phonemes, the second one being sonorant: consonant $\rightarrow$ vowel, consonant $\rightarrow$ consonant, vowel $\rightarrow$ vowel; at present we do not make use of the vowel $\rightarrow$ consonant transitions;

3) triphones, that is, larger events embracing three phonemes, of which the central one is sonorant but not stationary (/r/ or semivowel).

The use of diphone-like units instead of the commonly used whole-word templates seems to be advisable in CSR systems. In fact the rather small size of the diphone template dictionaries ensures a smaller storage requirement and a lower computation time for the recognition system than those needed in whole-word template matching. Moreover, the time necessary to train the system on a new speaker is fairly low, since generally not all the words of the lexicon need to be comprised in the training set. Even for small vocabularies, such as the digits, the training set dimension for diphones is smaller than that required for whole words, if coarticulation effects are taken into account. When whole-word templates are used, different pronunciations or phonological variations of a word can only be taken into account by collecting many different templates. Here, one of the advantages in the use of diphones becomes clear: instead of adopting a unique description of each word, alternative and optional paths are allowed in the network, so that a highly accurate representation, endowed with greater flexibility and economy, is supplied. This kind of representation has a higher discriminative power on similar words as well, as no spurious differences in phonetically identical portions of such words may override true discriminative information. The diphones also provide a very natural way of dealing with junctions between adjacent fluently spoken words: these can be adequately represented by inserting optional transitional diphones such as diphthongs (see also [1]). As a final remark, we point out that the use of diphone-like units causes no penalty on recognition performance: actually, comparative tests have displayed better results with diphones than with whole words.

3. DIPHONE PHONOLOGY

The description of any word of a language in terms of a sequence of sub-word units is a rather easy problem to solve for the Italian language with the diphone-like units defined in Section 2.

The determination of the sequence(s) of diphones corresponding to any given word is accomplished in two steps: first a translation is performed from the orthographic form to a *phonetic transcription*; then the diphones relating to the sequence of phonemes are obtained. Table I shows the set of phonemes [11] pertaining to the Italian language.

The orthography of Italian words is closely related to their pronunciation, so that the phonetic transcription is quite an easy task. Generally there is a one-to-one correspondence between the phonemes making up an uttered word and the alphabetic symbols making up the same written word. The very few exceptions are easily dealt with in an automatic way.

The *determination of the diphone sequences* making up each word starts from the phonetic string corresponding to the word. It is based on rules likely to be applied not only to Italian, but also to any other syllable-timed language (such as Spanish or even German).

With regard to the three above mentioned diphone types, we point out that steady-state sounds are vowels, fricatives, nasals and liquid consonants, as well as the portions of affricates after the beginning of frication. Plosives generally have no "stationary" parts (/k/ may constitute an exception, as its burst may be long), whilst /r/ and semivowels may or may not have some. Plosives are simply rendered by means of a phonetic silence plus the transition to the following sonorant sound. Final plosives in names or foreign words (such as stop) are adequately represented by a transition to a "neutral" vowel /ə/. A phonetic silence may also appear before affricates. When a semivowel (/j/, /w/ following the notation of [11]) has a short steady-state portion, it is rendered by means of the corresponding vowel (/i/, /u/). In other cases a triphone is present. Only

NAME	SYMB.	TYPE	EXAMPLE
A	ɑ	VOWEL	pane
E+	ɛ	"	sette
E−	e	"	cena
I	i	"	riso
O+	ɔ	"	storia
O−	o	"	pozzo
U	u	"	cura
L	l	LIQ.	lotta
L^	ʎ	"	glielo
R	r	"	ramo
M	m	NAS.	mano
N	n	"	notte
N^	ɲ	"	gnomo
F	f	FRIC.	folla
S	s	"	sano
S^	z	"	rosa
SH	ʃ	"	scia
V	v	"	vero
C	tʃ	AFFR.	ciao
J	dʒ	"	gioco
Z	ts	"	lenzuolo
Z^	dz	"	zero
B	b	PLOS.	bosco
D	d	"	donna
G	g	"	lega
K	k	"	cosa
P	p	"	parte
T	t	"	terra

TABLE I : The Italian phonemes.

very few triphones actually exist when the central phoneme is /j/, because of the intrinsic length of the overall transition "consonant → /j/ → vowel". Altogether, fewer than 400 different diphones are sufficient to cover all Italian words.

Each Italian syllable can be developed as a sequence of diphones by following the above mentioned rules. The development of each syllable contains:

1)   the stationary consonant(s) (if any)   and/or
2)   the phonetic silence preceding plosives (if any);
3)   the CC transition (if any)   and/or
4)   the CV transition;
5)   the steady-state vowel(s);
6)   the diphthong (if any).

For instance the syllables "sei", "ra", "ta", "spa", "fle" and "tro" can be decomposed as:

	sei	ra	ta	spa	fle	tro
1)	|S			|S	|F,L	
2)			|sil	|sil		|sil
3)					|FL	|TR
4)	|SE	|RA	|TA	|PA	|LE	|RO
5)	|E,I	|A	|A	|A	|E	|O
6)	|EI					

In the following we present the complete diphone sequences corresponding to the expansion of words containing the syllables of the above example. The diphones in parentheses (which correspond to diphthongs or "stationary" portions of /k/ or affricates) may be skipped. The couples of diphones in curly brackets can be replaced by the corrresponding triphones (i.e., "KUA", "TRO" and "ZIO").

serata   → S - SE - E - RA - A - sil- TA - A
sei   → S - SE - E -(EI)- I

quattro   → sil- (K)-{KU -UA}- A -sil-{TR -RO}- O

i.e.:

quattro   → sil- (K)$\underset{KUA}{\overset{KU\ \text{-}UA}{<}}$A -sil$\underset{TRO}{\overset{TR\ \text{-}RO}{<}}$O

spazio   → S -sil- PA - A -sil -(Z)-{ZI -IO}- O

i.e.:

spazio   → S -sil- PA - A -sil -(Z)$\underset{ZIO}{\overset{ZI\ \text{-}IO}{<}}$O

flebile   → F -FL - L -LE - E -sil-BI - I - L -LE - E

We have also developed length rules for the diphones, to be applied in the generation of the network representation of the language.

4. LANGUAGE MODEL AND NETWORK REPRESENTATION

The adopted language model refers to a simple language type, the finite-state one, that can be associated with a non-recursive state transition network or finite-state automaton [6].

We make use of a hierarchical transition network representation [7], in which all the knowledge is partitioned into several levels. The specific knowledge pertaining to each level is contained in one or more networks whose nodes are related to an appropriate kind of unit (that is words, diphones or spectra). In all the levels except the lowest one each node points to a network belonging to the adjacent lower level, which may be considered as the expansion of the node in terms of simpler units. This provides a link between adjacent levels. Fig. 2 shows an example of a portion of a simplified HTN representation of a mini command language, with only one node in each level fully expanded through a lower level subnetwork. The language of the application is represented in terms of words in one or more high-level networks, where the syntactic and linguistic knowledge defines the correct sequences of words. The highest level may simply correspond to a network of words, or it may be convenient to introduce a number of upper levels (as in the example), whose nodes represent syntactic groups, each one associated with a different network. For complex and large

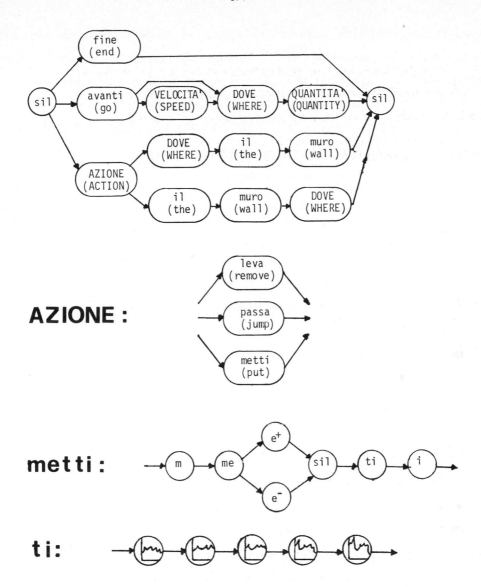

FIG. 2 :   Hierarchical Transition Network representation of a mini command language. Only one node at each level is fully expanded through a subnetwork in the immediately lower level.

languages, in which the same groups appear in different positions, the latter representation is particularly useful because the repetition of their network representation is avoided. In this case the storage requirements generally decrease, while the computation effort required to manage this more complex structure grows. The initial and final states of the language correspond to the silence that precedes and follows any utterance; in adddition, an optional silence state may be included between any two consecutive words.

At a lower level, each word is described in terms of a network, whose nodes correspond to diphones, and which is built according to the phonetic knowledge. All the information about the possible alternative sequences of units in the word and their duration is contained in this diphone-level network. A node corresponding to a diphone can be described by means of a structure containing:

→ the diphone identifier

→ the position of the diphone in the word (initial, intermediate or final)

→ a steadiness flag

→ lower and upper duration bounds (only for stationary diphones).

Each transitional diphone can be simply represented by a sequence of spectral states, with no need to duplicate or skip any of them. In fact it is well known that the very transition between two sounds has a basically fixed duration, mainly determined by the articulatory time constants [3]. A duration variability is however allowed for steady-state sounds. The duration bounds depend on the particular sound, on the position in the word and on the stress level. Their accurate determination is very important in avoiding the erroneous recognition of abnormally short or long phonetic events. This model of temporal variability offers a better time warping capability than the common whole-word template matching methods with 2:1 maximum duration ratio between templates and test words [10]. Indeed the time alignment between input signal and templates thus achieved avoids possible misrecognitions due to the insertion or deletion of spectral states in the transitions, whilst the steady-state sounds can be shrinked or stretched to a greater extent within reasonable limits.

Phonological rules are also applied at the diphone level, to deal with junctions between words.

At the lowest level, in which the acoustic knowledge is present, a parametric representation of each diphone is given as the sequence of spectral states that make up its templates. Steady-state diphones are represented by one-spectral-state templates, while transitional diphones are represented each by one multi-frame template of appropriate length which exactly covers the transition.

The HTN representation can be automatically derived for any language generated by a regular grammar [6]. A procedure has been developed for the generation of the word network(s) (expressing the linguistic knowledge of the system, as shown in Fig. 1) from a BNF representation of the grammar where the type of recursion allowed in regular grammars may be present. Either one-level or multi-level organizations can be chosen for this representation. The insertion of optional silence states between consecutive words and the elimination of redundant states are automatically performed.

We have also developed a transcription procedure, which picks out the sequence(s) of diphones making up any Italian word simply from the orthographic form of the word itself. It is based on the rules presented in Section 3. Given a recognition task, with its lexicon and grammar, the procedure permits us to determine all the units needed for the representation of the vocabulary (including possible junctions between fluently spoken words). This in turns allows us both to derive the definition of the template dictionary (that is, how many and which units are needed, and how many and which templates for each unit) and to generate the diphone networks (expressing the phonetic knowledge of the system).

5. THE LINGUISTIC DECODER

In our diphone-based CSR system the HTN language model adopted yields a tight integration between signal and symbol processing, resulting in a simple organization. The entire system consists of only two processes: the acoustic front-end, providing a parametric representation of the speech signal, and the linguistic decoder, producing the interpretation of the utterance as a correct sentence of the language.

The speech signal, collected with a close-talking microphone, is low-pass filtered at 4.6 KHz and sampled at 10 KHz. Every 10 ms a 256-point Hamming window is applied to the signal and a parametric representation is derived. Different kinds of acoustic analysis are allowed; in the experiments being currently run we make use of 12 cepstrum coefficients derived by LPC analysis [13].

The HTN representation of the language is the database where all the knowledge relating to the recognition task is present at different levels. The recognizer basically performs a dynamic-programming search to find the path through the HTN which attains the highest cumulative similarity score with the input sentence. This path corresponds to a sequence of basic units, chosen from among all the acceptable ones that make up a sentence of the language. The multi-level organization requires the search to start from the highest level network, and to go downwards through the levels from a node to its expansion at the adjacent lower level, till the lowest level is reached. Here the similarity can be computed between input and template frames. Then the information is conveyed upwards through the levels to the highest one, and at each level a piece of knowledge is worked out, based on the information coming from the adjacent lower level. Any decision is deferred to the full-message level, where all the pieces of information, from acoustic-phonetic to lexical and syntactic, and possibly semantic, are available. Delaying decisions to the highest level reduces errors and, in addition, avoids the complications that arise in recovering from segmentation errors.

The recognizer makes use of a best-few search strategy without backtracking to update at each step the paths of the network being currently explored. The number of paths explored is kept small by a beam-search strategy similar to the one developed in the Harpy system [9]: those paths whose cumulative similarity score falls below the locally best one by more than a given threshold are pruned out. Preliminary tests were carried out to find the best pruning threshold, and the one which most restricted the number of paths retained without lowering the performance was chosen.

At each time interval an input frame is processed; a similarity measure is only computed between this frame and one template frame of the diphones associated with the current paths. The cumulative similarity for these paths is updated, and the best-few strategy is then applied to cut off low-similarity paths. The similarity score between an input frame and a template frame can be interpreted as an evaluation of the possibility that the input frame belongs to the relevant phonetic event. It can be obtained by calculating a distance between the two patterns, and transforming it into a number ranging between 0 and 1 as a linear function between two predefined distance thresholds, whose values depend on the analysis adopted. The distance chosen when using LPC coefficients is the Euclidean one.

The algorithm described is real-time oriented, as the decoding proceeds along with the similarity measurement. This means that a partial interpretation of early words in a sentence can be available when the input speech is still being processed, even before the speaker has finished talking. Indeed the decision on the recognized diphones does not have to be delayed until the end of the sentence; as soon as only one interpretation remains possible for a time interval, that is, only one path in the network is "alive" for it, the relative diphones and words are given, and a cleanup procedure eliminates dead paths, thus keeping the required memory storage to a minimum. Of course such a decoder cannot make use of pieces of information such as the length of the sentence; the decoder itself detects the end of the sentence when the last node in the best path corresponds to a final silence whose duration is longer than a predefined value. The segmentation process performed by the recognizer can be represented in graphic form, as a waveform where the boundaries of each recognized diphone are marked. An example is shown in Fig. 3.

The method appears to be robust, so that no particular care is required in the way the sentences are uttered. Moreover the simple algorithms and control strategy make a custom hardware implementation possible. An approximate evaluation of the computational power necessary for large vocabularies has revealed that it is well within the capability of present multiprocessor hardware. At present the linguistic decoder is implemented on a general-purpose mini-computer by means of Fortran routines.

6. AUTOMATIC TRAINING

When performing CSR with whole-word templates, the training set must comprise all the words of the lexicon in one or more occurrences; indeed, in order to correctly handle coarticulation effects between adjacent words, a different template is required for each context situation. When using diphones, the training sentences are only expected to include one occurrence of each diphone. As the lexicon size increases, the whole-word template set becomes larger and larger, whereas a diphone template dictionary remains fairly small in size. In the latter case both the amount of training material and the computational load are greatly reduced. On the other hand, the template extraction from the training sentences is undoubtedly more complex in the case of sub-word units, where a reliable segmentation is required to correctly isolate very small portions of the signal.

Since a different dictionary is necessary for each speaker and each language, however, the problem of determining the set of diphones for a given application and extracting the templates for a test speaker becomes crucial. Moreover, making the training phase completely automatic not only avoids a lot of manual work, but is also necessary for practical applications, if the recognition system is

377

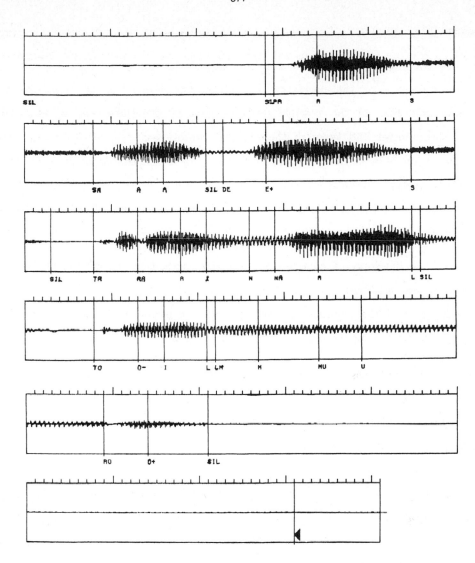

FIG. 3 :   Output of the recognition of the utterance "Passa a destra in alto il muro" ("Jump the wall up right").

actually to be used by persons with no skills in phonetics or linguistics.

The training procedure necessarily consists of the following steps:

1) determination of the necessary units from the lexicon of the language and, for each unit, of the possible different context situations, i.e., determination of the number and types of the required prototypes;

2) generation of a suitable set of training sentences containing occurrences of all the prototypes needed;

3) extraction of the templates from the training sentences uttered by the test speaker.

We have developed a completely automatic method of performing these steps. It includes two modules:

→ generation of the training sentences (GTS). It performs steps 1 and 2;

→ diphone bootstrapping (DB). It performs step 3.

The GTS and DB modules can be used separately. For a given application, it is necessary to perform the GTS procedure only once and the DB procedure every time templates by a new speaker are needed.

GENERATION OF THE TRAINING SENTENCES

The input to the GTS module (see Fig. 1) consists of the vocabulary of the language and of a BNF representation of the grammar of the application, which must be a regular grammar. The main task performed by the procedure is the creation of the set of training sentences which, uttered by the test speaker, will constitute the training set and supply the templates. The procedure also produces the new diphone dictionary scheme, and a file which provides the DB module with the information necessary, i.e., the context of the diphones in each word and the transitional diphones that may be present at the junction between two consecutive words. It should be noted that it is possible to create a training set containing only some of the diphones of the application. This is useful if a dictionary of templates for the test speaker is available but a different application is required. This means that a number of templates already existing need not be extracted again; in this case it is convenient to enlarge the old dictionary by simply adding the missing units.

The GTS procedure was developed in a modular way, so that different routines perform a part of the whole task.

First a list of the necessary units is derived from the vocabulary by generating diphone expansions for each word using the rules described in Section 3. The procedure also finds out which stationary diphones appear in different prosodic situations and thus require multiple templates. At present multiple templates are only derived for sonorant sounds (vowels, liquids and nasals) if they appear in different positions in the words of the lexicon (initial / intermediate / final). For vowels the stress level is also considered. Altogether about 500 templates can represent the whole Italian lexicon for an individual speaker. A list of the junction diphones is derived by examining all the possible couples of consecutive words in the language to find out when an optional transitional diphone can be present at their junction. The junctions between words generally correspond to diphthongs (as usually Italian words end with a vowel), but they may also be consonant-vowel or consonant-consonant transitions, as shown for instance in Fig. 3 ("NA", "LM").

Another routine generates the set of training sentences that are expected to include one occurrence of each diphone. If a diphone can appear in different prosodic situations, at least one occurrence corresponding to each of them will be present, and it will be possible to extract each junction diphone between consecutive words. It is not necessary for the training set language to be the same as that of the application. A different grammar can be used that includes all the words of the lexicon; shorter or fewer training sentences can be obtained with a more flexible, less constrained training grammar, including a greater number of permissible sequences of word. This can be done for instance by allowing the elimination of some portions of sentences.

The input to the procedure for generating the training sentences consists of the training grammar and of a table containing, for each necessary template, a list of all the words that contain it. The procedure repeatedly creates groups of words, parts of correct sentences of the language, each group corresponding to the expansion of a non-terminal symbol in the grammar. This process stops as soon as all the templates are present in one or other of the groups. To go into detail, at each step the set of templates that have not yet been included in any group is examined. Only the templates that appear in a minimal number of words of the lexicon are considered: for each of these templates one of the words containing it is selected, namely the one comprising the greatest number of unselected templates. The groups of words are then arranged into a set, which must contain all the selected words; each group includes two or if possible more selected words, plus others chosen in such a way as to minimize the length of the group, while extracting as many templates as possible from it. When all the templates are present in one or other of the groups a set of complete sentences including all the groups is generated by adding as few words as possible.

DIPHONE BOOTSTRAPPING

Having generated a set of sentences containing occurrences of all the units needed for a given task by means of the above described GTS procedure, we have a complete training set. The actual template extraction is accomplished for each speaker through the DB procedure described in [2] (another example of a bootstrapping technique for deriving sub-word units, namely Japanese syllables, can be found in [5]).

The DB procedure, which is sketched in Fig. 4, consists of four steps, namely:

1) the acquisition and analysis of the training set;

2) a forced recognition of the training sentences, with hand-cut or automatically derived templates from a training speaker, by means of which the signal is

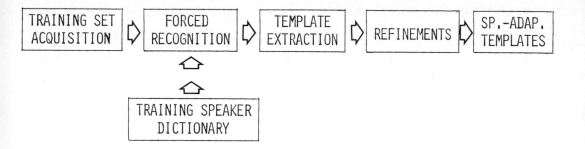

FIG. 4 :   The Diphone Bootstrapping procedure.

segmented into diphones;

3)   the template extraction;

4)   a refinement session, for a check on the bootstrapped templates and, if necessary, the addition of any missing templates.

With regard to the *acquisition* (step 1), we must point out that the GTS procedure not only generates a complete training set (that is, all the templates needed can be extracted from it), but also makes the training session short and easy relative to the application.   The training sentences are in fact fairly few; moreover, the fact that they are meaningful means that they can be uttered in a natural way.   However, the speaker is allowed to utter every training sentence without any constraint on pronunciation.   Each training utterance is sampled at 10 KHz and 12 Cepstrum coefficients are calculated every 10 ms.

The *forced recognition* of each training utterance (step 2) is accomplished by making use of one training speaker's prototypes as a reference set [2] and of a constrained network.   The latter is obtained from the general network representation of the language by forcing the word sequence to be uniquely the correct one, while within each word all the valid sequences of diphones are permitted, and the general junction rules between adjacent words apply. Fig. 5-a

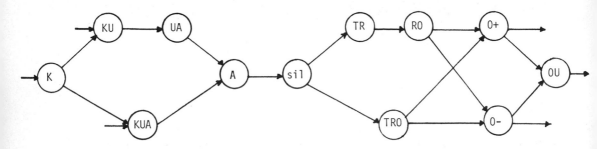

FIG. 5-a : Diphone network for the word "QUATTRO" ("four").

shows the network representation of the Italian digit "quattro" ("four"), with different paths corresponding to alternative allowed sequences of diphones. In particular, note at the end of the word the diphthong "OU" representing the possible junction with a word beginning with "U" (such as "uno"). The path in the network through "OU" is permitted but not forced, in order to take into account possible hesitations between words. Fig. 5-b shows a portion of a training utterance, containing the word "quattro", with the actual output of forced recognition. It corresponds to the sequence of diphones attaining the highest cumulative similarity score. Each diphone is delimited by its boundaries (marked with solid lines on the waveform). From each diphone occurrence a possible template for that diphone can be extracted.

The *template extraction* (step 3) is performed for a transitional diphone by taking the entire portion of signal corresponding to an occurrence, while for steady-state diphones only the central frame of an appropriate occurrence is

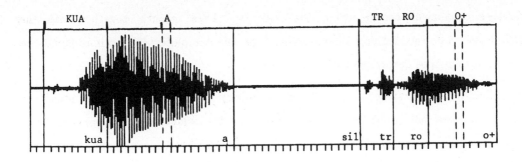

FIG. 5-b :   Templates for some diphones in the word "QUATTRO" as detected
by the forced recognition.

chosen (marked with dotted lines in Fig. 5-b). Only one template is derived for
each different context of each diphone; the template is extracted from the first
available occurrence of that diphone in the relevant context situation (for
steady-state diphones occurrences shorter than a given duration are discarded).
At present all diphones except steady-state ones corrresponding to sonorant sounds
are considered mono-context; therefore multiple templates are derived only for
vowels, nasals and liquids.

Finally (step 4) we apply two different kinds of *refinements*: template
checking and dictionary filling. Although the segmentation produced by forced
recognition is fairly accurate, we check the correctness of the location of the
automatically derived templates. For steady-state diphones the steadiness of the
intensity pattern and Cepstrum coefficients is checked against the surrounding
environment of the template: the variation must not exceed a given threshold.
For transitions the behaviour of spectral and energetic derivatives is examined.
Any bad template for a diphone is dropped and, if possible, replaced with

another convenient occurrence of the diphone. These checks, together with the reliability of forced segmentation, ensure that the templates for each diphone are derived from true occurrences of that diphone.

Finally, we provide a means for dictionary filling. In fact the procedure described does not guarantee the extraction of the whole set of templates from the training material. For instance a dropped template may not have been replaced, or none of the occurrences of a final vowel may be long enough, or a certain junction diphone may be missing due to non-fluent pronunciation. Missing templates (if any) are simply supplied by the training speaker's dictionary.

The output of the DB procedure is a manageable diphone template dictionary tailored for the speaker. This template dictionary provides a complete and correct representation of the lexicon relating to a given application and is part of the acoustic knowledge of the system.

7. EXPERIMENTAL RESULTS

Different applications are being tested in our Laboratory. Until now only one extensive experiment with automatically derived prototypes has been completed on the language of sequences of Italian digits. It was mainly performed in order to check the adequacy of the diphone bootstrapping procedure, but the whole described procedure of generation of the recognizer data bases was used. The recognition experiment with bootstrapped templates was done on 20 sequences of 5 connected digits, each uttered by 19 (9 male and 10 female) speakers. Each digit was present 10 times in different contexts in the test set. The training set was not acquired at the same time as the test set, thus proving that the efficacy of the template set was not influenced by environmental conditions. The three reference template dictionaries used for forced recognition contained hand-extracted prototypes from other speakers (two males and a female).

An average word recognition rate (WRR) of 99% corresponding to a rate greater than 98.5% with a confidence level of 99%, was obtained over the whole experiment, which included 1900 words. This corresponds to a 95.5% recognition rate on the 5-digit sequences. These results show the effectiveness of the training procedure, as they are only slightly below the average WRR of 99.5% obtained in a speaker-dependent recognition experiment with hand-extracted templates. Moreover they display a satisfactory improvement over the 88.9% average WRR obtained in a speaker-independent test with the training speakers' templates.

The above experimental results clearly show how our automatic training procedure produces reliable template sets (at least for small vocabularies). Moreover the procedure not only performed very well on the average, but also yielded homogeneous results on all the test speakers: even for the worst speaker 96 words out of 100 were correctly recognized.

8. CONCLUSIONS

We have presented a knowledge generation procedure for a diphone-based CSR system, which generates all the pieces of information relating to any given application in a completely automatic way. The procedure can also train the system on new speakers deriving a complete and correct template dictionary for each of them.

We make use of the procedure, which has proved to be both fast and reliable, as a tool for testing our system in new recognition tasks with a great number of different speakers. However, the main aim of the procedure is to enable the system to be used by unskilled users in practical applications. In fact none of the steps performed by the procedure require any intervention by the user, who only needs to supply the lexicon and a BNF representation of the grammar of the language.

The procedure has been developed in a modular way, so that it is possible to use the various modules separately, if only one specific task (such as the search for the diphone inventory, or the template bootstrapping) has to be performed.

REFERENCES

1. P. S. Cohen and R. L. Mercer, "The Phonological Component of an Automatic Speech Recognition System", in D. R. Reddy (Editor), *SPEECH RECOGNITION*, Academic Press, New York, p. 275, 1975.
2. A. M. Colla and D. Sciarra, "Automatic Diphone Bootstrapping for Speaker-Adaptive Continuous Speech Recognition", Proc. ICASSP 1984, (35.2), S. Diego, 1984.
3. J. L. Flanagan, C. H. Coker, L. R. Rabiner, R. W. Schafer and N. Umeda, "Synthetic Voices for Computers", IEEE Spectrum, 7, p. 22, 1970.
4. K. S. Fu, *SYNTACTIC METHODS IN PATTERN RECOGNITION*, Academic Press, New York, 1974.
5. H. Fujisaki, K. Hirose and T. Inoue, "Automatic Recognition of Connected Words from a Large Vocabulary Using Syllable Templates", Proc. ICASSP 1984, (26.9), S. Diego, 1984.
6. D. Hopkin and B. Moss, *AUTOMATA*, MacMillan, London, p. 5, 1976.
7. M. J. Hunt, M. Lennig and P. Mermelstein, "Experiments in Syllable Based Recognition of Continuous Speech", Proc. ICASSP 1980, Denver, p. 880, 1980.
8. D. H. Klatt, "SCRIBER and LAFS: Two New Approaches to Speech Analysis", in W. A. Lea (Editor), *TRENDS IN SPEECH RECOGNITION*, Prentice-Hall, Englewood Cliffs, p. 529, 1980.
9. B. T. Lowerre and D. R. Reddy, "The HARPY Speech Understanding System", in W. A. Lea (Editor), *TRENDS IN SPEECH RECOGNITION*, Prentice-Hall, Englewood Cliffs, p. 340, 1980.
10. C. S. Myers, L. R. Rabiner and A. E. Rosenberg, "On the Use of Dynamic Time Warping for Word Spotting and Connected Word Recognition", The Bell System Technical Journal, 60, 3, p. 303-325, 1981.
11. M. Onishi (Supervisor), *A GRAND DICTIONARY OF PHONETICS*, The Phonetic Society of Japan, p. 129, 1981.
12. J. E. Paul and A. S. Rabinowitz, "An Acoustically Based Continuous Speech Recognition System", IEEE Symposium on Speech Recognition, Carnegie-Mellon University, Pittsburgh, PA, p. 63, 1974.
13. L. R. Rabiner and R. W. Schafer, *DIGITAL PROCESSING OF SPEECH SIGNAL*, Prentice-Hall, Englewood Cliffs, p. 442, 1978.
14. C. Scagliola and L. Marmi, "Continuous Speech Recognition via Diphone Spotting: a Preliminary Implementation", Proc. ICASSP 1982, Paris, p. 2008, 1982.

15. C. Scagliola, "Continuous Speech Recognition Without Segmentation: Two Ways of Using Diphones as Basic Speech Units", Speech Communication, 2 (2-3), p. 199, 1983.
16. C. Scagliola, "Language Models and Search Algorithms for Real-Time Speech Recognition" (to appear on: International Journal of Man-Machine Studies).
17. J. E. Shoup, "Phonological Aspects of Speech Recognition", in W. A. Lea (Editor), *TRENDS IN SPEECH RECOGNITION*, Prentice-Hall, Englewood Cliffs, p. 125, 1980.

THE USE OF DYNAMIC FREQUENCY WARPING IN A SPEAKER-INDEPENDENT VOWEL CLASSIFIER

W. A. Ainsworth and H. M. Foster

Department of Communication & Neuroscience

University of Keele

Keele, Staffs., ST5 5BG

ENGLAND

ABSTRACT

A dynamic frequency warping algorithm has been used to match the spectra of the vowels of one speaker against the spectra of vowels of different speakers. Although the method resulted in a transformation which produced a good match, it was not accurate as a speaker-independent vowel classifier. With reference spectra from the vowels of male speakers and test spectra from the vowels of female speakers, and vice versa, the recogntion scores were only 33%, whilst with reference and test spectra from different utterances of the same speaker the mean score was 96%.

Various parameters of the spectra and the DFW algorithm have been studied. It was found that limiting the frequency range of the spectra to approximately telephone bandwidth (250-3200 Hz) increased the male-female scores by about 6%. Changing the frequency scale to barks or reducing the order of the linear prediction analysis reduced the recognition scores. Adjusting the warping window in the dynamic programming algorithm so that it was 160 Hz wide above the diagonal raised the male-female recognition score to 48.6%.

NATO ASI Series, Vol. F16
New Systems and Architectures for Automatic Speech
Recognition and Synthesis. Edited by R. De Mori and C. Y. Suen
© Springer-Verlag Berlin Heidelberg 1985

INTRODUCTION

The vowels of female speakers have higher formant frequencies than those of males because of their shorter vocal tracts. This causes no difficulty for a human listener, but the mechanism by which the compensation for different size vocal tracts occurs is not understood. It is possible that a value derived from the average fundamental frequency is used as a normalising factor, or that the average values of the formant frequencies are used. Perceptual experiments by Fujisaki and Kawashima (1968) and Ainsworth (1975) suggest that either or both of these factors are involved.

A more detailed examination of the formant frequencies of the vowels produced by male and female speakers, however, shows that a non-linear transformation is required to change the formant frequencies of a male vowel into those of a female vowel (Fant, 1975).

DYNAMIC TIME WARPING

In the time domain a superficially similar situation exists. Not only is the total duration of a fast utterance of a word shorter than that of a slow utterance of the same word, but the duration of certain sounds are relatively much shorter in the fast utterance. In automatic speech recognition systems it is possible to minimise the effects of these differences in duration by means of dynamic programming algorithms which compress and expand in the time scale of a test word in order to effect an optimal match with a reference word. This technique is known as dynamic time warping (Sakoe and Chiba, 1978; Myers, Rabiner and Rosenberg, 1980).

DYNAMIC FREQUENCY WARPING

In the present project a number of dynamic programming algorithms have been applied in the frequency domain to the problem of matching the vowels of one speaker against those of another speaker (Paliwal and Ainsworth, 1985).

Suppose that the log-power spectrum of a test vowel uniformly sampled at m frequency values, is:

$$\underline{a} = (a_1, a_2, \ldots a_i, \ldots a_m)$$

and the spectrum of a reference vowel (of another speaker) is:

$$\underline{b} = (b_1, b_2, \ldots b_j, \ldots b_m).$$

In order to obtain the optimum warping path between these spectra, the distance D $(\underline{a}, \underline{b})$ is computed along all possible warping paths between the points (1, 1) and (m, m) constrained by the warping window.

The distance D($\underline{a}, \underline{b}$) is computed as follows. The local distance between the ith component of the test spectrum and the jth component of the reference spectrum is given by:

$$d(i, j) = (a_i - b_j)^2.$$

The cumulative distance function at the point (i, j) is given by Sakoe and Chiba (1978):

$$g(i, j) = \min \begin{cases} g(i-1, j) + d(i, j) \\ g(i-1, j-1) + 2d(i,j) \\ g(i, j-1) + d(i,j) \end{cases}$$

with the initial condition g(1, 1) = 2d(1, 1).

The distance D($\underline{a},\underline{b}$) along the optimum warping path is computed from the final cumulative distance function by:

$$D(\underline{a}, \underline{b}) = g(m, m)/2m.$$

VOWEL ANALYSIS AND CLASSIFICATION

The eleven English vowels were spoken in /hVd/ context ten times by each of eight speakers (four male and four female). The waveforms were digitised at 10 kHz and displayed on a CRT. A 25.6 msec segment from the steady state part of each vowel was selected manually. The segment was weighted by a Hamming window function and a 10th order linear prediction analysis was performed using the autocorrelation method (Makhoul, 1975). The log-power spectrum was obtained from the resulting ten linear prediction coefficients by computing a 256-point discrete Fourier transform using the fast Fourier transform algorithm. Reference spectra were computed for each speaker by averaging the repetitions of the spectra of each vowel.

The above dynamic frequency warping (DFW) algorithm was applied to each pair of test and reference spectra. Vowel classification was achieved by choosing the reference class, p, for which:

$$D(\underline{a}, \underline{b}^{p}) < D(\underline{a}, \underline{b}^{q})$$

for all q except p = q.

A number of parameters affecting the vowel spectra and the warping window were varied in order to study their effects on the performance of the vowel classification system.

SPEAKER-DEPENDENT AND SPEAKER-INDEPENDENT RECOGNITION

In order to provide base-line data, the vowel classifier was tested in both speaker-dependent and speaker-independent modes. The test patterns were the 128-point log-power spectra from each speaker. The reference patterns were the averaged spectra from each speaker. The system was trained with the vowels of each speaker one at a time.

The warping window was a region parallel to the diagonal bounded by $j = i - r$ and $j = i + r$, where r is the warping window length. It had been shown previously (Paliwal and Ainsworth, 1985) that recognition performance does not depend greatly on warping window length in the rang $r = 0$ to 8. (The units of r are the spectrum range (5 kHz)/no. of points (128) $= 39$ Hz.) It was found that when trained with one male speaker and tested with another, the recognition score deteriorated with increase in r, whereas when trained with a male speaker and tested with a female, the recognition score increased slightly with increase in warping window length. In the present experiment a value of $r = 4$ was employed.

The results are shown in Table 1. In speaker-dependent mode a mean recognition score of 96.1% was obtained for both the male and female groups of speakers. In speaker-independent mode, where the reference vowels have been excluded from the test set, the performance dropped dramatically. With male reference vowel spectra and female test spectra, or vice versa, the mean recognition score was about 33%.

TABLE 1

Recognition scores obtained with speaker-dependent and speaker-independent vowel
classifiers using dynamic frequency warping.

Speaker	Reference vowels	Test vowels	Recognition score (%)
Dependent	Male	Same male	96.1
	Female	Same female	96.1
	Both	Same speaker	96.1
Independent	Male	Different male	53.4
	Female	Different female	44.0
	Male	Female	33.6
	Female	Male	32.2
	Both	Different speaker	39.7

NUMBER OF POINTS IN THE SPECTRUM

It has long been known that the most important factors for the discrimination of vowel sounds are frequencies of the first two formants (Pols, van der Kamp, and Plomp, 1969). These occupy the frequency range from about 200-3000 Hz. It is possible that only information in this range contributes to vowel recognition, and by ignoring information outside this range little deterioration in performance would result. The advantage of restricting the number of points is that the amount of computation is reduced.

The experiment described in the last section was repeated, but only using the first 80-points of each spectrum. This effectively reduces the frequency range to about 3200 Hz. The computation time was about halved.

The results are shown in Table 2. In speaker-dependent mode the recognition scores were reduced by about 3% to 93%. In speaker-independent mode, however, the mean recognition score increased by about 3% to 43%. The largest increase was found with male reference patterns and female test patterns, or vice versa, where the mean recognition scores increased by about 6% to 39%.

PSYCHOPHYSICAL SCALING

The points in the spectra are equally spaced in the physical frequency scale of Hertz. This was a consequence of employing the fast Fourier transform algorithm in the analysis. Perceptual studies, however, have shown that another frequency scale is more appropriate when listening to sounds. This is the Bark scale which effectively places the sampling points nearer together in the low frequencies and further apart in the high frequencies. An appropriate transformation is given by Schroeder, Atal and Hall (1979) as:

$$f = 650 \sink (x/7)$$

where f is the frequency in Hertz and x is the frequency in Barks.

TABLE 2

Recognition scores obtained for speaker-dependent and speaker-independent vowel classifiers using DFW with the frequency of the spectra limited to 0-3200 Hz.

Speaker	Reference	Test	Score
Dependent	Male	Same male	92.7
	Female	Same female	93.0
	both	Same	92.9
Independent	Male	Different male	48.7
	Female	Different female	46.4
	Male	Female	39.3
	Female	Male	39.2
	Both	Different speaker	42.8

Psychophysical spectra were constructed using this transformation, and the experiment with the vowel classifier was repeated with the vowels from all speakers forming the reference patterns and the vowels from the male speakers as the test pattern.

The results are given in Table 3. They show that the scores are about 5% less with the psychophysical spectra compared with the scores obtained with the physical spectra.

NUMBER OF LINEAR PREDICTION COEFFICIENTS

For the production of a neutral vowel the vocal tract can be modelled approximately by a uniform tube closed at one end (the glottis) and open at the other (the lips). The resonances of this tube are uniformly spaced. For a male speaker the formant frequencies are approximately at 500, 1500, 2500 Hz etc., making a total of five formants below 5000 Hz. For a typical female speaker the formant frequencies are about 20% higher, i.e. at 600, 1800, 3000 Hz etc. The female vowel has only four formants below 5000 Hz. One of the reasons why the male-female recognition scores are so low is that the DFW algorithm is attempting to match spectra having different numbers of formants, although they represent the same vowel class.

One way of reducing the number of apparent formants in a spectrum is to reduce the number of linear prediction coefficients in the analysis. This effectively models the vocal tract with a filter having less poles. In order to examine whether these simplified spectra are more useful for vowel recognition, the experiment was repeated with 6th order linear prediction analysis.

The results of this experiment are also shown in Table 3. It can be seen that 6th order linear prediction analysis is less useful than 10th order linear prdiction analysis for vowel spectra measured in either physical or psychophysical frequency units.

TABLE 3

Comparison of the recognition scores obtained with the spectra in Hz and in barks. The spectra obtained from the vowels of the male speakers were employed as the test patterns.

Reference patterns	10th order LPC		6th order LPC	
	Hz	Barks	Hz	Barks
Speaker-dependent males	92.7	86.1	88.0	78.4
Speaker-indpendent males	48.7	42.6	43.2	34.4
Females	39.2	33.2	36.4	33.5

LOW FREQUENCY LIMITATION

Although linear prediction analysis attempts to separate the source from the filter function of speech production, there are still major differences in the low frequency region of the spectra of vowels produced by different speakers. It is expected that the information in this region contributes little to the classification of the vowels of different speakers, so an experiment was performed in which the low frequency information was successively eliminated. The vowels from the male speakers were used to form the reference patterns and those from the female speakers were used as the test patterns.

The results are shown in Table 4. For the 3200 spectrum, there was a slight increase in the recognition score when the low frequency of the spectrum was limited to 250 Hz but this decreased at 500 and 1000 Hz. A similar pattern of results was obtained for the full spectrum (up to 5000 Hz) although there was little difference between 0 and 250 Hz.

SIZE OF THE WARPING WINDOW

All the experiments described so far have employed a warping window which is symmetrical about the diagonal. This is appropriate for a speaker-independent system. However, although the test speaker is unknown, the identity of the speaker who forms the reference patterns can be known. If he is a male speaker it might be expected that vowel spectra from another male speaker would need to be compressed or expanded with equal probability in order to obtain the test match. With vowel spectra from a female speaker, however, it would be expected that more compression than expansion would be required. To test this hypothesis an experiment was carried out with asymmetrric warping windows, with male reference patterns and female test patterns.

TABLE 4

The effect of low frequency limitation on recognition scores for the 3200 Hz and 5000 Hz spectra.   Vowels from the male speakers were used as the refernce patterns and those from the female speakers as tet patterns.

Low frequency (Hz)	Recognition scores (%)	
	3200 Hz	5000 Hz
0	39.3	33.6
250	40.1	33.2
500	37.8	29.3
1000	29.4	24.8

With a symmetric warping window bounded by $j = i - 4$ and $j = i + 4$, a recognition score of 39.3% was obtained. With a warping window bounded by $j = i$ and $j = i + 8$, the score increased to 47.0%. With a warping window bounded by $j = i - 8$ and $j = 0$, the score fell to 24.4%. Thus for male reference patterns and female test patterns an asymmetric warping window increases the recognition score.

A parametric study of the window size was performed next. The warping window was bounded by $j = i + r$ and $j = i$, where r is the window size. The spectra were limited to a frequency rage of 250 to 3200 Hz. The results are shown in Table 5. A maximum recognition score of 48.6% occurred with a warping window size of $r = 4$, i.e. with a warping window 160 Hz wide.

CONCLUSIONS

A dynamic frequency warping algorithm has been studied as a method of recognizing the vowel sounds of different speakers. It was found to give good results (96.1% recognition scores) for a speaker-dependent system, but poor results (39.7%) in a speaker-independent system. In particular with reference patterns obtained from the vowels of male speakers and test patterns from the vowels of female speakers, and vice versa, the recognition scores were only 33%.

Limiting the high frequency of the spectra to 3200 Hz raised the male-female recognition scores to 39%, and this was increased to 40% by limiting the frequency range to 250-3200 Hz. It was found that changing to a psychophysical frequency scale (barks) or reducing the order of the linear prediction analysis both had a deleterious effect on the recognition scores.

The greatest increase in recognition score, to 48.6%, ws obtained for the male reference patterns and female test patterns by using an asymmetric warping window in the dynamic programming algorithm. It is suggested that further investigation into the optimum shape of the warping window is required.

TABLE 5

Recognition scores obtained with an asymmetric warping window bounded by
$j = i + r$ and $j = i$. Vowels from the male speakers were used as the reference
patterns and vowels from the female speakers as the test patterns.

Warping window size (Hz)	Recognition score (%)
0	38.4
80	44.4
160	48.6
320	47.0
480	43.8

ACKNOWLEDGEMENTS

We are indebted to Dr. K. K. Paliwal for writing the computer programs and collaborating during the early experiments. The work was supported by the UK Science and Engineering Research Council.

REFERENCES

1. W. A. Ainsworth (1975) "Intrinsic and extrinsic factors in vowel judgements", *Auditory Analysis and Perception of Speech*, (G. Fant and M. Tatham, eds.), Academic Press, London, 103-113.
2. G. Fant (1975), "Nonuniform vowel normalisation", *STL QPR*, No. 2-3, RIT, Stockholm, Sweden, 1-19.
3. H. Fujisaki and T. Kawashima (1968), "The roles of pitch and higher formants in the perception of vowels", *IEEE Trans. Audio. Electroacoust.*, *AU-16*, 73-77.
4. J. Makhoul (1975), "Linear prediction, a tutorial review", *Proc. IEEE*, 63, No. 4, 561-580.
5. C. Myers, L. R. Rabiner and A. E. Rosenberg (1980), "Performance tradeoffs in dynamic time warping algorithms for isolated word recognition", *IEEE Trans.*, *ASSP-28*, No. 6, 623-635.
6. K. K. Paliwal and W. A. Ainsworth (1985), "Dynamic frequency warping for speaker adaptation in automatic speech recognition", J. Phonetics, Vol. 13, No. 1.
7. L. C. W. Pols, L. J. van der Kamp and R. Plomp (1969), "Perceptual and physical space for vowel sounds", *J. Acoust. Soc. Am.*, 46, 458-467.
8. H. Sakoe and S. Chiba (1978), "Dynamic programming algorithm for spoken word recognition", *IEEE Trans.*, *ASSP-26*, No. 1, 43-49.
9. M. R. Schroeder, B. S. Atal and J. L. Hall (1979), "Objective measure of certain speech signal degradations based on masking properties of human auditory perception", *Frontiers of Speech Communication Research*, (B. Lindblom and S. Ohman, eds.), Academic Press, London, 212-229.

DYNAMIC TIME WARPING ALGORITHMS FOR
ISOLATED AND CONNECTED WORD RECOGNITION

J. di Martino
C.R.I.N. – Université de Nancy I
B.P. 239 – 54506 Vandoeuvre

ABSTRACT

In this paper we present a new formulation of the dynamic programming recursive relations both for word and connected word recognition that permits relaxation of boundary conditions imposed on the warping paths, while preserving the optimal character of the dynamic time warping algorithms.

I. INTRODUCTION

One of the most interesting approach for word recognition and connected word recognition is based on the dynamic programming approach. Several studies have shown that the technique of dynamic programming is very well suited for compensating for time distorsions due to the variability of elocution speed [1]-[8]. However, most of the algorithms that have been presented until now assume that the extraction of the vocal forms from the ambiant noise is error free and that the end-words are not too much corrupted by parasite noises. Unfortunately in practice such conditions are not always respected. For instance most of the speech detectors have great difficulties in capturing weak energy end-phonemes. Some attempts [1] [3] [4] have been made to take into account these problems, but all the strategies used failed in trying to maintain the optimality of the dynamic matching.

In this paper, after a brief summary of the dynamic programming technique, we introduce new dynamic recursive relations both for isolated word recognition and connected word recognition. These relations compensate for distorsions that may affect the end-words and at the same time preserves the optimality of the dynamic time warping algorithms. Preliminary experimental results in the case of isolated word recognition are given.

II. SOME NOTIONS ON TIME ALIGNMENT

Let $\quad T = t(1), t(2), \ldots t(i), \ldots t(I)$
and
$\quad\quad R = r(1), r(2), \ldots r(j), \ldots r(J)$

be two speech patterns, where $t(i)$ and $r(j)$ are multidimentional feature vectors characterizing the speech signal at a given instant. The purpose of time alignment is to make a time registration between these vectors so as to synchronise the time scales of the two patterns. This registration can be formalized mathematically as the problem of finding among the functions :

$$W : \mathbb{N}_{I \times J} \to \mathbb{N}_I \times \mathbb{N}_J$$

$$k \longrightarrow W(k) = (i(k), j(k))$$

NATO ASI Series, Vol. F16
New Systems and Architectures for Automatic Speech
Recognition and Synthesis. Edited by R. De Mori and C. Y. Suen
© Springer-Verlag Berlin Heidelberg 1985

- where $\mathbb{N}p = \{1, 2, \ldots p\}$ and $W(k)$ indicates that the kth coincidence associates the feature vector $i(k)$ of the pattern T with the feature vector $j(k)$ of the pattern R -

the optimal one that realizes the best mapping between the two patterns. The mappings W are called warping functions. In order for the warping paths to respect time fluctuations of the speech signal, the following monotonic conditions must be applied to the warping paths :

$$(1) \quad \begin{cases} i(k - 1) \leqslant i(k) \\ j(k - 1) \leqslant j(k) . \end{cases}$$

Furthermore, to eliminate possible unrealistic contractions or dilatations, local constraints, introducing continuity and slope conditions, must be applied. Relation (2) is an exemple of a local constraint due to Itakura [8] :

$$(2) \quad \begin{cases} j(k + 1) - j(k) = 0, 1, 2 & \text{If} \quad j(k) \neq j(k - 1) \\ j(k + 1) - j(k) = 1, 2 & \text{If} \quad j(k) = j(k - 1) \end{cases}$$

Finally, to avoid omission of word-end feature vectors through warping the end-frames of the two patterns are matched by the following boundary conditions :

$$(3 - a) \quad \begin{cases} i(1) = 1 \\ j(1) = 1 \end{cases}$$

- where K is the number of points of the warping path -

$$(3 - b) \quad \begin{cases} i(K) = I \\ j(K) = J \end{cases}$$

The optimal warping path is determined using the following metric on the set of warping functions :

$$(4) \quad D(W) = \frac{\sum_{k=1}^{K} d(i(k), j(k)) * P(k)}{N(P)}$$

- where : . K is the number of points of the warping path,
  . $d(i(k), j(k))$ is a local distance between the $i(k)$'th vector of the pattern T and the $j(k)$'th vector of the pattern R ,
  . $N(P)$ is a normalization factor that depends on the type of the weighting function used. The purpose of this factor is to compensate for the effect of K that is to say to make the metric independent of the length of the warping path.

The optimal path is then defined by :

$$(5) \quad \hat{W} = \underset{W}{\text{ARGMIN}} \quad D(W) .$$

In combining relation (4) with relation (5) the problem of time normalization can be solved as :

$$(6) \quad D(\hat{W}) = \underset{K, i(k), j(k)}{\text{MIN}} \quad \frac{\sum_{k=1}^{K} d(i(k), j(k)) * P(k)}{N(P)} .$$

The typical weighting functions generally used are :

(7) $Pa(k) = i(k) - i(k - 1)$

(8) $Ps(k) = i(k) - i(k - 1) + j(k) - j(k - 1)$.

The first is asymmetric since it is only function of the index of the projection of the pattern into the horizontal axis while the second one is symmetric being function of the indices of both the two patterns.

The motivation of this choice stems from the fact that if we define the normalization factor $N(P)$ by :

(9) $N(P) = \sum_{k=1}^{K} P(k)$,

then it is easy to show, by substituting relations (7) and (8) in (9) and in taking into account relations (3-a) and (3-b) that $N(Pa) = I$ and $N(Ps) = I + J$. Consequently, $N(P)$, for $P = Pa$ or $P = Ps$, is a constant, so can therefore be factorized in relation (6) :

(10) $D(\hat{W}) = \dfrac{1}{N(P)} * \underset{K,\ i(k),\ j(k)}{MIN} \sum_{k=1}^{K} d(i(k),\ j(k)) * P(k)$.

Relation (10) can be solved by dynamic programming owing to the following local optimality principle introduced by Bellman [9]

- let $C[(1, 1), (i ,j)]$ be the optimal path joining the point (1, 1) and the point (i, j) , then for any point (i', j') belonging to $C[1, 1), (i, j)]$, the optimal path $C[(1, 1), (i', j')]$ is included in $C[(1, 1), (i, j)]$ as a portion of it.

Thus if we define $D(i, j)$ as the unnormalized distance associated with the optimal path $C[(1, 1), (i, j)]$, in applying the local optimality principle $D(i, j)$ can be expressed as :

(11) $D(i, j) = \underset{\substack{(i', j') \\ \in V(i, j)}}{MIN} D(i', j') + dp((i', j'), (i, j))$

where (i', j') belongs to the neighbourhood $V(i, j)$ of the point (i, j) defined by the local constraint - for example in the case of the local constraint defined by relation (2) , $V(i, j)$ is the set $\{(i - 1, j), (i - 1, j - 1), (i - 1, j - 2)\}$ - and $dp((i', j'), (i, j))$ is the weighted distance between the point (i', j') and the point (i, j) .

Consequently thanks to the recursive expression of $D(i, j)$ given by relation (11) the following simple algorithm evaluating $D(\hat{W})$ is easily obtained :

1) INITIALIZATION

$D(1, 1) = d(1, 1) * P(1)$
$D(1, j) = + \infty$ for $j = 2, \ldots, J$

2) DYNAMIC PROGRAMMING

FOR $2 \leqslant i \leqslant I$ Do
FOR $1 \leqslant j \leqslant J$ Do
COMPUTE RECURSIVELY $D(i, j)$
END FOR, END FOR

3) EVALUATION OF THE DISSIMILARITY DISTANCE

$$D(\hat{W}) = \frac{1}{N(P)} * D(I, J) .$$

III. GENERALIZATION OF THE DYNAMIC PROGRAMMING RECURSIVE RELATIONS

We have seen previously that if the weighting functions are Pa or Ps and if the boundary conditions expressed by relations (3-a) and (3-b) are applied to the warping paths, then the normalization factor is a constant. From this result and from the local optimality principle we get the standard dynamic programming recursive relation given by (11) . If now we are interested in relaxing the boundary conditions so that the DP matching algorithm compensates for distorsions that may corrupt the end-words, then as in this case the length constancy property is not guaranted, it results that (11) does not hold. To make clear this point it is interesting to show that in general when the boundary conditions are relaxed the length constancy property is no more valid.

Let us make the assumption that the initial boundary conditions are relaxed - in this discussion we shall not consider the terminal boundary conditions because the results would be the same - and let us consider first the case of a symmetric local constraint. If the relaxation of the boundary conditions is authorized on the vertical axis, see figure 1-a , the lengths of the paths Cv1, Cv2, Cv3 starting respectively at the points (1, v1), (1, v2), (1, v3) with vi ≠ vj if i ≠ j and ending at the fixe point (I, J) are :

(12) $\ell(Cvi) = I + J - vi + 1$ for i = 1, 2, 3

and as we have assumed that vi ≠ vj if i ≠ j we get $\ell(Cvi) \neq \ell(Cvj)$ if i ≠ j .

In the same way, if the relaxation of the initial boundary conditions is authorized on the horizontal axis, see figure 1-b, the lengths of the paths Ch1, Ch2, Ch3 starting respectively at the points (h1, 1), (h2, 2), (h3, 3) with hi ≠ hj if i ≠ j and ending at the point (I, J) are :

(13) $\ell(Chi) = I + J - hi + 1$

and as hi ≠ hj we get as previously $\ell(Chi) \neq \ell(Chj)$ if i ≠ j . From these results we can already conclude that if the local constraint is symmetric then the length constancy property does not hold if the initial boundary conditions are relaxed.

Let us now consider the case of an asymmetric local constraint. If the initial boundary conditions are relaxed on the vertical axis the lengths of Cv1, Cv2, Cv3 are :

(14) $\ell(Cvi) = I$ for i = 1, 2, 3 .

On the other hand if the relaxation is realized on the horizontal axis, the lengths of Ch1, Ch2, Ch3 are :

(15) $\ell(Chi) = I - hi + 1$

and here again we have $\ell(Chi) \neq \ell(Chj)$ if i ≠ j .

409

In conclusion we have seen that whatever the type of the local constraint the
length constancy property does not hold generally if the initial boundary conditions are relaxed. The only case where the property is still valid is when
the relaxation is done in the vertical axis with an asymmetric constraint.

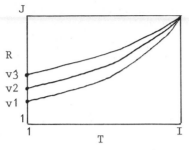

a- Vertical relaxation
of the initial
boundary conditions

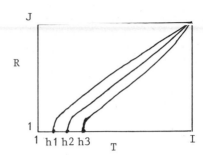

b- Horizontal relaxation
of the initial
boundary conditions

Figure 1 : RELAXATION OF THE INITIAL BOUNDARY CONDITIONS.

In order to take into account variations of the path lengths when the boundary conditions are relaxed, a generalization of the optimality principle is
needed :

- LET B be a sub-set of the matching planc PL , containing all the
points that can be starting points of the warping paths,
- LET p : PL → B the function that gives at each point (i, j) the
starting point of the optimal path ending at (i,j),
- LET $C[p(i, j), (i, j)]$ be the optimal going from the point $p(i, j)$
to the point (i, j) ,

THEN for each point (i', j') belonging to $C[p(i, j), (i, j)]$ we have

1. $p(i', j') = p(i, j)$
2. $C[p(i', j'), (i',j')]$ is included in $C[p(i, j), (i, j)]$, as a
portion of it

With this new local optimality principle, to evaluate the accumulated distance
D(i, j) recursively from the accumulated distances D(i', j') where the points
(i', j') belong to the neighbourhood V(i, j) of the point (i, j) defined
by the local constraint, it is necessary to use a two-phase dynamic programming
strategy $[10][11]$:

- in a first phase the point $(î', ĵ') \in V(i, j)$ through which the optimal path goes must be determined in taking into account the length differences
of the warping paths ending at (i, j). So a normalization of the accumulated
distances by the length of the warping paths must be realized :

$$(16) \quad (î', ĵ') = \underset{\substack{(i', j') \\ \in V(i, j)}}{ARGMIN} \frac{D(i', j') + dp((i', j'), (i, j))}{\ell(C[p(i', j'), (i',j')]) + \ell(C[(i', j'),(i,j)])}$$

(17) $D(i, j) = D(\hat{i}', \hat{j}') + dp((\hat{i}', \hat{j}'), (i, j))$

(18) $p(i, j) = p(\hat{i}', \hat{j}')$

(19) $\ell(C[p(i, j), (i, j)]) = \ell(C[p(\hat{i}', \hat{j}'), (\hat{i}', \hat{j}')])$
$\qquad\qquad\qquad\qquad + \ell(C[(\hat{i}', \hat{j}'), (i, j)])$.

Relations (16), (17), (18) and (19) can be considered as a generalization of relation (11).

For example if the local constraint used is the symmetric Sakoe and Chiba local constraint [7] and if $\ell(i, j)$ denotes an abbreviation of $\ell(C[p(i, j), (i, j)])$ then relations (16), (17), (18) and (19) can be evaluated in the following manner :

1. FIRST PHASE

$$d = \mathrm{MIN} \begin{cases} \dfrac{D(i-2, j-1) + 2 * d(i-1, j) + d(i, j)}{\ell(i-2, j-1) + 2 + 1} = d_1 \\[2mm] \dfrac{D(i-1, j-1) + 2 * d(i, j)}{\ell(i-1, j-1) + 2} = d_2 \\[2mm] \dfrac{D(i-1, j-2) + 2 * d(i, j-1) + d(i, j)}{\ell(i-2, j-1) + 2 + 1} = d_3 \end{cases}$$

2. SECOND PHASE

IF $(d = d_1)$ THEN $D(i, j) = D(i-2, j-1) + 2 * d(i-1, j) + d(i, j)$
$\qquad\qquad\qquad\qquad p(i, j) = p(i-2, j-1)$
$\qquad\qquad\qquad\qquad \ell(i, j) = \ell(i-2, j-1) + 3$

IF $(d = d_2)$ THEN $D(i, j) = D(i-1, j-1) + 2 * d(i, j)$
$\qquad\qquad\qquad\qquad p(i, j) = p(i-1, j-1)$
$\qquad\qquad\qquad\qquad \ell(i, j) = \ell(i-1, j-1) + 2$

IF $(d = d_3)$ THEN $D(i, j) = D(i-1, j-2) + 2 * d(i, j-1) + d(i, j)$
$\qquad\qquad\qquad\qquad p(i, j) = p(i-1, j-2)$
$\qquad\qquad\qquad\qquad \ell(i, j) = \ell(i-1, j-2) + 3$

Owing to relations (16), (17), (18) and (19) it is possible to use a symmetric local constraint even when the boundary conditions are relaxed. That is the reason why we call the algorithm based on relations (16), (17), (18) and (19) using a symmetric local constraint UESLS "Unconstrained End-points Symmetric Local Strategy".

But in fact (16), (17), (18) and (19) are more general than that because they permit the implementation of local constraints weighted by any kind of weighting functions. For example if we consider the Sakoe and Chiba constraint weighted by arbitrary coefficients as indicated by figure 2 then relations (16), (17), (18) and (19) can be evaluated as follows :

1. FIRST PHASE

$$d = MIN \begin{cases} \dfrac{D(i-2, j-1) + a * d(i-1, j) + b * d(i, j)}{\ell(i-2, j-1) + a + b} = d_1 \\[2ex] \dfrac{D(i-1, j-1) + c * d(i, j)}{\ell(i-1, j-1) + c} = d_2 \\[2ex] \dfrac{D(i-1, j-2) + d * d(i, j-1) + c * d(i, j)}{\ell(i-1, j-2) + d + e} = d_3 \end{cases}$$

2. SECOND PHASE

IF $(d = d_1)$ THEN $D(i, j) = D(i-2, j-1) + a * d(i-1, j) + b * d(i, j)$

$p(i, j) = p(i-2, j-1)$

$\ell(i, j) = \ell(i-2, j-1) + a + b$

IF $(d = d_2)$ THEN $D(i, j) = D(i-1, j-1) + c * d(i, j)$

$p(i, j) = p(i-1, j-1)$

$\ell(i, j) = \ell(i-1, j-1) + c$

IF $(d = d_3)$ THEN $D(i, j) = D(i-1, j-2) + d * D(i, j-1) + e * d(i, j)$

$p(i, j) = p(i-1, j-2)$

$\ell(i, j) = \ell(i-1, j-2) + d + e$

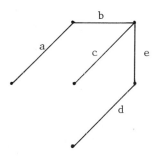

Figure 2 : THE SAKOE AND CHIBA LOCAL CONSTRAINT WEIGHTED
BY ARBITRARY COEFFICIENTS.

IV. EXTENSION OF THE GENERALIZED DYNAMIC PROGRAMMING RECURSIVE RELATIONS IN THE CASE OF THE CONNECTED WORD RECOGNITION PROBLEM

IV.1. Introduction

One of the first attempt to solve the problem of the connected word recognition was undertaken by Sakoe [12]. He showed that the minimization process could be broken down into two dynamic programming levels, a word level where any portion of the input pattern is matched to all the reference patterns, and a phrase level where the best string of reference patterns is found owing to the best partial distances obtained in the word level. Myers and Rabiner [13], later showed that a computationnally more efficient method can be obtained in determining the optimal warping path in a "level building" fashion. The Myers-Rabiner algorithm, although an interesting improvment of the Sakoe algorithm is not very well suited for real time recognition. Recently Bridle et al. [14] and Nakagawa [15], independently proposed an algorithm that eliminates the weaknesses of the level building algorithm. This new algorithm is a one-stage algorithm, that is to say no backward jumps on the input pattern are necessary during the matching process, as is the case for the level building algorithm. Furthermore all the local distances are evaluated only once. However this algorithm is difficult to grasp because the formalism used clouded the useful analogy with the word recognition problem. In a recent paper, Ney [16] has presented a new formalism relying on the use of certain path constraints both in the word interior and at the end-words that links tightly the connected word recognition problem and provides a new and simpler formulation of the algorithm designed by Bridle et al and Nakagawa -hence forward refered as the Bridle-Nakagawa algorithm-.

IV.2. The pattern matching problem

Let T be the test pattern of length I in frames and V a set of N reference patterns R_k of length J_k that have been obtained by an isolated training procedure. The purpose of the connected word recognition is to find the best "super-reference" pattern :

$$SR(\ell, q) = R_{q(1)} \oplus R_{q(2)} \oplus \dots \oplus R_{q(\ell)}$$

defined as the concatenation of ℓ reference patterns that best matches the input pattern. In this problem, ℓ and the boundaries of the words are not known.

IV.3. The dynamic recursive relations of a one-pass algorithm for connected word recognition

The main idea of the one-pass algorithm relies in determining the optimal path in a three-dimensional space as illustrated by figure 3.

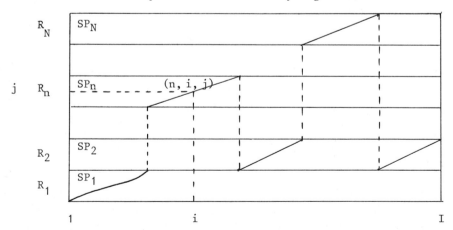

Figure 3 : ILLUSTRATION OF A WARPING PATH IN THE
BRIDLE-NAKAGAWA MATCHING ALGORITHM.

Each point in this matching space can be represented by a triple (n, i, j) where n designates the sub-space SP_n relative to the reference pattern R_n; i the current index of the input pattern, and j the j'th frame of R_n. With this formalism a warping path W is given as a sequence of points $(n(k), i(k), j(k))$ with $k = 1, 2, \ldots, K$, where K is the number of points of the warping path. The problem of the connected word recognition can now be stated in a similar manner as for the word recognition, that is to say, it can be solved by the following global metric minimization :

$$(17) \quad D(\widehat{W}) = \underset{K, \, n(k), \, i(k), \, j(k)}{\text{MIN}} \frac{\sum_{k=1}^{K} d(n(k), i(k), j(k)).P(k)}{N(P)}$$

where $d(n(k), i(k), j(k))$ is the local distance between the $i(k)$'th frame of the input pattern and the $j(k)$'th frame of $R_{n(k)}$.

In the case of a symmetric local constraint, (17) depends on the length of the super-reference patterns that is obviously not constant, so that the normalization factor $N(P)$ cannot be factorized. To get around the difficulty, only asymmetric local constraints with no relaxation of the boundary conditions has hitherto been considered. In that case $N(P)$ is equal to the length of the input pattern and the minimization problem can be expressed as :

$$(18) \quad D*(\widehat{W}) = \underset{K, \, n(k), \, i(k), \, j(k)}{\text{MIN}} \sum_{k=1}^{K} d(n(k), i(k), j(k))*P(k)$$

- the asterisk signifying that the global distance D is not normalized -

In order to solve (18) by a dynamic programming technique, by applying the optimality principle of Bellman, it is necessary to define for each point (n, i, j) of the matching space a minimum accumulated distance $D(n, i, j)$. And, as for the word recognition problem, the evaluation of this distance can be realized recursively as a function of the minimum distances associated to the points belonging to the neighbourhood $V(n, i, j)$ of the point (n, i, j) defined by the local constraint used :

$$(19) \quad D(n, i, j) = \underset{\substack{(n', i', j') \\ \in V(n, i, j)}}{\text{MIN}} D(n', i', j') + d_p((n', i', j'),(n, i, j))$$

where $d_p((n', i', j'),(n, i, j))$ denotes the weighted distance of the local path going from the point (n', i', j') to the point (n, i, j). As was clearly shown in Ney's excellent tutorial paper [16] two types of neighbourhood must be defined : a whitin-template neighbourhood at the interior of a word and a between-template neighbourhood at the boundaries of the words. Assuming the local constraint is the simple constraint with no slope conditions, shown in figure 4, then the within and between template neighbourhoods can be defined respectively by (20) and (21) :

$$(20) \quad V(n, i, j) = \{(n, i - 1, j), (n, i - 1, j - 1), (n, i, j - 1)\}$$
with $j > 1$

$$(21) \quad V(n, i, j) = \{(n, i - 1, j), (n, i - 1, Jn'), n' = 1, 2, \ldots N\}$$
with $j = 1$

Figure 4 : A SIMPLE LOCAL CONSTRAINT WITH NO SLOPE CONDITIONS.

For further details, see [16]. Owing to relations (19), (20) and (21) the connected word recognition problem can be solved in a similar manner as the word
recognition problem – the only differences lying in the introduction of another
loop all over the reference patterns and of backtraking pointers –. It is in
this last point that lies the original approach of Ney.

As now relation (19) can be regarded as just an extension of relation (11), the
generalization of relation (19) in the case of a relaxation of the boundary
conditions can be obtained by analogy with the relations we get for word recognition :

1. FIRST PHASE RELATION

$$(22) \quad (\hat{n}', \hat{i}', \hat{j}') = \mathop{\mathrm{ARGMIN}}_{\substack{(n',i',j') \\ \in V(n,i,j)}} \frac{D(n',i',j') + d_p((n',i',j'), (n, i, j))}{\ell(C[p(n',i',j'), (n',i',j')]) + \ell(C[(n',i',j'), (n, i, j)])}$$

2. SECOND PHASE RELATION

$$(23) \quad D(n, i, j) = D(\hat{n}', \hat{i}', \hat{j}') + d_p(\hat{n}', \hat{i}', \hat{j}'), (n, i, j))$$

$$(24) \quad p(n, i, j) = p(\hat{n}', \hat{i}', \hat{j}')$$

$$(25) \quad \ell(C[p(n, i, j), (n, i, j)]) = \ell(C[p(\hat{n}', \hat{i}', \hat{j}'), (\hat{n}', \hat{i}', \hat{j}')]) + \ell(C[(\hat{n}', \hat{i}', \hat{j}'), (n, i, j)])$$

where p(n, i, j) denotes the starting point of the optimal path going through
the point (n, i, j) .

In order to illustrate how relations (22), (23), (24) and (25) can be implemented in a practical case let us assume that the local constraint used is the simple local constraint with no slope conditions weighted by arbitrary coefficients
– figure 5 – and distinguish the two types of neighbourhoods. The notation
$\ell(n, i, j)$ is an abbreviation of $\ell(C[p(n, i, j), (n, i, j)])$.

Case of a within-template neighbourhood (j > 1) :

$$d = \mathrm{MIN} \begin{cases} \dfrac{D(n, i-1, j) + a * d(n, i, j)}{\ell(n, i-1, j) + a} = d_1 \\[2ex] \dfrac{D(n, i-1, j-1) + b * d(n, i, j)}{\ell(n, i-1, j) + b} = d_2 \\[2ex] \dfrac{D(n, i, j-1) + c * d(n, i, j)}{\ell(n, i, j-1) + c} = d_3 \end{cases}$$

IF $(d = d_1)$ THEN $D(n, i, j) = D(n, i - 1, j) + a * d(n, i, j)$

$p(n, i, j) = p(n, i - 1, j)$

$\ell(n, i, j) = \ell(n, i - 1, j) + a$

IF $(d = d_2)$ THEN $D(n, i, j) = D(n, i - 1, j - 1) + b * d(n, i, j)$

$p(n, i, j) = p(n, i - 1, j - 1)$

$\ell(n, i, j) = \ell(n, i - 1, j - 1) + b$

IF $(d = d_3)$ THEN $D(n, i, j) = D(n, i, j - 1) + c * d(n, i, j)$

$p(n, i, j) = p(n, i, j - 1)$

$\ell(n, i, j) = \ell(n, i, j - 1) + c$

Case of a between-template neighbourhood $(j = 1)$:

$$d = \text{MIN} \begin{cases} \dfrac{D(n, i - 1, j) + a * d(n, i, j)}{\ell(n, i - 1, j) + a} = d_1 \\[2ex] \underset{n'}{\text{MIN}} \quad \dfrac{D(n, i - 1, Jn') + b * d(n, i, j)}{\ell(n, i - 1), Jn') + b} = d_2 \end{cases}$$

IF $(d = d_1)$ THEN $D(n, i, j) = D(n, i - 1, j) + a * d(n, i, j)$

$p(n, i, j) = p(n, i - 1, j)$

$\ell(n, i, j) = \ell(n, i - 1, j) + a$

IF $(d = d_2)$ THEN $\hat{n}' = \underset{n'}{\text{ARGMIN}} \dfrac{D(n, i - 1, Jn') + b * d(n, i, j)}{\ell(n, i - 1, Jn') + b}$

$D(n, i, j) = D(\hat{n}, i - 1, J\hat{n}') + b * d(n, i, j)$

$p(n, i, j) = p(\hat{n}', i - 1, J\hat{n}')$

$\ell(n, i, j) = \ell(\hat{n}', i - 1, J\hat{n}') + b$

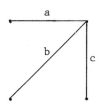

Figure 5 : THE LOCAL CONSTRAINT WITH NO SLOPE CONDITION
WEIGHTED BY ARBITRARY COEFFICIENTS.

V. SOME CONSIDERATIONS ON TIME-SPACE COMPLEXITY

In order to compare our algorithms with the classical DTW algorithms from the point of view of time space complexity we will restrict the discussion to the problem of isolated word recognition – the discussion relative to the connected word recognition would be similar –.

Let N be the number of references, I the length of the test utterance, J the mean length of the references, β the number of bytes necessary to represent a word of data of integer type in the machine used, α the ratio of the time necessary to carry out a floating point division to the time needed to evaluate a local distance. For the standard DTW algorithm, in the case of a full search of the optimal path in the matching $N*I*J$ local distances must be evaluated and $N*J*\beta$ bytes of data are necessary to store the accumulated distances. In the case of our algorithm $N*I*J(1+3\alpha)$ "local distances" must be evaluated and $2*N*J*\beta$ bytes of data are necessary to store both the accumulated distances and the lengths of the partial optimal path ending at each point. From the expression of the number of local distances for our algorithm, we see that the computational effort necessary to implement our algorithm depends critically on the parameter α. If the time necessary for calculating a floating point division is greater or equal than the time necessary for evaluating a local distance - as it is the case in a general computer- the computational effort is multiplied by a factor of 4 or more. It is clear that our algorithm needs a special hardware configuration including an array processor or a digital signal processor. The comparison of the expressions giving the space of the data memory both for the two algorithms shows that our algorithm needs twice as much memory space as the standard algorithm. This is the minimum memory space requirement imposed by our method and there is no way of compression it further.

VI. SOME PRELIMINARY EXPERIMENTAL RESULTS ON WORD RECOGNITION

We have implemented on a mini-computer, MITRA 125, the algorithm we have called previously UESLS using the symmetric Sakoe and Chiba local constraint. The speech signal was analysed by a 16 chanel vocoder with a sampling frequency of 50 Hz. The vocabulary of words considered was the ten french digits. The mismatch in duration, tm , was a parameter of the algorithm. Only one reference was used for each word. Each word was pronounced 20 times. For tm = 0 ms we get 3 % of error rate and for tm = 60 ms we get 1 % of error rate. Consequently an increase in performance seems to appear when the boundary conditions are relaxed. But these experiments are not sufficient to give a final judgment on the performance of the method employed. For a more precise evaluation of the accuracy of the new class of DTW algorithms, both for isolated and connected word recognition, proposed in this paper, extensive experiments are under course in our research group. Detailed results will be given in a companion paper.

VII. CONCLUSION

In this paper we have presented a new formulation of the DTW recursive relations both for word recognition and connected word recognition. The new recursive relations presented are able to take into account possible warping path length variation which may result either from a relaxation of the boundary conditions or from the assignment of arbitrary weighting coefficients to the arcs of the local constraint employed. Preliminary experiments for word recognition indicate an improvment in performance in the case of the ten frech digit vocabulary when the boundary conditions are relaxed.

REFERENCES

[1] L.R. Rabiner, A.E. Rosenberg, S.E. Levinson, "Considerations in Dynamic Time Warping Algorithms for Discrete Word Recognition", IEEE Trans. Acoust., Speech, Signal Processing, vol. ASSP-26, N° 6, pp. 575-582, December 1978.

[2] J.P. Haton, "Contribution à l'Analyse et à la reconnaissance Automatique de la Parole", Thèse d'Etat, Université de Nancy I, January 1974.

[3] S.K. Das, "Some Experiments in Discrete Utterance Recognition", Proc. ICASSP, Denver, Co, 1980, pp. 178-181.

[4] A. Waibel, B. Yegnanarayana, "Comparative Study of Nonlinear Time Warping Techniques in Isolated Word Speech Recognition", Carnegie-Mellon University, Computer Science Department, 1982.

[5] C. Myers, L.R. Rabiner, A.E. Rosenberg, "Performance Tradeoffs in Dynamic Time Warping Algorithms for Isolated Word Recognition", IEEE Trans. Acoust. Speech, Signal Processing, vol. ASSP-6, N° 6, pp. 623-635, December 1980.

[6] H. Sakoe, S. Chiba, "A Dynamic Programming Approach to Continuous Speech Recognition", In Proc. Int. Congr. Acoust., Budapest, Hungary, 1971.

[7] H. Sakoe, S. Chiba, "Dynamic Programming Algorithm Optimization for Spoken Word Recognition", IEEE Trans. Acoust., Speech, Signal Processing, vol. ASSP-26, pp. 43-49, February 1978.

[8] F. Itakura, "Minimum Prediction Residual Principle Applied to Speech Recognition", IEEE Trans. Acoust., Speech, Signal Processing, vol. ASSP-23, pp. 67-72, February 1975.

[9] R. Bellman, "Dynamic Programming", Princeton, N.F. : Princeton, Univ. Press, 1957.

[10] J. di Martino, J.P. Haton, M.C. Haton, "Evaluation d'Algorithmes en Reconnaissance Automatique de la Parole", In Proc. Int. Congr. Acoust., Paris, France, 1983.

[11] J. di Martino, "Contribution à la Reconnaissance Globale de la Parole : Mots Isolés et Mots Enchaînés", Dr. Ing. thesis, Université de Nancy I, April 1984.

[12] H. Sakoe, "Two-Level DP-Matching-A Dynamic Programming Based Pattern Matching Algorithm for Connected Word Recognition", IEEE Trans. Acoust., Speech, Signal Processing, vol. ASSP-27, pp. 588-595, December 1979.

[13] C.S. Myers, L.R. Rabiner, "A Level Building Dynamic Time Warping Algorithm for Connected Word Recognition", IEEE Trans. Acoust., Speech, Signal Processing, vol. ASSP-29, pp. 284-297, April 1981.

[14] J.S. Bridle, M.D. Brown , R.M. Chamberlain, "An Algorithm for Connected Word Recognition", in Proc. 1982, IEEE International Conference on Acoustics, Speech and Signal Processing, Paris, pp. 899-902, May 1982.

[15] S. Nakagawa, "A Connected Spoken Word Recognition Method by O(n) Dynamic Programming Pattern Matching Algorithm", In Proc. 1983, IEEE International Conference on Acoustics, Speech and Signal Processing, Boston, pp. 226-299, April 1983.

[16] H. Ney, "The Use of a One-Stage Dynamic Programming Algorithm for Connected Word Recognition", IEEE Trans. Acoust., Speech, Signal Processing, vol. ASSP-32, pp. 263-271, April 1984.

AN EFFICIENT ALGORITHM FOR RECOGNIZING ISOLATED TURKISH WORDS

Neşe Yalabık and Fatih Ünal
Department of Computer Engineering
Middle East Technical University
Ankara, Turkey

ABSTRACT

In this study, a computationally efficient speaker independent
isolated word recognition system for Turkish language is designed and implemented. The approach used is a combination of
whole-word matching techniques with segmentation into phonetic
units before classification. Linear Predictive Coding (LPC)
coefficients for an eight-pole model of the short-time signal
are used as feature vectors. Computational costs are reduced
by a two-step classification strategy where unlikely words are
eliminated in the first step by comparing only the first syllable. The Dynamic Time Warping (DTW) method is used in comparisons at both levels.

CPU time spent for word comparisons is reduced by about 40%
compared to the time that has to be spent for a one-step whole-
word classification without degrading the system performance.

I.   INTRODUCTION

Many isolated word recognition systems for single speaker case
process the incoming speech in real time. If speaker independence is also a desired feature, the extra processing that
is needed may raise the computational costs significantly.
This is caused by the fact that higher numbers of features and
higher numbers of training samples need to be used in the
classification to compensate for the variations among different

speakers' speech.

In the whole-word template matching classification approach this means that usually more than one template per word is needed for comparisons.

This study makes use of a two-step classification strategy to reduce the number of whole-word comparisons, thus obtaining significant reduction in computational costs. The vocabulary is segmented into groups of dissimilar words. In the first step, a candidate from each group is selected by considering only the first syllable, thus avoiding the comparison cost for the rest of the word. In the second step, selected candidates which are few in number are compared with the unknown word as a whole to select the most likely one.

The block diagram for the system is shown in Figure 1. It has an 18-word vocabulary consisting of Turkish digits and arithmetic operators like plus, equal, etc. The speech signal is filtered by an analog low-pass filter to eliminate high-frequency noise and to prevent aliasing effects before it is digitized and stored in an LSI 11/2 microcomputer. The system software can mainly be divided into learning and recognition phases, as will be discussed in the following sections.

II.   FEATURE EXTRACTION AND PATTERN SIMILARITY

Many different features are used for recognizing isolated words. Among them are short-time spectrum, cepstrum, LPC coefficients, etc. The LPC method, which was selected to be used in this work, is presently a widely used technique because it provides accurate estimates for spectral features of most sounds in a computationally feasible amount of processing time(1). LPC analysis relies on a model of the digitized speech signal s_n where it can be approximated by a linear combination of p past samples as follows:

$$s_n = \sum_{k=1}^{p} a_k \, s_{n-k} \tag{1}$$

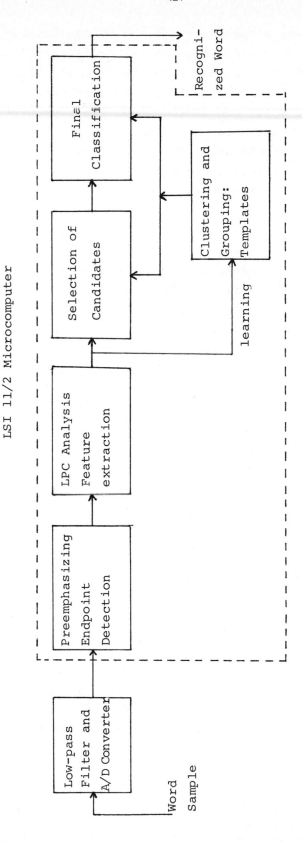

Figure 1. Sequential Speaker Independent Word Recognition System

This corresponds to a speech generation mechanism modeled as a
p-pole digital filter whose input is a periodic train of impulses
for voiced speech and a random sequence of noise for unvoiced
speech.   The filter is time invariant only for a short interval
of time (about 30 msec) due to the vocal-tract properties.   Hence
the signal for a whole word is divided into a number of frames.
Here, the frame width is selected to be 40 msecs, succesive frames
overlapping by two thirds to compansate with the filtering problems
at the sides.   The p parameters $a_1, a_2, \ldots, a_p$ represent the properties
of each frame. $p = 8$ is found to be good enough for this particular
application.

Fig.1. shows that the digitized speech signal is first preprocessed
for pre-emphasizing the high-frequency components and detecting the
endpoints.   The endpoint detection algorithm makes use of the zero
crossing rate and energy measures, which is described in (2).   After
the preprocessing operations, the LPC parameters for each frame are
estimated using the autocorrelation method of linear prediction(2,3)

Several distance measures between the two words which are represented
by a sequence of LPC parameters have been proposed in the literature
Initially a distance measure between the two compared frames of two
corresponding words has to be defined.   Here the Itakura distance(4)
is used, which is mainly the log ratio of the normalized autocorrelation functions of the LPC coefficients of test and learning samples

Once the distance measure between the two corresponding frames has
been determined, a time warping of two words to achieve an optimum
match is employed.   Main problems arise due to the fact that the
number of frames in two compared words may not be the same, in addition to the problem that repetitions of the same word might have
different durations for the same phonetic units.   These problems
were tackled by Dynamic Time Warping(DTW) alignment, which nonline-
arly shifts the frames to get a best match between the two words
or other compared units (5).   An optimum solution is found by
dynamic programming methods and allows different-length samples.

III.   CLUSTERING

The last step in learning is setting a classification rule which makes use of reference patterns. The Nearest-Neighbor Rule classifies the unknown sample as belonging to the category closest reference pattern belongs to. However, computational costs involved in comparisons and storage make it impossible to use this classifier without any modification for most of the applications, as it is the case in word recognition problems. Only a few representative ones between the learning samples of each category is selected. These patterns are called templates. In the speaker independent recognition problem it is desired that the number of templates be more than one for each word to obtain acceptable results. To select the representative templates, possible clusters of feature vectors are selected. Here, a clustering algorithm which is proposed by (6) is used. The original algorithm creates a variable number of templates according to the structure inherent in the training set. The total number of clusters need not be known or specified a priori.

For determining the first template, a single pattern is selected from all the replications of that word in such a way that the maximum distance to any other sample is minimum. This point is called the minimax center. After the first template is selected, a cluster is formed around this point by including all the points that are closer to it than a predefined threshold. The samples which are not covered by the first cluster are considered for the determination of the second template and the second cluster, using the same procedure. The procedure can be repeated until all the words in the same class are covered.

IV.   SEQUENTIAL CLASSIFICATION

One way to reduce the computational costs for the comparisons is to use a smaller number of frames. Obviously, this would cause some loss of information and an increase in the error rate. However, if the classification discriminates between distant (dissimilar) words, only a portion of the complete feature set might be used with acceptable results. The idea utilised here is as follows: Divide the words in the vocabulary into a number of groups such that mostly confused words fall into different groups. Table 1 shows such a grouping for the Turkish words that are in the vocabulary.

GR-1	GR-2	GR-3	GR-4	GR-5
SIFIR/səfər/	ALTI /ä l tə/	IKİ /iki/	BİR /bir/	DÖRT /dœrt/
YEDİ /jedi/	SEKİZ/sekiz/	DOKUZ/dokuz/	ÜÇ /yt /	BEŞ /beʃ /
NOKTA/noktä/	TOPLA/toplä/	EŞİT /eʃit/	AÇ /ä tʃ/	ÇARP /tʃärp/
KAPA/käpä /	ÇIKAR/tʃəkar/		BÖL /bœl/	

Table 1: Grouping of the Turkish words in the vocabulary.

This approach differs from other sequential methods in the sense
that dissimilar words, rather than similar are grouped together.
Once advantage of this is that it might give better results when
the vocabulary allows a uniform distribution of reference templates over the pattern space, rather than forming distinct clusters.
The grouping of words in Table 1 is performed by making use of
the confusion matrices obtained by the experiments performed on a
one-step classification process in a previous study(2). For example,
YEDİ,SEKİZ and EŞİT are found to be confused mostly so they fall in
different groups.

Here, one concern in determining the number of groups is to keep
it small enough to allow a considerable reduction is computational
cost but large enough so that the system performance is not degra-
ded. This is performed heuristically here. Other factors that

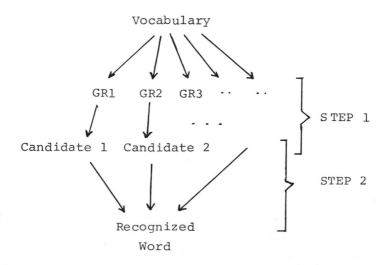

Figure 2. Two-Step Classification Procedure

affect the groupings are the syllabic properties of the Turkish language. Words that are in the same group have the same number of syllables. Also, it was shown in previous(7,8) that segmentation of a word into its syllables is not as difficult as in many other languages. This fact is utilised in forming the following two-step classification rule (Fig. 2): A candidate is selected from each group. The frames that are taken into account in this selection approximately correspond to the first syllable of each word. The syllabic segmentation is performed by making use of energy values during the endpoint detection procedure. The reason for selecting the first syllable arises from the fact that the average duration of the first vowel, and hence the first syllable is shorter than the following ones in general for the Turkish language. Also, plosives such as /p/ and /t/, which appear at the end of the words in general generate bursts of energy, which result in peaks and causes a confusion of these sounds with vowels. Considering only the beginning of a word will avoid this problem.

The candidate selection from each group is performed by dynamically time-warping the selected frames of the words as discussed above. Once this has been done, the final classification is performed among the selected candidates, this time making full use of all the frames, using DTW matching.

V. RESULTS AND CONCLUSION

The word templates were generated by 16 different speakers (8 males and 8 females of different ages). About 300 words generated by other speakers were used for testing. In an earlier study (2) using the single-step dynamic time warping approach with two templates per word, a recognition rate of 80% was obtained. The approach discussed in the previous sections allowed for an improvement of 40% in recognition time while keeping the recognition rate at the same level. The earlier experiments showed that using three templates rather than two improves the recognition rate considerably (to approximately 87%), so that the savings in time might be used to keep more templates for recognition.

REFERENCES

(1) Makhoul,J., 'Linear Prediction: A Tutorial Review', Proc. IEEE, 63, 1975, pp.583-587

(2) Ünal,F., 'A Speaker Independent Isolated Turkish Word Recognition System', M.S. Thesis, METU, Ankara, Turkey, 1983.

(3) Rabiner,L.R., Schafer,R.W., 'Digital Processing of Speech Signals', Prentice-Hall, 1978.

(4) Itakura,F., 'Minimum Prediction Residual Principle Applied to Speech Recognition', IEEE Trans. Acoust. Speech and Signal Processing, Vol. ASSP-23, 1975, pp. 67-72

(5) Sakoe,H., Chiba,S., 'Dynamic Programming Algorithm Optimization for Spoken Word Recognition', IEEE Trans. on Acoust. Speech and Signal Processing, Vol.ASSP-26, 1978, pp. 43-49.

(6) Rabiner,L.R., Wilpon,J.G., 'Considerations in Applying Clustering Techniques to Speaker Independent Word Recognition', J. Acoust. Soc. Am. 1979, pp. 663-673

(7) Töreci,E., 'Statistical Investigations on the Turkish Language Using Digital Computers', M.S. Thesis, METU, Ankara, Turkey, 1974

(8) Özmen,H., 'A Microcomputer Based System for the Recognition of Spoken Turkish Digits', M.S. Thesis, METU, Ankara, Turkey, 1981.

A GENERAL FUZZY-PARSING SCHEME FOR SPEECH RECOGNITION.

Enrique Vidal *
Francisco Casacuberta *
Emilio Sanchis *
Jose M. Benedi **

(*) CENTRO DE INFORMATICA
(**) DEP. ELECTRONICA E INFORMATICA FAC. FISICAS
UNIVERSIDAD DE VALENCIA
SPAIN

ABSTRACT.

In this paper a Speech Recognition Methodology is proposed which is based on the general assumption of "fuzzyness" of both speech-data and knowledge-sources. Besides this general principle, there are other fundamental assumptions which are also the bases of the proposed methodology: "Modularity" in the knowledge organization, "Homogeneity" in the representation of data and knowledge, "Passiveness" of the "understanding flow" (no backtraking or feedback), and "Parallelism" in the recognition activity.

The proposed methodology is formally presented, and algorithms to develop actual systems on general pourpose hardware are given. An implementation example as well as the results obtained with it are also presented.

1.- INTRODUCTION.

Automatic Speech Recognition (like other human-like perceptive and cognitive problems aimed at being solved by digital computers) has proved to be a dificult task. The main dimensions of the dificulty are <u>variability</u> and <u>noise</u> of data and <u>ambiguity</u> and <u>uncertainty</u> of knowledge; in fact, all these are of a nature which is very far from the exact-like principles under which all modern Von-Newman-machine based computers work. Most implementations of Speech Recognition Systems are, in reality, computer-simulated mathematical models which aim at accounting for the inexact nature of the problem. Among the theories which have been adopted as background for modeling inexactness is the Fuzzy-Sets Theory. It has been used in several Artificial Inteligence areas (12) and, in particular, it has proved to be a consitent mathematical support for quite different problems in Speech Recognition (1)(2)(3)(13)(14).

The work presented in this paper is based on the above introduced general assumption of _fuzzyness_ of both knowledge and data, and uses the Fuzzy-Sets Theory as the primary frame-work for developping a general model of perception and cognition with direct application to Speech Recognition.

Besides the fuzzyness principle there are four other fundamental assumptions under which the presented model is being developed: namely modularity, homogeneity, pasiveness and paralelism. "Modularity" stands for the organization of the knowledge, which is assumed to be structured into levels of understanding (acoustic, phonetic, lexical, etc.). The "Homogeneity" principle assumes knowledge and data to be uniformly represented at all the levels. "Passiveness" refers to the "understanding flow" which is thought to progress just as a parsimonious bottom-up systolic flow, without backtracking or feedback. The "Parallelism" principle, represents the way in which understanding activity is performed; both _inter_-level (all levels can work concurrently) and _intra_-level (several elements in each level can hold a parallel activity, cooperating to the in-level understanding process).

All these ideas agree closely with certain psycho-cognitive "connectionist" theories more or less based on speculative assumptions on the actual neuronal hardware (4) (5) (6). In these theories, it is considered that all encodings of importance are in terms of relative strengths of synaptic connections, and individual neurons do _not_ transmit large ammounts of symbolic information; rather they communicate with each-other in a simple way. Complex concepts are thought to be held by an appropiate interconection scheme between several elemental units, and the apparent rule-based nature of cognition is considered as an illusion based on statistical properties of mass neuronal interactions.

The cognitive model presented in this paper, like all those related to "connectionist" theories (and many other models of speech understanding), are especially well suited for implementing with massively parallel machine architectures which are not tecnologically available at present, but which seem to be the target of much recent research effort (7) (8) (9). Nevertheles, for the model introduced, algorithms have been developped which can run satisfactorily on present general-pourpose (mini) computers, and there seem to be many potential (and actual) applications which can run on general pourpose hardware.

Under a more classical perspective the work presented in this paper can be viewed as a "pasive" system with the different knowledge sources structured into levels. In general, this kind of system produces important information reductions at each level, by "interpreting" the data coming from the lower level(s). This information reduction (which is very interesting from a computational point of view) is the main cause of a degradation in results produced by the presence of ambiguity and noise, which makes it impossible to get the "clean" interpretations usually aimed for at each level. The alternative proposed renounces explicitly to handle "clean" data, and aims to reduce the degradation by minimizing the loss of information associated with the interpretation process at each level. Fig 1.1. shows an intuitive illustration of the proposed methodology. Level-0 is a special level which obtains a fuzzy symbolic description of the parametric representation of speech. Level-1 fuzzy-interprets this fuzzy-symbolic description in terms of (broad) phonetic categories. This fuzzy-interpretation is processed in its turn by Level-2 which fuzzy-interprets it in terms of lexical categories. The process continues in a similar manner at all the levels, "focalizing" the incoming data into the most likely interpretations in terms of the categories associated with each level, but without significative dropping of information about low-scored interpretations which will therefore be available for the higher levels if there is low compatibility of the most likely data with the corresponding knowledge sources.

For most applications, the knowledge associated with each level can be homogeneously represented by fuzzy finite-state networks, and the same fuzzy-parsing scheme can be (concurrently) applied to all levels.

2.- THEORY AND ALGORITHMS.

In this section we will deal with a formal presentation of the proposed general knowledge representation and fuzzy-parsing scheme.

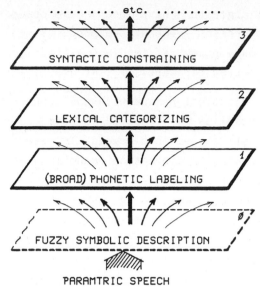

.... etc. ....

SYNTACTIC CONSTRAINING   3

LEXICAL CATEGORIZING   2

(BROAD) PHONETIC LABELING   1

FUZZY SYMBOLIC DESCRIPTION   Ø

PARAMTRIC SPEECH

Fig 1.1. Multilevel fuzzy-interpretation process.

PARAMETERS: CONTIN_MODE, STARTING_SCORE, STATE_THD, RECOGN_THD,
CONTINUITY_THD, NON_CONTINUITY_PENALTY.

INITIALIZATION:

Make all current_state scores = 0;
Make all next_state scores = 0;
Make initial_state score = STARTING_SCORE;
Make utterance_time = 0;

RECURSION:

repeat
input the current_fuzzy_label;
for all current_states with score > STATE_THD:
find all next_states;
for each next_state:
evaluate transition_evidence =
= T(current_state,current_fuzzy_label,next_state);
if next_state score < current_state score ◻
transition_evidence
then make next_state score = current state score ◻
transition_evidence;
end for;
end for;
for all next_states:
if next_state score - current_state score < CONTINUITY_THD
then decrement next_state score by NON_CONTINUITY_PENALTY;
if next_satate score < STATE_THD then make this score = 0;
end for;
make all current_state scores = next_state scores;
{prunning may be necesary for large networks}
for all final_states with score > RECOGN_THD:
output these states and their scores as the fuzzy set
of recognized categories;
end for;
{decimation can be applied for saving resources in next level}
if CONTIN_MODE then make initial_state score = STARTING_SCORE;
increment utterance_time by the time_unit;
until utterance_time is exhausted.

Fig 2.2. The fuzzy-parsing algorithm.

As introduced in first section, each level accepts a sequence of a certain class of fuzzy-symbols produced by the lower level(s), and outputs another sequence of "fuzzy-symbols" corresponding to the associated symbol repertory. All these "fuzzy-symbols" are modeled as fuzzy subsets over the output alphabet corresponding to the categories associated with each level.

The output sequences of fuzzy-symbols are produced at all the levels, by a general "fuzzy-interpretetion process" and the knowledge needed for this interpretation is assumed to be represented by fuzzy finite-state networks. The exception is the lowest level, which must extract its corresponding sequence by means of a different "fuzzy-description process" (14) applied to a parametric representation of speech.

Let Y be a finite alphabet, and G the set of all fuzzy subsets over Y. We define a Y-fuzzy-finite state machine as a five-tuple $\underset{\sim}{A}$

$$\underset{\sim}{A} = (Q, q_I, F, \underset{\sim}{R}, \underset{\sim}{T})$$

where:

1) Q is a finite set of states.
2) $q_I \in Q$ is the initial state.
3) $F \subseteq Q$ is the set of final states.
4) $\underset{\sim}{R}$: Q x Q $\longrightarrow$ G are the arcs with their confidence values.
5) $\underset{\sim}{T}$: Q x G x Q $\longrightarrow$ [0,1] defined as:

$$\underset{\sim}{T}(q_i, \underset{\sim}{D}, q_j) = \underset{\sim}{D} \Delta \underset{\sim}{R}(q_i, q_j) \; ; \; q_i, q_j \in Q; \; \underset{\sim}{D} \in G$$

The fuzzy relation $\underset{\sim}{T}$ aims at representing the "transition evidences" by considering the contribution of both the fuzziness of data $\underset{\sim}{D}$, and knowledge $\underset{\sim}{R}$. The simbol "Δ" is a generic composition operator which (depending on the requirements) can accept several different definitions:

- the max-min function:

$$\underset{\sim}{D} \Delta \underset{\sim}{R}(q_i, q_j) = \bigvee_{\forall e \in Y} \mu_{\underset{\sim}{D}}(e) \wedge \mu_{\underset{\sim}{R}(q_i, q_j)}(e)$$

- a normalized Hamming distance:

$$\underset{\sim}{D} \Delta \underset{\sim}{R}(q_i, q_j) = \frac{1}{card(Y)} \sum_{\forall e \in Y} | \mu_{\underset{\sim}{D}}(e) - \mu_{\underset{\sim}{R}(q_i, q_j)}(e) |$$

- a normalized euclidean distance:

$$\underline{D}\Delta\underline{R}(q_i,q_j) = \frac{1}{\sqrt{card(\Psi)}}\left[\sum_{\forall e \in \Psi} (\mu_{\underline{D}}(e) - \mu_{\underline{R}(q_i,q_j)}(e))^2\right]^{1/2}$$

Over $\underline{A}$ we can define a "configuration" $\underline{C}$ as a fuzzy subset of Q, and a state $q \in Q$ is said to be "λ-active" in a configuration $\underline{C}$ if $\mu_{\underline{C}}(q) > \lambda > 0$. A "move" between configurations can be defined as a function M: L x G $\longrightarrow$ L, where L is the set of configurations over $\underline{A}$.

$$\underline{C}_j = M(\underline{C}_i,\underline{D}) : \mu_{\underline{C}_j}(q) = \bigvee_{\forall q' \in Q} (\mu_{\underline{C}_i}(q') \square \underline{T}(q,\underline{D},q')) \; ; \; \forall q \in Q$$

where "$\square$" is another generic composition operator. A simple definition of this operator is the min function; however, this definition is not adequate to describe the evolution of configurations in all the cases, since it is too "local": that is, the configuration $\underline{C}_j$ at a given time is made to be only dependent on the last configuration $\underline{C}_i$ and the present transition evidence $\underline{T}$. In order to enable more "global" operator definitions, a new concept must be introduced:

A trellis X_a over $\underline{A}$ for an input string $a \in G^*$ ($a=\underline{D}_1 \underline{D}_2 \cdots \underline{D}_{|a|}$) is defined recursively as the sequence of configurations of $\underline{A}$:

$$\underline{C}_0 = \left\{(q,\mu_{\underline{C}_0}(q)) \; / \; \mu_{\underline{C}_0}(q) = \left< \begin{array}{l} 1 \; \text{if } q = q_I \\ 0 \; \text{if } q \neq q_I \end{array} \right\} \right.$$

$$\underline{C}_{k+1} = M(\underline{C}_k,\underline{D}_{k+1}) \; , \; k=0,1,\ldots,|a|-1$$

In this case other alternative formulations for the operator can be given:

* The "global" running average:
$$\mu_{\underline{C}_k}(q') \square \underline{T}(q,\underline{D}_{k+1},q') = \frac{k\,\mu_{\underline{C}_k}(q') + \underline{T}(q,\underline{D}_{k+1},q')}{k+1}$$

* The "time decaying" windowed local average:
$$\mu_{\underline{C}_k}(q') \square \underline{T}(q,\underline{D}_{k+1},q') = \alpha(\mu_{\underline{C}_k}(q') + \gamma\underline{T}(q,\underline{D}_{k+1},q')); \; 0<\alpha<1; \; \gamma = 1/\sum_{n=1}^{\infty}\alpha^n$$

In most cases it is of great importance to constrain the set of λ-active states to those which receive <u>continuous</u> evidence aportations from their incomming transitions. To achieve this goal a modification can be applied to the definition of M:

$$\underset{\sim}{C}_j = \hat{M}(\underset{\sim}{C}_i, \underset{\sim}{D}): \hat{\mu}_{\underset{\sim}{C}_j}(q) = \begin{cases} \mu_{\underset{\sim}{C}_j}(q) & \text{if } \mu_{\underset{\sim}{C}_j}(q) - \mu_{\underset{\sim}{C}_i}(q) > \varepsilon \\ \mu_{\underset{\sim}{C}_j}(q) - \eta & \text{if } \mu_{\underset{\sim}{C}_j}(q) - \mu_{\underset{\sim}{C}_i}(q) \leqslant \varepsilon \text{ and } \mu_{\underset{\sim}{C}_j}(q) - \eta \geqslant \lambda \\ 0 & \text{otherwise.} \end{cases}$$

where $\mu_{\underset{\sim}{C}_j}(q)$ is the above defined membership funcion, and ε and η are a "continuity-threshold" and a "non-continuity-penalty" respectively.

With this formulation, the trellis for a given input string can be interpreted as the time evolution of activity of states and the concept of λ-active states can be used as a pruning criterium for implementing the parsing algorithms. Depending on the definition of the "move" function M, the set of λ-active states can be reduced to a small subset of Q which changes dynamically with the evolution of configurations in the trellis. As will be shown later, this feature allows the implementation of efficient fuzzy-parsing algorithms over sequential general-pourpose hardware. It is worth-noting that the pruning methods introduced here have nothing to do with the well known beam-search technique used for parsing in large finite-state networks like Harpy (10); morever, this technique could be further applied over the methods presented in this paper.

In some cases it may be of interes to know how well a given input string is accepted by the Fuzzy-Automata $\underset{\sim}{A}$; in these cases we can say that a $\in G^*$ is λ-recognized by $\underset{\sim}{A}$, if the configuration $\underset{\sim}{C}_{|a|}$ of X_a contains at least one final state $q \in F$ such that $\mu_{\underset{\sim}{C}_{|a|}}(q) > \lambda$.

The fuzzy parsing scheme here presented can be easily extended for the aimed <u>fuzzy-interpretation process</u>. Let $\underset{\sim}{Z}$ be a fuzzy translation scheme defined as the triplet $\underset{\sim}{Z} = (\Phi, \underset{\sim}{A}, H)$ where:

1) $\underset{\sim}{A}$ is a fuzzy finite state machine.
2) Φ is an output alphabet.
3) $H : Q \longrightarrow \Phi^*$.

H represents the asignement of at most one string over the output alphabet for each state of $\underset{\sim}{A}$.

Let $\mathcal{L}_{\underset{\sim}{Z}}$ be the finite language defined by H, that is $\mathcal{L}_{\underset{\sim}{Z}} = \{b/b \in \Phi^*, \exists q \in Q: H(q) = b\}$. If $a \in G$ $(a = D_1 D_2 \cdots D_{|a|})$, and the corresponding trellis X_a over $\underset{\sim}{A}$ are given, then a $\underset{\sim}{Z}$-translation of a is said to be a sequence of fuzzy subsets $(\underset{\sim}{E}_i)$ of $\mathcal{L}_{\underset{\sim}{Z}}$, defined as

$$\mu_{\underline{E}_i}(H(q)) = \mu_{\underline{C}_i}(q) \qquad \forall q \in Q \;, \; 1 < i < |a|$$

In most cases, this translation scheme can be simplified by modelling the network to have one final state per considered category at the corresponding level. In this case the output alphabet can be mapped with these categories, the langage is reduced to single-simbol strings, and (relaxing the notation) the definition of H can be simplified to: H : F $\longrightarrow \Phi$, where F is the set of final states of $\underline{A}$.

Fig 2.1 summarizes the fuzzy interpretation process introduced above: for a sequence of fuzzy subsets over a finite input alphabet Ψ, the <u>interpretetion process</u> produces another sequence of fuzzy subsets over another finite output alphabet Φ. Although the length of both sequences is the same, in most cases the output categories can be described with a much coarser time resolution than the input ones (e.g. a 0.05 sec. resolution for phonemic-labeling versus 0.5 sec. for word-labeling). To take advantage of this feature, subsampling can be used for saving resources at the next level.

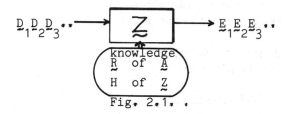

$$\underline{D}_1 \underline{D}_2 \underline{D}_3 \cdot \cdot \longrightarrow \boxed{\underset{\approx}{Z}} \longrightarrow \underline{E}_1 \underline{E}_2 \underline{E}_3 \cdot \cdot$$

knowledge
$\underline{R}$ of $\underline{A}$
H of $\underline{Z}$

Fig. 2.1. .

The Fuzzy-parsing and translation scheme introduced above, is implicitly associated with an abstract massively parallel machine. Though much recent research effort is being spent on such a kind of parallel hardware (8) (9), at present, only more or less sequential general-pourpose hardware is practically available. The algorithm developed for an efficient implementation of the methods presented in this section on general-pourpose computers (fig. 2.2) is based on the Viterbi algorithm (11), from which we have taken the structure of the trellis. The main differences in our algorithm are: 1) The weights of the arcs, which here represent the transition evidences $\underline{T}$, and 2) The score accumulation method, which is based on the definitions of the "move" function M between configurations. The latter (which is the main contribution to the aimed fuzzy-parsing task) leads to a formalized pruning method which can be used both for memory and processor-time saving, and is the base of the real efficiency of the algorithm.

3.- THE LEVEL STRUCTURE: CURRENT DEVELOPEMENTS.

The fuzzy interpretation process introduced in last section can be applied to Automatic Speech Recognition in two basic ways: 1) Encoding all the knowledge into a single network which interprets the speech data directly in terms of syntactic-semantic categories, or 2) Structuring the knowledge into levels of understanding, and modeling each level as a local small network. The first alternative would lead to a large network system with all its well known advantages and drowbacks. The second alternative, which is the one adopted in this work, has the attractive features of modularity and (potential) inter-level parallelism, without dropping the general principles of passiveness and homogeneous representation of knowledge and data.

Structuring knowledge into levels of understanding is not a straight-forword task, and usually responds more to implementational reasons then to fundamental assumptions. Some of the levels which have been assumed in modern Speech Understanding Systems are the following: microphonetic, pseudophonetic, phonetic, diphonetic, pseudosyllabic, syllabic, lexical, syntactic, semantic and pragmatic. Not all the systems have used all the levels, rather, a subset of them has been implemented in each system. In the work presented in this paper some different structures will be suggested; however, in order to make a preliminary test of the theoretical assumptions above presented, only a very simple example has been implemented. In this implementation just three levels (microphonetic, lexical and syntactic-semantic) are assumed, and a very crude parametric representation of speech is used; this permits an easy test of different issues without spending too much effort in implementational aspects. In the rest of this section some details and results of this implementation will be given and different alternatives that arise will be discussed.

3.1.- Parameter extraction.

This is the first step in all Speech Recognition Systems. In that presented here, only three elemental short-time parameters have been used: signal average-magnitude (Amplitude) (A), Signal Zero-Crossing (Z), and signal-derivative zero-crossing (D). These parameters are extracted through a non-overlapping 15 ms. rectangular window, using a previously estimated threshold to avoid fluctuations in Z and D due to environnemental noise, and normalizing A to the most stressed vowel contained in the signal input buffer. This crude representation has been adopted for two main reasons: computation simplicity, which allows easy and efficient implementation on general pourpose hardware, and low spectral descriptive power, which is a challenge for the recognition methods, which must then work mainly on the basis of accurate temporal feature description of the acoustic patterns. As these temporal features of speech data respond basically to general phonological constraints, multispeaker operation is expected to be achieved easily. The drawbacks of this kind of representation are obvious, and for many real-applications the use of a more powerfull spectral representation would be necessary.

3.2.- Fuzzy-symbolic description.

The first task after a parametric representation of speech is obtained, is to derive an elemental Fuzzy-symbolic description of this representation. This description can be obtained by the methods introduced in (14). Each parameter must be divided into (several) overlapping intervals, and each interval must be assigned both a name and a membership function. The number of intervals, and the shapes of the membership functions, depends on the parameters to be described and also on the categories which must be derived from this description in next level. Fig 3.1 shows these functions and names for each of the three parameters used in the example presented. These functions have been obtained by hand-smoothing-and-merging the results of the statistical distributions over the three parameters of the different microphonetic categories to be used.

3.3.- Fuzzy microphonetic labeling.

Once a fuzzy-symbolic description is available, the general fuzzy-interpretation process presented in section 2 can be applied to interpret this description in terms of the categories wanted. In the example presented a set of broad-phonetic classes, which corresponds to the phonetic-labels to be assigned to each frame, is associated with the first level.

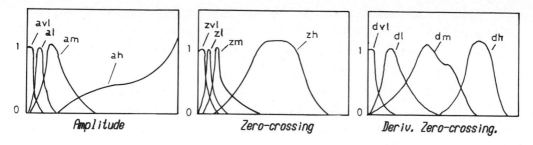

Fig 3.1. Membership functions for the fuzzy-description of parameters a,z,d.

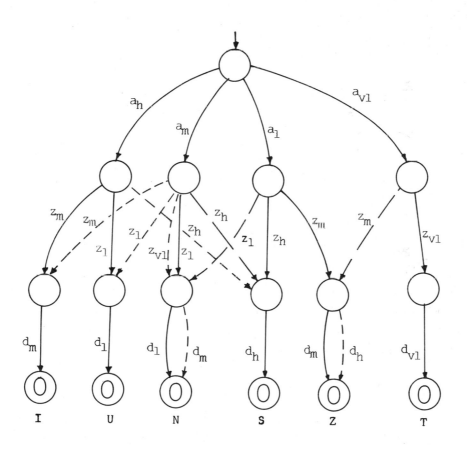

Fig 3.2. Broad-phonetic categories network.

(evidences of the arcs are represented by the diferent dashing of lines).

The broad-phonetic categories and symbols are the following:

"I": Front-vowel (/i/, /e/, /a/, some segments of /l/).

"U": Back-vowel (/u/, /o/).

"N": Weak-sonorant (/n/, /m/, /η/, /ʎ/, some segments of /l/, most segments of voiced stops).

"S": Strong-fricative (/s/, hissing segments of /c/).

"Z": Weak-fricative (/θ/, /f/, /x/, some segments of /β/).

"T": Silence (/p/, /t/, /k/, some voiced stops, stop segments of /c/) .

Fig 3.2. shows the network used to obtain an interpretation of each frame in terms of the categories considered above. It must be pointed-out that the interpretation process at this level is "parameter-indexed" in opposition to the following levels in which the process is "time-indexed". The general operators used in this level are:

$$\triangle = \underline{\text{max-min}} \text{ function;} \quad \square = \underline{\text{min}} \text{ function.}$$

3.4 The lexical level: isolated and connected word recognition.

The output of the micro-phonetic-labeling level is a time series of fuzzy-broad-phonetic labels. From this series, several phonetic-like or syllabic-like intrerpretations are possible. However, for moderate lexical sizes (as considered in the example), it is also possible to achieve a direct lexical categorizing without intermediate levels. Fig. 3.3 shows the network used for the spanish digits lexicon.

The fuzzy lexical access obtained at this level, can be used as an input to higher levels. Nevertheless, there are also applications in which the results of this level can be used directly: namely, isolated and connected word recognition (IWR, CWR). For IWR, the silence anterior and posterior to the words can be modelled as part of the network (dashed-line final states and T-arc in initial state of fig. 3.3), and the "systolic-like" progression of the configurations is restricted to just one "systole" per expected word; that is, activity in the network is initiated just once, at the beginning of recognition by making λ-active the initial state at the initial time. The activity (score) of the final states at the end of the uttered word, represents the evidence values of the fuzzy-set of recognized words, and the recognized word is assumed to

439

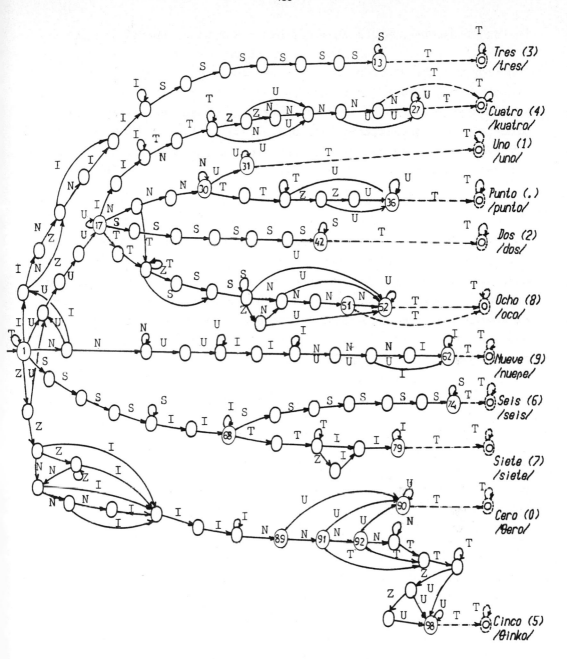

Fig 3.3. The spanish digits lexicon network.

be the word coresponding to the final state with greatest activity. For the IWR and CWR tasks the Δ operator is again the max-min function and the $\square$ operator can be implemented as either the "global running average" or as the "time-decaying" local average with delays (α) greater than the maximum expected word duration. Since neither normalization nor upper-limit bounding are necesary for IWR, it is also posible in this case to implement $\square$ as a global accumulation (algebraic summation).

The problem of connected word recognition can be aproached via the metodology introduced in two ways. The first and easier way is to extend the lexical network by introducing a "nil" labeled arc from each final state (like the ones drown with continous lines in Fig. 3.3) to the initial state. This allows the one "systole" activity flow, to feed-back the initial state every time some final-state has become λ-active, thus efectivelly initiating a new "systole" of recognition activity. The main and obvious drawback of this method is that recognition activity may be stopped if recognition fails for some word and no final-state becomes λ-active. The other way is to use the lexical network for continuously fuzzy-hypotesizing words in the continuous string of fuzzy microphonetic labels, producing an output string of fuzzy sets of recognized words ("multiword spotting"). This goal can be easily achieved by continuously making the initial state λ-active, thus allowing a continuous flow of systolic recognition activity, which starts a new "systole" whenever some compatibility of the data with the network is found. The errors of the output string can be minimized at the next level if syntax is associated with the language. For the CWR problem, no syntax is available, but a pragmatic-like level can be implemented to take into account the durational constraints of the string of connected words (e.g. the "presence" of the spanish word /kuatro/ is not possible before 0.6 sec. after the "presence" of any other word, etc.).

Fig. 3.4 shows the complete description and interpretation process for the spanish connected words /nueβepuntooco/ ("nine-point-eight"). The state-space evolution is also represented, showing the systolic-like progression of configurations and the time-decaying non-continuity-punished state deactivation feature. This deactivation feature reduces the ammount of λ-active states to a small subset of the state-space, leading to the high efficiency

441

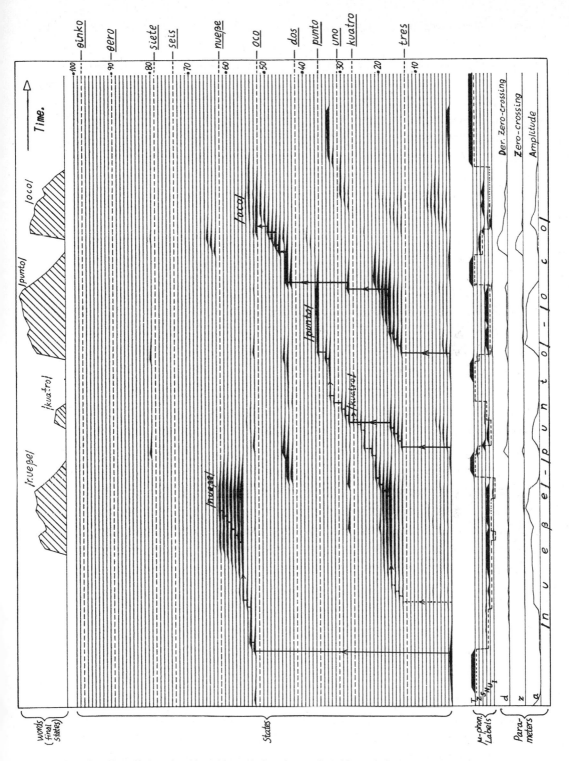

Fig 3.4. Activity at different levels while uttering the connected words
/nueβepuntoοco/ (nine-point-eight).

achieved by the recognition algorithm.

3.5.- Syntactic-Semantic level in task-oriented applications.

This level is usually assumed to have word-hipothesis as an input and must supply the phrase structure and the "corrected" words in the phrase as output. For many moderate-requirement applications the syntax of the language can be adequately modelled as a regular grammar or finite state network and, in most cases, the semantics (and/or pragmatics) of the task can also be embedded in the same network.

The general fuzzy-interpretation process introduced so far can be directly applied at this level. In this case the networks are usually free of fuzzyness; that is, the fuzzy relation $\underline{R}$ is simplified to the classical δ-function of non-fuzzy automatas. However, one can take advantage of fuzzyness to obtain better descriptions of language syntaxes, in which certain phrase structures are less common than others.

In most cases, the pragmatics of the task at hand allow the modelling of the network to group together, in one final state, all the semantically equivalent syntactic constructs, and to have one final state per semantic category. Fig. 3.5 shows a simple example of this kind, corresponding to the protocol of a small telephone-exchange. In this case the semantics of the langage can be reduced to the understanding of the thelephone-extension to be connected. In some other cases, the semantics of the application does not allow the above mentioned semantic categorizing. In those cases, the recognition algorithm presented in section 2 must be somewhat modified to maintain at each time and for each state, the trace of the partially accepted string of words up to this time. At the end of the utterance, each final state will supply (besides its score or activity) the string of words which, having reached it, have matched the network best.

Concernig the general operators used at this level, the max-min function for Δ and the global average or the global accumulation for $\square$ seem appropiate. As different utterances can easilly be isolated from each-other at the acoustic level (inter-phrase silences), it is adequate to select the "one systole" type recognition flow, which is achieved, as in IWR, by making the initial state λ active just once

443

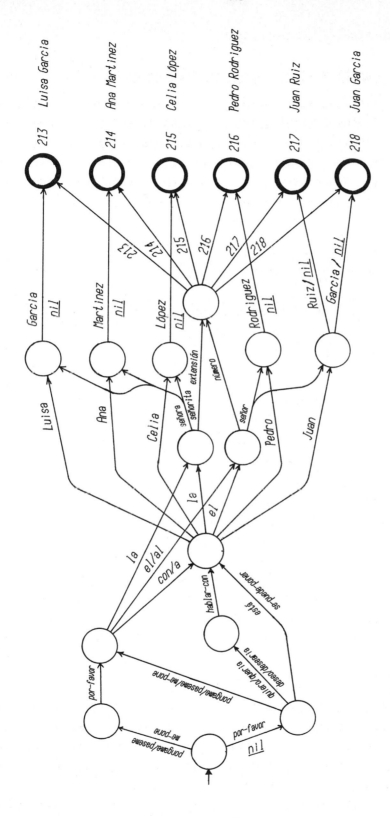

Fig 3.5. A simple example of syntactic-semantic level network; the "telephonist language".

444

at the initial time.

3.6.- <u>The problem of building the networks.</u>

The networks associated with the different levels must be built
on the basis of phonological/grammatical rules, and/or inferred from
actual speech data. At some levels (syntactic-semantic) the network
can be obtained from the language grammar in a straight-forward
enough way; at other levels (microphonetic-labeling, phonetic,
syllabic, lexical) the network can also be obtained by the use of
phonological rules. However, in these cases, several problems arise
which make the task difficult. The first problem is that the
fuzzyness of the network must be accurately generated, due to the
dependance of the performance of these levels on it. The second
problem is that the rules needed to obtain the networks, are usually
<u>not</u> very well known, and depend on the type of parameters and
categories associated with the different levels. The third problem
arises from the fact that, even if the rules needed were well known,
there are always non-standard phonological phenomena which are not
accounted for by the rules.

One way of resolving the problem of network building is to
proceed in two stages: 1) top-down rule-based arquetype
network-building, and 2) bottom-up learning-based refinement of the
built networks.

The first stage can be performed by means of an expert-systems
methodology. For the example presented in this paper, a production
system has ben implemented which supplies the regular expressions
needed to build the lexical-level arquetypical networks. These
expressions are automatically obtained from the ortographic
word-spelling, by applying a set of ~100 phonological rules. These
rules (which summarize expert-like knowledge abaut the problem) can
be easilly updated, and so the problem of partial knowledge of the
rules is somewhat minimized.

The second learning-based refinement stage is much more
difficult and, at present, is not performed automatically.
Nevertheless, the importance of this stage is realized, and some
research effort is being spent in order to develop good
learning-based refinement methods.

4.- RESULTS AND DISCUSSION.

The simple examples which are being implemented on the basis of the methods presented so far, show very encouraging performance results. At lexical level, recognition results are in the range of 94-99% for the speakers involved in the process of inferring the different knowledge sources (membership functions, microphonetic network, lexical network), and are greater than 85% for the other speakers tried. These results are obtained in IWR experiments with three lexicons of similar complexity (spanish digits, catalan digits, telephone-exchange protocol), and with reconition times of the order of real time with a general pourpose 16 bits 0.7 mips minicomputer. For connected words, no reliable results are available at this moment, because the tests have been made with the same lexicon networks used for IWR, which should have been significantly modified for the CWR task. Nevertheless, the preliminary experiments show an adequate and efficient behaviour of the fuzzy-parsing algorithm, though the need of finer speech parameters and phonetic-labeling has been manifested for some of the lexicons tested. The need of an intermediate level between the micro-phonetic and lexical levels, which would alleviate the work of building the lexical networks, has also been detected.

This level is being introduced in the next system implementation, aimed to support realistic applications. This implementation also incorporates a finer spectral parameter set, as well as a more complete phonetic repertory at the microphonetic level. The intermediate level has diphones as output chategories and so, the lexical networks will be built (from the ortographic word-spelling) in terms of diphones. One of the conveniences of the introduction of this level is that the set of rules through which the lexical networks must be built, are much better known than the phonological rules at present required for the microphonetic-based lexical nets. All the problems of partial knowledge of rules and learning-based network-refinements are thus shifted one level down, but with the advantage that the diphonetic level network has to be correctly built just once, while the lexical nets are application-dependent and must then be able to be changed easily.

Other issues which have arisen through the development of the model introduced here, and which are currently under investigation are: 1) the need of a learning method, able to carry-out the network refinement procedure; and 2) the extension of the fuzzy-parsing scheme with an "inhibitory" mechanism, which has been found to be necessary for accurate modeling of durational constraints, and is thought to lead to improved results in all the levels.

REFERENCES.

(1) R. De Mori, P. Laface, "Use of fuzzy algorithms for phonetic and phonemic labeling of continuous speech", IEEE Trans. PAMI-2, 136-138, 1980.

(2) M.Allerhard, F. Fallside, P. Hinds, "Constrained recognizer using duration", 11-ICA, Toulouse Satellite Symposium, 1983.

(3) R.K. Moore, M.J. Russell, M.J. Tomlinson, "Locally constrained Dynamic Programming in Automatic Speech Recognition", ICASSP-82, pp 1270-1273.

(4) J.R. Anderson, "Cognitive psicology", Artificial Intelligence, 23(1984) 1-11.

(5) J.A. Feldman, D.H. Ballard, "Connectionist models and their properties", Cognitive Sciences 6(1982), 205-254.

(6) D.H. Ballard, "Parameter nets" Artificial Inteligence 22(1984) 235-267.

(7) J.A. Feldman, "A connectionist model of visual memory", in G.E. Hinton and J.A. Anderson (Eds.) Parallel models of associative memory, 1981.

(8) W.D. Hillis, "The connection machine (Computer architecture for the new wave)", AI memo 646, MIT, Cambridge, MA, 1981.

(9) G.E. Hinton, "Shape representation in parallel systems", Proc. 7th. IJCAI, Vancouver, B.C. (1981) 1088-1096.

(10) B. Lowerre, "The HARPY speech recognition system", Carnegie-Mellon Univ. memo, 1976.

(11) G.D. Forney, "The Viterbi Algorithm", IEEE proc. 3(1973), 268-278.

(12) L.A. Zadeh, "Fuzzy Sets and Their Applications to Cognitive and Decision Processes", Academic Press, 1975.

(13) E. Vidal, E.Sanchis, F.Casacuberta, "A speaker-independent Isolated Word Recognition System for specific dictionaries", SWSPA proc., 1,pp.B2/3(8p) Sitges, 1983.

(14) R. De Mori, L. Saitta, "Automatic Learning of fuzzy Naming Relations over finite languages". Information Sciences, Vol. 21, pp 83-139, 1980.

LINGUISTICS AND AUTOMATIC PROCESSING OF SPEECH

John J. Ohala

Phonology Laboratory

Department of Linguistics

University of California

Berkeley, CA   94720, U.S.A.

INTRODUCTION

To build a bridge it is helpful to know something about the physics of stress and vibration, about materials science, and so on. To cure sickness, it is helpful to know something about the nature and causes of disease, i.e., microbes, metabolism, etc. This is not to say that it is impossible to build bridges and cure sickness without such knowledge. Indeed, some bridges were built and some sicknesses cured centuries before anyone knew anything about the physical and physiological principles involved. However, it must be admitted that the bridges were modest, most sickness was not alleviated and successes in both areas owed more to trial and error or an intuitive understanding of the relevant principles than to any sort of systematic, scientific, knowledge. From the time that knowledge in these areas was put on a firm scientific basis, taking into account the factors underlying the behavior of materials and microbes, much more impressive bridges and cures were possible.

Similarly, to automate the production and the recognition of speech, it will be helpful to know something about the structure of speech and language and about the processes used by humans to produce and understand speech. Again, it may be possible to achieve limited success in these practical areas without knowing very much about the nature of speech but if the history of bridge

NATO ASI Series, Vol. F16
New Systems and Architectures for Automatic Speech
Recognition and Synthesis. Edited by R. De Mori and C. Y. Suen
© Springer-Verlag Berlin Heidelberg 1985

building and medicine is any guide, progress should be greater once this knowledge is obtained and applied to the solutions of these problems.

Although some information about the nature and behavior of speech has been accumulating for some 2300 years since the time of the Hindu grammarian Panini and the early Greek philosophers, it was only in the beginning of the 19th century that linguists had their first success in providing answers to some of the questions that had occupied them — answers which, I think it is safe to say, may properly be characterized as being "scientific", i.e., obtained with care and provided with rigorous empirical support. The question they answered was "how do languages evolve?", i.e., they were able for the first time to reconstruct the history of languages, especially their phonological history. Since that time a considerable treasure of data about changes in pronunciation has accumulated.

Change in pronunciation over time, or *sound change*, as it is usually called, manifests itself in many ways. Discrepancies between the pronunciation implied by a conservative orthography and the actual pronunciation, e.g., English *laugh*, pronounced [læf],[1] is an indication of sound change. Differences in the pronunciation of cognate words in different dialects or languages is another, for example, in the history of French the original Latin word *cantus* changed to [tʃant] and then to [ʃã], the modern pronunciation. English borrowed this word from French when it had the intermediate form (at the time of the Norman invasion in 1066 A.D.), and has not changed it substantially since then; thus we have the current English pronunciation [tʃænt]. Variation in the phonetic form of

---

[1] The phonetic transcription used throughout this paper follow the principles of the International Phonetic Association as of 1979, except that retroflex consonants are indicated by a dot underneath the letter. The arrows '>' and '<' stand for 'changes to' and 'comes from', respectively. Citation of cognate forms from sister dialects lack arrows because, strictly speaking, one is not derived from the other but both are derived from a common parent, not cited. In this case, however, it is assumed that the form on the left reflects the phonetic form of the parent language. Other expository simplifications have also been made, e.g., the citation of Classical Latin, instead of the more appropriate Vulgar Latin, as the origin of words in French and other Romance languages.

the same morpheme in different grammatical contexts is yet another example, e.g., the English words *native, nature,* and *natural* have the same stem in the different phonetic shapes [neı̆t], [neı̆tʃ], and [nætʃ], respectively. (For further examples, see Ohala, 1980, 1983a.)

In this paper I suggest how this wealth of information might be harvested and put to use in automatic speech recognition (ASR) and in the synthesis of speech (SS). One motivation for doing this is that although there is relatively wide (but by no means universal) recognition of the applicability of many other areas of linguistics for tasks in automatic processing of speech and language, e.g., syntax, semantics, pragmatics, sociolinguistics, lexicography, morphology (see, e.g., Lea, 1980), there seems to be little awareness of the applicability of historical linguistics, especially historical phonology, to the same tasks.

It is understandable that historical phonology would be overlooked in this domain. First, the documentation of language change is expressed in a rather obscure jargon, using an inconsistent notation, and based on an intricate set of (usually) unstated assumptions. It is therefore very difficult for the newcomer to penetrate this literature. Second, many of the speculations on the causes of sound change were such as would suggest that the phenomenon held little interest for ASR and SS. For example, some suggested that sounds change because speakers' vocal anatomy changes over time, because the climate or terrain affects speech, because infants with their immature vocal organs are incapable of pronouncing words in the same way as adults and some infantile pronunciations persevere, because speakers tend to adopt "easier" articulations or articulations which are more distinct and thus easier to hear, because speakers try to simplify or optimize their grammars, or because pronunciation is subject to the whims of fashion in the same way that styles of clothing or furniture are.

Although there is little I can do about the first problem — the impenetrability of the historical phonological literature — the second problem I propose to deal with by offering a different account of the nature of sound change. Specifically, I propose that the majority[2] of sound changes result from errors of transmission of pronounciation from one speaker to another. Most of these errors are perceptual. If this is accepted, then the relevance of a study of sound change to the tasks of ASR and SS is obvious: in the same way that destructive tests are of value in materials science, sound change, being a breakdown of normal speech behavior, can give us valuable clues about the structure of speech production and perception. Of course, these clues must always be followed up by systematic laboratory investigations.

There are good reasons for rejecting the earlier theories of sound change which propose that it stems from factors specific to a given terrain, a given time, culture, etc. or that it is introduced willfully by speakers (i.e., that it is at heart a teleological phenomenon). These reasons are the following:

1. The majority of sound changes occur in virtually the same form in languages distant from each other in time, geography, family history, and structure (Ohala, 1974, 1983a; Hombert, Ohala, & Ewan, 1979). Examples will be provided below.

2. The "seeds" of many such sound changes can be found in presentday speech. That is, laboratory study of a modern speaker of virtually any language which possesses the relevant sounds reveals the *same* kind of variation (either randomly or conditioned by rate of speaking, the phonetic context, etc.) as is found in sound change.

3. These "seeds" can, in most cases, be attributed to universal physical and physiological causes (or, in some cases, to universal psychological causes).

---

[2] I say 'majority' because there are changes in pronunciation due to such factors as spelling (e.g., English *sound* with a final [d] even though its source, Norman French *soun*, had no [d]), and the regularization of grammatical paradigms (e.g., the past tense of English *dream* as *dreamed* [drimd], replacing the earlier irregular form *dreamt* [drɛmpt].

The implication of this is that universal "extralinguistic" factors exist which are responsible for variation in speech; some of these variations eventually get "fixed" or "fossilized" (in ways to be described below) and thus lead to sound change.

The way this happens, I suggest, is similar to the way that noise invades electronically-transmitted signals, as schematized in Fig. 1. A message source sends a message, x, to an encoder which emits a signal x' which is an encoded

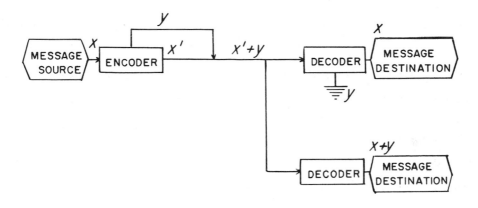

Figure 1.   Schematic representation of a transmission line used as an anologue of speech production and perception; see text.

form of x. Added to the signal x', however, is noise, y. Usually communication engineers are concerned with noise added from the environment but to make the analogy applicable to the present case the noise arises from the workings of the encoder itself. The composite signal $x' + y$ is received by a decoder which ideally must factor out the noise y and then translate the encoded signal x' back into the intended message x and deliver it to the message destination. If the decoder is not able to factor out the noise y from the composite signal, then the message sent to the message destination will be contaminated with this noise component (see the lower branch of Figure 1).

By the analogical connections I wish to draw, the message source and message destination are the brains of the speaker and listener, respectively. The encoder is the anatomical elements used to produce speech, including not only the peripheral anatomical structures such as lips, tongue, soft palate, and larynx, but also the underlying muscular, neuromuscular, and neurological structures which control them. It is these structures which, due to their inherent physical and physiological constraints, impose certain distortions on the intended speech signal. The decoder is the listener's auditory system, including higher-level neurological structures. (These have their own physical constraints which may also distort the signal they receive but this is not represented in the figure.)

An example may clarify some of this. Consider a case where a speaker intends to produce the sequence /tju/. When encoded, i.e., articulated, the stop frequently becomes slightly affricated to [tʃju]. This occurs due to the physical constraint whereby the degree of turbulence and thus the amplitude of the noise spectrum increases as the channel through which airflow is forced becomes smaller. Glides and high, close, vowels provide the narrow channel which leads to increased turbulence. Normally the listeners are accustomed to such distortions (due to their long experience in listening to speech) and they factor out the inadvertent affrication, thus reconstructing the intended /tju/. However, if the listener fails to factor out this distortion, then the pronunciation is taken to be /tʃju/ and this is the pronunciation the listener aims at when he/she produces this word. Originally the amplitude and duration of turbulence would vary continuously as a function of the peculiar aerodynamic conditions created by the sequence of *stop + glide*; after this change the turbulence (affrication) would be an invariable part of the pronunciation of the word. In fact, this very sound change is quite common. It is responsible for the dialectal variants in American English of [tjuzdi] and [tʃuzdi] *Tuesday*, for the pronunciation [æktʃuəl] for *actual* (originally [æktjuəl]) as well as many changes from Latin to French, e.g., *fortia* > *force* (i.e., [fɔʀs]) and *palatium* > *palais* (where the final *s* was once pronounced). In the latter two cases we assume the sequence of sound changes [tj] > [ts] > [s].

It must not be supposed that because the term 'distortion' is used to describe these physically-caused excrescences on the speech signal, and because the experienced listener is said to factor them out, that these perturbations are therefore completely ignored by the listener. On the contrary, the more we investigate the acoustic cues utilized by listeners, the more we find that they are able to take advantage of any acoustic details which show some greater-than-chance probability of being associated with given contrasts. In a somewhat similar way, although the characteristic "hum" of an automobile engine is not what the engineer designing the engine was intending to produce, this sound is still used by the experienced motorist to diagnose its malfunctions. These features are 'distortions' in speech in the sense that they are variable in their appearance and therefore listeners must learn not to incorporate them purposely in their own mental lexicons where the instructions for pronunciation are stored.

The imporant aspect of this account of sound change is that the changes are non-purposeful (i.e., non-teleological). We may assume that speakers speak in a way which, as far as they know, conveys the pronunciation of words that is "standard" in the given speech community and conveys them in a way such that other listeners will be able to figure out the intended pronunciation.

What has been given above is an account of what might best be called "mini-sound changes" because as described they would only apply to changes that occurred due to the misapprehension of a single listener about the pronunciation of a single word. To link this with the "maxi-sound changes" that linguists study, i.e., sound changes characteristic of whole linguistic communities or even whole languges and affecting typically a vast number of words with similar phonetic shape, requires in addition the following assumptions:

1. That the listener's misapprehensions are not corrected. Although this type of misapprehension due to a failure in the error-correcting process is fairly common, most such errors eventually get corrected by virtue of the listener usually having access to other sources of information about how words are

pronounced, e.g., other speakers, the orthography. Nevertheless, it seems safe to assume that some small fraction of such errors escape eventual correction.

2. That the speech of the person who initiated the change serves as the model for other speakers' pronunciation. The extent to which a given speaker's speech is imitated by others depends on their social position, how much they meet other people, etc. Again, it seems safe to assume that situations will arise where a single speaker will influence the speech of a great many other speakers who will therefore copy and perpetuate any innovation this speaker may have initiated.

3. That, optionally, the change which manifested itself on one word then spreads to other similar words in the vocabulary. How this would occur is not precisely clear, although several hypothetical "scenarios" can be constructed (but will not be discussed here).

It might seem that if sound changes are similar across languages and are due to universal physical and physiological factors, then languages should converge towards the same phonological shape. It is fair to say that the macro-structure of all human language *is* quite similar (e.g., all languages use stops, all languages' vowels are roughly equally distributed in the vowel space) but differ largely in their micro-structure (e.g., whether they permit consonant clusters or not). The reason for the variation is that there are so many degrees of freedom in the "design" of a vocal communication system that languages' phonologies can be modified — and are modified by sound change — in numerous ways and still not converge. Likewise, although all living things are similar in being based on chemical processes involving carbon, oxygen, and hydrogen, nevertheless a great variety of different life forms, showing no tendency towards convergence, can be found in any given habitat even though the physical and environmental constraints are uniform. It sometimes happens that in the history of a given language, what one sound change creates, another destroys, and vice-versa. For example, in the evolution of Sanskrit into Prakrit, and its other descendants, almost all intervocalic consonant clusters were eliminated, see Table 1a (based on data from Misra 1967). However, in Hindi, one of the modern descendants of Sanskrit, medial consonant clusters have re-appeared due to the action of a sound change which deleted the vowel [ə] in certain environments, see Table 1b (from M. Ohala, 1983). Such cyclicity of phonological processes is not the rule in linguistic history but neither is it rare.

TABLE 1

A. The loss of Sanskrit medial consonant clusters in its linguistic descendants (data from Misra 1967; a macron above a vowel signifies it is long).

Sanskrit		Prakrit		Hindi		Translation
ʃuska	>	sukk^{h}a	>	sūk^{h}a		dry
karpūra	>	kappūra	>	kapūr		camphor
asta-	>	att^{h}a	>	āt^{h}õ (oblique plural)		eight
karma-	>	karma-	>	kāmõ (oblique plural)		deed

B. Creation of medial consonant clusters in Modern Hindi (data from M. Ohala 1933).

Stem	Translation		Inflected/Derived Form	Translation
nəmək	salt	>	nəmkin	salty
purəb	east	>	purbi	Easterner
sɪsək	to sob	>	sɪski	a sob

To summarize: variations or distortions in the speech signal start out as phonetically dependent and potentially continuous. Then, due to the misapprehension of the listener these distortions become independent of the phonetic causation and they manifest themselves in an invariable way.

I will now list some of the clues a study of sound change provides us which may be of use in the tasks of ASR and SS.

CLUE 1:   The sources of variation in speech.

The first clue provided us may seem obvious:

Variation in speech may be due to two different causes: (a) the physically-caused variation arising from the physical constraints (inertial, aerodynamic, etc.) of the speech mechanism and (b) sound change.

As mentioned, although basically similar (since the latter are drawn from the set comprised of the former), these will have different characters.   The former will generally be a continuous function of phonetic context (rate of speaking, loudness, etc.).   They will also be potentially universal in that, e.g., all sequences of /tj/ in any language will be subject to affrication if the /t/'s and /j/'s are articulated in similar ways.   Therefore the rules for implementing this type of variation in synthesized speech (to achieve greater naturalness) will have the form of equations referring to parameters which may vary continuously e.g., that in (1), from Lindblom (1963) which predicts the F2 value of a vowel, given the target F2 of the vowel ($F2_{target}$), the F2 of the flanking consonants ($F2_{cons}$), the duration of the vowel (t), and two constants (k,b).

(1) $F2 = k(F2_{cons} - F2_{target}) \cdot e^{-bt} + F2_{target}$

The same rules — perhaps with different constants — could be used in different languages.

Variation due to sound change, however, will be discrete (the change is implemented or not — it would not have intermediate values) and might be a function of such non-phonetic factors as speaking style.   The rule in (2) is an example; this involves the change in English of the vowel /ɚ/ to /ə/ when it

(2)   ɚ → ə   / -- Cr̥

appears before a cluster of *consonant* ('C' in (2)) + /r̩/, e.g., *surprise* as [sɚpraɪz] or [səpraɪz]. (The motivation for this rule will be discussed below.) Such rules, which reflect the action of sound changes, although found in numerous languages, will be language-, dialect-, and possibly speaker-specific. It might be imagined that it should be a simple matter to differentiate these two types of variation in speech but this is not the case. It may be easy to detect the action of sound change when variants occur in different languages, or different dialects but not necessarily when they occur within a given language in different grammatical or stylistic environments. Who can say whether the intrusive stops in words like *warmth* [wɔrmpθ] and *strength* [strɛŋkθ] are physically caused or due to a sound change (see Ohala, 1981c)? Nevertheless, this is the kind of determination that must be made for optimal ASR and SS.

CLUE 2: Secondary Cues.

It is well known that many phonemic contrasts, although characterized by linguists as differing primarily by a single phonetic distinction, in actual fact show several phonetic differences. For example, in English the words *pat* and *bat* differ in the ways listed in Table 2. Presumably the more such features are included in synthetic speech, the more natural and the more intelligible it will be. Likewise, if these features can be detected it will enhance the success of a feature-based ASR effort. The problem is, how does one find out what these features are? A study of sound change can help. Many sound changes are of the type where a feature which was previously physically-caused and accessory to a sound is re-interpreted as a primary feature of the sound or sound sequence. A survey of the kind of re-interpretations which are possible for a given distinction will reveal what some of these accessory features are. For example, it is well documented that in the evolution from Middle Chinese to the pre-cursors of the modern Chinese languages, what was previously a contrast of voicing in initial stops changed into a tonal distinction on the following vowels. Table 3 gives comparable data from dialects of Kammu, spoken in Laos (data from Lindell, Svantesson & Tayanin, 1976).

TABLE 2

Some of the differences between the initial stops in *pat* and *bat*.

pat	*bat*
c. 60 msec VOT	c. 0 msec VOT
short transitions	long transitions
higher burst intensity	lower burst intensity
high falling FO	level or low rising FO
on following vowel	on following vowel
lower starting amplitude of	higher starting amplitude
of following vowel	of following vowel

TABLE 3

Data showing that tone in Northern Kammu corresponds to a voicing contrast in Southern Kammu (from Lindell et al. 1976).

Southern Kammu	Northern Kammu	Translation
klaaŋ	kláaŋ	eagle
glaaŋ	klàaŋ	stone

All languages which have segments contrasting in voicing and which have been subjected to instrumental study, show an FO difference of just this sort on the following vowels (Meyer, 1895; Hombert et al., 1979). Evidence exists that in the absence of other cues, English listeners can differentiate syllables such as /kɛ/ and /gɛ/ on the basis of the former having a falling FO on the vowel and the latter a rising FO (Fujimura, 1971). Apparently in the languages immediately descendant from Middle Chinese and the parent language of Northern Kammu, listeners took the FO contour as the intended difference between syllables with voiced and voiceless initial consonants. Perhaps this happened when the voicing contrast was made weakly or was not detected for some other reason.

The evidence which sound change provides us on the interaction of consonants and FO is quite specific, in fact. It also can tell us that sonorants like /m, n, l, j, w/ do not perturb FO, that implosives /ɓ ɗ/ in spite of their being heavily voiced, elevate the FO on following vowels, and that only glottal consonants such as /h ?/ affect the FO of both the preceding and following vowels (Hombert et al., 1979; Ohala, 1979).

Another similar case involves consonantal effects on vowels. There is much data of the sort in Table 4, which presents samples of sound changes in Tibetan

TABLE 4

Data from Tibetan showing the fronting influence of apical consonants on back vowels.

Written Tibetan (c. 8th century)		Lhasa Tibetan	Translation
drug	>	thuu	six
thog	>	thɔɔ	roof
nub	>	nuu	west
but:			
bod	>	phøø	Tibet
ston	>	tø̃	autumn
lus	>	lyy	body
spos	>	pøø	incense

(from Michailovsky, 1975). The forms in the left column are those of written

Tibetan which reflect pronunciation in the 8th century; those in the right column, the pronunciation of present-day Lhasa Tibetan. The data show what happens to back rounded vowels when a final consonant is lost: when it was labial or velar there was no substantial change in the quality of the vowel, but when it was dental the preceding back vowel became fronted, retaining its rounding, i.e., /u/ to /y:/ and /o/ to /ø:/. The "seed" of this particular sound change has been phonetically documented in a variety of languages, e.g., English (Stevens, House & Paul, 1966), Swedish (Lindblom, 1963), French (Chollet, 1976), and Japanese (Umeda, 1960). The addition of the apical constriction to that proper to the back rounded vowel causes the F2 of the resulting sound to raise; the resulting vowel sound is not articulated as a front rounded vowel but it *sounds* like one. For the sound change to have taken place, some listeners must not have been able to factor out this fronting distortion (quite an understandable failure if this final consonant was weakly articulated and thus not readily detected — which must have been the case since the final consonant was lost) and so reinterpreted what they heard as a front rounded vowel (see also Ohala, 1981a).

Other sound changes reveal that labial consonants tend to make front vowels more back, especially labial velar consonants like /k͡p g͡b w ʍ/; /l/, especially the velarized or "dark" lateral, tends to shift vowels toward a mid or high back position; various types of /r/ tend to centralize vowels and/or make them lax.

CLUE 3. What are the units of speech perception?

It is a striking fact that most sound changs usually occur in very specific environments. Consider, for example, the fate of the Latin /l/ in French, as presented in a simplified way in Table 5. The /l/ changed to an [u]-like sound only in the environment *vowel_____consonant*: in intervocalic position and word-initial position it was preserved without change.

From this we can conclude that it is not phonemes which change (otherwise the phoneme /l/ would have suffered the same fate no matter what the environment). On the other hand, whole syllables or words are not the typical domain of change, either. The likely candidates which remain are something in

TABLE 5

Data showing the fate of /l/ in the evolution of Latin to French.

Latin		French
alter	>	autre
caldus	>	chaud
but:		
malus	>	mal
lactis	>	lait

between, i.e., drawn from a set intermediate in size between these two extremes; perhaps allophones or diphones (and related constructs). Without reviewing the literature which might bear on this question, I would venture the opinion that the primary units of speech perception are those regions where rapid acoustic modulations occur, i.e., what are commonly called the "transitions" between phonemes. (This does not mean that phonemes have no reality; they may be inferred from the evidence presented by these more basic perceptual units in the same way as objects like cups, faces, and tables may be inferred by cognitive processing of what are undoubtedly the primary elements of visual perception: edges, shadings of light and dark, etc. Phonemes are also very possibly the units used to represent words in the mental lexicon.)

Units of this sort, i.e., diphone, demi-syllables, etc., which consist of those stretches of speech *between* the periods of minimum rate of change and which therefore include the transition, have been quite successful as a basis for SS, even though they require an order of magnitude more stored units than would be the case with phonemes. It is often thought that their success is due to the fact that they sidestep the problems inherent in figuring out how phonemes are to be joined in the acoustic domain since they "pre-compile" these junctions. However, if my guess is right, their success may be due to the fact that, more than any other unit used in SS, they closely match the units human listeners' ears are tuned to.

CLUE 4:   Sounds and Features have Varying Degrees of Salience and Confusability.

If communication engineers were set the task of designing a signalling system using the vocal-auditory channel, they would no doubt select units or ciphers for transmission which were as different from each other as possible in order to avoid confusions or other errors of reception.   Human speech wasn't designed this way and it turns out that, based on the evidence of sound change, some sounds or features are more susceptible to reception errors than others.   The cues for *manner of articulation* seem to be more robust than those for *place of articulation*.   *Nasal consonants* in initial position survive unchanged more often than oral obstruents in the same position (Ohala, 1975).   Weak fricatives, e.g., [f, v, θ, ð, x, ɣ], change more often than strong fricatives, e.g., [s, z, ʃ, ʒ, ʂ, ʐ]. These patterns may all reflect the high degree of salience of the amplitude parameter in comparison to other acoustic parameters and, obviously, the greater salience of any spectral parameter when it occurs on a part of the signal that has high intensity.

Also, although many sounds are salient by themselves, they are acoustically similar to other sounds and are thus susceptible of being confused.   Table 6 provides one example, the shift of palatalized labials to apical or palatal sounds because the two have similar spectral patterns.[3]

CLUE 5:   Perceptual Confusions tend to be Asymmetrical.

---

[3] When reading this and subsequent tables, it should be kept in mind that consonants can become phonetically palatalized or labialized by being adjacent to palatal and rounded vowels, respectively.

TABLE 6

Examples of the sound change whereby palatalized labials are confused with and become apical or palatal sounds (Ohala 1978).

Standard Czech	East Bohemian	Translation
m^{j}ɛstɔ	nɛstɔ	town
p^{j}ɛt	tɛt	five

Lungchow	T'ien-chow	
pjaa	tʃaa	fish

Latin		Intermediate Form		Spanish	
amplu	>	ampju	>	antʃo	large, spacious

Roman Italian	Genoese	
pjeno	tʃena	full
bjaŋko	dʒaŋku	white

Latin		French	
sapiens	>	saʒ	wise
rubeus	>	ʁuʒ	red

Proto-Bantu		Zulu	
pia	>	-tʃha	new

A puzzling meta-pattern found in sound change is the frequent asymmetry in the direction of change (see also Ohala, 1983b, c). Table 6, above, presents one such case; shifts in the reverse direction, of palatal or apical sounds to palatalized labials, are much less common. Other such asymmetrical sound changes are the shift of labialized velars to labials (e.g., Proto-Indo-European *ekwōs* became *hippos* in Classical Greek) and the shift of palatalized velars to apical affricates (e.g., Latin *radikina* "root" became /raditšinə/, and subsequently, French *racine* [ʁasin]). Such shifts are understandable given the great similarity in the spectral patterns of the sounds involved in each pair (Durand, 1955; Halle, Hughes & Radley, 1957).

These same asymmetries have been found in speech perception experiments (which reinforces the claim that these sound changes have a phonetic basis). Table 7 presents some results from a study by Winitz, Scheib and Reeds (1972) involving listeners' identification of CV sequences.

TABLE 7

Asymmetries of confusion in a speech perception study by Winitz et al. (1972), where ' > ' means 'was misidentified as'.

Error type			Incidence		Error type			Incidence
[pi]	>	[ti]	34%	but	[ti]	>	[pi]	6%
[ki]	>	[ti]	32%	but	[ti]	>	[ki]	6%
[ku]	>	[pu]	27%	but	[pu]	>	[ku]	16%

If one of these pairs of sounds changes into the other because they are acoustically similar and listeners mistake which one they are hearing, then it should be the case that the sound changes could go in either direction. The fact that they don't requires some explanation. A clue to the solution to this puzzle may be found in analyses of data from visual perception studies which also exhibit asymmetrical confusions. Gilmore, Hersh, Caramazza and Griffin (1979), for example, found the following kinds of asymmetries in subjects' misidentification of the capital Roman letters when presented under conditions which degrade perceptual performance, as shown in (3), (where '>' means the letter on the left was misidentified as that on the right more often than the reverse):

(3)   Q > O   E > F   R > P

         B > P   P > F   J > I

The letters in each pair are structurally similar to each other except for some extra distinguishing feature. In the case of E and F, for example, both are identical except for the "foot" of the E — missing in the case of F. If this distinguishing feature is missed when the letter on the left is viewed, then it will appear to be the letter on the right. When the righthand letter is viewed, however, it is less likely that this extra distinguishing feature will be mistakenly "filled in". Herein lies the basis for the asymmetry in confusion (Garner, 1978).

Pursuing the implications of this clue, it must therefore be the case that the pairs of speech sound sequences which exhibit asymmetries in sound change and in speech perception studies are acoustically similar except that the ones which are more susceptible to change have one or more extra distinguishing features which are lacking in the more stable sounds. Research is needed to identify these features but some candidates features immediately suggest themselves. For example, comparison of the smoothed spectra of the bursts of [gi] and [di] (see Fig. 2 from Stevens and Blumstein, 1978) reveals that each pair is quite similar except for a sharp peak at about 3 kHz in the case of [gi].

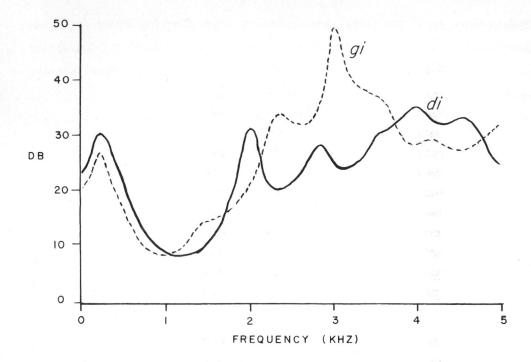

Figure 2. Spectra of the stop bursts of the syllables [di] (solid line) and [gi]
(dashed line). (Redrawn from Stevens and Blumstein, 1978.)

It is obvious that these features which distinguish one sound from another
must be discovered if SS is to be successful. But these perceptual asymmetries
have more profound implications for ASR. The metric which compares the
unknown input with a series of known templates should be capable of
accommodating or reflecting this inherently asymmetrical nature of speech
perception. That is, it should be the case that an input [di] would be shown to
be more similar to a reference [gi] than would an input [gi] when referred to a
[di]. This reflects the fact that it is easier to turn a [gi] into a [di] (by deleting
the sharp peak in the burst) than it is to turn a [di] into a [gi] (which could
only be done by *adding* that spectral peak). The assumption is made that
accidental loss of certain features is more likely than their accidental introduction.

Current comparison metrics used in ASR, e.g., dynamic time warping, can be
made inherently asymmetric by attaching different weights to paths which skip
over or which repeat frames in the reference template (cf. R. Moore, this volume).

This is certainly a step in the right direction but the evidence I have reviewed here suggests that the asymmetrical comparison must also apply to the comparison of individual spectral frames or arrays of distinctive features (which cannot be done by just skipping or repeating spectral frames) and that the asymmetries — the differential weights attached to permitted operations which transform the input into the reference template — may be specific to certain sounds or sound sequences.

CLUE 6: Many Distinctive Features may be Non-Orthogonal.

In a maximally efficient signalling system the values assumed by any parameter should be completely independent of other parameters. Speech, by this criterion, is not maximally efficient. An examination of the record of sound changes in the history of many languages — including their segment inventories, which have been shaped by sound change — reveals a number of interdependencies among features.

Place of articulation and the feature of voicing interact as shown by, among other evidence, the stop inventories of over 570 languages (surveyed by Sherman, 1975; see also Gamkrelidze, 1975); Table 8 shows the incidence of stop gaps among languages which used a voicing contrast in at least one place of articulation for stops.

TABLE 8

Incidence of gaps in the indicated place of articulation in the stop inventories of over 570 languages (from Sherman 1975).

Place of articulation:	Labial	Apical	Velar
Voiceless	34	0	0
Voiced	2	21	40

(Many of these languages did not have a voicing contrast on stops; in the vast majority of these cases the stops were voiceless. This also demonstrates interdependence between the features 'stop' and 'voice'.) As can be seen, among voiceless stops, the labial stop /p/ is most often missing; among voiced stops, the velar, /g/ is the most common gap. Among languages lacking a /p/ (in native vocabulary) are Arabic, Yoruba and Vietnamese; Japanese uses a [p] only in very restricted phonological environments. Some languages lacking a /g/ are Dutch, Czech and Thai. Insofar as we know the history of these languages, the missing sounds were present at one time but subsequently changed either in the feature of voicing or stoppedness. What was once a [g] in Dutch, for example, is now an uvular fricative [χ].

The physical causes of these patterns are reasonably well understood: In the case of the voiceless consonants, the stop burst, which is one of the major cues to the presence of a stop, is of much lower intensity in the case of /p/ since, unlike the other stops, it has little or no resonating cavity in front of the point of release (where the burst is created) to reinforce it. In the case of the voiced consonants, the smaller air cavity behind back-articulated stops is less able to accommodate the glottal airflow with the result that the rapid accumulation of air behind the constriction diminishes the transglottal pressure drop and hence the rate of glottal airflow and thus voicing (Ohala, 1983a).

Voicing also doesn't sit comfortably on fricatives. Voiced fricatives require a delicate aerodynamic balancing act: for optimal frication the pressure drop across the consonantal constriction should be high; for the sake of optimal voicing, the pressure drop across the glottis should be high. These two requirements are represented in (4). Since atmospheric pressure cannot be manipulated and

(4)   For optimal frication: P atmospheric < P oral

          For optimal voicing: P oral < P subglottal

subglottal pressure cannot be easily altered in the short interval (c. 60 msec) required for the production of a single obstruent, the only one of these pressures that is amenable to modification is the oral pressure. But for one purpose it should be as high as possible while for the other as low as possible. Both cannot be done simultaneously. Therefore, to the extent that voiced fricatives have intense frication, e.g., [s,z,ʃ,ʒ] the so-called "strong fricatives", they have a tendency to become devoiced, while to the extent that they have robust voicing, e.g., [β, v, ð, ɣ, ʁ, ʕ], the "weak fricatives", they tend not to have very much frication.

Rules for SS need to take account of these non-orthogonalities by, e.g., modifying the degree of voicing or noise intensity depending on what other features they co-occur with. Natural sounding synthetic /g/'s in American English will not only be typically voiceless but will even have up to 20 msec of aspiration, even in pre-stress intervocalic position (Ohala, 1981b). Feature-extracting algorithms for ASR will not be able to use quite the same methods in the detection of, say, all voiced obstruents or all fricatives.

It should also be mentioned that non-orthogonality of features may appear not only due to articulatory, but also acoustic-auditory factors. It is not physiologically difficult to add pharyngealization (a secondary constriction in the pharyngeal region) to consonants having primary place of constriction in the labial and apical regions. However, Arabic, noted for its pharyngealized or "emphatic" sounds, uses this contrast primarily (some would say 'exclusively') on apical sounds. The reason is that the acoustic manifestation of pharyngealization is a lowering of some of the higher formants but labials already have lowered formants and so would not manifest this effect in an optimal way; apical sounds, on the other hand, have maximally high F2 and so would manifest pharyngealization's lowered formants quite clearly. (For further discussion, see Ohala, in press b; Ohala & Kawaskai, in press.)

CLUE 7: Listeners Perform Error-Correction in Speech Perception

In the introduction I suggested that the speech signal is a composite of the intended message (pronunciation) plus unintended distortions caused by the physical constraints of the speech production apparatus and that one of the tasks of the listener is to strip away the distortions in order to recover the canonical form of the message. If this is accepted, it has rather important implications for

ASR, namely, that successful speech recognition by machine will have to duplicate the listener's performance. Given that variability is at the heart of the problems facing ASR, developing this error-correcting capacity may be the key to successful ASR. That human listeners *do* have this capacity need not be simply assumed; there is evidence for it from sound change. I argue that some sound changes, those said to exhibit "dissimilation", are caused by the listeners inappropriately applying their error-correcting rules.

To begin discussion of this topic, we note first that assimilation can sometimes extend over relatively long stretches of speech. In a $C_1 VC_2$ sequence, for example, not only the intervening V but also C_1 can assimilate to some of the features of C_2. An example of this may be found in Kaiwa, an indigenous language of Brazil (Harrison & Taylor, 1971). The phrase $/d^y u\textʔi \ \textŋ^w e/$ "frog" may appear in casual speech as $[\textɲũ\textʔĩ \ \textŋ^w e]$ where the nasalization of the $[\textŋ^w]$ has spread all the way to the beginning of the phrase to change $/d^y/$ to $[\textɲ]$ (the palatal nasal). We assume that this kind of distortion presents no difficulty for listeners because they can factor it out. Now, however, consider the evolution of the Latin word *quīnque* [kwĩŋkwe] in its various daughter languages; see (5a). The stages in the evolution of this word from Latin to Italian, for example, is as given in (5b).

(5) (a) Latin *quīnque*

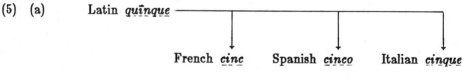

French *cinc*   Spanish *cinco*   Italian *cinque*

(b) kwĩŋkwe

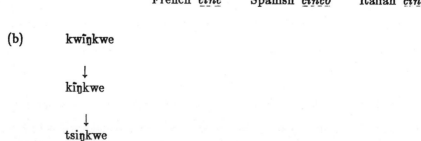

kĩŋkwe

tsiŋkwe

The initial labialized velar lost its labialization (and subsequently changed to an apical affricate — for the reasons discussed earlier). The second labialized velar survived a bit longer. Why should this dissimilation, a /kw/ changing to /k/ before another /kw/, occur? I claim it is due to the listeners erroneously attributing the labialization on the first syllable as due to the spreading labialization from the second syllable. In other words, they treated this labialization as a distortion and factored it out. In their own most careful pronunications, this word would not have any labialization in the first syllable. Presumably, similar reasons underlie the sound change mentioned above in (2) whereby a retroflex vowel [ə] becomes de-retroflexed before another retroflex sound.

In the terms of the schematization given above in Fig. 1, the process of dissimilation may be represented as in Fig. 3. Here the intended pronunciation includes $x + y$ but the decoder interprets y as noise and so strips it from the reconstructed signal x.

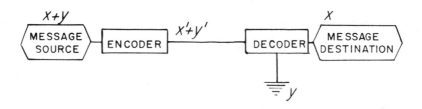

Figure 3. Schematic representation of a transmission line used as an analogue of speech production and perception to explain the process of dissimilation; see text.

There are a number of pieces of evidence supporting this account of dissimilation. First, it would predict that the only phonetic features which could be subject to dissimilation would be those features which are known to spread like a prosody over large stretches of speech, e.g., palatalization, retroflexion, aspiration, labialization, etc., but not features like stop or affricate which by their nature cannot spill over onto adjacent segments. By and large, this prediction is borne out (see Ohala, 1981a, 1983b, in press a). Second, there is supporting evidence from speech perception studies. Ohala, Kawasaki, Riordan, & Caisse (forthcoming) (as reported in Ohala, 1981a) had listeners identify as /i/ or /u/ stimuli of the sort /sVt/, /fVp/ where the vowel, V, was one of 9 steady-state vowels synthesized to range at regular increments between (and including) /i/ and /u/. Naturally listeners' judgements shifted from being predominantly /i/ to predominantly /u/ somewhere in the middle of this continuum. However, the location of this crossover point was further towards the front of the vowel space (i.e., towards /i/) when the vowels appeared in the /s__t/ context than the /f__p/ context. That is, a more front vowel was accepted as a good /u/ when it appeared in a phonetic environment known to cause fronting of back vowels (see above). Presumably, listeners attributed some of the frontness of the vowels to the surrounding apical consonants, /s/ and /t/, and thus factored it out in deducing its intended quality. Several other speech perception studies have also shown that listeners identify speech sounds after taking into account possible distorting effects of the phonetic environment they are found in (see Ohala, 1981a, 1983b, in press a, for references).

There is as yet no suggestion as to how human listeners perform this error-corrrection but a number of approaches are possible for algorithms that would do the same thing in an ASR task. One might be to take equations such as those of Lindblom's, presented above in (1), and turn them around so that target formant frequency of vowels could be computed given the rate of speaking, the formant frequencies of the adjacent consonants, and the measured formant frequencies of the spoken vowel. Another, more qualitative, approach — appropriate, perhaps, to an "expert system" for ASR — would be statements of the sort in (6).

(6) If: F2 of vowel > 1500 Hz and preceding or following consonants are alveolar or palatal,

Then: vowel has .60 probability of being a back vowel.

CONCLUSION

Some very challenging goals face those working in speech synthesis and automatic speech recognition: in speech synthesis, natural-sounding speech from unlimited text and in machine recognition of speech, the accurate recognition of large vocabulary continuously-spoken speech by any native speaker. I believe that the solution to these problems will entail learning as much as possible about how speech is structured and how human speakers and listeners accomplish their tasks in handling spoken language. One largely untapped but very rich source of clues about how speech works is the documentation linguists have accumulated over the past 2 centuries of *sound change*, i.e., the changes in pronunciation over time. I regard sound change as Mother Nature's speech perception experiment. All we have to do is to try to interpret the record of sound change for our purposes. In this paper I have given some examples of how one might do this.

ACKNOWLEDGEMENTS

I gratefully acknowledge the helpful comments, data, and bibliographical advice given by Mariscela Amador and those attending the NATO ASI at Bonas, July 1984, especially Renato De Mori and Manjari Ohala.

REFERENCES

1. G. Chollet, "Effects of coarticulation, syllable type and stress on acoustic French vowel targets", J. Acous. Soc. Am., Vol. 60, S44, 1976.
2. M. Durand, "Du rôle de l'auditeur dans la formation des sons du langage", J. de Psych., Vol. 52, pp. 347-355, 1955.
3. O. Fujimura, "Remarks on stop consonants: Synthesis experiments and acoustic cues", in L. L. Hammerich, R. Jakobson & E. Zwirner (eds.), *Form and substance. Phonetic and linguistic papers presented to Eli*

474

Fischer-Jørgensen. Copenhagen: Akademisk Forlag, pp. 221-232, 1971.

4. T. V. Gamkrelidze, "On the correlation of stops and fricatives in a phonological system", Lingua, Vol. 35, pp. 231-261, 1975.

5. W. R. Garner, "Aspects of a stimulus: features, dimensions and configurations", in E. Rosch & B. B. Lloyd (eds.), *Cognition and Categorization*, Hillsdale, N. J., Erlbaum, pp. 99-133, 1978.

6. G. C. Gilmore, H. Hersh, A. Caramazza and J. Griffin, "Multidimensional letter similarity derived from recognition errors", Perception & Psychophysics, Vol. 25, pp. 425-431, 1979.

7. M. Halle, G. W. Hughes and J.-P. A. Radley, "Acoustic properties of stop consonants", J. Acous. Soc. Am., Vol. 29, pp. 107-116, 1957.

8. C. H. Harrison and J. M. Taylor, "Nasalization in Kaiwa", in D. Bendor-Samuel (ed.), *Tupi studies I*, Norman, Oklahoma: Summer Institute of Linguistics, pp. 15-20, 1971.

9. J.-M. Hombert, J. J. Ohala and W. G. Ewan, "Phonetic explanations for the development of tones", Language, Vol. 55, pp. 37-58, 1979.

10. W. A. Lea (ed.), *Trends in Speech Recognition*, Englewood Cliffs: Prentice-Hall, 1980.

11. B. Lindblom, "Spectrographic study of vowel reduction", J. Acous. Soc. Am., Vol. 35, pp. 1773-1781, 1963.

12. K. Lindell, J-O. Svantesson and D. Tayanin, "Phonology of Kammu dialects", paper presented at the 9th International Conference on sino-Tibetan Languages and Linguistics, Copenhagen, 1976.

13. E. A. Meyer, "Zur Tonbewegung des Vokals", Phonetische Studien, Vol. 10, pp. 20ff, 1896.

14. B. Michailovsky, "On some Tibeto-Burman sound changes", Proceedings of the Annual Meeting, Berkeley Linguistics Society Vol. 1, pp. 322-332, 1975.

15. J. J. Ohala, "Experimental historical phonology" in J. M. Anderson & C. Jones (eds.), *Historical Linguistics II. Theory and Description in Phonology*. Amsterdam: North Holland, pp. 353-389, 1974.

16. J. J. Ohala, "Phonetic explanations for nasal sound patterns", in C. A. Ferguson, L. M. Hyman and J. J. Ohala (eds.), *Nasalfest: Papers from a symposium on nasals and nasalization*, Stanford: Language Universals Project, pp. 289-316, 1975.

17. J. J. Ohala, "The production of tone", in V. A. Fromkin (eds.), *Tone: A Linguistic Survey*, New York: Academic Press, pp. 5-39, 1978.

18. J. J. Ohala, "The application of phonological universals in speech pathology", in N. J. Lass (ed.), *Speech and Language. Advances in Basic Research and Practice*, Vol. 3, New York: Academic Press, pp. 75-97, 1980.

19. J. J. Ohala, "The listener as a source of sound change", in C. S. Masek, R. A. Hendrick and M. F. Miller (eds.), *Papers from the Parasession on Language and Behavior*. Chicago: Chicago Linguistic Society, pp. 178-203, 1981a.

20. J. J. Ohala, "Articulatory constraints on the cognitive representation of speech", in T. Myers, J. Laver and J. Anderson (eds.), *The Cognitive Representation of Speech*, Amsterdam: North Holland, pp. 111-122, 1981b.

21. J. J. Ohala, "Speech timing as a tool in phonology", Phonetica, Vol. 38, pp.

204-212, 1981c.

22. J. J. Ohala, "The origin of sound patterns in vocal tract constraints", in P. F. MacNeilage (ed.), *The Production of Speech*, New York: Springer-Verlag, pp. 189-216, 1983a.

23. J. J. Ohala, "The direction of sound change", in A. Cohen & M. P. R. v. d. Broeck (eds.), *Abstracts of the Tenth International Congress of Phonetic Sciences*, Dordrecht: Foris, pp. 253-258, 1983b.

24. J. J. Ohala, "The phonological end justifies any means", in S. Hattori & K. Inoue (eds.), *Proceedings of the XIIIth International Congress of Linguists, August 29 — September 4, 1982, Tokyo.* Distributed by Sanseido Shoten, pp. 232-243, 1983c.

25. J. J. Ohala, "Phonological evidence for top-down processing in speech perception", in J. Perkell et al. (eds.), *Invariance and Variability in Speech Processes*, Hillsdale, N. J.: Erlbaum, in press, a.

26. J. J. Ohala, "Around *flat*", in V. Fromkin (ed.), *Phonetic Linguistics*, New York: Academic Press, in press, b.

27. J. J. Ohala and H. Kawasaki, "Phonetics and prosodic phonology," *Phonology Yearbook*, in press.

28. J. J. Ohala, H. Kawasaki, C. Riordan & M. Caisse, Forthcoming. The influence of consonantal environment upon the perception of vowel quality.

29. M. Ohala, *Aspects of Hindi Phonology*, Delhi: Motilal Banarsidass, 1983.

30. D. Sherman, "Stop and fricative systems: A discussion of paradigmatic gaps and the question of language sampling", Stanford Working Papers in Language Universals, Vol. 17, pp. 1-31, 1975.

31. K. N. Stevens and S. E. Blumstein, "Invariant cues for place of articulation in stop consonants", J. Acous. Soc. Am., Vol. 64, pp. 1358-1368, 1978.

32. K. N. Stevens, A. S. House and A. P. Paul, "Acoustical description of syllabic nuclei: an interpretation in terms of a dynamic model of articulation", J. Acous. Soc. Am., Vol. 40, pp. 123-132, 1966.

33. N. Umeda, "Influence of consonants on vowels", J. Acous. Soc., Japan, Vol. 16, pp. 87-93, 1960.

34. H. Winitz, M. E. Scheib and J. A. Reeds, "Identification of stops and vowels for the burst portion of /p,t,k/ isolated from conversational speech", J. Acous. Soc. Am., Vol. 51, pp. 1309-1317, 1972.

SYNTHESIS OF SPEECH BY COMPUTERS AND CHIPS

Ching Y. Suen and Stephen B. Stein

Dept. of Computer Science

Concordia University

1455 de Maisonneuve Blvd., West

Montreal, Quebec H3G 1M8

Canada

ABSTRACT

Speech of unlimited vocabulary can be synthesized from systems which can produce the basic set of about 40 phonetic sounds of a language. However, the quality of the speech output is highly dependent on the method used in the system. Good synthesized speech requires good phonetic rules to give an accurate transcription of the input texts. A description of an accurate unrestricted text-to-speech algorithm will be described. An evaluation of speech synthesizers and the experimental results will be discussed. Further addition of prosody features will make the synthesized sound more and more natural. Some new systems developed in recent years and their characteristics will be presented.

INTRODUCTION

Speech is the primary mode of human communication. The great variety of applications of synthetic speech has already been described in the literature, see e.g. references [5-7, 10, 13-15, 19, 21, 22, 30, 33]. In this paper, we examine the role that synthetic speech can play in the man-machine interface.

NATO ASI Series, Vol. F16
New Systems and Architectures for Automatic Speech
Recognition and Synthesis. Edited by R. De Mori and C. Y. Suen
© Springer-Verlag Berlin Heidelberg 1985

Methods of synthetic speech production may be grouped in the following manner:

1. Those which involve the storage, processing and coding of actual human speech such as those using linear predictive coding, see e.g. [3, 13, 17, 20, 23].

2. Those which involve the synthetic production of speech from formant type of synthesizer (usually equipped with flexible filters) and speech from a set of rules, see e.g. references [1, 2, 4-6, 8, 9, 12, 21, 25, 26, 28, 29, 31, 32, 34].

The former method may employ magnetic tape recordings or the digitization and machine processing of speech stored in solid state memory. In either case, with or without an encoding process, these methods which are commonly used in the manufacturing of talking toys, calculators, and watches are appropriate to only those applications where a small finite vocabulary is needed.

The latter method must be used where the ability to produce a large number of different vocabulary items is required. Such is the case in the development of reading machines for the blind or an auditory component to a computer assisted learning package.

The Concordia Speech Project (CSP) is involved in the development of a "speech by rule" system that produces speech with a high degree of intelligibility, yet is compact enough to be run on a microcomputer. The software was developed on a large mainframe, CDC's Cyber 172 computer, and drives a Votrax VS-6 synthesizer [26, 28, 29].

The Votrax synthesizer is an electronic analogue to the human vocal tract. It consists of two sound generator circuits. One produces voiced sounds and the other produces fricative sounds. These two outputs are joined and passed through a set of filters to simulate the vocal tract's resonance. The synthesizer has the ability to produce any of sixty-one phonemes, and is hardware controlled. All that is required to run it is a sequence of phonetic codes represented in six bit words. The VS-6 model which is used for this research has four set levels of intonation which control the phonemes, pitch and amplitude, requiring an additional two bits. Therefore, the entire command word has eight bits.

The Votrax synthesizer was chosen for this research because its operation requires a bit rate of only 70 bits per second and it provides a valuable research tool to develop phonetic rules to make it speak unlimited English. In microcomputer applications Votrax's single chip synthesizer (the SC-01) can be substituted for the VS-6 to which it is supposed to be identical. The major shortcoming of the synthesizer is that the lack of software control over pitch, speech rate and amplitude makes control of the suprasegmental aspects of speech rather limited.

This paper will present the speech rule system developed at Concordia University with experimental results and a comparison of performance with another synthesizer, the Type 'N Talk text-to-speech synthesizer. It also gives a description of new devices and speech synthesis chips available in the market. This paper is mainly addressed to the synthesis of spoken English, synthesis of other languages may be found in references [27, 16, 18].

PRINCIPLE OF TEXT TO SPEECH CONVERSION

The development of an algorithm to convert a string of orthographic symbols to a string of phonetic symbols needed by the Votrax synthesizer presents a problem with many facets. This is particularly true if the algorithm must be small enough to be run on a microcomputer.

Perhaps the simplest workable approach to the problem is that taken by Elovitz et al. [6]. In this system, a word is scanned from left to right and letters are assigned phonetic symbols solely on the basis of 329 letter-to-sound rules. The algorithm is very compact and can be easily implemented on practically any microcomputer. The absence of stress rules and problems of phonetic accuracy, however, impair the general intelligibility of the output.

At the other end of the simplicity continuum are systems such as those developed by Allen [2] and Hertz [8, 9]. Both these systems employ parametric synthesizers rather than the Votrax synthesizer used in the CSP. A parametric synthesizer is typically more expensive to run but allows much greater control over the realization of stress and intonation. In Allen's system words are broken up into their constituent morphemes. The pronunciation of these morphemes is checked against a dictionary of 12,000 entries. In the final output, adjustments are made in the cases where affixation affects the pronunciation of root morphemes. Those words for which no entries are found are sounded out as a human would upon encountering a new word.

While there can be little doubt that Allen's system is an excellent one, incorporating all known aspects of speech production, its size and complexity precludes its implementation on a small microcomputer.

THE CSP SYSTEM

The CSP system must be considered as one based on stress. It became apparent in the early stages of the project that much of the variation in a vowel's pronunciation depends more upon whether it is stressed than on its immediate segmental environment. The stress assignment algorithm used in CSP has three major functions:

1) It aids in the overall intelligibility of words,
2) It allows for the separate application of rules to stressed and unstressed vowels,
3) It enables the system to capture the most salient characteristic of English phonology: namely, that unstressed vowels generally reduce to "schwa".

In the CSP system, a word is first read in and checked against a prelexicon. The prelexicon contains the phonetic code for words which are exceptions to both the rules of English pronunciation and affixation. An example of this is the word "island", for which the correct pronunciation cannot be established by sounding out the word as a whole or by removing the suffix "land" and pronouncing "is" in isolation.

If the word is found in the prelexicon, the phonetic code is sent to the Votrax synthesizer. If it is not found, the word is syllabified by counting the number of vowel clusters. Of course, not all sequences of vowels are vowel clusters, and the system employs a set of rules to distinguish between words such as "noun" and "neon" assigning the former a syllable count of one, and the latter a syllable count of two. In addition, the detection of final silent "e" is necessary to avoid an inflation of the syllable count. It should be noted here that because the assignment of stress requires only that the number of syllables be known, the system does not establish syllable boundaries within a word.

Following syllabification, all external affixes are removed from the word. An external affix is defined as one which does not affect the placement of stress. Examples of these are the suffixes "ness" and "ment". This procedure has the advantages of simplifying stress assignment and aiding in the detection of silent medial "e". In the word "basement", for example, removal of "ment" places the silent "e" in final position where the final silent "e" rule can apply to the word "base". In addition, the removal of external affixes makes it possible to limit the size of the lexicon. The lexicon is consulted after affixes are removed, and therefore need only contain root words. The lexicon entries are words whose pronunciations are exceptions to general English rules, but allow for external affix removal. Therefore, although a word like "island" must be placed in the prelexicon, the correct pronunciation of "Thailand" requires only that "Thai" be a lexicon entry.

If a root word is not found in the lexicon, stress is assigned to it. The rules of stress assignment are based on principles of English stress described in Chomsky and Halle [4] as well as those in Wijk [32]. Although the Chomsky and Hall rules are rather elegant, they could not be taken over wholesale because of their reliance on the part-of-speech values of words. The CSP system, which does no grammatical parsing could not employ them.

Once stress has been established, two sets of text to speech rules translate letters to phonetic codes. One set of rules is reserved solely for stressed vowels, and the other provides phonetic code for unstressed vowels and consonants. Detailed descriptions of these rules can be found in Stein's thesis [26].

Before the final output, the phonetic code for any affixes that were removed is attached to the word. The code for affixes is derived using the same set of rules as the root word.

Finally, the entire word is sent to the Votrax buffer. The synthesized speech is produced using normal audio speakers.

Although the sets of stressed and unstressed rules specify different phonetic codes for the orthographic representation of vowels, they are identical in organization. The rules are organized by grapheme. Thus, there are blocks of 'A' rules, 'B' rules, etc.

For example, to determine the phonetic code for the word 'CAT', the system must first search linearly through the 'C' rules, then the stressed 'A' rules and finally the 'T' rules. The fact that a linear search is carried out through a rule block enables us to control the application of rules by ordering them within the block. In our example, the 'C' rule that applies is: [C] = /K/. This rule is simply read: "The letter 'C' is pronounced /K/". Because the rule specifies no special environment for its application, it must occupy the last position in the rule block. Otherwise, it would traverse through all other rules which come below it. All rules must be ordered, therefore, from the most specific to the most general.

In addition to specifying the pronunciation of a single letter, a rule may specify the pronunciation of a cluster of letters. The rule block into which such a rule is placed, however, must correspond to the first letter of the cluster. For example, the rule that states that [CHR] at the beginning of a word is pronounced /KR/ is found in the 'C' rules.

The fact that rules must be placed in letter blocks leads to some interesting consequences when one tries to capture some of the generalizations of English phonology. This can be seen in Figure 1 in which the system's output for the word 'COMPUTERS' is displayed. Here the palatalization of the letter 'P' is captured by the 'U' rule that is read: "If a stressed letter 'U' is preceded by one or more consonants but not (TH,ST,SH,CH,N,X,Y,S,Z,J,L or R) and if it is followed by one and only one consonant followed by at least one vowel, then it is pronounced /YU/.

FIGURE 1
EXAMPLE 1 (using the word 'computers')

WORD % 'COMPUTERS'
C C
V O
C MP
V U
C T
V E
C RS

THERE IS/ARE 3 SYLLABLE(S)

PREFIX/SUFFIX RULE(S) NUMBER(S)-7
3 SYLLABLE(S) IS/ARE CONSIDERED IN RULE
AFTER STRESS RULE, WORD BECAME % COMPUTER
STRESS 1 AFTER THE PREFIX % U
RULE 19

MAIN WORD
[C]=/K/
[/0(S1);0/]=/UH3/
[M]=/M/
[P]=/P/
(C1)/TH;ST;SH;CH;N;X;Y;S;Z;J;L;R/^[U](C1,1)(V1)=/Y U/
[T]=/T/
[/E(V1);E/]=/EH3/
[R]=/R/
SUFFIX
%(C1)/T'/^[S]#=/Z/

Figure 1 exemplifies the operation of the algorithm described above. The word is first divided into consonant and vowel clusters. All affixes are identified and stress is assigned to the appropriate vowel. It is the knowledge that all vowels except the 'U' are unstressed that allows the lax pronunciation to be assigned to the 'O' and 'E'.

In this case the plural morpheme 'S' is seen as an external affix because it does not affect the placement of stress within the main word 'COMPUTER'.

PERFORMANCE

All of the first five thousand most frequently used words in the Brown corpus are pronounced correctly by the CSP system, within the hardware limitations of the Votrax synthesizer.

This was ascertained by listening to the synthesized version of each word and by looking at the phonetic transcription that was being produced to drive the synthesizer.

It was decided, however, that if the true performance of the CSP system were to be evaluated, a test situation more closely approximating the actual conditions under which the system would be used was needed. An experiment was therefore devised to test the performance of the CSP system against that of a human speaker and another, simpler, system — Votrax's Type 'N Talk. This synthesizer is based on the SC 01 chip, and its repertoire of phonemes is nearly identical to that of the VS 6. Both synthesizers are made by the same company. However, the Type 'N Talk contains its own built-in algorithm for text to speech conversion.

It was envisioned that the comparison of the CSP system to the Type 'N Talk would yield information on whether the greater complexity of our system actually produces significantly more intelligible output than a simpler, and therefore less expensive, algorithm.

they do not allow the listener to successfully employ any word expectancy strategy.

The nine lists of ten words were presented by means of a tape recording at approximately 60 dB to three randomly assigned groups of subjects. Three lists were read by a human, three by the Type 'N Talk, and three by the CSP. After each sentence was read, the subjects were required to write down exactly what they had heard. The test situation was therefore very similar to a standard dictation exercise.

The variables being manipulated were speaker (CSP, Type 'N Talk, human) and practice for each condition (first, second and third set of trials).

The design was a fully counter-balanced 3 x 3 factorial design with repeated measures on both factors.

After the subjects had completed the dictation task, each group was asked to subjectively rate the reading of an article from Time magazine by one of the three speakers in terms of overall intelligibility. The subjects were given a numerical rating range from zero to one hundred.

Results

A two way analysis of variance with factor trial (1st, 2nd, 3rd) and system (CSP, Type 'N Talk, human) with repeated measures on both factors was done. The main effect for system was $F(2,178) = 4231, .001$. The main effect for trial was $F(2,178) = 95, .001$, while the interaction between system and trial was $F(4,356) = 9.96, .001$.

These results are represented graphically in Figure 2.

The subjective ratings of the magazine article reading for each of the three speakers yielded the following results on a scale of 1 to 100: Human = 91; CPS = 64; Type 'N Talk = 32.

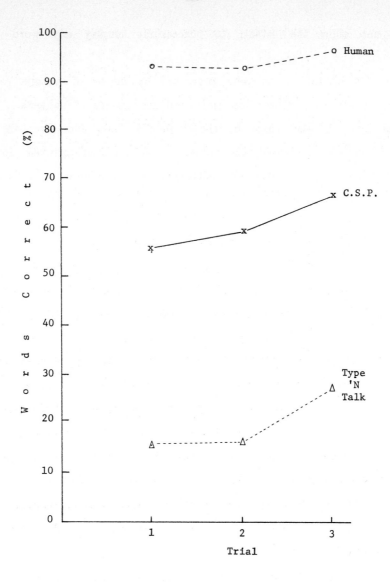

Percentage of correct words for each system.

Figure 2

DISCUSSION AND PRELIMINARY ERROR ANALYSIS

The large difference in words correct for CSP and "Type 'N Talk" was not expected. It would be convenient to attribute all the difference between the two systems to the fact that CSP uses a more sophisticated algorithm. Although this certainly is an important factor it does not account for all the results obtained in the experiment.

Spectrographs taken of the sentence "The tiny girl took off her hat.", spoken by all three systems show some important differences between systems. The spectrographs were made from the tapes actually used in the performance test.

The formant transitions produced by the Votrax VS-6 synthesizer, used in the CSP, tend to be smoother than those of the "Type 'N Talk". Much more information is available from the speech produced by the Votrax VS-6 at the higher frequencies than that of the "Type 'N Talk".

It is our aim at the CSP to use the results of this experiment to point to areas in which improvement to the CSP system is most needed. Preliminary analyses have revealed some interesting tendencies. It seems to us that the vast majority of errors are a result of 'semantic filling'. It is probable that in processing the sentences, the cadets did not recognize each word as they heard it, but rather, formed a general impression of the meaning of the sentence based on the key words that they did recognize. For each sentence then, the previously unrecognized words were filled in to construct a syntactically correct sentence that would be consistent with this meaning. The use of this strategy can be detected precisely because it did not work. The sentences used in the experiment were constructed so as not to allow the listener to build the entire sentence using only partial information. Had normal sentences been used, the semantic filling strategy would have undoubtedly been more successful.

Our observations have thus far been consistent with this explanation. Relatively few errors were made in the recognition of open-class words (nouns, verbs, adjectives and adverbs) whereas errors were frequently the result of the substitution of one preposition for another or the switching of article forms (a, the). Even where errors in open-class words were made, evidence points to semantic filling. In the sentence, "The Friendly gang left the drug store", 'gang' was changed to 'man' by a great many subjects listening to the CSP version. The most plausible explanation for this is that one generally does not expect a gang to be friendly.

Although we must emphasize that our error analysis results are preliminary, the concept of comprehension threshold promises to play an important role in the evaluation of synthetic speech systems. The Type 'N Talk system seems to be below the threshold for the recognition of open-class words. The CSP system seems to be at present below the threshold for the complete comprehension of closed-class words, in the absence of syntactic or semantic redundancy. We are currently investigating the role that increased phonetic redundancy could play in improving the intelligibility of the CSP output.

NEW SPEECH SYNTHESIS SYSTEMS AND CHIPS

As research and technologies advance in the field of speech synthesis and micro-electronics, new integrated circuit chips have been developed by a number of manufacturers [22]. Some of them perform the specific function of speech synthesis while others also include a text-to-speech algorithm. Obviously those presented in the following table do not necessarily exhaust all the speech synthesis systems and chips which exist in this rapidly growing market, anyhow, this list should provide the readers with sufficient leads to explore them further., As expected, most speech synthesizers accept ASCII texts and convert them to spoken English or other languages. they also provide controls (either discrete levels by software or external adjustment) on both pitch, speed and amplitude. These devices can be interfaced to most computers easily through the serial port. Several speech synthesis systems incorporating the synthesizer chips already exist in the market, e.g. the Type 'N Talk by Votrax, Intex-Talker by Intex Micro Systems Inc., and the Sweet Talker II by The Micromint Inc., all built around the Votrax SC-01A chip; while the SynPhonix speech articulator by Artic Technologies is built from a Silicon Systems Inc. SSI 263 phoneme synthesizer.

TABLE 1 New speech synthesis systems and chips from different manufacturers.

Manufacturer	Model	Synthesis Technique	Vocabulary	Feature
Covox, Inc.	Voice Master	Waveform processing and coding	Up to 64 numbered words or phrases, or other sounds	
Digital Equipment Corp.	DECtalk	Computer model of the vocal tract	Unlimited	Can produce voices from old male to a female, to a young child
General Instrument	VSM 2032	Linear prediction		
Hewlett-Packard Co.	82967A	Linear prediction	1500 words	
Infovox, Sweden	SA101	Formant synthesis	Unlimited	English, French Spanish, Italian German, Swedish
National Semiconductor	Digitalker	Waveform processing and synthesis	256 words or phrases	
	Microtalker	Concatenation of waveforms and processing	256 words	
NEC America, Inc.	AR-10	ADPCM coding		
Oki Semi-conductor	MSM 6202 MSM 6212	ADPCM	Ability to select up to 125 phrases stored on chip ROM	Can store 12-40 sec. of speech

Silicon Systems Inc.	SSI 263	Formant synthesis	Unlimited	64 phonemes each with 4 different duration settings
Speech Plus Inc.	Prose 2000 Prose 2020		Unlimited	
	Text 5000		Unlimited	IBM PC compatible also through toned telephone
Street Electronics Corp.	ECHO GP		Unlimited	Stand-alone unit with own on-board microcomputer
Texas Instruments Inc.	TMS 5200	Linear prediction	Unlimited	
Vynet Corp.			Information "Spoken" by the computer as predetermined voice messages from a program or database	For IBM PC as a voice response unit
Votrax Division, Federal Screw Works	SC-01A	Formant synthesis	Unlimited	64 phonemes plus 3 silences
	VS-B	Formant synthesis	Unlimited	64 phonemes plus 3 silences, French and German

CONCLUDING REMARKS

Speech synthesis by computer has been investigated by many researchers in the past two decades. This field has advanced from the simple method of split and concatenation to highly sophisticated methods of coding and employing powerful phonetic rules. As demonstrated in this paper, computer synthesis of spoken English, probably the most difficult one among European languages [25], due to immense variations and inconsistencies between English spelling and pronunciation, has been developed successfully. Additional research on prosodic and suprasegmental features will improve the naturalness of synthetic speech. Syntheses of other languages also exist in the market. The emergence of VLSI (Very Large Scale Integrated) circuits has added a new dimension to the field of speech synthesis. Indeed, as shown in this paper, several speech synthesizer chips have been manufactured. This new era has widely opened up the consumer market for speech synthesizers in toys, cars, teaching aids, computer terminals, automatic telephone answering, alarm systems, disabled aids and message systems [19]. The consumer market has attracted the attention of several leading computer manufacturers. It is anticipated that speech synthesizers will become popular built-in attachments to computers and peripherals, and daily utilities. It is not surprising that they will form standard peripherals to most personal computers in the near future.

ACKNOWLEDGEMENTS

This research was supported by the Department of Education of Quebec. The authors wish to thank Ms. T. Rossman, Mr. C. L. Yu, Mr. G. Liben, and Prof. N. Segalowitz for their help and comments in the experimental study of this project.

REFERENCES

1. W. A. Ainsworth, "A system for converting English text into speech", IEEE Trans. Audio Electroacoust., Vol. AU-21, 288-290, 1973.
2. J. Allen, "Synthesis of speeach from unrestricted text", Proc. IEEE, Vol. 64, 433-442, April 1976.
3. B. S. Atal and S. L. Hanauer, "Speech analysis and synthesis by linear prediction of the speech waveform", J. Acoust. Soc. Amer., Vol. 50, 637-655, August 1971.
4. N. Chomsky and M. Halle, *The Sound Pattern of English*, Harper and Row, New York, 1968.
5. S. Ciarcia, "Build a third-generation phonetic speech synthesizer", Byte, 28-46, March 1984.
6. H. S. Elovitz, R. W. Johnson, A. McHugh and J. E. Shore, "Letter-to-sound

rules for automatic translation of English text to phonetics", IEEE Trans. Acoust., Speech, Signal Processing, Vol. 24, 446-459, December 1976.

7. J. L. Flanagan, "Talking with computers: synthesis and recognition of speech by machines", IEEE Trans. Bio-Med. Engng., Vol. BME-29, 223-232, April 1982.

8. S. R. Hertz, "The 'morthology' of English spelling: a look at the SRS text-modification rules for English", Working Papers of the Cornell Phonetics Laboratory, No. 1, 17-28, December 1983.

9. S. R. Hertz, "From text to speech with SRS", J. Acoust. Soc. Am., Vol. 72, 1155-1170, 1982.

10. D. R. Hill, "Spoken language generation and understanding by machine: a problems and applications oriented overview", in J. C. Simon (ed.), *Spoken Language Generation and Understanding*, Proc. NATO Advanced Studies Institute, D. Reidel Publishing Co., Dordrecht, 3-38, 1980.

11. J. N. Holmes, "Formant synthesizers: cascade or parallel", Speech Communication, Vol. 2, 251-273, 1983.

12. S. Hunnicutt, "Phonological rules for a text-to-speech system", Technical Report, Research Lab of Electronics, MIT, 1979.

13. L. M. Koehler and T. C. Mackey, "Speech output for HP series 80 personal computers", Hewlett-Packard Journal, 29-36, January 1984.

14. J. A. Kuecken, *Talking Computers and Telecommunications*, Van Nostrand Reinhold, New York, 1983.

15. D. L. Lee and F. H. Lochovsky, "Voice response systems", Computing Surveys, Vol. 15, 351-374, December 1983.

16. S. C. Lee, S. Xu and B. Guo, "Microcomputer-generated Chinese speech", Computer Procesing of Chinese & Oriental Languages, Vol. 1, 87-103, December 1983.

17. K.-S. Lin, K. M. Goudie, G. A. Frantz and G. L. Brantingham, "Text-to-speech using LPC allophone stringing", IEEE Trans. Consumer Electronics, Vol. CE-27, 144-152, May 1981.

18. W. C. Lin and T.-T. Luo, "On synthesis of Mandarin by means of Chinese phonemes and phoneme-pairs (JIFH)", to appear in Computer Processing of Chinese and Oriental Languages, an international journal of the Chinese Language Computer Society.

19. G. C. Lyman, III, "Voice messaging comes of age", Speech Technology, Vol. 2, 45-49, August/September 1984.

20. J. D. Markel and A. H. Gray, *Linear Prediction of Speech*, Springer-Verlag, New York, 1976.

21. M. D. McIlroy, "Synthetic English by rule", Computer Science Tech. Report 14, Bell Laboratories, Murray Hill, Ner Jersey, March 1974.

22. N. Morgan, *Talking Chips*, McGraw-Hill Book Co., New York, 1984.

23. F. S. Mozer, "Method and apparatus for speech synthesizing", US Patent No. 4,214,125, July 1980.

24. *1965 Revised List of Phonetically Balanced Sentences (Harvard Sentences)*, IEEE Trans. Audio Electro-acoust., Vol. AU-17, 238-246, 1969.

25. B. A. Sherwood, "Fast text-to-speech, algorithms for Esperanto, Spanish, Italian, Russian and English", Int. J. Man-Machine Studies, Vol. 10, 669-692,

1978.

26. S. B. Stein, "A unrestricted text-to-speech algorithm for the Votrax synthesizer", M. Comp. Sc. Thesis, Concordia University, Montreal, March 1982.

27. C. Y. Suen, "Computer synthesis of Mandarin", Proc. IEEE Int. Conf. Acoustics, Speech and Signal Processing, 698-700, April 1976.

28. C. Y. Suen, T. Rossman, S. Stein, M. G. Strobel, C. Charbonneau and L. Santerre, "Computer speech synthesis at Concordia University", Proc. Int. Electrical, Electronics Conf. & Expo, 176-177, 1981.

29. C. Y. Suen, S. B. Stein, M. G. Strobel and L. Santerre, "An unrestricted text-to-speech algorithm for the Votrax synthesizer", Proc. 10th Int. Cong. Phonetic Sciences, 394, August 1983.

30. E. R. Teja, *Teaching Your Computer to Talk*, TAB Books Inc., Blue Ridge Summit, PA, 1981.

31. N. Umeda, "Linguistic rules for text-to-speech synthesis", Proc. IEEE, Vol. 64, 443-451, 1976.

32. A. Wijk, "Rules of pronunciation for the English language", London, 1966.

33. I. H. Witten, *Principles of Computer Speech*, Academic Press, New York, 1982.

34. I. Witten and J. Abbess, "A microcomputer-based speech synthesis-by-rule system", Int. J. Man-Machine Studies, Vol. 11, 585-620, 1979.

PROSODIC KNOWLEDGE IN THE RULE-BASED SYNTHEX EXPERT SYSTEM FOR SPEECH SYNTHESIS

A. Aggoun, C. Sorin, F. Emerard, M. Stella

C.N.E.T. — Lannion

Route de Trégastel

BP 40

22301 Lannion Cedex

France

1. INTRODUCTION

Speech synthesis is the transformation of a written text into an acoustic signal.

The speech synthesis system by diphones developed at C.N.E.T. (Centre National d'Etudes des Télécommunications de LANNION) is complete and is described in [14, 23]. The synthetic speech produced by the system is intelligible, but lacks more naturalness. The improvement of the intelligibility and naturalness depends in particular on progress carried out in segmental and prosodic rules. At the moment, experiments with new rules and in particular prosodic rules are not easy.

During the last few years, different speech synthesis systems from a written text have emerged. Some of these systems are written in classical programming languages (FORTRAN, etc...), which makes modification and improvement difficult.

More recently, the use of knowledge based systems as a framework has spread into new areas, such as speech recognition [15] and natural language understanding; the methodology of the expert systems facilitates an incremental

NATO ASI Series, Vol. F16
New Systems and Architectures for Automatic Speech
Recognition and Synthesis. Edited by R. De Mori and C. Y. Suen
© Springer-Verlag Berlin Heidelberg 1985

transfer of knowledge from the human to the machine.

In this paper, we discuss the SYNTHEX (System SYNTHesis EXpert) system developed at C.N.E.T. The design of SYNTHEX is an example of the use of Artificial Intelligence techniques in order to study various problems related to speech synthesis from a written text [1, 2]. The main aim of this project is to develop a tool able to formalize knowledge related to the problem of speech synthesis from written text and to improve this knowledge.

II. TEXT-TO-SPEECH

Speech synthesis systems combine a given method with a given technique [9, 11, 23]. The technique permits the reconstruction of the acoustic signal containing the characteristics of the speech sound from certain parameters. The "text-to-speech" method consists of generating the above parameters from a given written text, such as synthesis by word, synthesis by rule [3, 7, 8, 16] or synthesis by concatenation of preanalysed units [14].

The speech synthesis system (fig. 2) is composed of:

— a grapheme-to-phoneme conversion module [12] which produces a string of phonetic symbols based on information in the written text;
— a prosodic module [14, 20, 24] which processes rules (expert rules) to produce prosodic parameters (pitch, duration and loudness);
— a conversion module which converts prosodic parameters into appropriate parameters in order to drive the synthesizer;
— a synthesizer to reconstruct the acoustic signal using various techniques [23].

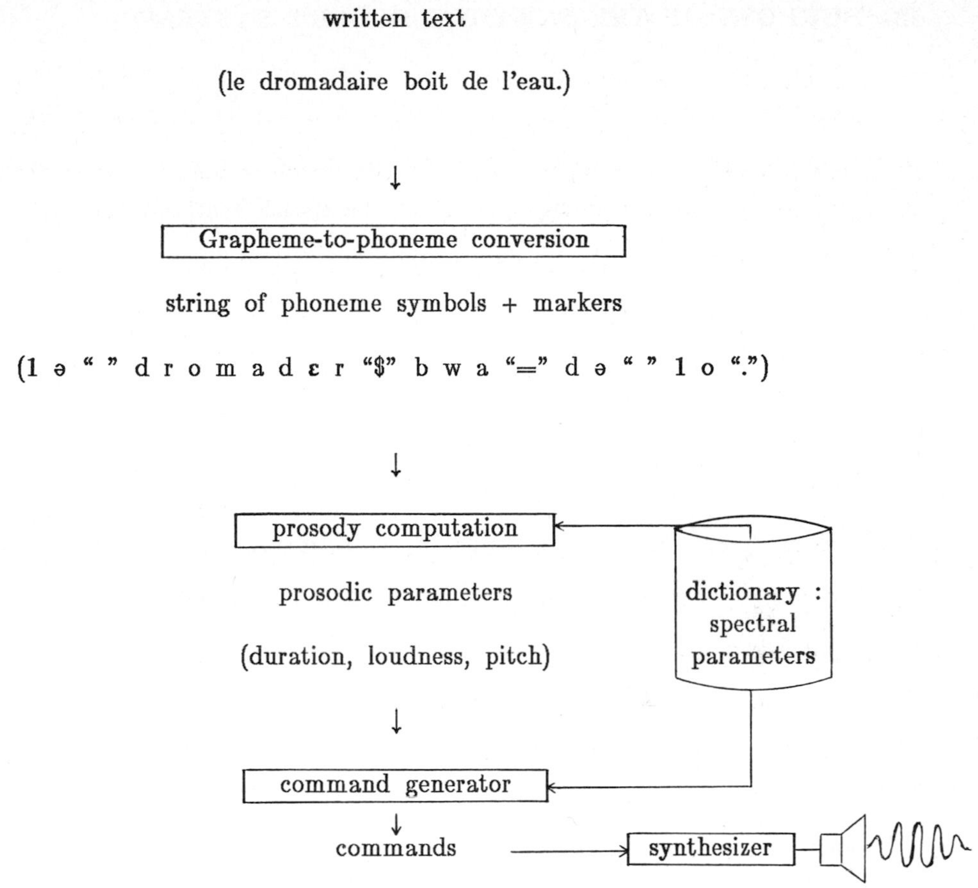

written text

(le dromadaire boit de l'eau.)

↓

| Grapheme-to-phoneme conversion |

string of phoneme symbols + markers

(l ə " " d r o m a d ɛ r "$" b w a "=" d ə " " l o ".")

↓

| prosody computation | ← ┌─────────────┐
                            | dictionary : |
prosodic parameters | spectral |
                            | parameters |
(duration, loudness, pitch) └─────────────┘

↓

| command generator | ←
↓
commands ──────→ | synthesizer |

Fig. 1: Text-to-speech synthesis
The translation of the french sentence "le dromadaire boit de l'eau." is "the dromedary drinks water."

N.B.: Phoneme codification used in the example:
phonemes: l, d, r, m, b, w, ə, o, a, ɛ,
markers: " ", "$", "=", "."

III. PURPOSE OF THE SYNTHEX EXPERT SYSTEM

The SYNTHEX system has been developed originally to provide investigation in the speech synthesis domain. From the beginning, the goal of this system was to formalize the prosodic module (fig. 1) of the speech synthesis system.

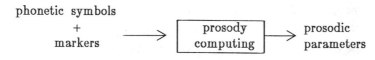

Fig. 2   Prosodic module

The system accepts as input a string of phonetic symbols (grapheme-to-phoneme conversion) and prosodic markers, and delivers as output prosodic parameters such as pitch, loudness and duration. Some markers are delivered implicitly in the text, such as punctuation markers and spaces between words. The remaining markers indicate syntactic points in the sentence such as the end of the preverbal group.

Some of the existent systems are written in an ad hoc manner, so their adaptation and maintenance are difficult. Other software packages are parameterized, but they can not solve problems caused by adding new knowledge, neither those caused by modifications of the existing rules.

In recent years, different languages adapted to phonetic and linguistic terminology have been proposed for synthesis by rules [3, 7, 8, 16, 22]. These languages are easy to use, but it is difficult to take into account the syntactic structure of the sentence.

The SYNTHEX expert system has been developed to fulfil the following goals:

— simplicity is essential, since speech synthesis experts are not necessarily programming specialists;

— independence from the language being synthesized (French, English, etc...) and the synthesis technique;

— paraphrase and reformulation of the rules expressed by the speech experts to avoid any ambiguity;

— explanation of the reasoning adopted by the system during execution;

— formalization of the speech experts knowledge;

— introduction of methods for improving this knowledge.

IV GENERAL ARCHITECTURE OF THE SYSTEM

SYNTHEX is an expert system based on production rules [4, 17, 19, 21]. These rules defined by the user are stored in knowledge bases. Briefly an expert system is composed of:

— knowledge bases (methods, facts, assertions, relevant assertions, metaknowledges, etc...)

— inference engine (pattern matcher, knowledge modifiers, etc...)

— working memories (current goals, current hypotheses, etc....)

V KNOWLEDGE EXPRESSION LANGUAGE

To facilitate the transfer of the experts synthesis knowledge in the system, we have devloped a formalism adapted to the expert's needs. One of the basic criteria of this system is its simplicity. It should be easy to use by non programming specialists.

In this chapter we describe the external formalism.

The corresponding internal formalism will be illustrated in V. 2.

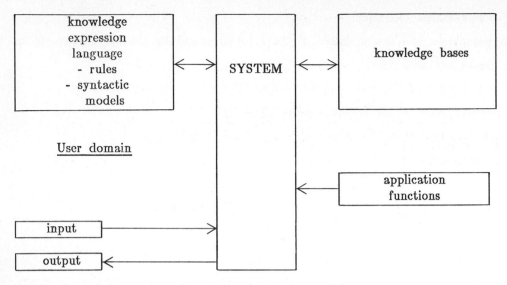

Fig. 3:   General architecture of the SYNTHEX system

V.1   EXTERNAL FORMALISM

This formalism permits the expression of the two following entities:

— syntactic models which express the application concepts

— prosodic rules, as production rules.

V.1.1 SYNTACTIC MODELS

Those are essentially composed of syntactic structures, definitions, object descriptions and dictionaries containing the specific application data.

The "syntactic structure", "definition" and "object description" models should allow for the construction of a syntactic tree from a sentence composed of phonetic symbols and markers.

The various prosodic rules are applied to this tree. These concepts are derived from the study of speech synthesis. The syntax is carefully chosen to be as close as possible to the formalism used by synthesis experts.

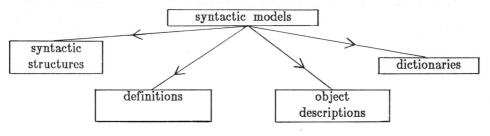

Fig. 4: Syntactic models

SYNTACTIC NOTATION

— the strings of underlined lower characters represent terminals,

— the strings of upper case characters represent non-terminals

— {A} n, *   if n =   0 => the symbol A is optional

if n ≠   0 => 1 or many times the symbol A

* => means many times

V.1.1.1 - SYNTACTIC STRUCTURE

syntax :   (syntax: ({OBJECT} 1, *)

Where: OBJECT :: string-of-characters

EXAMPLE :

(syntax : (sentence word syllable phoneme frame))

(syntax : (sentence marker))

This example describes a syntactic tree where the root (ancestor) is sentence. The descendants of the root are either word nodes or marker nodes. Each word node can be broken down into smaller descendants, for example syllables, etc...

This syntax permits the user to define the different structures required for his application.

V.1.1.2 - DESCRIPTIONS

syntax :   (description : OBJECT {ATTRIBUT} 0, *)
Where   ATTRIBUT :: string-of-characters.
EXAMPLES:
                 (description : word (number-of-syllables type))

This model describes in terms of attributes each object declared in the syntactic structures. In the above example, the object "word" is characterized by the two attributes "number-of-syllables" and "type" (the type of a word may be lexical, grammatical, etc...). The system uses these models which define each node and its attributes to generate the syntactic tree from a written text. The attributes of the objects are instantiated in the second phase when rules are applied.

V.1.1.3 - DEFINITIONS

syntax :   (definition : OBJECT
                              DOMAIN
                              REWRITING-RULES)
Where : DOMAIN : define the set of values of the object
REWRITING-RULES: these rules permit the input sentence to be structured in
                   accordance with the syntactic pattern described by the
                   user.

EXAMPLE:

In figure 7, the domain of the object marker is:

(belong to (" " "$" "=" "."))

The rewrite rules are expressed in an adequate formalism. The following rules are used to structure each word into syllables (Fig. 5).

EXAMPLE:

[consonant consonant vowel consonant vowel] →

[consonant consonant vowel) (consonant vowel]

|consonant vowel consonant vowel] →

[consonant vowel) (consonant vowel]

|consonant vowel consonant end} →

[consonant vowel consonant]

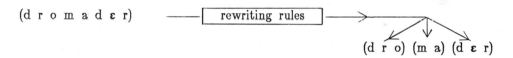

(d r o m a d ɛ r) ———— rewriting rules ————→

(d r o) (m a) (d ɛ r)

Fig. 5: Results once the rewrite-rules above are applied

phonetic symbols + markers

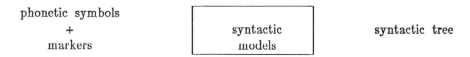

syntactic models

syntactic tree

Fig. 6: Syntactic models interpretation

As shown in fig. 7, the string of symbols placed at the first level of the tree represents the instance of the object "sentence". The system produces the descendants of the root derived from the object "sentence" and information obtained from syntactic models. The second level is composed of:

— objects of type "word": (l ə), (d r o m a d ɛ r), (b w a),

(d ə) and (l o)

504

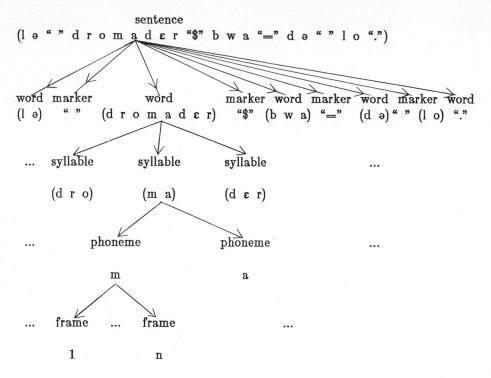

Fig. 7: The generated syntactic tree once syntactic models are performed the input of the interpreter system is:
(l ə " " d r o m a d ɛ r "$" b w a "=" d ə " " l o ".")

— objects of type "marker" : " ", "$", "=" and "."

Once objects of the second level are generated, the system performs rules to decompose each instance of word into syllables. In this example, "(d r o m a d ɛ r)" is composed of three syllables with their respective values "(d r o)", "(m a)" and (d ɛ r). The same process is repeated at each level until the syntactic tree is completed. The group of objects obtained constitute working data base to which prosodic rules can be applied.

V.1.1.4 - THE DICTIONARIES

The dictionary is a store of knowledge base which consists of the specific application data (the dictionary of diphones or phonemes, the phoneme features, etc...). The acquisition of this knowledge can be achieved by an adapted programming tool.

V.1.2 - PROSODIC RULES

As we have already indicated, all vocal synthesis systems include a prosodic module. In the SYNTHEX system this part is referred to as "prosodic rules". These rules take into account the statements of the syntactic models.

syntax:

```
(problem : IDENTIFIER
    {if
        {- PREMISE }n, *
    then} *
        {- ACTION }n, *)
```

Where :

IDENTIFIER :: string of characters which identifies the problem.

PREMISE : a condition which has to be satisfied

ACTION : an action to be carried out.

semantic:

case 1: the premises are not omitted

```
(problem : toto
    if
        - p1
        - p2
    then
```

                - a1

                - a2)

the associated semantic is :

           if (p1 and p2) then (a1 and then a2)

case 2:   the premises are omitted

           (problem : toto

           - a1

           - a2)

           The associated semantic is :

             do a1 and then a2.

SYNTHEX differs from other similar experiment systems in this domain in that it permits the speech synthesis expert to use his natural language when formalizing a problem. In fact, in the prosodic rules, the "PREMISES" and "ACTIONS" are expressed in a pseudo-natural language, i.e. in the form of sentences using a restricted french grammar (sub-grammar) augmented by variables. We know, based on the research done by several teams on the comprehension of natural languages [13, 10], that problems presented by "anaphoras" and pronominal reference are particularly difficult to carry out. The notion of variable allows such difficulties to be solved elegantly and simply without making speech synthesis expert's task more difficult. In a written text, a variable is a string of characters preceded by the special character "*". The "prosodic rules" component is organized as a set of knowledge bases, each one regrouping different problems. Each problem regroups a set of rules.

EXAMPLE:

exp-base is the name of the knowledge base in the figure below.

This knowledge base (fig. 8) includes four problems : number-of-syllables, first-consonant-duration, initial-duration and pause. Each of the first problems contains one related rule while the fourth one contains two rules.

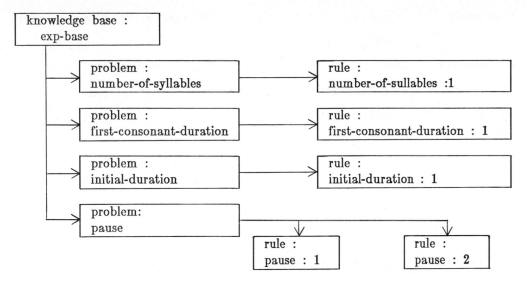

Fig. 8   Example of knowledge base

According to the external formalism, the first rule of the knowledge-base is described below:

(problem : number-of-syllables

if

    - there exists a word *x

then

      - count in *1 the number of phonemes whose instances are vowels

      - attribute to the number-of-syllables of the word *x the value of the variable *1)

Remarks :

*x is a variable used to reference the object typed "word",

*1 is another variable which contains intermediate results,

premise :

if there exists a word in the syntactic tree

actions :

first action :   count in the variable *1 the number of phonemes whose instances are vowels

section action :   gives to the attribute "number-of-syllables" of the word above the value of the variable *1.

V.1.3 - EXAMPLES

For reasons of simplicity, it is assumed the statement below is true:

         (description : phoneme (instance))

         (description : frame (duration))

         (description : marker (instance duration))

Example : 1

(problem : initial-duration

if

- there exists a word *m

then

- attributes to the duration of all frames of the word *m the value 26 multiplied by 0.85).

Remark

The rule gives to the attribute "duration" of all phoneme frames of each sentence's word the value 26 multiplied by 0.85.

Example : 2

(problem : first-consonant-duration

if

- the instance of the first phoneme *p1 of a word *w is consonant

- the instance of adjacent right phoneme *p2 of the phoneme *p1
  in the word *w is vowel.

<u>Then</u>

- print ("rule : frame's durations of the first phoneme")
- multiply the duration of all frames of the phoneme *p1 by the value 1.15
- display the instance of the phoneme *p1
- display the duration of all frames of the phoneme *p1).

<u>Remarks</u>

If the first phoneme of a word possesses the characteristic "consonant" and if its immediate successor in the same word has the characteristics "vowel", then the following actions can be applied successively. First print the parameter text of the primitive "print", then multiply by 1.15 the value of the attribute "duration" of all phoneme frames.

<u>Example : 3</u>

(<u>problem</u> : pause

<u>if</u>

- the instance of a marker *x belongs to the list ("*" "+" "&")

<u>then</u>

- attribute to the pause of the marker *x the value 65).

(<u>problem</u> : pause

<u>if</u>

- the instance of a marker *x belongs to the list ("." "?" "!").

<u>then</u>

- attribute to the pause of the marker *x the value 400)

Remarks

The problem "pause" contains the two rules : pause : 1 and pause : 2 (see fig. 8). The system tries all the problem rules scucessively, except those frozen dynamically by commands.

first rule :   if the value of a marker belongs to the list ("*" *+" "&"), then the associated pause is 65 ms.

second rule : if the value of a marker belongs to the list ("." "?" "!"), then the associated pause is 400 ms.

EXAMPLE 4 :

(problem : duration-and-pause
- execute initial-duration
- execute first-consonant-duration
- execute pause).

Remarks

This rule is not a prosodic rule, but is used to define the order in which the prosodic rules are applied, i.e. first the rules concerning initial-duration, next those concerning the first-consonant-duration and lastly those concerning pause. This approach allows several problems to be regrouped under the same name.

V.2 - INTERNAL FORMALISM

The internal formalism is the formalism of Horn clauses (PROLOG clause). The PROLOG language [18] is used as a knowledge representation language and also as a programming language to perform· the translation of external formalism into the internal formalism.

In fact the language used is LISLOG [5, 6] which integrates the two programming languages LISP and PROLOG.

The internal formalism is directly executable. The LISLOG interpreter plays the role of the inference engine of the system.

VI SPEECH SYNTHESIS : USER DOMAINS

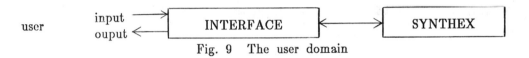

Fig. 9   The user domain

N.B.   : A speech synthesis expert can be a user.

We have shown that experts in speech synthesis express their knowledge in a pseudo-natural language, and the system generates the corresponding internal forms (HORN clauses).

As soon as the SYNTHEX system has gathered enough expertise, one can use the system to synthesize sentences (i.e. check rules, evaluate results obtained, etc...).

Example : By applying the rule which counts the number of syllables in each word, the attribute "number-of-syllables" of each word is given an appropriate value.

word : 1	number-of-syllables : 1
word : 2	number-of-syllables : 3
word : 3	number-of-syllables : 1
word : 4	number-of-syllables : 1
word : 5	number-of-syllables : 1

SYNTHEX provides a number of facilities for the development of synthesis rules. SYNTHEX's editor is interactive. The form of all commands is simplified.

Syntactic patterns and prosodic rules are structured in knowledge bases. The user can define, store, edit, execute and then (possibly) improve the rule.

The user can also change by commands the ordering of the rules to be applied. The system possesses control commands which permits dynamically to freeze, activate and execute rules.

SYNTHEX's debugger facilitates the check of rules; it permits to display the text of the rule with the instances of the variables of applied rules.

Example : assume that we want to apply the "pause" rules to the sentence (fig. 7) and we specify by command to debug the pause : 2 rule, the debugger display the following text :

(problem : pause : 2
if
    - the instance of a marker 5 belongs to the list ("." "?" "!")
then
    attribute to the pause of the marker 5 the value 400).

VII CONCLUSION

The main aims of the development of the SYNTHEX system are : to give a method for formalizing the knowledge in the speech synthesis domain (prosody of vocal synthesis) and to study methods for improving this knowledge.

The system is written entirely in LISLOG which allows us to use logic programming in different forms.

The SYNTHEX system is being experimented on. Different extensions are being studied in order to explain the rules and the control mechanisms.

The translation of the written rule to the internal formalism takes about five seconds of run time (the run time for the rule in example V.1.3 is about 2 seconds on a DPS/8 machine) for each rule. The run time of each applied rule is about one second.

SYNTHEX was designed on the multics system.

ACKNOWLEDGEMENTS

The authors thank M. Dincbas, S. Bourgault, J. P. Le Pape and M. Guyomard for helpful discussions.

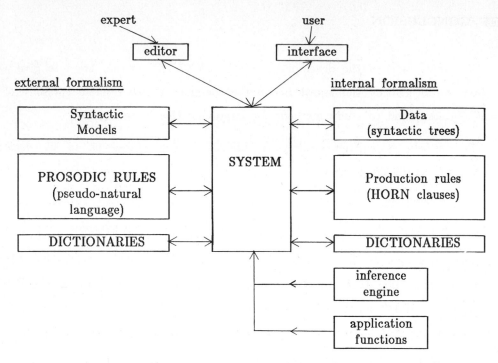

Figure 10: The complete architecture of the system SYNTHEX

REFERENCES

1. A. Aggoun, "A computer language adapted to the programming of prosodic rules". Arabic school on science and technology, Applied Arabic linguistics and signal and information processing. September 26 - October 1983, p. 208 à 210, RABAT (Maroc).

2. A. Aggoun, S. Bourgault, M. Guyomard, "SYNTHEX: un système expert pour la synthèse vocale à partir du texte". Séminaire sur la programmation en logique. Avril 1984, Plestin-les-Greves, France.

3. M. Barioglio, "Progetto di un compilatore per un linguaggio diserittiro di regole prosodicke struttura del sistema di sintesi". Thèse soutenue à l'Université de Turin, 1980.

4. A. Bonnet, "Applications de l'intelligence artificielle : les systèmes experts". Rairo Informatique/Computer Science, Vol. 15, no. 4, 1981, p. 325 à 341.

5. S. Bourgault, M. Dincbas, J. P. Le Pape, "Manuel Lislog". Note Technique NT/LAA/SLC/159, Janvier 1984, CNET LANNION, France.

6. S. Bourgault, M. Dincbas, D. Feuerstein, J. P. Le Pape, "LISLOG: l'an II", Séminaire sur la programmation en logique, PERROS-GUIREC, 22-23 mars 1983, France.

7. C. P. Browman, "Rules for demisyllabic synthesis using lingua, a language interpreter", Proc. 1980, conf. ASSP, p. 561-564.

8. R. Carlson, B. Granstrom, S. Hunnicutt, "A multi-language text-to-speech-module", Proc. 1980, conf. ASSP, p. 1604-1607.

9. R. Carre, J. P. Haton, J. S. Lienard, "Reconnaissance et synthèse de la parole, état de la recherche et du développement, IRIA - 1979.

10. A. Colmerauer, "Un sous-ensemble intéressant du Français", RAIRO Informatique, Theoretical Informatics, Vol. 13, No. 4, 1979, p. 309 à 336.

11. R. Descout, "Les techniques de synthèse de la parole, Note Technique NT/LAA/TSS/RCP, avril 1982, CNET LANNION - France.

12. M. Divay, M. Guyomard, "Conception et réalisation sur ordinateur d'un programme de transcription graphemo-phonétique du Français", Thèse troisième cycle, Université de Rennes, avril 1977.

13. P. Saint-Dizier, "Contribution à la transformation des langues naturelles en logique", Thèse troisième cycle 1983, Université de Rennes.

14. F. Emerard, "Synthèse par diphones et traitement de la prosodie", Thèse troisième cycle, Université de Grenoble, mars 1977.

15. M. Gilloux, F. Hautin, C. Tarridec, A. Vailly, D. Gillet, G. Mercier, "Note avant-projet d'un Système Expert en Reconnaissance Acoustico-phonétique : SERAC", Note Technique NT/LAA/SLC/119, NT/LAA/SLC/151, janvier 1983, CNET LANNION, France.

16. S. Hertz, "From text to speech with S.R.S.", J.A.S.A. 72(4), October 1982.

17. D. Kayser, "Examen de diverses méthodes utilisées en représentation des connaissances", Quatrième congrès de reconnaissance des formes et intelligence artificielle, 25-27 janvier 1984, Paris, p. 115 à 144.

18. R. Kowalski, "Predicate logic as programming language", Proceeding IFIP 74.
19. J. L. Lauriere, "Les systèmes experts, représentation et utilisation des connaissances, T.S.I. no. 1, 1982, p. 25-42, T.S.I. no. 2, 1982, p. 109-133.
20. P. Martin, "Phonetic realisations of prosodic contours in french", Speech Communication, Vol. 1, no. 34, December 1982.
21. S. Pinson, "Représentation des connaissances dans les systèmes experts", Rairo Informatique/Computer Science, Vol. 15, No. 4, 1981, p. 343-367.
22. S. Sandri, E. Vivalda, "A formal language for the generation of prosodic rules", The fourth F.A.S.E. symposium 81, Venezia, Italy.
23. M. Stella, "Synthèse de parole", l'Echo des Recherches No. 15, 1er trimestre, p. 21-32, 1984.
24. J. Vaissière, "The search for language-independent prosodic features", A paper presented at the first international congress on the perception of speech, No. 7-20, December 1980, Florence, Italy.

SYNTEX - UNRESTRICTED CONVERSION OF TEXT TO SPEECH FOR GERMAN

Wolfgang Kulas
Hans-Wilhelm Rühl
Ruhr-Universität Bochum
Lehrstuhl für Allgemeine Elektrotechnik und Akustik
Federal Republic of Germany

ABSTRACT

This paper is intended to give an overview over the SYNTEX system, a text-to-speech software for the German language designated to control phoneme synthesizers. Descriptions of the algorithms used for word structure analysis, letter-to-sound conversion, computing of word accent, sentence parsing, and generating an intonation contour are given. The software runs on a small microprocessor system much faster than real-time.

GENERAL DESCRIPTION

The general structure of SYNTEX is depicted in fig. 1. It is a construction of modules for text preprocessing, for processing at word level, for sentence level analysis and for control of prosodics and coarticulations. It is designed to drive phoneme or allophone based synthesizers.

The text preprocessing module converts unrestricted German text into a limited set of characters containing only upper case letters and some word boundary markers like blanks, commas, periods, etc. This means for example

NATO ASI Series, Vol. F16
New Systems and Architectures for Automatic Speech
Recognition and Synthesis. Edited by R. De Mori and C. Y. Suen
© Springer-Verlag Berlin Heidelberg 1985

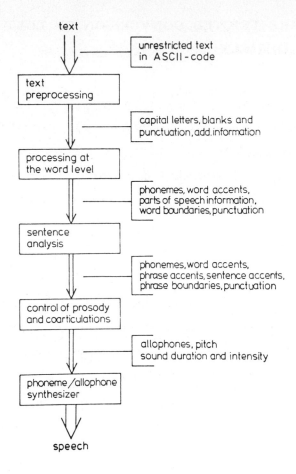

Fig. 1:   The concept of the SYNTEX text-to-speech software

that strings of digits used to code integer, decimal or ordinal numbers, date, time, year or price are "spelled out" as strings of letter characters in the appropriate format.   Input may be in upper case or lower case only, like a usual computer dialogue, or preferably in standard German orthography with initial capital letters for nouns and for the beginning of a sentence, lower case letters elsewhere. Standard orthography with nouns marked by capitals is useful for sentence analysis.

The input may be in standard ASCII code or in the German ASCII character set, which means that the German "Umlaute" 'Ä' , 'Ö', 'Ü' and the character 'ß' may be either represented as national ASCII characters or in standard ASCII as 'AE', 'OE', 'UE' and 'SS'. The set of characters may be selected statically by escape sequences as well as dynamically by software. In the dynamic mode rules based on adjacent characters are used to determine the meaning of characters having different meanings in both character sets.

Word level processing includes an analysis of word structure, a letter-to-sound algorithm and a generation of word accent patterns. As the German language tends to form compound words, the word structure analysis is based on an algorithm for finding morpheme boundaries by rules which employ a recognition of affixes. As the pronunciation of German words is based on a morpheme decomposition, 72 rather simple rules are sufficient to convert letters to phonemes. Word accent is computed by rules as well as by data included in the affix dictionaries.

At the sentence level we have been concentrating on the generation of an $F\emptyset$-contour by rule. The calculated intonation is a function of utterance length, sentence type and number of phrases within a sentence. To detect phrases, we use an incomplete sentence parsing, as time is limited for real-time text-to-speech conversion. Parsing is done in three steps: first by assigning valences to function words, then by combining words to groups with paying attention to valences and third by verifying these phrases. The parser also determines the most significant word for each phrase and the most significant phrase of a sentence which is to carry the sentence accent. Having parsed a sentence in this way, each group is associated an $F\emptyset$-contour which is similar to the hat-shaped patterns proposed by Cohen and t'Hart [7] to describe intonation.

ANALYSIS OF WORD STRUCTURE

German pronunciation rules are rather simple compared to English ones, provided that the rules can be expresssed at the morpheme level. Unfortunately, parsing words into morphemes is a rather difficult task, as German tends to form compounds more frequently than English. Expressions written in English as separate words (e.g. "word structure") are written as one word ("Wortstruktur") in German. Compounds acccount only for about 4% of the content words in running text, but most of the less frequent words are compounds, and they make up more than 50% of the words in a standard dictionary. Hence, for a low error rate, an analysis of the word structure is absolutely necessary.

Simple words containing one root can be decomposed by stripping off affixes only. But a compound processed by this affix detection remains as an unsolved cluster that starts and ends with roots, and perhaps contains affixes and further roots between the bracketing roots. Morpheme based pronunciation rules applied to such a cluster of morphemes will produce a lot of errors.

To perform a word structure analysis including a root recognition, algorithms based on a complete grammar and a large morpheme dictionary have been used, e.g. by Allen [1,2] for American English. This proceeding results in complex and slow programs with an extensive need for memory. For this reason we developed a decomposition algorithm which is not based on the recognition of all morphemes but on the recognition of affixes. It is used together with an algorithm called cluster analysis which is able to find boundaries between morphemes.

CLUSTER ANALYSIS

This algorithm called cluster analysis is based on the findings of W. Kästner [3], who decomposed all German morphemes into basic clusters. Basic clusters are strings of adjacent vowels or consonants. The morpheme "Flasche" for example decomposes into fl — initial basic consonant cluster

a — medial basic vowel cluster

sch — medial basic consonant cluster

e — final basic vowel cluster.

Kästner found that only 52 different basic initial consonant clusters and 120 basic final or medial consonant clusters are used to form German morphemes and that only few of the initial consonant clusters may be used in medial or final positions. He also found some twenty vowel clusters in different positions but these are not important for word analysis because most of the German roots have consonant clusters in initial and final position. Hence most of the morpheme boundaries fall between consonants.

In order to find morpheme boundaries within a word the cluster analysis tries to find medial clusters that are no basic ones. In the word "Weinflasche" for example, this test would find the cluster "nfl". Clusters like "nfl" are called boundary areas, because there has to be a morpheme boundary within the area of this cluster. In order to determine the exact position of the boundary, all possibilities are evaluated to split the cluster into basic initial and final clusters. "nfl" is neither an initial nor a final basic consonant cluster, hence boundaries before or after "nfl" are impossible. But "n-fl" and "nf-l" both split the medial cluster into basic clusters. In many cases, only one boundary leads to a valid basic cluster, which is a clear result and causes the cluster analysis to stop. But with several possible boundaries as in the example "Weinflasche", additional rules have to be employed for a decision.

In cases where there is more than one valid boundary, there can be no decision about the correct boundary without further knowledge and context-dependent rules. But even without knowledge of the context, a decision can be taken which boundary will produce least errors by examining the frequencies of the basic clusters. In our example, the basic clusters "n" and "l" have a very high frequency in German morphemes, "fl" is rather frequent and "nf" occurs seldom. Therefore a boundary between "n" and "fl" would be correct in more cases than a boundary between "nf" and "l". This relationship can be represented by attaching a number to each basic cluster representing a logarithmic frequency of occurrence. To get the most plausible boundary only the logarithmic frequencies of the resultant basic clusters have to be added for each possible boundary, and the boundary with the highest result will be selected. For our example, this decision algorithm marks a correct boundary between "Wein" and "Flasche".

The cluster analysis is able to find most boundaries between roots, due to the fact that most German roots begin and end with consonant clusters. For this reason, about 90% of the boundaries between roots are detected. Less than one third of the undetected boundaries cause pronunciation errors that reduce intellegibility. A main accent on a wrong syllable occurs very seldom, a mismatched boundary usually only causes a missing secondary accent. The typical pronunciation error that has to be expected when applying morpheme based letter-to-sound rules to words is a wrong vowel length for vowels preceding a final consonant cluster or a morpheme boundary. This error is very rare when cluster analysis is used.

THE ARCHITECTURE OF THE WORD STRUCTURE ANALYSIS BASED ON CLUSTER ANALYSIS

Cluster analysis is well suited to find morpheme boundaries between consonants. But a lot of German affixes either start or end with a vowel cluster, hence many boundaries adjacent to affixes are not detected. This would be a severe problem if there were no other ways of finding the missing boundaries. But not every boundary needs to be marked. The affix recognition starts at the beginning and at the end of a word recursively looking for the longest affix. It is also capable of starting at the boundaries detected by the cluster analysis looking to the left and the right for the longest affix. So all we need is one detected boundary within or adjacent to an affix cluster embedded between roots, and every affix within this cluster can be recognized. Examining every possible

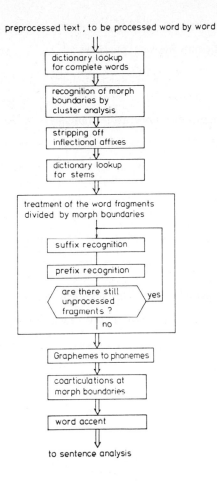

preprocessed text , to be processed word by word

- dictionary lookup for complete words
- recognition of morph boundaries by cluster analysis
- stripping off inflectional affixes
- dictionary lookup for stems
- treatment of the word fragments divided by morph boundaries
  - suffix recognition
  - prefix recognition
  - are there still unprocessed fragments ? yes / no
- Graphemes to phonemes
- coarticulations at morph boundaries
- word accent

to sentence analysis

Fig. 2 Processing at the word level

combination of affixes between roots in the expressions

    root1 — 1 or more suffixes — root2
    root1 — 1 or more prefixes — root2
    root1 — 1 or more suffixes — 1 or more prefixes — root2

we found that in the worst cases 'root1 — prefix — root2' the chance of detecting at least one boundary is 89%, in every other case the chance is more than 90%, which is sufficient for our purposes.

Hence, the general proceeding of word structure analysis is:

— Mark morpheme boundaries by cluster analysis

— Strip off inflectional affixes appearing only at the end of the word.

— Strip off prefixes at the beginning of the word and suffixes at the end of the word.

— Look for morpheme boundaries marked by the cluster analysis. If you find one, look for prefixes and suffixes to the right and to the left of the boundary.

This procedure is depicted in fig. 2. The chances of finding every affix within a word by using this procedure are very high. For this reason, every fragment not matched by affix recognition and not split by morpheme boundaries can be treated as a root.

AFFIX RECOGNITION

In a word decomposition algorithm based on a morpheme dictionary, the usual way of getting the correct decomposition of a word is to evaluate every possible combination of morphemes and then to score which combination fits best [2]. In most cases, there will be just one sequence of morphemes that matches the whole word and the algorithm to resolve ambiguities will be needed only in exceptional cases.

In our word structure analysis the problem of how to match morphemes within a word is different: we do not have all the "chips" to completely solve the "puzzle", nevertheless the few "chips" (= affixes) we have should be placed correctly. Attempts to match affixes are supported by word and morpheme boundaries and the beginnings and endings of recognized affixes that serve as points of departure for the matching process. But in each word there has to be at least one gap (= root) that cannot be verified by looking it up in a dictionary nor can it be decided without further rules whether the affixes to the right and to the left of a gap are correct. For this reason when recognizing affixes, the affix and the remaining word fragment have to fulfill some conditions for the recognition to be correct.

If the remaining word fragment is considered to be a root, it has to fulfill some general conditions: it should consist at least of one consonant cluster and one vowel cluster; it should at least consist of three letters (roots with only two letters are very rare), and it should start with a basic initial cluster and end with a basic final cluster. These general rules sometimes prevent incorrect matches, but in many special cases they still allow the recognition of parts of a root as an affix.

Hence special rules have been introduced for affixes to be recognized. These rules define an environment at the boundaries of the affixes, and by controlling the environment of the actual match it can be decided whether an affix is recognized or not. This leads to an organization of the affix recognition in the following way.

— Start at a marked boundary and look for the longest affix.
— When a character string is found that is a potential affix, apply the environmental rules in order to verify the affix.
— If the affix is verified, mark the resultant boundary and return to the first step.
— If the affix is not verified, look for shorter matches.
— If a shorter match is found, return to the second step, else finish the search.

The verificiation rules which examine the environment are different for every affix, and they are enclosed in the dictionary together with the affix they belong to and additional information. The rules have the general form:

$$(\text{action}) \ (\text{environment data})$$

where (action) describes, what to do with the following environment data and how the results of the action have to be interpreted. A typical rule e.g. is

$$\text{Comp-R-N, ber, kul, ren, rin}$$

which is used for the prefix 'her' to reject the recognition of an affix in the words "Herberge", "Herkules", "Herren" and "Herrin". The first part of the action describes the class of instruction, which in our example is a 'compare'-instruction. The next letter 'R' tells the instruction to search at the 'R'ight boundary, and the last letter 'N' specifies that if a match is found the string to be verified is 'N'ot an affix. Other instructions examine the morpheme class of adjacent morphemes and test whether the following inflectional affixes contain a vowel or similar things.

The number of rules to verify an affix is somehow dependent on the string length of the affix. While long affixes are rather unambiguous and need only few rules, affixes consisting of two or three characters often correspond to parts of a root, and therefore they need more rules to be verified. Our current affix dictionaries are based on some two thousand frequent words including 32 prefixes and 57 suffixes. The dictionaries occupy about 2 kbyte. An improved version based on a German standard dictionary will have several hundred entries and is in progress.

As the analysis of word structure is partially based on statistical rules, it has to be equipped with dictionaries for exceptions that include words which would cause pronuncation errors if they were decomposed and pronounced according to the rules. Currently, we use two dictionaries for exceptions, one for entire words and the second one for stems, i.e. words with their inflectional suffixes stripped off. Both lists currently contain only function words used for sentence analysis and a few very frequent exceptions.

Word structure analysis based on cluster analysis is insufficient as a linguistic tool for word decomposition, but it is a fast and very effective tool for purposes of speech synthesis. No root lexicon is needed, only a list of the basic clusters and an affix dictionary. Decomposition is done in far less time than is used to pronounce the word, and the analysis written in assembler needs only 3 kbytes of memory. A version written in C is in progress.

LETTER-TO-SOUND RULES AND WORD ACCENTS

Due to the preceding word structure analysis, well known letter-to-sound rules may be used. We chose a conversion of letters to sounds in two steps. This means for vowels, that in the first step only a vowel quality is computed while in the second step the same rules are applied to all vowels to determine whether the vowel is long or short. 23 rules are needed for the first step and 4 rules for the second step. For consonants, most part of the conversion is done in the first step with 36 rules, while in the second step 9 rules govern the devoicing of voiced fricatives and plosives, the selection of two 'r'-variants and the change of 'n' to 'ng'. These 72 rules have proved to be sufficient for a conversion based on morphemes.

The generation of word accent patterns is a three stage process. At first, with the aid of information provided by affix dictionaries and word structure, it is decided which affixes can carry an accent. Then for each root and its adjoined affixes, accent patterns are generated. The last step is to combine these accent patterns in order to form a word accent pattern for compound words.

While there are few and simple rules to perform the second and the last step, a lot of computation is needed in the first stage to get the accent for affixes. The "accentability" of affixes depends on the order of affixes within a word as well as on context rules. Frequently, German affixes in some words may carry the main accent and in other words they may have no accent at all. To resolve such ambiguities, similar rules as for the affix verification are being used.

These rules have the same limitations as the rules for affix verification: currently they are based on several thousand words only, but they will be improved to match a complete standard dictionary.

SENTENCE ANALYSIS

In the SYNTEX system, the syntactical analysis of a sentence is the presupposition for generating its prosody. When the syntactical analysis has identified the parts of the sentence, its constituents can be determined. On the basis of these constituents or phrases, the prosodic features of the spoken utterance are calculated. We decided to use only syntax for prosody, because there are considerable difficulties in taking content and context into account. The two main reasons for this are, that it is not yet possible to describe and detect semantic relations under unrestricted text conditions, and that too much processing time would be required to allow real-time text-to-speech conversion.

Earlier research on German syntax analysis with unrestricted text [4] demonstrated processing intervals of several minutes on a mainframe for the complete parsing of a single main clause. Most of the time was spent determining the parts of speech of content words and detecting the correct syntactical relations between the constituents of a sentence. As processing time of that order of magnitude is not acceptable for real-time applications, we decided to do without a complete syntax analysis. We gained evident savings in processing time, because we need not detect the part of speech for every word of the sentence, and because detecting one possible syntactical structure for a sentence is sufficient.

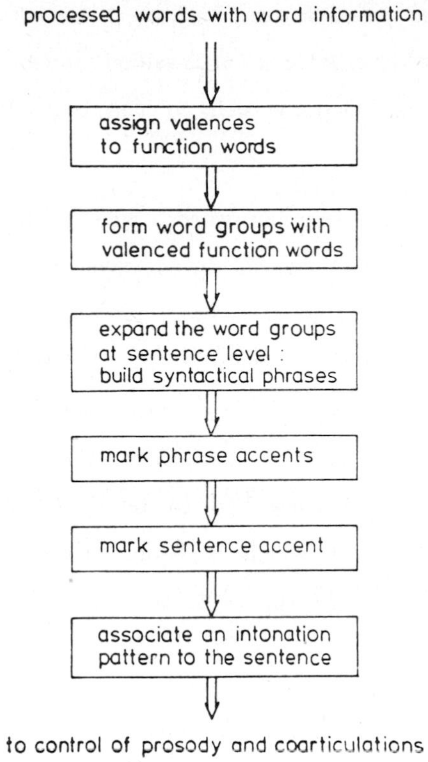

processed words with word information

```
        ┌─────────────────────────┐
        │ assign valences         │
        │ to function words       │
        └─────────────────────────┘
                    │
                    ▼
        ┌─────────────────────────┐
        │ form word groups with   │
        │ valenced function words │
        └─────────────────────────┘
                    │
                    ▼
        ┌─────────────────────────┐
        │ expand the word groups  │
        │ at sentence level :     │
        │ build syntactical phrases│
        └─────────────────────────┘
                    │
                    ▼
        ┌─────────────────────────┐
        │ mark phrase accents     │
        └─────────────────────────┘
                    │
                    ▼
        ┌─────────────────────────┐
        │ mark sentence accent    │
        └─────────────────────────┘
                    │
                    ▼
        ┌─────────────────────────┐
        │ associate an intonation │
        │ pattern to the sentence │
        └─────────────────────────┘
                    │
                    ▼
```

to control of prosody and coarticulations

Fig. 3   Sentence analysis

INCOMPLETE SENTENCE PARSING

In written German only 512 words form about 60% of normal orthographic text
[5].   Most of these words are function words to which we assign a valence.
Valences mark the tendency of a word to be followed by certain parts of speech.
With the help of function words and their valences sentences are decomposed into
word groups (see fig. 3), by combining a function word and, dependent on the
specified valence, some of the following unclassified words.   There are 7 types of

valences: no valence, and valences over 1, 2 or 3 words, which may be extended in a further step by adding trailing unclassified words to the valence group. These word groups correspond quite well to the beginning of German nominal phrases.

The problem arising with function words, which can carry either no valence or one or more valences, was solved by always assigning them no valence. Therefore, in order to determine the final length of a nominal phrase, an expansion of the word groups at sentence level is necessary. Looking at a whole sentence, sentence level rules are used to guess how far a word group can be expanded, provided that the group is marked with an extendable valence. The definition of the sentence level rules had to be done carefully, as they depend very much on the sort of text which is being processed. We determined our rules on the basis of German newspaper texts and found them to fit quite well for any kind of text.

Up to this point the sentence has been decomposed into a sequence of marked noun groups with unclassified words between them. In forming groups with these unknown words too, we define the groups marked so far to be the syntactically relevant phrases of the sentence.

MARKING ACCENTS ON PHRASE AND SENTENCE LEVEL

In German nominal phrases, there is a tendency to place the most important word of the phrase, which usually carries an accent, at the end. The nominal phrases of a sentence are detected by valence assignment to function words. So in every phrase detected with the help of valences the rightmost unclassified word, which is nearly always a contend word, is assigned a phrase accent.

The sentence accent can only be carried by a phrase which already has a phrase accent. If there is only one phrase accent, it automatically will be the sentence accent. If there are two phrase accents, the last phrase will get the sentence accent. If there are more than two phrase accents, the sentence accent is calculated on the basis of the rules given by J. Pheby [6], which rely on regularities in the sequence of German nominal phrases. For example, if there are two nominal phrases, one in the dative and the other in the accusative, the accusative phrase gets the sentence accent. The cases can be determined by analysing the function words and the word suffixes.

PROSODICS

At the prosodic level (see fig. 4) our main work concentrated on generating an FØ-contour by rule for a sentence. Therefore only simple timing rules like the shortening of the duration of function words are implemented at the moment. For the future, modules are planned, that control the speech rhythm depending on the speech rate and the number of phrases within a sentence. These modules will also consider coarticulations on the phrase and sentence level.

So at the moment, phoncme duration is determined by table only by considering the word structure, which means that sound lengthening occurs if there is a word accent. As function words carry no accent in the SYNTEX system, they are always shortened to a minimum length. This can be interpreted as a rhythmic component on phrase level which occurs in thc system's output.

GENERATION OF AN FØ-CONTOUR

For the generation of an FØ-contour, we adapted a modified form of the hat-shaped pattern strategy proposed by Cohen and t'Hart [7]. For each utterance we calculate FØ by using a logarithmic scale which is measured in Cent (doubling FØ = 1200 Cent). The reference point for this scale is the lowest fundamental frequency normally produced in speech (55 Hz). This enables us to describe FØ-values that can be produced by the phoneme synthesizer.

SETTING THE BASELINE

In almost any language, there is a gradual fall of FØ in the course of an utterance. This is often explained by the decreasing air pressure in a speaker's lung which results in a diminishing of vocal cord tension [8]. We take account of this physiological effect by calculating an FØ-baseline which falls gradually with 200 cents per second in the first 1.5 seconds of an utterance and after that with 50 cents per second. A reduction of the FØ-fall in the second part of an utterance is necessary to prevent a too low FØ-value at the end of long utterances, that would affect the perception of the produced speech.

BUILDING FØ-PATTERNS

Like Cohen and t'Hart, we build the FØ-contour of an utterance by adding predefined FØ-movements to the baseline, in order to construct all perceptually relevant FØ-movements. We distinguish four FØ-movements:

— a steep fall with a fixed slope of 1200 cent per second and the FØ-change limited to 150 cent

— a steep rise with a fixed slope of 1200 cent per second and the FØ-change limited to 150 cent

— a gradual rise with variable slope and the FØ-change limited to 300 cent

— a gradual fall with variable slope and the FØ-change limited to 300 cent

Further on, there are two possible constant courses: one at baseline level ("low"), and the other 300 cent above the baseline ("high"). Frequently occuring sequences of FØ-movements may be combined to FØ-patterns. Among these FØ-patterns is the important "hat" shaped pattern" (low course - steep rise - high course - steep fall - low course).

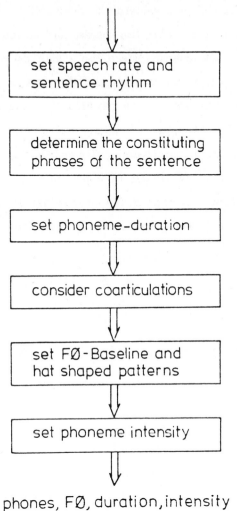

processed sentence
with word- and sentence information

set speech rate and
sentence rhythm

determine the constituting
phrases of the sentence

set phoneme-duration

consider coarticulations

set FØ-Baseline and
hat shaped patterns

set phoneme intensity

phones, FØ, duration, intensity

Fig. 4   Control of prosody and coarticulations

APPLICATION OF THE FØ-PATTERNS

Changing FØ at the end of a sentence is important for the perception of the characteristics of the sentence. The last phrase of an interrogative sentence is assigned the FØ-pattern "low course - steep rise - high course" and the preceding phrase has the pattern "high course - steep fall - low course". The two last phrases of a terminating sentence get the patterns "low course - steep rise - high course" and "high course - steep fall - low course". that means, that at the end of sentences there is always a hat shaped pattern either inverted or not. While developing the final patterns, we found that perception is increased by a slight modification of the patterns: a gradual fall or rise has to be added to the last syllable of a terminating or interrogative sentence respectively.

All preceding phrases of a sentence, if there are any, are handled by assigning the pattern "low course - steep rise - high course" without regard of the sentence characteristics. In the special case of a sentence consisting of only one phrase, this phrase is assigned the pattern "low course - steep rise -high course" for an interrogative sentence, or "high course - steep fall - low course' for a terminating sentence.

CURRENT STATUS

SYNTEX is a software system designed for microprocessors. Most routines have been written in assembler and are running on the Motorola 68XX microprocessors family. The software currently needs about 30 kbytes including 10 kbytes for dictionaries. Conversion of text to speech is done in less than 30% of the time used to pronounce the text. A 'C' version of the system is in progress.

While the development of algorithms at the word level is almost finished, the dictionaries are rather preliminary yet and have to be updated to match the whole German language. Analysis on sentence level and generation of intonation contours will be refined, too. Control of the prosodic features sound duration and intensity is planned.

Although up to date no high quality phoneme synthesizers for the German language are available, SYNTEX will not be expanded by the development of a phoneme synthesizer; only available phoneme synthesizers will be used to fill the gap between the phonemes and the spoken output. Up to now, driver programs for e.g. the Votrax VS6-G and the Votrax SC01 have been developed.

ACKNOWLEDGEMENTS

The authors wish to thank J. Blauert, who made this work possible at the Acoustics Laboratory of the Ruhr-University Bochum. We also thank M. Kugler, who helped us writing this paper, and the Deutsche Forschungsgemeinschaft (DFG), that supported essential parts of the research work.

REFERENCES

1. J. Allen, "Speech synthesis from unrestricted text" in J. L. Flanagan, L. R. Rabiner (eds.), *Speech Synthesis*, Dowden, Hutchinson and Ross Inc., Stroudsburg, pp. 416-428, 1973.
2. J. Allen, M. S. Hunnicutt and D. H. Klatt, MITalk-79, Notes for the M.I.T. summer course 6.69s, 1979.
3. W. Kästner, "Phonemisierung orthographischer Texte" im Deutschen, Helmut Buske Verlag, Hamburg, 1972.
4. Arbeitsgruppe MasA, "Zur maschinellen Syntaxanalyse", Forschungsberichte des Instituts für deutsche Sprache, Vol. 18.1, 18.2, 19, Mannheim, 1974.
5. H. Meier, *Sprachstatistik I/II*, Georg Olms Verlag, Hildesheim, 1964.
6. J. Pheby, "Phonologie: Intonation", in K. E. Heidolph et al, *Grundzüge einer Deutschen Grammatik* Akademie Verlag, Berlin, pp. 839-897.
7. A. Cohen and J. t'Hart, "Intonation by rule: a perceptual quest", J. of Phonetics, Vol. 1, pp. 309-327, 1973.
8. R. Collier, "Perceptual and linguistic tolerance in intonation", Int. Rev. Appl. Linguistics in Language Teaching, Vol. XIII/4, pp. 292-308, 1975.

CONCATENATION RULES FOR DEMISYLLABLE SPEECH SYNTHESIS

Helmut Dettweiler* and Wolfgang Hess

Lehrstuhl für Datenverarbeitung

Technische Universität München

Munich

Federal Republic of Germany

ABSTRACT

A system for speech synthesis by rule is described which uses demisyllables as phonetic units. The problem of concatenation is discussed in detail; the pertinent stage converts a string of phonetic symbols into a stream of speech parameter frames. For German about 1650 demisyllables are required to permit synthesizing a very large vocabulary. Synthesis is controlled by 18 rules which are used for splitting up the phonetic string into demisyllables, for selecting the demisyllables in such a way that the size of the inventory is minimized, and — last but not least — for concatenation. The quality and intelligibility of the synthetic signal is very good; in a subjective test the median word intelligibility dropped from 96.6% for a LPC vocoder to 92.1% for the demisyllable synthesis, and the difference in quality between the demisyllable synthesis and ordinary vocoded speech was judged very small.

---

* Dr. Dettweiler is now with BMW, Munich.

NATO ASI Series, Vol. F16
New Systems and Architectures for Automatic Speech
Recognition and Synthesis. Edited by R. De Mori and C. Y. Suen
© Springer-Verlag Berlin Heidelberg 1985

1. PHONETIC UNITS AND THE PROBLEM OF CONCATENATION

Concatenation is a central problem in any system for speech synthesis by rule. It provides the link between the phonetic level, where the information to be synthesized is represented as a sequence of discrete phonetic and/or linguistic units, and the parametric level where the information is coded (Fig. 1).

In practice concatenation is controlled by a set of rules that act upon a data base of speech data. This data base may contain experimental data, such as a table of formant frequencies, but it may also consist of (parameterized) natural speech. The design of the concatenation component of a speech synthesis system is determined by a tradeoff between the number and complexity of the concatenation rules on the one hand and the size of the memory required for the data base on the other hand. The most important question in this respect is that of the phonetic units to be applied.

Viable phonetic units for speech synthesis are words, syllabic units, and phonemic units. Words as units for synthesis require a minimum of rules but a maximum of data memory; they are not realistic for synthesis of large or unlimited vocabularies. Phonemes, on the other hand, require a minimum of data memory since their number is limited to about 40, and their duration is rather short. It is well known, however, that phonemes cannot be simply concatenated; due to coarticulation effects, the information relevant for understanding speech is realized in the transitions between phonemes, and a great number of (language-dependent) concatenation rules are necessary to realize the transitions and to provide an acceptable quality and intelligibility. A lot of human work is thus required to establish and to test these rules (Allen, 1976; Klatt, 1980); nevertheless, the quality of the resulting speech is limited.

Considerable efforts have therefore been made towards designing speech synthesis systems that use larger phonetic units. In such systems many of the transitions and coarticulation effects are intrinsic to the stored data and need no longer be explicitly generated by rule. The number of concatenation rules necessary can thus be drastically reduced; this reduces the overall system

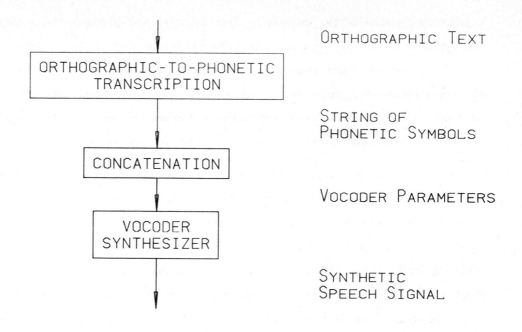

ORTHOGRAPHIC TEXT

STRING OF
PHONETIC SYMBOLS

VOCODER PARAMETERS

SYNTHETIC
SPEECH SIGNAL

Fig. 1.   Block diagram of a speech synthesis system by rule. The components necessary for prosodic analysis and generation of prosodic control information have been omitted.

complexity (in spite of the increase in data memory) and improves the quality of the synthetic speech at the same time, since any rule, even a very sophisticated one, can never completely replace natural speech. Diphones, i.e., units consisting of transitions between adjacent phonemes, have been applied in various systems, such as the one by Olive (1980) for American English, the one by Emerard (1977) for French, or the one by Endres and Wolf (1980) for German.

Besides diphones, syllabic units supply a viable data base for high-quality speech synthesis by rule. It has been shown that the influence of coarticulation strongly diminishes when a syllable boundary is crossed (Fujimura, 1981; Öhman, 1966). The number of complete syllables, however, is still too large (and, in addition, difficult to determine) to permit synthesizing an unlimited vocabulary with a reasonably small amount of memory. The number of elements, however, is drastically reduced when a syllable is split up into two *demisyllables* (DSs), as first proposed by Fujimura (1975, 1976a).

How can we suitably split up a syllable into two demisyllables? Usually a syllable is defined to consist of the *nucleus* (in German this is always a vowel or a diphthong) which is preceded and followed by a number of consonants, the so-called *consonant clusters* (CCs). The consonants preceding the syllabic nucleus form the *initial consonant cluster*, and the consonants following the nucleus represent the *final consonant cluster*. According to Fujimura's proposal a syllable is now split up into demisyllables in such a way that the initial CC and the beginning of the syllabic nucleus form the *initial demisyllable*, whereas the remainder (i.e., the second part of the nucleus and the final CC make up the *final demisyllable*.

As already mentioned, demisyllables as units of speech processing were first proposed by Fujimura both for speech recognition (Fujimura, 1975) and for speech synthesis purposes (Fujimura, 1976a), and an experimental system for demisyllable synthesis of American English was designed and implemented (Fujimura et al., 1977; Macchi, 1980; Browman, 1980). For German demisyllables were taken up by Ruske and Schotola (1978) in connection with a speech recognition system; for speech synthesis they were first used by Dettweiler (1980, 1981).

There are two advantages of the demisyllable approach. First, due to linguistic constraints, the number of demisyllables actually used in a language is only a small fraction of the number of demisyllables one could think of just by arbitrarily combining consonants and vowels. Second, since the experiments suggest (Fujimura et al., 1977; Dettweiler, 1980) that the boundaries of the demisyllables coincide with temporal minima of coarticulation effects, a small number of relatively simple rules will be sufficient to concatenate the individual elements. In this paper we will show that about 18 rules and about 1650 demisyllables requiring a data memory of less than 0.5 MByte is sufficient to synthesize (nearly) unrestricted German text.

The remainder of this paper is organized as follows. In Sect. 2 the complete demisyllable inventory will be established, and we will develop the concatenation rules for the syllabic nucleus which enable us to synthesize monosyllabic words. In Sect. 3 suitable reductions of the inventory will be discussed. Section 4 describes a major part of the concatenation rules for CCs in order to synthesize words with more than 1 syllable. Section 5 finally presents the results of intelligibility tests for a list of about 180 frequent meaningful German words.

2. THE DEMISYLLABLE INVENTORY. SYNTHESIZING MONO-SYLLABIC WORDS

A representative list of demisyllables for the German language was compiled by Ruske and Schotola (Schotola, 1980, 1984; Ruske, 1984; Ruske and Schotola, 1978) based on a list of the 8000 most frequent German words (Meier, 1967) and other investigations (cf. Schotola, 1984). The initial consonant clusters contain from zero to three consonants, whereas up to 5 consonants may be encountered in a final CC. Nevertheless, the number of CCs is extremely limited due to linguistic constraints: there are only 47 initial and 159 final CCs, a list of which is given in this volume (Ruske, 1984). Concerning the syllabic nuclei, 23 vowels and 3 diphthongs must be dealt with; a list is given in Table 1.

LONG VOWELS									
Tense	Closed	e:	i:	o:	u:	ø:	y:	a:
	Open	ɛ:						
SHORT VOWELS									
Tense	Closed	e	i	o	u	ø	y	a
Lax	Open	ɛ	ɪ	ɔ	ʊ	œ	ʏ	
	schwa	ə						
DIPHTHONGS		a^{e}	a^{o}	$\text{ɔ}^{\text{ø}}$				

Table 1. German vowels and diphthongs. After Martens and Martens (1965).

Contrary to speech recognition, where syllabic nuclei and CCs can be treated separately (Ruske and Schotola, 1978), the transitions between the syllabic nuclei and the CCs are essential for the quality of the synthesized speech; they cannot be generated by rule and must thus be available as stored data. That means that the number of elements required for the complete demisyllable inventory* amounts to

$$N_C = 26.51 \text{ initial DSs} + 26.159 \text{ final DSs} = 5460.$$

This number is considerable so that efforts are necessary in order to reduce the number of elements without degrading the resulting synthetic speech. This question will be further dealt with in Section 3.

Each DS now consists of a CC and part of a syllabic nucleus. Concatenation of DSs at boundaries within the syllabic nuclei and within CCs are principally different tasks and must be treated by separate rules. For synthesizing monosyllabic words, we only need to concatenate demisyllables within the syllabic nucleus. This problem shall thus be treated first.

Since coarticulation shows a strong tendency toward anticipating future articulatory gestures (Öhman, 1966; Fujimura, 1981), it is adequate to locate the demisyllable boundary within the first part of the vowel. As the experiment shows, Fujimura's proposal (1976a) to place the boundary 50 ms after the beginning of the vowel can be applied to German as well (Dettweiler, 1980). This means that all the problems of vowel duration as well as the question of the diphthongs are confined to the final demisyllables. This leads to concatenation rule #1 (Fig. 2):

---

* The number of initial CCs rises from 47 to 51 due to four CCs which do not occur in word-initial position, but must be added to the set of initial CCS due to rule SR2. for more details see Section 4.1.

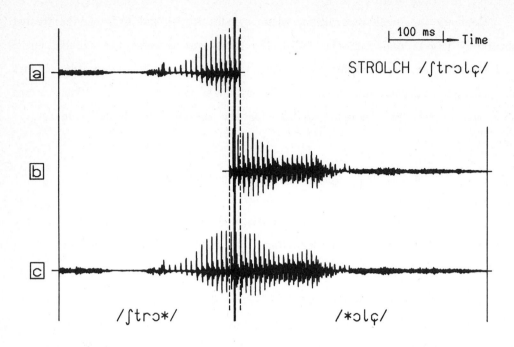

Fig. 2 a-c. Concatenation within the syllabic nucleus (rule CR1). (a) Initial DS, (b) final DS; (c) complete word after concatenation. The example shows the word "Strolch" ("lounger"); /ʃtrɔlɕc/ -- > /ʃtrɔ*/ ‖ /* lɕ/. In this and the following figures, the thick vertical line indicates the interconnection point; the smoothing interval is indicated by the dashed lines. The asterisk in the phonetic transcription refers to the position of the syllabic nucleus. All the signals were synthesized from the demisyllable data base (speaker HTD) using an LPC vocoder.

An initial demisyllable and a final demisyllable are concatenated after the first 50 ms of the vowel. Parameters are smoothed within ± 10 ms around the interconnection point. (CR1)

Like the system for American English (Fujimura et al., 1977), our system smoothes the transition by means of interpolation; i.e., frames within the smoothing area are obtained by interpolating between the parameter values of the adjacent frames on either side of the interpolation interval (which pertain to different demisyllables). A smoothing interval of ± 10 ms around the interconnection point has proved adequate.

3. INVENTORY REDUCTION

To reduce the number of demisyllables, two ways seem feasible: 1) vowel substitution, and 2) further splitting of consonant clusters. Both these possibilities have been implemented in our system. Three inventory reduction rules (RR1-3) and one splitting rule (SR1) have been developed for this purpose. Contrary to the concatenation rules that act on the parametric level, inventory reduction rules and splitting rules act on the phonetic level; they influence the selection of the demisyllables for a given input string of phonetic symbols.

3.1 VOWEL AND DIPHTHONG SUBSTITUTION

Inventory reduction rule #1, dealing with diphthongs, is a direct consequence of rule CR1:

Given a diphthong, CR1 states that most of it will be located in the final DS. The initial DS of the diphthong can thus be replaced with the initial DS containing the initial vowel of the diphthong. (RR1)

In standard German this is possible since the initial vowel of the diphthong is always well pronounced. If the substituted initial DS and the final DS which contains the diphthong do not match perfectly, this does not matter since the audible result of this mismatch will only be a further diphthongization.

The second rule refers to the short tense vowels which are always unstressed in German (and rather rare). Usually in German the long (stressed) vowels are tense, and the short vowels (whether stressed or unstressed) are lax and thus more open. These two categories of vowels must remain separated. The short tense vowels, however, can be derived from the corresponding long ones according to reduction rule #2:

A short tense vowel is obtained by concatenating the demisyllables with the corresponding long vowels and adequately decreasing the duration of the vowel.

(RR2)

The correspondence in German between the features "long" and "tense" on the one hand and "short" and "lax" on the other hand leads to a number of additional, well-known similarities between German vowels (Endres, 1971; Hess, 1972, 1976): /I/ and /e:/, /Y/ and /ø:/, /ʊ/ and /o:/ as well as /a/ and /a:/. In speech recognition, for instance, these vowel pairs become almost indistinguishable when duration is omitted as a cue (Hess, 1972). As the experiment shows, however, these vowel pairs are still somewhat different. Extending rule RR2 to them would thus lead to an undesirable diphthongization except for the case of /a/ and /a:/ where applying the rule does not degrade the synthetic speech. Hence, the two rules RR1 and RR2 reduce the number of vowels from 23 to 15 and eliminate the diphthongs from the initial demisyllables.

3.2 SPLITTING UP CONSONANT CLUSTERS. RUDIMENT AND SUFFIX

According to a later paper by Fujimura (1976b), certain consonants, when occurring in final position of a DS, may be split off from the DS and form separate units, the so-called *affixes*. According to Fujimura's proposal these are the consonants /θ/, /s/, /t/, /z/, and /d/ . Whereas for English this indicates a considerable inventory reduction, the effect is rather small for German since of these consonants only /s/ and /t/ occur in final position (the others do not exist in German, or they only occur in initial position). The fact that such a splitting is possible at all, however, indicates that fricatives and stops in final position, like vowels in the syllabic nuclei, represent a natural coarticulation barrier; i.e., sounds following this barrier do not (substantially) affect previous sounds. Looking for a different splitting scheme which is more efficient for German, Dettweiler (1980, 1981), arrived at the principle of rudiment and suffix (splitting rule #1; Fig. 3):

If a final demisyllable ends with /t/, /s/, /f/, /ʃ/ or a combination thereof, this part is split off and separately treated as a suffix. The remainder is defined to be the rudiment.   (SR1)

It is obvious that /t/ and /s/ can be treated in a common way since their places of articulation - and with it the anticipatory coarticulation effects - are almost identical. In addition, the experiments have shown that there is no loss of intelligibility or quality when the rule is extended to /f/ and /ʃ/.

In practice the rudiment* is formed by uttering a demisyllable that contains

---

* According to the definition given in rule SR1, the term *rudiment* is used in connection with final demisyllables. For reasons of simplification, we also use this term in connection with final consonant clusters. To distinguish between a rudiment and an ordinary final DS or CC, any rudiment is marked by a '.' at the end.

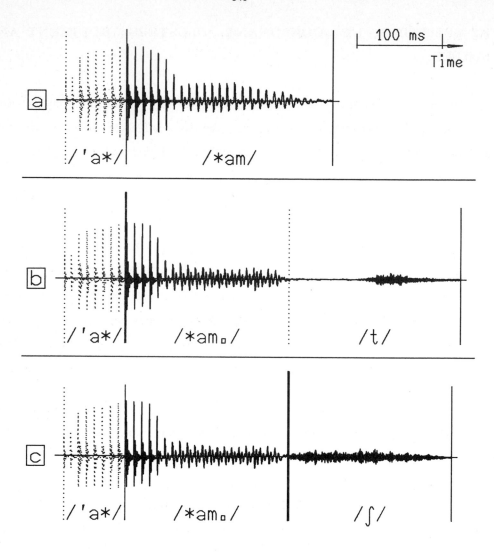

Fig. 3 a-c. The principle of rudiment and suffix. (a) Ordinary consonant cluster: example /*am/. (b) Rudiment and suffix: the demisyllable /*amt/ is split up into the rudiment /*am./ and the suffix /t/ (the dotted line represents the boundary). (c) Concatenation using rudiment and suffix (rule CR2): /*am./ || /ʃ/ -- /*amʃ/. The difference between the ordinary consonant cluster and the rudiment is clearly seen. The rudiment is shorter and ends more abruptly. In this and the following figures, signals drawn with dotted lines represent demisyllables that are needed to complete the word, but do not pertain to the demisyllables involved in the particular rule being explained.

the remainder of the consonantal cluster [without the suffix consonant(s)] plus a final /t/ and then removing the /t/ together with the pertinent silence before the burst (Fig. 3b). Since the rudiment contains all the coarticulatory influences by the following /t/, it is easy to see that the rudiment and the final DS containing an identical consonant cluster without the /t/ are different (cf. Fig. 3a,b). The concatenation rule for a rudiment and its suffix is simple:

A rudiment and a suffix are directly concatenated without any smoothing.

(CR2)

Applying the principle of rudiment and suffix thus leads to inventory reduction rule #3:

A final consonant cluster is split up into a rudiment and a suffix whenever possible, i.e., when it ends with /ʃ/, /s/, /ʃ/, /t/ or a combination thereof.

(RR3)

This rule reduces the number of (ordinary) final consonant clusters from 159 to 23; in addition we obtain 23 rudiments and 26 suffixes (any combination of /f/, /s/, /t/, and /ʃ/ that occur in the final DSs of the full-size inventory). Table 2 contains a list of the reduced inventory of final CCs, rudiments, and suffixes. The total number of elements of the reduced inventory now amounts to

$$N_R = 51 \cdot 15 \text{ initial DSs} + 23 \cdot 19 \text{ final DSs} + 23 \cdot 19 \text{ rud.} + 26 \text{ suff.} = 1665 .$$

With an average duration of 0.3 s per element, the memory required for this inventory will be less than 0.5 MByte if a vocoder at or below 7.2 kbits/s is used.

FINAL CONSONANT CLUSTERS / RUDIMENTS	—	r	l	m	n	ŋ	p	k	ç	x
	— —ₐ	r rₐ	l lₐ	m mₐ	n nₐ	ŋ ŋₐ	p pₐ	k kₐ	ç çₐ	x xₐ
			rl rlₐ	rm rmₐ	rn rnₐ		rp rpₐ	rk rkₐ	rç rçₐ	
				lm lmₐ	ln lnₐ		lp lpₐ	lk lkₐ	lç lçₐ	
							mp mpₐ	ŋk ŋkₐ	ŋç ŋçₐ	

REDUCED SUFFIXES / SUFFIXES	f	s	ʃ	t	fs	fts	sts	st	ft	ts	tʃ
SUFFIXES	f	s	ʃ	t tₐ	fs	fts	sts	st stₐ	ft ftₐ	ts	tʃ
REDUCED SUFFIXES	fst fstₐ						ʃst ʃstₐ	tst tstₐ	tʃt tʃtₐ	ʃt ʃtₐ	tʃt tʃstₐ

Table 2a,b. #(a) Final consonant clusters and rudiments, (b) suffixes for demisyllable synthesis of German text after inventory reduction (Dettweiler, 1980). The reduced suffixes represent some kind of "rudiment of a suffix"; they may be needed when a concatenation rule requires a rudiment in connection with a final demisyllable that ends with a suffix.

4. SYNTHESIZING POLYSYLLABLE WORDS

Polysyllabic words contain intervocalic consonant clusters between subsequent syllabic nuclei. This requires additional rules for the concatenation of consonant clusters (Dettweiler, 1980, 1984). The procedure is carried out in two steps. First (Sect. 4.1) an intervocalic CC is split up into a final CC followed by an initial CC, and the CCs are joined to the respective syllabic nuclei to form demisyllables. In the second step (Sect.4.2) the two DSs are concatenated. As in Sect. 3, the three splitting rules described in Sect. 4.1 act on the phonetic level where they define the syllable boundaries; the concatenation rules presented in Sect. 4.2, on the other hand, operate on the parametric level.

4.1 SPLITTING UP INTERVOCALIC CONSONANT CLUSTERS

The first rule (splitting rule #2) is necessary for the demisyllable principle to be applicable at all.

Given an intervocalic consonant cluster, this cluster must always be split up into a valid final consonant cluster and a valid initial consonant cluster. (SR2)

A CC is regarded as *valid* if it is contained in the demisyllable inventory.

If rule SR2 does not yield a solution, the inventory must be enlarged* so that a viable splitting can be provided. In German this applies to the four consonant "clusters" /s/, /x/, /ç/, and /ŋ/ which occur in final and intervocalic position, but not at the beginning of a word; these clusters must be added to the

---

* In order to enlarge the DS inventory, one must enter the new demisyllable(s) as specified in Section 5.1. This requires manual interaction and cannot be done at the same time as the (automatic) synthesis.

initial demisyllable inventory. If rule SR2, on the other hand, provides several solutions, the following experimental rule is applied:

If SR2 provides more than one valid solution, then the one is taken where as many consonants as possible are grouped within the initial consonant clu

This experimental boundary need not be identical to the syllable boundary requested by morphologic constraints (which, by the way, can be different for different words containing the same intervocalic CC). Inmost cases, however, the two boundaries are identical. The rule takes into account the anticipatory effect of coarticulation; a loss of quality was not registered when a demisyllable boundary, as established by Rule SR3, differed from a given morph boundary. The rule thus represents an adequate means to split up intervocalic CCs without requiring morphologic knowledge at this level.

A special case is given when the intervocalic CC only contains one consonant:

If the intervocalic CC contains one consonant only, and if this is neither a plosive nor /s/, /f/, or /ʃ/ (i.e., if it is a sustained consonant other than a suffix), then this consonant pertains to both the initial and the final demisyllables, and rule SR3 does not apply. (SR4)

This rule actually switches the system into a diphone mode.

The three splitting rules SR2-4 enable the system to split up any intervocalic CC into a final CC followed by an initial CC and to combine them with the preceding and subsequent syllabic nuclei to form a final DS followed by an initial one.

4.2 CONCATENATING CONSONANT CLUSTERS

The way in which an intervocalic CC is concatenated strongly depends on the consonants involved. Three principally different cases must be regarded: 1) the intervocalic CC contains at least one consonant, and there is no plosive at the interconnection point (Sect. 4.2.1); 2) the intervocalic CC is empty, i.e., two vowels that do not represent one of the diphthongs immediately follow each other (Sect. 4.2.2); and 3) the intervocalic CC contains one or several plosives at the interconnection point (Sect. 4.2.3).

4.2.1 THE INTERVOCALIC CC IS NOT EMPTY AND DOES NOT CONTAIN A PLOSIVE AT THE INTERCONNECTION POINT.

This case is handled by three concatenation rules which are rather self-explanatory. The most important point is that the anticipatory coarticulation effects within the initial DS are preserved; i.e., parts of the initial DS which are perceptually important must not be dropped nor smoothed out. The interval to be smoothed is thus situated asymmetrically around the interconnection point.

If the diphone mode applies, i.e., if the intervocalic CC contains one consonant other than /s/, /ʃ/, /ʃ/, or a plosive, then the demisyllables are concatenated by cutting off the onset of the consonant in the initial DS and as much of the consonant in the final DS as necessary to obtain correct consonant duration. Smoothing is performed starting 30 ms before and ending at the first frame after the interconnection point. (CR3)

If the initial DS begins with /s/, /ʃ/, /ʃ/, /z/, or /v/, and if the final DS does not end with one of these consonants, then the coarticulation effects between the demisyllables correspond to the case of Rule CR2. Therefore the final DS is replaced with the pertinent rudiment, and the initial DS is appended without smoothing. (CR4)

As this rule shows, the rudiment is not only suitable for inventory reduction; it can also be advantageously applied in such context where it represents a quasi natural way of coarticulation.

> *In all cases where rules CR3 and CR4 do not apply, the demisyllables are concatenated in such a way that the final part of the final DS (about 60 ms) and the onset of the initial consonant of the initial DS are dropped. Smoothing is performed in the same manner as in rule CR3, i.e., within -30 and +10 ms from the interconnection point.* (CR5)

Figures 4-6 show examples for these rules.

It is obvious that neither of these rules can be applied if there is a plosive at the interconnection point, i.e., if the initial DS starts or the final DS ends with a plosive. If a plosive, however, occurs only in internal position of a DS, then it is totally embedded in that demisyllable and does not pose any problems. For instance, the German word "Anspruch" ("claim"; see Fig. 5) is concatenated as

$$/\text{'an}\text{ʃprʊx}/ \; < \; -- \; /\text{'a*}/ \; || \; /\text{*an.}/ \; || \; /\text{ʃprʊ*}/ \; || \; /\text{*ʊx}/$$

according to the rules CR1 and CR3. The asterisk in the phonetic transcription of the demisyllables indicates the position of the syllabic nucleus, and the sign "||" stands for concatenation.

4.2.2 THE CONSONANT CLUSTER IS EMPTY

In this case two syllabic nuclei form a vowel cluster. A vowel cluster has to be distinguished from a true diphthong; the diphthong per definition represents a single syllabic nucleus (although in German a diphthong is orthographically represented by two letters), whereas a vowel cluster always represents a syllable with an empty final CC followed by a syllable with an empty initial CC. Acoustically such a cluster is realized by a rather long and slow transition; it can

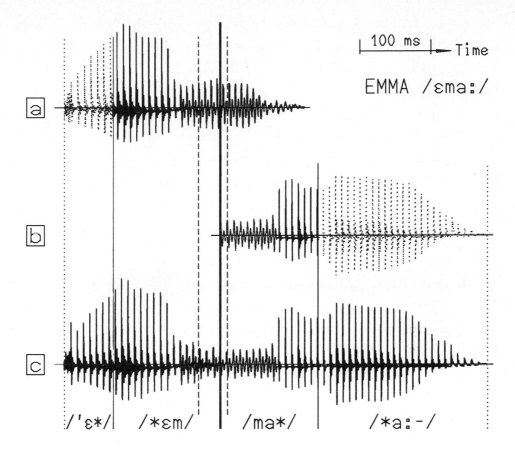

Fig. 4 a-c. Concatenation of consonant clusters in diphone mode (rule CR3). (a) First syllable; (b) second syllable; (c) complete word after concatenation. The final consonant /m/ of the first syllable was shortened by 120 ms prior to concatenation. Example: /*ɛm/ ‖ /ma*/ from the name "Emma" /'ɛma/.

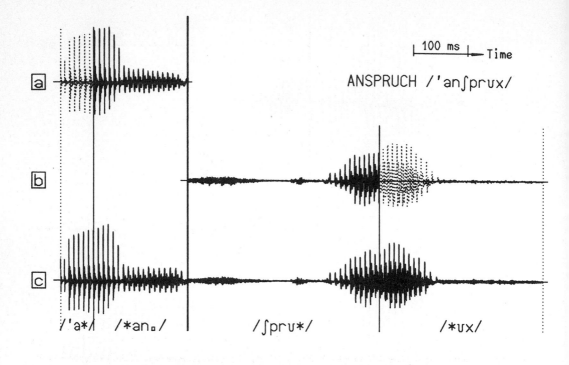

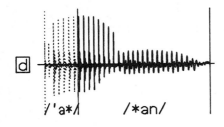

Fig. 5 a-d. (a-c) Concatenation of consonant clusters by rudiment (concatenation rule CR4). Example: /*an./ || /ʃprʊ*/ --> /*anʃprʊ*/ from "Anspruch" ("claim") /'anʃprʊx/; (d) DS with ordinary CC /*an/ for comparison. The thick vertical line indicates the interconnection point; there is no smoothing since a rudiment is involved.

557

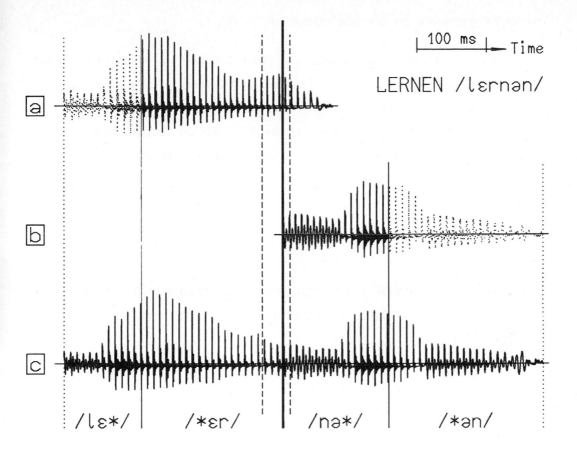

Fig. 6 a-c.   Standard case of consonant cluster concatenation (rule CR5). Example: /*ɛr/ ‖ /nɛ*/ -- /*ɛrnɛ*/ from "lernen" ("to learn") /lɛrnɛn/.

easily be synthesized by extended interpolation.

In the case of a vowel cluster the final DS consists of the first vowel followed by an empty final CC; the initial DS consists of the second vowel preceded by an empty initial CC. The two components are concatenated in such a way that the last 40 ms of the final DS are dropped. Smoothing by linear interpolation is performed within ± 30 ms of the interconnection point.

(CR6)

4.2.3 THE INTERVOCALIC CONSONANT CLUSTER CONTAINS ONE OR SEVERAL PLOSIVES AT THE DEMISYLLABLE BOUNDARY

German has 6 plosives: /b/, /d/, /g/, /p/, /t/, and /k/. All of them may occur in initial position whereas plosives in final position are always voiceless. In intervocalic as well as in final position two plosives may immediately follow each other.

Concatenating intervocalic CCs with plosives at the demisyllable boundary represents the most delicate case of demisyllable synthesis. The problems mainly result from the fact that plosives in initial and in final position are differently realized. A plosive in final or intervocalic position is characterized by 1) the sequence of the preceding transition, 2) the silent interval before the burst (which may be substituted by a voice bar in the case of a voiced plosive), 3) the burst, and - in nonfinal position - 4) the subsequent transition. In initial position, however, a (measurable) silent interval before the burst does not exist; it must therefore be substituted when an initial DS starting with a plosive is used for synthesizing an intervocalic CC. Five concatenation rules (CR7-11) are necessary to cover this task (Dettweiler, 1981, 1984). We first have to look at the position of the plosive (in the case of several subsequent plosives at the DS boundary we regard the last one). Three cases have to be distinguished.

1) The plosive pertains to the initial DS; appending it to the final DS, however, will result in a valid final CC as well. This case is also assumed to apply if the plosive is voiced (and therefore does not occur in final position) and the pertinent voiceless plosive (for instance, /p/ instead of /b/) can be appended to the final DS.

2) The plosive pertains to the initial DS and cannot be appended to the final DS.

3) The plosive pertains to the final DS and cannot be assigned to the initial DS.

Cases 1 and 2 must be further subdivided. In case 1 we must distinguish according to whether a) the plosive is voiceless, or b) the plosive is voiced; in case 2 we must look whether the final DS ends with another plosive or not.

The resulting five concatenation rules CR7-11 are not self-explanatory; discussing them in detail is not possible in this paper due to lack of space. Hence the discussion will be confined to case 1a (concatenation rule CR7) which is another good example how the rudiment can be advantageously applied.

If the initial DS starts with a voiceless plosive that can also be assigned to the final DS, the plosive is doubled, i.e., it is assigned to both the final and the initial DSs. The (extended) final DS is then replaced by the pertinent rudiment, and the initial DS is appended without smoothing.(CR7)

The performance of this rule is illustrated using an example (Fig. 7) Rule SR2 splits the intervocalic CC /rk/ of the German word "Wirkung" ("effect") into the final CC /r/ and the initial CC /k/; this leads to the task of concatenating the DSs /*Ir/ and /kʊ*/. It is obvious that the silent interval before the /k/ is not contained in either of these DSs; it must thus be inserted. The concatenation

560

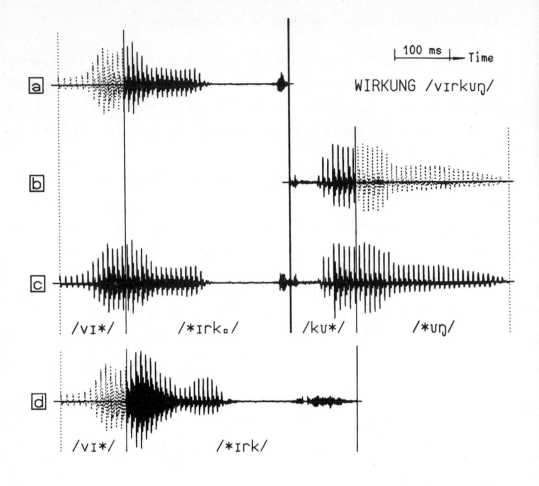

Fig. 7 a-d.   Example of plosive processing (rule CR7). The rule applies when a voiceless plosive that can be assigned to both the initial and the final DSs occurs at the DS boundary. (a-c) Example: /*Irk./ ‖ /kʊ*/ -- /*Irkʊ*/ from "Wirkung" ("effect") /vIrkʊŋ/; (d) DS with ordinary CC /*Iirk/ for comparison. Note that the /v/ in German represents a glide rather than a fricative.

$$/\text{*Ir}/ \;\; \| \;\; \text{``silence''} \;\; \| \;\; /\text{ku*}/ \;\; \text{--} \;\; /\text{*Irku*}/ \;\;,$$

however, is not a good solution since the coarticulatory influence of the /k/ on the demisyllable /* r/ is disregarded. If we concatenate the final DS /*Irk/

$$/\text{*Irk}/ \;\; \| \;\; /\text{ku*}/ \;\; \text{--} \;\; /\text{*Irku*}/,$$

contains both the silent interval and the coarticulatory influence of the /k/ on the /*Ir/ . However, the burst of the /k/ is now realized twice; it must thus be removed from one of the DSs, preferably from the final one. In this case, however, the beginning of the burst in the final DS must be exactly measured and marked. Of course this is undesirable.

A better solution is given when the rudiment /*Irk./ is taken instead of the true final DS /*Irk/. In the rudiment /*Irk./ the speaker is prepared to utter a /t/ subsequently to the /k/ so that the burst of the /k/ is very short (Fig. 7b). Removing the burst of the /k/ in the rudiment is thus unnecessary; if it is concatenated with the burst of the /k/ in the initial DS /ku*/, the two bursts are perceptually merged into one with slightly greater duration which only emphasizes the voiceless character of the plosive (Delattre, 1968). Therefore the concatenation

$$/\text{*Irk.}/ \;\; \| \;\; /\text{ku*}/ \;\; \text{-->} \;\; /\text{*Irku*}/ \;\;,$$

as specified by rule CR7, represents the optimal solution.

5.   ACOUSTIC REALIZATIONS AND INTELLIGIBILITY TESTS

5.1 ACOUSTIC REALIZATION

An experimental system was realized using a 12th-order standard LPC vocoder with a constant frame interval of 10 ms and a signal sampling frequency of 10 kHz. Besides the 12 PARCOR coefficients which were available in unquantized form for the experiments, amplitude and normalized fundamental frequency were stored.

In principle it is not necessary to store fundamental frequency in a speech synthesis system since any prosodic effect of linguistic significance, regardless whether it influences amplitude, fundamental frequency, or duration, must be generated by a special rule system. Microprosodic effects, however, such as small F_0 inflections before and after plosives (which are rather difficult to be controlled by rule), as well as intrinsic pitch of vowels can be covered this way at the cost of a modest increase of the memory required (Dettweiler, 1980). As the experiments have shown, the use of microprosody as a stored parameter not only increases the naturalness of the synthesized speech, but also its intelligibility (Dettweiler, 1982).

For data acquisition the demisyllables were embedded in two-syllable meaningless words of the form /<initial DS>tYr/ and /gYt<final DS>/; the demisyllables were always in stressed position except for the demisyllables containing a schwa which were recorded in the form <initial CC> te:r/ and /ge:t <finalCC>/ in unstressed position. The data were LPC analyzed using a 20-ms Hamming window and the autocorrelation method of linear prediction (Markel and Gray, 1976). F_0 was determined by autocorrelation analysis of the LPC residual (Wagner, 1981); the influences of word prosody were removed from the F_0 contour, and the values of F_0 were normalized in order to yield equal values at the interconnection points within the syllabic nuclei. The DSs were then manually extracted using a display program and an interactive segmentation procedure.

5.2 INTELLIGIBILITY TESTS

A first test was carried out to investigate whether the use of rudiments and suffixes decreases intelligibility. For this test meaningless words of the form /gəa./|||/<suffix>/ were offered to the listeners; the single consonants /t/, /f/, /s/, and /ʃ/ were used as suffixes. In a control experiment (which covered a part of the material) the same words were presented in a quasi-natural environment, i.e., LPC-analyzed and resynthesized by the same vocoder without further processing. The test showed systematic confusions between /f/ and /s/ which were mainly due to the high-frequency band limitation (5 kHz) of the vocoder. The two phonemes /ʃ/ and /t/ were clearly intelligible.

The main intelligibility test was carried out with a phonetically balanced list of 179 words (Dettweiler, 1984) pertaining to the 1000 most frequent German words (Meier, 1967; Ruske and Schotola, 1978); 9 meaningless words were added. The listeners were asked to exactly transcribe (phonetically or orthographically) what they heard; they were further told that there was a minority of meaningless words in the list (but not how many); so they could feel free to declare any word meaningless when they did not clearly understand it. In a control experiment the same words were offered as LPC-analyzed and resynthesized speech.

In the evaluation the meaningless words were excluded, and the transcription errors were counted with reference to the number of words, i.e., a word was regarded as wrong even when the transcription error was confined to a single phoneme. The result was very encouraging: for 18 listeners the median rate of correctly transcribed words was 92.5% for the demisyllable-synthesized speech and 96.6% for the vocoder alone. The median deviation from this value was 4.1%, and the median intelligibility loss per listener for the demisyllable-synthesized speech with reference to the vocoded speech was 3.4%. A number of errors were again due to the LPC vocoder, some more errors were due to incorrect demisyllable extraction and segmentation, particularly in connection with weak fricatives, and some additional errors might be due to the speaker who was not a professional speaker but one of the authors (HTD).

In summary, this test clearly shows that the degradation of intelligibility due to the concatenation by rule is almost negligible. This result is underligned by a subjective quality test where the subjective ranking of quality on a 10-rank scale (from "completely unnatural and unintelligible" to "fully natural") differed only by 0.3 points for synthetic and vocoded speech.

6. SUMMARY AND CONCLUSIONS

The concatenation component of an experimental speech synthesis system by rule was presented which uses demisyllables as phonetic units. The component consists of a rule framework and a data base with parameterized natural speech; it converts text given as a string of phonemes into a stream of parameter frames which control an LPC vocoder. The rule framework for demisyllable concatenation comprises 4 rules for splitting up the intervocalic consonant clusters into demisyllables, 3 substitution rules for demisyllable inventory reduction, and 11 concatenation rules. The data base comprises 1665 demisyllables which need less than 0.5 MByte of memory when used in conjunction with a 7.2-kbit/s vocoder. The quality of the synthetic speech was found nearly undistinguishable from vocoded speech using the same vocoder as the synthesis system; the degradation in word intelligibility (median value: 3.1%), compared to the vocoded speech, is rather small. Most of the errors found in understanding the synthetic speech were due to the LPC vocoder and to the stored demisyllable data, but not to the rules.

Future work thus will first aim at improving the quality of the vocoder in connection with the stored data. Since this kind of vocoder application needs a sensitive, high-quality vocoder rather than a robust or a fast one, complex speech analysis methods with high computing effort can be applied during the data acquisition phase. In particular, a signal bandwidth of 7 kHz requiring a sampling frequency of 16 kHz will eliminate the systematic confusions between the fricatives /f/ and /s/ present in the actual 5-kHz system, and a variable-frame-rate vocoder (Heiler, 1982) permitting a minimum frame rate of less than 5 ms without increasing the overall amount of memory will particularly improve the quality of synthetic stop consonants.

The question of prosody has been kept apart from the problem of concatenation as completely as possible. Microprosody, however, which influences the speech signal on a short-time basis very much alike to that of coarticulation, has been taken into account by adding normalized F_0 values to the stored data. On the syllabic level prosodic rules are necessary only to separate stressed and unstressed syllables. Since the whole material (except those DSs containing a schwa) was recorded using stressed syllables, one primitive rule (which has not been discussed in this paper) is necessary to reduce stressed demisyllables to unstressed ones whenever needed. All other questions of prosody must be dealt with at levels above that of concatenation.

The work described in this paper concentrates on the problem of concatenation, and in our opinion the experiments have shown that the use of demisyllables as phonetic units for speech synthesis solves the problem of concatenation to such an extent that the contribution of the concatenation component to the overall degradation of the quality and intelligibility of the synthetic signal becomes almost negligible.

ACKNOWLEDGEMENTS

The major part of this paper was extracted from the Dr.-Ing. dissertation of the first author (Dettweiler, 1984). The authors wish to thank Dr. G. Ruske for many fruitful discussions.

REFERENCES

1. J. Allen, "Synthesis of speech from unrestricted text", Proc. IEEE 64, 433-442, 1976.
2. C. P. Browman, "Rules for demisyllable synthesis using LINGUA, a language interpreter", Proc. IEEE Intern. Conf. on Acoustics, Speech, and Signal Processing (ICASSP-80), 561-564 (IEEE, New York), 1980.
3. P. Delattre, "From acoustic cues to distinctive features", Phonetica 18, 198-230, 1968.
4. H. Dettweiler, "Versuche zur Sprachsynthese deutscher Woerter mit Halbsilben", in Fortschritte der Akustik, Plenarvorträge und Kurzreferate der 7, Tagung der Deutschen Arbeitsgemeinschaft für Akustik (DAGA '80), München (VDE-Verlag, Berlin), 703-706, 1980.
5. H. Dettweiler, "An approach to demisyllable synthesis of German words", Proc. IEEE ICASSP-81, Atlanta, GA, 110-113 (IEEE, New York), 1981.
6. H. Dettweiler, "Sprachsynthese deutscher Woerter mit Halbsilben", in Fortschritte der Akustik (FASE/DAGA'82); 3. Kongress der FASE, 9. Tagung der DAGA, Goettingen 1982 (Goettingen), 1039-1042, 1982.
7. H. Dettweiler, Automatische Sprachsynthese deutscher Woerter mit Hilfe von silbenorientierten Segmenten (Diss., Technische Universität München), 1984.
8. F. Emerard, Synth ese par diphones et traitement de la prosodie (CNET, F-22301 Lannion), 1977.
9. W. K. Endres, "Die Uebergangslaute der deutschen Sprache als verbindende Elemente für eine Sprachsynthese", Proc. 7th Int. Congr. on Acoustics, Budapest 1971, Vol. 3, paper 25C14, 301-304, 1971.
10. W. K. Endres, "Speech synthesis for an unlimited vocabulary, a powerful tool for inquiry and information service", in Spoken Language Generation and Understanding, Proceedings of the NATO Advanced Study Institute held at Bonas, France, June 23 - July 5, 1979; ed. by J. C. Simon, (Reidel, Dordrecht), 1980.
11. O. Fujimura, "Syllable as a unit of speech recognition." IEEE Trans. ASSP-23, 82-87, 1975.
12. O. Fujimura, "Syllable as the unit of speech synthesis", unpublished Bell memorandum (Bell Labs, Murray Hill, NJ), 1976a.
13. O. Fujimura, "Syllables as concatenated demisyllables and affixes", J. Acoust. Soc. Am. 59 (Suppl.); paper XX3, 91st Meet. ASA, 1976b.
14. O. Fujimura, "Temporal organization of articulatory movements as a multidimensional phrasal structure", Phonetica 38, 66-83, 1981.
15. O. Fujimura, "Syllables as concatenative phonetic units", in Syllables and Sequences, ed. by A. Bell and J. B. Hooper (North-Holland, Amsterdam), 107-120, 1978.
16. O. Fujimura,
    M. J. Macchi, J. B. Lovins, "Demisyllables and affixes for speech synthesis", Proc. 9th Int. Congr. on Acoustics, Madrid 1977, paper I107, 1977.
17. J. Heiler, "Optimized frame selection for variable frame rate synthesis", Proc. IEEE ICASSP-82, Paris 1982, 586-589 (IEEE, New York), 1982.
18. W. J. Hess, Digitale grundfrequenzsynchrone Analyse von Sprachsignalen als

Teil eines automatischen Spracherkennungssystems (Diss., Technische Universität München), 1972.

19. W. J. Hess, "A pitch-synchronous digital feature extraction system for phonemic recognition of speech", IEEE Trans. ASSP-24, 14-25, 1976.

20. D. H. Klatt, "Software for a cascade/parallel formant synthesizer", J. Acoust. Soc. Am. 67, 971-980, 1980.

21. J. B. Lovins, M. Macchi, O. Fujimura, "A demisyllable inventory for speech synthesis", in Speech communication papers presented at the 97th Meeting of the Acoustical Society of America, Cambridge MA, June 12-16, 1979, ed. by. J. J. Wolf and D. H. Klatt, 519-522 (Acoustical Society of America New York, NY), 1979.

22. M. J. Macchi, "A phonetic dictionary for demisyllabic speech synthesis", Proc. IEEE ICASSP-80, Denver, CO., 565-567 (IEEE, New York), 1980.

23. M. J. Macchi, O. Fujimura, "The syllable and speech synthesis", J. Acoust. Soc. Am. 59 (Suppl.), 34; paper R3, 89th Meet. ASA, 1976.

24. J. D. Markel, A. H. Gray, "Linear prediction of speech", Communications and Cybernetics, Vol. 12 (Springer, Berlin), 1976.

25. C. Martens, P. Martens, *Phonetik der deutschen Sprache*, (Max Hueber, München), 1965.

26. I. G. Mattingly, "Syllable Synthesis", Speech Research 49, 111-119, (Haskins Labs., New Haven, CT), 1977.

27. H. Meier, *Deutsche Sprachstatistik*, (Olms, Hildesheim), 1967.

28. S. E. G. Öhman, "Coarticulation in VCV utterances: Spectrographic measurements", J. Acoust. Soc. Am. 39, 151-166, 1966.

29. J. P. Olive, "A scheme for concatenating units for speech synthesis", Proc. IEEE ICASSP-80, Denver, CO, 568-571 (IEEE, New York).

30. L. C. W. Pols, "Consonant intelligibility of speech produced by dyadic rule synthesis", unpublished Bell memorandum (Bell Laboratories, Murray Hill, NJ) 1979.

31. G. Ruske, "Demisyllables as processing units for automatic speech recognition and lexical access", this volume, 1984.

32. G. Ruske, Th. Schotola, "An approach to speech recognition using syllabic decision units", Proc. IEEE ICASSP-78, Tulsa, OK, 722-725 (IEEE, New York), 1978.

33. Th. Schotola, "Silbenanlautende und silbenauslautende Konsonantenfolgen als Entscheidungseinheiten für die automatische Spracherkennung (Diss., Technische Universität München), 1980.

34. Th. Schotola, "On the use of demisyllables in automatic speech recognition", Speech Commun. 3, 63-87, 1984.

35. M. Wagner, "Automatic labelling of continuous speech with a given phonetic transcription using dynamic programming algorithms", Proc. IEEE ICASSP-81, Atlanta, GA (IEEE New York), 1981.

ON THE USE OF PHONETIC KNOWLEDGE FOR AUTOMATIC SPEECH RECOGNITION

Renato De Mori
Concordia University
Department of Computer Science
1455 de Maisonneuve Blvd., West
Montreal, Quebec
H3G 1M8
Canada

Pietro Laface
Politecnico di Torino
Cens-Dipartimento di Automatica e Informatica
Corso Duca degli Abruzzi 24
10129 Torino
ITALY

ABSTRACT

A distributed rule-based system for automatic speech recognition is described.

Acoustic property extraction and feature hypothesization are performed by the application of sequences of operators. These sequences, called plans, are executed by cooperative expert programs.

Experimental results on the automatic segmentation and recognition of phrases, made of connected letters and digits are described and discussed.

NATO ASI Series, Vol. F16
New Systems and Architectures for Automatic Speech
Recognition and Synthesis. Edited by R. De Mori and C.Y. Suen
© Springer-Verlag Berlin Heidelberg 1985

INTRODUCTION

Machines for the automatic recognition of spoken words are now available. They perform well in a speaker-dependent mode on vocabularies of hundreds of words. Some of them may operate in a speaker-independent mode on more limited vocabularies. Some results have been obtained on the recognition of connected words for limited tasks, mostly in a speaker-dependent way [1,2].

Interesting results have also been achieved in researches on continuous speech in a speaker-dependent mode [3] or on highly constrained tasks in a speaker-independent mode [4].

Most of the systems proposed so far take advantage of the *redundancy* of the protocols they use. The most difficult and unsolved problems arise when tasks have little redundancy or when speaker-independence is required on complex tasks. Examples of such complex tasks are the recognition of letters and digits (isolated or connected) or of large vocabularies. In these cases, the use of a large variety of acoustic properties extracted with specific signal processing algorithms seem to be promising [5,6].

In many cases, acoustic property extraction is context-dependent. Context-dependencies impose precedence relations on the extraction processes. For example (see Demichelis et al. [7] for details), formant pseudo-loci are important cues for the recognition of plosive consonants in a Consonant Vowel (CV) or in a VC context, but their extraction can be performed only after having hypothesized the existence of a plosive sound before or after a vowel and having detected the voice onset interval and the formant loci of the vowel. Kopec [8] in a recent report on the speaker-independent recognition of unvoiced plosive consonants at the beginning of a syllable, has shown that the point of consonant release has to be detected before applying efficient recognition algorithms. Furthermore, acoustic properties of burst spectra, useful for the recognition of plosive consonants, can also be extracted with a specific algorithm in parallel with vowel formant loci.

Systems for extracting acoustic properties can be conceived in the framework of *distributed problem solving* in which acoustic properties are facts that drive computational processes to the achievement of goals consisting in hypothesis generation.

One motivation in favour of distributed systems is that they can be implemented with parallel computer architectures capable of reaching real-time performances that cannot be achieved by classical sequential computers.

Another important motivation is that if knowledge for problem solving is distributed into various sources, it is possible to update separately the knowledge of each source when new scientific results or new experience pertinent to it become available. Furthermore, different data structures and learning algorithms can be used for each source of knowledge. These algorithms can be, for example, syntactic or parametric.

A third motivation is that powerful control strategies can be used, for example, capable of scheduling the parallel execution of sensory procedures which extract new properties from the data when this is requested.

Based on these motivations, a system has been implemented for which the extraction of acoustic properties and generation of syllabic hypotheses is the result of a plurality of cooperating activities performed by many processes. This cooperation of computational activities has been conceived using the paradigm of an *Expert System Society* [9,10].

Each Expert is associated with a *Long Term Memory* (LTM) containing the specific Expert's knowledge and a *Short Term Memory* (STM) where data interpretations are written.

Experts are computing agents which execute reasoning programs using structural and procedural knowledge. The knowledge of each Expert is expressed by a set of *plans* some of which can be executed in parallel. Communication between cooperating tasks is performed by message passing. Some plans are executed as a result of a spontaneous data-driven activity. Other plans are executed on a request. In any case, each perceptual plan achieves a *goal* set by the system strategy. Plan definition will be given later on in this section.

The novelty of the knowledge based approach proposed here is that, descriptions of acoustic properties are extracted and related with phonetic feature interpretations using plans that are the result of a long learning effort in which a large number of patterns has been analyzed in order to extract invariant properties using knowledge about speech analysis, production and perception. For example, it is known that the burst spectrum of an alveolar plosive consonant should be compact but rules have to be inferred for detecting burst spectra and for characterizing compactness and statistics about their performances have to be collected.

Furthermore, rules may specify strategies for speech analysis that depend on incomplete feature hypotheses and model-driven predictions. These strategies involve variable-resolution spectral analysis (in the time and in the frequency domain), morphological analysis of the speech waveform, its loudness and pitch contour as well as the choice of a transfer function expression (selection of number of poles and zeros) for vocal tract modelling.

With this approach a phoneme PH_i is expressed by a set of phonetic features, i.e.

$$PH_i = (pf_{i1}, pf_{i2},...,pf_{ij},...,pf_{iJ}) \qquad (1)$$

Each phonetic feature pf_x is represented by a relation R_x with a set of acoustic properties ap_x, i.e.

$$pf_x = R_x (ap_{x1}, ap_{x2},....ap_{xk},....ap_{xK}) \qquad (2)$$

For example, the phoneme /p/ is represented as follows:

/p/ =

(nonsonorant-interrupted-consonant,tense,labial) =

(nit,labial).

The phonetic feature 'labial' in the context of 'nit' features is represented by the following relation R_k :

(relation R_k
(left-side
(feature (labial))
    (feature context (nit))
    (temporal context (followed-by front vowel)))
(right-side
(suprasegmental and time-domain properties)
(formant-transition properties)
(burst—spectra properties)))   (3)

The rule for 'labial' takes into account different types of *contextual dependencies*. One contextual dependency is represented by the other features that appear with 'labial' in a plosive phoneme. The other contextual dependences are represented by the class of phonemes that can follow or precede the plosive phoneme under consideration. Relations are used by *plans* executed by the Expert System.

A *plan* is a sequence of items. Each item may contain a *precondition expression* for applying rules of the type R_k, *operators* containing sensory procedures, for extracting the properties used by R_k and an *algorithm* for evaluating the evidence of the hypothesis generated by R_k. In practice, a plan is a sequence of operators. Each operator is assoicated with a precondition and an action.

Sequences of phonetic feature hypotheses generated under the control of rules can be compared with prototypical sequences automatically generated from the orthographic form of a sentence using *Dynamic Programming* (DP). The result of the comparisons can be used for recognition or for segmenting continuous speech into words and for automatically learning different feature sequences corresponding to different pronounciation of a word. Sequences of phonetic feature hypotheses can also be used for computing the likelihood that a Markov source generates them when a sentence is pronounced. Bahl et al. [3] have proposed algorithms for this purpose.

STRUCTURE OF THE EXPERT SOCIETY

Interpretations of the speech waveform are generated by an Expert Society implemented on a VAX 11/780. Its structure is shown in Fig. 1.

EXP_1 is the Acoustic Expert (AE). It has the task of sampling and quantizing the signal, performing various types of signal transformations, extracting and describing acoustic cues. The term *acoustic cues* will be used for indicating spectral or signal properties describing aspects that are relevant for hypothesizing phonetic features. Examples of acoustic cues are formant loci, characteristics of burst spectra like "compactness", peaks and valleys of signal energy.

EXP_1 can perform, for example, an analysis based on Linear Prediction Coefficients (LPC) for segments labelled with vocalic hypotheses in order to find formant loci capable of describing the place and manner of articulation. EXP_1 can also perform a broad-band spectral analysis based on a Fast Fourier Transformation (FFT) when hypotheses of nonsonorant-continuant sounds have been made. EXP_1, as any Expert, may perform "spontaneous" *data-driven* activities and *expectation-driven* activities based on requests issued by other Experts.

Requests and control messages are exchanged among Experts through the "message exchange network" shown in Fig. 1. Data, cues, descriptions and hypotheses are written by an Expert into its own Short Term Memory (STM). Only the Expert that owns the STM can write into it, but any Expert can read any STM.

EXP_2 is the Phonetic and Syllabic Expert (PSE). It translates descriptions of acoustic cues into *phonetic feature hypotheses*. These features describe the *manner* and the *place* of articulation of each segment of the spoken language. This translation may involve the extraction of new acoustic cues by asking EXP_1

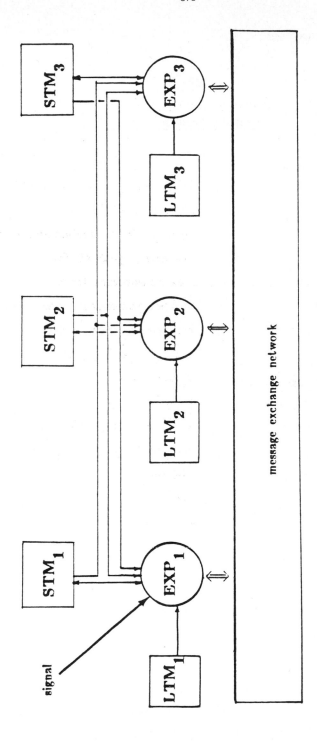

Fig. 1 - Structure of the Expert Society.

to execute sensory procedures.

Table I

Primary Acoustic Cues

Symbol	Attributes	Description
LPK	tb,te,m1,zx,	long peak of total energy (TE)
SPK	"	short peak of TE
MPK	"	peak of TE of medium duration
LOWP	"	low energy peak of TE
LNS	tb,te,zx	long nonsonorant tract
MNS	"	medium nonsonorant tract
LVI	tb,te,m1,zx	long vocalic tract adjacent to a LNS or a MNS in a TE peak
MVI	tb,te,m1,zx	medium vocalic tract adjacent to a LNS a MNS in a TE peak
LDD	emin,tb,te,zx	long deep dip of total energy
SDD	"	short deep dip of total energy
LMD	"	long dip of total energy with medium dep
SMD	"	short dip of total energy with medium de
LHD	"	long non-deep dip of total energy
SHD	"	short non-deep dip of total energy

Table II

Attribute description

Attribute	Description
tb	time of beginning
te	time of end
ml	maximum signal energy in the peak
emin	minimum total energy in a dip
zx	maximum zero-crossing density of the signal derivative in the tract

Table III

Primary Phonetic Features

Symbol	Primary Phonetic Feature
VF	Front vowel
VC	Central vowel
VB	Back vowel
VFC	Front or central vowel
VCB	Central or back vowel
VW	Uncertain vowel
NI	Nonsonorant interrupted consonant
NA	Nonsonorant affricate consonant
NC	Nonsonorant continuant consonant
SON	Sonorant consonant
SONV	A sonorant or the /v/ consonant
PP	Possible pause

There are some acoustic cues, like peaks and valleys of time evolutions of energies in fixed bands of the signal that can be extracted by context-independent algorithms. These acoustic cues will be called *Primary Acoustic Cues* (PAC) and the phonetic features related to them will be called *Primary Phonetic Features* (PPF). A definition of primary cues and features used in the system described in this paper is given in Tables I, II, III. These algorithms for extracting PACs generate descriptions of a time interval of the signal without being constrained by contextual information extracted from adjacent segments.

Examples of various types of PACs are shown in Fig. 2. The two curves in Fig. 2a represent the time evolution of the signal energy (---) and the zero-crossings counts (---) in successive intervals of 10 msec of the first derivative of the signal. The phrase is the sequence of letters and digits ECB3V. Fig. 2b shows the corresponding PAC description. Time unit is 0.01 sec. LONG and SHORT refer to the dip duration. DEEP, MEDIUM and HIGH refer to the height of the minimum energy in the dip with respect to background noise energy.

Other functions of EXP_2 are those of segmenting the speech signal into Pseudo Syllabic Segments (PSS) and of producing evidence measurements about phonetic hypotheses. The activity of generating PPFs is *data-driven*, the activities of extracting other phonetic features are *expectation-driven*. Expectations can be generated by a strategy inside EXP_2 or they can be requests transmitted by EXP_3.

EXP_3 is the Lexical Expert (LE) that generates lexical hypotheses based on prosodic features, phonetic hypotheses, syntactic and semantic constraints. As the design of the lexical component is still under development, it will be described in a future paper.

The behavior of the Expert Society can be summarized by the following algorithm written in Concurrent Pascal-like form.

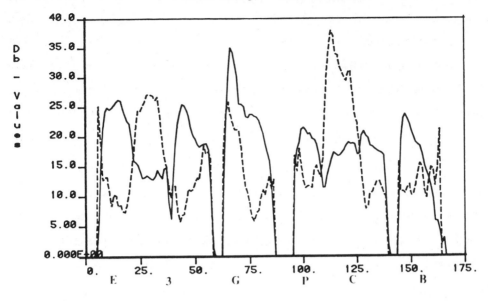

Fig. 2a   Total energy (—) and zero-crossing counts (---) divided by 6 of the pronounciation of the sequence E3G PCB (time references are in tenth of milliseconds)

PAC	t_b	t_e
LDD	1	7
LPK	8	28
LNS	29	38
SPK	39	41
LPK	42	60
SDD	61	65
MNS	66	72
LPK	73	89
LDD	90	98
LPK	99	111
SMD	112	113
LNS	114	126
LVI	127	141
SDD	142	145
LPK	146	168

Fig. 2b   Examples of PAC description for the sequence ECB3V

"Expert Society"

    <u>cobegin</u>

        acoustic-expert;

        phonetic-and-syllabic-expert;

        lexical-expert

    <u>coend</u>

A more detailed task-decomposition can be performed for each Expert. This decomposition can either describe the parallel execution of operations on different segments of the speech signal or the parallel application of different pieces of knowledge stored into an Expert's LTM to the same segment. Details of EXP_1 and EXP_2 are given in [17]. An implementation of EXP_3 is described in the following section.

A PLANNING SYSTEM FOR CONNECTED WORD RECOGNITION

Canadian postal codes consisting of three sequences of one letter and one digit were considered. For this experiment, one speaker pronounced in English 500 postal codes randomly generated by a computer program. A finite state automaton for each symbol to be hypothesized was automatically generated. This knowledge source contains acceptable degradations of sequences of PPFs for each symbol. Segmentation was performed using dynamic programming for aligning sequences of corrupted strings of PPFs with sequences of prototypes. Coarticulation effects were taken into account in generating sequences of prototypes. The set of automata contains 250 states. The automata were merged into a network. Arcs of the network were labelled with PPF symbols. Some nodes of the network were associated actions for generating letter or digit hypotheses. At the beginning there is only one pointer that points to the root of the network.

As EXP_1 and EXP_2 generate PPF hypotheses, pointers move along the network. When a pointer cannot move from a node it is suppressed. When a pointer reaches a node with an output action associated to it, it generates an arc in a chart phase and a new pointer to the root of the network is created. Generation of hypotheses were performed on another 200 sequences using a parsing algorithm that generates a chart-parse for each analyzed sequence.

The following results were obtained:

Average number of partially overlapping hypotheses:
Percent of times the right hypothesis was missed:
Average number of branches in the chart-parse:

Results seem to be encouraging even if a more extensive training has to be done on coarticulation instances especially for very difficult cases like I1O and Y1I.

In order to reduce the number of branches of the chart-parse to 1 and to eliminate partially overlapping hypotheses, special disambiguation plans have to be developed.

PSS representations in terms of PPFs are used for preselecting a disambiguation plan. As the recognition of connected letters and digits is an extremely difficult problem, it was decided to investigate one disambiguation plan at a time. A plan PE1 was developed for recognizing the letters and digits described by sequences of PPFs corresponding to consonant-vowel syllables with consonants described by PPFs of the following set :

$$C1 = (PP, NI, NA, NC)$$

and vowels described as VF or VFC. The purpose of PE1 is thus that of discriminating among the elements of the following E1 set:

$$E1 = (P,T,K,B,D,G,C,V,E,3).$$

For the sake of generality plan PE1 was conceived in such a way that it is executed whenever PSS of the type C1 VF or C1 VFC are detected and it does not take into account any syntactic (top-down) constraint.

The idea behind the conception of plan PE1 is that a redundant set of acoustic properties for each phonetic feature is extracted by a chain of operators such that *redundancy* can compensate for lack of knowledge in using the properties or for errors in property extraction. With the actual system, it is easy to add or delete properties and a program is provided for collecting statistics about properties.

As the main purpose of this paper is that of describing the system, the choice of strategies for using detected properties will be discussed in a future work.

An overview of plan PE1 for the recognition of the E1 set is shown in Fig. 3. The plan is subdivided into sub-plans (Pe11, Pe12, ... , PE15).

PE11   produces an envelope description by analyzing the signal amplitude before and after preemphasis. Envelope samples are obtained every msec by and the absolute minimum of the signal in a 3 msec interval. The envelope description is made by the following alphabet . (~ represents negation) :

EDA := SHORT—STEP(ST),
          LONG—STEP(LST),
          NO—STEP(NST),
          STEP WITH HIGH LOW FREQUENCY ENERGY(BZ),
          BURST—PEAK(BUR),
          POSSIBLE—BURST(PBU),
          NBZ=~BZ,
          NBU =~BUR,
          NPB=~PBU.

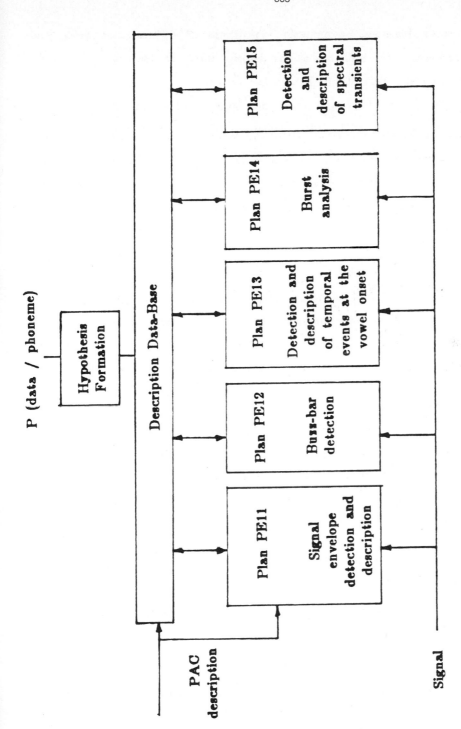

Fig. 3 Overview of plan PE1

PE12   detects a buzz-bar by analyzing the shape of FFT spectra before the voice onset. The alphabet of the descriptions it produces is :

BZA = {NOB,BU1,BU2,BU}

NOB means no buzz and the other three symbols describe degrees of buzz-bar evidence (BU1 : little evidence, BU : strong evidence)

PE13   analyzes temporal events at the voice onset. These events are related to voice onset time. They are :

D   :   the delay between the onset of low and high frequency energies,

ZQ   :   the duration of the largest zero-crossing interval of the signal at the onset,

ZR   :   the number of zero-crossing counts in the largest sequence of sucessive zero-crossing intervals with duration less than 0.5 msecs.

PE14 and PE15 perform respectively burst and formant transition analysis.

PE14 was not used in the experiment described in this sub-section.

PE15 was described in section V.

D is extracted and used according to a suggestion by Delgutte [15].

Preconditions for plan execution are learned with a general-purpose algorithm whose details are given in [13]. The following precondition expressions PRE_j $(1 \leq j \leq 5)$ have been inferred.

PRE1 = (LDD+SDD) * (LPK+SPK+MNS LPK)

PRE2 = LDD * (LPK+SPK)

PRE3 = (LDD+SDD) * (LPK+SPK)

PRE4 = SPK+BUR+PBU

PRE5 = LDD+LPK

Notice that '+' represents logical disjunction and A*B means that A preceeds B in time.

Expressions made of symbols extracted by subplans PE11 and PE12 and representing positive and negative information have been inferred for each PAC description and for each phoneme.

An example of such rules is given in the following :

E	:=	NBU	NBZ	NST	NBU	NPB
K	:=	NBU	NBZ	ST	BUR	PBU
B	:=	BU	BZ	ST	y	PBU

There are 96 of such rules in the plan corresponding to 24 sequences of PAC descriptions; y is a don't care condition.

A PAC description is used for indexing a set of rules that is matched against the input description produced by the plans. As rules and descriptions contain the same number of symbols, a similarity index S1 between a rule and a description is easily computed by the Algorithm Similarity that will be described in the following.

The parameters extracted by PE13 and PE15 are used in fuzzy relations. There is a fuzzy relation for each phoneme and the invocation of a fuzzy relation is conditioned by PAC, PE11 and PE12 descriptions. Fuzzy relations are conjunctions of disjunctions of fuzzy sets. A fuzzy relation computes another similarity index between phonemes and data extracted by subplans PE13 and PE15. A fuzzy relation can be seen as a conjunction of clauses. Each clause contains a disjunction of fuzzy sets defined over a parameter extracted by the planning system.

Fuzzy sets have been derived from a-priori probability distributions of parameters extracted by the plans. For each phoneme F, the membership function in the disjunction used in the relation of F is 1 in the interval in which 70% of the parameter values obtained by the pronounciation of F fall. The membership function then decreases toward zero and remains different from zero only in the interval in which fall 90% of the parameter values obtained by the

<u>Algorithm</u> Similarity (rule,description)

 <u>begin</u>

  c := 0;

  d := 0;

  <u>for</u> each i <u>do</u>

   <u>begin</u>

    <u>if</u> rule-symbol(i) matches

     description-symbol(i)

      <u>then</u> d := d + 1

      <u>else</u> d := d - 1;

    c := c + 1

   <u>end</u>

  similarity := $\dfrac{d + c}{2c}$

 <u>end</u>

pronounciation of F.

A similarity index S2 is computed by using the *max* operator for disjunctions and by summing the contributions of each clause and then dividing the sum by the number of clauses.

An example of clauses involved in fuzzy relations is the following :

E	:=	(short D)	(short ZQ)	(low ZR)
K	:=	(long D)	(short ZQ)	(high ZR)

where "short, long, high, low" are fuzzy sets. There are 43 such relations.

A-priori probabilities of the two similarity indices can be inferred from experiments for every phoneme. These probabilities can be supplied to the language model for further preprocessing or, they can be used in a Bayesian classifier. In the application described in this sub-section a simpler recognition strategy was used. It is described in the next sub-section.

Similarity measurements for the hypotheses generated by PE1 are averaged and the parameter S12 $= \frac{1}{2}$ (S1 + S2) is used for selecting the three candidates having the highest similarity with the data. Formant transitions are analyzed and a new similarity value S3 is computed for the three candidates. If the algorithm for analyzing formant transitions did not find plausible and unambiguous candidates, then S3 is not used, otherwise S3 is used for changing or confirming the ordering established based on S12.

S3 is used according to the rules of the following type. Horizontal formant patterns give a high S3 for E and bring E in the first position if E was second after B or P or third after both of them. There are five of such rules. Their details are omitted for the sake of brevity.

Bayesian classifiers or tree classifiers could be used for this approach. Nevertheless it was decided to experiment with a strategy in which expectation are built up using a-priori knowledge and parameter histograms. Candidates are then ranked according to how well they match expectations based on a voting criterion. Experimenting with other strategies is easy in this framework and will be done in the future. Various type of a-priori probabilities can be learned in this system and used in a recognition process based on an information theoretic approach as in [3].

Experiments on 1,000 samples of sequences of symbols in the E1 set pronounced by five male and five female speakers have given an error rate of 0.5% in *segmentation* without requiring any speaker adaptation.

Performances are shown in Fig. 4.

CONCLUSIONS

The following points summarize the most interesting aspects emerging from the experience described in this paper.

1) A distributed knowledge base system allows one to find a detailed

PRONOUNCED

	P	T	K	B	D	G	C	V	E	3
P	93		1	2					2	
T		92	4		2	2			1	1
K		2	94						1	
B	5			93	4			3	1	
D		2		2	90			2		
G		3		1	2	97		1		1
C						1	100			
V				2	2			92		1
E	2		1					1	95	
3		1						1		97

(Row label at left, read vertically: R E C O G N I Z E D)

INSERTION ERROR RATE: 0.5%
DELETION ERROR RATE : 0

Fig. 4 Performances on the recognition of the E1 set

explanation of the errors indicating along which directions the system should grow.

2) Speaker-dependent knowledge can be separated from the speaker-independent one.

3) Morphological features are useful ingredients for plan preconditions and for recognition.

4) Segmentation and recognition of place of articulation for vowels do not appear to be speaker dependent.

5) The good segmentation performances allows one to partition the difficulty of continuous speech recognition. Segmentation error are well explained.

6) Vectors of phonetic features can be mapped into symbols making this system similar to a vector quantizer where output can be used as an input to a recognizer based on DP-matching or on stochastic decoders.

7) Robust statistical algorithms can be used for clustering parameters used by plans. Clusters can be characterized by fuzzy sets.

8) Phonetic features are characterized by acoustic properties. Redundancies in this representation improve the recognition accuracy.

9) The research on connected letters and digits has potential applications in postal code recognition, in file directory access and in directory listing retrieval [16].

10) Planning can be systematically developed by listing the acoustic properties of phonetic features and the corresponding acoustic cues. Acoustic cues have to be described with a suitable formation (i.e. predicate calculus). Descriptions can be used for inductively learning rules [13].

ACKNOWLEDGEMENTS

This research was supported by the National Science and Engineering Research Council of Canada with grant no. A2439.

REFERENCES

1. G. R. Doddington and T. B. Schalk, "Speech Recognition, Turning Theory To Practice", IEEE Spectrum, Vol. 18, pp. 26-32, Sept. 1981.

2. L. R. Rabiner and S. L. Levinson, "Isolated and Connected Word Recognition. Theory and Selected Applications", IEEE Trans. on Communications, Vol. COM-29, No.5, pp. 621-659, 1981.

3. L. R. Bahl, F. Jelinek and R. L. Mercer, "A Maximum Likelihood Approach to Continuous Speech Recognition", IEEE Trans. on Pattern Analysis and Machine Intelligence, Vol. PAMI-5, No. 2, pp. 179-190, 1983.

4. L. R. Rabiner, J. G. Wilpon, A. M. Quinn and S. G. Terrace, "On the Application of Embedded Digit Training to Speaker Independent Connected Digit Recognition", IEEE Trans. on Acoustics, Speech and Signal Processing, Vol. ASSP-32, No. 2, pp. 272-279, 1984.

5. R. A. Cole, R. M. Stern, M. S. Phillips, S. M. Brill, A. P. Pilant and P. Specker, "Feature-Based Speaker-Independent Recognition of Isolated English Letters", IEEE Int. Conference on Acoustics, Speech and Signal Processing, Boston, Mass., pp. 731-734, 1983.

6. D. P. Huttenlocher and V. W. Zue, "A Model of Lexical Access Based on Partial Phonetic Information", IEEE Int. Conference on Acoustics, Speech and Signal Processing, San Diego, Cal., pp. 26.4.1-16.4.4, 1984.

7. P. Demichelis, R. De Mori, P. Laface and M. O'Kane, "Computer Recognition of Plosive Sounds Using Contextual Information", IEEE Trans. on Acoustics, Speech and Signal Processing, Vol. ASSP-31, pp. 359-377, 1983.

8. G. E. Kopec, "Voiceless Stop Consonant Identification Using LPC Spectra", IEEE Int. Conference on Acoustics, Speech and Signal Processing, San Diego, Cal., pp. 4211-4214, 1984.

9. M. Minsky, "A Framework for Representing Knowledge", In The Psychology of Computer Vision, Ed. by P. Winston, McGraw-Hill, 1975.

10. L. D. Erman, F. Hayes-Roth, V. R. Lesser and D. R. Reddy, "The HEARSAY-II Speech Understanding System. Integrating Knowledge to Resolve Uncertainty", Computing Surveys, Vol. 12, pp. 213-253, 1980.

11. R. De Mori, A. Giordana, P. Laface and L. Saitta, "An Expert System for Speech Decoding", Proc. AAAI Conference, Pittsburg, PA, pp. 107-110, 1982.

12. R. De Mori and P. Laface, "Use of Fuzzy Algorithms for Phonetic and Phonemic Labelling of Continuous Speech", IEEE Trans. on Pattern Analysis and Machine Intelligence, Vol. PAMI-2, pp. 136-148, 1980.

13. R. De Mori and M. Gilloux, "Inductive Learning of Phonetic Rules for Automatic Speech Recognition", Proc. CSCSI-84, London, Ont., pp. 103-105, 1984.

14. K. C. You and K. S. Fu, "A Syntactic Approach to Shape Recognition Using Attributed Grammars", IEEE Trans. on System, Man and Cybernetics SMC-9, pp. 334-345, 1979.

15. B. Delgutte, "Some Correlates of Phonetic Distinctions at the Level of the Auditory Nerve", in The Representation of Speech in the Peripheral Auditory System, Ed. by R. Carlson and B. Granstrom, Elsevier Biomedical, Amsterdam, pp. 131-149, 1982.

16. L. R. Rabiner, J. G. Wilpon and S. G. Terrace, "A Directory Listing Retrieval System Based on Connected Letter Recognition", IEEE Int. Conference on Acoustics, Speech and Signal Processing, San Diego, Cal., pp. 3541-3544, 1984.

17. R. De Mori, P. Laface, Y. F. Mong, "Parallel Algorithms for Syllable Recognition in continuous Speech IEEE Transctions on Pattern Analysis and Machine Intelligence. In press.

DEMISYLLABLES AS PROCESSING UNITS FOR AUTOMATIC SPEECH RECOGNITION AND LEXICAL ACCESS

G. Ruske
Division of Data Processing
Technical University of Munich
Federal Republic of Germany

1. INTRODUCTION

This paper describes a number of experimental investigations into syllable-based acoustic-phonetic analysis of German words; these methods can be used as a basic processing stage in a system for automatic speech recognition as well as for speech understanding. In this connection the importance of the syllable in speech processing by man and machine will first be discussed. Then several methods and experiments are presented involving segmentation into syllables and recognition of vowels and consonant clusters, as well as two methods for lexical access and lexical search using these units. The search in the lexicon is necessary in order to find the word in a word-list corresponding to the units recognized, or alternatively to determine the most similar word. The most salient feature of this system is that so-called demisyllables are used as the processing units.

A fundamental problem faced by every system is that of defining suitable segments in the speech signal which can be used for the analysis algorithms of the spoken utterance. Particularly when processing continuous speech and large vocabularies, some kind of segmentation is necessary, whether explicitly or implicitly. The introduction of smaller subword-units reduces the amount of training data and comes nearer to a phonetic description of the spoken utterance.

NATO ASI Series, Vol. F16
New Systems and Architectures for Automatic Speech
Recognition and Synthesis. Edited by R. De Mori and C. Y. Suen
© Springer-Verlag Berlin Heidelberg 1985

It could be shown in previous experiments [1] that the use of smaller units in fact results in better performance than whole-word recognition when the vocabulary size increases.

If the segmentation is carried out explicitly in the signal domain or its parametric representation, the segmentation procedure is required to provide segments which on the one hand are readily found and isolated in the speech signal, and which on the other hand can be dealt with as independently of each other as possible. It is important to realize that the syntactic and semantic interpretation of a sentence can be carried out to best advantage at word level, since words fulfill grammatical functions as well as conveying the meaning. Seen in this light, it is thus advantageous at the first stage to aim to recognize words, or to form hypotheses about words. However, the explicit separation of words in continuous speech is an impossible task since words are linked and coarticulated with one another in much the same way as syllables. This leads immediately to the possibility of regarding syllables, and not words, as the elements with the greatest temporal extent from which every spoken utterance can be built up.

2. THE ROLE OF THE SYLLABLE IN SPEECH PROCESSING

In fact, there are a number of good reasons for regarding the syllable as the basic unit in speech processing. Evidence can be found from the areas of

— speech production (articulation)
— speech perception
— technical realizability of the segmentation

In the following, each of these areas will be discussed briefly in turn. The basic gesture performed in speaking consists of a repeated opening and closing, or constriction, of the vocal tract. This is what lies behind the definition of the spoken syllable [2]. This basic speech gesture is responsible among other things for increased loudness within the syllable nucleus, a typical pitch contour, and a typical development in the quality of the speech sounds; this quality contour is most clear in the middle of the syllable. Finally, this production mechanism causes the strong coarticulatory effects, and thus the interdependency of the acoustic cues within the initial and final parts of the syllable.

Speech perception must also face the question of what units can be assumed. A variety of experiments indicate that consonants and vowels are not perceived independently of one another. For instance, experiments with consonant-vowel-consonant sequences (CVC) showed that both consonant and vowel information in a syllable is exploited to identify the vowel [3]. Such findings provide grounds for believing that consonants and vowels are not analyzed separately from each other, and that perception operates on units having at least the extent of a syllable. Of crucial importance is the practical realizability of the segmentation procedure in a speech recognition system if we intend to perform an explicit segmentation. Two facts facilitate the localization of syllable nuclei quite considerably: Firstly, a maximum in the sound pressure level, or to be more precise, in the psycho-acoustically defined 'loudness' can be expected [4,5,6]; secondly, the vocalic part of the syllable nucleus can be identified quite readily from the spectral distribution. These two procedures can be combined to produce a simple syllable detector; further details will be presented below. In contrast, the precise separation of consecutive syllables presents some problems. However, relative minima in the loudness contour can be regarded as suitable candidates for syllable boundaries [4,6].

3. DEMISYLLABLES AS PROCESSING UNITS

Since the inventory of syllables is very large, it seems sensible to divide every syllable into two *demisyllables*, namely into one extending from syllable boundary to syllable nucleus, and into one extending from syllable nucleus to the next syllable boundary, see fig. 1. The German language possesses more than 1000 initial and final demisyllables each. Demisyllable segments retain practically

Segmentation:

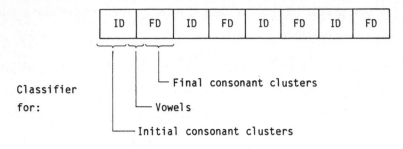

Fig. 1   Principle of demisyllable segmentation and recognition (ID = initial demisyllable; FD = final demisyllable).

all the advantages of complete syllables, are easy to locate, and include the strongest coarticulatory effects; in comparison, coarticulation between adjacent demisyllables is fairly weak.

A dramatic reduction in the number of classes can be achieved if the internal structure of a demisyllable is taken into account: Each demisyllable contains a part of the vowel forming the syllable nucleus as well as a *consonant cluster*, which can consist of any sequence of consonants permitted in syllable-initial or syllable-final position. It is thus appropriate to incorporate different classifiers, namely one each for the vocalic part forming the syllable nucleus, for the consonantal part at the beginning of the syllable, and for the consonantal part at the end of the syllable [4,6]. The decision units (classes) are thus defined to be vowels and consonant clusters. A precise separation of vocalic and consonantal parts is not absolutely essential for this purpose. It is sufficient for the part of interest to be emphasized and fed to the appropriate classifier.

In German, only about 47 initial consonant clusters occur [6,7], see fig. 2a. If extremely rare combinations (such as /dv/) and foreign words are included, the size of this inventory increases somewhat of course, but still remains within strict limits.

The number of final consonant clusters is significantly larger since a number of inflections can be appended. As depicted in fig. 2b, the inventory can amount to a maximum of 159 final consonant clusters, with many occurring very rarely indeed. If the vocabulary is limited to 8000 words then 103 final consonant clusters are enough, and with a vocabulary consisting of the 1001 most frequent German words this number drops to only 50 final consonant clusters [7]. With the consonant cluster inventory just described plus a maximum of 20 vowels (long vowels, short vowels, and diphthongs) it is possible to represent an almost unlimited German vocabulary, for both isolated words and continuous speech.

4. EXPERIMENTS WITH A SYLLABLE-BASED SPEECH RECOGNITION SYSTEM

A series of basic experiments with a syllable-based speech recognition system is described below; the system consists of the following stages: segmentation of individual words into demisyllables, classification of consonant clusters and vowels, and the subsequent correction of the recognition results with a phonetic lexicon.

Segmentation: Syllable-based segmentation is made easier if auditorily based pre-processing of the speech wave is carried out. Psycho-acoustic investigations have shown that the vowels in the syllable nucleus are normally experienced as being noticeably louder than their neighbouring consonants. In the following experiments a functional model of loudness sensation was thus implemented [8]. The analysis starts from a decomposition of the audible frequency range into 24 'critical bands' [9]. In each band (channel of a filter bank) the 'specific' loudness

(a)

| 'p t k b d g h f z ʃ m n l r v j |
| ʃpr pr ʃtr tr kr br dr gr pfr fr ʃr |
| ʃpl pl kl bl gl pfl fl ʃl ʃm ʃn kn gn |
| tsv ʃv kv   ʃp ʃt pf ts |

(b)

r l m n ŋ p t k f s ʃ ç x –	
rl rm rn rp rf rt rʃ rk rç	
lm ln lp lf lt lʃ lk lç	usually also with suffixes -s -t -st -ts
ŋk nf nʃ nç mp mpf mʃ	
pf pʃ ft tʃ	

Fig. 2   Inventory of German initial consonant clusters (a), and final consonant clusters (b).

component $N_\nu(t)$ is calculated. We use 22 channels covering the range from 50 Hz to 8.5 kHz. The (total) loudness $N(t)$ is formed from the sum of the specific loudness components over all 22 channels. In addition, a 'modified' loudness function $N_m(t)$ is derived as the difference between a lower (channels 3 to 15) and a higher (channels 20 to 22) frequency range. This modified loudness function is then smoothed by a low-pass filter with a cut-off frequency of about 10 Hz. Taken together with a rough vowel/non-vowel classification and a lower bound for the overall loudness it is then possible to infer the locations of the syllable nuclei directly from the maxima in the function $N_m(t)$. Fig. 3 shows as an example the German word 'Spracherkennung'; here the syllable nuclei (vowels) /a:/, /ɛ/, /ɛ/ and /u/ were picked out in this way. The maximum at /ʃ/ was

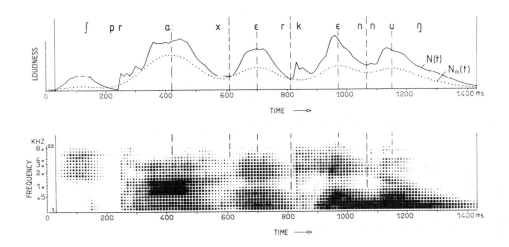

Fig. 3   Segmentation of the German word 'Spracherkennung' using the modified loudness function $N_m(t)$ and the (total) loudness $N(t)$.

rejected since it did not fulfill the conditions for a vowel. The minima in the loudness contour $N(t)$ show possible positions for the syllable boundaries. The experiments with a vocabulary of 1001 words spoken in isolation produced error rates of about 4% in the correct identification of the syllable nuclei.

Classification of consonant clusters and vowels: When classifying consonant clusters we are faced with the problem that the vocalic part must be suppressed or masked out as far as possible. The problem was solved in the following way. Each demisyllable segment covers a series of loudness spectra, which are measured at 10 ms intervals, the segments being of varying lengths. Using a so-called 'dynamic interpolation' procedure [4,6], this series is converted into a series with a fixed number of loudness spectra. Experiments show that conversion by interpolation into 12 spectra is sufficient. Suppression of the vocalic part is then achieved by dropping 3 interpolated spectra on the vocalic side; the 9 remaining spectra now represent the actual pattern for the consonant cluster. Classification of the interpolated patterns of the consonant clusters was carried out with the help of a geometrical distance measurement by using the 1-nearest-neighbour rule and a city-block metric. Previous experiments with German consonant clusters had resulted in recognition scores for initial consonant clusters in the order of 75% on average [6]; the average recognition scores for final consonant clusters amounted to 85%. Overall these results show that good recognition accuracy can be achieved using the concept of consonant cluster recognition and classification by template matching.

Classification of consonant clusters using feature vectors: Since knowledge about the phonetic structure could considerably reduce the dimensionality of the consonant cluster templates a second method was developed starting from a description of the relevant acoustic events within each demisyllable segment [10]. In a first step those spectral and temporal features or 'cues' are evaluated which can be objectively measured in the signal. The cues describe: the 'loci' of the first 3 formants of the syllable vowel, the formant transitions, formant-like 'links' for nasals and liquids, duration and spectral distribution of bursts and fricative noise ('turbulences'), pauses and the presence of voicing during pauses or turbulences.

A main problem is the dependency of most of the features on phonetic context; in this approach the context dependencies are taken into consideration by collecting the results of feature extraction within each demisyllable segment. This enables the contextual dependencies between the acoustic features to be determined statistically from representative speech material. The feature vector for an initial consonant cluster as well as for a final consonant cluster have a fixed number of components. In syllable-initial position 1 nasal, liquid or glide, and up to 2 fricatives or plosives are possible; in syllable-final position the maximum number of plosives or fricatives in the test speech material was 3.

Therefore, initial consonant clusters are completely described by 24 feature components and final consonant clusters by 31 components [10].

Feature extraction starts from a voiced/unvoiced/silence-decision for each spectral frame. Additionally, formant tracking is performed within voiced parts. Acoustic parameters are then derived from the energy in selected frequency bands, which allow a gross characterization of the spectral shape. Based on these parameters, a set of rules has been established in order to detect voiced and unvoiced turbulences and bursts, pauses, and liquid and nasal links. After detection the individual features are characterized by gross measurements of their spectral and temporal distribution (e.g. center of gravity as well as upper and lower cut-off frequency for turbulences, and the frequency values of spectral peaks for links) and used as components of the common demisyllable feature vector.

Classification of the feature vectors was based on Euclidean distance measurements within the feature space. For this purpose a special 'average normalized distance' was defined which allows the comparison of all feature vectors even if they differ quite considerably as to their current composition. For comparison, the same speech material was processed by a template matching method using a very fine temporal and spectral resolution; in this experiment 22 spectra with all 24 loudness components were used for each template giving 528 components altogether. The recognition results showed that the recognition scores for the feature representations were about 5-7% lower as compared to the template matching approach [10]. But when comparing both methods it has to be borne in mind that the feature vector for a consonant cluster has only 24 or 31 components whereas a corresponding template constructed from a series of consecutive spectra needs on average more than 500 components which have to be time normalized and compared by appropriate distance measurements. Therefore the two methods differ drastically in storage requirements and computation time. Thus feature components can in fact be seen as an efficient way of representing the units.

5. SYLLABLE-BASED SEARCH IN THE LEXICON

The quality of the search in the lexicon is decisively important for the performance of a recognition system. The effectiveness of the correction of wrongly recognized words is largely determined by the extent to which a-priori knowledge about the distribution of the classifier's wrong decisions can be utilized. The experiments to be described next will contrast two procedures, namely:

a)   The words are stored in the lexicon in phonetic transcription in groups of consonant clusters and vowels (comparison based on phonetic symbols);

b)   The individual demisyllables are given a spectral representation ('prototypes') both in the lexicon and at the output of the classifier.

In fig. 4a and 4b the two methods are contrasted. In the first procedure (fig. 4a), the similarity between recognition output and lexical entry is measured by using alternatives from a confusion matrix containing the a-posteriori probabilities; these typical confusions have been obtained in a training phase. The confusion matrices are set up separately for initial consonant clusters, final consonant clusters and vowels; the lexical entries are in phonetic transcription.

In the second procedure (fig. 4b), a geometric distance measurement using spectral representations ('prototypes') is carried out. The prototypes each consist of several consecutive loudness spectra from a complete demisyllable, and thus include the consonant cluster and the vowel up to the middle of the syllable [11]. The test material consisted of the 1001 most frequent German words and were spoken by one speaker three times.

The reference patterns for the classification of the consonant clusters and vowels were obtained from a training set. The classification was carried out using a distance measurement (1-NN rule with a city block metric). For each classified, unknown word the result is a sequence of labels (phonetic symbols) for initial consonant clusters, vowels and final consonant clusters. In this primary classification stage the average recognition rate for complete words amounted to

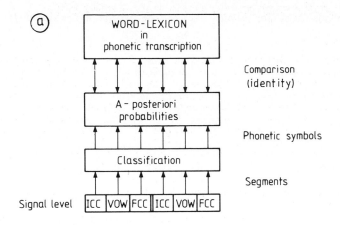

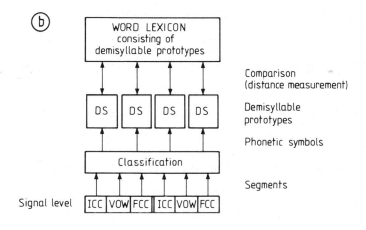

Fig. 4   Principle of the lexical search, (a) using a-posteriori probabilities and (b) using spectral prototypes; (ICC=initial consonant cluster, FCC=final consonant cluster, VOW=Vowel, DS=demisyllable).

50.1%; this means that for about half of the words every label in the complete word was correct.

Lexical search with a-posteriori probabilities: The confusion matrices were etablished by observing the confusions made by the classifier. If the given ('true') class membership of a unit is denoted by c, and the recognition result by k, the classification of a large sample of these units provides an estimate for the conditional probability p(k|c). This result can be used to determine the a-posteriori probability of c for a given recognition result k:

$$p(c|k) = p(k|c) \cdot p(c)/p(k),$$

with

p(c) and p(k) : A-priori probabilities

p(k|c) : Conditional probabilites

(decisions of the classifier).

Let us consider now as an example the search for a monosyllabic word consisting of the 3 units: $C = \{c_1, c_2, c_3\}$. The classification output is given by: $K = \{k_1, k_2, k_3\}$. The lexical search has to find the word possessing the greatest overall a-posteriori probability for this particular recognition result. The a-posteriori probability for the word C of the lexicon when K was recognized, is expressed as:

$$p(C|K) = p(c_1, c_2, c_3 | k_1, k_2, k_3) .$$

Assuming statistical independence of the three classification results we obtain the following expression:

$$p(K|C) = p(k_1, k_2, k_3 | c_1, c_2, c_3) = p(k_1|c_1) \cdot p(k_2|c_2) \cdot p(k_3|c_3) .$$

Using Bayes' formula we get:

$$p(c_1,c_2,c_3|k_1,k_2,k_3) = \frac{p(k_1,k_2,k_3|c_1,c_2,c_3) \cdot p(c_1,c_2,c_3)}{p(k_1,k_2,k_3)}$$

$$= \frac{p(k_1|c_1) \cdot p(k_2|c_2) \cdot p(k_3|c_3) \cdot p(c_1,c_2,c_3)}{p(k_1,k_2,k_3)}$$

$$= \frac{p(c_1|k_1)p(c_2|k_2)p(c_3|k_3) \cdot p(k_1)p(k_2)p(k_3) \cdot p(c_1,c_2,c_3)}{p(c_1)p(c_2)p(c_3) \cdot p(k_1,k_2,k_3)}$$

The term $p(k_1,k_2,k_3)$ in the denominator and the product $p(k_1)p(k_2)p(k_3)$ in the numerator can be disregarded for the following considerations since they remain constant in the search. The expresion $p(c_1,c_2,c_3) = p(C)$ is the probability of occurrence of word C in the lexicon. Assuming the same probability of occurrence for all M words in the lexicon this term can also be left out for the search. In addition, it may be admissible to assume that the probabilities of occurrence of the classes $p(c_1)$, $p(c_2)$ and $p(c_3)$ in the lexicon are equally distributed, so that no class is preferred; in this case the lexical search becomes independent of the current distribution of the classes in the lexicon.

Let the j-th word in the lexicon be designated by $C_j = \{c_{1j}, c_{2j}, c_{3j}\}$. Based on the conditions outlined above, the lexical search chooses the word C_i for which the product of the a-posteriori probabilities is greatest:

$$\{k_1,k_2,k_3\} \epsilon C_i, \text{ if } p(c_{1i}|k_1)p(c_{2i}|k_2)p(c_{3i}|k_3) > p(c_{1j}|k_1)p(c_{2j}|k_2)p(c_{3j}|k_3)$$

for j = 1...M, i ≠ j ; M = Number of words in the lexicon

This expression means that the maximum of the products for all words in the lexicon must be determined. To this end, the individual classification results k_1, k_2 and k_3 are expanded to include all those 'alternatives' offered by the confusion matrices for these recognized units. The list of alternatives contains all those words to which an inference would be possible. Fig. 5 shows as an example the list of alternatives for the recognition result /' ai ls/. We see that several words in the lexicon will fit in here, e.g. 'als' (/'als/), 'teils' (/tails/),

RECOGNITION RESULT	ˈ	aɪ	ls

ALTERNATIVES FROM CONFUSION MATRICES						
ˈ	94.0	aɪ	73.0	ls	83.0
p	1.4	ə	9.0	ts	6.0
t	1.2	ɐ	7.0	s	6.0
b	1.1	ɛ	6.5	nts	5.0
d	.9	a:	1.6		
g	.8	e:	1.2		
fr	.6	ɔʏ	.9		
		ɛ:	.7		
	[%]		[%]		[%]

Fig. 5   Expansion of the recognition result /ˈ ai ls/ by using alternatives from confusion matrices together with their a-posteriori probabilities.

'Tanz' (/tants/) etc. Every word in the lexicon must now be compared with this list of alternatives to check for a match. The recognized word will be the one with the highest joint probability calculated from the product of the individual a-posteriori probabilities in the columns of this table.

In the present experiment with the 1001 word vocabulary a total recognition score of about 89.0% was achieved, see fig. 6a. The main problem resides in the determination of sufficiently precise confusion matrices and the corresponding a-posteriori probabilities.

Lexical search with spectral representations: When spectral prototypes are used it is also desirable for the confusions of the preceding classification to be represented as well as possible during the lexical search in order to make the best correction. This can be realized if the prototypes are represented in a feature space similar to the one underlying the classification. Representation in the form of demisyllable prototypes is particularly simple. A similar approach using

a)

EXPERIMENT 1 (Lexical search with phonetic symbols):

— Total recognition score (1001 words):   89.0%

b)

EXPERIMENT 2 (Lexical search with spectral prototypes):

— Total recognition score (1001 words):   90.3%

Number of components:	22	12	6	3
10	90.3	90.3	89.9	85.3
Number of 5	90.2	90.3	89.9	85.1
spectra 2	90.0	90.1	89.5	84.1

Fig. 6   (a) Recognition score of experiment 1 and (b) recognition scores of experiment 2 as a function of the temporal and spectral resolution of demisyllable prototypes for lexical search (in %).

diphone prototypes has already been proposed for English [12].

An example for the generation of demisyllable prototypes is depicted in fig. 7; the demisyllable segmentation procedure and dynamic interpolation is applied to each reference word.   After that, the prototypes were constructed by averaging all demisyllables with the same label from the 2x1001 words of the training set.   To handle the lexicon mentioned here about 200 prototypes each are required for the initial and final demisyllables.   In the first trial each demisyllable prototype (in

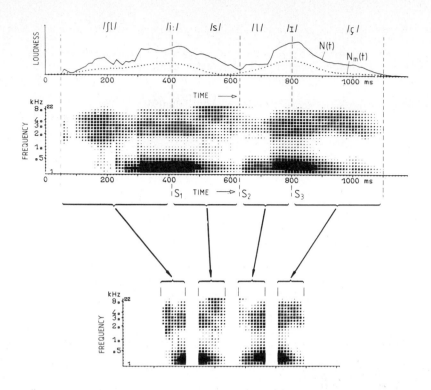

Fig. 7   Generation of demisyllable prototypes from the German word 'schließlich'.

the lexicon and the classification result) was represented by 10 spectra with 22 components.   The total recognition rate was 90.3%, see fig. 6b.

It is not possible to improve the performance further by increasing the resolution of the prototypes, and this thus represents an upper bound.   On the other hand, the table in fig. 6b shows that the spectral and temporal resolution of the prototypes can be reduced considerably without significant deterioration in correction performance.   Even when the demisyllable prototypes were reduced to 2 spectra with six components, an overall recognition rate of 89.5% was still achieved [11].   In the present experiment lexical search with spectral representations thus attained practically the same recognition performance as a lexical search based on a-posteriori probabilities; the spectral representation method is even slightly superior as long as extremely low resolution in the prototypes is avoided. When judging the performance of the correction stage it must always be borne in mind that uncorrectable confusions and segmentation errors mean that the highest recognition result actually obtainable was 94.7%.

6. OUTLOOK

It is interesting to compare this 2-stage approach with whole-word recognition methods which can be considered as 1-stage methods. In other experiments we were able to show that the 2-stage method using a demisyllable segmentation and classification and a lexical correction stage, yielded better recognition scores when compared with whole-word recognition /1/. Further, it is an important advantage of the two-stage method that the recognition task is split up into two individual tasks, each of which can be realized with a substantially smaller number of components. The demisyllable segments thus consist of no more than 220 components (i.e. 10 spectra with 22 channels). The number of classes in the 1001-word list used here does not rise above an average of 41 consonant clusters and 19 vowels (with diphthongs); the representatives in the lexicon may consist of as few as 12 components (2 spectra with 6 channels). Within this feature space the classification can be realized easily using straightforward procedures. In contrast, for whole-word recognition a high-dimensional space is required in which the classification is to be performed.

The experiments discussed here were based on the speech material of one speaker, and were carried out with words spoken in isolation. The applicability of the demisyllable concept to the recognition of continuous speech has however already been demonstrated in some preliminary experiments [13]; under these conditions the number of syllable segmentation errors increases slightly.

Demisyllables have proven to be an appropriate choice of unit for the different processing stages. In sentence recognition syllable-based segmentation also has advantages for the subsequent processing stages. Pilot experiments have shown that it is advantageous to take well identified syllables as anchor points when generating hypotheses about words; on average, the first syllable only allows 40 words out of 1001 to be picked out as hypotheses. On this level it is possible to employ procedures which allow wrongly indicated syllables to be skipped or missing syllables to be inserted. For example, the comparison of the word hypotheses can be carried out back on the parametric level, this time without segmentation.

ACKNOWLEDGEMENTS

This research was supported by the 'Deutsche Forschungsgemeinschaft' (DFG).

REFERENCES

1. G. Ruske and T. Schotola, "The efficiency of demisyllable segmentation in the recognition of spoken words," IEEE Int. on Acoustics, Speech and Signal Processing, Atlanta, 971-974, 1981.
2. G. Hammarström, "Linguistische Einheiten im Rahmen der modernen Sprachwissenschaft," in *Kommunkation und Kybernetik in Einzeldarstellungen*, (H. Wolter and W. D. Keidel eds.), Volume 5, Springer-Verlag, 1966.
3. P. Mermelstein, "On the relationship between vowel and consonant identification when cued by the same acoustic information," Percept. Psychophys. 23, 331-336, 1978.
4. G. Ruske and T. Schotola, "An approach to speech recognition using syllabic decision units," IEEE Int. Conf. on Acoustics, Speech and Signal Procesing, Tulsa, 722-725, 1978.
5. M. J. Hunt, M. Lennig and P. Mermelstein, "Experiments in syllable-based recognition of continuous speech," IEEE Int. Conf. on Acoustics, Speech and Signal Processing, Denver, 880-883, 1980.
6. G. Ruske, "Auditory perception and its application to computer analysis of speech," in *Computer Analysis and Perception, Vol. II, Auditory Signals* (C. Y. Suen and R. De Mori, eds.), CRC-Press, Boca Raton, Florida, 1-42, 1982.
7. T. Schotola, "On the use of demisyllables in automatic word recognition," Speech Communication 3, North-Holland Publ., 63-87, 1984.
8. E. Zwicker, E. Terhardt and E. Paulus, "Automatic speech recognition using psychoacoustic models," JASA 65, 487-498, 1979.

9. E. Zwicker, "Subdivision of the audible frequency range into critical bands (Frequenzgruppen)", JASA 33, 248, 1961.

10. G. Ruske, "On the usage of demisyllables in automatic speech recognition," in *SIGNAL PROCESSING II: Theoreies and Applications*, H. W. Schüßler (Ed.), Elsvier Science Publishers B. V. (North-Holland), 419-422, 1983.

11. W. Schiele, "Korrektur falsch klassifizierter Halbsilben in einem Worterkennungssystem durch geometrische Abstandsmessungen", Report of the Division of Data Processing, Technical University of Munich, Germany, 1981.

12. D. H. Klatt, "Speech perception: A model of acoustic-phonetic analysis and lexical access," Journal of Phonetics 7, 279-312, 1979.

13. H.-J. Geywitz, "Automatische Erkennung fließender Sprache mit silbenorientierten Einheiten", Doctoral thesis, Division of Data Processing, Technical University of Munich, Germany, 1984.

DETECTION AND RECOGNITION OF NASAL CONSONANTS IN CONTINUOUS SPEECH - PRELIMINARY RESULTS

R. Gubrynowicz

L. Le Guennec

G. Mercier

Centre National d'Etudes des Telecommunications

22301 Lannion, France

1. INTRODUCTION

The problem of the detection, recognition or perception of nasal consonants in continuous speech signals is not frequently treated in the literature. Among the most significant works on this subject should be mentioned the classical ones such as [5,9,4] or more recently [11,3,2]. The principal reason that there are relatively few papers devoted to this subject is, perhaps, its complexity. In fact, from the acoustical point of view, the spectral structure of nasal consonants is rather complicated because their spectral envelope is formed not only by the resonants of the pharyngeal and nasal cavities but also by the anti-resonants of the oral cavity, which is closed during the articulation of nasals.

In general, the variations of resonants frequencies are not very great and are independent of the place of articulation. Only the variation of antiresonant frequencies are strictly connected with changes of articulatory parameters, which,

---

R. Gubrynowicz is also invited professor at Institut de Phonétique, Université de Provence, Aix-en-Provence, France.

NATO ASI Series, Vol. F16
New Systems and Architectures for Automatic Speech
Recognition and Synthesis. Edited by R. De Mori and C. Y. Suen
© Springer-Verlag Berlin Heidelberg 1985

in the first approximation, determine the length of the oral cavity branching the pharyngeal and nasal parts of the vocal tract. It is very often that the first anti-resonant (whose frequency is, for example for /m/, around 1,2 kHZ) involves the diminution or even total annihilation of the second formant which frequently is in the proximity of this anti-resonant. In addition, the individual voice characteristics of speaker can have a significant influence on the final form of the nasal consonant spectrum. In fact, the anatomical structure of nasal cavities varies from one speaker to the other, so it is difficult to identify the nasal consonant from their static acoustic properties determined mainly by the transfer function of pharyngo-nasal part of the vocal tract. The inadequacy of the approach based only on static parameters of speech is particularly evident in recognition systems, especially in those which are based only on general description of spectral properties as is the case with the vocoder, for example.

The purpose of our paper is to present a general scheme of the procedure for detecting and, in some particular conditions, for recognition of three French nasal consonants /m, n, gn/ spoken in continuous speech. This procedure is designed for the speech understanding system described in [8].

2. ARTICULATORY AND ACOUSTIC PROPERTIES OF NASAL CONSONANTS

In French, three nasal consonants are essentially distinguished, namely bilabial /m/, alveo-dental /n/ and palatal /gn/. The velar /gn/ is present only in words of English origin as it is in the case of the word "parking" (car-park). These consonants belong to the class of interrupted ones, for which the airflow in the oral cavity is stopped by closing lips or by forming lingual obstruction (with tongue blade or another part of the tongue body). This attribute is also characteristic of nasal consonants as a constant cue. In general, the articulatory properties of the same consonant spoken in a stream of sounds are modified by the context. In the case of nasals, the most important modifications are in the horizontal plane, especially concerning the place of articulation. But there are also some indications that alterations of the aperture in vertical plane are possible. The general rule, well established, says that the greater the important difference between the articulation forms of adjacent sounds, the more considerable is the influence of the following (or in specific cases, of the preceding) sound segment. In the case of nasals which are very sensitive to context. This influence is most visible for the nasal /n/, for example, pronounced in the vicinity of sounds with posterior place of articulation than of those with a more central configuration of the tongue body. Similarly, the palatal /gn/ as in the french word "agneau" (lamb) the place of articulation is more displaced to central region of the vocal tract in the vicinity of frontal sounds than for the others.

From an articulatory point of view, the basic attribute of nasals is the closing of the oral cavity and the opening of the velo-pharyngeal part which allows air to flow through nasal cavity. On the other hand, between pharyngo-nasal and oral cavities we observe a coupling which varies with the velum position and oral cavity configuration.

These articulatory properties result, in the acoustic domain, in the apparition of a very low first formant, typically between 200-300 Hz for adult's voices. Some acoustical attributes of nasals are independent of the adjacent vowel and are marked by a sharp change of total energy level at the release of the nasal segment, but this discontinuity is not very great (about 4 dB). The spectral changes are also rather sharp and generally, cover the total frequencies so that the presence of the nasal in sounds the stream is often easy to discriminate by eye on sonagrams, with one exception perhaps for the liquid /l/ which is frequently confused with this category of speech sounds. The spectral variations at the release of the nasal segment (in CV syllables) can be used for the distinction of its place of articulation, as suggested by [1] who demonstrated that the place of articulation can be characterized by the spectral energy distribution at the consonant release which in the case of alveolars is tilted towards high frequencies and for labials is either flat or else tilted towards lower frequencies. This tendency is visible on Figures 1 and 2 with sonagrams of bisyllabic

616

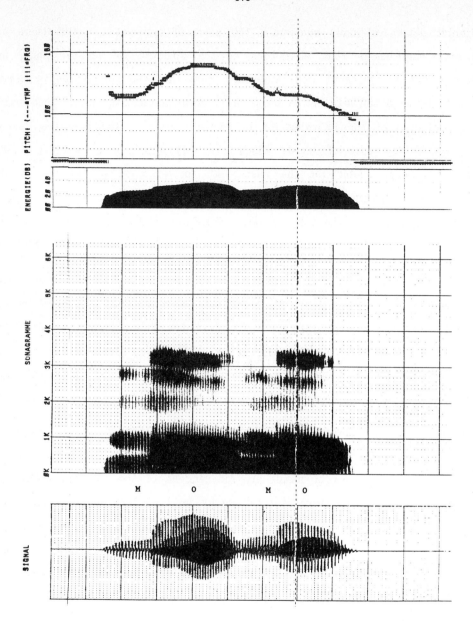

Fig. 1 Sonagram of the bisyllabic sequence /momo/ spoken in isolation by male speaker.

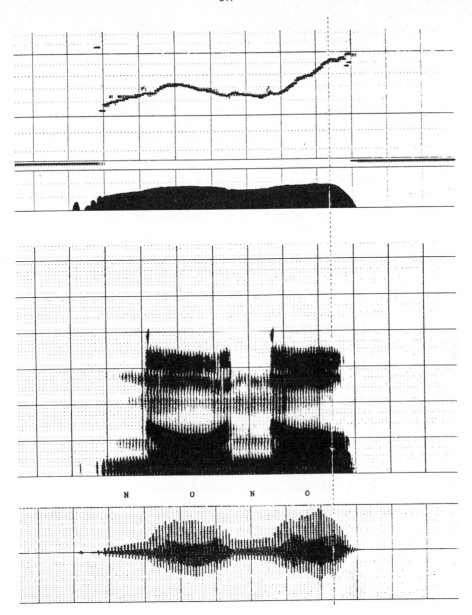

Fig. 2   Sonagram of the bisyllabic sequence /nono/ spoken in isolation by the same as in Fig. 1 speaker.

sequences /momo/ and /nono/ pronounced in isolation by a male speaker.

However, the system which we have used for speech signal analysis is based on a channel vocoder which does not permit a vry fine measurement of temporal and spectral parameters. So we consequently have additional difficulties in developing the algorithms that will reliably detect and recognize nasal consonants in continuous speech.

Some examples of spectra given by the 14 channel vocoder used in the continuous speech understanding system developed in the National Center of Telecommunication Studies (CNET) are presented in Figure 3.

These spectra were measured at the consonantal release of /m/ and /n/ spoken in continuous speech, in the same intervocalic context /a-i/, by three male subjects. From this example it is evident that the distinction between the two nasals is not obvious and is strongly dependent on individual voice characteristics.

3. SPEECH MATERIAL

In our study we used two sets of sentences. The first was composed of 44 sentences pronounced by five male speakers (two of them with a slurring articulation) and one female. The sentences were constructed in such a way that a maximum of possible coarticulations of nasals with 11 oral and 4 nasal vowels were obtained. Other coarticulations with some consonants were also taken into account and particular attention was paid to sequences of two nasals /mn/ and /nm/, nasals followed or preceded by a liquid /l/ or by a voiced fricative and stop consonants, because these cases turned out to be the most difficult for the nasal segment discrimination. The second set was composed of phonetically balanced sentences and of some other pronounced in Breton language for which the frequency of occurrence of nasals is relatively high. The overall number of subjects was equal to 8 male and 3 female speakers.

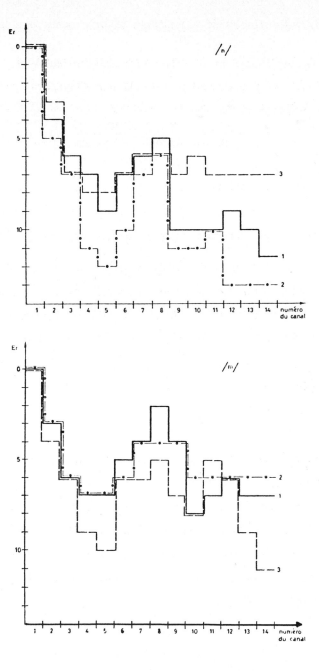

Fig. 3   Some examples of the nasal consonants' spectra evaluated at the release: a) of the /n/, of the /m/. The two nasals were spoken in the same intervocalic context /a-i/ by 3 male subjects.

In our study we distinguished three types of intervocalic contexts:

1) with no important change of the place of vocalic articulation,

2) with a relatively weak backward of forward movement,

3) with a strong change of the place.

In all we have analyzed 236 realizations of nasals: 108 of /m/, 109 of /n/ and 19 of /gn/.

4. SPEECH SIGNAL PROCESSING AND FEATURE PARAMETER EVALUATION

The speech signal was recorded in a sound treated studio, digitalized and coded by a 14 channel vocoder implemented on a VAX computer. After conversion each sentence is represented by a string of samples of 13.3 ms duration, each of them characterized by a set of 14 numbers which describes the spectral energy distribution. The data provided by vocoder were memorized and processed using a set of elaborate procedures.

Several features parameters were used for detecting nasals:

1) total energy of analyzed sample, obtained as a simple sum of channels' energy

2) a parameter called "pente" ('slope'-temporal derivative) which characterizes dynamic the spectral variations on two consecutive *samples* and was calculated by summing up the energy differences in corresponding channels,

3) the center of spectral gravity determined by formula:

$$ CDGNO = \frac{\sum_{j=1}^{14} j \cdot (E_j - E_{min})}{\sum_{j=1}^{14} (E_j - E_{min})} $$

where $E_{min} = MIN(E_1, E_2, ..., E_{14})$ for a given sample.

Our procedure is composed of two parts. The first, for segments previously classified as consonantal, determines the samples as potentially nasal. The detection of this class of samples is based on the gross spectral shape parameters, independently of the context. The principal condition which must be satisfied to consider the analyzed sample as potentially nasal, is the presence in the first channel (frequency band 250-450 Hz) of an energy peak dominating the others. Moreover, this peak in the case of nasals has a characteristic configuration which is described using some level differences (in the range of low frequencies, mainly below 1000 Hz, as it is presented on Figure 4. In Figure 5, the complete specification of parameters with the context-independent detection rule potentially nasal sample is given.

The following step of our analysis of the sequences of nasal samples is applied only for those segments whose duration is greater than 27 ms. Some realizations of the liquid /l/, a small perceptage of voiced stop /b, d, g/ and in individual cases voiced fricatives as /v/ and /z/ are classified as potentially nasal. In the last two last cases, the results of labelling are strongly speaker dependent. As mentioned, a stationary segment is labelled "nasal" if it is composed of enough "potentially nasal" spectral frames and if the following contextual and temporal criteria hold for each frame:

1. The energy within the 250-450 Hz bandwidth is less than or equal to that computed on the frame corresponding to the following vocalic energy peak.

2. The energy within the 450-650 Hz bandwidth is at least 65% of the energy in the same bandwidth computed on the vocalic energy peak.

3. At the point j corresponding to the maximum of instability between the nasal segment and the following (or preceding) vocalic segment the jump of energy is not too high: $E_{j+1} / E_j < 2.4$ where E_j is the energy of the jth frame.

SPECTRAL NASAL CONSONANT CUES

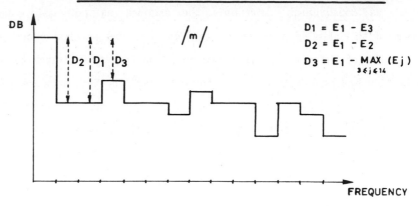

/m/

$D_1 = E_1 - E_3$
$D_2 = E_1 - E_2$
$D_3 = E_1 - \underset{3 \leqslant j \leqslant 14}{MAX} (E_j)$

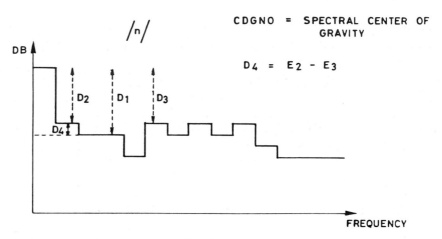

/n/

CDGNO = SPECTRAL CENTER OF GRAVITY

$D_4 = E_2 - E_3$

CONDITIONS FOR DETECTING THE NASAL FEATURE :

$D_1 \geqslant 12$ DB $D_2 \geqslant 0$

$D_3 > 4$ DB $D_4 \geqslant 0$

$3 < CDGNO \leqslant 7$

E_j = Energy within the Jth CHANNEL

Fig. 4   Schematic representation of some spectral cues used for detection of 'potentially nasal' frames with examples of vocoder spectra obtained for /m/ and /n/.

NASAL 1: CALCULATED PARAMETERS

$D1 = E1 - E3 \iff E_{250-450} - E_{650-850}$

$D2 = E2 - \underset{2 \leq j \leq 6}{MAX(Ej)} \iff E_1 - \underset{450-1600}{MAX(Ej)}$

$D3 = E1 - \underset{7 \leq j \leq 14}{MAX(Ej)} \iff E1 - \underset{1600-4200}{MAX(Ej)}$

$D4 = E2 - E3 \iff E_{450-650} - E_{650-850}$

$D5 = E1 - E4 \iff E_{250-450} - E_{850-1050}$

$D6 = E1 - E5 \iff E_{250-450} - E_{1050-1300}$

RULE USED FOR NASAL SAMPLE DETECTION

$(3 \leq CDGNO \leq 7) \wedge (D1 > 12DB) \wedge (D2 > 4DB) \wedge (D3 > 8DB) \wedge (D4 \geq 4DB) \wedge [(D5 \geq 8DB) \vee (D6 \geq 8DB)]$

$\wedge$ — AND
$\vee$ — OR
E1: Energy in the channel 1 (250 to 450 HZ)

Fig. 5 Specification of static spectral cues used for detection of nasal frames.

4. The increase in energy within the 250-450 Hz bandwidth between the end of the "nasal" segment and the vocalic peak must not be too large (< 12 dB).

The conditions 1, 3, 4 are schematically presented in Figure 6.

This part of the algorithm eliminates most of voiced stops and fricatives classified previously as potentially nasal.

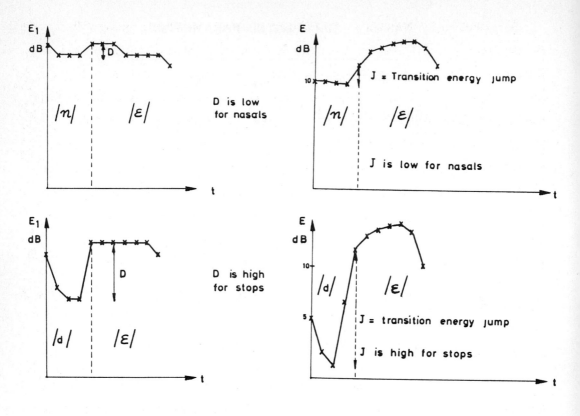

Fig. 6   Temporal cues used for detection of nasal consonants.

A preliminary study on the possibility of nasal consonants recognition has recently been begun. The first approach is based on a more detailed analysis of the spectral part in the frquencies band 820-1660 Hz. The algorithm is contextually dependent and begins with the analysis of time movements of the maximum in this frequency range, which in this case is divided in four bands (16 channel vocoder was used). The description of the peak movements is preceded by the evaluation of the place of articulation of the vowel which follows the nasal. Next, three types of time evolution, in the intervals starting 50 ms before and ending 50 ms after the limit separating the nasal and vocalic segments (determined by segmentation procedure of G. MERCIER with time sampling of 13,3 ms), in this range of frequencies are distinguished:

a)   with rising frequency of the peak
b)   with no changes
c)   with frequency falling.

Another procedure was used to evaluate the mean level of energy in the 1180-1400 Hz band which in most cases is the region where the second formant and the first anti-resonant appear for the bilabial nasal /m/. The time variations of this parameter at the vicinity of the vocalic onset (30 ms before and after) were taken into account.

We have noted that for the nasal /n/ the rising of the peak frequency is more accentuated than for /m/, with exception however, for frontal vocalic context. In this case, no important variations were observed. It seems, that the mean relative level of nasal samples evaluated with regard to the energy spectral density can be used for final discrimination of nasals pronounced in prevocalic or intervocalic context. In the first approximation we have found that the samples of the nasal /n/, in most cases have an energy level in this frquency band higher than other nasals. A final version of the recognition procedure is under preparation.

5. RESULTS

The procedure of nasals detection based on the analysis of gross spectral shape parameters was tested on a relatively large sample of speech material in which about 240 nasal consonants realized in different contexts were present. Most cases of non-detection of nasals were due to the flatness of the low-frequency maximum, what is sometimes observed for opened and nasalized vowels context. In all the detection score of nasal consonants averaged of 80% ranging from one speaker to the other from 70% to 90%. Some difficulties in the discrimination of the liquid /l/ from the nasal, spoken in sequence have been noted, especially in the cases when these consonants were not separated by a schwa. Also for post-vocalic articulations, before a pause or at the end of the sentence similar problems were present. The mean error score for /l/ was about 20%. For other consonants such as voiced fricatives and stops the errors were less frequent, not exceeding 7%.

Some preliminary results of nasal consonants recognition obtained very recently for one male subject are presented on Figure 7.

Before the final recognition decision a weighting coefficient was calculated taking into account temporal variations of analyzed parameters evaluated in the vicinity of the following vowel onset. The results obtained for the nasal /gn/ are not satisfactory but we hope that some improvements of elaborated algorithms are possible, especially by introducing finer spectral description.

6. CONCLUSION

In our paper, we have presented some results of nasal consonants detection in continuous speech and of their recognition for the case when they were pronounced in bi-syllabic non-sense words. In the first case context-independent rules were used. It seems, that some improvements of nasal detection can be obtained by taking into account the properties of the adjacent vowel. In the

SPOKEN		RECOGNIZED			SPOKEN		RECOGNIZED		
		M	N	GN			M	N	GN
ma	:	6	0	4	ma	:	7	2	0
na	:	4	10	9	na	:	5	13	2
mi	:	10	2	7	mi	:	20	9	1
ni	:	2	5	4	ni	:	4	5	14
mo	:	7	3	6	mo	:	7	2	12
no	:	2	20	1	no	:	4	8	0
mu	:	7	2	7	mu	:	8	0	4
nu	:	0	11	4	nu	:	5	6	4
mon	:	6	0	2	mon	:	10	2	7
non	:	2	19	2	non	:	5	8	0
man	:	6	0	4	man	:	6	4	3
nan	:	3	16	1	nan	:	4	18	3
mou	:	9	3	11	mou	:	7	2	4
nou	:	2	15	1	nou	:	8	7	8
meu	:	7	0	8	meu	:	7	0	0
neu	:	2	9	1	neu	:	2	6	1
mei	:	9	0	5	mei	:	9	0	5
nei	:	3	8	4	nei	:	1	8	2
mai	:	6	0	0	mai	:	7	0	5
nai	:	0	8	1	nai	:	0	8	1
gna	:	8	5	18	gna	:	8	5	15
gni	:	4	5	8	gni	:	3	8	15
gno	:	4	5	6	gno	:	6	6	8
gnon	:	3	6	7	gnon	:	8	5	7
gnan	:	5	5	7	gnan	:	8	2	8
gnou	:	6	3	6	gnou	:	10	3	10
gneu	:	7	2	7	gneu	:	5	9	9
gnei	:	7	8	9	gnei	:	8	6	10
gnai	:	5	8	9	gnai	:	6	6	5

Fig. 7   Preliminary results of nasal consonants recognition in bisyllabic sequences /CVCV/.

case of nasal recognition the knowledge of context is strictly necessary, especially, for multi-speaker systems.

The algorithms for detection and recognition of nasals, are very simple and are based on the analysis of broad spectral cues, which generally make the elaborated rules more reliable than algorithms which make use of too precise and detailed acoustic properties which are often more context and speaker dependent.

REFERENCES

1. S. E. Blumstein and K. N. Stevens, "Acoustic invariance in speech production: Evidence from measurements of the spectral characteistics of stop consonants", JASA, Vol. 66, pp. 1001-1017, 1979.
2. P. Demichelis, "The automatic recognition of some sonorant consonants in continuous speech", Speech Communication, Vol. 1, No. 3-4, pp. 231-255, 1982.
3. R. De Mori, R. Gubrynowicz and P. Laface, "Influence of a knowledge source for the recognition of nasals in continuous speech", IEEE Trans. ASSP, Vol. ASSP-27, Vol. 5, pp. 538-549, 1979.
4. O. Fujimura, "Analysis of nasal consonants", JASA, Vol. 34, No. 12, pp. 1865-1875, 1962.
5. A. Malecot, "Acoustic cues for nasal consonants", Language, Vol. 32, No. 2, pp. 274-284, 1956.
6. G. Mercier, "Evaluation des acoustiques utilisés dans l'analyseur phonétique du système KEAL, ACTES 9èmes Journées d'Etudes sur la Parole, Lannion, pp. 231-242, 1978.
7. G. Mercier, "Acoustic-phonetic decoding and adaptation in continuous speech recognition, in: *Automatic Speech Analysis and Recognition*, Proc. NATO ASI Bonas, J.-P. Haton (ed.), Dordrecht, D. Reidel, pp. 69-99, 1981.
8. G. Mercier, "From KEAL to SERAC: a new based expert system for speech recognition", (see this book), 1984.
9. K. Nakata, "Synthesis and perception of nasal consonants, JASA, Vol. 31, No. 6, pp. 661-665, 1959.
10. K. N. Stevens, "Constraints imposed by auditory system on the properties used to classify speech sounds: .Data from phonology, acoustics and psychoacoustics, in : *The Cognitive Representation of Speech*, T. Myers, J. Laver and J. Anderson (eds), North-holland, New York, 1981.
11. S. Takeuchi, H. Kasuya and K. Kido, "A method for extraction of the spectral cues of nasal consonants", J. Acoust. Soc. Jap. Vol. 31, No. 12, pp. 739-740, 1975.

AUTHOR INDEX

Aggoun, A.	495	Lawrence, S. G. C.	343
Ainsworth, W. A.	389	Le Guennec, L.	613
Alderson, P. R.	343	Mercier, G.	303,613
Benedi, J. M.	427	Moore, R. K.	73
Bisiani, R.	169	Mühlfeld, R.	271
Brietzmann, A.	271	Niemann, H.	271
Casacuberta, F.	427	Ohala, J. J.	447
Cavazza, M.	215	Pacifici, R.	215
Ciaramella, A.	215	Quinton, P.	145
Colla, A. M.	361	Regel, P.	271
De Mori, R.	569	Rühl, H. W.	517
Dettweiler, H.	537	Ruske, G.	593
di Martino, J.	405	Sanchis, E.	427
Dours, D.	225	Schukat, G.	271
Emerard, F.	495	Sciarra, D.	361
Facca, R.	225	Sinclair, D. A.	343
Foster, H. M.	389	Sorin, C.	495
Frison, P.	145	Stein, S. B.	477
Fu, K. S.	191	Stella, M.	495
Gilloux, M.	303	Suen, C. Y.	477
Gubrynowicz, R.	613	Tarridec, C.	303
Haton, J.-P.	249	Ünal, F.	419
Hess, W.	537	Vaissiere, J.	303
Hugli, H.	1	Vidal, E.	427
Kaye, G.	343	Williams, B. J.	343
Kulas, W.	517	Wolff, G. J.	343
Kunt, M.	1	Wood, D.	233
Laface, P.	569	Yalabik, N.	419

NATO ASI Series F

Vol. 1: Issues in Acoustic Signal – Image Processing and Recognition. Edited by C. H. Chen. VIII, 333 pages. 1983.

Vol. 2: Image Sequence Processing and Dynamic Scene Analysis. Edited by T. S. Huang. IX, 749 pages. 1983.

Vol. 3: Electronic Systems Effectiveness and Life Cycle Costing. Edited by J. K. Skwirzynski. XVII, 732 pages. 1983.

Vol. 4: Pictorial Data Analysis. Edited by R. M. Haralick. VIII, 468 pages. 1983.

Vol. 5: International Calibration Study of Traffic Conflict Techniques. Edited by E. Asmussen VII, 229 pages. 1984.

Vol. 6: Information Technology and the Computer Network. Edited by K. G. Beauchamp. VIII, 271 pages. 1984.

Vol. 7: High-Speed Computation. Edited by J. S. Kowalik. IX, 441 pages. 1984.

Vol. 8: Program Transformation and Programming Environments. Report on an Workshop directed by F. L. Bauer and H. Remus. Edited by P. Pepper. XIV, 378 pages. 1984.

Vol. 9: Computer Aided Analysis and Optimization of Mechanical System Dynamics. Edited by E. J. Haug. XXII, 700 pages. 1984.

Vol. 10: Simulation and Model-Based Methodologies: An Integrative View. Edited by T. I. Ören, B. P. Zeigler, M. S. Elzas. XIII, 651 pages. 1984.

Vol. 11: Robotics and Artificial Intelligence. Edited by M. Brady, L. A. Gerhardt, H. F. Davidson. XVII, 693 pages. 1984.

Vol. 12: Combinatorial Algorithms on Words. Edited by A. Apostolico, Z. Galil. VIII, 361 pages. 1985.

Vol. 13: Logics and Models of Concurrent Systems. Edited by K. R. Apt. VIII, 498 pages. 1985.

Vol. 14: Control Flow and Data Flow: Concept of Distributed Programming. Edited by M. Broy. VIII, 525 pages. 1985.

Vol. 15: Computational Mathematical Programming. Edited by K. Schittkowski. VIII, 451 pages. 1985.

Vol. 16: New Systems and Architectures for Automatic Speech Recognition and Synthesis. Edited by R. De Mori, C.Y. Suen. XIII, 630 pages. 1985.

HOPE 3454

DATE LOANED

HIGHSMITH   # 45222